SolidWorks 20[illegible] Tutorial with MultiMedia CD

A Step-by-Step Project Based Approach Utilizing 3D Solid Modeling

David C. Planchard & Marie P. Planchard

ISBN: 978-1-58503-338-6

SDC
PUBLICATIONS

Schroff Development Corporation

www.schroff.com
www.schroff-europe.com

Trademarks and Disclaimer

SolidWorks and its family of products are registered trademarks of the Dassault Système. Microsoft Windows, Microsoft Office and its family of products are registered trademarks of the Microsoft Corporation. Other software applications and parts described in this book are trademarks or registered trademarks of their respective owners.

Dimensions of parts are modified for illustration purposes. Every effort is made to provide an accurate text. The authors and the manufacturers shall not be held liable for any parts or drawings developed or designed with this book or any responsibility for inaccuracies that appear in the book. World Wide Web and company information was valid at the time of the printing.

Examination Copies

Books received as examination copies are for review purposes only and may not be made available for student use. Resale of examination copies is prohibited.

Electronic Files

Any electronic files associated with this book are licensed to the original user only. These files may not be transferred to any other party.

INTRODUCTION

SolidWorks 2007 Tutorial with MultiMedia CD is written to assist students, designers, engineers and professionals. The book provides an introduction to the user interface, menus, toolbars, concepts and modeling techniques of SolidWorks to create parts, assemblies, and drawings.

Follow the step-by-step instructions and develop multiple assemblies that combine over 80 extruded machined parts and components. Formulate the skills to create, modify, and edit sketches and solid features. Learn the techniques to reuse features, parts, and assemblies through symmetry, patterns, copied components, design tables, and configurations.

Desired outcomes and usage competencies are listed for each project. Know your objective up front. Follow the steps in Project 1 through Project 4 to achieve your design goals. Work between multiple documents, features, commands, and custom properties that represent how engineers and designers utilize SolidWorks in industry.

The book is designed to compliment the Online Tutorials and Online Help contained in SolidWorks 2007. The goal is to illustrate how multiple design situations and systematic steps combine to produce successful projects.

The authors developed the industry scenarios by combining their own industry experience with the knowledge of engineers, department managers, vendors, and manufacturers. These professionals are directly involved with SolidWorks everyday. Their responsibilities go far beyond the creation of just a 3D model.

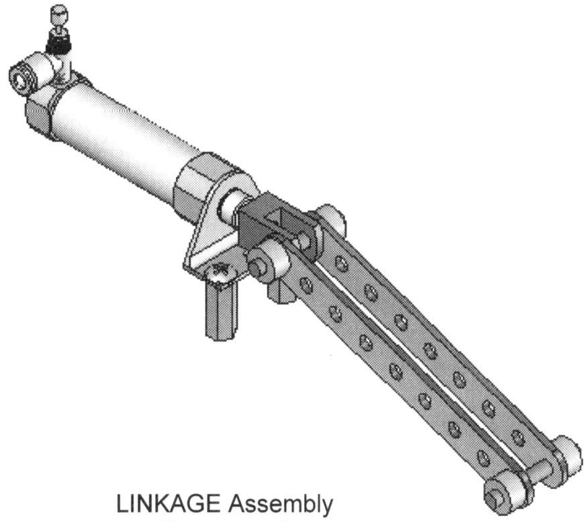

LINKAGE Assembly
Courtesy of
Gears Educational Systems & SMC
Corporation of America

About the Cover

Displayed on the front cover is the Pneumatic-Test-Module Assembly. The Pneumatic-Test-Module Assembly is developed in the book.

The pneumatic components are manufactured by SMC Corporation of America, Indianapolis, IN.

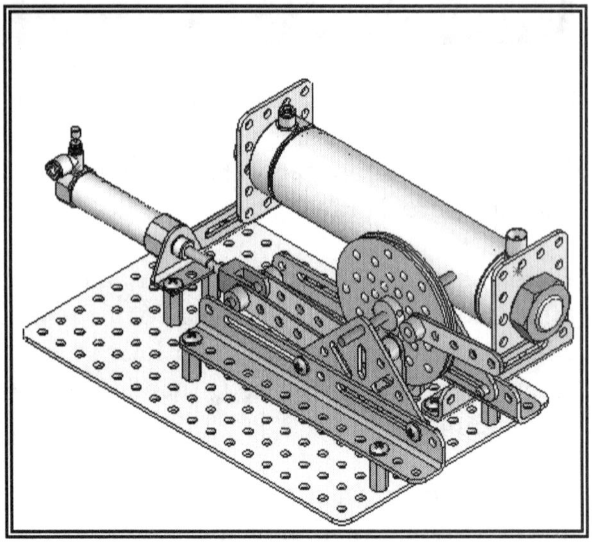

Pneumatic Components Diagram
Courtesy of SMC Corporation of America
and Gears Educational Systems.

About the Authors

Marie Planchard is the Director of Education Marketing at SolidWorks Corporation. Before she joined SolidWorks, Marie spent over 10 years as an engineering professor at Mass Bay College in Wellesley Hills, MA. She has 13 plus years of industry software experience and held a variety of management and engineering positions including Beta Test Manager for CAD software at Computervision Corporation. As a Certified SolidWorks Professional (CSWP), she presented at SolidWorks World. Marie was the founder of the New England SolidWorks Users Group.

David Planchard is the President of D&M Education, LLC. Before starting D&M Education LLC, he spent over 23 years in industry and academia holding various Engineering, Marketing, and teaching positions and degrees. He has five U.S. patents and one International patent. He has published and authored numerous papers on equipment design. David is also a technical editor for Cisco Press. He is a member of the New England Pro/Users Group, New England SolidWorks Users Group, and the Cisco Regional Academy Users Group. David Planchard is an active industry and education consultant. David is a SolidWorks Research Partner and SolidWorks Solution Partner.

David and Marie Planchard are co-authors of the following books:

- **A Commands Guide Reference Tutorial for SolidWorks 2007.**
- **Engineering Design with SolidWorks 1999, 2000, 2001, 2001Plus, 2003, 2004, 2005, 2006, and 2007.**
- **SolidWorks Tutorial with Multimedia CD 2001/2001Plus, 2003, 2004, 2005, 2006, and 2007.**
- **SolidWorks The Basics, with Multimedia CD 2004, 2005, and 2006.**
- **Assembly Modeling with SolidWorks 2001Plus, 2003, 2004-2005, and 2006.**
- **Drawing and Detailing with SolidWorks 2001/2001Plus, 2002, 2003, 2004, and 2006.**
- **Applications in Sheet Metal Using Pro/SHEETMETAL & Pro/ENGINEER.**
- **An Introduction to Pro/SHEETMETAL.**

Dedication

A special acknowledgment goes to our loving daughter, Stephanie Planchard, who supported us during this intense and lengthy project. Stephanie continues to support us with her patience, love, and understanding.

Contact the Authors

This is the 7th edition of this book. We realize that keeping software application books current is imperative to our customers. We value the hundreds of professors, students, designers, and engineers that have provided us input to enhance our book. We value your suggestions and comments. Please contact us with any comments, questions, or suggestions on this book or any of our other SolidWorks books. David and Marie Planchard, D & M Education, LLC, dplanchard@msn.com.

Note to Instructors

Please contact the publisher **www.schroff.com** for additional materials and the Instructor's Guide that support the usage of this text in the classroom. The physical parts and assemblies utilized in the exercises in this book are available through Gears Educational Systems, Hanover, MA (www.gearseds.com). The parts and assemblies provide students the ability to design, build and test pneumatic and electro-mechanical systems with industrial components. Incorporate concepts in mathematics, physics, engineering mechanics, machine design, robotics, and analysis.

Trademarks, Disclaimer, and Copyrighted Material

References

- SolidWorks Users Guide, SolidWorks Corporation, 2007.
- ASME Y14 Engineering Drawing and Related Documentation Practices.
- Beers & Johnson, Vector Mechanics for Engineers, 6th ed. McGraw Hill, Boston, MA.
- Betoline, Wiebe, Miller, Fundamentals of Graphics Communication, Irwin, 1995.
- Earle, James, Engineering Design Graphics, Addison Wesley, 1999.
- Hibbler, R.C, Engineering Mechanics Statics and Dynamics, 8th ed, Prentice Hall, Saddle River, NJ.
- Hoelscher, Springer, Dobrovolny, Graphics for Engineers, John Wiley, 1968.
- Jensen, Cecil, Interpreting Engineering Drawings, Glencoe, 2002.
- Jensen & Helsel, Engineering Drawing and Design, Glencoe, 1990.
- Olivo C., Payne, Olivo, T, Basic Blueprint Reading and Sketching, Delmar, 1988.
- Planchard & Planchard, Drawing and Detailing with SolidWorks, SDC Pub., Mission, KS 2006.
- Walker, James, Machining Fundamentals, Goodheart Wilcox, 1999.
- 80/20 Product Manual, 80/20, Inc., Columbia City, IN, 2006.
- Reid Tool Supply Product Manual, Reid Tool Supply Co., Muskegon, MI, 2006.
- Simpson Strong Tie Product Manual, Simpson Strong Tie, CA, 2006.
- Ticona Designing with Plastics – The Fundamentals, Summit, NJ, 2006.
- SMC Corporation of America, Product Manuals, Indiana, 2006.
- Gears Educational Design Systems, Product Manual, Hanover, MA, 2006.
- Emhart – A Black and Decker Company, On-line catalog, Hartford, CT, 2006.

TABLE OF CONTENTS

Appendix

What is SolidWorks?

SolidWorks is a design automation software package used to produce parts, assemblies and drawings. SolidWorks is a Windows native 3D solid modeling CAD program. SolidWorks provides easy to use, highest quality design software for engineers and designers who create 3D models and 2D drawings ranging from individual parts to assemblies with thousands of parts.

The SolidWorks Corporation, headquartered in Concord, Massachusetts, USA develops and markets innovative design solutions for the Microsoft Windows platform. Additional information on SolidWorks and its family of products can be obtained at their URL, www.SolidWorks.com.

In SolidWorks, you create 3D parts, assemblies and 2D drawings. The part, assembly and drawing documents are related.

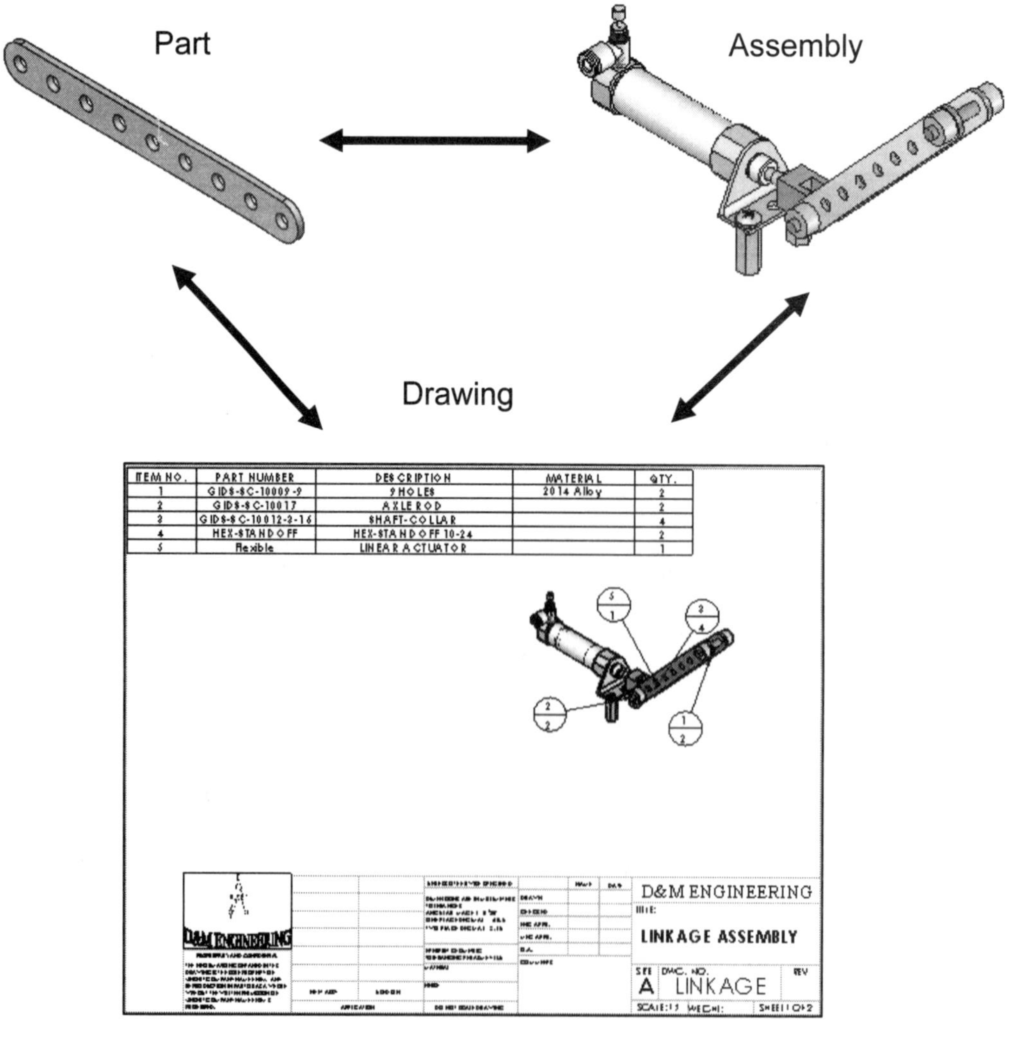

Features are the building blocks of parts. Use features to create parts, such as: Extruded Boss and Extruded Cut. Extruded features begin with a 2D sketch created on a Sketch plane.

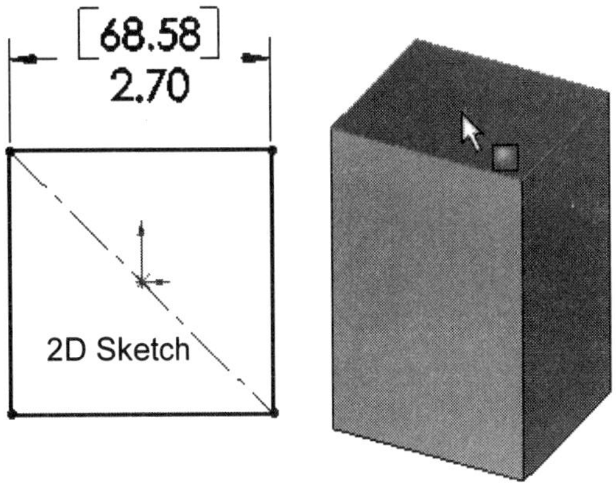

The 2D sketch is a profile or cross section. Sketch tools such as: lines, arcs, and circles are used to create the 2D sketch. Sketch the general shape of the profile. Add geometric relationships and dimensions to control the exact size of the geometry.

Create features by selecting edges or faces of existing features, such as a Fillet. The Fillet feature rounds sharp corners.

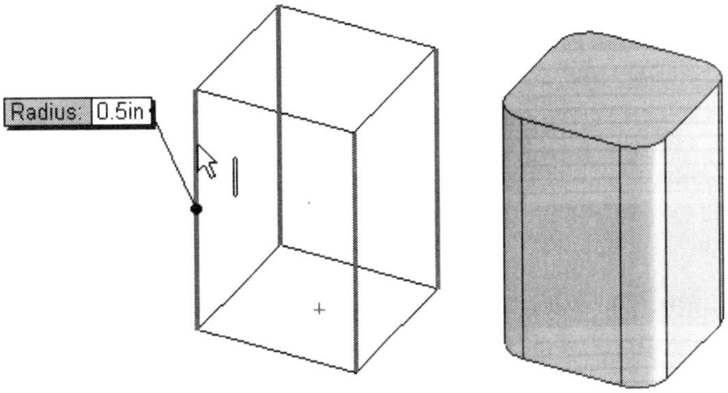

Dimensions drive features. Change a dimension, and you change the size of the part.

Use Geometric relationships: Vertical, Horizontal, Parallel, etc. to maintain Design intent.

Create a hole that penetrates through a part. SolidWorks maintains relationships through the change.

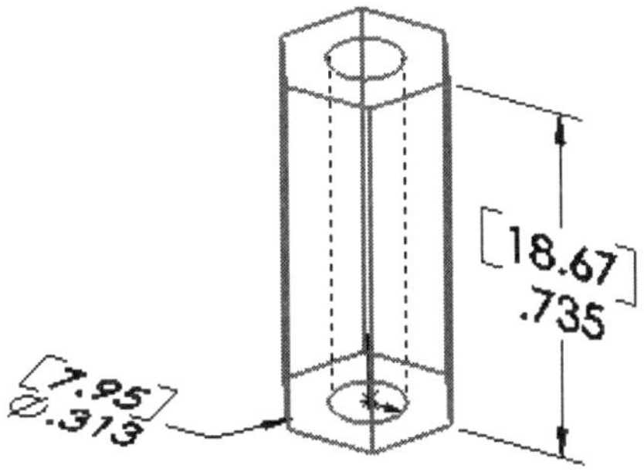

The step-by-step approach used in this text allows you to create parts, assemblies, and drawings.

The text allows you to modify and change all components of the model. Change is an integral part of design.

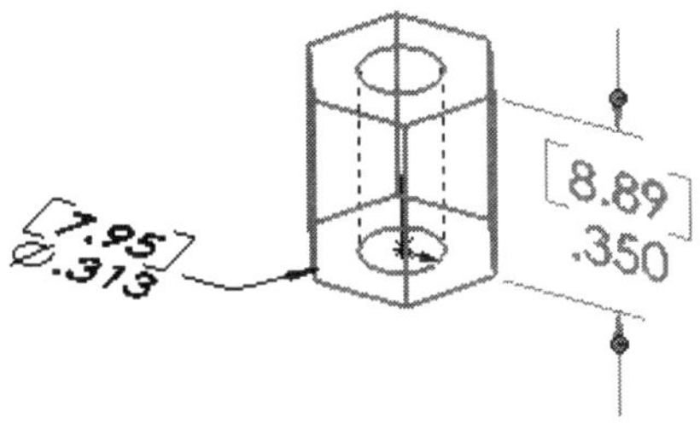

Design Intent

The SolidWorks definition of design intent is the process in which the model is developed to accept future changes.

Models behave differently when design changes occur. Design for change.

Utilize geometry for symmetry, reuse common features and reuse common parts.

Build change into the following areas:

1. Sketch.
2. Feature.
3. Part.
4. Assembly.
5. Drawing.

1. Design Intent in the Sketch.

Build the design intent in the sketch as the profile is created.

A profile is determined from the sketch tools, Example: rectangle, circle and arc.

Build symmetry into the profile through a sketch centerline, mirror entity and position about the Reference planes and Origin.

Build design intent as you sketch with automatic relationships.

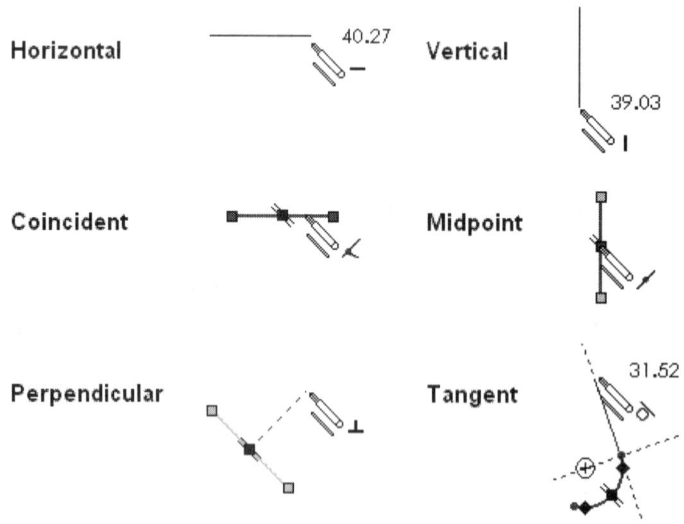

A rectangle contains horizontal, vertical and perpendicular automatic relations.

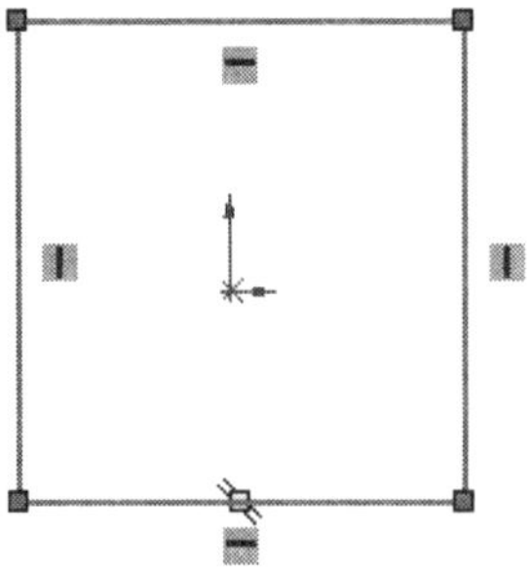

Build design intent using added geometric relations. Example: horizontal, vertical, coincident, midpoint, intersection, tangent and perpendicular.

Example A: Develop a square profile.

Build the design intent to create a square profile.

Sketch a rectangle. Insert a centerline. Add a midpoint relation. Add an equal relation between the two perpendicular lines. Insert a dimension to define the width of the square.

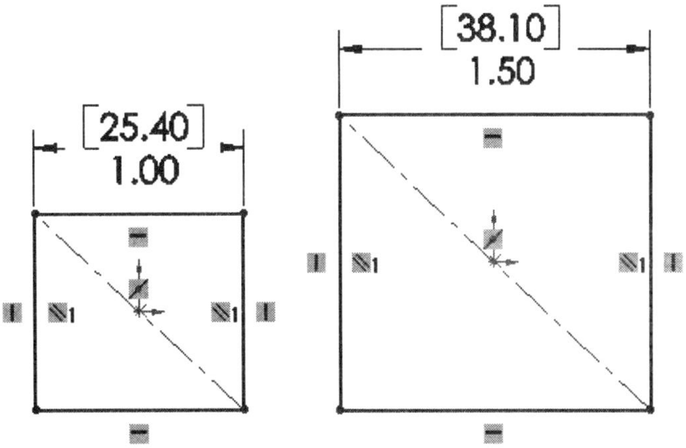

Example B: Develop a rectangular profile.

The bottom horizontal midpoint of the rectangular profile is located at the Origin.

Sketch a rectangle.

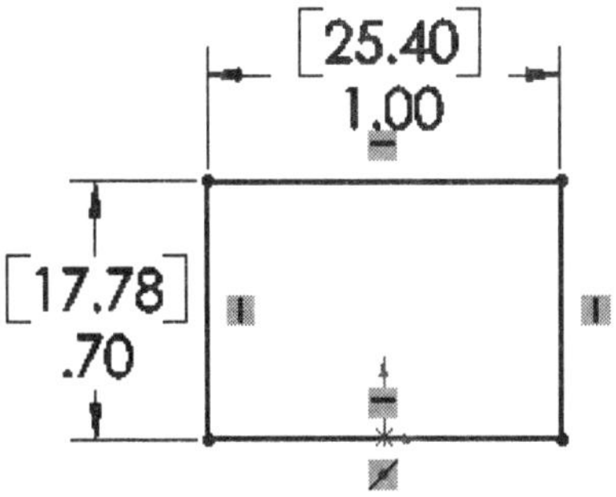

Add a midpoint relation between the horizontal edge of the rectangle and the Origin.

Insert two dimensions to define the width and height of the rectangle.

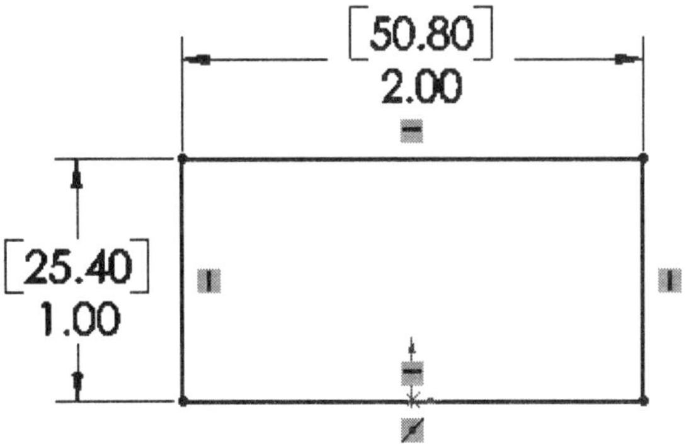

2. Design Intent in the Feature.

Build design intent into a feature by addressing symmetry, feature selection and the order of feature creations.

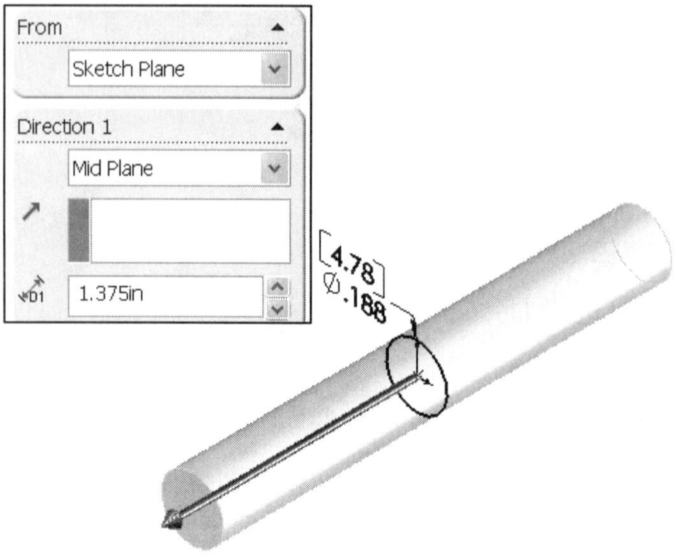

Example A: Extruded feature remains symmetric about a plane.

Utilize the Mid Plane Depth option. Change the depth and the feature remains symmetric about the Front Plane.

Example B: Create six holes for a pattern.

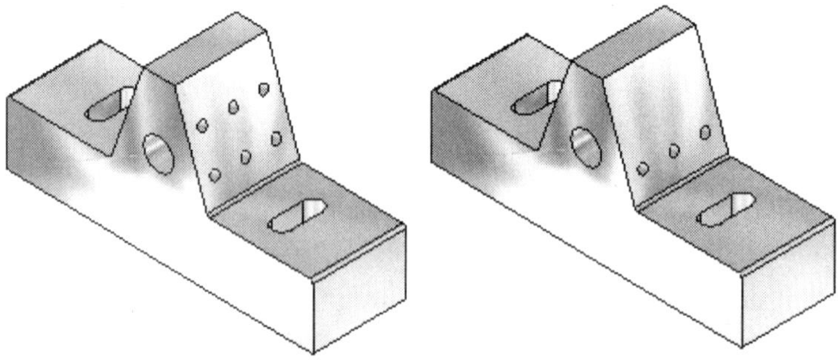

Do you create six separate Extruded Cuts? No. Create one hole with the Hole Wizard.

Insert a Linear Pattern.

Change the number of holes from six to three.

3. Design Intent in the Part.

Utilize symmetry, feature order and reusing common features to build design intent into the part.

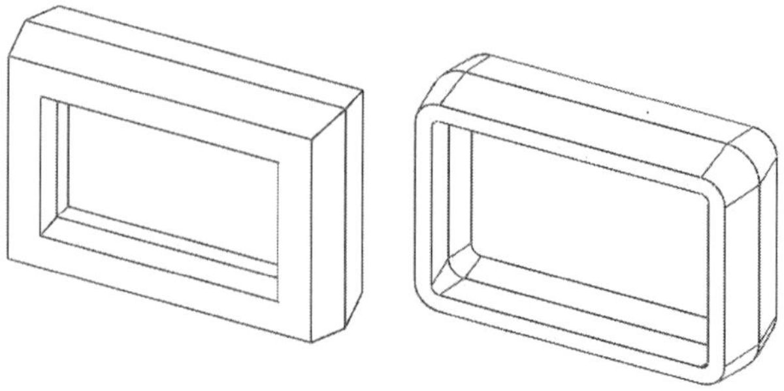

Example A: Feature Order.

Is the entire part symmetric?

Feature order affects the part. Apply the Shell feature before the Fillet feature and the inside corners remain perpendicular.

4. Design Intent in the Assembly.

Utilizing symmetry, reusing common parts and using the Mate relationship between parts builds the design intent into an assembly.

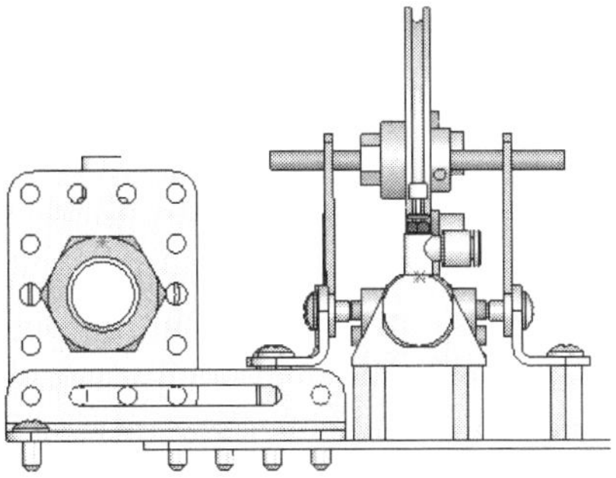

Example A: Reuse Geometry in an assembly.

The PNEUMATIC-TEST-MODULE Assembly contains a Linear Pattern of holes. Insert one SCREW into the first Hole. Utilize Component Pattern to copy the SCREW to the other holes.

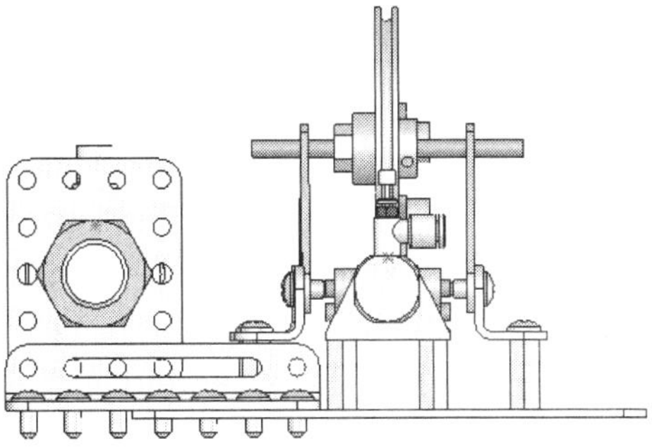

5. Design Intent in the Drawing.

Utilize dimensions, tolerance and notes in parts and assemblies to build the design intent into the Drawing.

Example A: Tolerance and material in the drawing.

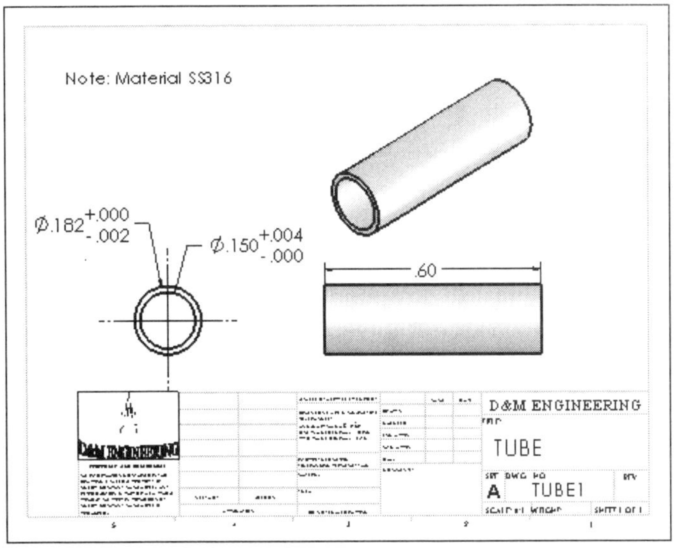

Insert an outside diameter tolerance +.000/-.002 into the TUBE part. The tolerance propagates to the drawing.

Define the Custom Property MATERIAL in the Part. The MATERIAL Custom Property propagates to the drawing.

Additional information on the design process and design intent is available in Online Help.

Overview of Projects

Project 1: Linkage Assembly

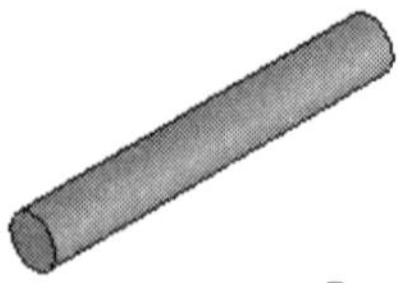
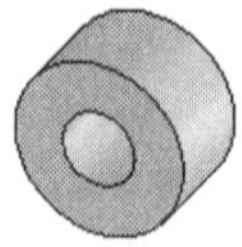

Project 1 introduces the basic concepts behind SolidWorks and the SolidWorks user interface.

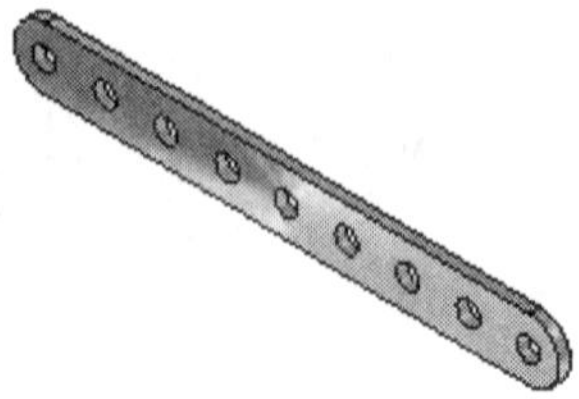

Create a file folder to manage projects. Create three parts: AXLE, SHAFT-COLLAR, and FLATBAR. Utilize the following features: Extruded Base, Extruded Cut, and Linear Pattern.

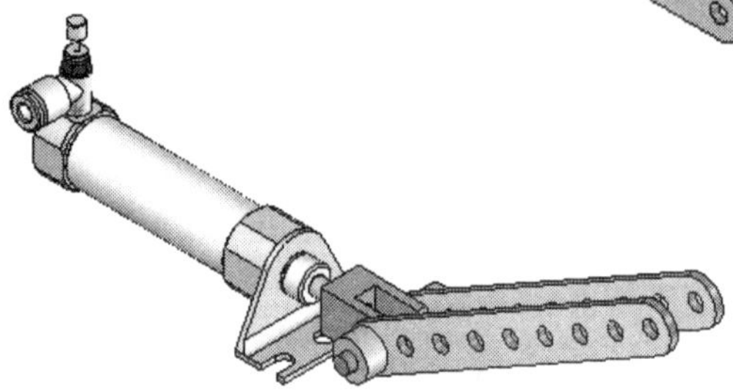

Create the LINKAGE assembly. The LINKAGE assembly utilizes the SMC AIRCYLINDER component located on the enclosed book CD.

Project 2: Front Support Assembly

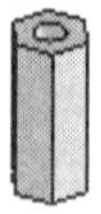
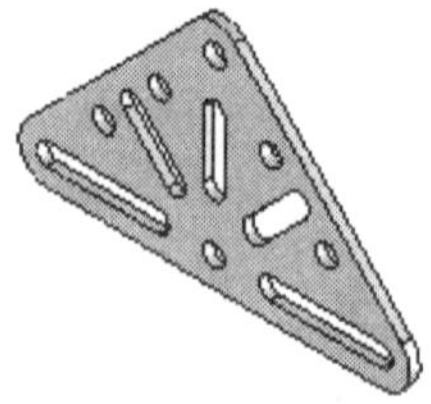

Project 2 introduces various Sketch planes to create parts. The Front, Top, and Right Planes each contain the Extruded Base feature for the TRIANGLE, HEX-STANDOFF, and ANGLE-13HOLE parts. Sketches utilize geometric relationships.

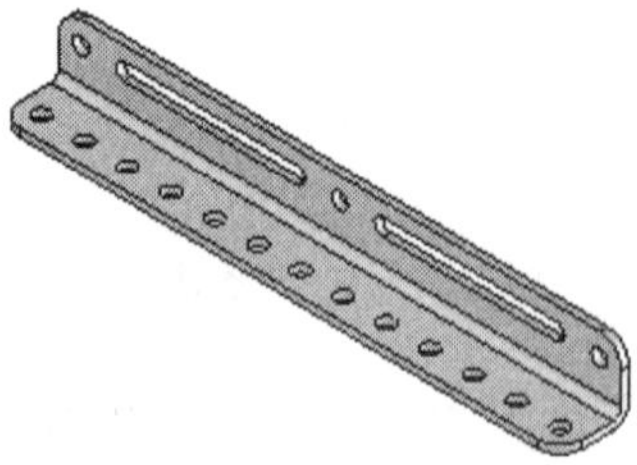

Create the SCREW part using the following features: Revolve Base, Extruded Cut, Fillet, and Circular Pattern.

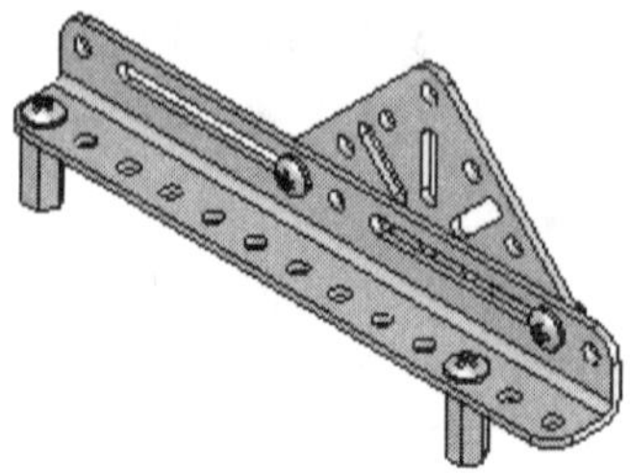

Create the FRONT-SUPPORT assembly. Utilize additional parts from the World Wide Web or the enclosed CD to create the RESERVOIR SUPPORT assembly in the project exercises.

Project 3: Fundamentals of Drawing

Project 3 covers the development of a customized sheet format and drawing template.

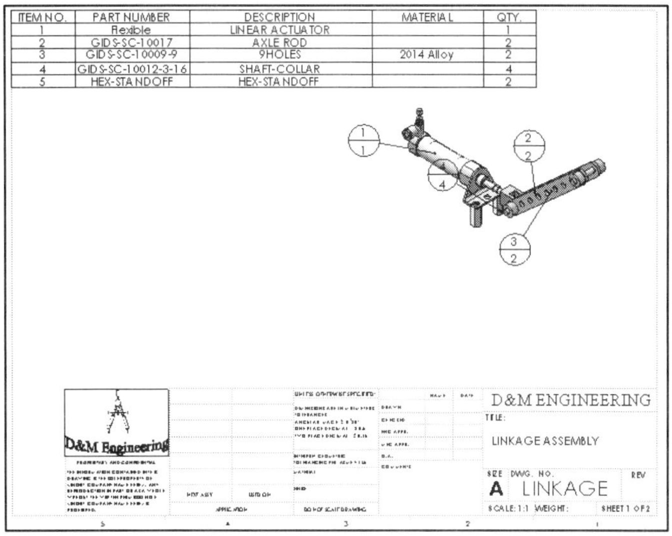

Review the differences between the sheet and the sheet format. Develop a company logo from a bitmap or picture file.

Create a FLATBAR drawing. Insert dimensions created from the part features. Create the LINKAGE assembly drawing with multiple views and assemblies.

Develop and incorporate a Bill of Materials into the drawing Custom Properties in the parts and assemblies. Add information to the Bill of Materials in the drawing. Insert a Design Table to create multiple configurations of parts and assemblies.

Project 4: Pneumatic Test Module Assembly

Project 4 focuses on the final PNEUMATIC-TEST-MODULE assembly.

Create the WHEEL-AND-AXLE parts and assembly. Utilize the following features: Loft, Sweep, Dome, Circular Pattern, and Sweep Cut. Utilize assembly features to mirror components and pattern components.

Comprehend the process to work with multiple documents in an assembly.

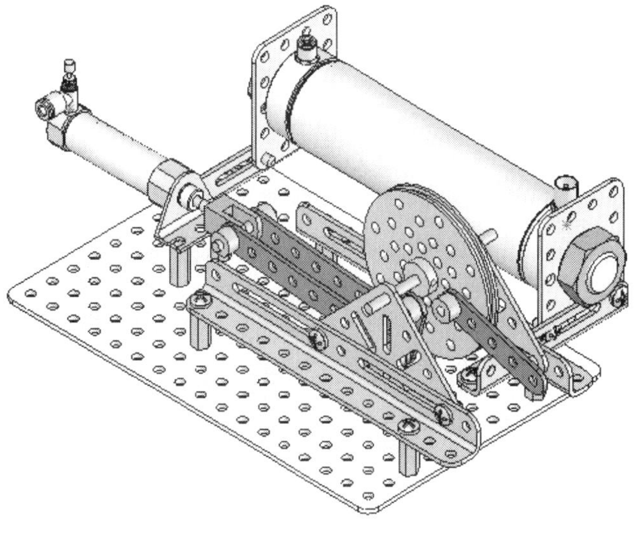

About the Book

The following conventions are used throughout this book:

- The term document is used to refer to a SolidWorks part, drawing, or assembly file.
- The list of items across the top of the SolidWorks interface is the Main menu. Each item in the Main menu has a pull-down menu. When you need to select a series of commands from these menus, the following format is used: Click **Insert**, **Reference Geometry**, **Plane** from the Main menu. The Plane PropertyManager is displayed.
- The book is organized into 4 Projects. Each Project is focused on a specific subject or feature.
- Use the enclosed Multimedia CD to obtain parts and models that are used in this book, and to view the features created in Projects.

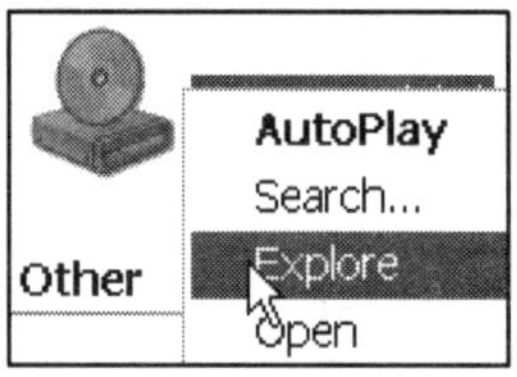

The following command syntax is used throughout the text. Commands that require you to perform an action are displayed in **Bold** text.

Format:	Convention:	Example:
Bold	• All commands actions. • Selected icon button. • Selected geometry: line, circle. • Value entries.	• Click **Tools**, **Options** from the Main menu. • Click **Rectangle** from the Sketch toolbar. • Select the **centerpoint**. • Enter **3.0** for Radius.
Capitalized	• Filenames. • First letter in a feature name.	• Save the **FLATBAR** assembly. • Click the **Fillet** feature.

Windows Terminology in SolidWorks

The mouse buttons provide an integral role in executing SolidWorks commands. The mouse buttons execute commands, select geometry, display Shortcut menus and provide information feedback.

A summary of mouse button terminology is displayed below:

Item:	Description:
Click	Press and release the left mouse button.
Double-click	Double press and release the left mouse button.
Click inside	Press the left mouse button. Wait a second, and then press the left mouse button inside the text box. Use this technique to modify Feature names in the FeatureManager design tree.
Drag	Point to an object, press and hold the left mouse button down. Move the mouse pointer to a new location. Release the left mouse button.
Right-click	Press and release the right mouse button. A Shortcut menu is displayed. Use the left mouse button to select a menu command.
ToolTip	Position the mouse pointer over an Icon (button). The tool name is displayed below the mouse pointer.
Large ToolTip	Position the mouse pointer over an Icon (button). The tool name and a description of its functionality are displayed below the mouse pointer.
Mouse pointer feedback	Position the mouse pointer over various areas of the sketch, part, assembly or drawing. The cursor provides feedback depending on the geometry.

A mouse with a center wheel provides additional functionality in SolidWorks. Roll the center wheel downward to enlarge the model in the Graphics window. Hold the center wheel down. Drag the mouse in the Graphics window to rotate the model. Review various Windows terminology that describes: menus, toolbars, and commands that constitute the graphical user interface in SolidWorks.

Notes:

Project 1

LINKAGE Assembly

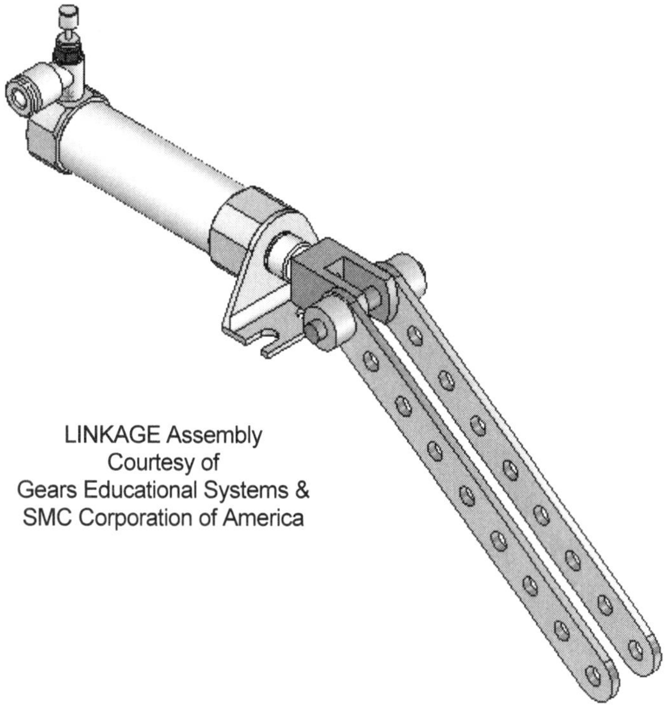

LINKAGE Assembly
Courtesy of
Gears Educational Systems &
SMC Corporation of America

Below are the desired outcomes and usage competencies based on the completion of Project 1.

Desired Outcomes:	Usage Competencies:

• Create three parts:
  ○ AXLE.
  ○ SHAFT-COLLAR.
  ○ FLATBAR.
	• Establish a SolidWorks session.
	• Understand the SolidWorks Interface.
	• Develop new parts.
	• Apply the following features: Extruded Base, Extruded Cut, and Linear Pattern.

• Create an assembly: ○ LINKAGE assembly.	• Insert Components into an Assembly. • Insert the following Standard Mates: Concentric, Coincident, and Parallel.

Notes:

[redacted]

Project 1 – LINKAGE Assembly

Project Objective

Provide a basic understanding of the SolidWorks User Interface: Menus, Toolbars, System feedback, System options, Keyboard shortcuts, and Document Properties.

Obtain the knowledge of the following SolidWorks features: Extruded Base, Extruded Cut and Linear Pattern.

Create three individual parts:

- AXLE.
- SHAFT-COLLAR.
- FLATBAR.

Create an assembly using the three created parts and a sub-assembly downloaded from the CD in the book:

- LINKAGE assembly.

On the completion of this project, you will be able to:

- Establish a SolidWorks session.
- Set units and dimensioning standards for a SolidWorks document.
- Generate a 2D sketch.
- Add and modify dimensions.
- Create a 3D model.
- Insert Geometric Relations.
- Download an assembly into SolidWorks.
- Create an assembly.
- Insert Coincident, Concentric, and Parallel Mates into an assembly.
- Use and understand the following SolidWorks Features:
  - Extruded Base, Extruded Cut, and Linear Pattern.

Project Overview

SolidWorks is a design automation software package used to produce and model parts, assemblies, and drawings.

SolidWorks is a 3D solid modeling CAD program. SolidWorks provides design software to create 3D models and 2D drawings.

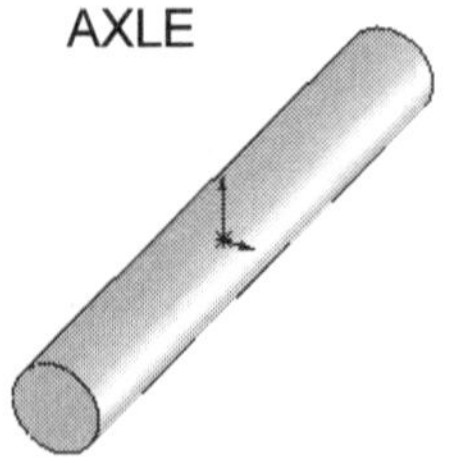
AXLE

SHAFT-COLLAR

Create three parts in this project:

- AXLE.
- SHAFT-COLLAR.
- FLATBAR.

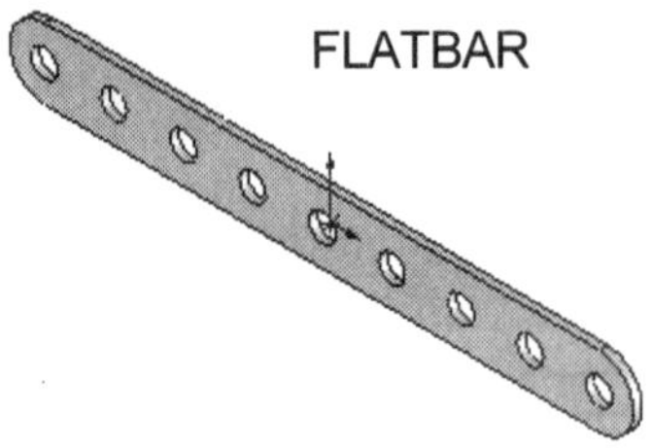
FLATBAR

Download the AIRCYLINDER assembly from the enclosed CD.

The AIRCYLINDER assembly is also available to download from the World Wide Web.

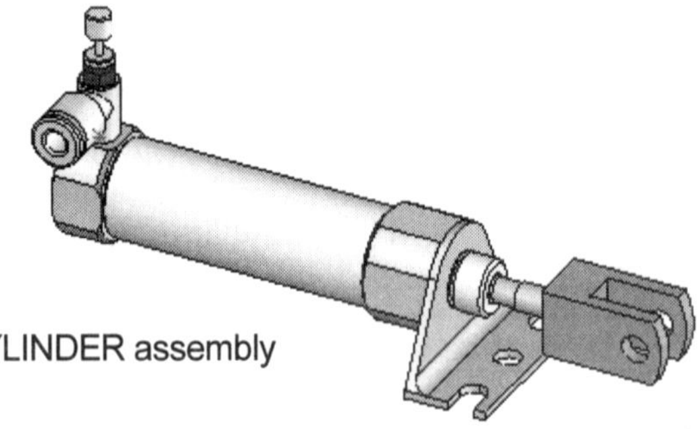
AIRCYLINDER assembly

Combine the created parts and the downloaded AIRCYLINDER assembly to create the LINKAGE assembly.

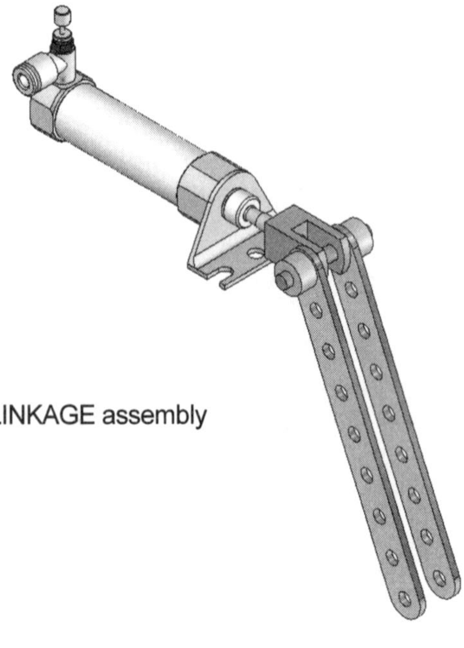
LINKAGE assembly

AXLE Part

The AXLE is a cylindrical steel rod. The AXLE supports the two FLATBAR parts.

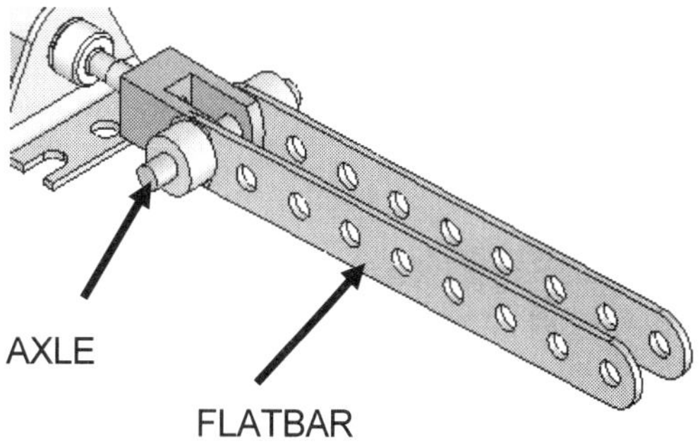

The AXLE rotates about its axis. The dimensions for the AXLE are determined from the other components in the LINKAGE assembly.

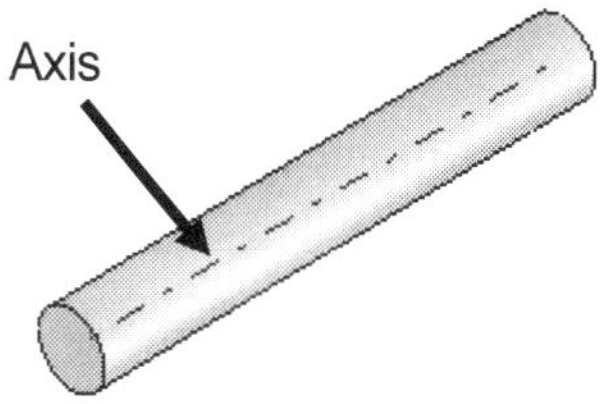

Start a new SolidWorks session. Create the AXLE part.

Use features to create parts. Features are the building blocks that add or remove material.

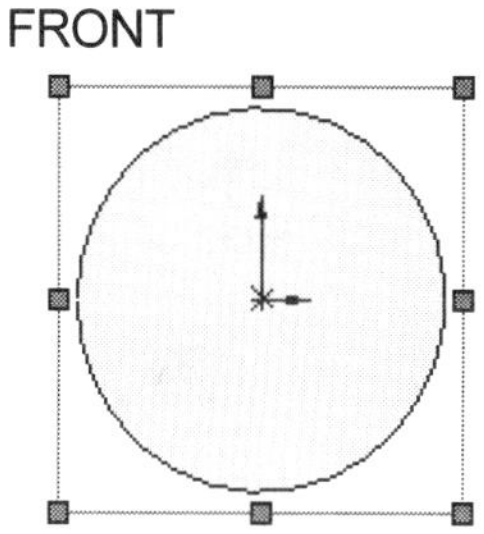

Utilize the Extruded Base feature. The Extruded Base feature adds material. The Base feature is the first feature of the part. The Base feature is the foundation of the part. Keep the Base feature simple!

The Base feature geometry for the AXLE is an extrusion. How do you create a solid Extruded Base feature for the AXLE?

- Sketch a circular profile on the Front plane, centered at the Origin.
- Extend the profile perpendicular (⊥) to the Front plane.

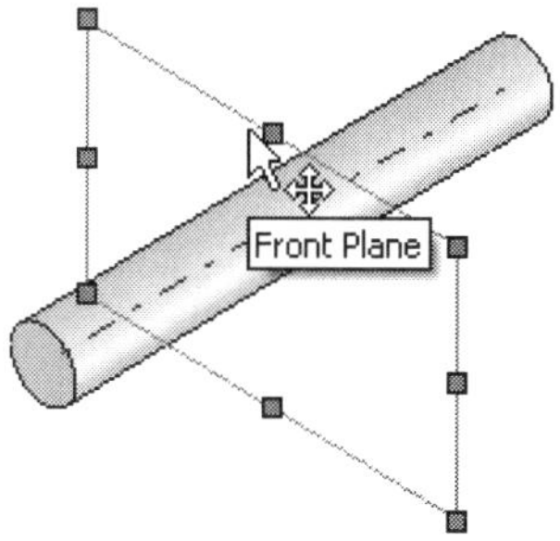

Utilize symmetry. Extrude the sketch with the Mid Plane End Condition in Direction 1. The Extruded Base feature is centered on both sides of the Front plane.

Start a SolidWorks session. The SolidWorks application is located in the Programs folder.

SolidWorks displays the Tip of the Day box. Read the Tip of the Day to obtain additional knowledge on SolidWorks.

Open a new part. Select File, New from the Main menu. There are two options for new documents: Novice and Advanced. Select the Advanced option. Select the Part document.

Activity: Start a SolidWorks Session

Start a SolidWorks 2007 session.

1) Click **Start** from the Windows Taskbar. Click **All Programs** All Programs ▶.

2) Click the **SolidWorks 2007** folder.

3) Click the **SolidWorks 2007** SolidWorks 2007 application. The SolidWorks program window opens. Note: Do not open a document at this time.

If available, double-click the SolidWorks 2007 icon on the Windows desktop to start a SolidWorks session.

Read the Tip of the Day dialog box.

4) Click the **Collapse arrow** » in the Task Pane to close the Tip of the Day. If you do not see this screen, click the SolidWorks **Resources** icon on the right side of the Graphics window located in the Task Pane.

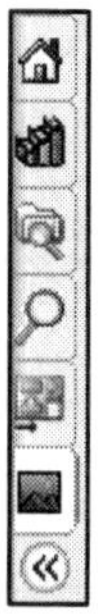

The SolidWorks 2007 Task Pane is displayed when a SolidWorks session starts. The Task Pane can be displayed in the following states: Visible or hidden, expanded or collapsed, pinned or unpinned, docked or floating. The Task Pane contains the following standard tabs: SolidWorks Resources, Design Library, File Explorer, Search, View Palette, and PhotoWorks Items.

If you do not see the PhotoWorks Items tab, click Tools, Add-Ins from the Main menu. Check the PhotoWorks box. Click OK.

SolidWorks Resources

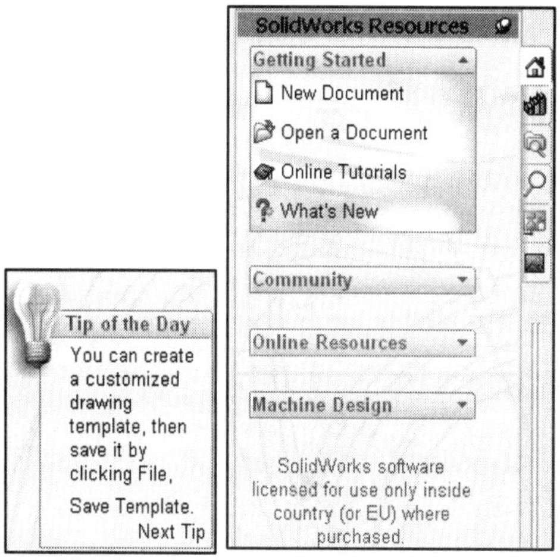

Utilize the left/right arrows to expand or collapse the Task Pane options. The basic SolidWorks Resources menu displays the following default selections:

- Getting Started.
- Community.
- Online Resources.
- Tip of the Day.

Other user interfaces are available to be displayed during the initial software installation selection: Machine Design, Mold Design, or Consumer Products Design. The illustration displays the Machine Design user interface.

Design Library

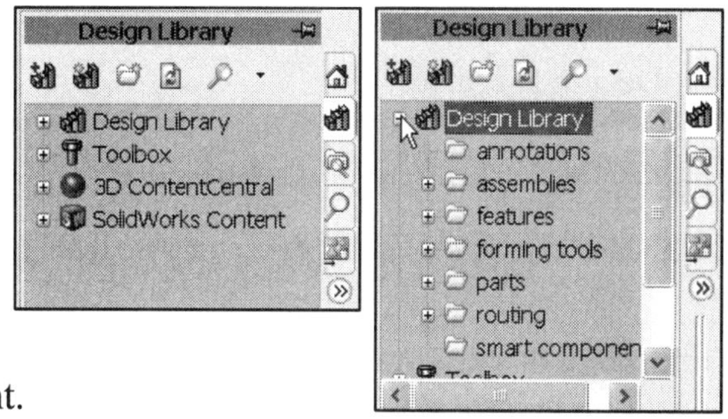

The Design Library contains reusable parts, assemblies, and other elements, including library features.

The Design Library tab contains four default selections. Each default selection contains additional sub categories. The selections are: Design Library, Toolbox, 3D ContentCentral, and SolidWorks Content.

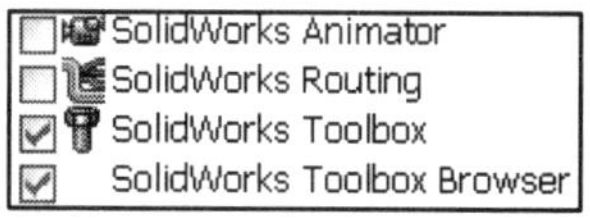

Click Tools, Add-Ins.., SolidWorks Toolbox and SolidWorks Toolbox Browser to active the SolidWorks Toolbox.

To access the Design Library folders in a non network environment, click Add File Location, enter: C:\Program Files\SolidWorks\data\design library. Click OK. In a network environment, contact your IT department for system details.

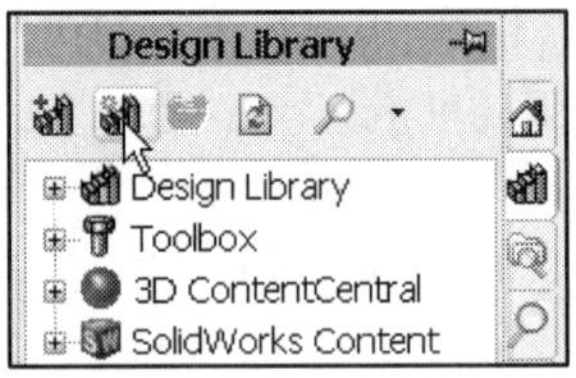

SolidWorks File Explorer

File Explorer in the Task Pane duplicates the function of Windows Explorer from your local computer and displays the recent and open documents in the SolidWorks directories.

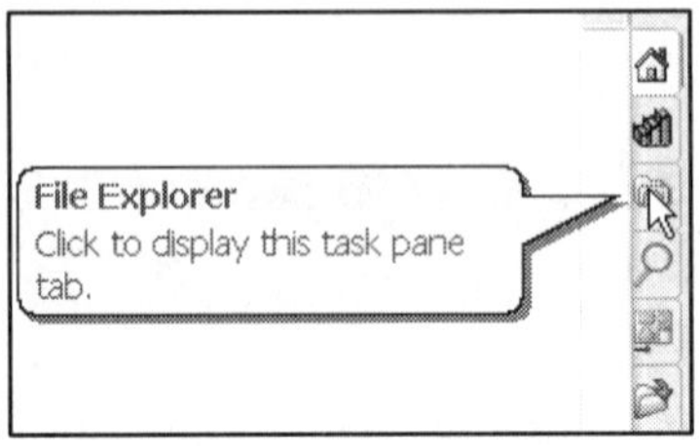

SolidWorks Search

Microsoft Windows Search is installed with SolidWorks and indexes the resources once before searching begins, either after installation, or when you initiate the first search.

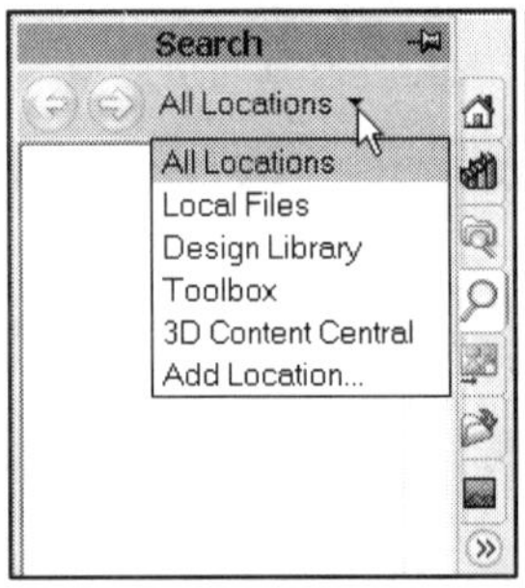

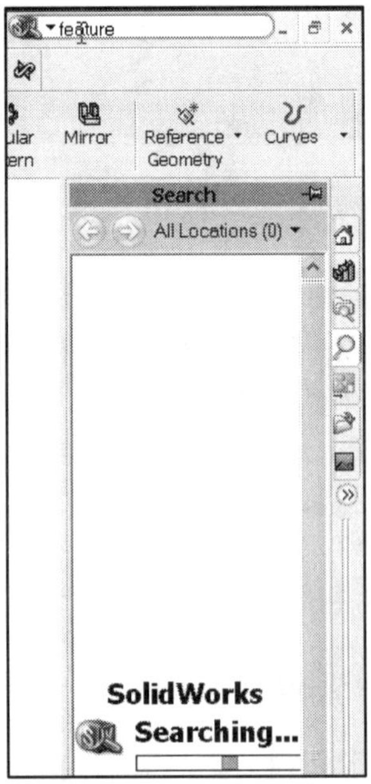

The SolidWorks Search box is displayed in the upper right corner of the SolidWorks Graphics window. Enter the text or key words to search. Click the drop down arrow to view the last 10 recent searches.

The Search tool in the Task Pane searches the following locations:

- All locations.
- Local Files.
- Design Library.
- SolidWorks Toolbox.
- 3D ContentCentral.
- Added location.

Select any or all of the above locations. If you do not select a file location, all locations are searched.

View Palette

Use the View Palette, located in the Task Pane, to insert drawing views of an active part, or click the Browse button to locate the desired model. Click and drag the desired view from the View Palette into an active drawing sheet to create a drawing view.

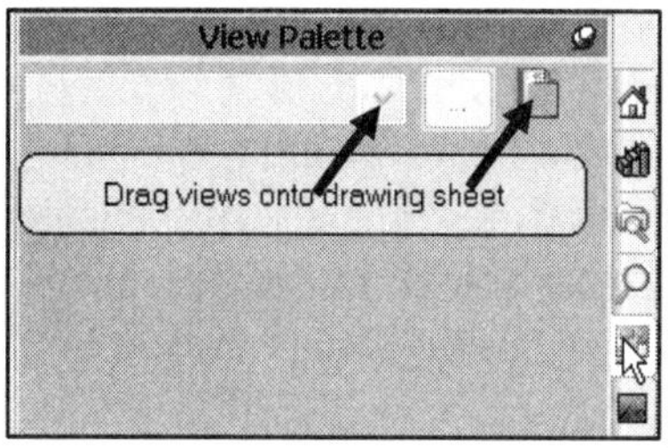

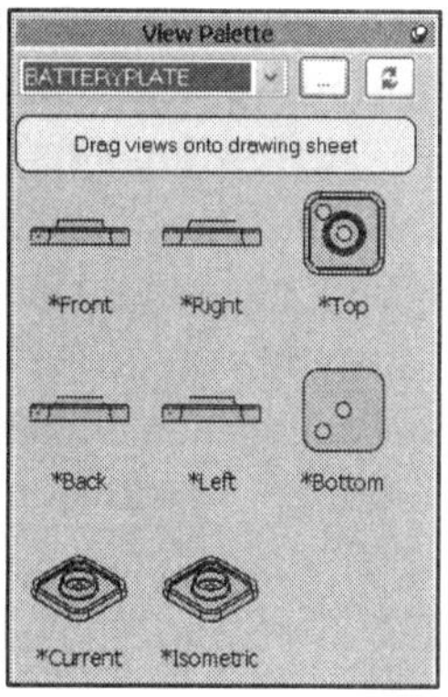

Auto Recovery

If auto recovery is initiated in the System Options section and the system terminates unexpectedly with an active document, the saved information files are available on the Task Pane Document Recovery tab.

PhotoWorks

PhotoWorks Items create photo-realistic images of SolidWorks models. PhotoWorks provides many professional rendering effects. PhotoWorks contains the following default folders: Scene, Materials, Decals, and Lighting.

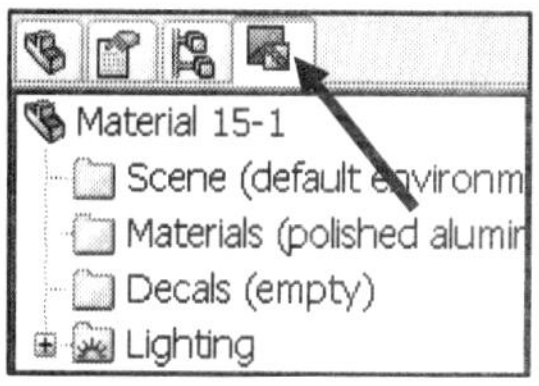

Click Tools, Add-Ins.., PhotoWorks from the Main menu to activate the PhotoWorks feature.

Drop-Down Menu

SolidWorks takes advantage of the familiar Microsoft Windows® graphical user interface. Communicate with SolidWorks either through the drop-down menus or the application toolbars. A command is an instruction that informs SolidWorks to perform a task.

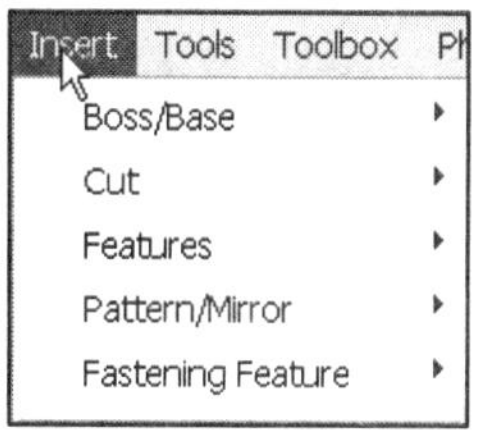

To close a SolidWorks drop-down menu, press the Esc key. You can also click inside the SolidWorks Graphics window, or click another drop-down menu. The drop-down menu options perform three basic functions. They are:

- Displays a SolidWorks dialog box.
- Submits a command to create or modify a model or drawing.
- Offers an expanded set of tools located in the SolidWorks toolbars.

Fly-out FeatureManager

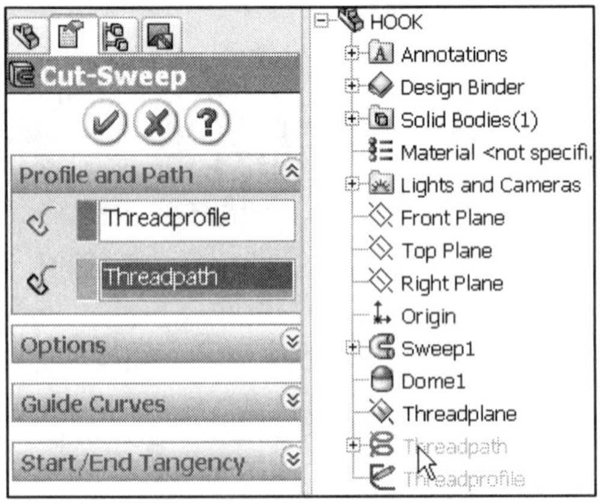

The fly-out FeatureManager design tree allows you to view and select items in the PropertyManager and the FeatureManager design trees at the same time. The fly-out FeatureManager provides the ability to select items which may be difficult to view or select from the Graphics window. You can hide, modify the transparency of, go to, or zoom to selected items.

You cannot suppress items or roll back the build.

Throughout the book, you will select commands and command options from the drop-down menus, fly-out FeatureManager, or from the SolidWorks main toolbars.

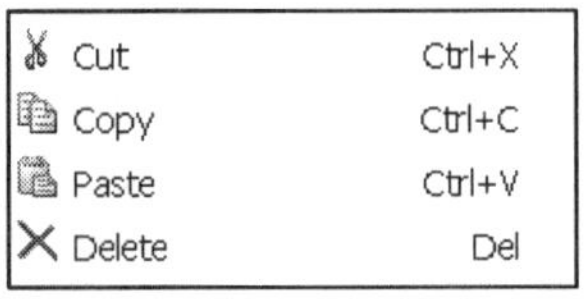

Another method for accessing a command is to use an accelerator key. Accelerator keys are special keystrokes which activate the drop-down menu options. Some commands in the menu bar and items in the drop-down menus have an underlined character. Pressing the Alt key followed by the key corresponding to the underlined character activates that command or option.

Right Click Pop-up menus

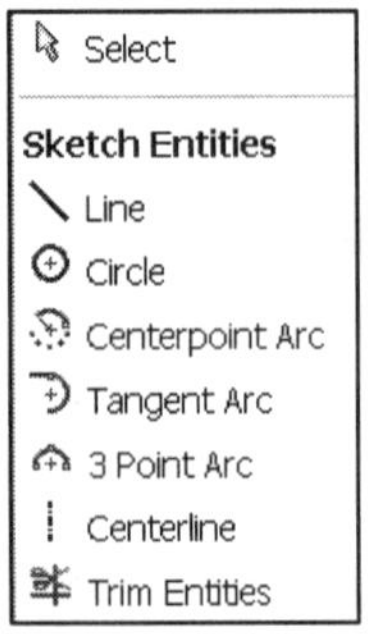

Right-click in the Graphics window to display a context-sensitive shortcut menu. If you are in the middle of a command, this menu displays a list of options related to that command. Example: if you right-click your mouse before picking the first point of the Rectangle tool, a menu is displayed in the Graphics window. The menu displays Sketch Entities, Selected Entity, and other Relations and menu options.

FeatureManager design tree

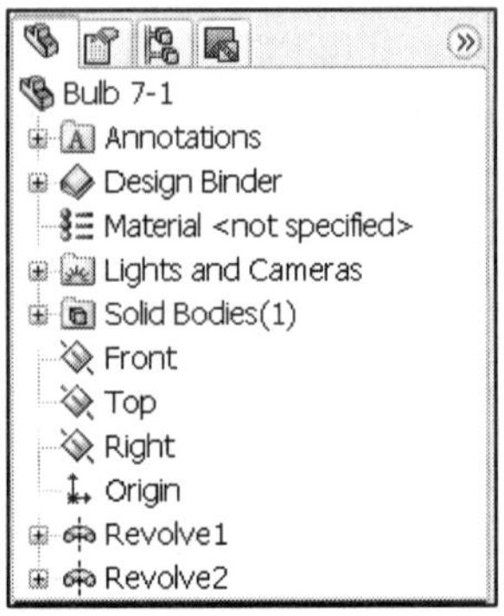

The FeatureManager design tree is located on the left side of the SolidWorks Graphics window. The FeatureManager design tree provides a summarized view of the active part, assembly, or drawing. The FeatureManager displays the details on how your part, assembly, or drawing was created.

Understand the FeatureManager design tree to troubleshoot your model. The FeatureManager is used extensively throughout this book. Expand, collapse, and scroll the FeatureManager design tree.

To collapse all items in the FeatureManager, right-click and select Collapse items, or press the Shift+C keys.

Confirmation Corner

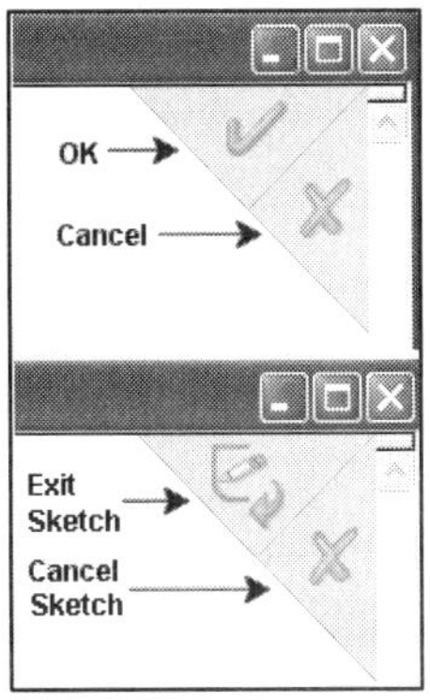

When numerous SolidWorks commands are active, a symbol or a set of symbols is displayed in the upper right corner of the Graphics window. This area is called the Confirmation Corner.

When you activate or open a sketch, the confirmation corner box displays two symbols. The first symbol is the sketch tool icon. The second symbol is a large red X. These two symbols supply a visual reminder that you are in an active sketch.

There are two modes in the New SolidWorks Document dialog box: Novice and Advanced. The Novice option is the default option with three templates. The Advanced option contains access to more templates.

Create a new part.

5) Click **File**, **New** from the Main menu.

Select Advanced Mode.

6) Click the **Advanced** button to display the New SolidWorks Document dialog box in Advanced mode.

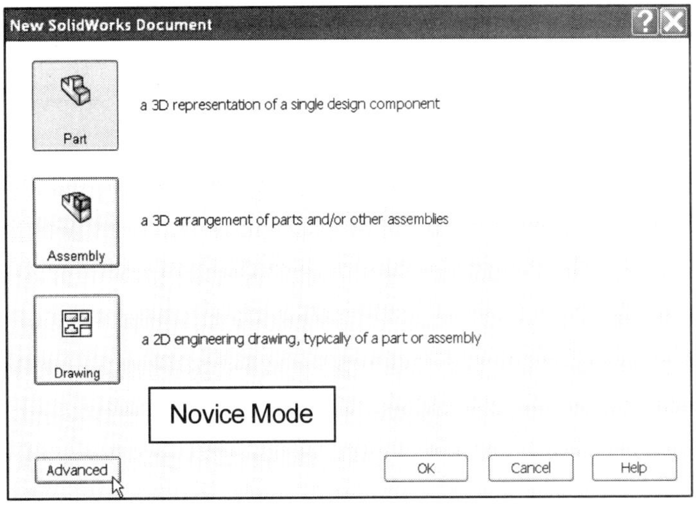

7) The Templates tab is the default tab. Part is the default template from the New SolidWorks Document dialog box. Click **OK**.

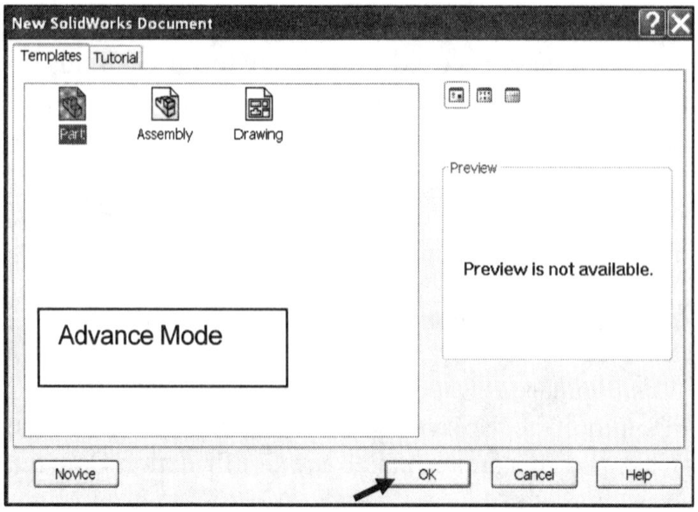

The Advanced mode remains selected for all new documents in the current SolidWorks session. When you exit SolidWorks, the Advanced mode setting is saved.

The default SolidWorks installation contains two tabs in the New SolidWorks Document dialog box: Templates and Tutorial. The Templates tab corresponds to the default SolidWorks templates. The Tutorial tab corresponds to the templates utilized in the Online Tutorials.

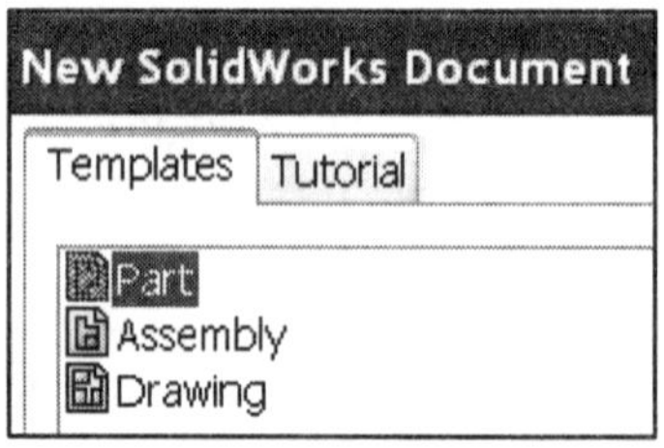

User Interface and CommandManager

The user interface combines the menus, toolbars, and commands with graphic display and Microsoft Windows properties.

Part1 is displayed. Part1 is the new default part window name. The Main menu, Standard Toolbar, View Toolbar, and CommandManager are displayed above the Graphics window.

The part Origin  is displayed in blue in the center of the Graphics window. The Origin represents the intersection of the three default reference planes: Front plane, Top plane, and Right plane. The positive X-axis is horizontal and points to the right of the Origin in the Front view. The positive Y-axis is vertical and point upward in the Front view.

The FeatureManager contains a list of features, reference geometry, and settings utilized in the part.

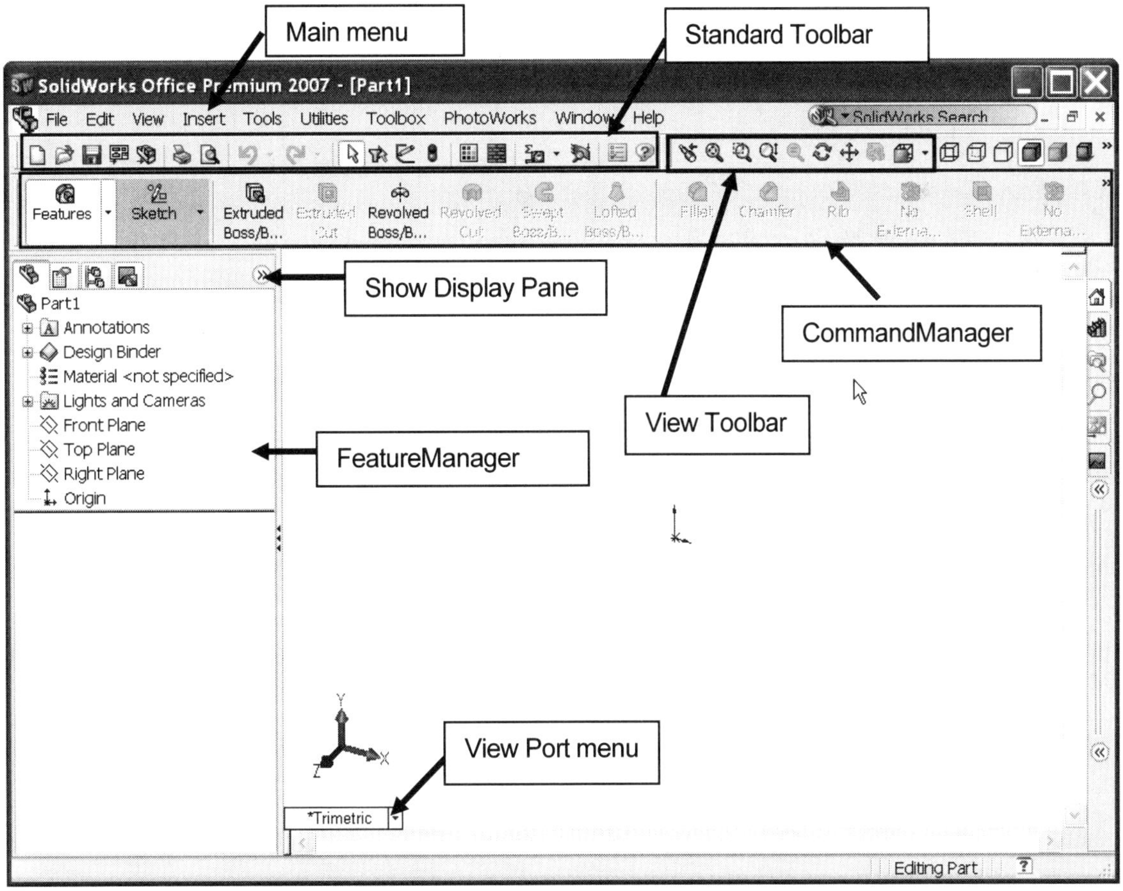

The CommandManager is divided into the Control Area and an expanded toolbar. Select a Control Area icon to display the corresponding toolbar. The Features icon and Features toolbar are selected by default in Part mode.

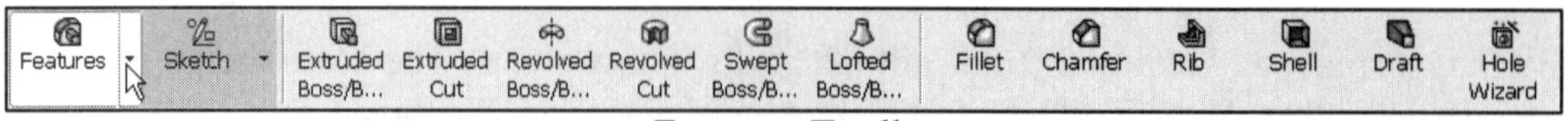

Features Toolbar

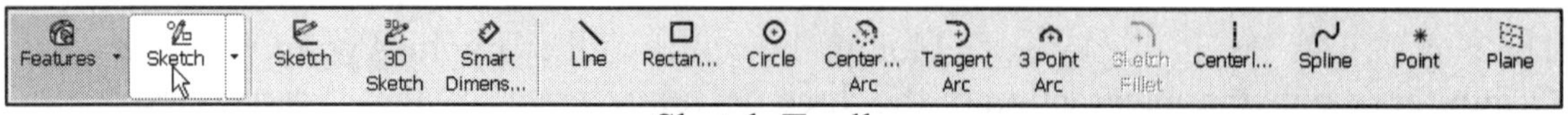

Sketch Toolbar

The CommandManager is utilized in this text. Control the CommandManager display. Right-click in the gray area to the right of the Help entry, in the Main menu. A complete list of toolbars is displayed. Check CommandManager if required.

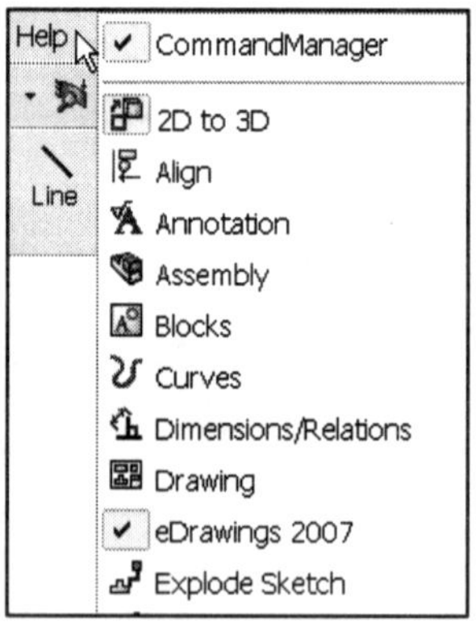

Select individual toolbars from the toolbar list to display in the Graphics window. Reposition toolbars by clicking and dragging their drag handle.

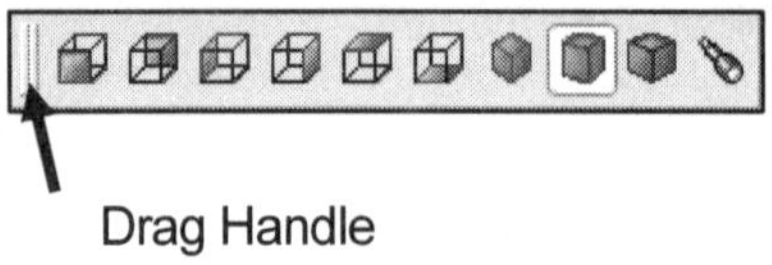

Enter commands from the CommandManager, individual toolbars, and Main menus.

Example:

- Click Extruded Boss/Base in the CommandManager.
- Click Extruded Boss/Base from the Features toolbar.

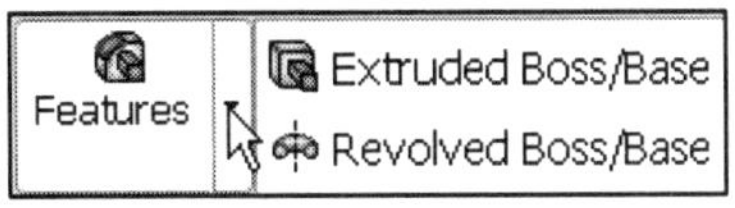

- Click Insert, Boss/Base, Extrude from the Main menu.

Enter additional commands through Shortcut keys and the Right Mouse button Pop-up menus.

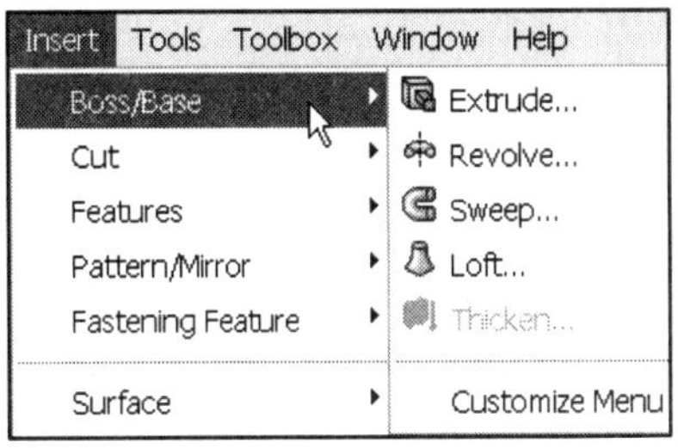

Activity: AXLE Part

Set the Document Properties.

8) Click **Tools**, **Options**, **Document Properties** tab from the Main menu.

9) Select **ANSI** from the Dimensioning standard box.

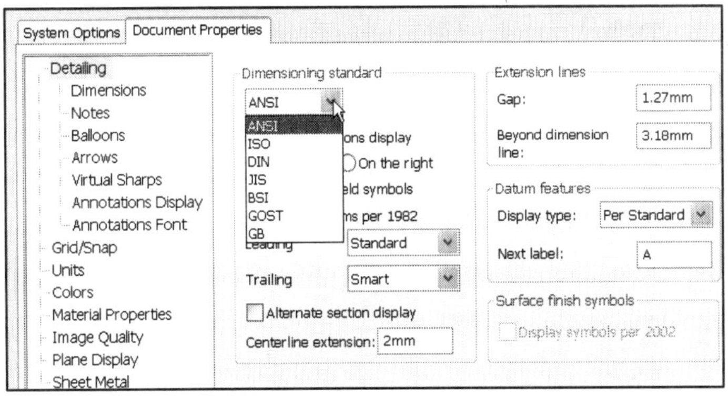

Various detailing options are available depending on the selected standard.

The Dimensioning standard determines the display of dimension text, arrows, symbols, and spacing. Units are the measurement of physical quantities. Millimeter dimensioning and decimal inch dimensioning are the two most common unit types specified for engineering parts and drawings.

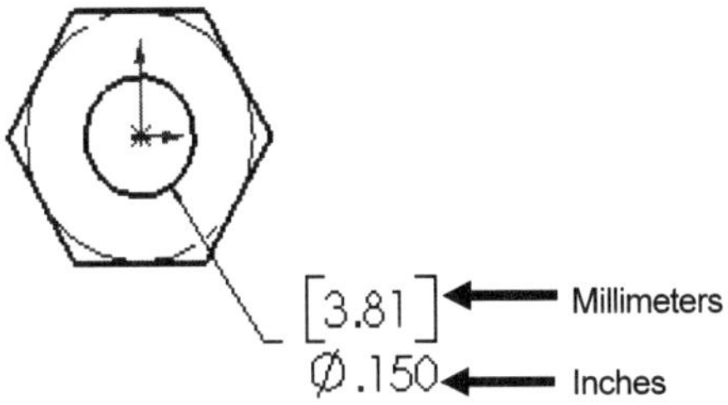

The primary units in this book are provided in IPS, (inch, pound, seconds). The optional secondary units are provided in MMGS, (millimeters, grams, second) and are indicated in brackets [ ].

Illustrations are provided in both inches and millimeters.

Set the part units.

10) Click **Units**. Click **IPS**, (inch, pound, second) [**MMGS**] for Unit system.

11) Select **3**, [**2**] for Length units Decimal places.

12) Select **0**, [**0**] for Angular units Decimal places.

13) Click **OK** from the Document Properties - Units dialog box. The Part FeatureManager is displayed.

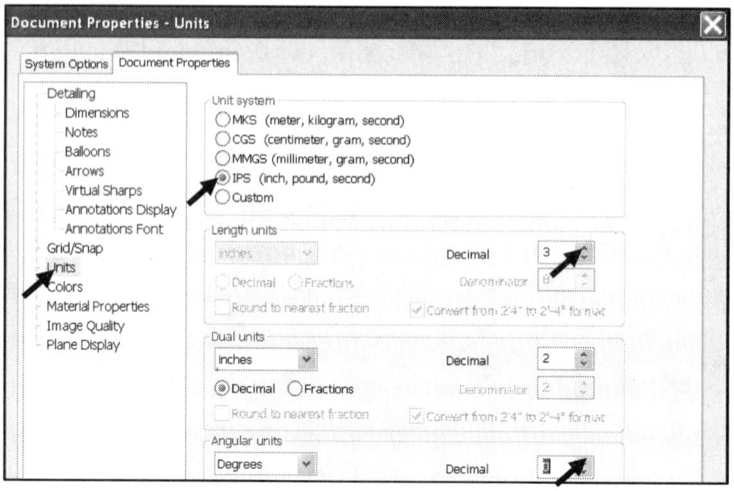

Activity: AXLE Part-Extruded Base Feature

Insert a new Sketch for the Extruded Base feature.

14) Click **Front Plane** from the FeatureManager. This is your Sketch plane.

15) Click **Sketch** Sketch from the Control Area.

16) Click **Circle** Circle from the Sketch toolbar. The Circle PropertyManager is displayed.

17) Drag the **mouse pointer** into the Graphics window. The cursor displays the Circle feedback symbol. The center point of the circle is positioned at the Origin.

18) Click the **Origin** of the circle. The cursor displays the Coincident to point feedback symbol.

19) Drag the **mouse pointer** to the right of the Origin to create the circle as illustrated.

20) Click a **position** to create the circle.

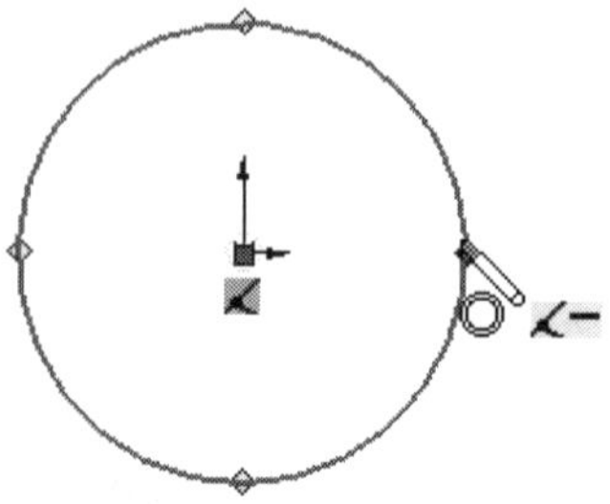

Add a dimension.

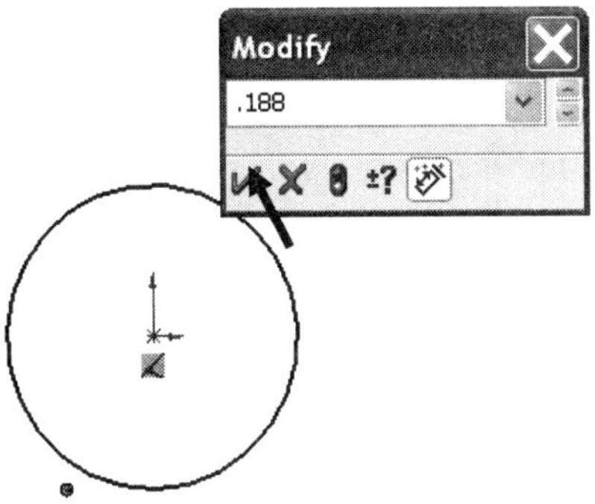

21) Click **Smart Dimension** Smart Dimens... from the Sketch toolbar.

22) Click the **circumference** of the circle. The cursor displays the diameter feedback symbol.

23) Click a **position** diagonally above the circle in the Graphics window.

24) Enter **.188**in, [**4.78**] in the Modify dialog box.

25) Click the **Green Check mark** in the Modify dialog box. The diameter of the circle is .188 inches.

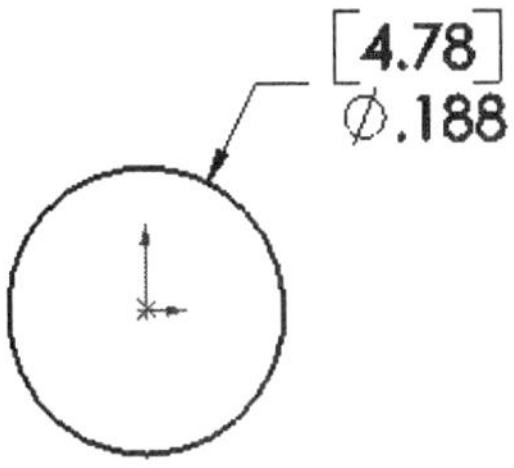

The circular sketch is centered at the Origin. The dimension indicates the diameter of the circle.

If your sketch is not correct, select the UNDO tool. To fit your sketch to the Graphics window, press the f key.

Extrude the sketch to create the Extruded Base Feature.

26) Click **Features** Features from the CommandManager.

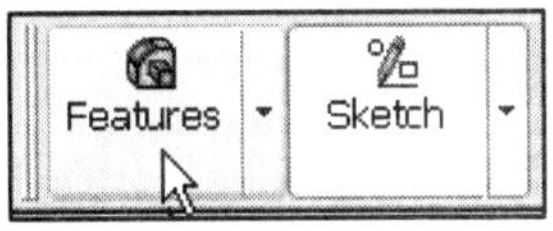

27) Click **Extruded Boss/Base** Extruded Boss/B... from the Features toolbar. The Extrude PropertyManager is displayed.

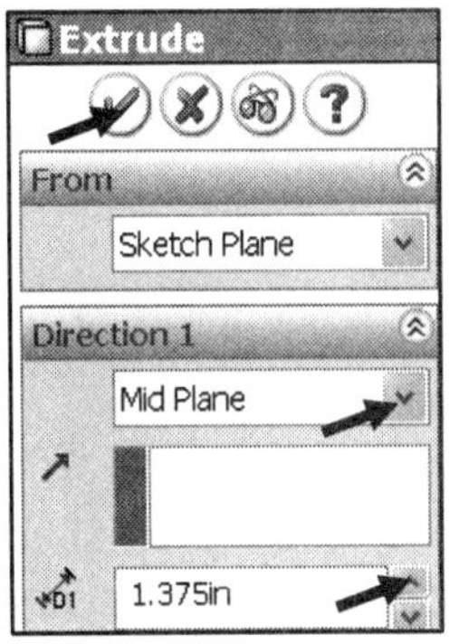

28) Select **Mid Plane** for End Condition in Direction 1.

29) Enter **1.375**in, [**34.93**] for Depth in Direction 1. Accept the default conditions.

30) Click **OK** from the Extrude PropertyManager. Exturde1 is displayed in the FeatureManager.

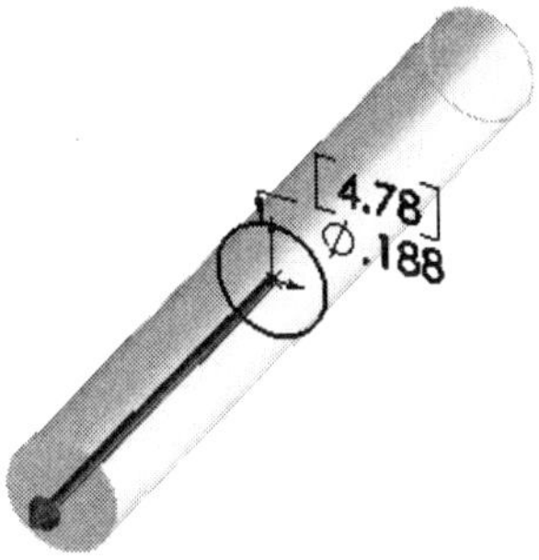

Fit the model to the Graphics window.

31) Press the **f** key.

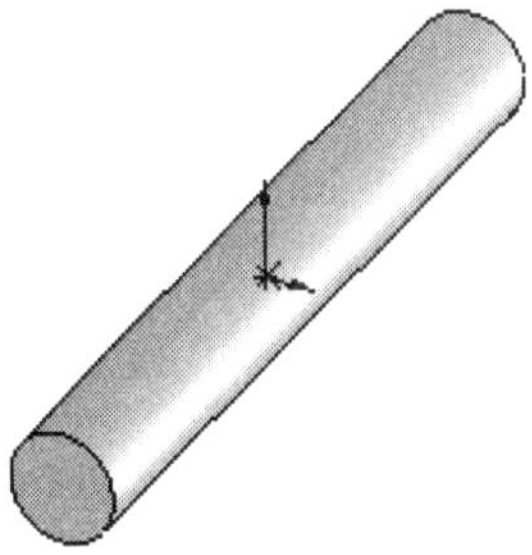

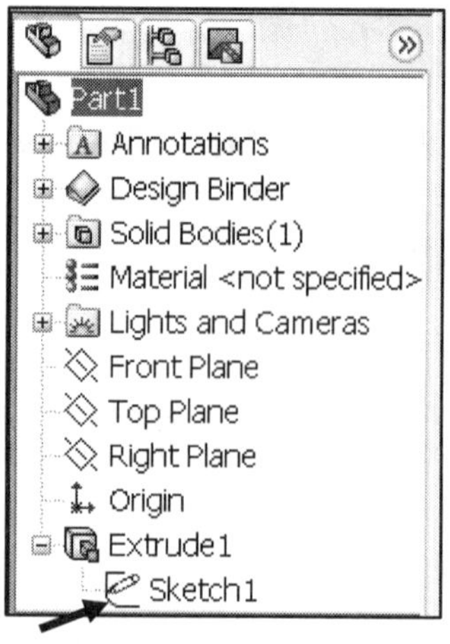

The Extrude PropertyManager displays the parameters utilized to define the feature. The Mid Plane End Condition in the Direction 1 box extrudes the sketch equally on both sides of the Sketch plane. The Depth defines the extrude distance.

The Extrude1 feature name is displayed in the FeatureManager. The FeatureManager lists the features, planes and other geometry that construct the part. Extrude features add material. Extrude features require the following:

- Sketch plane.
- Sketch.
- Depth.

The Sketch plane is the Front plane. The Sketch is a circle with the diameter of .188in, [4.76]. The Depth is 1.375in, [34.93].

Activity: AXLE Part-Save

Save the part.

32) Click **File**, **Save As** from the Main Menu.

33) Double-click the **MY-DOCUMENTS** file folder.

34) Click **Create New Folder**.

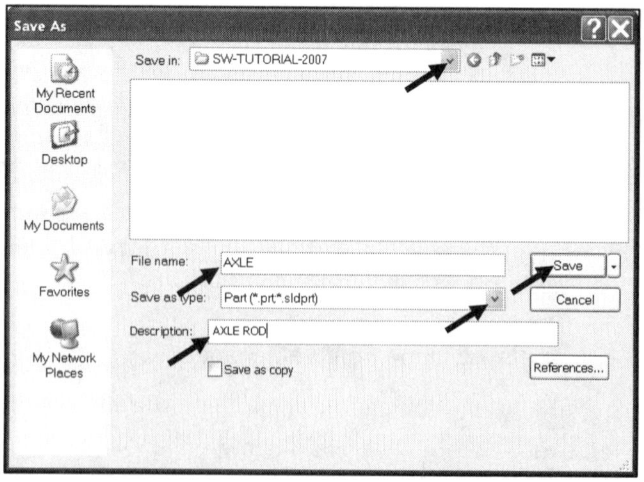

35) Enter **SW-TUTORIAL-2007** for the file folder name.

36) Double-click the **SW-TUTORIAL-2007** file folder. SW-TUTORIAL-2007 is the Save in file folder name.

37) Enter **AXLE** for the File name.

38) Enter **AXLE ROD** for the Description.

39) Click **Save**. The AXLE FeatureManager is displayed.

Organize parts into file folders. The file folder for this project is named: SW-TUTORIAL-2007. Save all documents in the SW-TUTORIAL-2007 file folder. Copy all files from the CD in the book to the SW-TUTORIAL-2007 folder.

Activity: AXLE Part-Edit Color

Modify the color of the part.

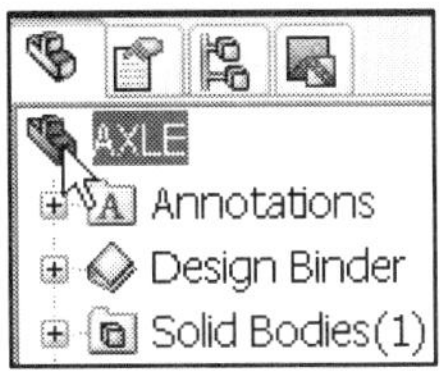

40) Click the **AXLE** AXLE icon at the top of the FeatureManager.

41) Click **Edit Color** from the Standard toolbar. The Color And Optics PropertyManager is displayed. AXLE is displayed in the Selection box.

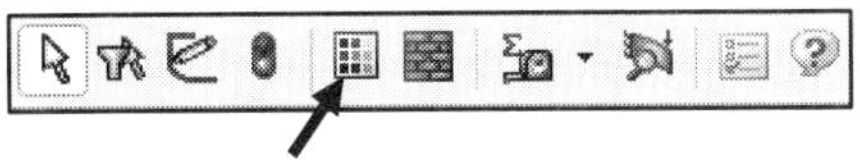

42) Select a **light yellow** color from the Edit Color box.

43) Click **OK** from the Color And Optics PropertyManager.

The SolidWorks FeatureManager design tree provides an indicator informing you on the status of your sketch. The sketch can either be:

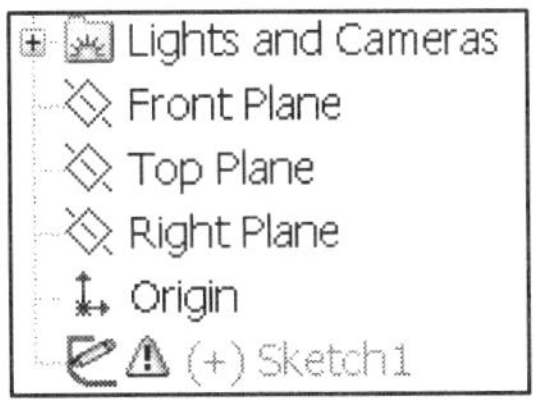

1.) (+) Over defined. The sketch is displayed in red.

2.) (-) Under defined. The sketch is displayed in blue.

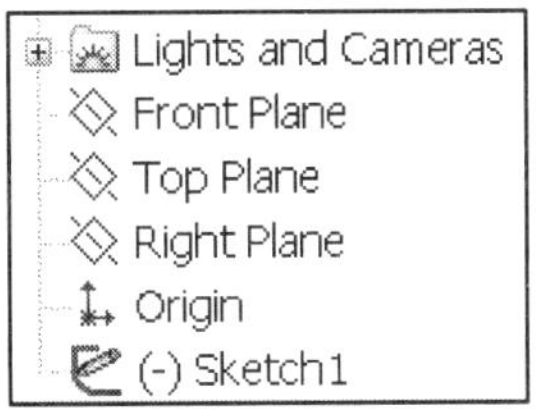

3.) (?) Cannot be solved.

4.) No prefix: the sketch is fully defined. This is the ideal state. A fully defined sketch has complete information and is displayed in black.

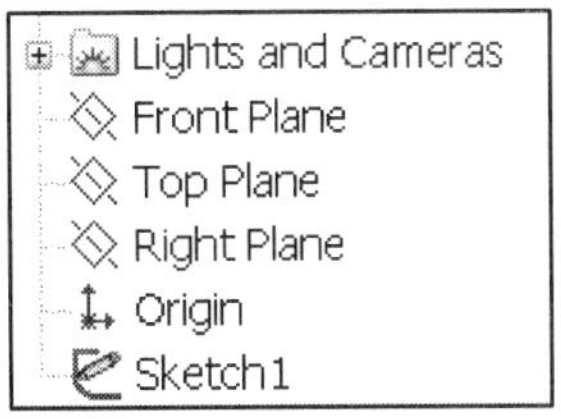

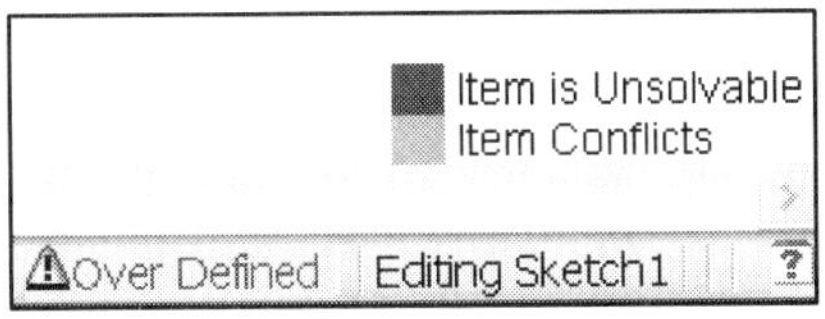

A new feature for 2007 is the SketchXpert PropertyManager. The SketchXpert PropertyManager provides the ability to diagnose an over defined sketch to create a fully defined sketch. Click Over Defined at the bottom of the Graphics window toolbar. The SketchXpert PropertyManager is displayed. Click the Diagnose button.

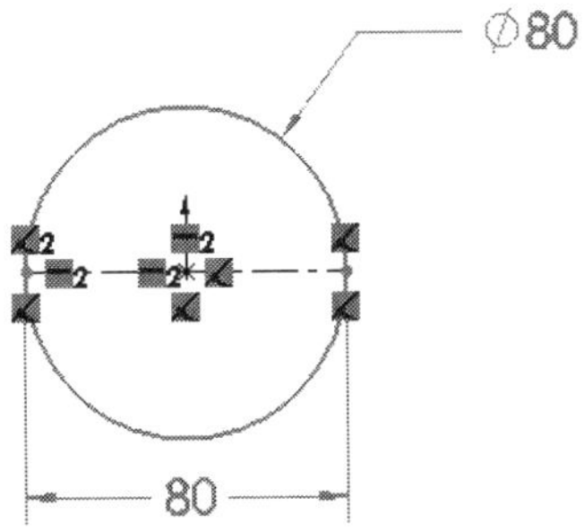

Select the desired solution and click the Accept button from the Results box.

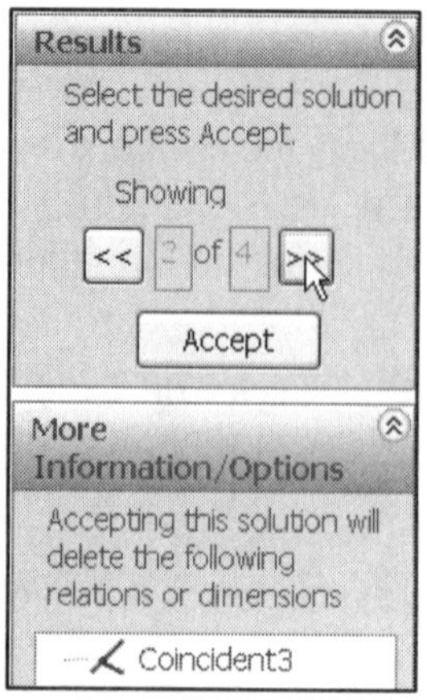

Activity: AXLE Part-Standard Views and View Modes

Display the Standard Views toolbar.

44) If required, click **View**, **Toolbars**, **Standard Views** from the Main menu. The Standard Views toolbar is displayed below the Main menu.

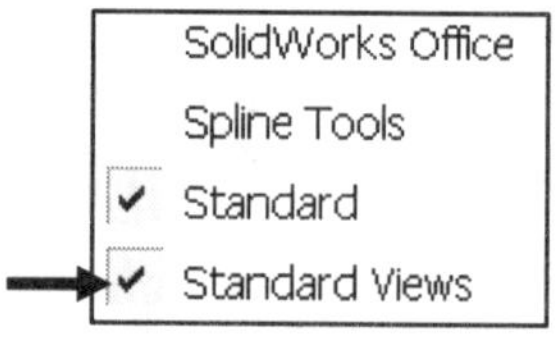

45) Position the **mouse pointer** on an individual toolbar icon to receive a ToolTip.

Orthographic projection is the process of projecting views onto parallel planes with ⊥ projectors. The default reference planes are the Front, Top and Right side viewing planes.

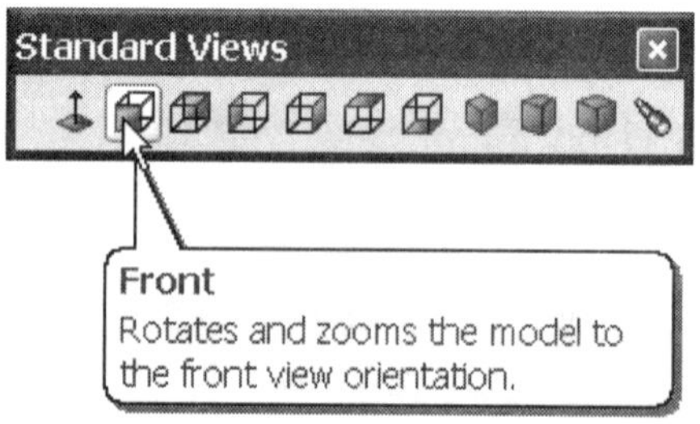

The Isometric view displays the part in 3D with two equal projection angles.

Display the Standard Views for the AXLE.

46) Click **Front view** Front from the Standard Views menu or from the View Port Menu in the Graphics window.

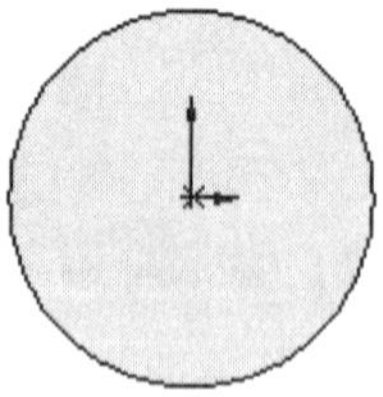

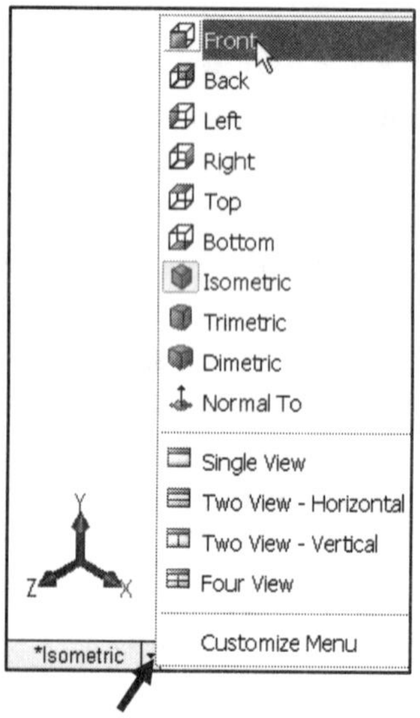

47) Click **Top view** Top.

48) Click **Right view** Right.

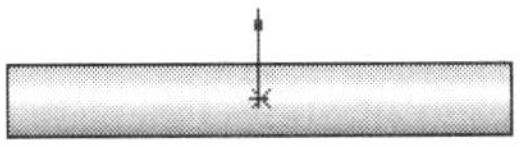

49) Click **Isometric view** Isometric.

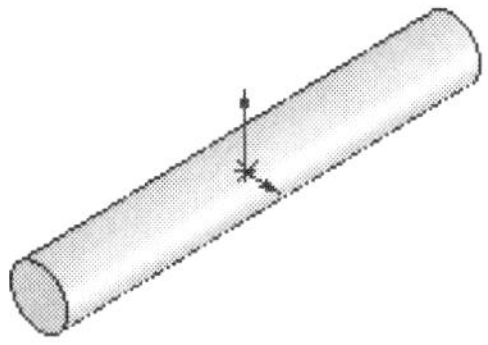

View modes manipulate the model in the Graphics window.

Display the various View modes.

50) Click **Zoom to Fit** to display the full size of the part in the current window.

The defined view fits to the current window.

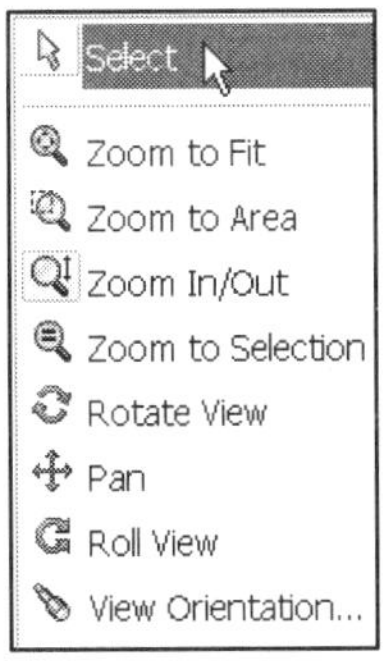

51) Click **Zoom In/Out**. Drag upward to **zoom in**.

52) Drag downward to **zoom out**. Press the lower case **z** key to zoom out. Press the upper case **Z** key to zoom in.

53) **Right-click** in the Graphics window. Click **Select**. Click the **front circular edge** of the AXLE in the Graphics window.

54) Click **Zoom to Selection**. The selected geometry fills the current window.

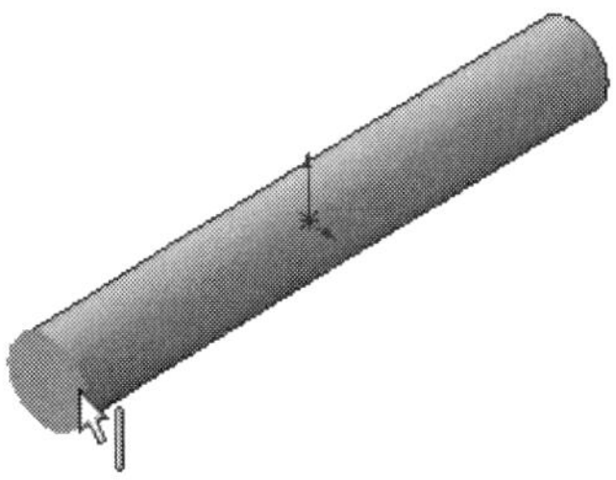

55) Click **Rotate**. Drag the **mouse pointer** to rotate about the screen center.

56) Use the computer keyboard **arrow keys** to rotate in 15-degree increments.

57) Click **Pan**. Drag the **mouse pointer** up, down, left, or right. The model scrolls in the direction of the mouse.

58) Right-click in the **Graphics window** area to display the zoom options.

59) Click **Zoom to Fit**.

Note: View modes remain active until deactivated from the View toolbar or unchecked from the pop-up menu.

Utilize the center wheel of the mouse to Zoom In/Zoom Out and Rotate the model in the Graphics window.

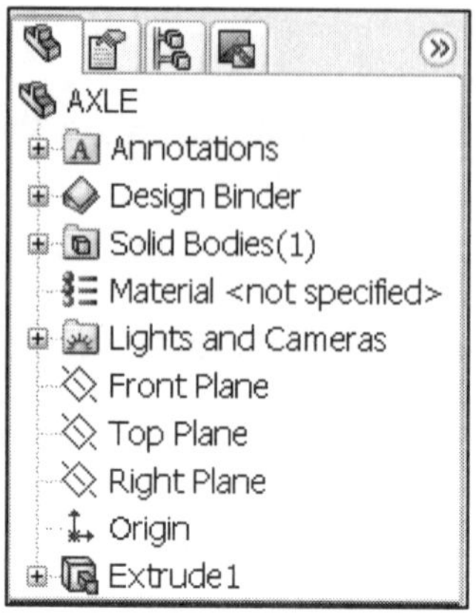

Display the Isometric view.

60) Click **Isometric view** from the Standard Views toolbar.

Save the AXLE part.

61) Click **Save**. The AXLE part is complete.

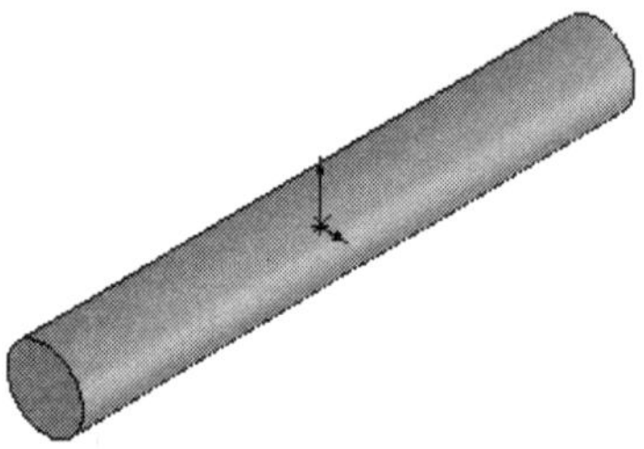

Review the AXLE Part.

The AXLE part utilized an Extruded Base feature. The Extruded Base feature adds material. The Extruded feature required a Sketch plane, Sketch, and Depth. The AXLE Sketch plane was the Front plane. The 2D circle was sketched centered at the Origin. A dimension defined the overall size of the sketch based on the dimensions of mating parts in the LINKAGE assembly.

The name of the feature is Extrude1. Extrude1 utilized the Mid Plane End Condition. The Extrude1 feature is symmetrical about the Front plane.

The Edit Color option modified the part color. Select the Part icon in the FeatureManager to modify the color of the part. Color and a prefix defines the sketch status. A blue sketch is under defined. A black sketch is fully defined. A red sketch is over defined.

The default Reference planes are the Front, Top, and Right side viewing planes. Utilize the Standard Views toolbar or the View Port menu in the lower left side of the Graphics window to display the principle views of a part. The View modes manipulate the model in the Graphics windows. Utilize Zoom, Pan, and Rotate from the View toolbar.

SHAFT-COLLAR Part

The SHAFT-COLLAR part is a hardened steel ring fastened to the AXLE part.

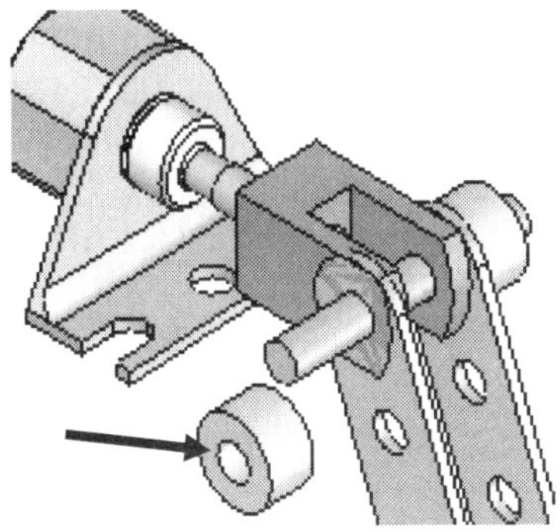

Two SHAFT-COLLAR parts are used to position the two FLATBAR parts on the AXLE.

Create the SHAFT-COLLAR part.

Utilize the Extruded Base feature. The Extruded Base feature requires a 2D circular profile.

Utilize symmetry. Sketch a circle on the Front plane centered at the Origin.

Extrude the sketch with the Mid Plane End Condition. The Extruded Base feature is centered on both sides of the Front plane.

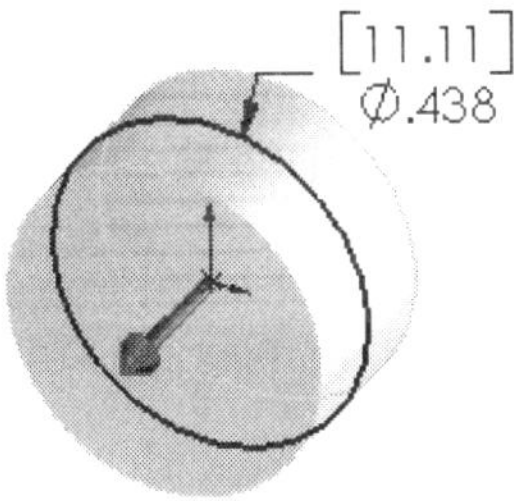

The Extruded Cut feature removes material. Utilize an Extruded Cut feature to create a hole. The Extruded Cut feature requires a 2D circular profile. Sketch a circle on the front face centered at the Origin.

The Through All End Condition extends the Extruded Cut feature from the front face through all existing geometry.

SHAFT-COLLAR

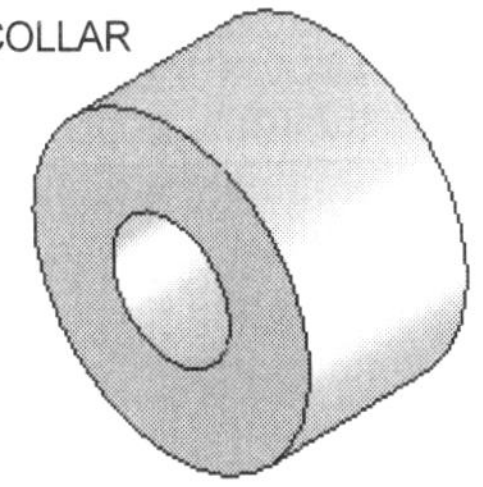

Activity: SHAFT-COLLAR Part-Extruded Base Feature

Create a new part.

62) Click **File**, **New** from the Main Menu. The Templates tab is the default tab. Part is the default template from the New SolidWorks Document dialog box.

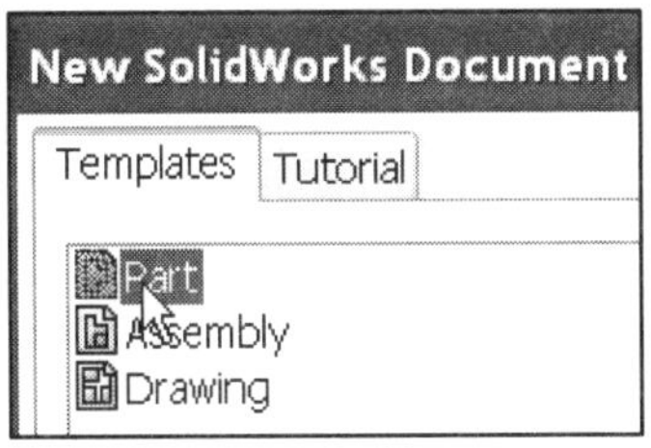

63) Double-click **Part**. The Part FeatureManager is displayed.

Save the Part.

64) Click **File**, **Save As** from the Main menu.

65) Enter **SHAFT-COLLAR** for File name in the SW-TUTORIAL-2007 folder.

66) Enter **SHAFT-COLLAR** for Description.

67) Click **Save**. The SHAFT-COLLAR FeatureManager is displayed.

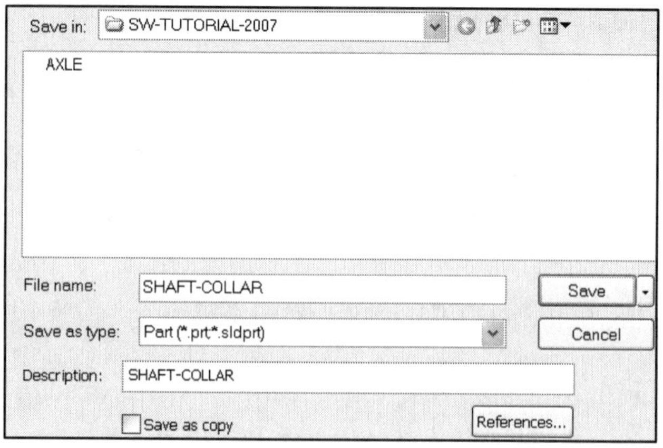

Set the Dimension standard and part units.

68) Click **Tools**, **Options**, **Document Properties** tab from the Main menu.

69) Select **ANSI** from the Dimensioning standard box.

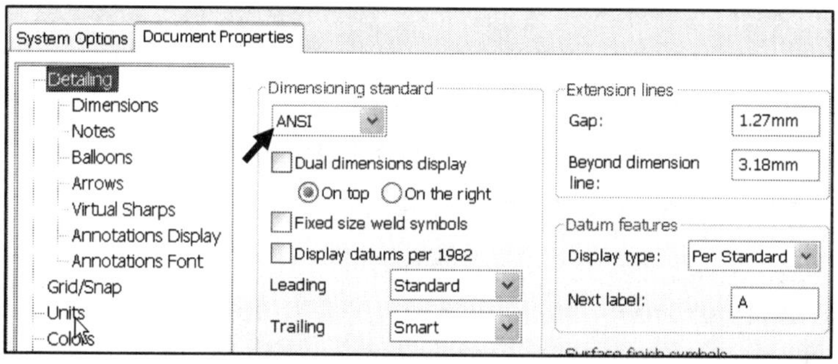

70) Click **Units**.

71) Click **IPS** (inch, pound, second), [**MMGS**] for Unit system.

72) Select **3**, [**2**] for Length units Decimal places.

73) Select **0**, [**0**] for Angular units Decimal places.

74) Click **OK** from the Document Properties - Units dialog box.

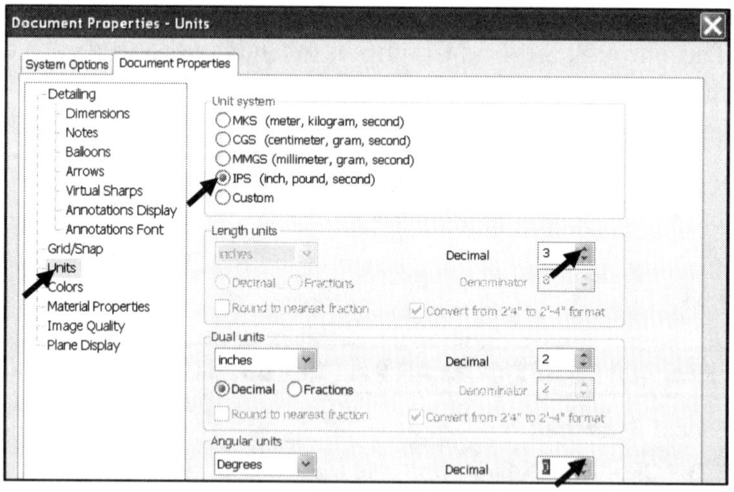

Insert a new Sketch for the Extruded Base feature.

75) Click **Front Plane** from the FeatureManager. This is the Sketch plane.

76) Click **Sketch** Sketch from the Control Area.

77) Click **Circle** Circle from the Sketch toolbar. Click the **Origin**. The cursor displays the Coincident to point feedback symbol.

78) Drag the **mouse pointer** to the right of the Origin as illustrated. Click a **position** to create the circle.

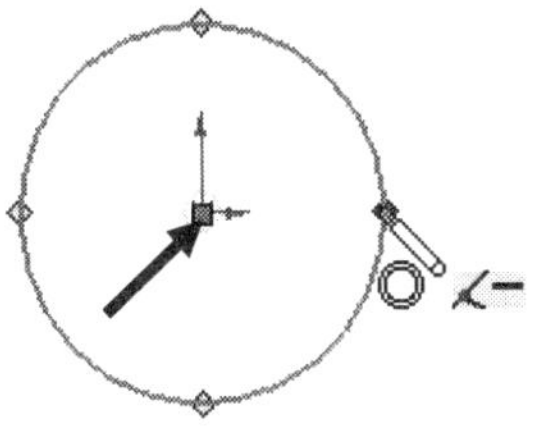

Add a dimension.

79) Click **Smart Dimension** Smart Dimens... from the Sketch toolbar. Click the **circumference** of the circle. The cursor displays the diameter feedback symbol.

80) Click a **position** diagonally above the circle in the Graphics window.

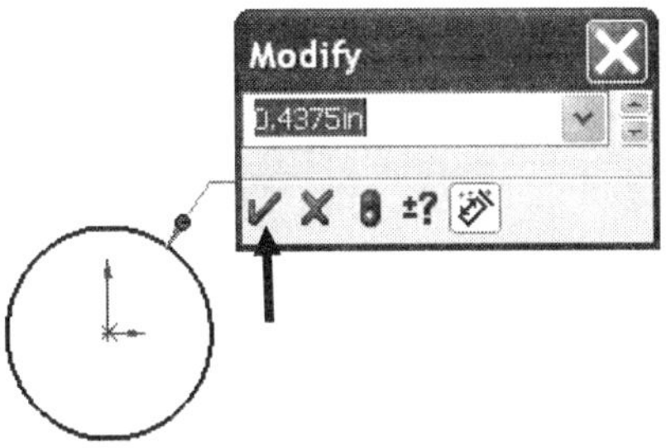

81) Enter **.4375**in, [**11.11**] in the Modify dialog box.

82) Click the **Green Check mark** in the Modify dialog box. The black sketch is fully defined.

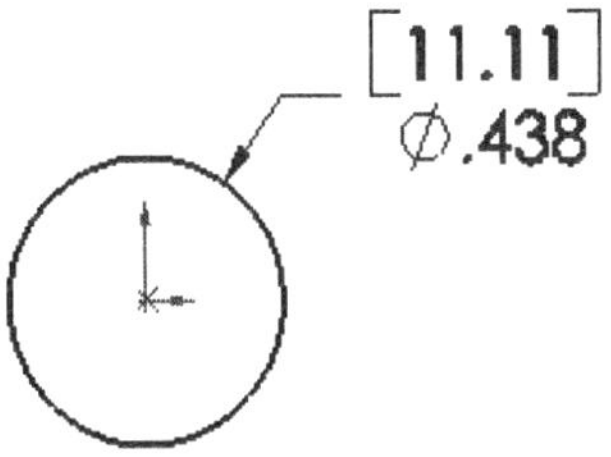

Note: Three decimal places are displayed. The diameter value .4375 rounds to .438.

Extrude the sketch to create the Base feature.

83) Click **Features** Features from the CommandManager.

84) Click **Extruded Boss/Base** Extruded Boss/B... from the Features toolbar. The Extrude PropertyManager is displayed.

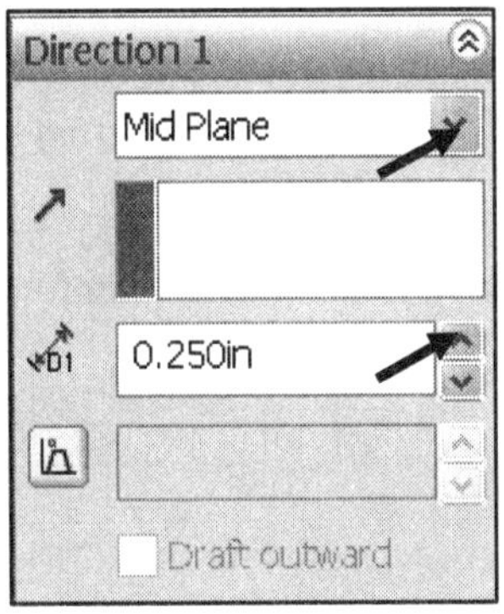

85) Select **Mid Plane** for End Condition in Direction 1.

86) Enter .**250**in, [**6.35**] for Depth. Accept the default conditions.

87) Click **OK** from the Extrude PropertyManager. Extrude1 is displayed in the FeatureManager.

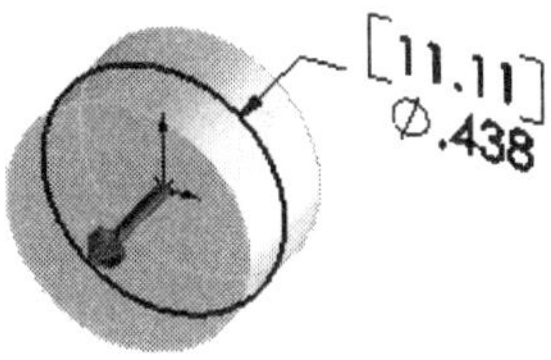

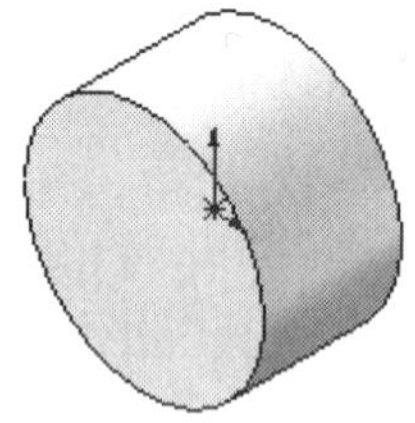

Fit the model to the Graphics window.

88) Press the **f** key.

89) Click **Isometric view** .

Save the model.

90) Click **Save** .

Activity: SHAFT-COLLAR Part-Extruded Cut Feature

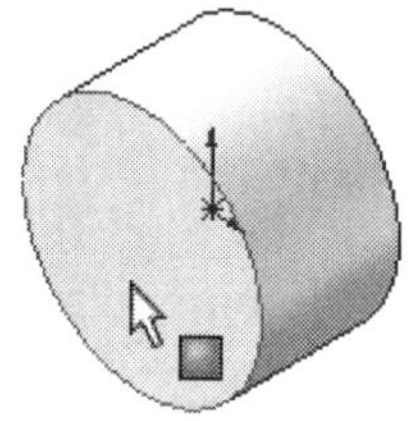

Insert a new sketch for the Extruded Cut feature.

91) Click the **front circular face** of the Extrude1 feature for the Sketch plane. The mouse pointer displays the face feedback icon.

View the mouse pointer for the correct geometry: line, face, point, or vertex.

92) Click **Sketch** Sketch from the Control Area.

93) Click **Circle** Circle from the Sketch toolbar. The Circle PropertyManager is displayed.

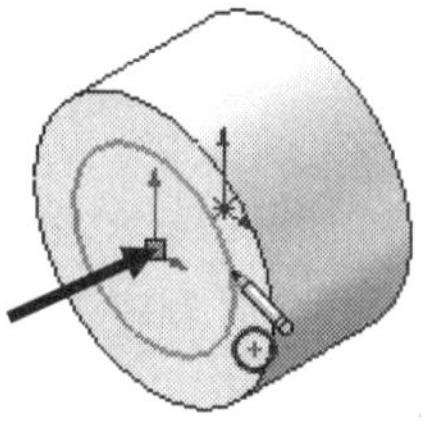

94) Click the **Origin** . The cursor displays the Coincident to point feedback symbol.

95) Drag the **mouse pointer** to the right of the Origin.

96) Click a **position** to create the circle as illustrated.

Add a dimension.

97) Click **Smart Dimension** Smart Dimens... from the Sketch toolbar.

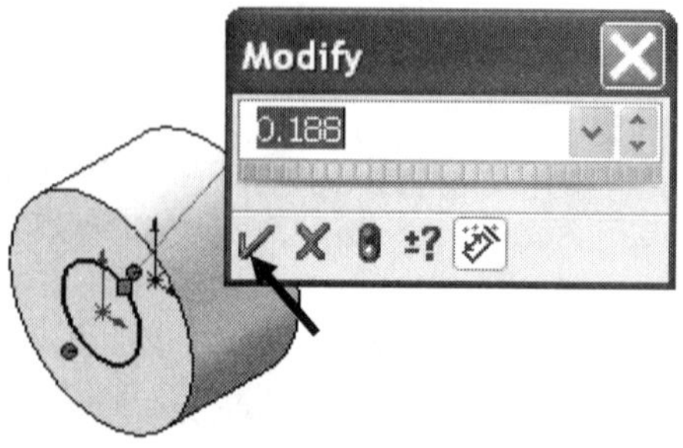

98) Click the **circumference** of the circle.

99) Click a **position** diagonally above the circle in the Graphics window.

100) Enter **.188**in, [**4.78**] in the Modify dialog box.

101) Click the **Green Check mark** in the Modify dialog box.

Insert an Extruded Cut feature.

102) Click **Features** Features from the CommandManager.

103) Click **Extruded Cut** Extruded Cut from the Features toolbar. The Cut-Extrude PropertyManager is displayed.

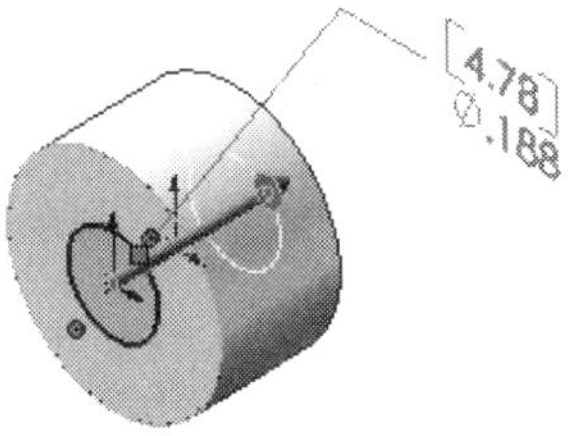

104) Select **Through All** for End Condition in Direction 1. The direction arrow points to the right. Accept the default conditions.

105) Click **OK** from the Cut-Extrude PropertyManager. Cut-Extrude1 is displayed in the FeatureManager,

The Extruded Cut feature is named Cut-Extrude1. The Through All End Condition removes material from the Front plane through the Extrude1 geometry.

Activity: SHAFT-COLLAR-Modify Dimensions and Edit Color

Modify the dimensions.

106) Click **Trimetric view**. Double-click the **outside face** of the SHAFT-COLLAR. The Extrude1 dimensions are displayed. Sketch dimensions are displayed in black. The Extrude depth dimensions are displayed in blue.

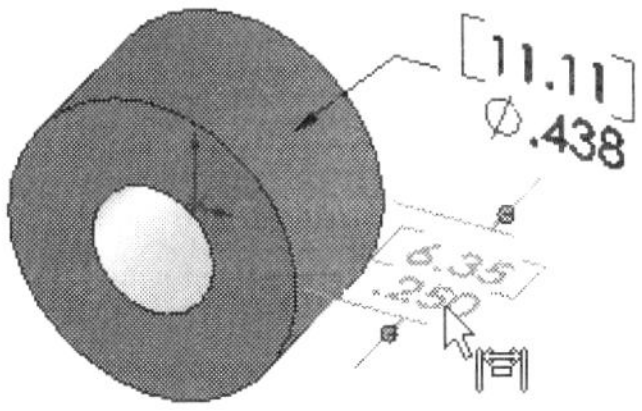

107) Double-click the .**250**in, [**6.35**] depth dimension.

108) Enter .**500**in, [**12.70**].

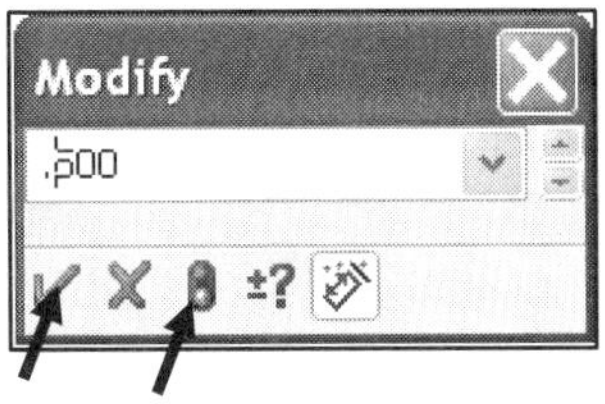

109) Click **Rebuild** from the Modify pop-up box.

110) Click the **Green Check mark** from the Modify dialog box.

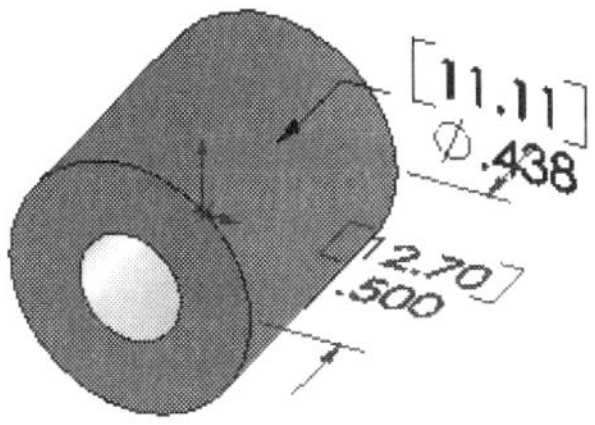

The Extrude1 and Cut-Extrude1 features are modified.

Return to the original dimensions.

111) Double-click the .**500**in, [**6.35**] depth dimension.

112) Enter .**250**in, [**6.35**] in the Modify dialog box.

113) Click **Rebuild** from the Modify dialog box.

114) Click the **Green Check mark** .

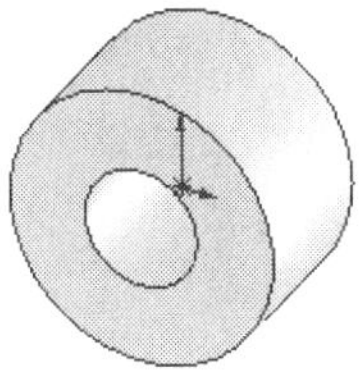

115) Click **OK** from the Dimension PropertyManager.

Modify the part color.

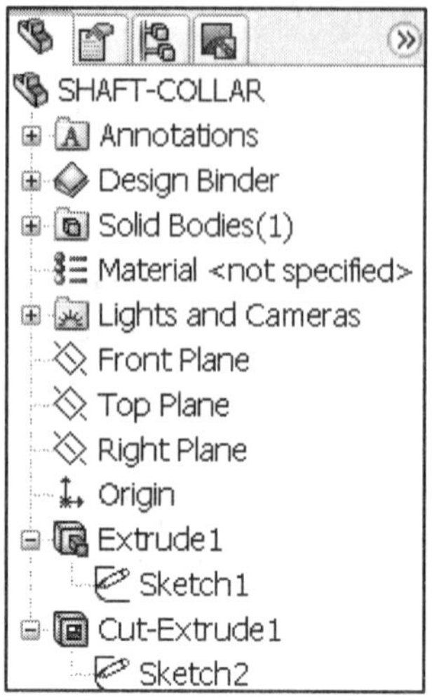

116) Click the **SHAFT-COLLAR Part** SHAFT-COLLAR icon at the top of the FeatureManager.

117) Click **Edit Color** from the Standard toolbar.

118) Select a **light blue** color from the Color and Optics PropertyManager.

119) Click **OK** from the Color And Optics PropertyManager.

Save the SHAFT-COLLAR part.

120) Click **Save** . The SHAFT-COLLAR part is complete.

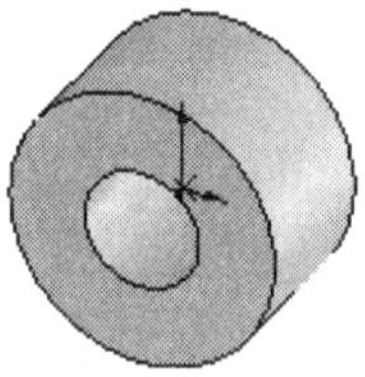

Review the SHAFT-COLLAR Part.

The SHAFT-COLLAR utilized an Extruded Base feature. The Extruded Base feature adds material. An Extruded feature required a Sketch plane, Sketch, and Depth.

The Sketch plane was the Front plane. The 2D circle was sketched centered at the Origin. A dimension defined the overall size of the sketch.

The name of the feature was Extrude1. Extrude1 utilized the Mid Plane End Condition. The Extrude1 feature was symmetric about the Front plane.

The Extruded Cut feature removed material to create the hole. The Extruded Cut feature was named Cut-Extrude1. The Through All End Condition option created the Cut-Extrude1 feature. Feature dimensions were modified. The Edit Color option was utilized to modify the part color.

Additional details on Circle, Modify, Smart Dimensions, Sketch Color, Extruded Base and Extruded Cut are available in SolidWorks Help. Keywords: Circle, Modify, Sketch (color), Dimension, and Extrude.

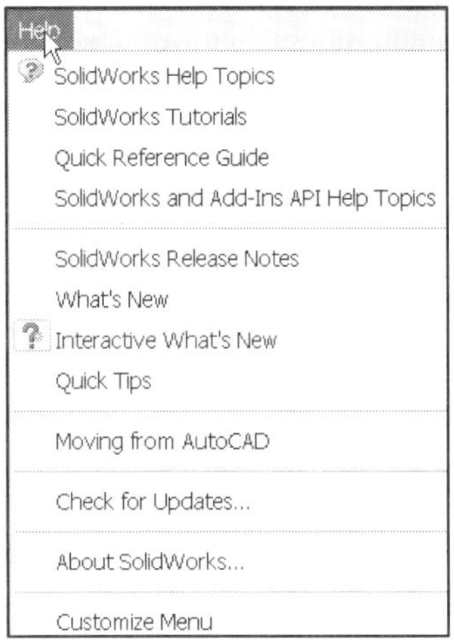

The SolidWorks Help Topics contains step-by-step instructions for various commands. The Help icon is displayed in the dialog box or in the PropertyManager for each feature.

Display Help for a rectangle.

121) Click **Help** from the Main menu.

122) Click **SolidWorks Help Topics** SolidWorks Help Topics.

123) Click the **Index** tab.

124) Enter **rectangle**. The description is displayed in the right window.

125) Click **Close** to close the Help window.

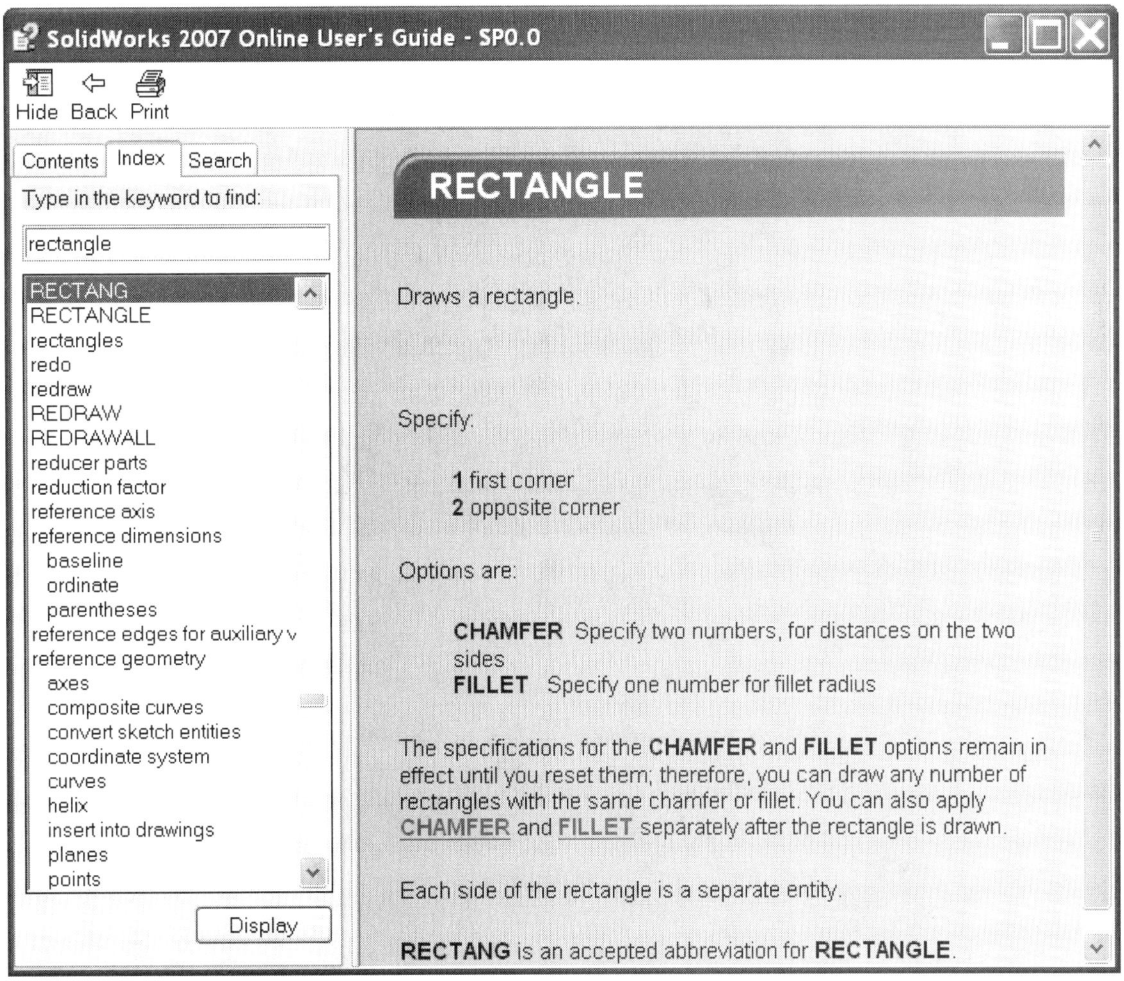

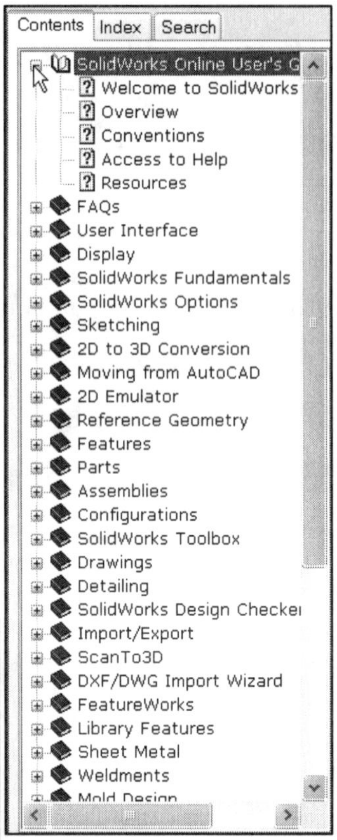

The Help option contains tools to assist the user. The SolidWorks Help Topics contain:

- **Contents** tab: Contains the SolidWorks Online User's Guide documents.
- **Index** tab: Contains additional information on key words.
- **Search** tab: To locate information.

Display the SolidWorks Tutorials.

126) Click **Help** from the Main menu.

127) Click **SolidWorks Tutorials**. The SolidWorks Tutorials are displayed. Review Lesson 1. This is a great location for additional information.

128) Click **Close** from the Online Tutorial dialog box. Return to the Graphics window.

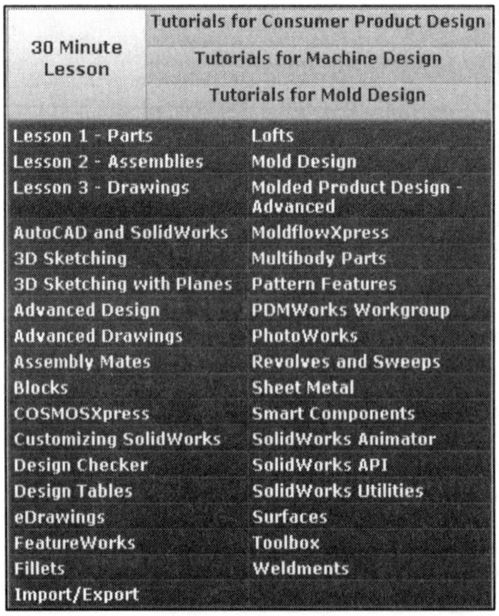

FLATBAR Part

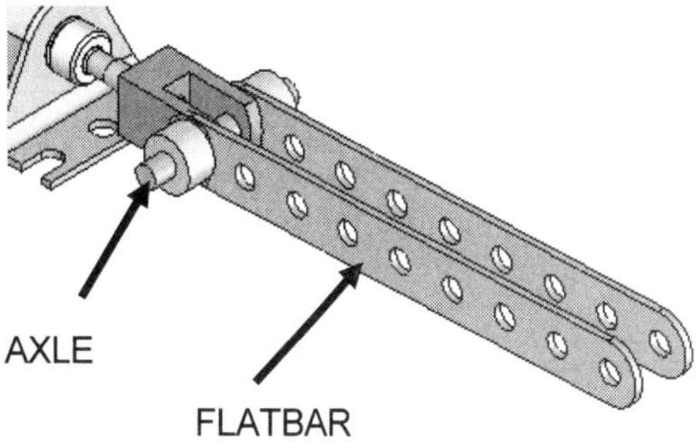

The FLATBAR part fastens to the AXLE. The FLATBAR contains nine, ∅.190in holes spaced 0.5in apart.

The FLATBAR part is manufactured from .060in stainless steel.

Create the FLATBAR part. Utilize an Extruded feature.

The Extruded feature requires a 2D profile sketched on the Front plane.

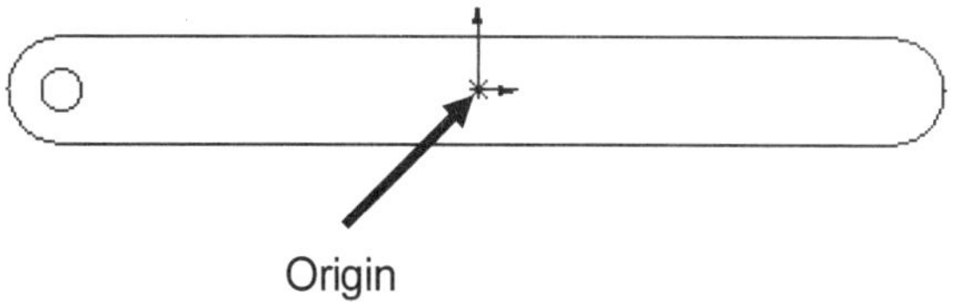

Utilize symmetry. Create the 2D profile centered about the Origin.

Relations control the size and position of entities with constraints.

Utilize the Add Relations sketch tool to define a Midpoint geometric relation in the sketch.

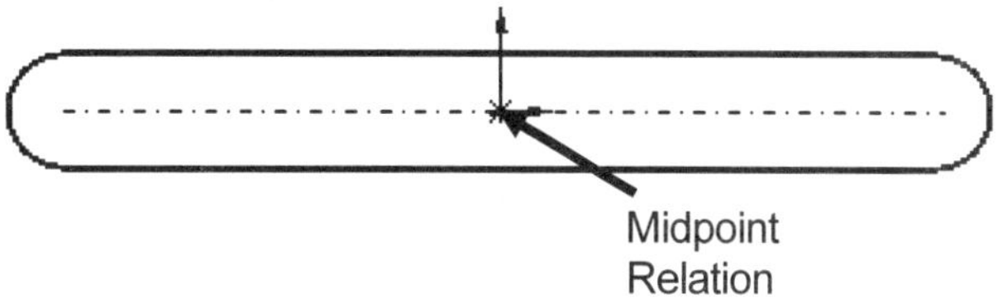

Utilize an Extruded Cut feature to create the first hole.

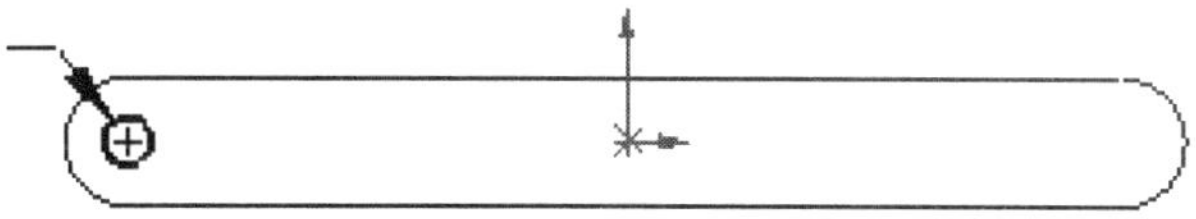

Utilize a Linear Pattern to create the remaining holes. A Linear Pattern creates an array of features in a specified direction.

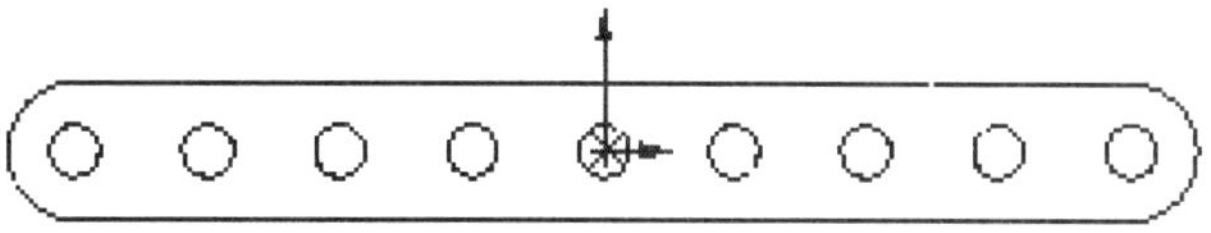

Activity: FLATBAR Part-Extruded Base Feature

Create a new Part.

129) Click **File**, **New** from the Main menu. The Templates tab is the default tab. Part is the default template from the New SolidWorks Document dialog box.

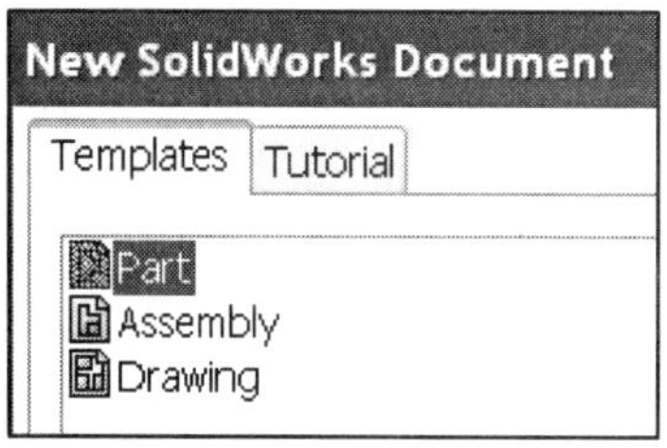

130) Double-click **Part**. The Part FeatureManager is displayed.

Save the part.

131) Click **File**, **Save As** from the Main menu.

132) Enter **FLATBAR** for File name in the SW-TUTORIAL-2007 folder

133) Enter **FLAT BAR 9 HOLES** for Description.

134) Click **Save**. The FLATBAR FeatureManager is displayed.

Set the Dimension standard and part units.

135) Click **Tools**, **Options**, **Document Properties** tab from the Main menu.

136) Select **ANSI** from the Dimensioning standard box.

137) Click **Units**.

138) Click **IPS**, [**MMGS**] for Unit system.

139) Select **3**, [**2**] for Length units Decimal places.

140) Select **0**, [**0**] for Angular units Decimal places.

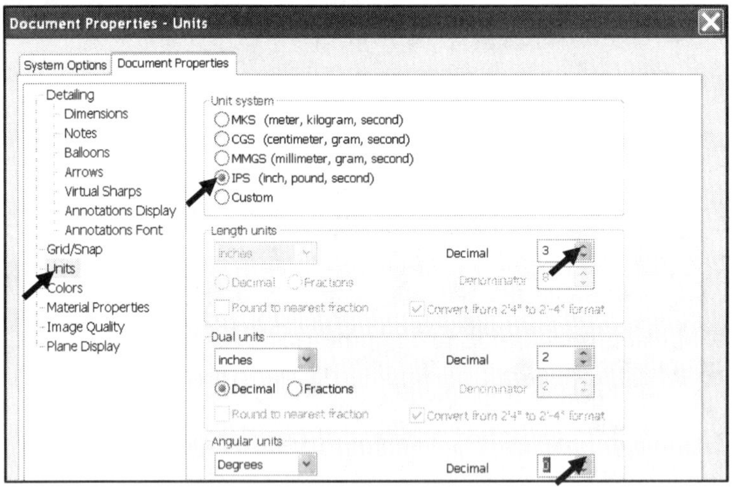

141) Click **OK** to set the document units.

Insert a new Sketch for the Extruded Base feature.

142) Click **Front Plane** from the FeatureManager. This is the Sketch plane.

143) Click **Sketch** Sketch from the Control Area.

144) Click **Rectangle** Rectan... from the Sketch toolbar.

145) Click the **first point** of the rectangle below and to the left of the Origin in the Graphics window.

146) Drag the **mouse pointer** up and to the right of the Origin. Release the **mouse button** to create the second point of the rectangle as illustrated.

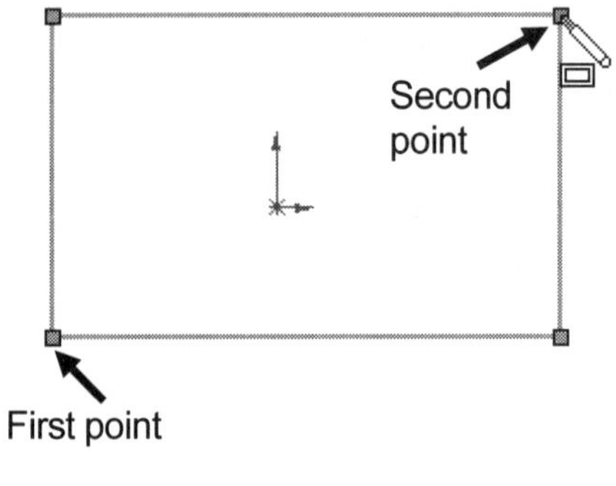

Trim the vertical lines.

147) Click **Trim Entities** Trim from the Sketch toolbar. The Trim PropertyManager is displayed.

148) Click **Trim to closest** from the Options box.

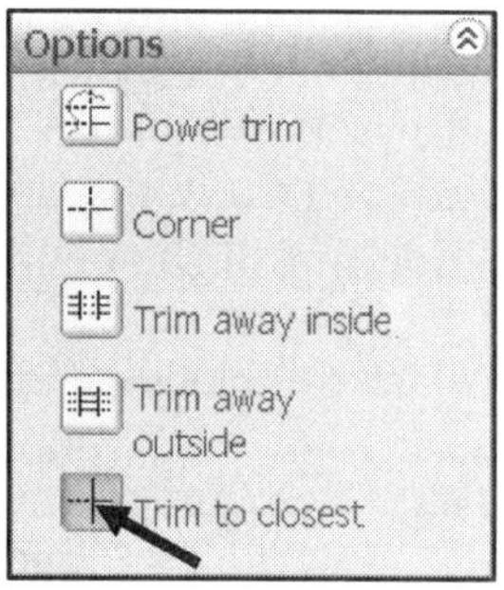

149) Click the **left vertical** line. The left vertical line is removed.

150) Click the **right vertical** line. The right vertical line is removed.

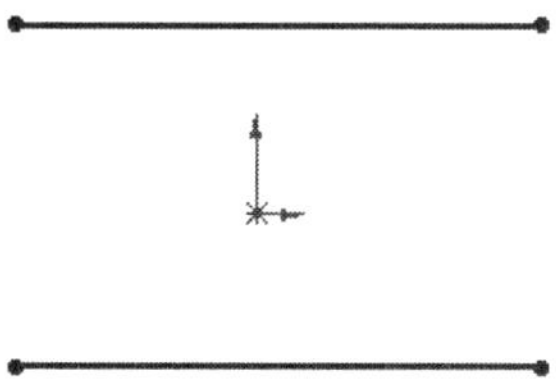

151) Click **OK** from the Trim PropertyManager.

Sketch the right 180 degree Tangent Arc.

152) Click **Tangent Arc** Tangent Arc from the Sketch toolbar.

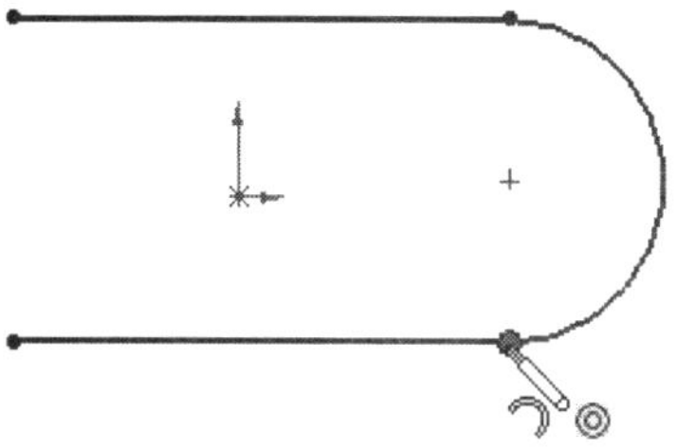

153) Click the **top right** endpoint of the top horizontal line.

154) Drag the **mouse pointer** to the right and downward.

155) Click the **bottom right endpoint** to complete the arc.

Sketch the left 180 degree Tangent Arc.

156) Click the **top left** endpoint of the top horizontal line.

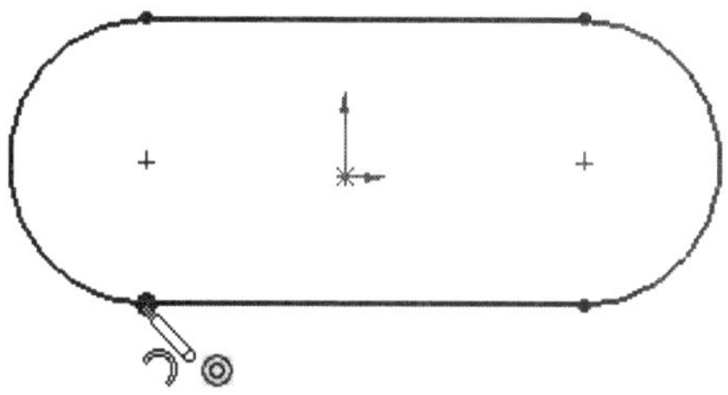

157) Drag the **mouse pointer** to the left and downward.

158) Click the **bottom left endpoint** to complete the arc.

Window-select geometry in the Graphics window.

159) Right-click **Select** Select in the Graphics window.

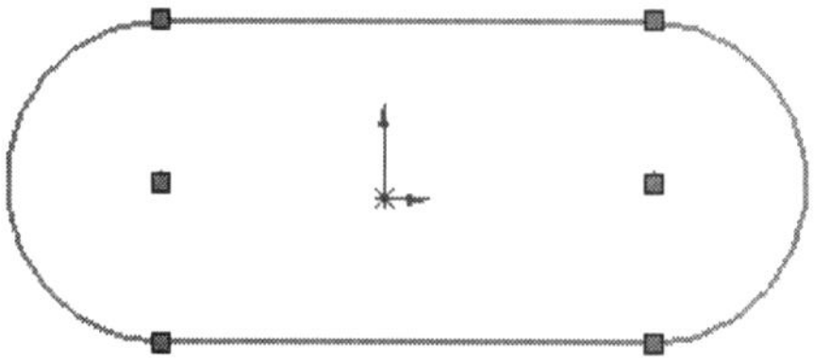

160) Click a **position** in the upper left corner of the Graphics window.

161) Drag the **mouse pointer** to the lower right corner of the Graphics window.

162) Release the **mouse pointer**. The selected geometry is displayed in the Selected Entities box. The selected geometry is displayed in green in the Graphics window.

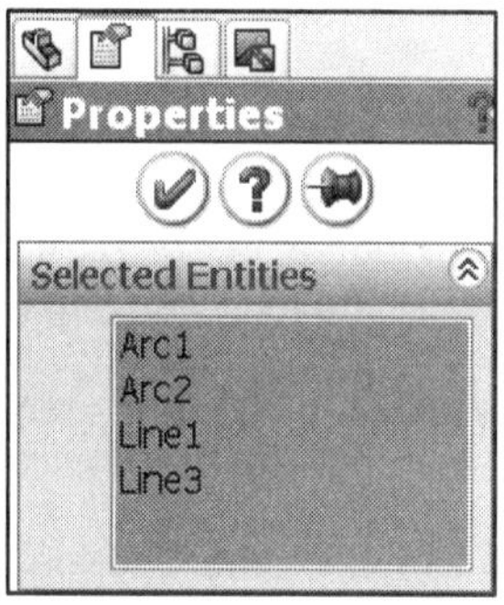

Maintain the slot sketch symmetric about the Origin. Utilize relations. A relation is a geometric constraint between sketch geometry. Position the Origin at the Midpoint of the centerline.

Sketch a centerline.

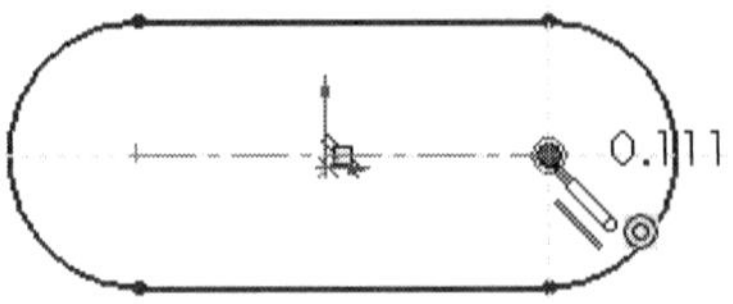

163) Click **Centerline** Centerl... from the Sketch toolbar. The Insert Line PropertyManager is displayed.

164) Sketch a **horizontal centerline** from the left arc center point to the right arc center point.

165) Right-click **Select** Select.

Add a Midpoint relation.

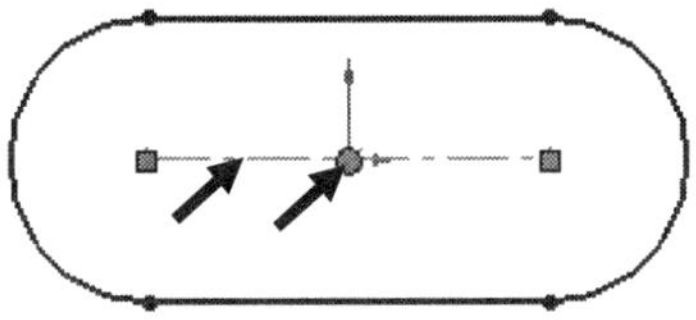

166) Click the **Origin**. Hold the **Ctrl** key down.

167) Click the **centerline**. The Properties PropertyManager is displayed. Release the **Ctrl** key. The Origin and the centerline is displayed in the Selected Entities box.

168) Click **Midpoint** from the Add Relations box.

169) Click **OK** from the Properties PropertyManager.

Add an Equal relation.

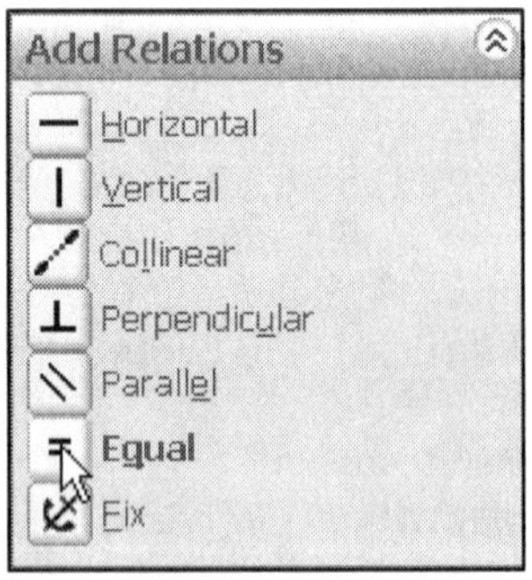

170) Click the **top horizontal line**. Hold the **Ctrl** key down.

171) Click the **bottom horizontal line**. The Properties PropertyManager is displayed. Release the **Ctrl** key.

172) Click **Equal** = from the Add Relations box.

173) Click **OK** from the Properties PropertyManager.

Add a dimension.

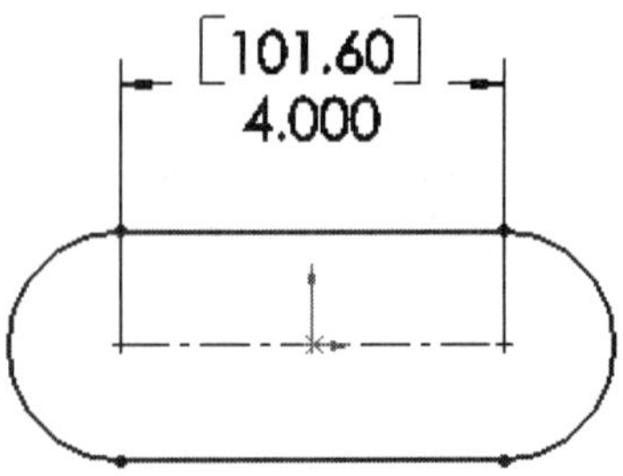

174) Click **Smart Dimension** Smart Dimens... from the Sketch toolbar.

175) Click the **horizontal centerline**. Click a **position** above the top horizontal line in the Graphics window.

176) Enter **4.000**in, [**101.60**] in the Modify dialog box.

177) Click the **Green Check mark** in the Modify dialog box.

178) Click the **right arc** of the FLATBAR.

179) Click a **position** diagonally to the right in the Graphics window.

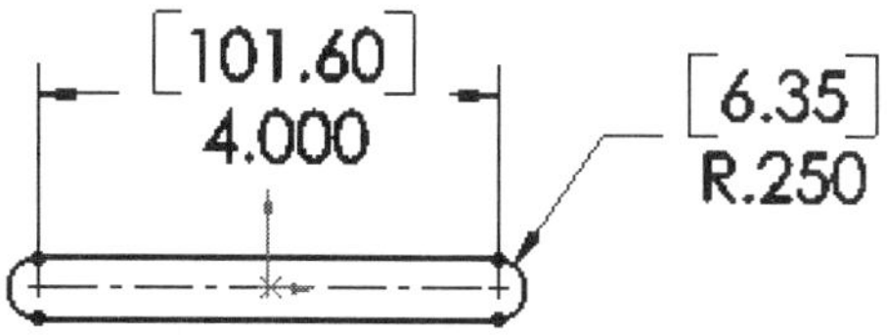

180) Enter **.250**in, [**6.35**] in the Modify dialog box.

181) Click the **Green Check mark**. The black sketch is fully defined.

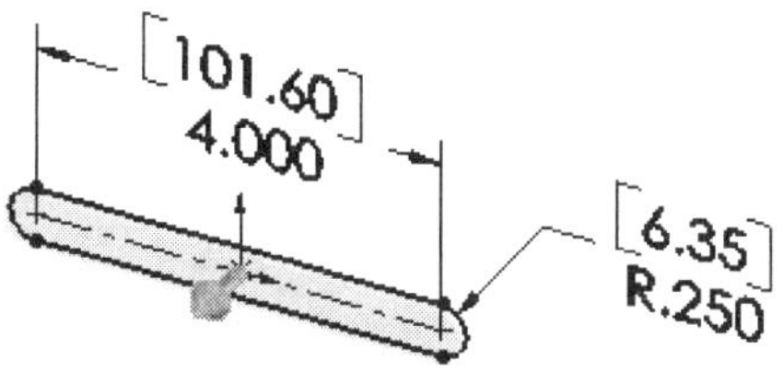

Extrude the sketch to create the Base feature.

182) Click **Extruded Boss/Base** Extruded Boss/B... from the Features toolbar. The Extrude PropertyManager is displayed.

183) Enter .**060**in, [**1.5**] for Depth. Accept the default conditions.

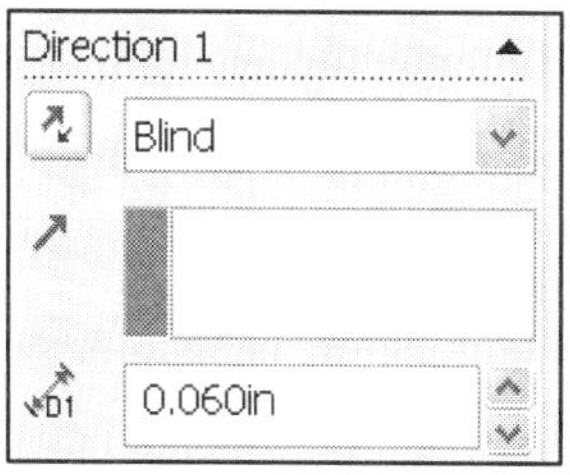

184) Click **OK** from the Extrude PropertyManager. Extrude1 is displayed in the FeatureManager.

Fit the model to the Graphics window.

185) Press the **f** key.

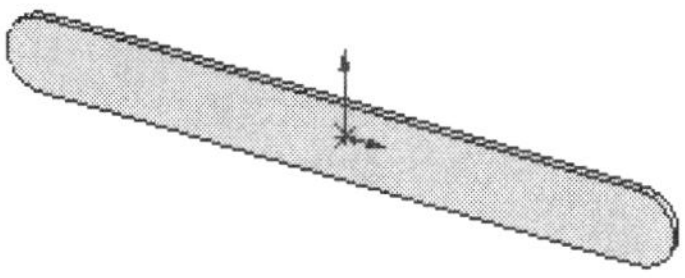

Save the FLATBAR part.

186) Click **Save**.

Activity: FLATBAR Part-Extruded Cut Feature

Insert a new sketch for the Extruded Cut Feature.

187) Click the **front face** of the Extrude1 feature in the Graphics window. This is the Sketch plane. Extrude1 is highlighted in the FeatureManager.

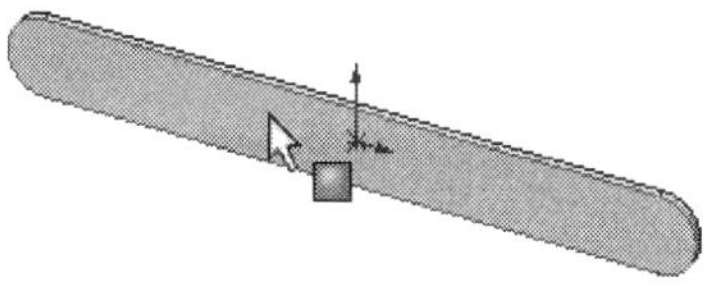

188) Click **Sketch** Sketch from the Control Area.

Display the Front view.

189) Click **Front view**.

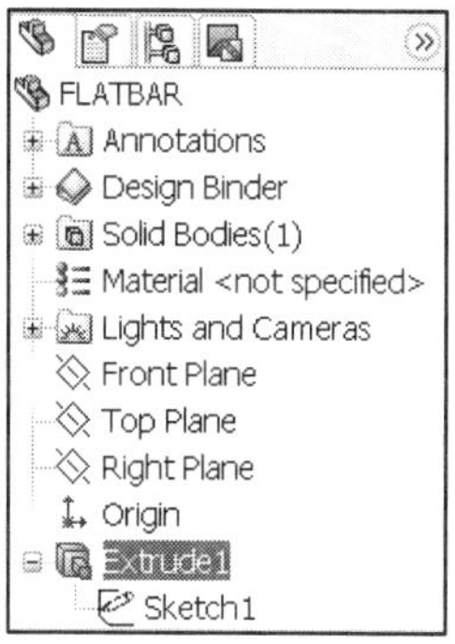

The process of placing the mouse pointer over an existing arc to locate its center point is called "wake up".

Wake up the center point.

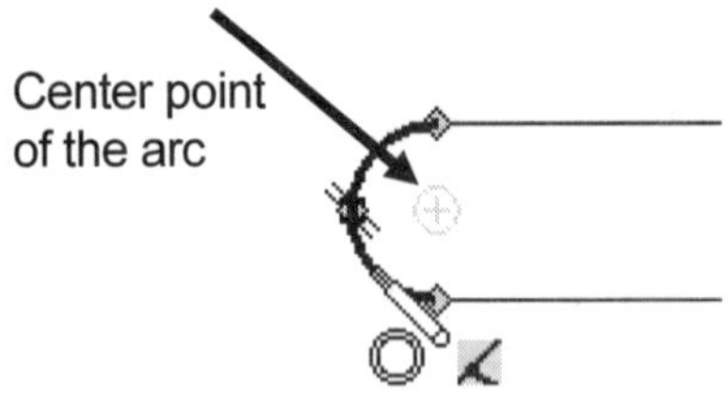

190) Click **Circle** Circle from the Sketch toolbar. The Circle PropertyManager is displayed.

191) Place the **mouse pointer** on the left arc. Do not click. The center point of the slot arc is displayed.

192) Click the **center point** of the arc.

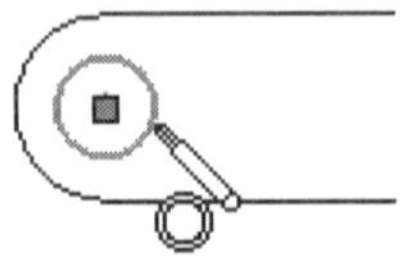

193) Click a **position** to the right of the center point to create the circle as illustrated.

Add a dimension.

194) Click **Smart Dimension** Smart Dimens... from the Sketch toolbar.

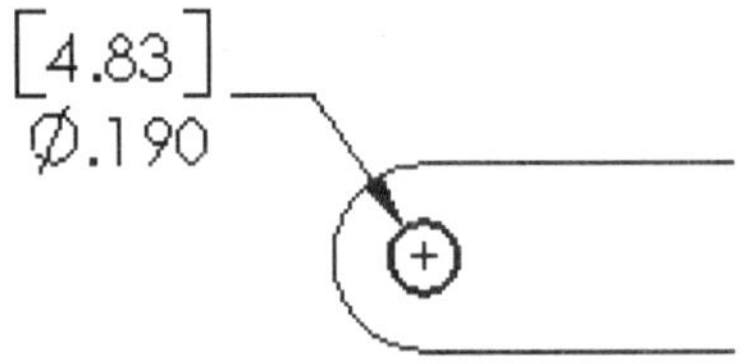

195) Click the **circumference** of the circle.

196) Click a **position** diagonally above and to the left of the circle in the Graphics window.

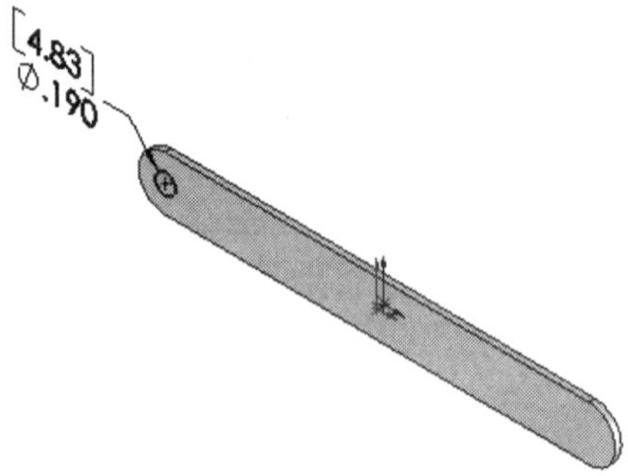

197) Enter **.190**in, [**4.83**] in the Modify box.

198) Click the **Green Check mark**.

199) Click **Isometric view**.

Insert an Extruded Cut feature.

200) Click **Extruded Cut** Extruded Cut from the Features toolbar. The Cut-Extrude PropertyManager is displayed.

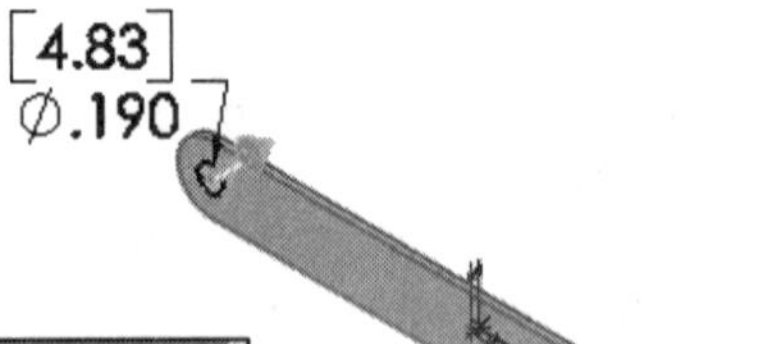

201) Select **Through All** for End Condition in Direction 1. The direction arrow points to the right. Accept the default conditions.

202) Click **OK** from the Cut-Extrude PropertyManager. The Cut-Extrude1 feature is displayed in the FeatureManager.

Save the FLATBAR part.

203) Click **Save**.

The blue Cut-Extrude1 Cut-Extrude1 icon indicates that the feature is selected.

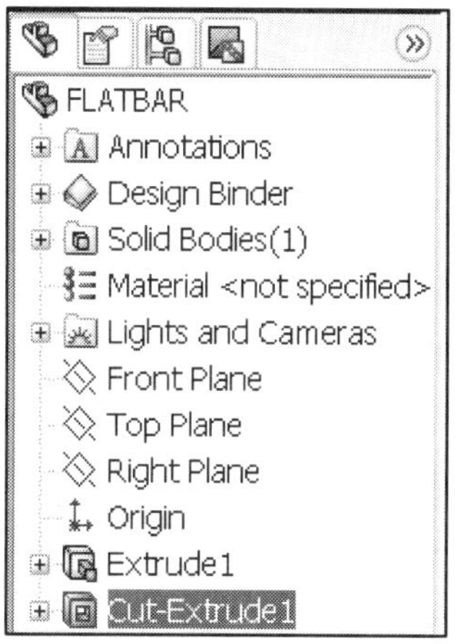

Select features by clicking their icons in the FeatureManager or by selecting their geometry in the Graphics window.

Activity: FLATBAR Part-Linear Pattern Feature

Create a Linear Pattern.

204) Click **Linear Pattern** Linear from the Features toolbar. The Linear Pattern PropertyManager is displayed.

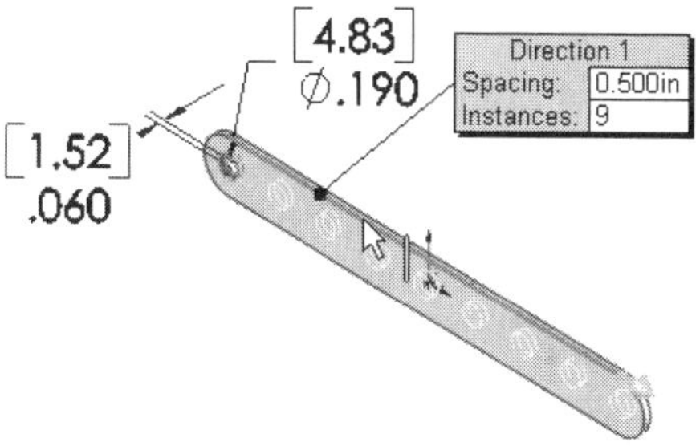

205) Click the **top edge** of the Extrude1 feature for Direction1. Edge<1> is displayed in the Pattern Direction box.

206) Enter **0.5**in, [**12.70**] for Spacing.

207) Enter **9** for Number of Instances. Instances are the number of occurrences of a feature.

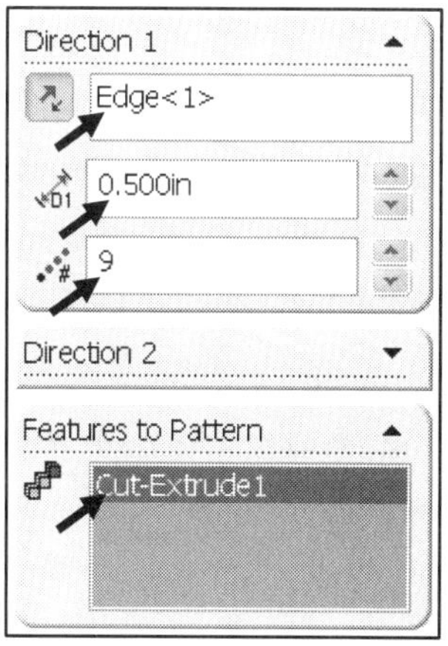

208) The Direction arrow points to the right. Click the **Reverse Direction** button if required.

209) Cut-Extrude1 is displayed in the Features to Pattern box. Click **OK** from the Linear Pattern PropertyManager. The LPattern1 feature is displayed in the FeatureManager.

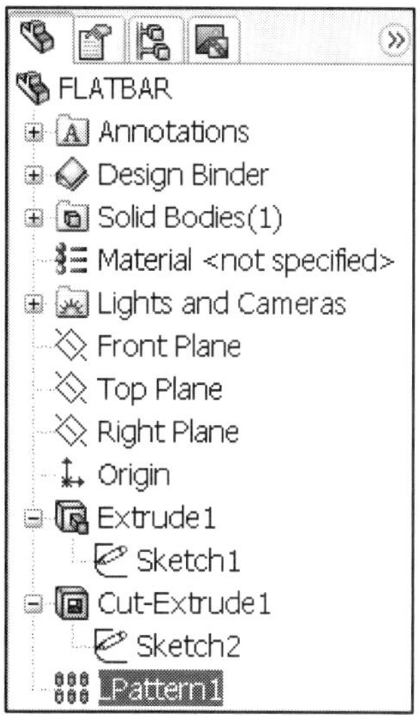

Save the FLATBAR part.

210) Click **Save**. The FLATBAR part is complete.

Close all documents.
211) Click **Windows, Close All** from the Main menu.

Review the FLATBAR Part.

The FLATBAR utilized an Extruded Base feature. The Sketch plane was the Front plane. The 2D sketch utilized the Rectangle and Tangent Arc Sketch tools to create the slot profile. You created a centerline between the two arc center points.

The Midpoint relation maintained the slot profile symmetric about the Origin. Linear and radial dimensions were added to define the overall size of the sketch. The name of the feature was Extrude1. Extrude1 utilized the Blind End Condition.

The Extruded Cut feature removed material to create the hole. The Extruded Cut feature was named Cut-Extrude1. The Through All End Condition option created the Cut-Extrude1 feature from the Front plane. The Linear Pattern created an array of 9 holes, equally spaced along the length of the FLATBAR Part.

Additional details on Rectangle, Trim Entities, Extruded Base, Extruded Boss, Extruded Cut and Linear Pattern are available in SolidWorks Help. Keywords: Rectangle, Trim, Extruded Features, and Linear Pattern.

LINKAGE Assembly

An assembly is a document that contains two or more parts. An assembly inserted into another assembly is called a sub-assembly. A part or sub-assembly inserted into an assembly is called a component. The LINKAGE assembly consists of the following components: AXLE part, SHAFT-COLLAR part, FLATBAR part, and AIRCYLINDER sub-assembly.

Establishing the correct component relationship in an assembly requires forethought on component interaction. Mates are geometric relationships that align and fit components in an assembly. Mates remove degrees of freedom from a component.

Mate Types

Mates reflect the physical behavior of a component in an assembly. The components in the LINKAGE assembly utilize Standard Mate types. Review the Standard and Advanced Mates types.

Standard and Advanced Mates:

The Mate Property Manager displays Standard Mate types and Advanced Mate types. Components are assembled with various Mate types. The Standard Mate types are:

Standard Mate Types:	
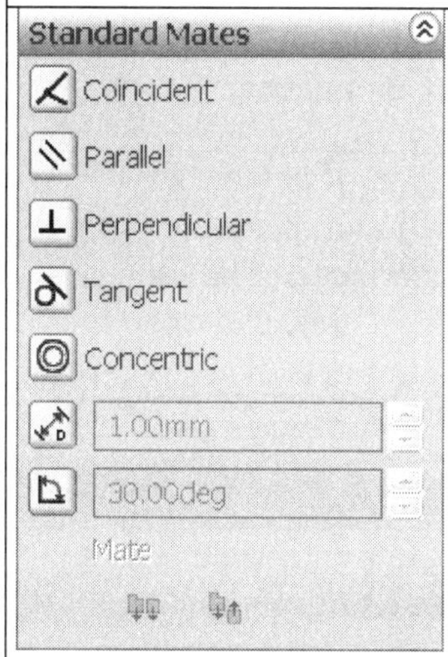	**Coincident**: Positions selected faces, edges, and planes so they share the same infinite line. Positions two vertices so they touch.
	Parallel: Positions the selected geometry so they lie in the same direction and remain a constant distance apart.
	Perpendicular: Positions the selected geometry at 90°.
	Tangent: Positions the selected items in a tangent mate (at least one selection must be a cylindrical, conical, or spherical face).
	Concentric: Positions the selected geometry so that they share the same center point.
	Distance: Positions the selected geometry at a specified distance between them.
	Angle: Positions the selected geometry at a specified angle between them.

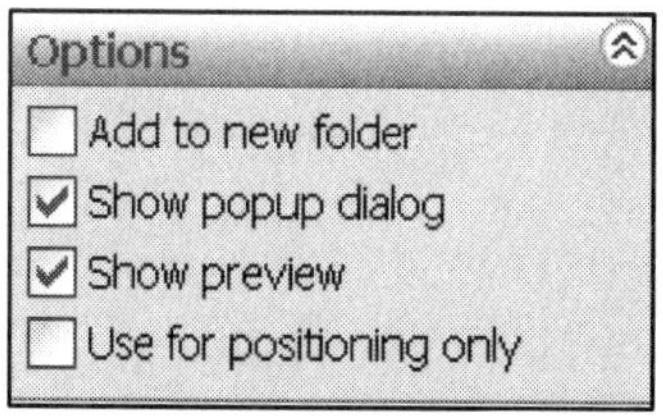

The Mate dialog box displays the Pop-up toolbar during the Mate procedure. The Standard Mate types, Aligned/Anti-Aligned, Undo, and OK are displayed in the Pop-up toolbar.

There are two Mate Alignment options. The Aligned option positions the components so that the normal vectors from the selected faces point in the same direction. The Anti-Aligned option positions the components so that the normal vectors from the selected faces point in opposite directions.

Advanced Mates:

The Advanced Mate types are:

Advanced Mate Types:	
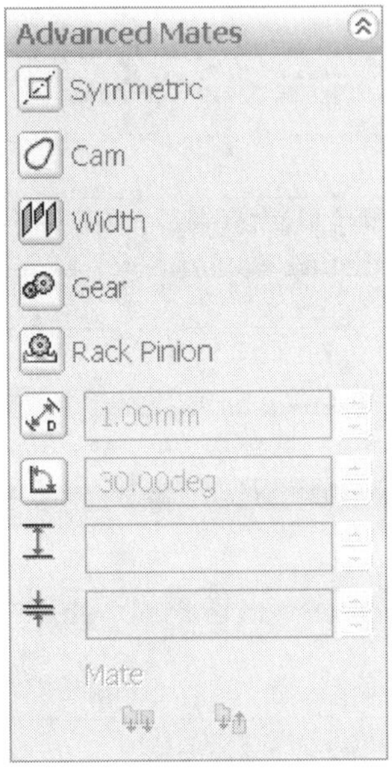	**Symmetric**: Positions two selected entities to be symmetric about a plane or planar face. A Symmetric Mate does not create a Mirrored Component.
	Cam: A cam-follower mate is a type of tangent or coincident mate. It positions a cylinder, plane, or point to a series of tangent extruded Cam faces. The Cam profile is comprised of tangent lines, arcs, and/or splines in a closed loop.
	Width: Centers a tab within the width of a groove.
	Gear: Positions two components to rotate relative to one another about selected axes. The axis of rotation includes cylindrical and conical faces, axes, and linear edges. Gear components are not required for a Gear Mate; example, two rolling cylinders.
	Rack Pinion: Linear translation of one part (the rack) causes circular rotation in another part (the pinion), and vice versa.
	Limit: Defines a range of motion for a Distance Mate or Angle Mate. Specify a starting value, minimum value and maximum value.

SolidWorks Help Topics list the rules governing Mate Type valid geometry. The valid geometry selection between components in a Coincident Mate is displayed in the Coincident Mate Combinations Table.

SolidWorks Help Topics also display Standard Mates by Entity. Specific combinations of geometry create valid Mates.

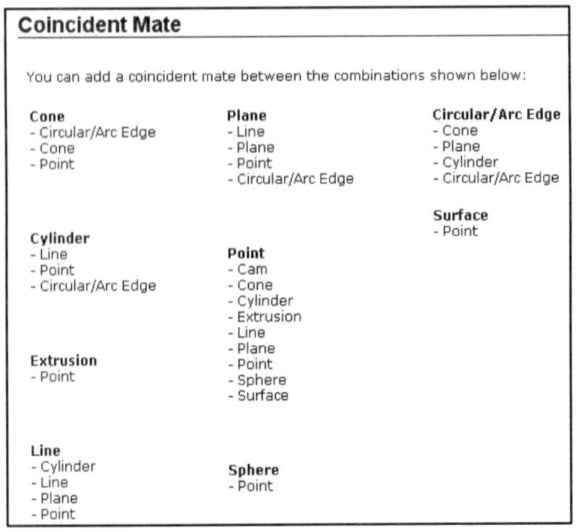
Coincident Mate

You can add a coincident mate between the combinations shown below:

Cone
- Circular/Arc Edge
- Cone
- Point

Cylinder
- Line
- Point
- Circular/Arc Edge

Extrusion
- Point

Line
- Cylinder
- Line
- Plane
- Point

Plane
- Line
- Plane
- Point
- Circular/Arc Edge

Point
- Cam
- Cone
- Cylinder
- Extrusion
- Line
- Plane
- Point
- Sphere
- Surface

Sphere
- Point

Circular/Arc Edge
- Cone
- Plane
- Cylinder
- Circular/Arc Edge

Surface
- Point

Example: Utilize a Concentric Mate between the AXLE cylindrical face and the FLATBAR Extruded Cut (hole). Utilize a Coincident Mate between the SHAFT-COLLAR back face and the FLATBAR front flat face.

The LINKAGE assembly requires the AIRCYLINDER assembly. The AIRCYLINDER assembly is located on the SolidWorks Tutorial Multimedia CD in the pneumatic components folder.

Activity: AIRCYLINDER Assembly-Open and Save As option

Open the AIRCYLINDER assembly.

212) Click **File**, **New** from the Main menu.

213) Double-click **Assembly** from the New SolidWorks Document dialog box. The Insert Component PropertyManager is displayed.

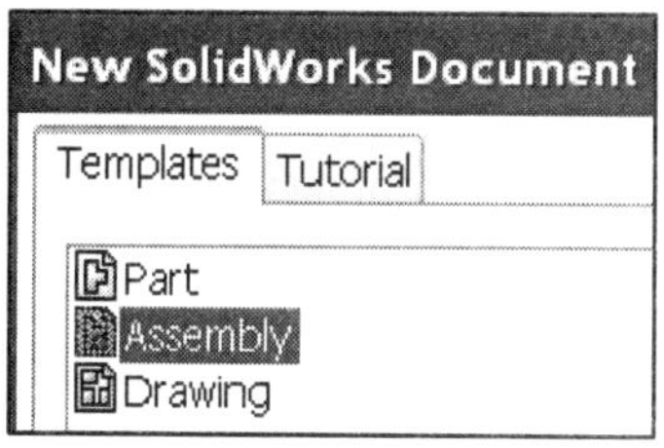

214) Click **View**; check **Origins** from the Main menu.

215) Click **Browse** from the Insert Component PropertyManager.

216) Select the **pneumatic components** folder from the CD in the book.

217) Double-click the **AIRCYLINDER** assembly. The AIRCYLINDER assembly is displayed in the Graphics window.

218) Click the **Origin** to fix the AIRCYLINDER assembly in the Graphics window. The (f) symbol is placed in front of the AIRCYLINDER name in the FeatureManager.

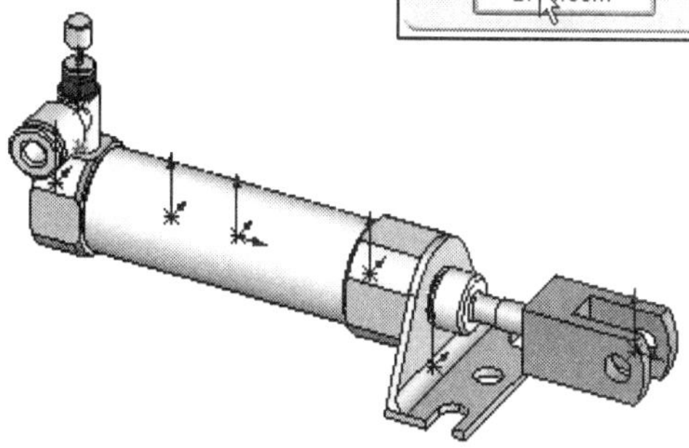

The AIRCYLINDER assembly is displayed in the Graphics window. Copy the AIRCYLINDER assembly with the Save As command. Save all sub-assemblies and part references to the SW-TUTORIAL-2007 folder.

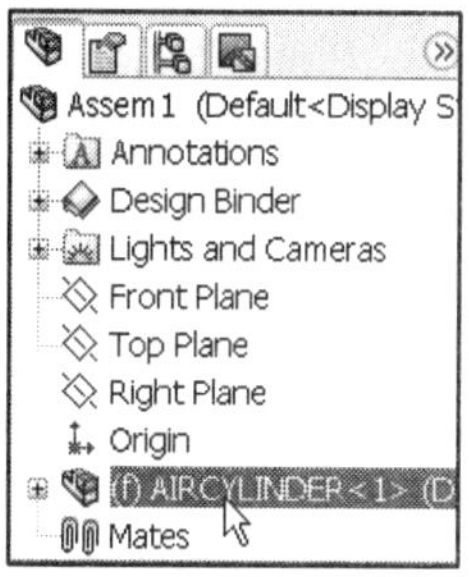

Save the AIRCYLINDER assembly to the SW-TUTORIAL-2007 folder.

219) Click **File**, **Save As** from the Main menu.

220) Select **SW-TUTORIAL-2007** for Save in folder.

221) Click the **References** button.

222) Click the **Select All** button to check all components contained in the AIRCYLINDER assembly.

223) Click the **Browse** button from the Edit Referenced File Locations.

224) Select the **SW-TUTORIAL-2007** folder. Click **OK** from the Browse for Folder dialog box.

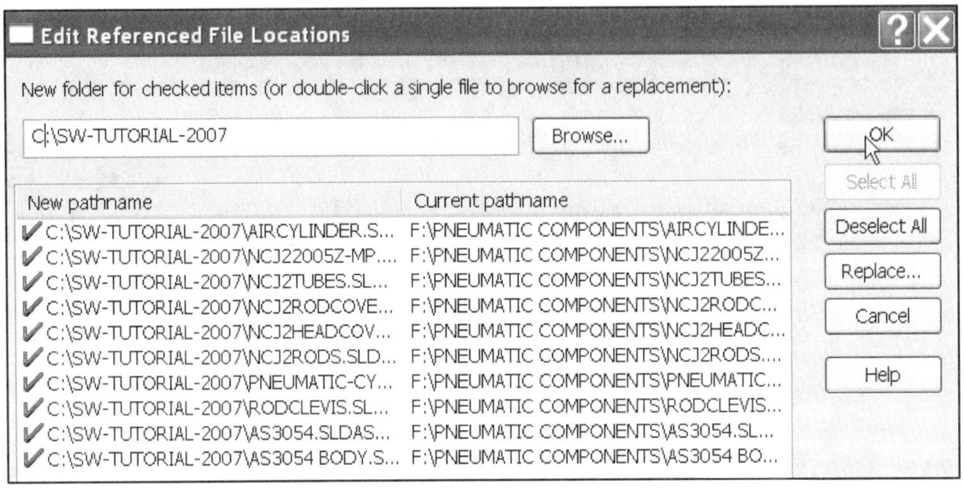

225) Click **OK** from the Edit Referenced File Locations dialog box.

226) Enter **LINKAGE** for File name.

227) Click **Save**.

228) Click **YES**.

The AIRCYLINDER assembly and its references are copied to the SW-TUTORIAL-2007 folder. Assemble the AXLE to the holes in the RodClevis.

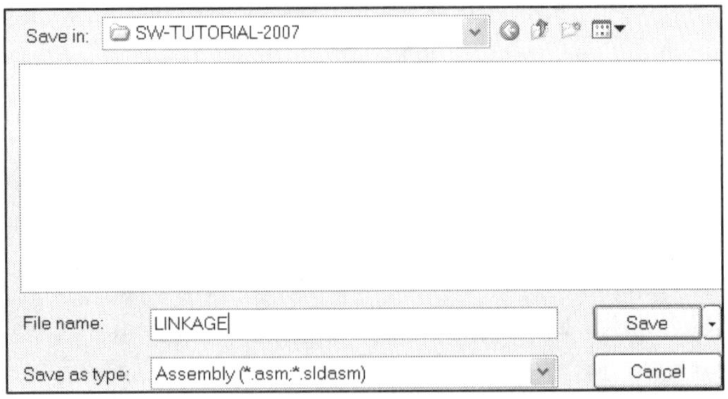

Display the RodClevis Component.

229) **Expand** the AIRCYLINDER assembly in the FeatureManager.

230) Click **RodClevis<1>** from the FeatureManager. Note: The RodClevis is displayed in green in the Graphics window.

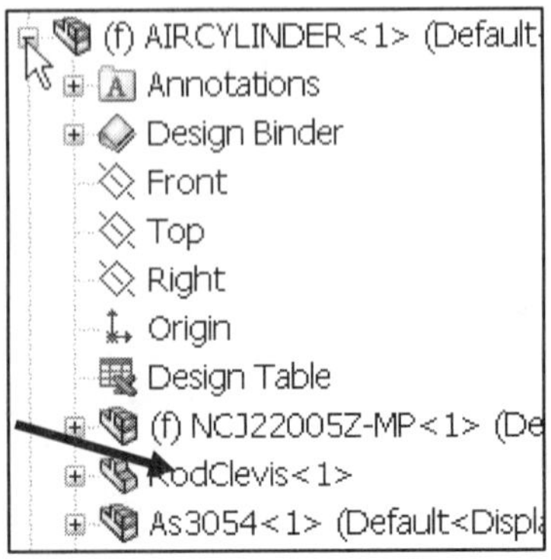

Hide the Origins.

231) Click **View**; uncheck **Origins** from the Main menu.

The AIRCYLINDER is the first component in the LINKAGE assembly and is fixed (f) to the LINKAGE assembly Origin.

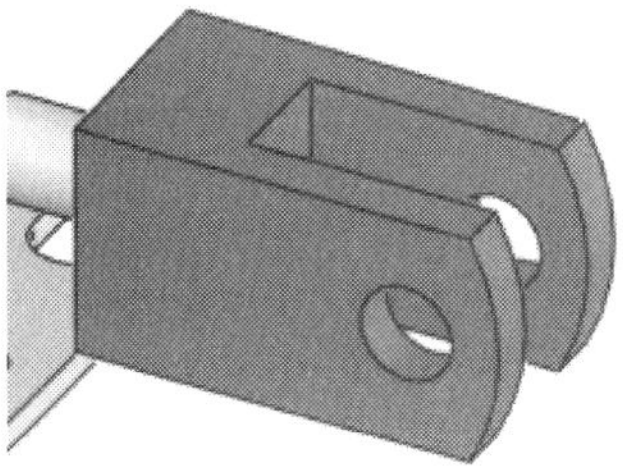

Display the Isometric view.

232) Click **Isometric view** .

Insert the AXLE part.

233) Click **Insert Component** Insert Compo... from the Assembly toolbar. The Insert Component PropertyManager is displayed.

234) Click **Browse**. Select **All Files** from the Files of type box.

235) Double-click **AXLE** from the SW-TUTORIAL-2007 folder.

236) Click a **position** to the left of the AIRCYLINDER assembly as illustrated.

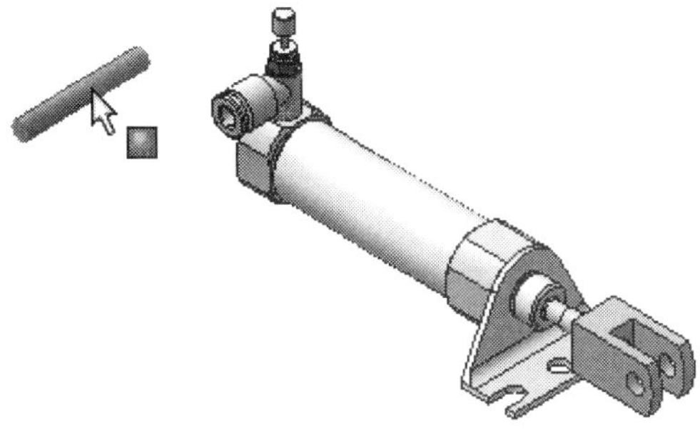

Move the AXLE component.

237) Click and drag a **position** in front of the RODCLEVIS.

Enlarge the view.

238) Click **Zoom to Area** on the RodClevis and the AXLE.

Insert a Concentric Mate.

239) Click **Mate** Mate from the Assembly toolbar. The Mate PropertyManager is displayed.

240) Click the inside **left hole face** of the RodClevis.

241) Click the **long cylindrical face** of the AXLE. The cursor displays the Face feedback symbol. The selected faces are displayed in the Mate Selections box. Concentric Mate is selected by default. The AXLE is positioned concentric to the RodClevis hole.

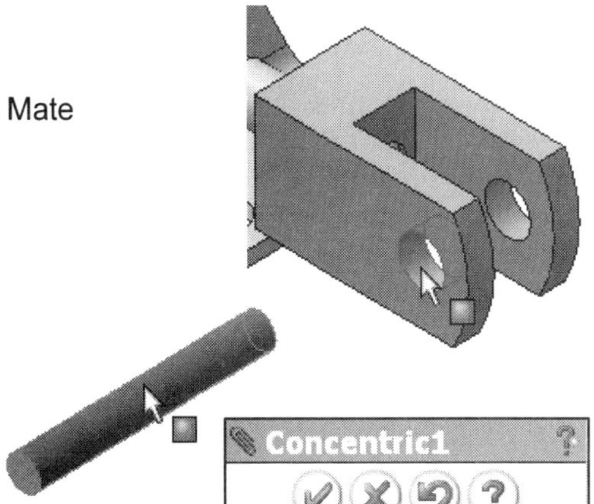

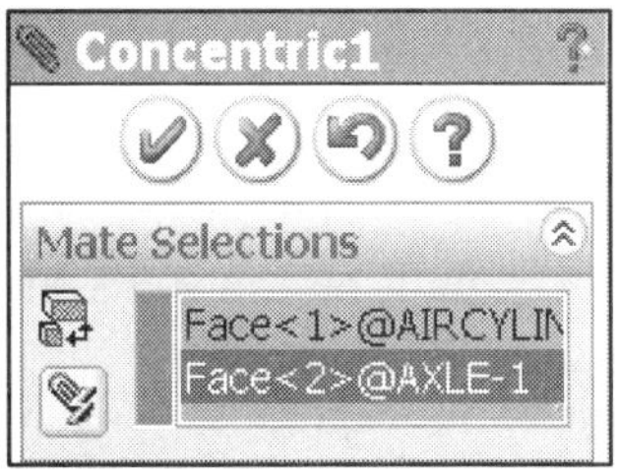

242) Click the **Green Check mark** .

Move the AXLE.

243) Click and drag the **AXLE** left to right. The AXLE translates in and out of the RodClevis holes.

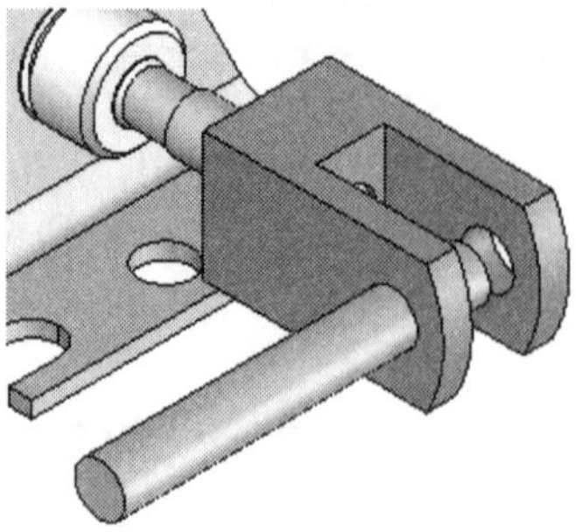

The Mate Pop-up toolbar is displayed after selecting the two cylindrical faces. The Mate Pop-up toolbar minimizes the time required to create a Standard Mate.

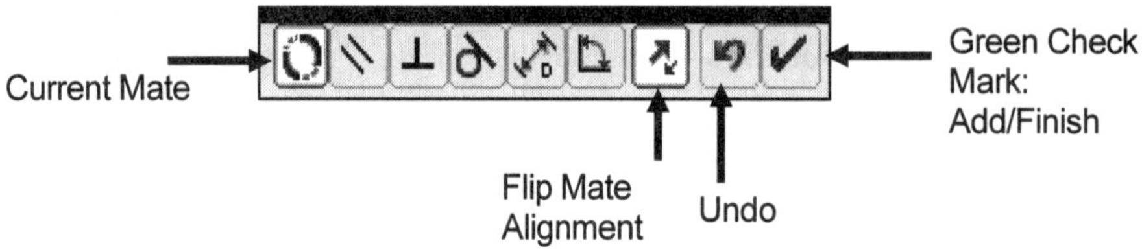

Position the mouse pointer in the middle of the face to select the entire face. Do not position the mouse pointer near the edge of the face. If the wrong face or edge is selected, perform one of the following actions:

- Click the face or edge again to remove it from the Items Selected text box.
- Right-click in the Graphics window. Click Clear Selections to remove all geometry from the Items Selected text box.
- Utilize the UNDO button to begin the Mate command again.

Display the Top view.

244) Click **Top view** .

Expand the LINKAGE assembly and components in the fly-out FeatureManager.

245) **Expand** the LINKAGE assembly from the fly-out FeatureManager.

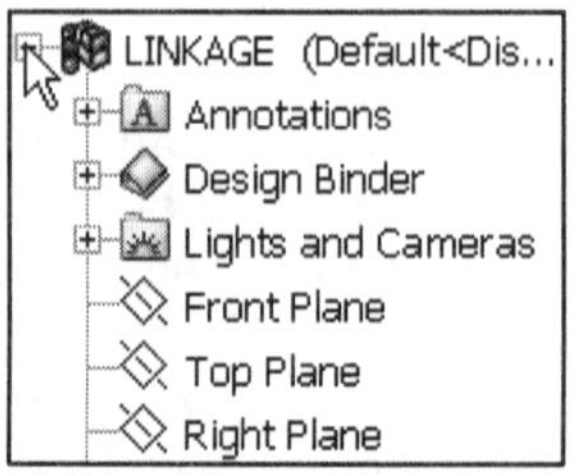

246) **Expand** the AIRCYLINDER assembly from the fly-out FeatureManager.

247) **Expand** the AXLE part from the fly-out FeatureManager.

Clear all sections from the Mate Selections box.

248) Right-click **Clear Selections** inside the Mate Selections box.

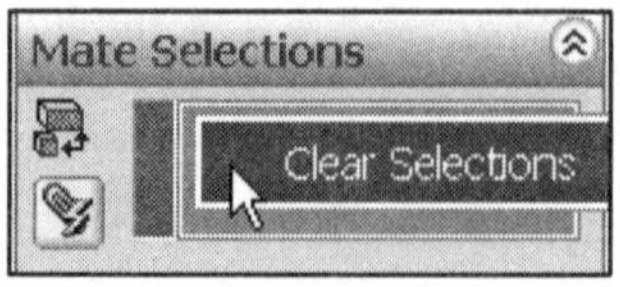

Insert a Coincident Mate.

249) Click the **Front Plane** of the AIRCYLINDER assembly from the fly-out FeatureManager.

250) Click the **Front Plane** of the AXLE part from the fly-out FeatureManager. The selected planes are displayed in the Mate Selections box. Coincident Mate is selected by default.

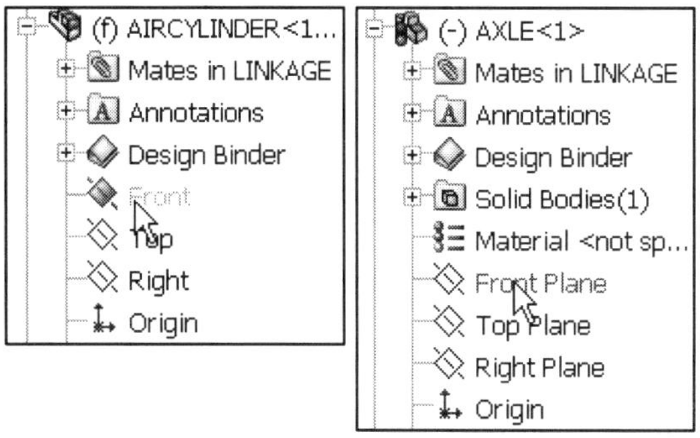

251) Click the **Green Check mark** in the Modify dialog box.

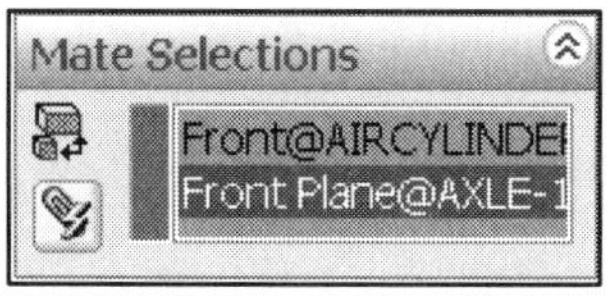

252) Click **OK** from the Mate PropertyManager.

The AIRCYLINDER Front plane and the AXLE Front plane are Coincident. The AXLE is centered in the RodClevis.

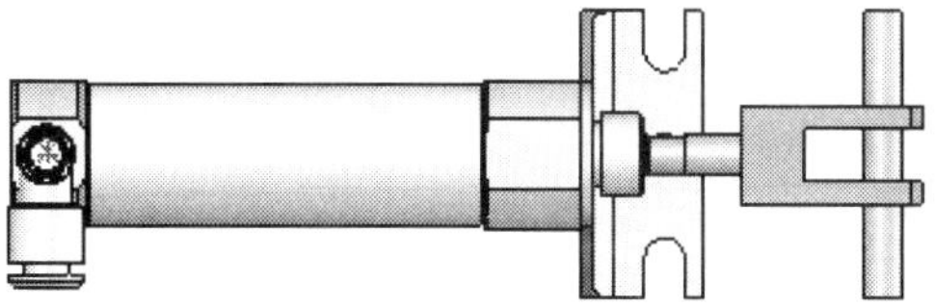

Display the Mates in the FeatureManager to check that the components and the Mate Types correspond to the design intent. Note: If you delete a Mate and then recreate it, the Mate numbers will be in a different order.

Display an Isometric view.

253) Click **Isometric view**.

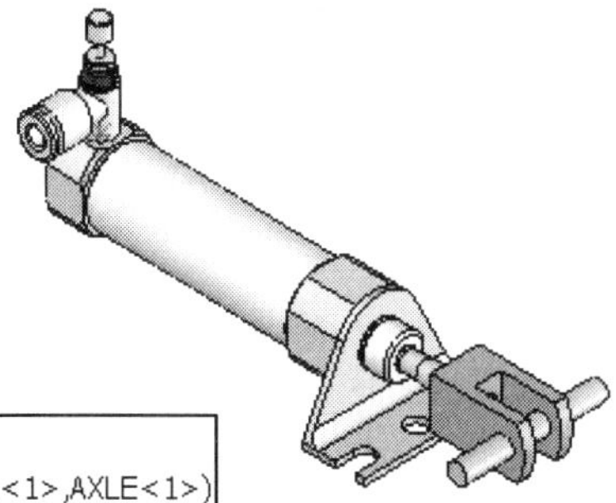

Display the Mates.

254) **Expand** the Mates folder in the FeatureManager.

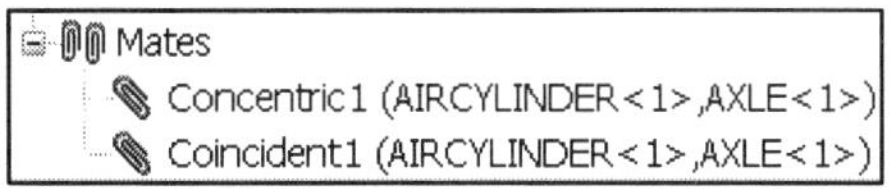

Save the LINKAGE assembly.

255) Click **Save**.

Activity: LINKAGE Assembly-Insert FLATBAR Part

Insert the FLATBAR part.

256) Click **Insert Component** Insert Compo... from the Assembly toolbar. The Insert Component PropertyManager is displayed.

257) Click **Browse**.

258) Select **Part** for Files of type from the SW-TUTORIAL-2007 folder.

259) Double-click **FLATBAR**.

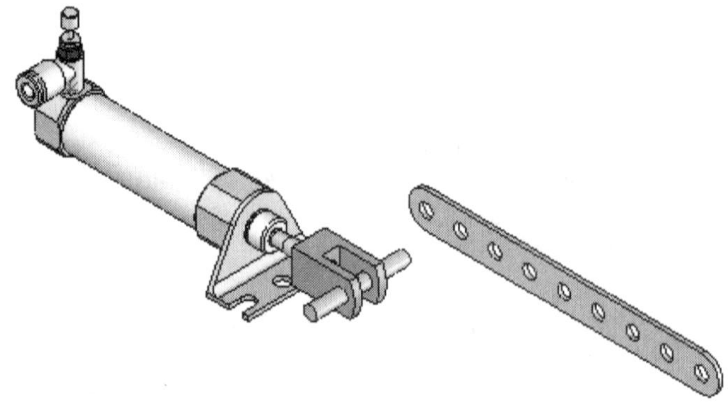

Place the Component.

260) Click a **position** in the Graphics window as illustrated.

Enlarge the view.

261) Click **Zoom to Area** on the AXLE and the left side of the FLATBAR to enlarge the view.

Insert a Concentric Mate.

262) Click **Mate** from the Assembly toolbar. The Mate PropertyManager is displayed. If required, right-click **Clear Selections** inside the Mate Selections box.

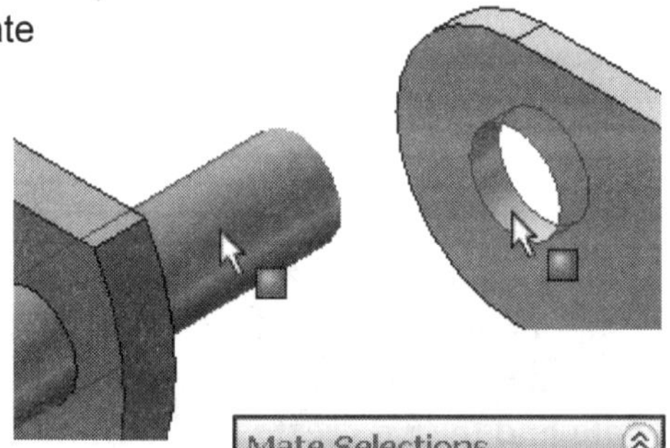

263) Click the inside **left hole face** of the FLATBAR.

264) Click the **long cylindrical face** of the AXLE. The selected faces are displayed in the Mate Selections box. Concentric is selected by default.

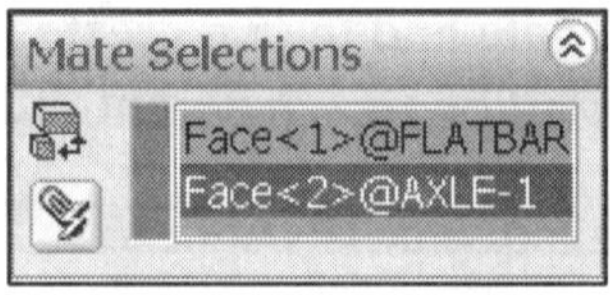

265) Click the **Green Check mark**.

Fit the model to the Graphics window.

266) Press the **f** key.

Move the FLATBAR.

267) Click and drag the **FLATBAR**. The FLATBAR translates and rotates along the AXLE.

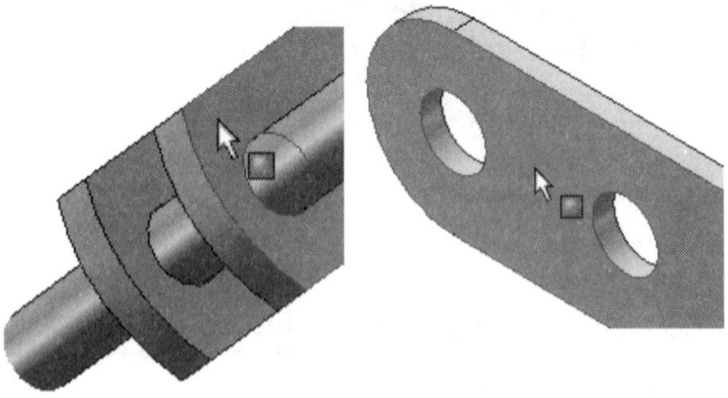

Insert a Coincident Mate.

268) Click the **front face** of the FLATBAR.

269) Press the **left arrow key** approximately 5 times to rotate the model and to view the back face of the RodClevis. Click the **back face** of the RodClevis as illustrated. The selected faces are displayed in the Mate Selections box. Coincident is selected by default.

270) Click the **Green Check mark**.

271) Click **OK** from the Mate PropertyManager.

Display the Isometric view.

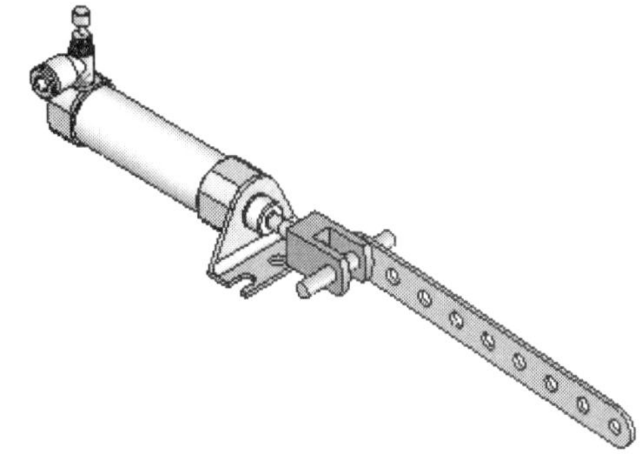

272) Click **Isometric view**.

Insert the second FLATBAR Component.

273) Click **Insert Component** Insert Compo... from the Assembly toolbar. The Insert Component PropertyManager is displayed.

274) Click **Browse**.

275) Select **Part** for Files of type from the SW-TUTORIAL-2007 folder.

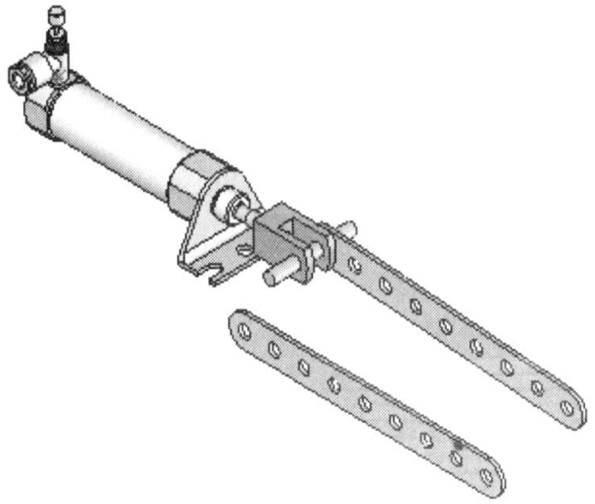

276) Double-click **FLATBAR**.

277) Click a **position** to the left of the AIRCYLINDER in the Graphics window as illustrated.

Enlarge the view.

278) Click **Zoom to Area** on the second FLATBAR and the AXLE.

Insert a Concentric Mate.

279) Click **Mate** Mate from the Assembly toolbar. The Mate PropertyManager is displayed.

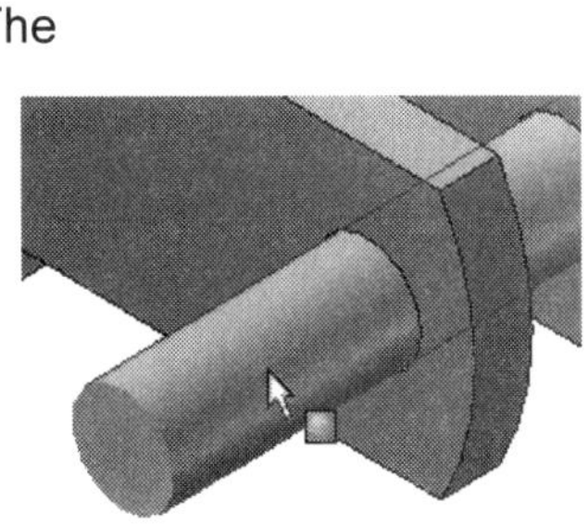

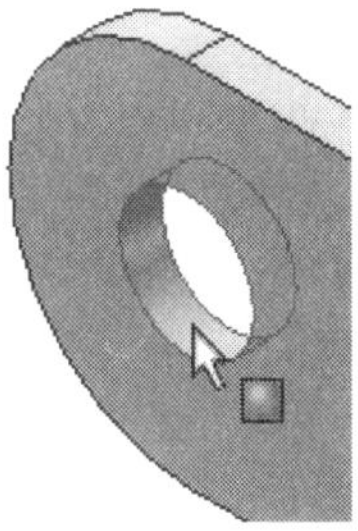

280) Click the **left inside hole face** of the second FLATBAR.

281) Click the **long cylindrical face** of the AXLE. The selected faces are displayed in the Mate Selections box. Concentric is selected by default.

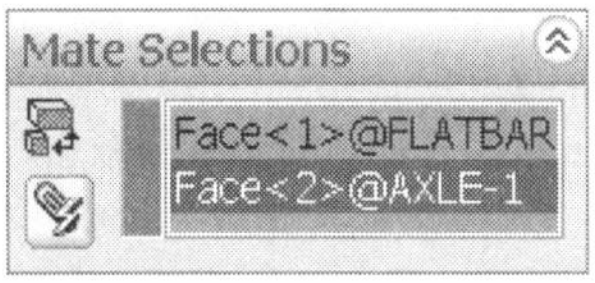

282) Click the **Green Check mark**.

283) Press the **f** key to fit the model to the Graphics window.

Insert a Coincident Mate.

284) Press the **left arrow key** approximately 5 times to rotate the model to view the back face of the second FLATBAR.

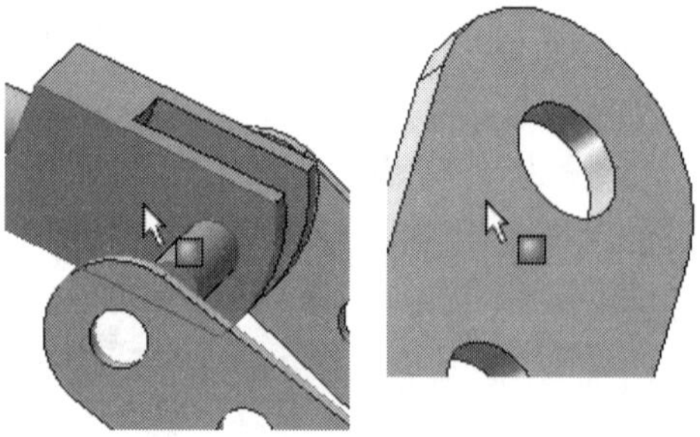

285) Click the **back face** of the second FLATBAR.

286) Press the **right arrow key** approximately 5 times to rotate the model to view the front face of the RodClevis.

287) Click the **front face** of the RodClevis. The selected faces are displayed in the Mate Selections box. Coincident is selected by default.

288) Click the **Green Check mark** ✔.

Create a Parallel Mate.

289) Press the **Shift-z** keys to Zoom in on the model.

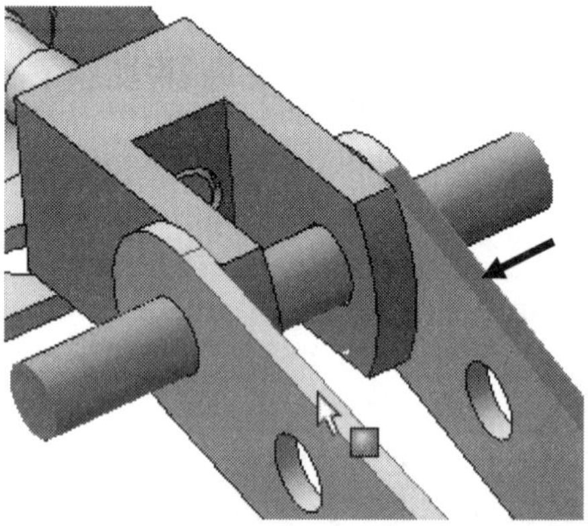

290) Click the **top narrow face** of the first FLATBAR.

291) Click the **top narrow face** of the second FLATBAR. The selected faces are displayed in the Mate Selections box.

292) Click **Parallel**.

293) Click the **Green Check mark** ✔.

294) Click **OK** from the Mate PropertyManager.

295) Click **Isometric view**.

Move the two FLATBAR parts.

296) Click and drag the **second FLATBAR**. Both FLATBAR parts move together.

View the Mates.

297) **Expand** the Mates folder from the FeatureManager.

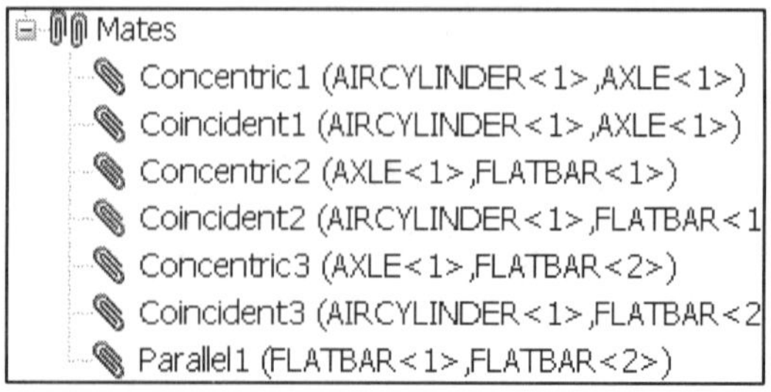

Activity: LINKAGE Assembly-Insert SHAFT-COLLAR Part

Insert the first SHAFT-COLLAR.

298) Click **Insert Component** Insert Compo... from the Assembly toolbar. The Insert Component PropertyManager is displayed.

299) Click **Browse**.

300) Select **Part** for Files of type from the SW-TUTORIAL-2007 folder.

301) Double-click **SHAFT-COLLAR**.

302) Click a **position** to the right of the AXLE as illustrated.

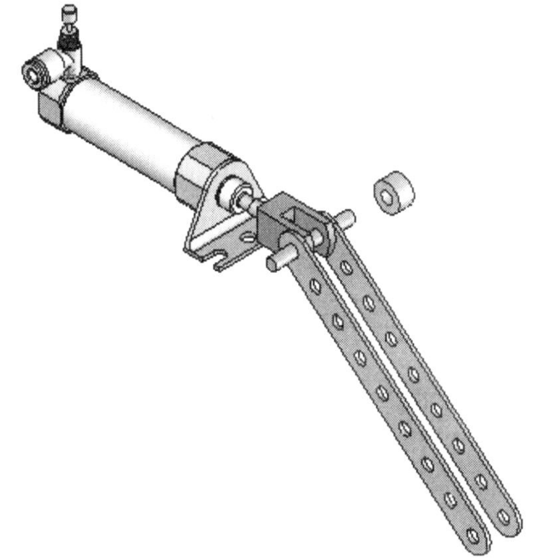

Enlarge the view.

303) Click **Zoom to Area**. **Zoom-in** on the SHAFT-COLLAR and the AXLE to enlarge the view.

Insert a Concentric Mate.

304) Click **Mate** Mate from the Assembly toolbar. The Mate PropertyManager is displayed.

305) Click the inside **hole face** of the SHAFT-COLLAR.

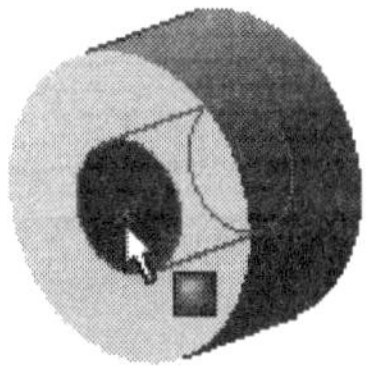

306) Click the **long cylindrical face** of the AXLE. The selected faces are displayed in the Mate Selections box. Concentric is selected by default.

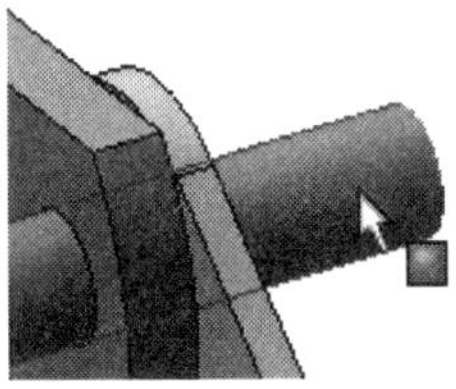

307) Click the **Green Check mark** ✔.

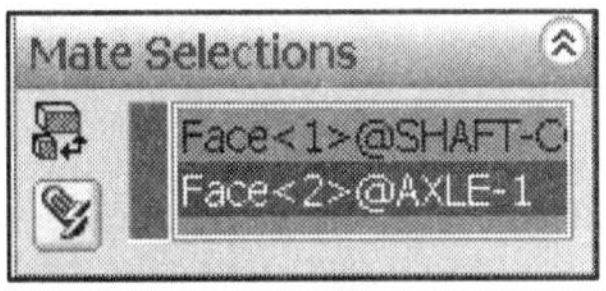

Insert a Coincident Mate.

308) Press the **Shift-z** keys to Zoom in on the model.

309) Click the **front face** of the SHAFT-COLLAR as illustrated.

310) Press the **left arrow key** approximately 5 times to rotate the model to view the back face of the first FLATBAR.

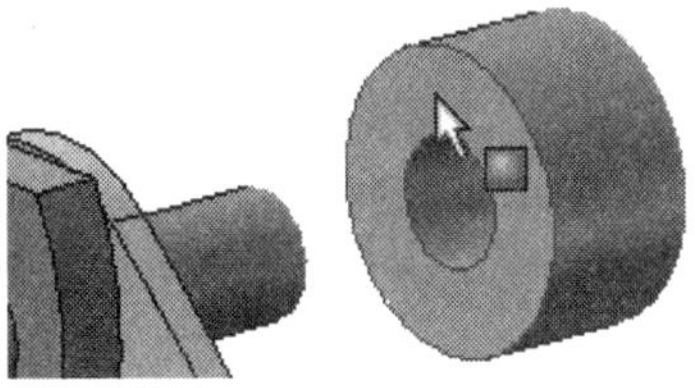

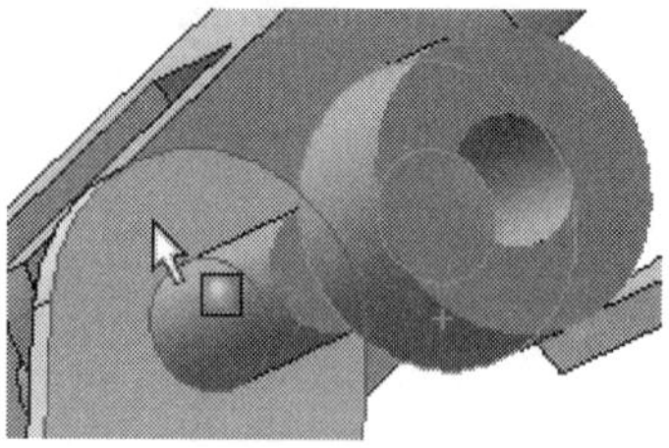

311) Click the **back face** of the first FLATBAR. The selected faces are displayed in the Mate Selections box. Coincident is selected by default.

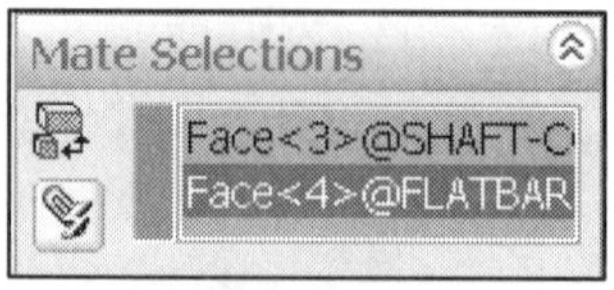

312) Click the **Green Check mark**.

313) Click **OK** from the Mate PropertyManager.

Display the Isometric view.

314) Click **Isometric view**.

Insert the second SHAFT-COLLAR.

315) Click **Insert Component** Insert Compo... from the Assembly toolbar. The Insert Component PropertyManager is displayed.

316) Click **Browse**.

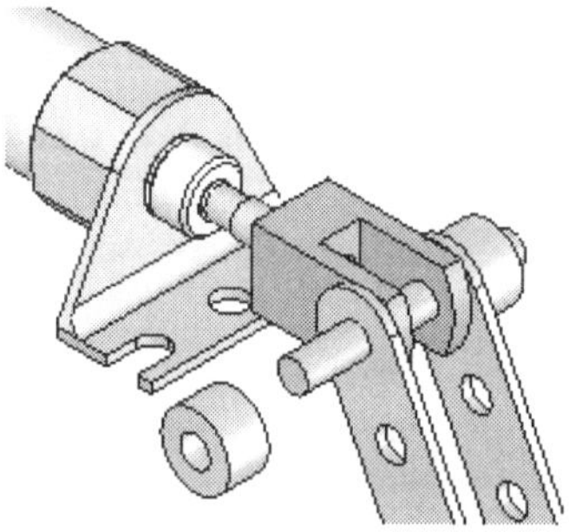

317) Select **Part** for Files of type from the SW-TUTORIAL-2007 folder.

318) Double-click **SHAFT-COLLAR**.

319) Click a **position** near the AXLE as illustrated.

Enlarge the view.

320) Click **Zoom to Area**. Zoom-in on the second SHAFT-COLLAR and the AXLE to enlarge the view.

Insert a Concentric Mate.

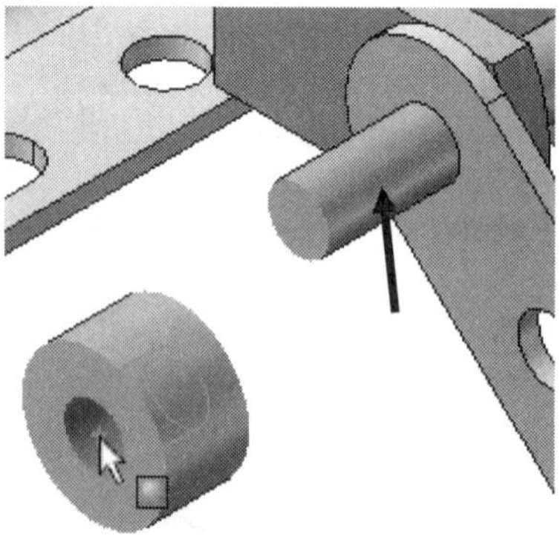

321) Click **Mate** Mate from the Assembly toolbar. The Mate PropertyManager is displayed.

322) Click the **inside hole face** of the second SHAFT-COLLAR.

323) Click the **long cylindrical face** of the AXLE. Concentric is selected by default. The selected faces are displayed in the Mate Selections box.

324) Click the **Green Check mark**.

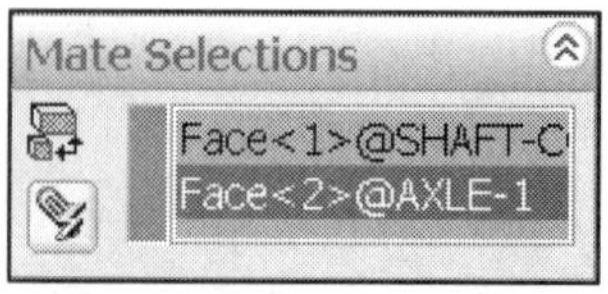

Insert a Coincident Mate.

325) Press the **f** key to fit the model to the Graphics window.

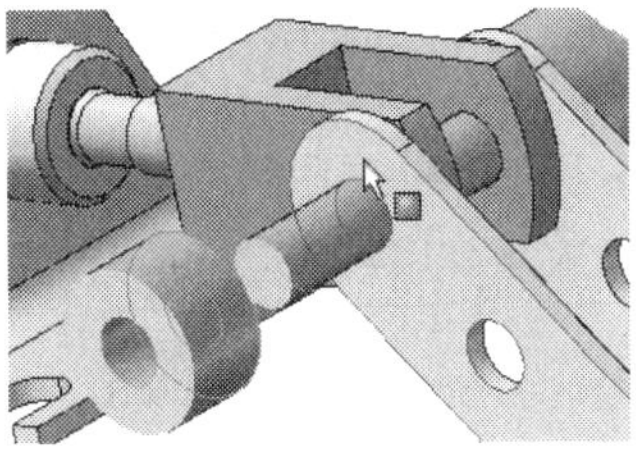

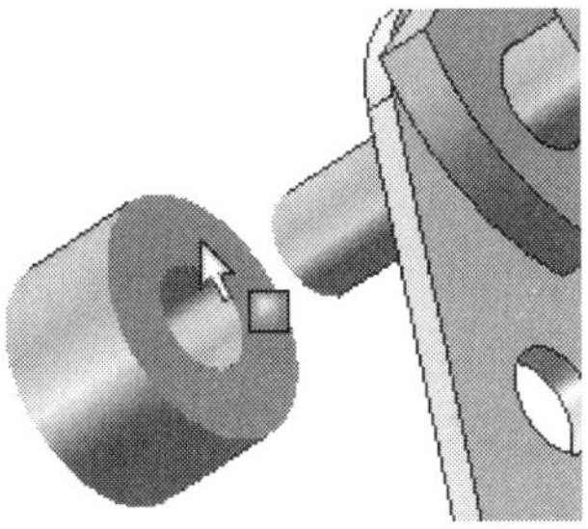

326) Click the **back face** of the second SHAFT-COLLAR.

327) Click the **front face** of the second FLATBAR. The selected faces are displayed in the Mate Selections box. Coincident is selected by default.

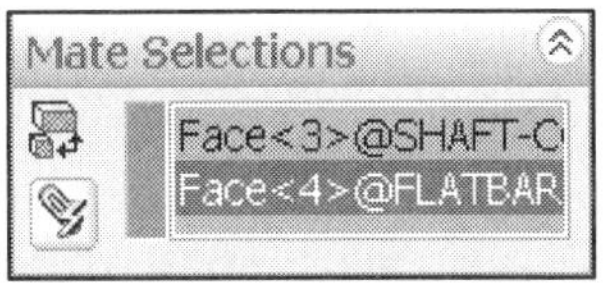

328) Click the **Green Check mark**.

329) Click **OK** from the Mate PropertyManager.

Display the Isometric view.

330) Click **Isometric view**.

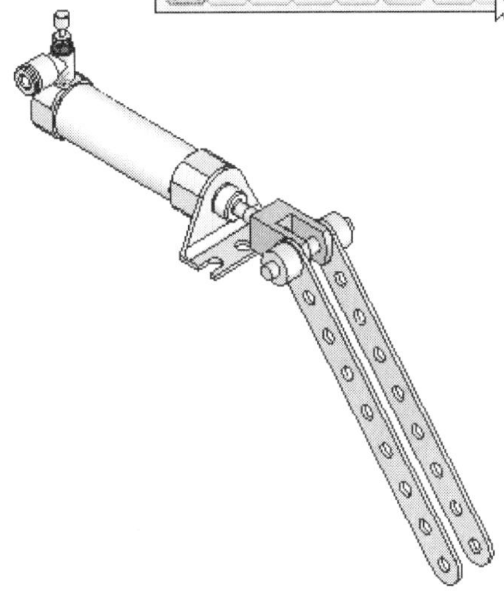

Fit the model to the Graphics window.

331) Press the **f** key.

Save the LINKAGE assembly.

332) Click **Save**. The LINKAGE assembly is complete.

Review the LINKAGE Assembly.

An assembly is a document that contains two or more parts. A part or sub-assembly inserted into an assembly is called a component. You created the LINKAGE assembly.

The AIRCYLINDER sub-assembly was the first component inserted into the LINKAGE assembly. The AIRCYLINDER assembly was obtained from the CD in the book and copied to the SW-TUTORIAL-2007 folder.

The AIRCYLINDER assembly was fixed to the Origin. The Concentric and Coincident Mates added geometric relationships between components in the LINKAGE assembly.

The AXLE part was the second component inserted into the LINKAGE assembly. The AXLE required a Concentric Mate between two cylindrical faces and a Coincident Mate between two Front planes.

The FLATBAR part was the third component inserted into the LINKAGE assembly. The FLATBAR required a Concentric Mate between two cylindrical faces and a Coincident Mate between two flat faces. A second FLATBAR was inserted into the LINKAGE assembly. A Parallel Mate was added between the two FLATBARs.

Two SHAFT-COLLAR parts were inserted into the LINKAGE assembly. Each SHAFT-COLLAR required a Concentric Mate between the two cylindrical faces and a Coincident Mate between two flat faces.

Physical Simulation Tools

The Physical Simulation tools represent the effects of motors, springs, and gravity on an assembly. The Physical Simulation tools are combined with Mates and Physical Dynamics to translate and rotate components in an assembly.

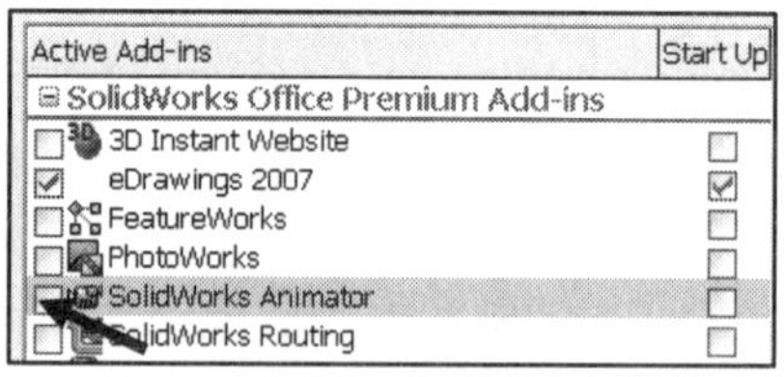

The Simulation Toolbar contains four simulation tools: Linear Motor, Rotary Motor, Spring, and Gravity. Activate SolidWorks Animator. Select Tools, Add-Ins, SolidWorks Animator from the Main menu.

Activity: LINKAGE Assembly-Physical Simulation

Insert a Rotary Motor Physical Simulation Tool.

333) Click **View**, **Toolbars**, **Simulation** from the Main menu. The Simulation toolbar is displayed

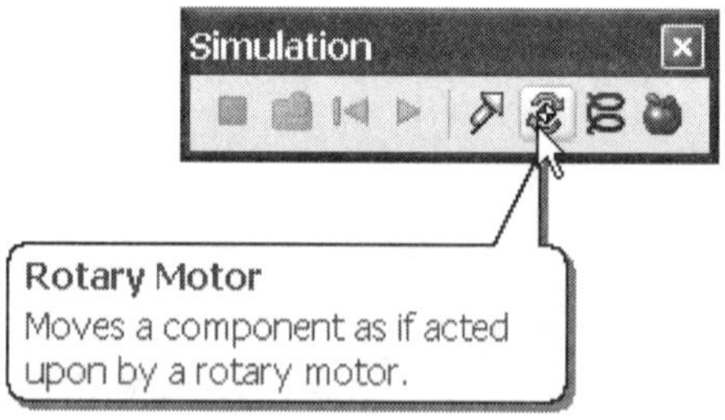

334) Click **Rotary Motor** from the Simulation toolbar. The Rotary Motor PropertyManager is displayed.

335) Click the **FLATBAR front face** as illustrated. A red Rotary Motor icon is displayed. The red direction arrow points counterclockwise.

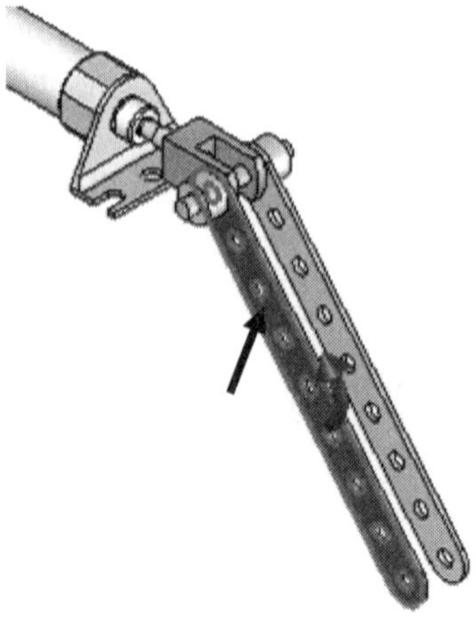

336) Position the **Velocity Slide bar** in the middle of the Rotary Motor PropertyManager.

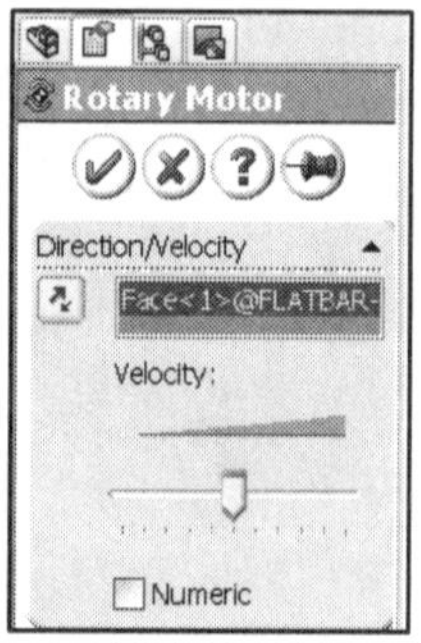

337) Click **OK** from the Rotary Motor PropertyManager. Note: Recording the simulation to an avi file requires the SolidWorks Animator application.

Record the Simulation.

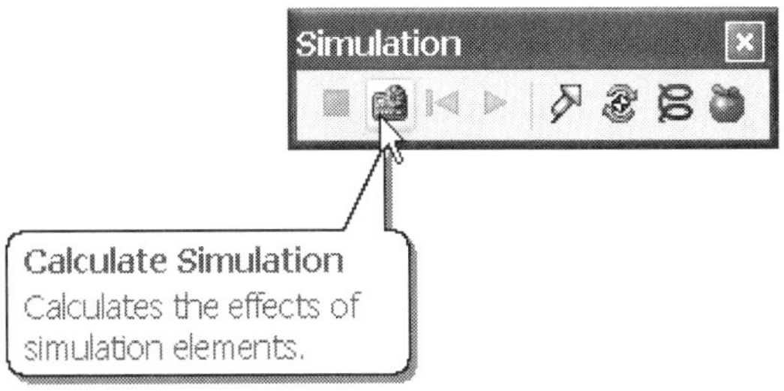

338) Click **Calculate Simulation**. The FLATBAR rotates in a counterclockwise direction.

339) Click **Replay Simulation** from the Simulation toolbar.

340) Click **Play** from the Animation Controller.

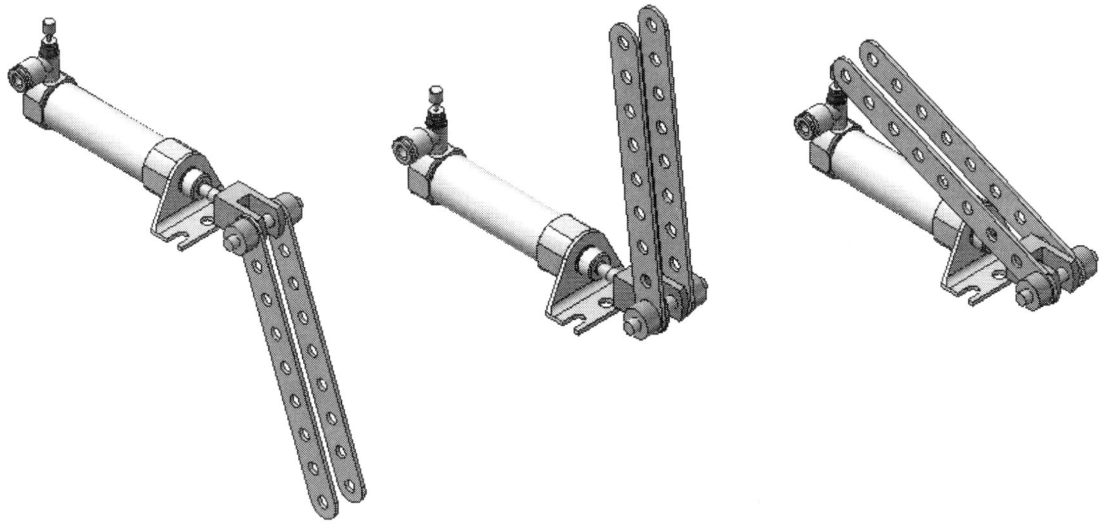

Linear Assembly Physical Simulation

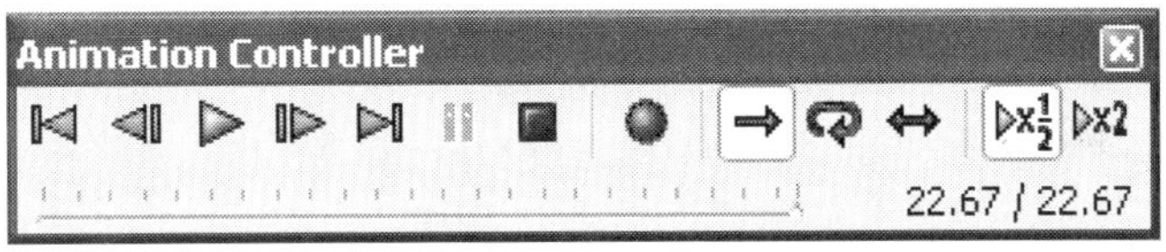

Stop the Simulation.

341) Click **Stop** from the Animation Controller.

342) Save the simulation in an AVI file to the SW-TUTORIAL-2007 folder. Click **Save**. Note: SW Animator is required to save the simulation in an .AVI file. Accept the default file name.

343) Click **Save**.

344) Click **OK** from the Video Compression box. Note: This should take approximately 2 minutes.

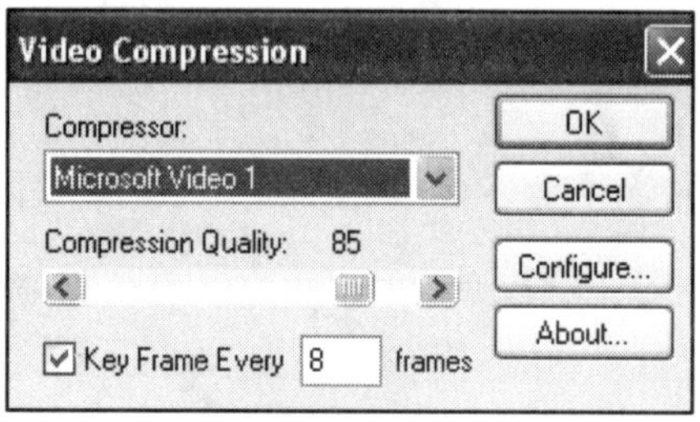

Close the Simulation.

345) Click **Close** from the Animation Controller.

Fit the assembly to the Graphics window.

346) Press the **f** key.

Save the LINKAGE assembly.

347) Click **Save**.

Exit SolidWorks.

348) Click **Windows**, **Close All** from the Main menu.

The LINKAGE assembly project is complete.

Review the Physical Simulation.

The Rotary Motor Physical Simulation tool combined Mates and Physical Dynamics to rotate the FLATBAR components in the LINKAGE assembly. The Rotary Motor was applied to the front face of the FLATBAR. You utilized the Calculate option to play the simulation. You saved the simulation in an .AVI file. Note: SW Animator is required to save the simulation in an .AVI file.

Additional details on Assembly, Mates, and Simulation are available in SolidWorks Help. Keywords: Standard Mates, Mate PropertyManager, Design Methods in Assembly, and Physical Simulation.

Review the Keyboard Short Cuts in the Appendix. Utilize the Keyboard Short Cuts to save modeling time.

Project Summary

In this project you created three parts, copied the AIRCYLINDER assembly from the CD in the book, and created the LINKAGE assembly.

You developed an understanding of the SolidWorks User Interface: Menus, Toolbars, Task Pane, System icon feedback, Keyboard shortcuts, Document Properties, Parts, and Assemblies.

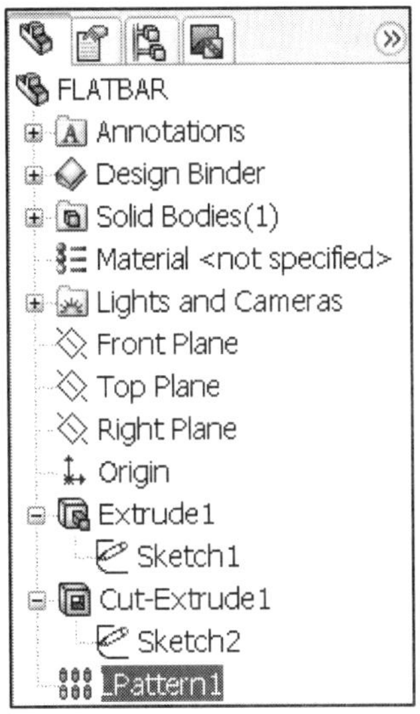

You created 2D sketches and addressed the three key states of a Sketch: Fully Defined, Over Defined, and Under Defined. Note: Always review your FeatureManager for the proper Sketch state.

You obtained the knowledge of the following SolidWorks features: Extruded Base, Extruded Cut, and Linear Pattern. Features are the building blocks of parts. The Extruded Base feature required a Sketch plane, Sketch, and Depth.

The Extruded Base feature added material to a part. The Extruded Base feature was utilized in the AXLE, SHAFT-COLLAR, and FLATBAR parts.

The Extruded Cut feature removed material from the part. The Extruded Cut feature was utilized to create a hole in the SHAFT-COLLAR, and FLATBAR parts.

The Linear Pattern feature was utilized to create an array of holes in the FLATBAR part.

When parts are inserted into an assembly, they are called components. You created the LINKAGE assembly by inserting the AIRCYLINDER assembly, AXLE, SHAFT-COLLAR, and FLATBAR parts.

Mates are geometric relationships that align and fit components in an assembly. Concentric, Coincident, and Parallel Mates were utilized to assemble the components.

The Rotary Motor Physical Simulation tool combined Mates and Physical Dynamics to rotate the FLATBAR components in the LINKAGE assembly.

Project Terminology

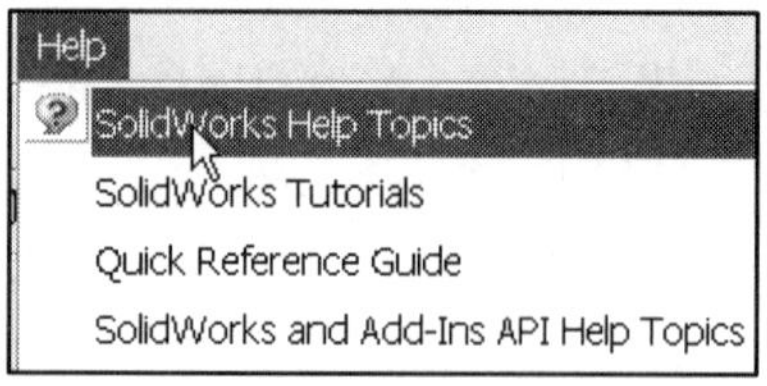

Utilize SolidWorks Help for additional information on the terms utilized in this project.

Assembly: An assembly is a document which contains parts, features, and other sub-assemblies. When a part is inserted into an assembly it is called a component. Components are Mated together. The filename extension for a SolidWorks assembly file name is .SLDASM.

Component: A part or sub-assembly within an assembly.

Cursor Feedback: Feedback is provided by a symbol attached to the cursor arrow indicating your selection. As the cursor floats across the model, feedback is provided in the form of symbols, riding next to the cursor.

Dimension: A value indicating the size of feature geometry.

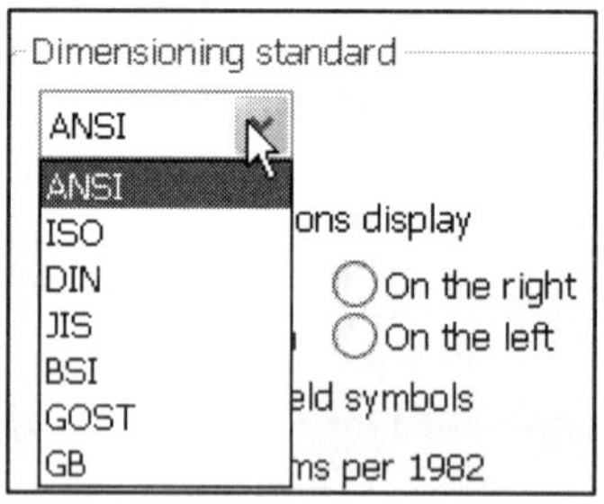

Dimensioning Standard: A set of drawing and detailing options developed by national and international organizations. The Dimensioning standard options are: ANSI, ISO, DIN, JIS, BSI, GOST, and GB.

Features: Features are geometry building blocks. Features add or remove material. Features are created from sketched profiles or from edges and faces of existing geometry.

Mates: A Mate is a geometric relationship between components in an assembly.

Menus: Menus provide access to the commands that the SolidWorks software offers.

Mouse Buttons: The left and right mouse buttons have distinct meanings in SolidWorks. Left mouse button is utilized to select geometry. Right-mouse button is utilized to invoke commands.

Part: A part is a single 3D object made up of features. The filename extension for a SolidWorks part file name is .SLDPRT.

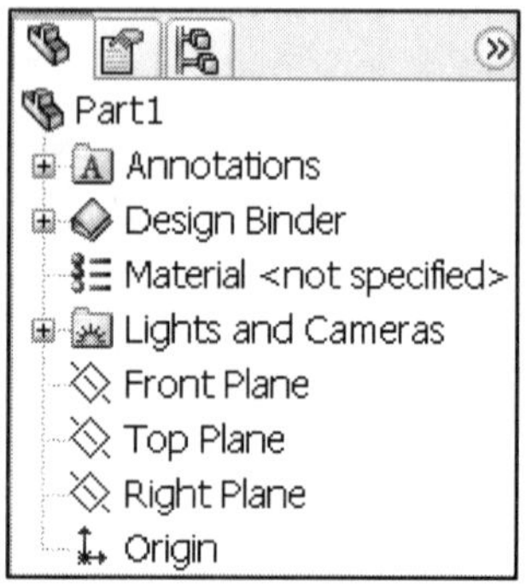

Plane: To create a sketch, select a plane. Planes are flat and infinite. They are represented on the screen with visible edges. The reference plane for this project is the Front plane.

Relation: A relation is a geometric constraint between sketch entities or between a sketch entity and a plane, axis, edge, or vertex. Utilize Add Relations to manually connect related geometry.

Sketch: The name to describe a 2D profile is called a sketch. 2D Sketches are created on flat faces and planes within the model. Typical geometry types are lines, arcs, rectangles, circles, polygons and ellipses.

Status of a Sketch: Three states are utilized in this Project:

- Fully Defined: Has complete information, (Black).
- Over Defined: Has duplicate dimensions, (Red).
- Under Defined: There is inadequate definition of the sketch, (Blue).

Toolbars: The toolbar menus provide shortcuts enabling you to quickly access the most frequently used commands.

Trim Entities: Deletes selected sketched geometry. Extends a sketch segment unit it is coincident with another entity.

Units: Used in the measurement of physical quantities. Millimeter dimensioning and decimal inch dimensioning are the two types of common units specified for engineering parts and drawings.

Project Features

Extruded Boss/Base: An Extruded Base feature is the first feature in a part. An Extruded Boss feature occurs after the Extruded Base feature. The Extruded Boss/Base feature adds material by extrusion.

Steps to create an Extruded Boss/Base Feature:

- Select the Sketch plane; Sketch the profile; Add Dimensions and Relations; Select Extruded Boss/Base from the Features toolbar; Select an End Condition and/or options; Enter a depth; Click OK from the Extrude PropertyManager.

Extruded Cut: The Extruded Cut feature removes material from a solid. The Extruded Cut feature performs the opposite function of the Extruded Boss/Base feature. The Extruded Cut feature starts with either a 2D or 3D sketch and removes material by extrusion.

Steps to create an Extruded Cut Feature:

- Select the Sketch plane; Sketch the profile, Add Dimensions and Relations; Select Extruded Cut from the Features toolbar; Select an End Condition and/or options; Enter a depth; Click OK from the Cut-Extrude PropertyManager.

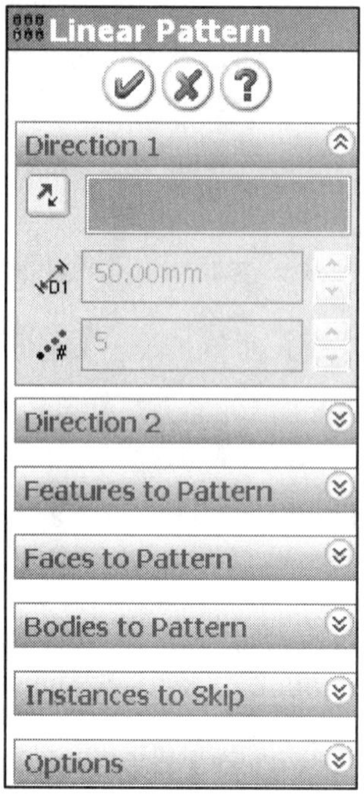

Linear Pattern: A Linear Pattern repeats features or geometry in an array. A Linear Patten requires the number of instances and the spacing between instances.

Steps to create a Linear Pattern Feature:

- Select the features to repeat; Select Linear Pattern from the Feature toolbar; Enter Direction of the pattern; Enter Number of pattern instances in each direction; Enter Distance between pattern instances; Optional: Pattern instances to skip; Click OK from the Linear Pattern PropertyManager.

Engineering Journal

Engineers and designers utilize mathematics, science, economics and history to calculate additional information about a project. Answers to questions are written in an engineering journal.

1. Volume of a cylinder is provided by the formula, $V = \pi r^2 h$. Where:

- V is volume.
- r is the radius.
- h is the height.

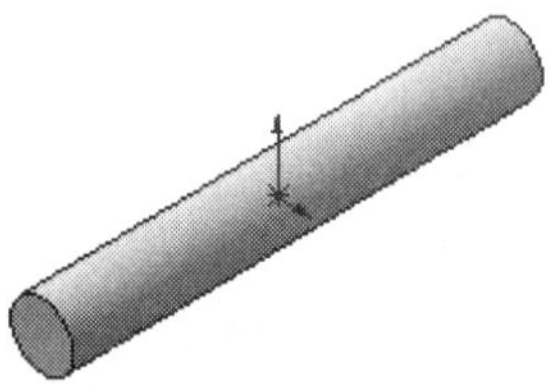

a) Determine the radius of the AXLE in mm.

b) Determine the height of the AXLE in mm.

c) Calculate the Volume of the AXLE in mm^3.

2. Density of a material is provided by the formula: $\rho = m/V$. Where:

- ρ is density.
- m is mass.
- V is volume.

a) Determine the mass of the AXLE in grams if the AXLE is manufactured from hardened steel. The density of hardened steel is .007842 g/mm^3.

______
______

3. The material supplier catalog lists Harden Steel Rod in foot lengths.

Harden Steel Rod (Ø 3/16):		
Part Number:	Length:	Cost:
23-123-1	1 ft	$10.00
23-123-2	2 ft	$18.00
23-123-3	3ft	$24.00

Utilize the table above to determine the following questions:

How many 1-3/8 inch AXLES can be cut from each steel rod?

Twenty AXLE parts are required for a new assembly. What length of Harden Steel Rod should be purchased?

______
______
______
______
______

4. Air is a gas. Boyle's Law states that with constant temperature, the pressure, P of a given mass of a gas is inversely proportional to its volume, V.

- $P_1 / P_2 = V_2 / V_1$
- $P_1 \times V_1 = P_2 \times V_2$

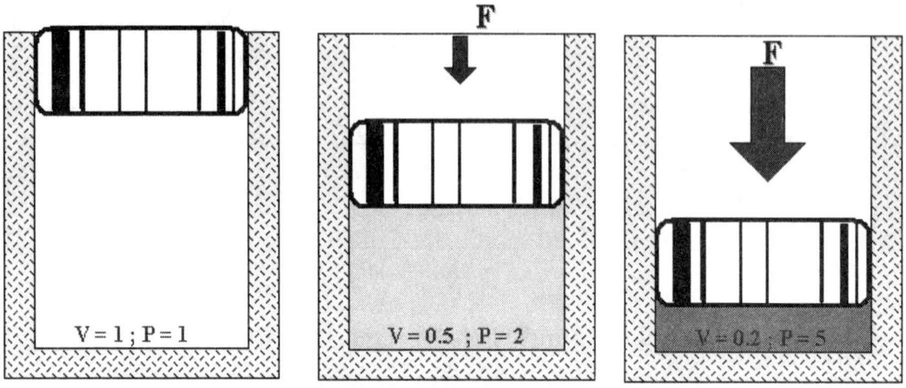

Illustration of Boyle's Law
Courtesy of SMC Corporation of America

The pressure in a closed container is doubled. How will the volume of air inside the container be modified?

Robert Boyle (1627-1691) was an Irish born, English scientist, natural philosopher and a founder of modern chemistry. Boyle utilized experiments and the scientific method to test his theories. Along with his student, Robert Hooke (1635-1703), Boyle developed the air pump.

Research other contributions made by Robert Boyle and Robert Hooke that are utilized today.

Questions

1. Explain the steps in starting a SolidWorks session.
2. Describe the procedure to begin a new sketch.
3. Explain the steps required to change part unit dimensions from inches to millimeters.
4. Describe a part.
5. Identify the three default reference planes.
6. What is the Base feature? Provide an example.
7. Describe the differences between an Extruded Base feature and an Extruded Cut feature.
8. The sketch color black indicates a sketch is ___________ defined.
9. The sketch color blue indicates a sketch is ___________ defined.
10. The sketch color red indicates a sketch is ___________ defined.
11. Describe the procedure to "wake up" a centerpoint.
12. Define a relation. Provide an example.
13. What is a Linear Pattern? Provide an example.
14. Describe an assembly or sub-assembly.
15. What are Mates and why are they important in assembling components?
16. In an assembly, each component has_______# degrees of freedom? Name them.
17. True or False. A fixed component cannot move in an assembly.
18. Review the Design Intent section in the book. Identify how you incorporated design intent into the parts and assembly.

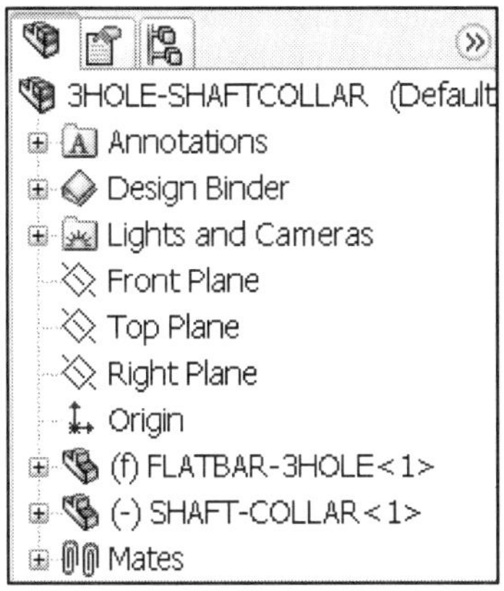

Exercises

Exercise 1.1: FLATBAR-3HOLE.

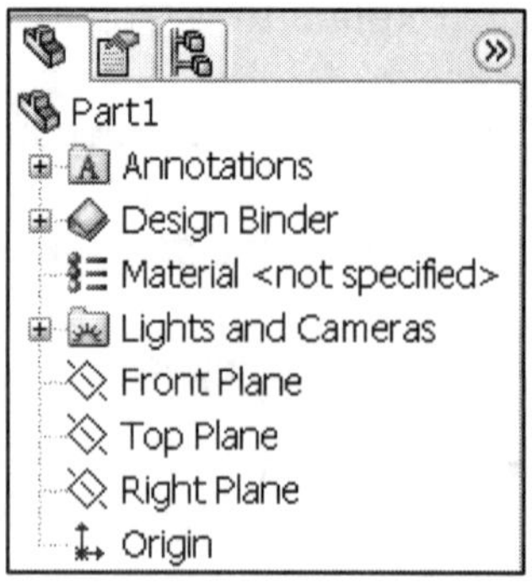

Create the FLATBAR-3HOLE part.

- Utilize the Front plane for the Sketch plane.
- Utilize a Linear Pattern for the three holes. The FLATBAR–3HOLE part is manufactured from 0.060in, [1.5mm] Stainless Steel.

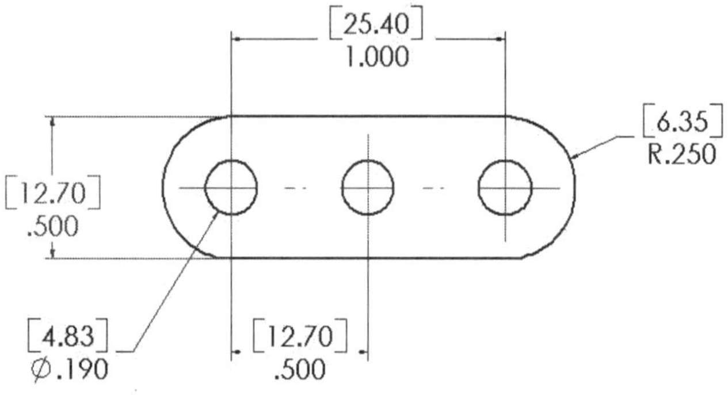

FLATBAR-3HOLE

Exercise 1.2: FLATBAR-5HOLE.

Create the FLATBAR-5HOLE part.

- Utilize the Front plane for the Sketch plane.
- Utilize a Linear Pattern for the five holes. The FLATBAR–5HOLE part is manufactured from 0.060in, [1.5mm] Stainless Steel.
- Calculate the required dimensions for the FLATBAR-5HOLE part. Use the following information:

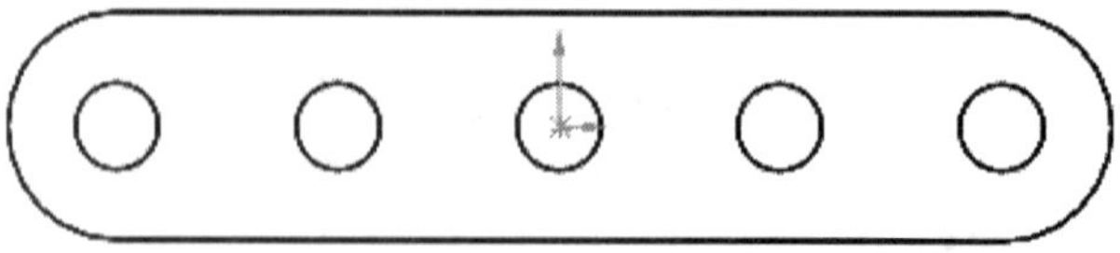

FLATBAR-5HOLE

- Holes are .500in on center.
- Radius is .250in.
- Hole diameter is .190in.

Exercise 1.3a: **LINKAGE-2 Assembly**.

Create the LINKAGE-2 assembly.

- Open the LINKAGE assembly.
- Select File, Save As from the Main menu.
- Check the Save as Copy check box.

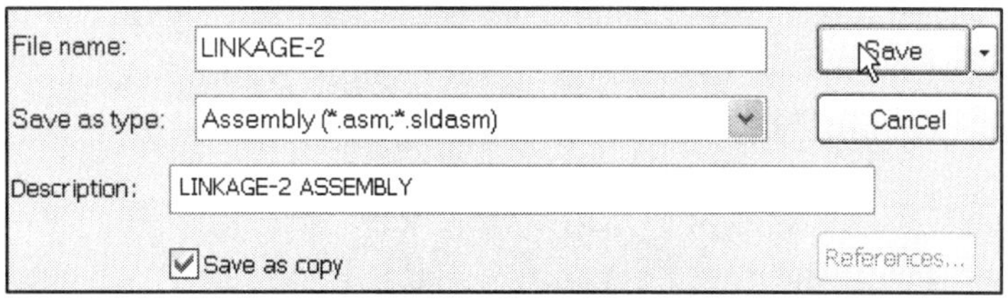

- Enter LINKAGE-2 for file name. LINKAGE-2 ASSEMBLY for Description.

The FLATBAR-3HOLE part was created in Exercise 1.1. Utilize two AXLE parts, four SHAFT COLLAR parts, and two FLATBAR-3HOLE parts to create the LINKAGE-2 assembly as illustrated.

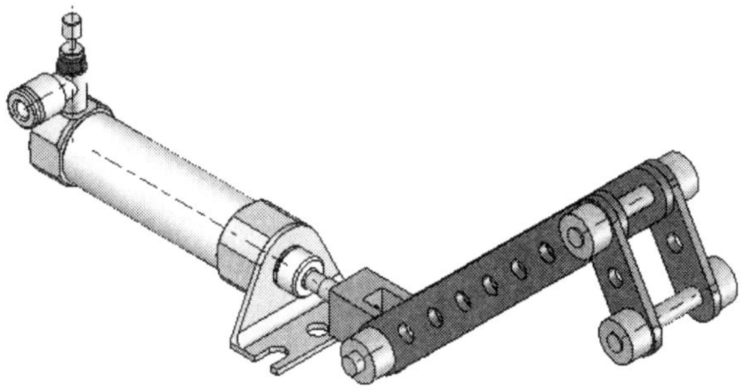

- Insert the first AXLE part.
- Insert a Concentric Mate.

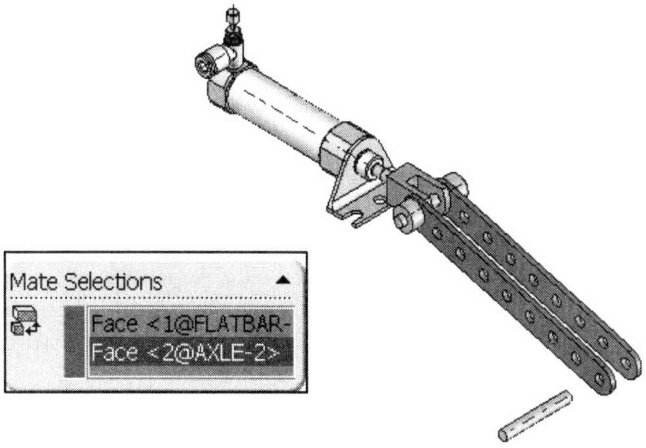

- Insert a Coincident Mate.

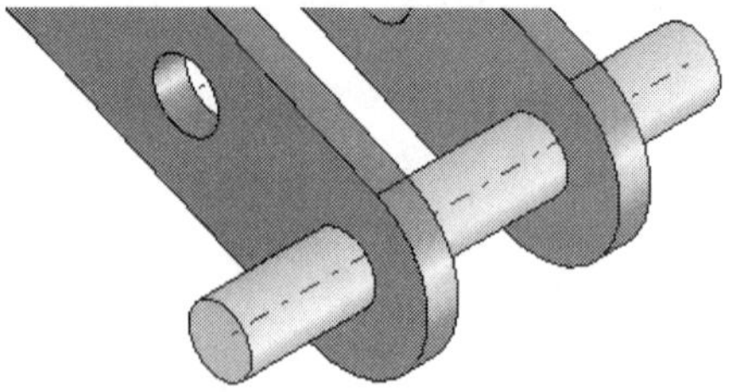

- Insert the first FLATBAR-3HOLE part.

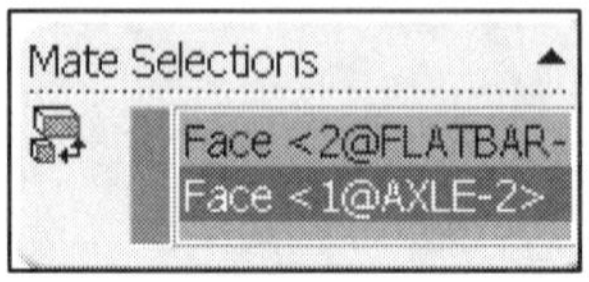

- Insert a Concentric Mate.

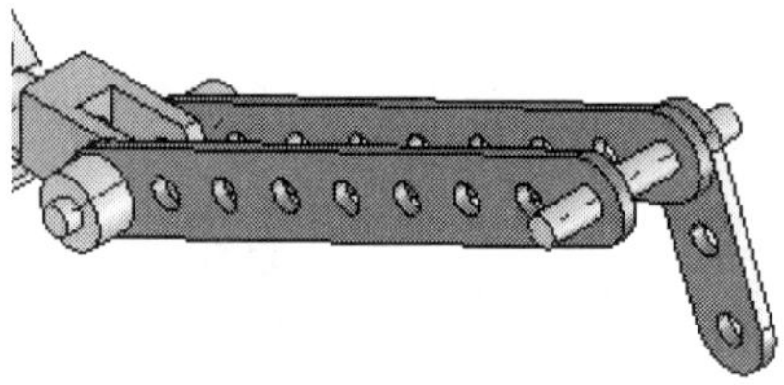

- Insert a Coincident Mate. Perform the same procedure for the second FLATBAR-3HOLE part.

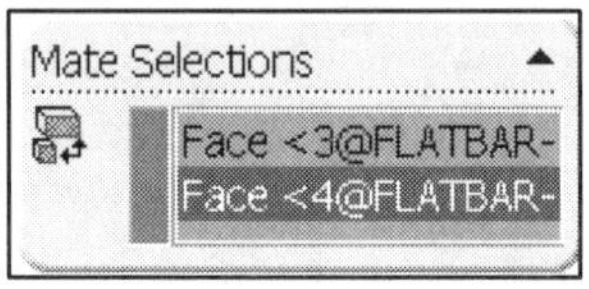

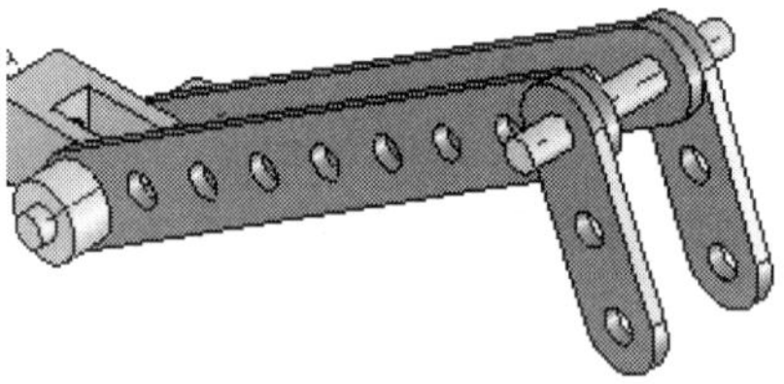

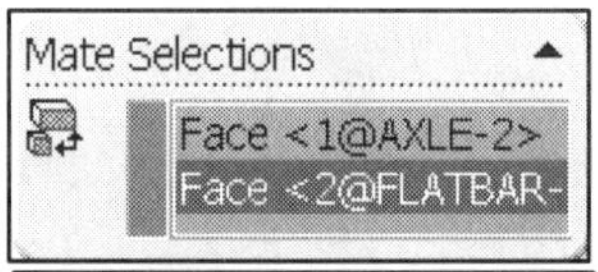

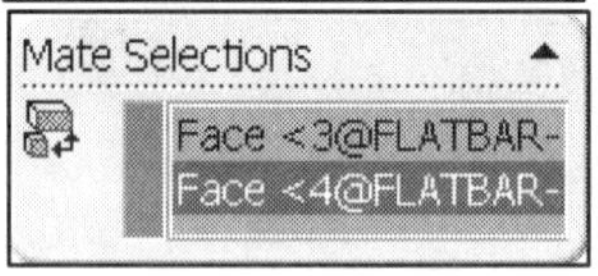

- Insert a Parallel Mate between the 2 FLATBAR-3HOLE parts. Note: The 2 FLATBAR-3HOLE parts move together.

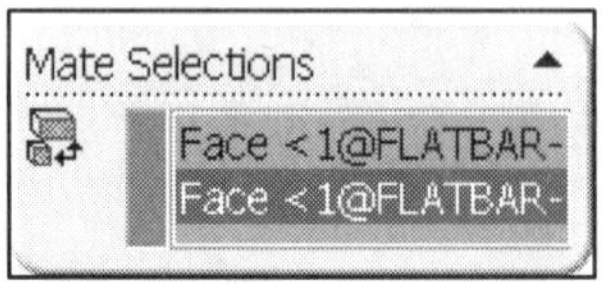

- Insert the second AXLE part.

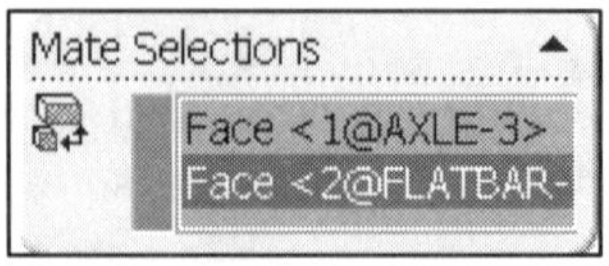

- Insert a Concentric Mate.

- Insert a Coincident Mate.

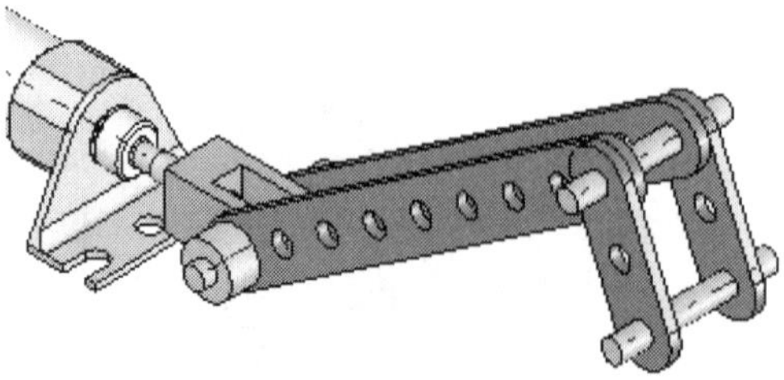

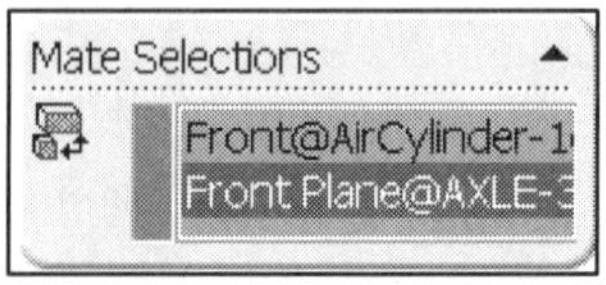

- Insert the first SHAFT-COLLAR part.

- Insert a Concentric Mate.

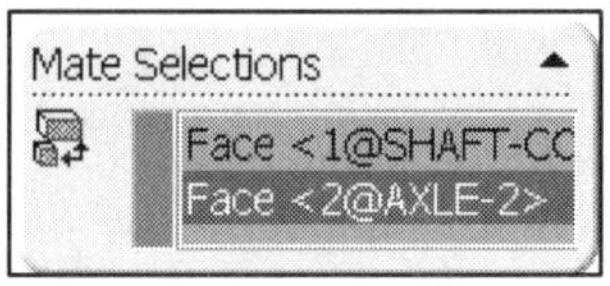

- Insert a Coincident Mate.
- Perform the same tasks to insert the other three required SHAFT-COLLAR parts.

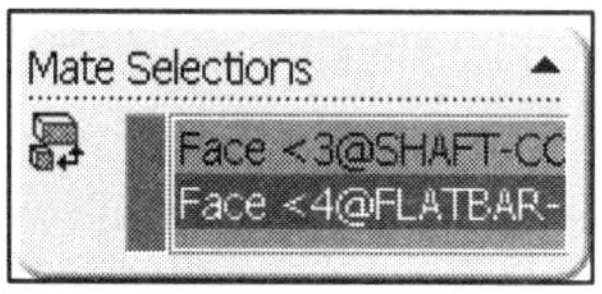

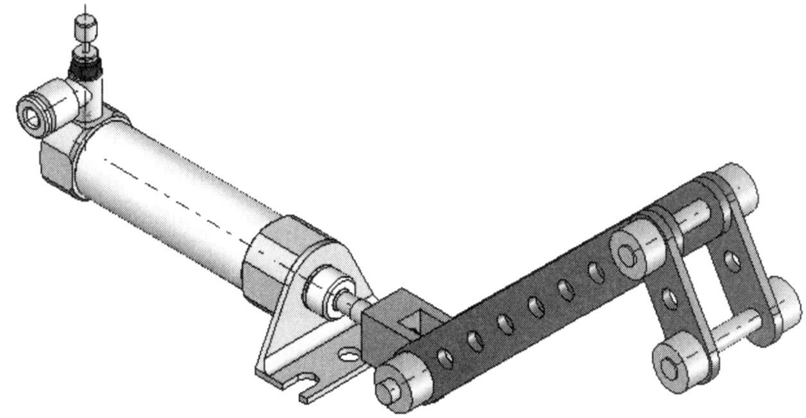

Exercise 1.3b: LINKAGE-2 Assembly Simulation.

Use the LINKAGE-2 assembly created in the previous exercise for the simulation

- Apply a Rotary Motor to the front FLATBAR-3HOLE.
- Record the Simulation.
- Play the Simulation.

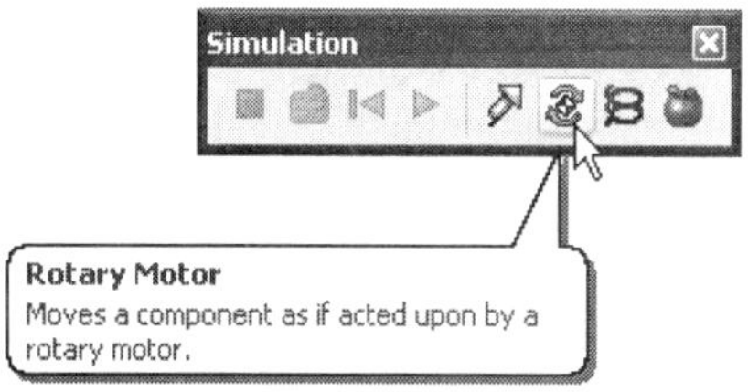

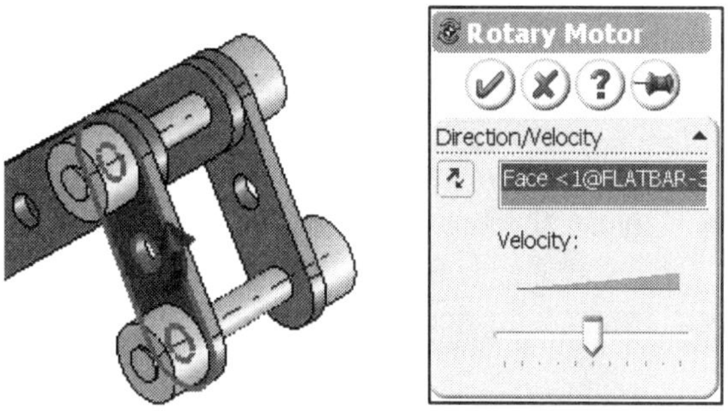

Exercise 1.4a: **ROCKER Assembly**.

Create a ROCKER assembly. The ROCKER assembly consists of two AXLE parts, two FLATBAR-5HOLE parts, and two FLATBAR-3HOLE parts.

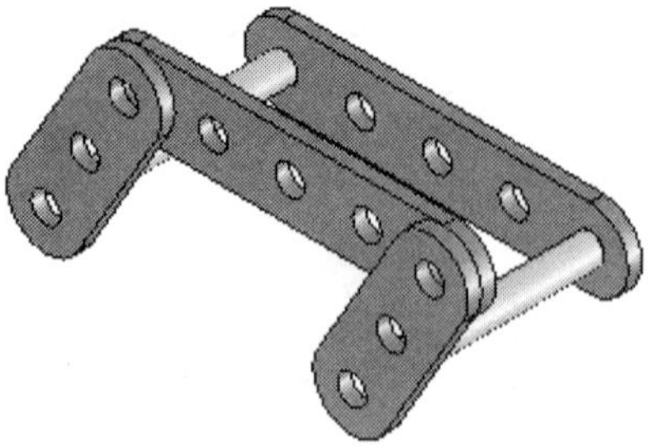

The FLATBAR-3HOLE parts are linked together with the FLATBAR-5HOLE.

The three parts rotate clockwise and counterclockwise, above the Top plane. Create the ROCKER assembly.

- Insert the first FLATBAR-5HOLE part. The FLATBAR-5HOLE is fixed to the Origin of the ROCKER assembly.

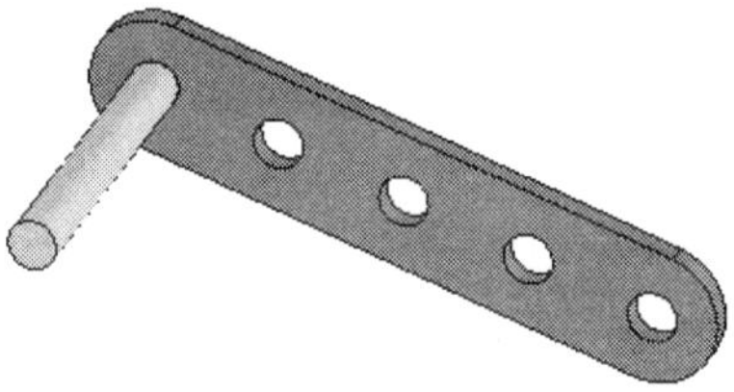

- Insert the first AXLE part.
- Insert a Concentric Mate.
- Insert a Coincident Mate.

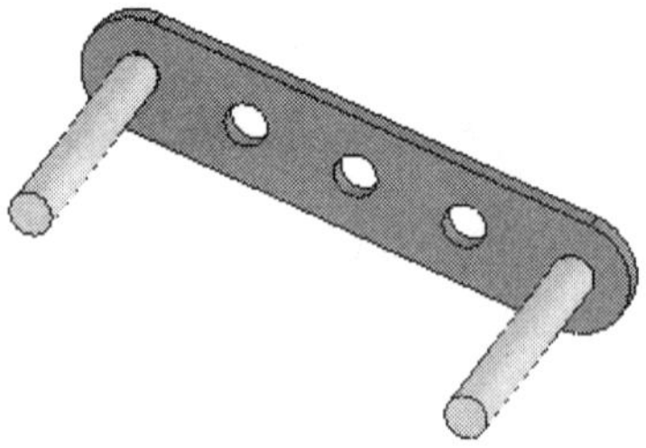

- Insert the second AXLE part.
- Insert a Concentric Mate.
- Insert a Coincident Mate.
- Insert the first FLATBAR-3HOLE part.

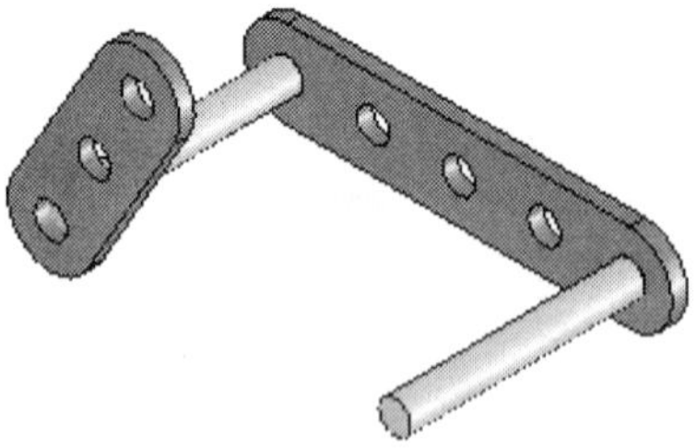

- Insert a Concentric Mate.
- Insert a Coincident Mate.
- Insert the second FLATBAR-3HOLE part.

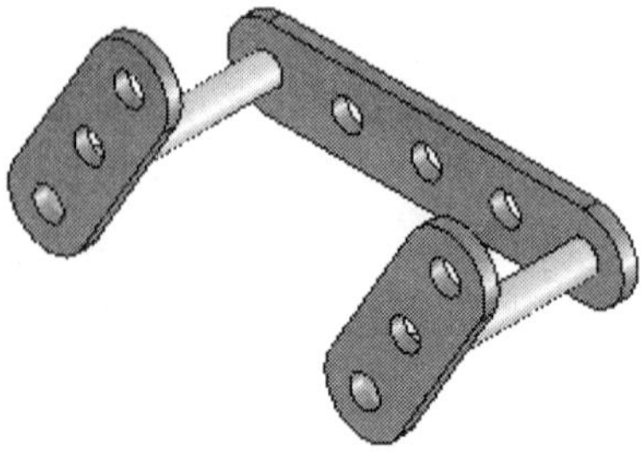

- Insert a Concentric Mate.
- Insert a Coincident Mate.

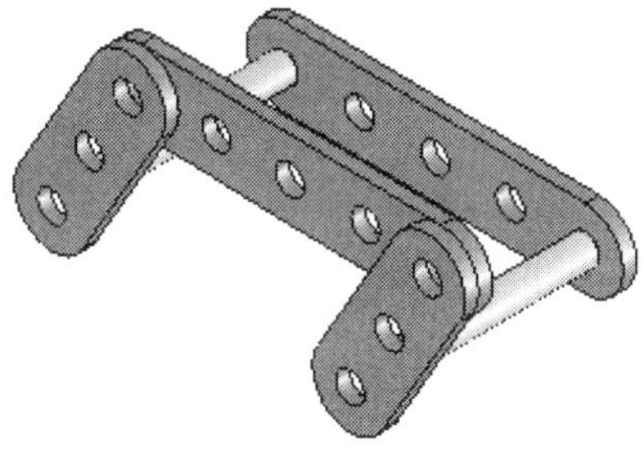

- Insert the second FLATBAR-5HOLE part.
- Insert a Concentric Mate.
- Insert a Coincident Mates.

Note: The end holes of the second FLATBAR-5HOLE are concentric with the end holes of the FLATBAR-3HOLE parts.

Exercise 1.4b: ROCKER Assemby Physical Simulation.

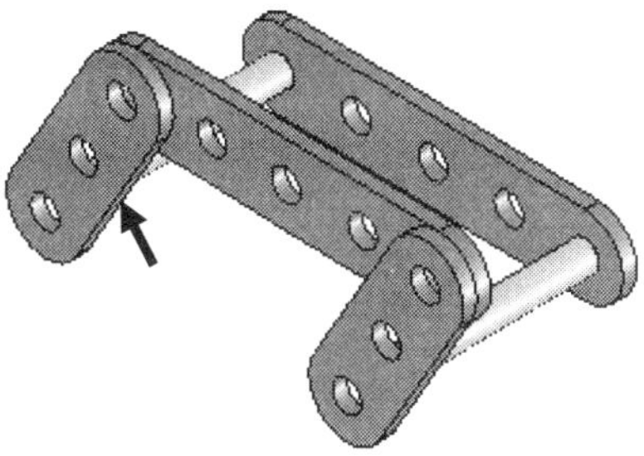

Create the ROCKER Physical Simulation.

- Apply a Rotary Motor to the left FLATBAR-3HOLE in a counterclockwise direction.
- Record the simulation.
- Select Reciprocating Replay .
- Select Play. The Reciprocating Replay continuously plays the simulation from the beginning to the end and then from the end to the beginning.

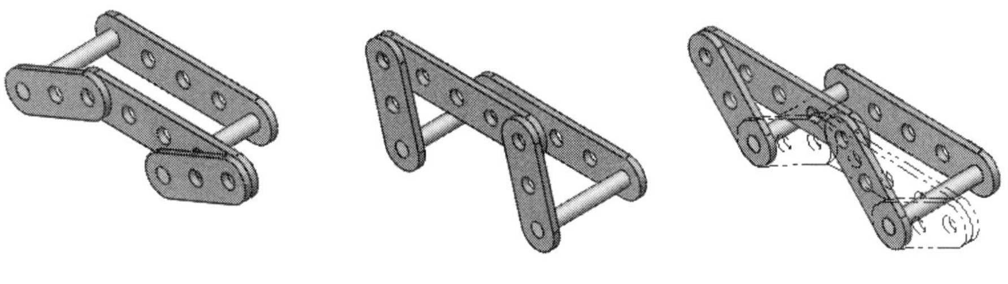

ROCKER Assembly Physical Simulation

In mechanical design, the ROCKER assembly is classified as a mechanism. A Four-Bar Linkage is a common mechanism comprised of four links.

Link1 is called the Frame.

The AXLE part is Link1.

Link2 and Link4 are called the Cranks.

The FLATBAR-3HOLE parts are Link2 and Link4. Link3 is called the Coupler. The FLATBAR-5HOLE part is Link3.

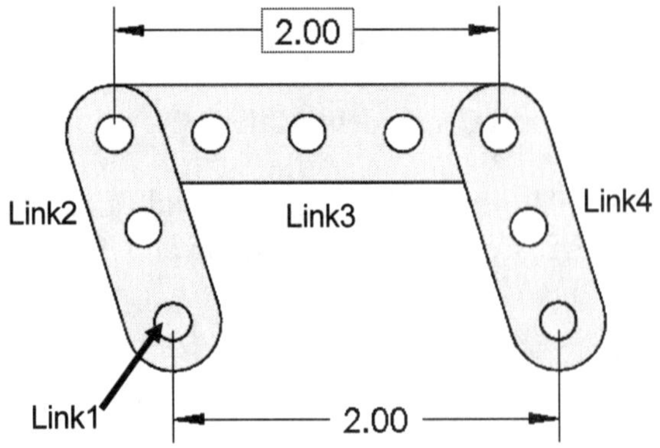

The Injection Molded Process

Lee Plastics of Sterling, MA is a precision injection molding company. Through the World Wide Web (www.leeplastics.com), review the injection molded manufacturing process.

The injection molding process is as follows:

An operator pours the plastic resin in the form of small dry pellets, into a hopper. The hopper feeds a large auger screw. The screw pushes the pellets forward into a heated chamber. The resin melts and accumulates into the front of the screw.

At high pressure, the screw pushes the molten plastic through a nozzle, to the gate and into a closed mold, (Plates A & B). Plates A and B are the machined plates that you will design in this project.

The plastic fills the part cavities through a narrow channel called a gate.

The plastic cools and forms a solid in the mold cavity. The mold opens, (along the parting line) and an ejection pin pushes the plastic part out of the mold into a slide.

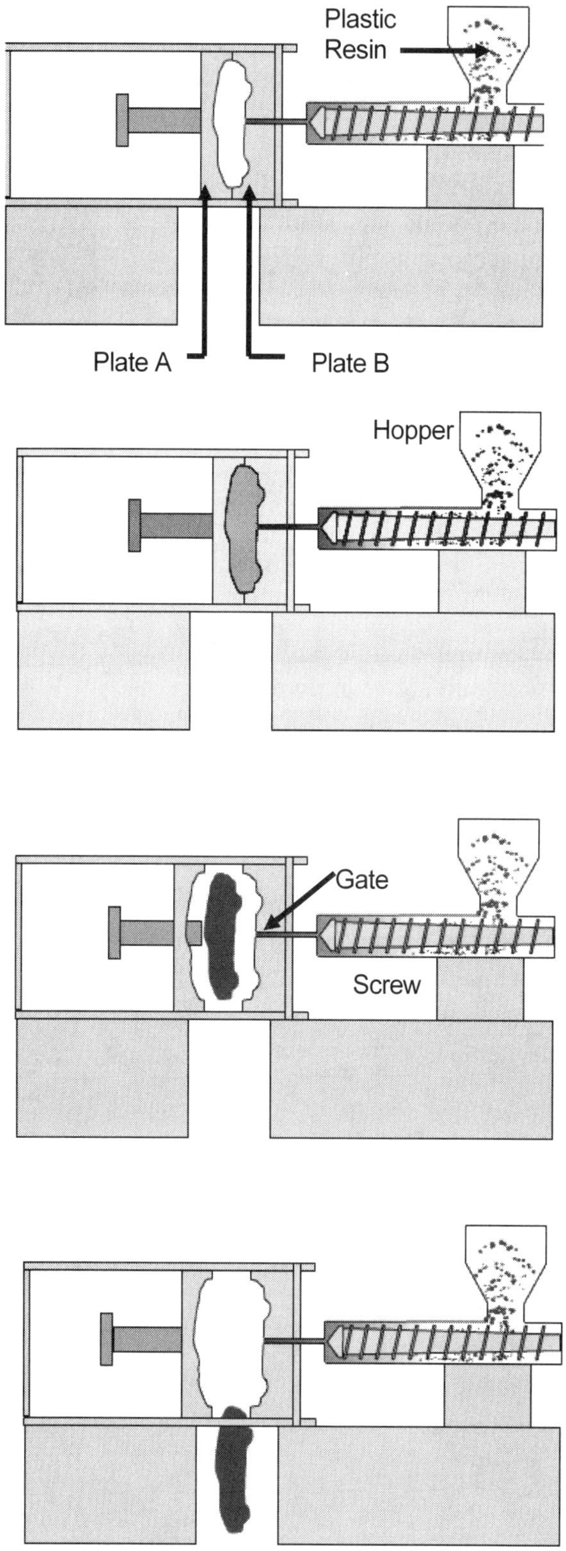

Injection Molded Process
(Courtesy of Lee Plastics, Inc.)

Exercise 1.5: Industry Application

Engineers and designers develop a variety of products utilizing SolidWorks.

Model information is utilized to create plastic molds for products from toys to toothbrushes.

- Utilize the World Wide Web and review the following web sites: mikejwilson.com and zxys.com.

The models obtained from these web sites are for educational purposes only.

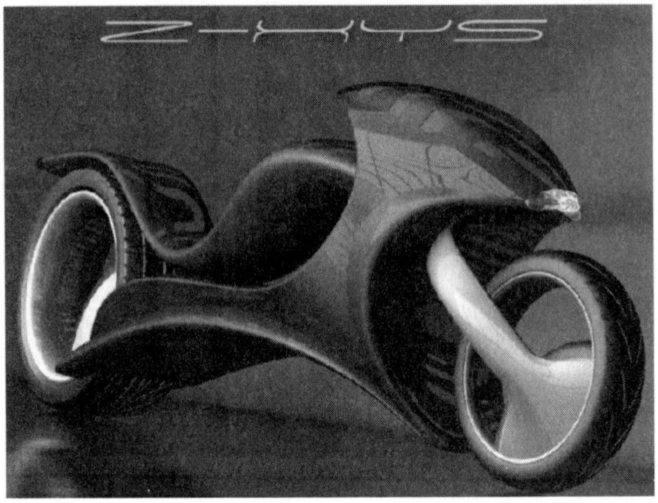

Model Courtesy of Mike J. Wilson, CSWP

Learn modeling techniques from others; create your own designs. A common manufacturing procedure for plastic parts is named the Injection Molding Process. Today's automobiles utilize over 50% plastic components.

Engineers and designers work with mold makers to produce plastic parts. Cost reduction drives plastic part production.

Project 2

FRONT-SUPPORT Assembly

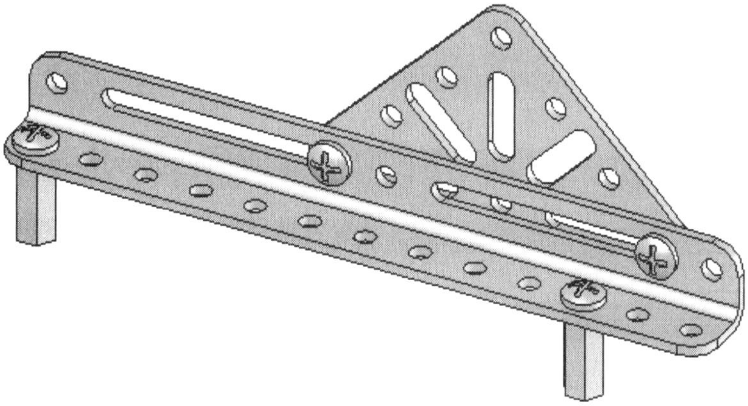

Below are the desired outcomes and usage competencies based on the completion of Project 2.

Desired Outcomes:	**Usage Competencies**:
• Create four parts: o HEX-STANDOFF. o ANGLE-13HOLE. o TRIANGLE. o SCREW.	• Apply the following model features: Extruded Boss/Base, Extruded Thin, Extruded Cut, Revolved Boss/Base, Hole Wizard, Linear Pattern, Circular Pattern, Mirror, Fillet, and Chamfer. • Apply Sketch techniques with various Sketch tools and Construction geometry.
• Create an assembly: o FRONT-SUPPORT assembly.	• Comprehend the assembly process and insert the following Mate types: Concentric, Coincident, Parallel, and Distance.

Notes:

Project 2 – FRONT-SUPPORT Assembly

Project Objective

Create four new parts utilizing the Top, Front, and Right planes. Determine the Sketch plane for each feature. Obtain the knowledge of the following SolidWorks features: Extruded Boss/Base, Extruded Thin, Extruded Cut, Revolved Boss/Base, Hole Wizard, Linear Pattern, Circular Pattern, Fillet, and Chamfer.

Apply Sketch techniques with various Sketch tools: Line, Circle, Rectangle, Centerline, Polygon, Parallelogram, Dynamic Mirror, and Convert Entities. Utilize centerlines as construction geometry to reference dimensions and relationships.

Create four new parts:

1. HEX-STANDOFF.
2. ANGLE-13HOLE.
3. TRIANGLE.
4. SCREW.

Create the FRONT-SUPPORT assembly.

On the completion of this project, you will be able to:

- Select the correct Sketch plane required for the Extruded Base feature.
- Create four new parts.
- Generate a 2D sketch.
- Add Dimensions and Geometric Relations.
- Use the following SolidWorks Features:
  - Extruded Base.
  - Extruded Cut.
  - Extruded Thin.
  - Revolved Base.
  - Linear and Circular Pattern.
  - Mirror.
  - Fillet.
  - Hole Wizard.
  - Chamfer.

Project Overview

The FRONT-SUPPORT assembly supports various pneumatic components and is incorporated into the final PNEUMATIC-TEST-MODULE in Project 4.

Create four new parts in this Project:

1. HEX-STANDOFF.
2. ANGLE-13HOLE.
3. TRIANGLE.
4. SCREW.

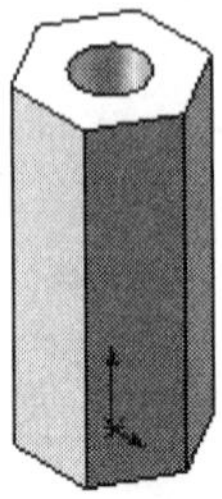

HEX-STANDOFF

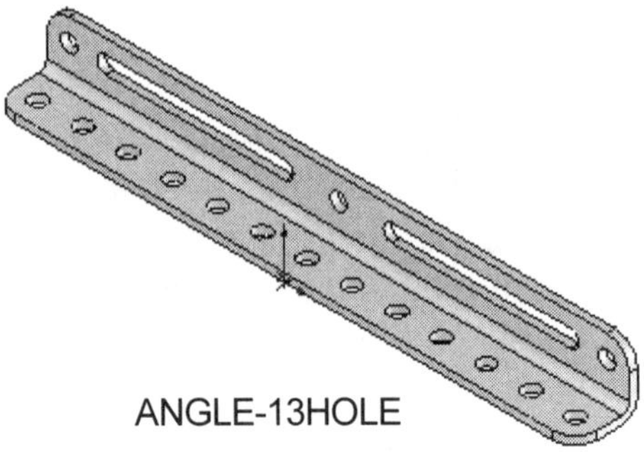

ANGLE-13HOLE

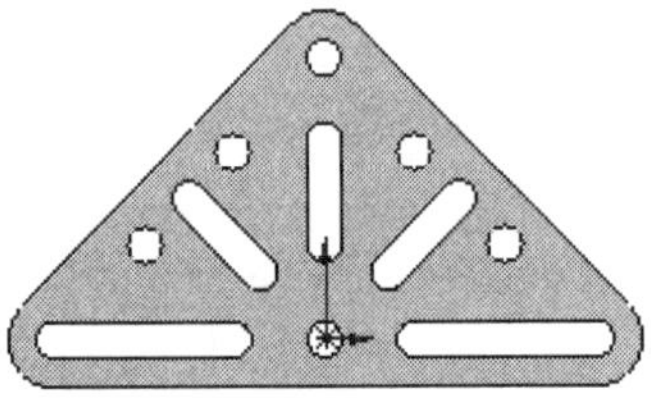

TRIANGLE

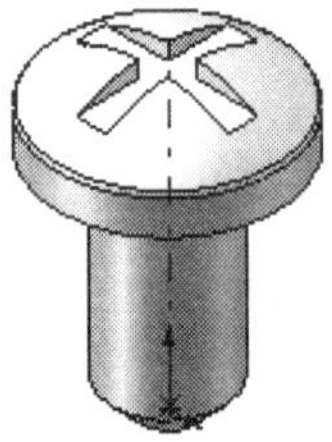

SCREW

Create the FRONT-SUPPORT assembly using the four new created parts.

The FRONT-SUPPORT assembly is used in the exercises at the end of this Project and in Project 4 of the book.

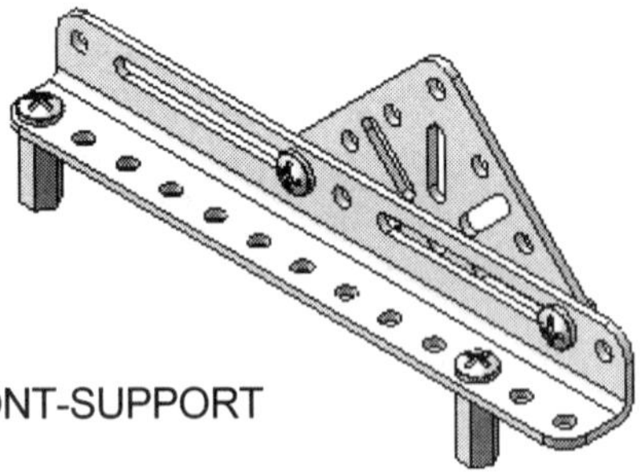

FRONT-SUPPORT

Reference Planes and Orthographic Projection

The three default ⊥ reference planes represent infinite 2D planes in 3D space:

- Front.
- Top.
- Right.

Planes have no thickness or mass.

Orthographic projection is the process of projecting views onto parallel planes with ⊥ projectors.

Default ⊥ datum planes are:

- Primary.
- Secondary.
- Tertiary.

These are the planes used in manufacturing:

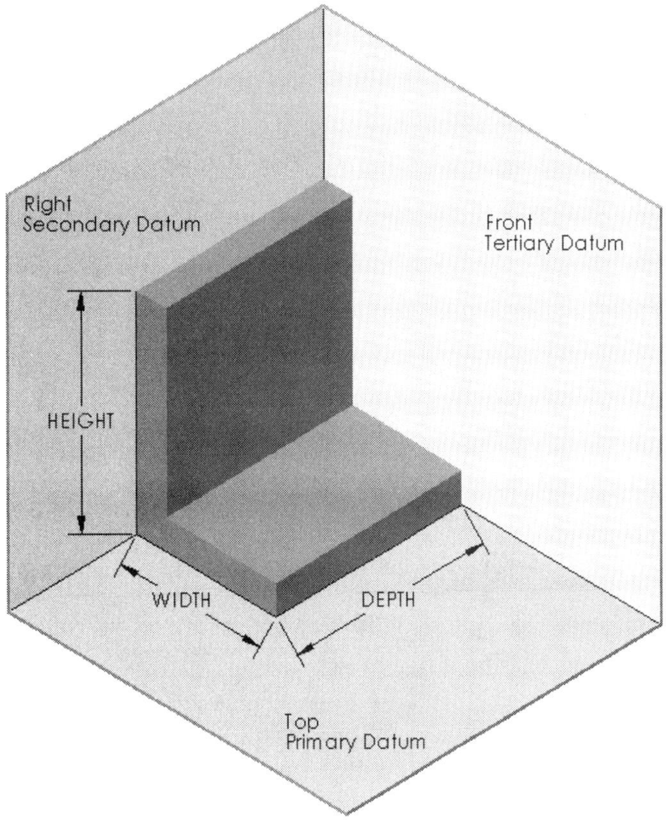

- Primary datum plane contacts the part at a minimum of three points.
- Secondary datum plane contacts the part at a minimum of two points.
- Tertiary datum plane contacts the part at a minimum of one point.

The part view orientation depends on the Base feature Sketch plane.

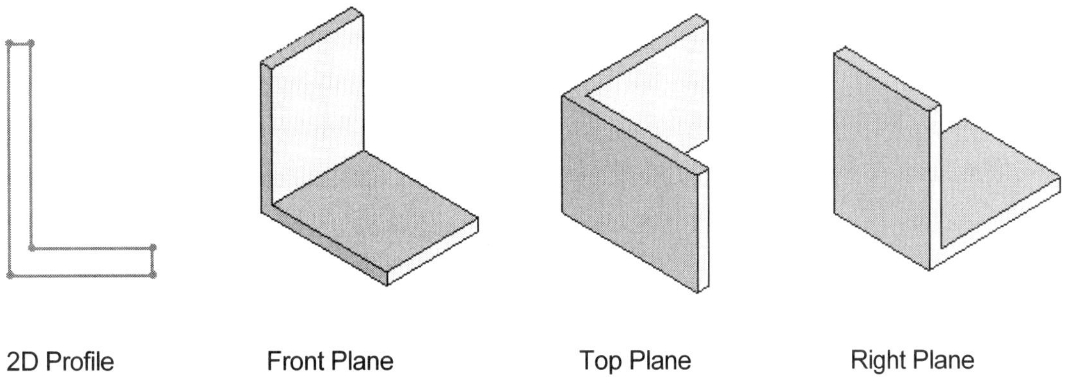

Compare the Front plane, Top plane, and Right plane. Each Extruded Base feature is created with an L-shaped 2D profile.

The six principle views of Orthographic projection listed in the ASME Y14.3M standard are: Top, Front, Right side, Bottom, Rear, & Left side. SolidWorks Standard view names correspond to these Orthographic projection view names.

ASME Y14.3M Principle View:	SolidWorks Standard View:
Front	Front
Top	Top
Right side	Right
Bottom	Bottom
Rear	Back
Left side	Left

In the Third angle Orthographic projection example, the standard drawing views are; Front, Top, Right, and Isometric.

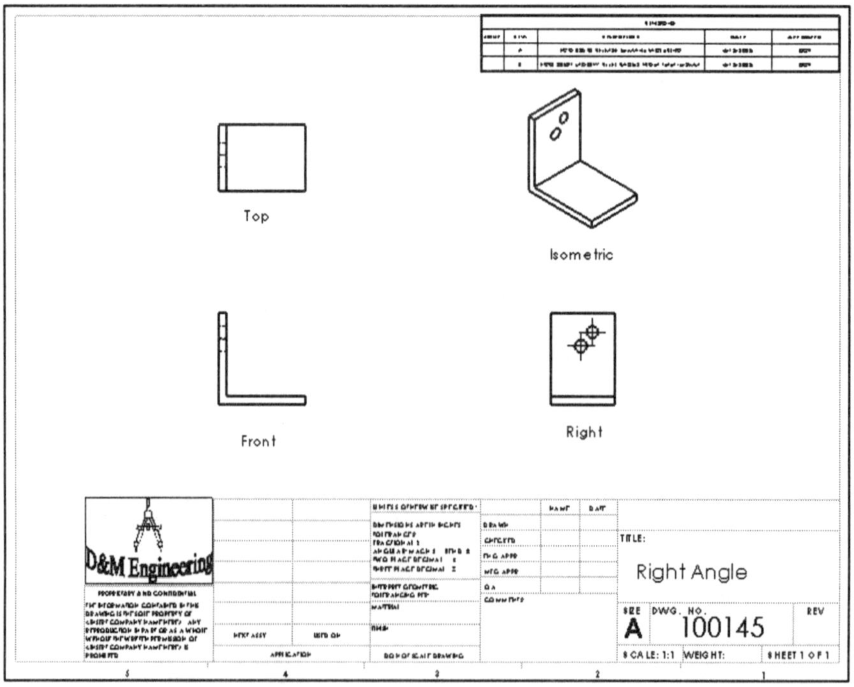

There are two Orthographic projection drawing systems. The first Orthographic projection system is called the Third angle projection.

The second Orthographic projection system is called the first angle projection. The systems are derived from positioning a 3D object in the third or first quadrant.

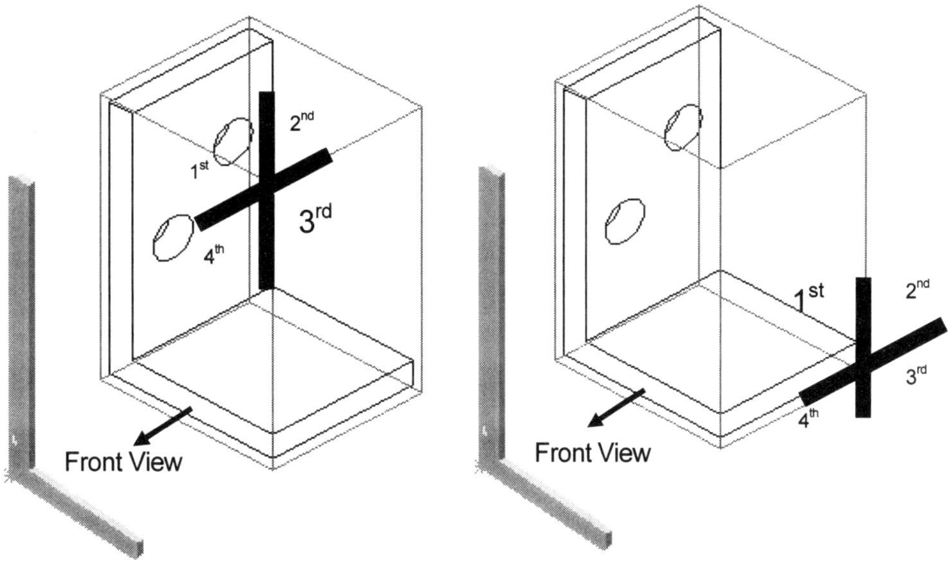

In Third angle projection, the part is positioned in the third quadrant. The 2D projection planes are located between the viewer and the part.

The projected views are placed on a drawing.

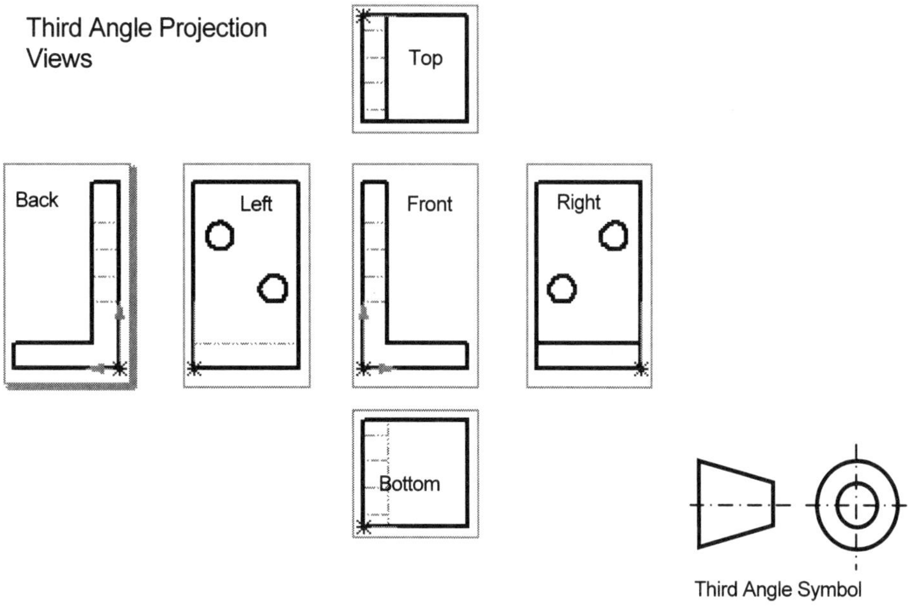

In first angle projection, the part is positioned in the first quadrant. Views are projected onto the planes located behind the part. The projected views are placed on a drawing.

First angle projection is primarily used in Europe and Asia. Third angle projection is primarily used in the U.S. & Canada and is based upon the ASME Y14.3M Multi and Sectional View Drawings standard. Designers should have knowledge and understanding of both systems.

There are numerous multi-national companies. Example: A part is designed in the U.S., manufactured in Japan and destined for a European market.

Third angle projection is used in this text. A truncated cone symbol appears on the drawing to indicate the projection system:

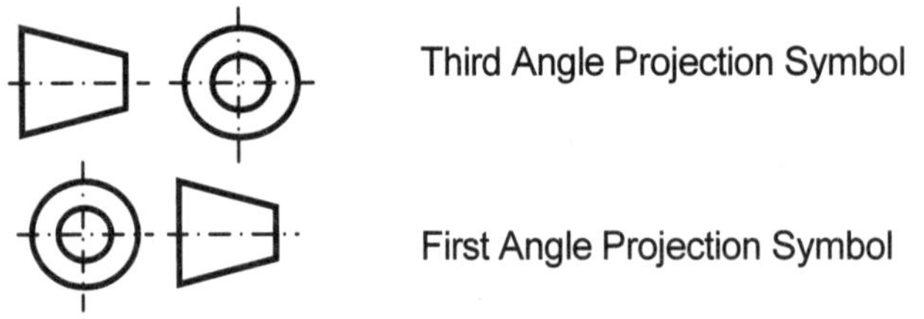

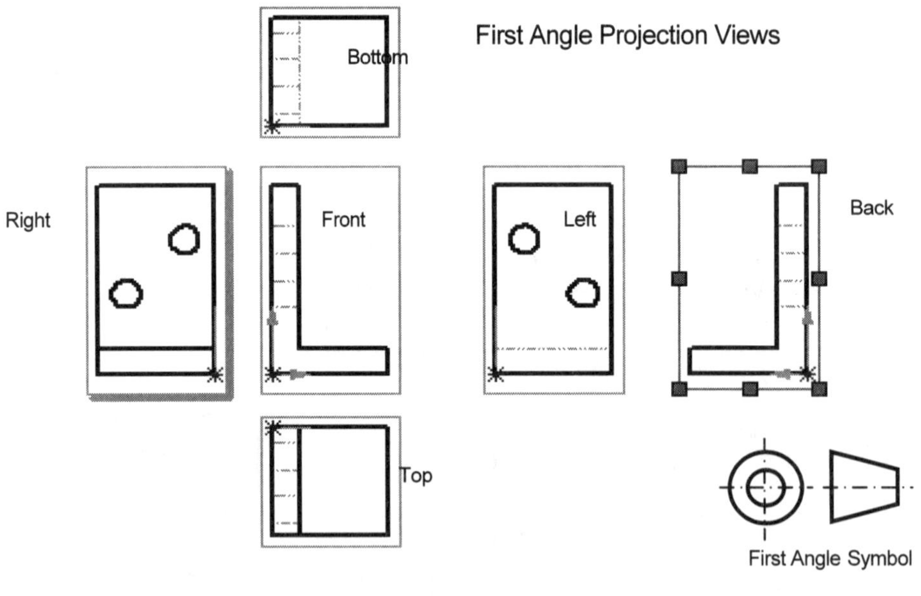

Utilize different planes for the Extruded Base feature.

- HEX-STANDOFF part – Top plane.
- ANGLE-13HOLE part – Right plane.

- TRIANGLE part – Front plane.
- SCREW part – Front plane.

Select the Sketch plane based on symmetry and orientation of the part in the FRONT-SUPPORT assembly. Utilize the standard views: Front, Back, Right, Left, Top, Bottom, and Isometric to orient the part. Create the 2D drawings for the parts in Project 3.

HEX-STANDOFF Part

The HEX-STANDOFF part is a hexagonal shaped part utilized to elevate components in the FRONT-SUPPORT assembly. Machine screws are utilized to fasten components to the HEX-STANDOFF.

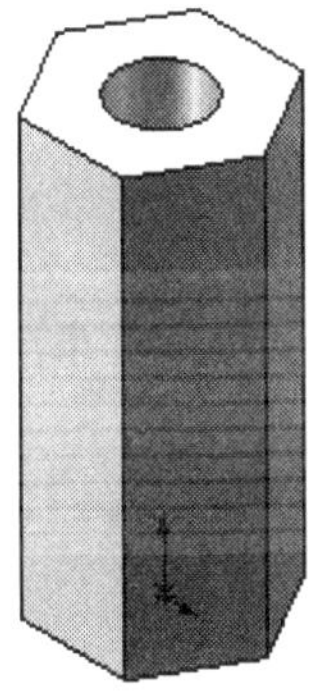

Create the HEX-STANDOFF part with the Extruded Base feature. The Sketch plane for the HEX-STANDOFF Extruded Base feature is the Top plane.

Create the HEX-STANDOFF in the orientation utilized by the FRONT-SUPPORT assembly. The Front and Right plane creates the Extruded Base feature.

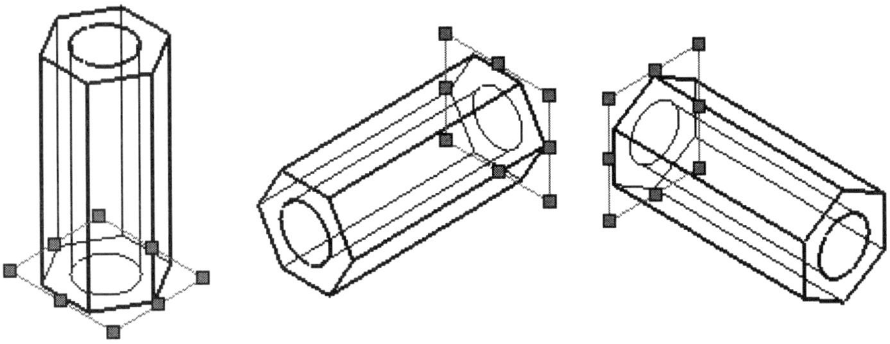

Top Plane Front Plane Right Plane

Utilize the Top plane for the Sketch plane.

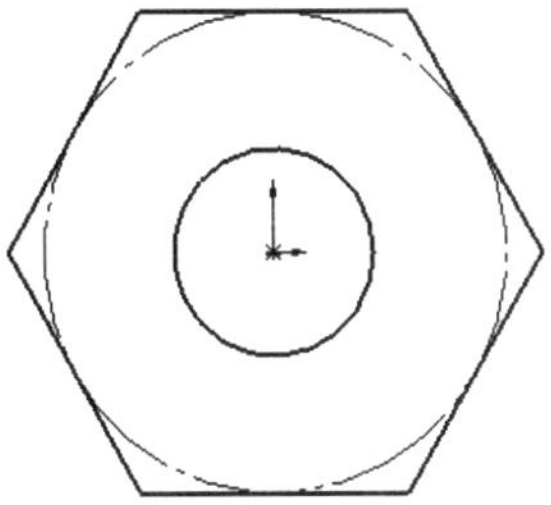

The Extruded Base feature sketch consists of two profiles. The first sketch is a circle centered at the Origin on the Top plane.

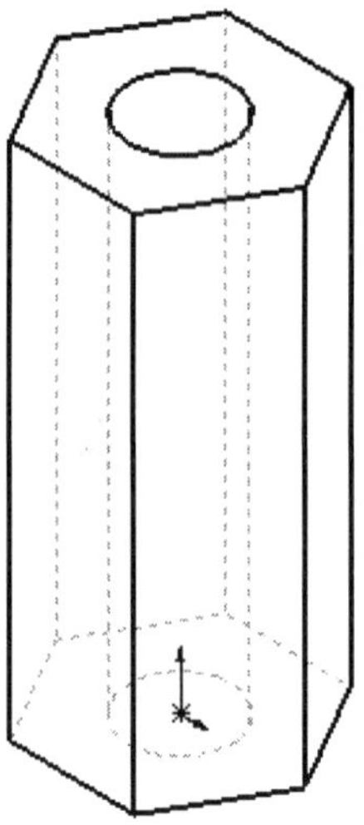

The second sketch is a polygon with 6 sides centered at the Origin. The polygon utilizes an inscribed circle to construct the geometry. Relations are constraints that control the size and position of entities. Utilize the Add Relations sketch tool to define a Horizontal relation in the polygon sketch.

Extrude the sketch perpendicular to the Top plane. Utilize the Edit Sketch tool to modify the sketch.

The Hole Wizard feature creates complex and simple Hole features. Utilize the Hole Wizard feature to create a Tap Hole.

The Tap Hole depth and diameter are based on Drill Size and Screw Type parameters. Use a Coincident relation to position the Tap Hole aligned with the Origin.

Activity: HEX-STANDOFF Part-Extruded Base Feature

Create a new part.

1) Click **File**, **New** from the Main menu. The Templates tab is the default tab. Part is the default template from the New SolidWorks Document dialog box.

2) Double-click **Part**. The Part FeatureManager is displayed.

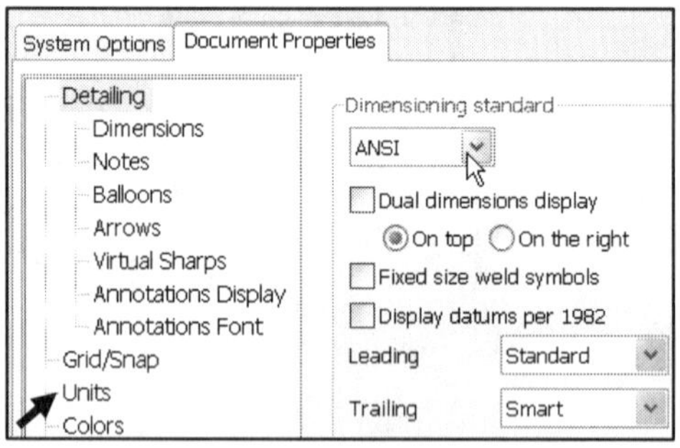

Set the dimensioning standard and part units.

3) Click **Tools**, **Options**, **Document Properties** tab from the Main menu.

4) Select **ANSI** from the Dimensioning standard box.

Set units.

5) Click **Units**.

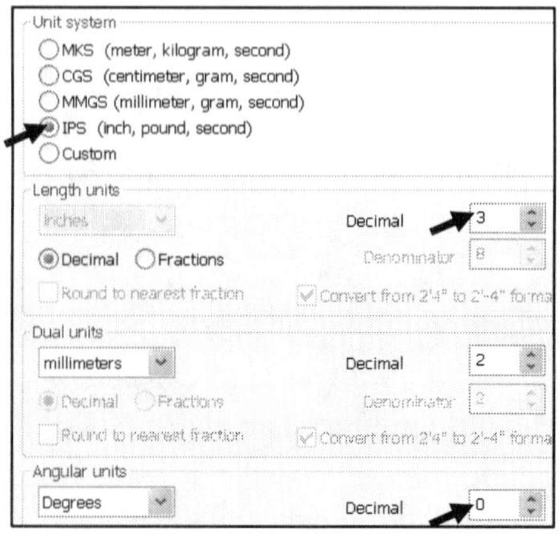

6) Select **IPS**, [**MMGS**] for Unit system.

7) Select **3**, [**2**] for Length units Decimal places.

8) Select **0**, [**0**] for Angular units Decimal places.

9) Click **OK**.

The primary units are provided in IPS, (inch, pound, seconds). The optional secondary units are provided in MMGS, (millimeter, gram, second) and are indicated in brackets [ ]. Illustrations are provided in inches and millimeters.

Save the part.

10) Click **File**, **Save As** from the Main menu.

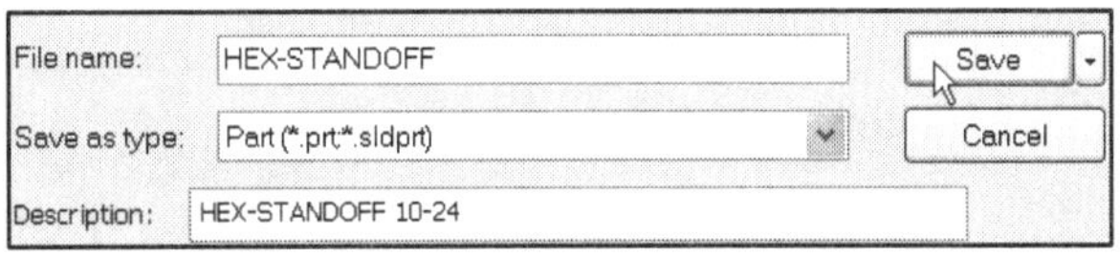

11) Select the **SW-TUTORIAL-2007** folder. Enter **HEX-STANDOFF** for File name.

12) Enter **HEX-STANDOFF 10-24** for Description.

13) Click **Save**. The HEX-STANDOFF FeatureManager is displayed.

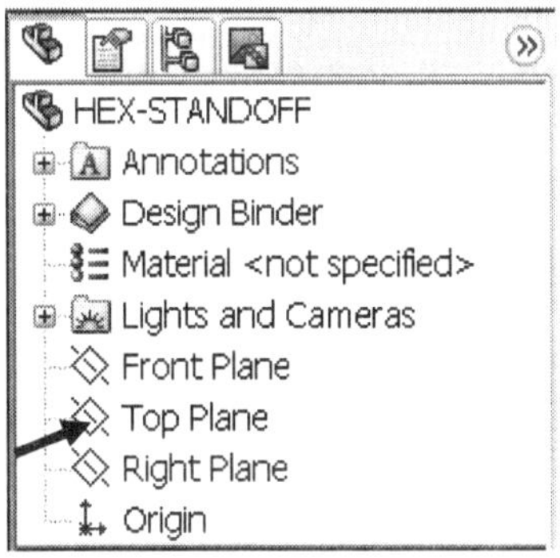

Select the Sketch plane.

14) Click **Top Plane** from the FeatureManager. This is the Sketch plane.

Insert an Extruded Base feature sketched on the Top plane. Note: A plane is an infinite 2D area. The green boundary is for visual reference.

Insert a new sketch.

15) Click **Sketch** from the Control Area.

16) Click **Circle** from the Sketch toolbar. The Circle PropertyManager is displayed.

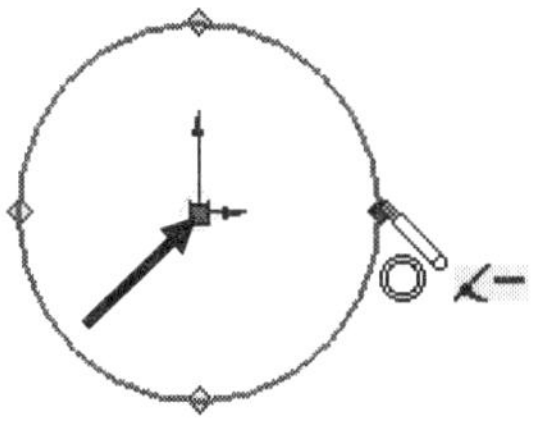

17) Drag the **mouse pointer** into the Graphics window. The cursor displays the Circle feedback symbol. Click the **Origin**. Drag the **mouse pointer** to the right of the Origin.

18) Click a **position** to create the circle as illustrated.

Insert a Polygon.

19) Click **Tools**, **Sketch Entities**, **Polygon** from the Main menu. The Polygon PropertyManager is displayed.

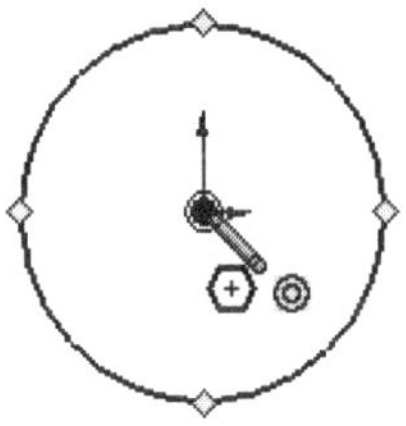

20) Click the **Origin**.

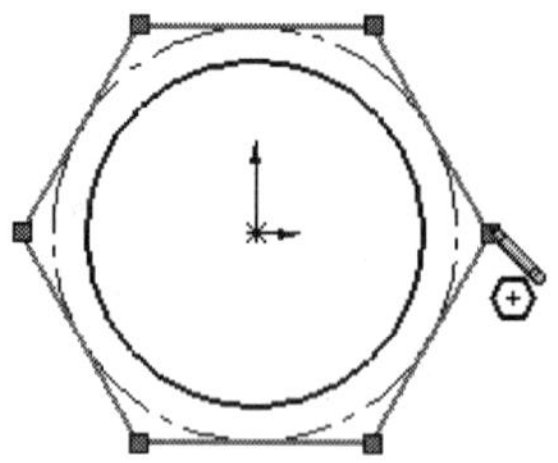

21) Drag the **mouse pointer** horizontally to the right.

22) Click a **position** to the right of the circle to create the hexagon as illustrated.

Add a dimension.

23) Click **Smart Dimension** Smart Dimens... from the Sketch toolbar. Click the **circumference** of the first circle.

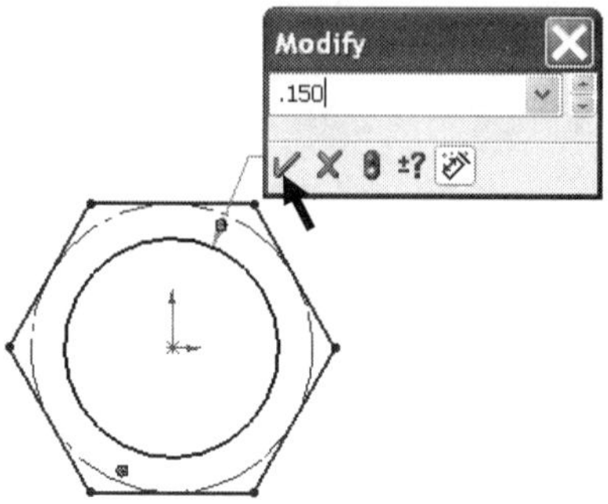

24) Click a **position** diagonally above the hexagon to locate the dimension.

25) Enter **.150**in, [**3.81**] in the Modify pop-up box.

26) Click the **Green Check mark**.

27) Click the **circumference** of the inscribed circle.

28) Click a **position** diagonally below the hexagon to locate the dimension. Enter **.313**in, [**7.94**] in the Modify pop-up box.

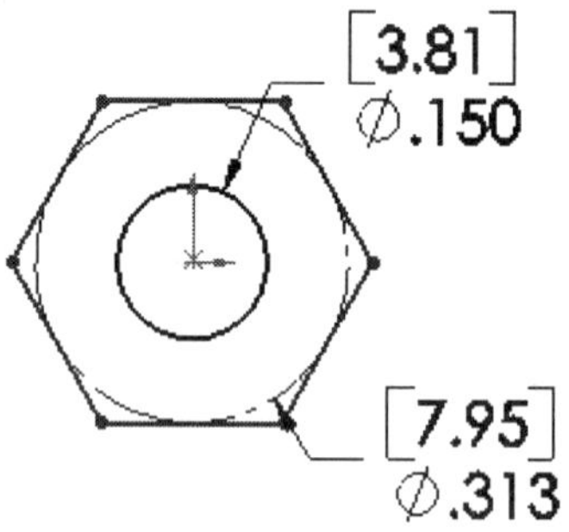

29) Click the **Green Check mark**. The black sketch is fully defined. Press the **f** key to fit the Model to the Graphics window.

30) Click **OK** from the Dimension PropertyManager.

Add a Horizontal relation.

31) Click the **Origin**. Hold the **Ctrl** key down.

32) Click the right most **point** of the hexagon. The Properties PropertyManager is displayed. Release the **Ctrl** key.

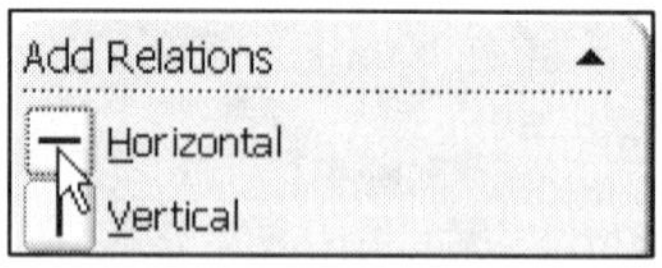

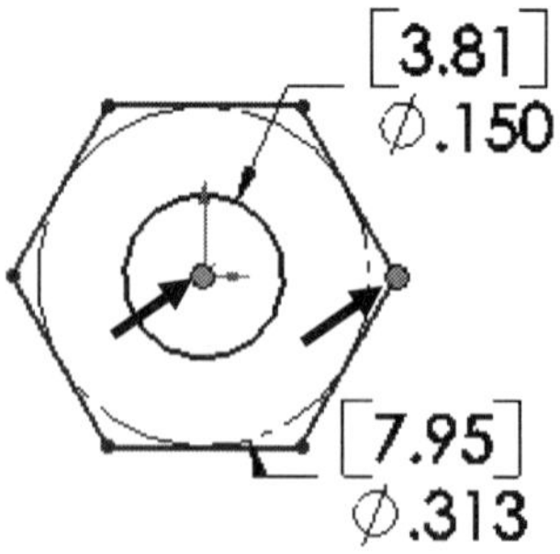

33) Click **Horizontal** from the Add Relations box.

34) Click **OK** from the Properties PropertyManager.

Extrude the sketch.

35) Click **Extruded Boss/Base** Extruded Boss/B... from the Features toolbar. The Extrude PropertyManager is displayed. Blind is the default End Condition in Direction1. The direction arrow points upward.

36) Enter **.735**in, [**18.67**] for Depth.

37) Click **OK** from the Extrude PropertyManager. Extrude1 is displayed in the FeatureManager.

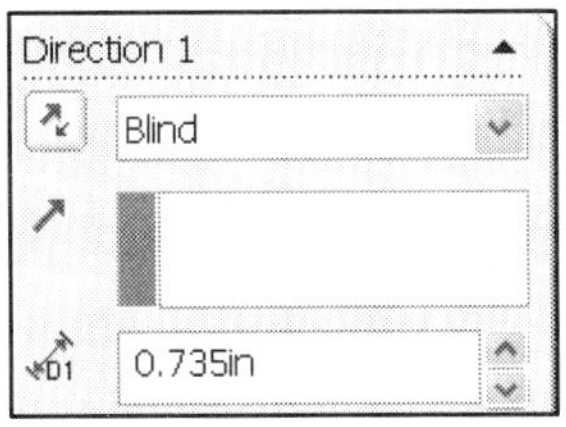

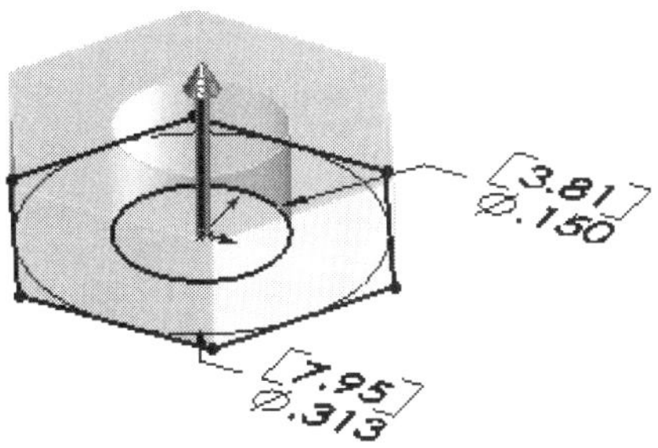

Fit the model to the Graphics window.

38) Press the **f** key.

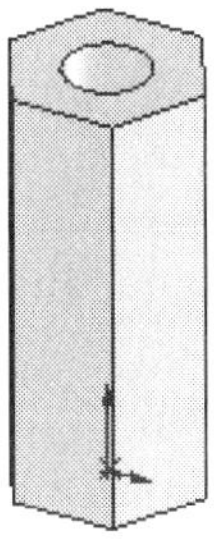

The Extruded Base feature was sketched on the Top plane. Changes occur in the design process. Edit the sketch of Extrude1. Delete the circle and close the sketch. Use the Hole Wizard feature to create a Tap Hole.

Edit Sketch1

39) **Expand** Extrude1 in the FeatureManager.

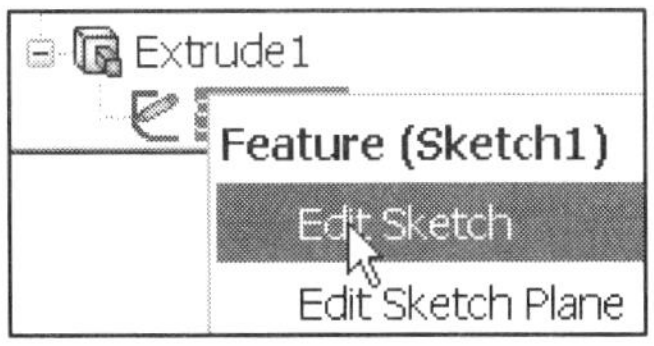

40) Right-click **Sketch1**.

41) Click **Edit Sketch**.

Delete the inside circle.

42) Click the **circumference** of the inside circle. The Circle PropertyManager is displayed.

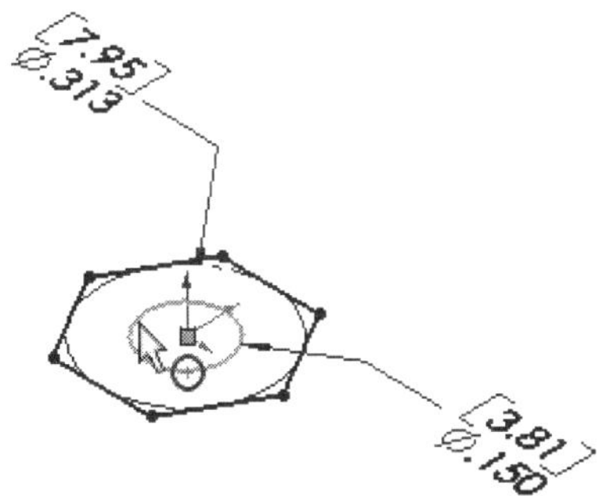

43) Press the **Delete** key.

44) Click **Yes** to the Sketcher Confirm Delete. Both the circle geometry and its dimension are deleted.

Save and close the sketch.

45) Click **Save**.

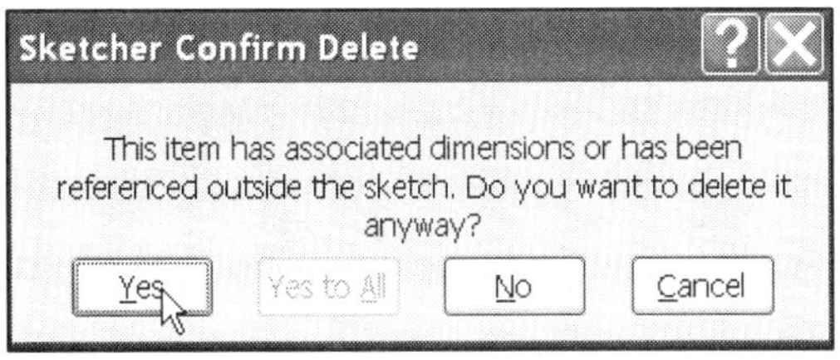

46) Click **OK** to Rebuild.

The Extrude1 feature is updated.

Fit the Model to the Graphics window.

47) Press the **f** key.

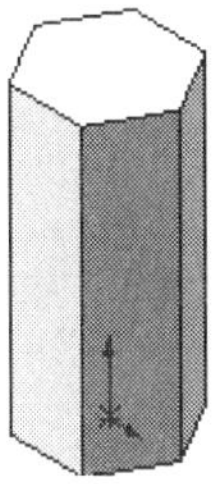

Activity: HEX-STANDOFF Part-Hole Wizard Feature

Insert a Tap Hole with the Hole Wizard Feature.

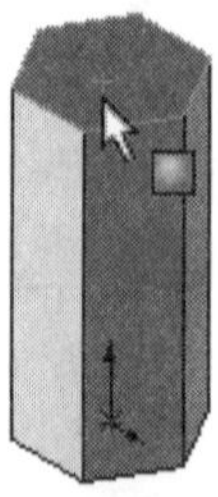

48) Click the **top face** of Extrude1 in the Graphics window.

49) Click **Hidden Lines Visible** from the View toolbar.

50) Click **Hole Wizard** from the Features toolbar. The Hole Specification PropertyManager is displayed.

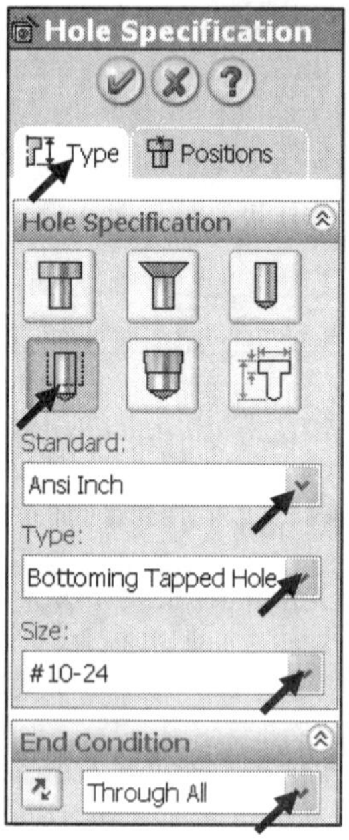

Note: For metric, utilize ANSI Metric and M5x0.8 for size.

51) Click the **Type** tab. Click **Tap** for Hole Specification.

52) Select **Ansi Inch**, [**Ansi Metric**] for Standard.

53) Select **Bottoming Tapped Hole** for Type.

54) Select **#10-24**, [**Ø5**] for Size.

55) Select **Through All** for End Condition. Accept the default conditions.

56) Click the **Positions** tab.

The Tap Hole is displayed in yellow. Yellow is a preview color. The Tap Hole center point is displayed in blue. The Sketch Point tool is automatically selected. No other holes are required. Note: Utilize a Coincident Relation to locate the center point of the Tap Hole in the Top view.

Add a Coincident relation.

57) Right-click **Select**. Click the **Origin**.

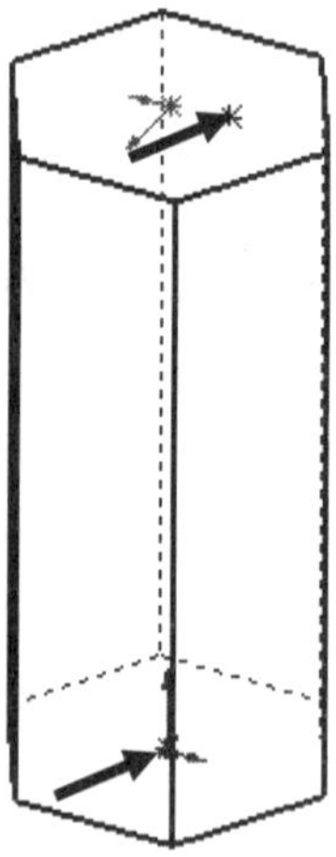

58) Hold the **Ctrl** key down.

59) Click the blue **center point** of the Tap Hole. The Properties PropertyManager is displayed. Release the **Ctrl** key.

60) Click **Coincident** from the Add Relations box.

61) Click **OK** from the Properties PropertyManager.

62) Click **OK** from the Hole Position PropertyManager.

The #10-24 Tapped Hole1 feature is displayed in the FeatureManager. Sketch3 determines the center point location of the Tap Hole. Sketch2 is the profile of the Tap Hole.

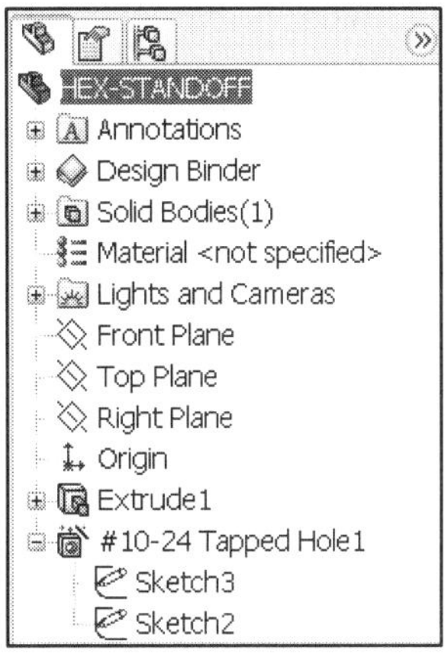

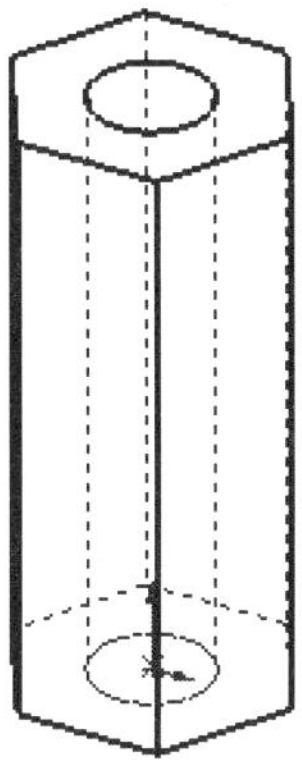

Save the HEX-STANDOFF part.

63) Click **Save**. The HEX-STANDOFF is complete.

Review the HEX-STANDOFF Part.

The HEX-STANDOFF part utilized an Extruded Base feature. The Extruded Base feature required a sketch on the Top plane. The first profile was a circle centered at the Origin on the Top plane. The second profile used the Polygon Sketch tool. You utilized Edit Sketch to modify the Sketch profile and to delete the circle.

The Hole Wizard feature created a Tap Hole. The Hole Wizard feature required the Extruded Base top face as the Sketch plane.

A Coincident relation located the center point of the Tap Hole aligned with respect to the Origin.

Additional details on Hexagon, Add Relations, Centerline, Delete, Hole Wizard, and Extruded Base are available in SolidWorks Help. Keywords: Polygon, Relations, Delete, Sketch Entities, Sketch Tools, Hole Wizard, and Extruded Boss/Base.

ANGLE-13HOLE Part

The ANGLE-13HOLE part is an L-shaped support bracket. The ANGLE-13HOLE part is manufactured from 0.090in, [2.3] aluminum.

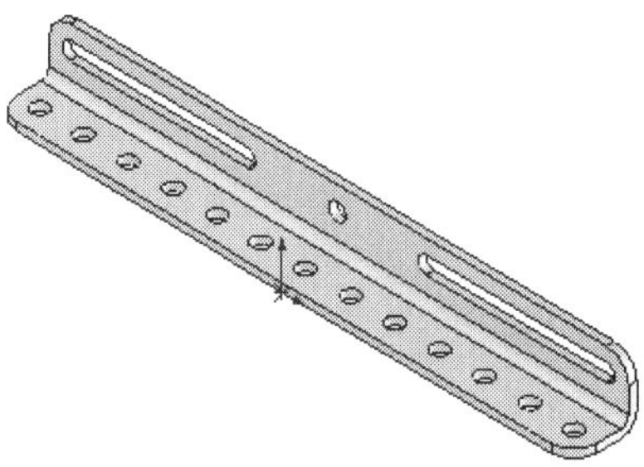

There ANGLE-13HOLE part contains fillets, holes, and slot cuts.

Simplify the overall design into seven features. Utilize symmetry and Linear Patterns.

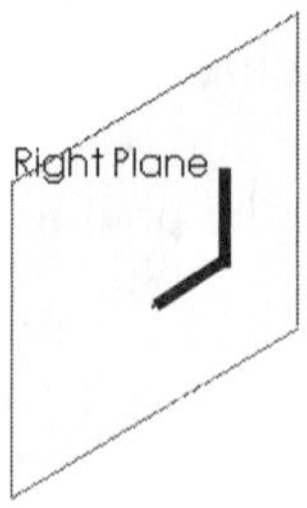

The open L-Shaped profile is sketched on the Right plane.

Utilize an Extruded Thin feature with the Mid Plane option to locate the part symmetrical to the Right plane.

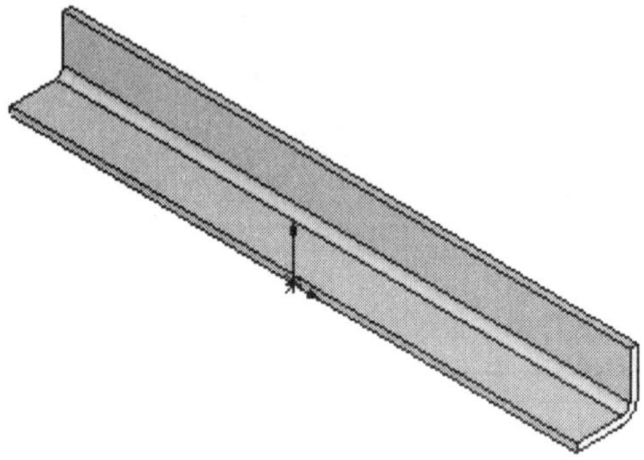

Insert the first Extruded Cut feature for the first hole. The first hole is sketch on the top face of the Extruded Thin feature.

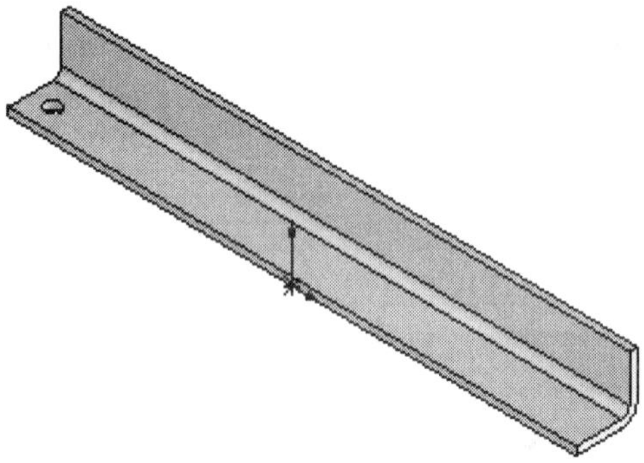

Insert a Linear Pattern to create an array of 13 holes along the bottom horizontal edge.

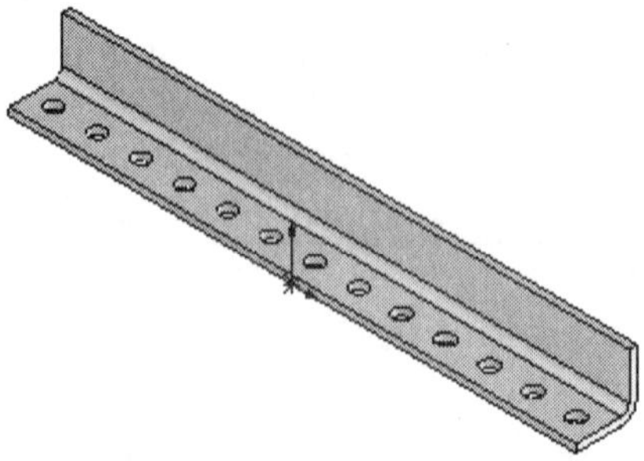

Insert a Fillet feature to round the four corners.

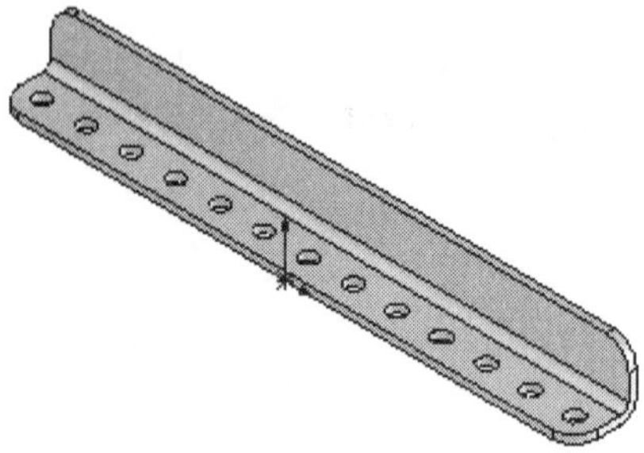

Insert the second Extruded Cut feature on the front face of the Extruded Thin feature.

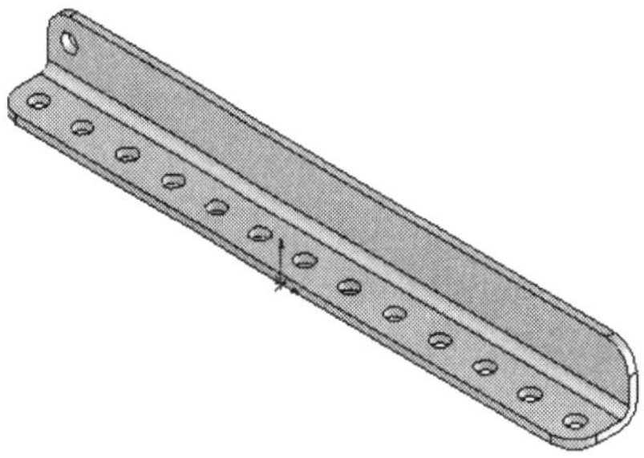

Insert a Linear Pattern feature to create an array of 3 holes along the top horizontal edge.

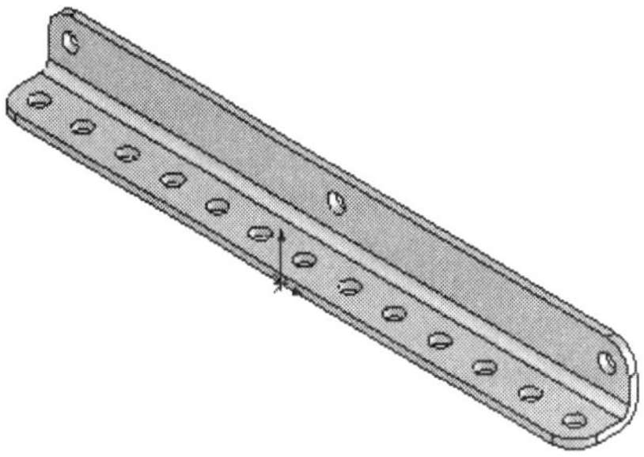

Utilize the Sketch Mirror tool to create the slot profile.

Insert the third Extruded Cut feature to create the two slots.

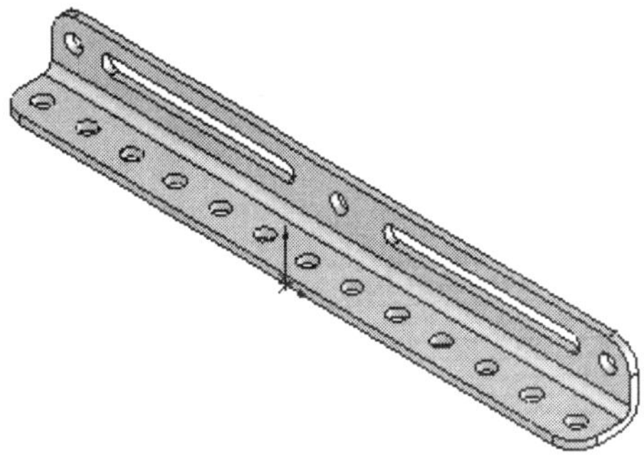

Select the Sketch plane for the Base feature that corresponds to the parts orientation in the assembly.

Activity: ANGLE-13HOLE Part-Documents Properties

Create a new part.

64) Click **File**, **New** from the Main menu. Part is the default template from the New SolidWorks Document dialog box.

65) Double-click **Part**. The Part FeatureManager is displayed.

Set the dimensioning standard and part units.

66) Click **Tools**, **Options**, **Document Properties** tab from the Main menu.

67) Select **ANSI** from the Dimensioning standard box.

68) Click **Units**. Select **IPS**, [**MMGS**] for Unit system.

69) Select **3**, [**2**] for Length units Decimal places.

70) Select **0**, [**0**] for Angular units Decimal places.

71) Click **OK**.

Save the part.

72) Click **File**, **Save As** from the Main menu.

73) Select the **SW-TUTORIAL-2007** file folder.

74) Enter **ANGLE-13 HOLE** for File name.

75) Enter **ANGLE BRACKET-13 HOLE** for Description.

76) Click **Save**. The ANGLE-13 Hole FeatureManager is displayed.

Activity: ANGLE-13HOLE Part-Extruded Thin Feature

Insert an Extruded Thin feature sketched on the Right plane.

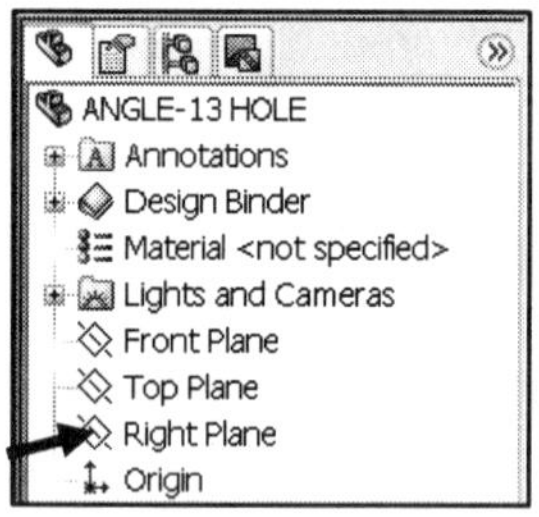

Select the Sketch plane.

77) Click **Right Plane** from the FeatureManager.

Sketch a horizontal line.

78) Click **Sketch** Sketch from the Control Area.

79) Click **Line** Line from the Sketch toolbar.

80) Click the **Origin**. Click a **position** to the right of the Origin.

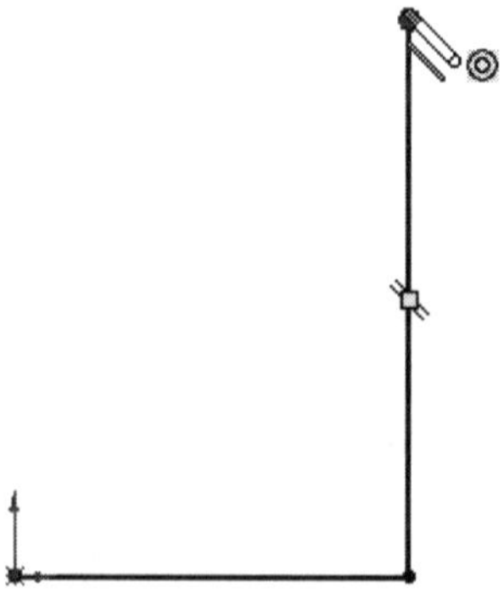

Sketch a vertical line.

81) Click a **position** directly above the right end point.

82) **Double-click** to end the line as illustrated.

83) Deactivate the Line tool. Click **Line** Line from the Sketch toolbar.

Add an Equal relation.

84) Click the **vertical** line. Hold the **Ctrl** key down. Click the **horizontal line**. Release the **Ctrl** key.

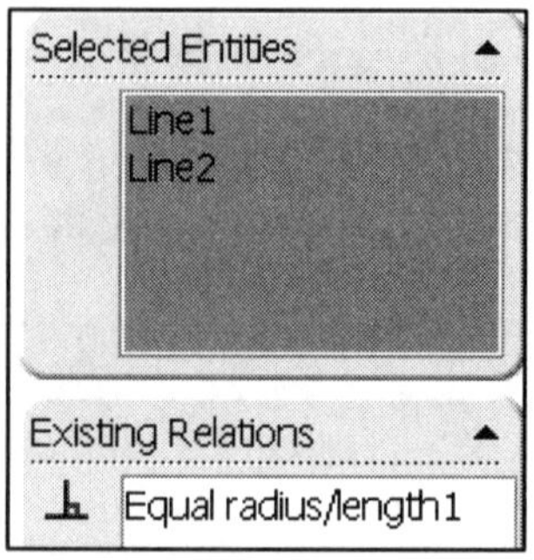

85) Click **Equal** = from the Add Relations box.

86) Click **OK** from the Properties PropertyManager.

Add a dimension.

87) Click **Smart Dimension** Smart Dimens... from the Sketch toolbar.

88) Click the **horizontal** line. Click a **position** below the profile.

89) Enter .**700**in, [**17.78**] in the Modify box.

90) Click the **Green Check mark**. The black sketch is fully defined.

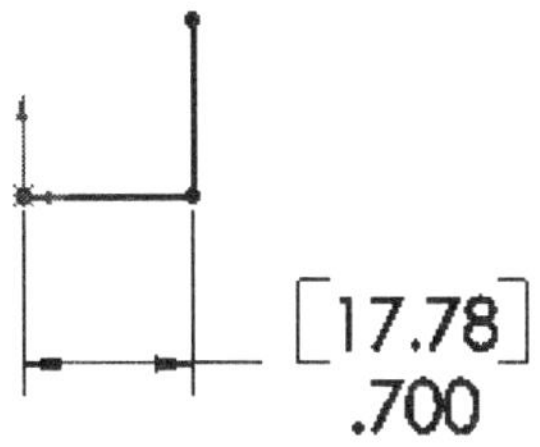

Save rebuild time. Add relations and dimensions to fully define a sketch. Fully defined sketches are displayed in black.

Extrude the sketch.

91) Click **Extruded Boss/Base** Extruded Boss/B... from the Features toolbar. The Extrude PropertyManager is displayed.

92) Select **Mid Plane** for End Condition in Direction 1.

93) Enter **7.000**in, [**177.80**] for Depth. Note: Thin Feature is checked.

94) If required, click the **Reverse Direction Arrow** button for One-Direction. Material thickness is created above the Origin.

95) Enter **.090**in, [**2.3**] for Thickness.

96) Check the **Auto-fillet corners** box.

97) Enter **.090**in, [**2.3**] for Fillet Radius.

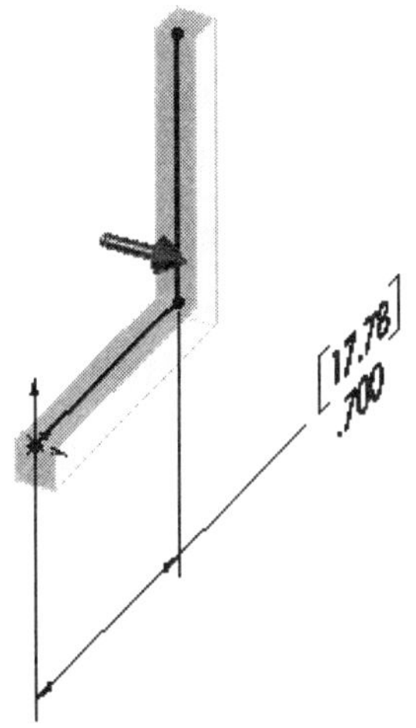

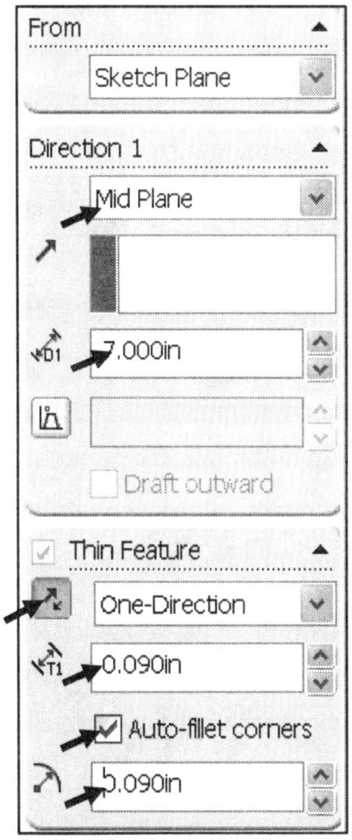

98) Click **OK** from the Extrude PropertyManager. Extrude-Thin1 is displayed in the FeatureManager.

Fit the model to the Graphics window.

99) Press the **f** key.

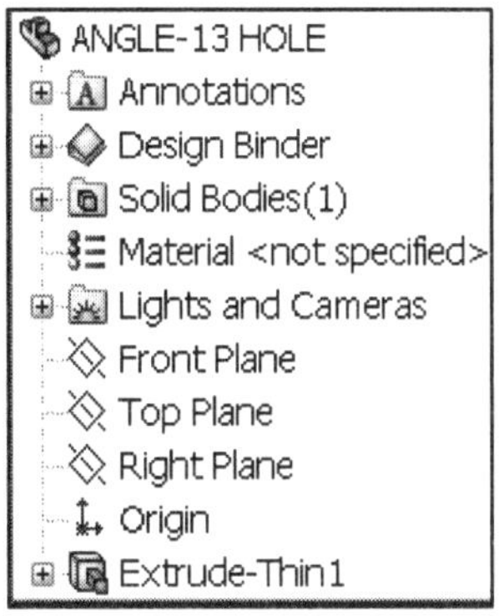

Clarify the Extrude-Thin1 feature direction and thickness options. Utilize multiple view orientations and Zoom In before selecting OK from the Extrude PropertyManager.

Modify feature dimensions.

100) Double-click **Extrude-Thin1** in the FeatureManager.

101) Double-click the **7.000**in, [**177.80**] dimension in the Graphics window.

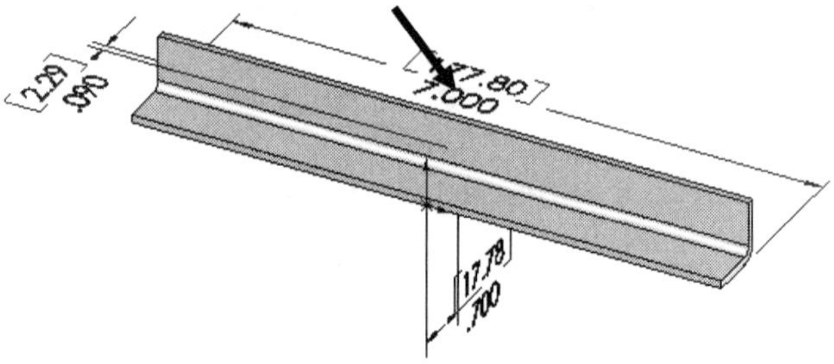

102) Enter **6.500**in, [**165.10**] in the Modify dialog box.

103) Click the **Green Check mark**.

104) Click **Rebuild** from the Standard toolbar.

Save the model.

105) Click **Save**.

Activity: ANGLE-13HOLE Part-Extruded Cut Feature

Insert a new sketch for the Extruded Cut.

106) Click the **top face** of Extrude-Thin1. This is the Sketch plane.

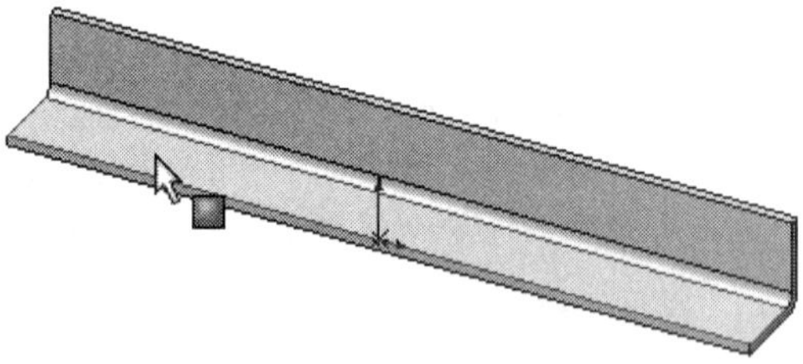

107) Click **Sketch** Sketch from the Control Area.

108) Click **Top view**.

109) Click **Circle** Circle from the Sketch toolbar.

110) Sketch a **circle** on the left side of the Origin as illustrated.

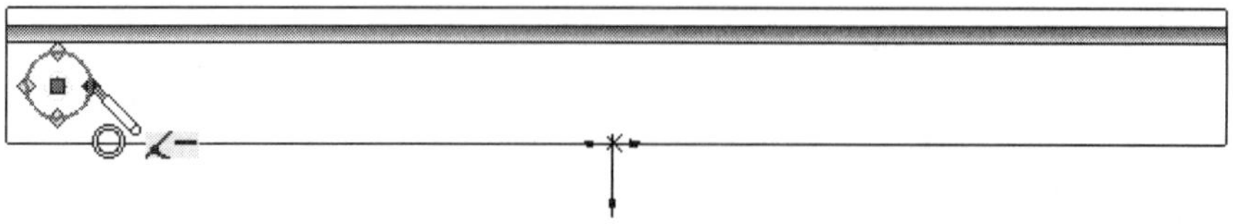

Add dimensions.

111) Click **Smart Dimension** Smart Dimens... from the Sketch toolbar.

112) Click the **Origin**. Click the **center point** of the circle.

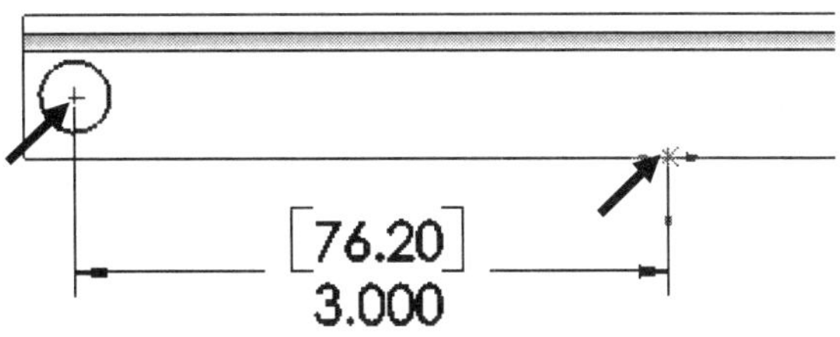

113) Click a **position** below the horizontal profile line.

114) Enter **3.000**in, [**76.20**]. Click the **Green Check mark**.

115) Click the **bottom horizontal line**.

116) Click the **center point** of the circle.

117) Click a **position** to the left of the profile.

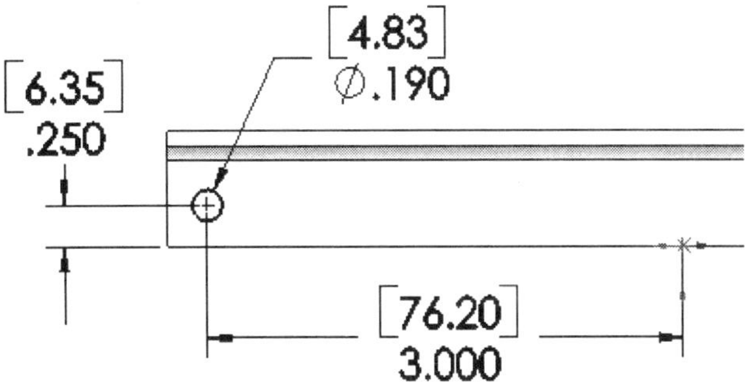

118) Enter **.250**in, [**6.35**]. Click the **Green Check mark**.

119) Create a diameter dimension. Click the **circumference** of the circle.

120) Click a **position** diagonally above the profile.

121) Enter **.190**in, [**4.83**]. Click the **Green Check mark**.

Insert an Extruded Cut Feature.

122) Click **Extruded Cut** Extruded Cut from the Features toolbar. The Cut-Extrude PropertyManager is displayed.

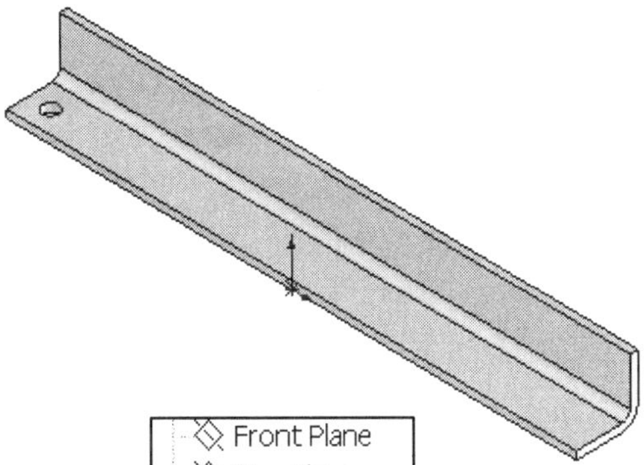

123) Select **Through All** for End Condition in Direction 1. Accept the default conditions.

124) Click **OK** from the Cut-Extrude PropertyManager. Cut-Extrude1 is displayed in the FeatureManager.

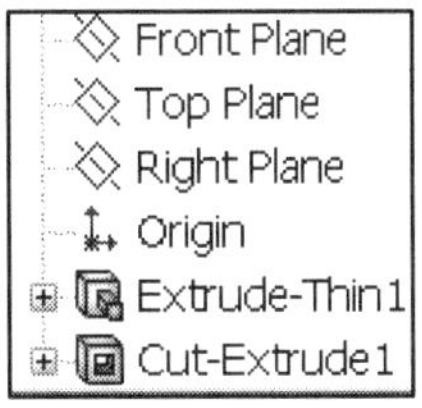

125) Click **Isometric view**.

Save the model.

126) Click **Save**.

Activity: ANGLE-13HOLE Part-Linear Pattern Feature

Insert a Linear Pattern.

127) Click **Top View**.

128) Click **Linear Pattern** Linear from the Features toolbar. The Linear Pattern PropertyManager is displayed.

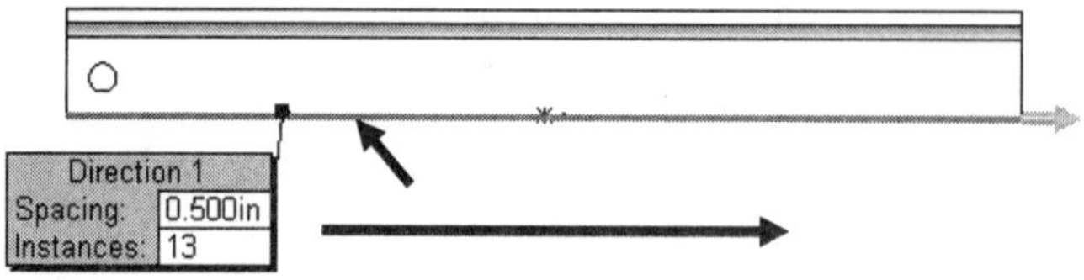

129) Click the **bottom horizontal edge** of the Extrude-Thin1 feature for Direction1. Edge<1> is displayed in the Pattern Direction box. The direction arrow points to the right. If required, click the Reverse Direction button.

130) Enter **0.5**in, [**12.70**] for Spacing.

131) Enter **13** for Number of Instances.

132) Click inside the **Features to Pattern** box.

133) **Expand** ANGLE-13 HOLE from the fly-out FeatureManager.

134) Click **Cut-Extrude1**. Cut-Extrude1 is displayed in the Features to Pattern box.

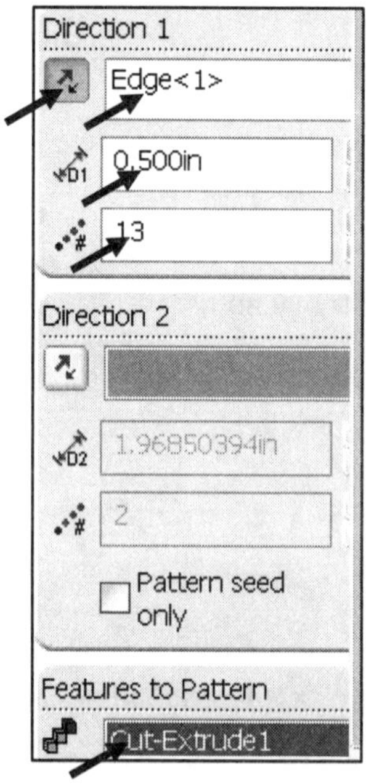

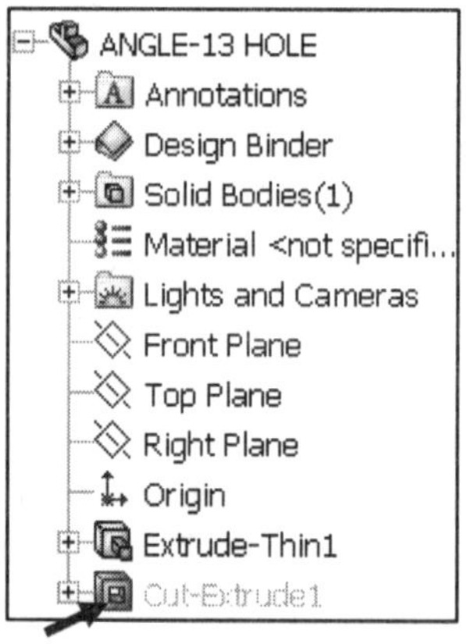

135) Click **OK** from the Linear Pattern PropertyManager. LPattern1 is displayed in the FeatureManager.

136) Click **Isometric view**.

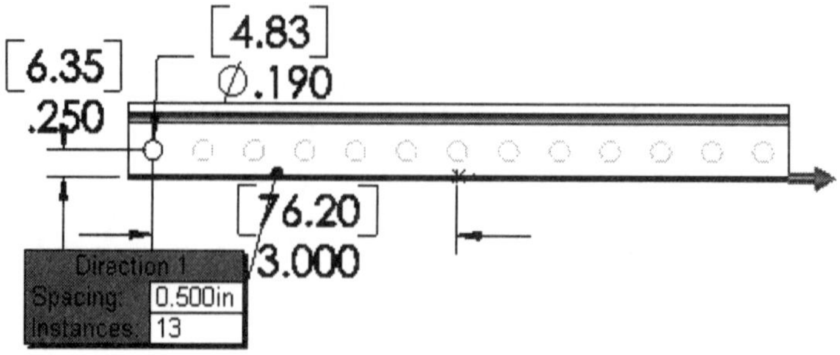

Save the ANGLE-13HOLE part.

137) Click **Save**.

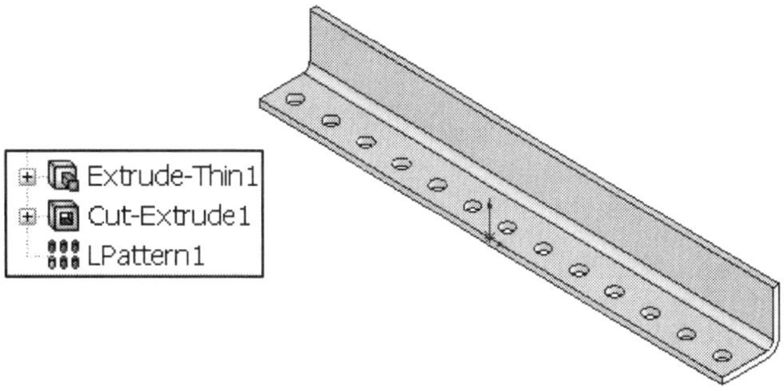

Activity: ANGLE-13HOLE Part-Fillet Feature

Insert a Fillet Feature.

138) Click **Zoom to Area**.

139) Click the **right top edge** of the Extrude-Thin1 feature. Click **Fillet** Fillet from the Features toolbar. The Fillet PropertyManager is displayed.

140) Constant radius is the default Fillet Type. Enter **.250** [**6.35**] for Radius.

141) Click the **right bottom edge**. Edge<1> and Edge<2> are displayed in the Items To Fillet box.

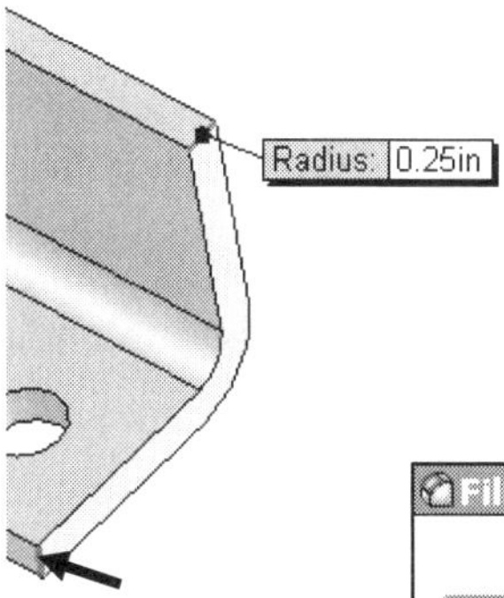

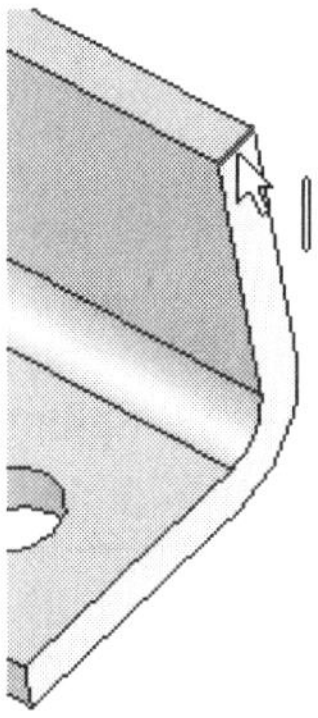

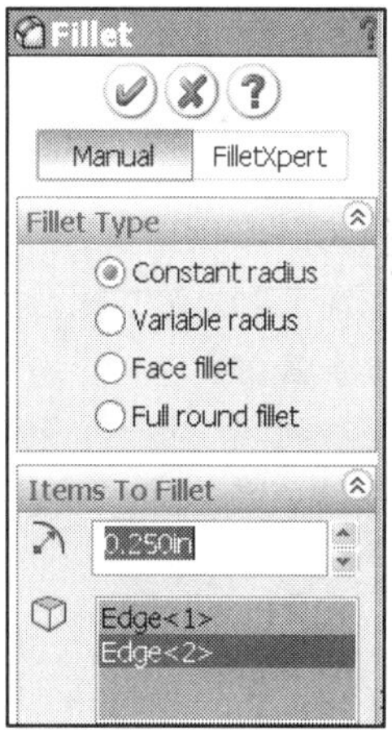

142) Click **OK** from the Fillet PropertyManager. Fillet1 is displayed in the FeatureManager.

Two Fillet PropertyManager tabs are available. Use the Manual tab to control features for all Fillet types. Use the FilletXpert tab when you want SolidWorks to manage the structure of the underlying features only for a Constant radius Fillet type. Click the button for additional information.

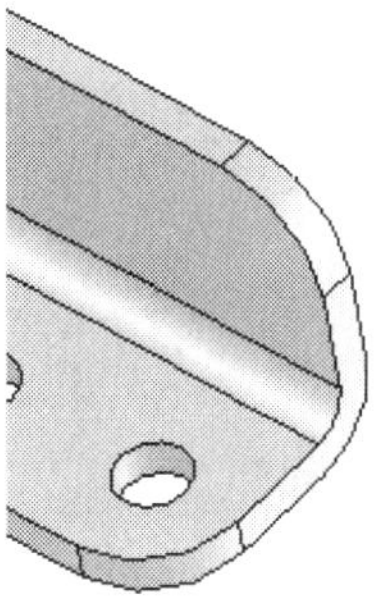

Fit the model to the Graphics window.

143) Press the **f** key.

Edit the Fillet feature.

144) Zoom to Area on the left side of the Extrude-Thin1 feature. Right-click **Fillet1** in the FeatureManager.

145) Click **Edit Feature**. The Fillet1 PropertyManager is displayed.

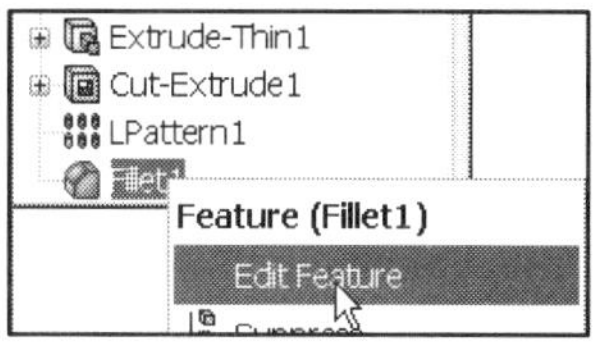

146) Click the **left top edge** and **left bottom edge**. Edge<3> and Edge <4> are added to the Items To Fillet box.

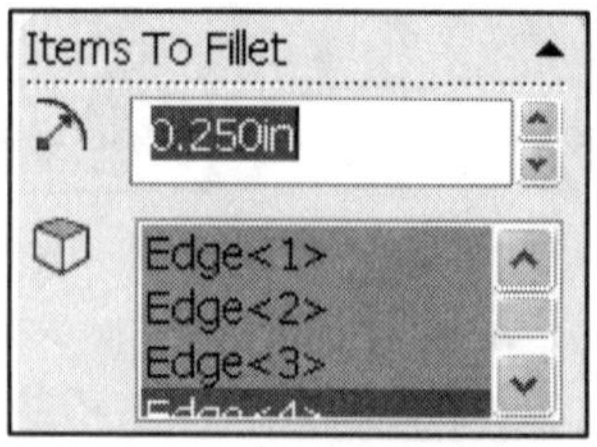

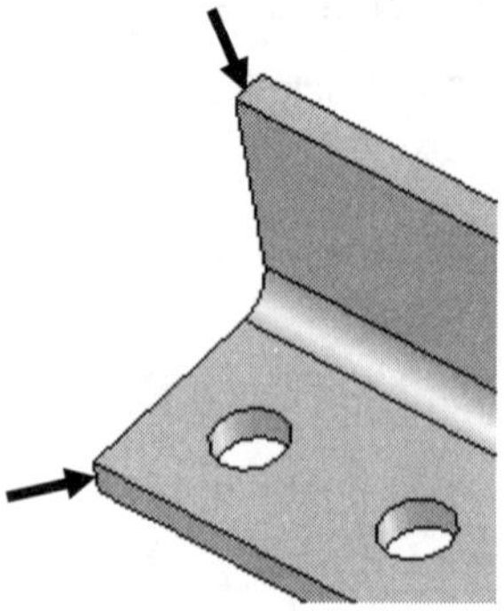

147) Click **OK** from the Fillet1 PropertyManager.

Display the Isometric view.

148) Click **Isometric view**.

Save the ANGLE-13HOLE part.

149) Click **Save**.

Activity: ANGLE-13HOLE Part-Second Extruded Cut / Linear Pattern

Insert a new sketch for the second Extruded Cut.

150) Click the **front face** of the Extrude-Thin1 feature in the Graphics window. The front face is the Sketch plane.

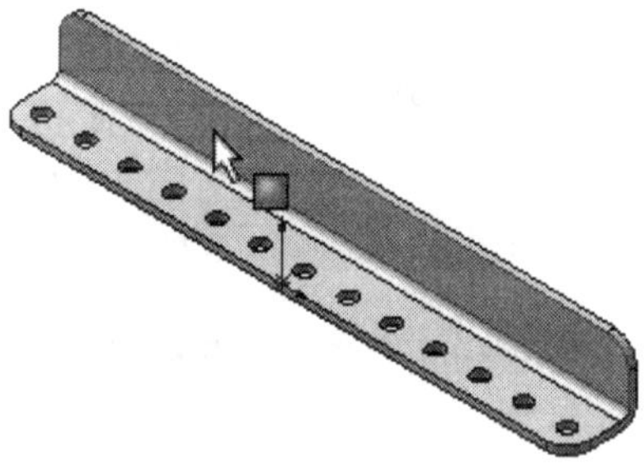

151) Click **Sketch** Sketch from the Control Area.

152) Click **Front view**.

153) Click **Wireframe** to display the Linear Pattern1 feature.

Note: Do not align the center point of the circle with the center point of the LPattern1 feature. Do not align the center point of the circle with the center point of the Fillet radius. Control the center point position with dimensions.

154) Click **Circle** Circle from the Sketch toolbar.

155) Sketch a **circle** on the left side of the Origin between the two LPattern1 holes as illustrated.

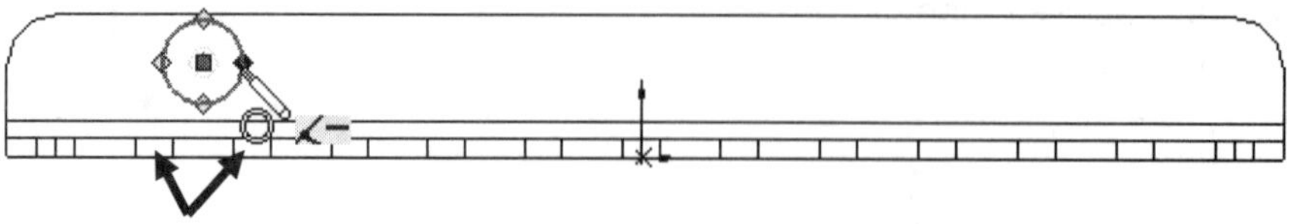

Add dimensions.

156) Click **Smart Dimension** Smart Dimens... from the Sketch toolbar.

157) Click the **Origin**. Click the **center point** of the circle.

158) Click a **position** below the horizontal profile line. Enter **3.000**in, [**76.20**].

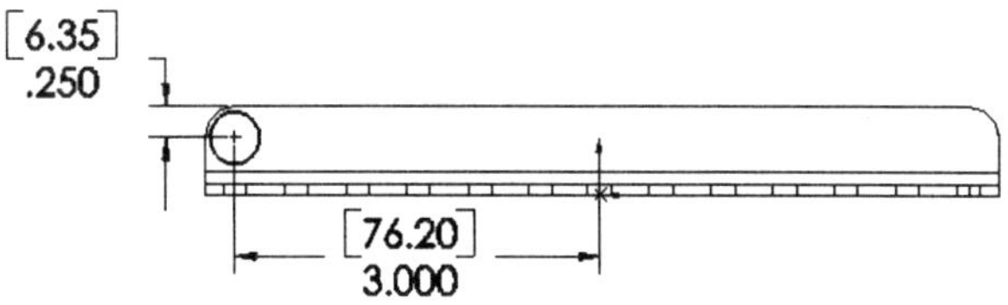

159) Click the **Green Check mark**.

160) Click the **top horizontal line**.

161) Click the **center point** of the circle.

162) Click a **position** to the left of the profile. Enter **.250**in, [**6.35**].

163) Click the **Green Check mark**.

164) Click the **circumference** of the circle.

165) Click a **position** above the profile.

166) Enter **.190**in, [**4.83**].

167) Click the **Green Check mark**.

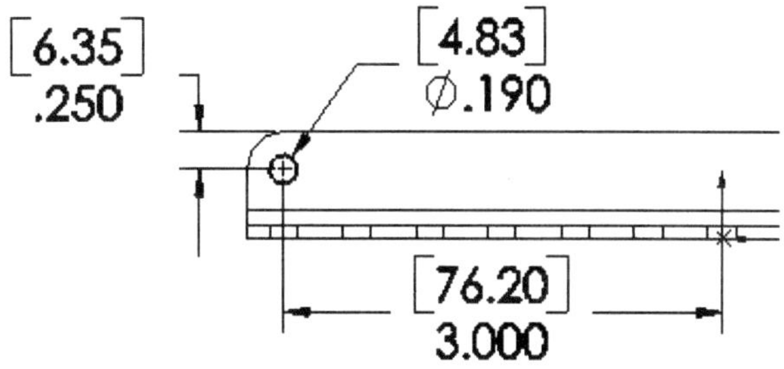

Insert an Extruded Cut Feature.

168) Click **Extruded Cut** Extruded Cut from the Features toolbar. The Cut-Extrude PropertyManager is displayed

169) Select **Through All** for End Condition in Direction1. Accept the default conditions.

170) Click **OK** from the Cut-Extrude PropertyManager. Cut-Extrude2 is displayed in the FeatureManager.

Create the second Linear Pattern Feature.

171) Click **Linear Pattern** Linear from the Features toolbar. The Linear Pattern FeatureManager is displayed. Click inside the **Pattern Direction** box.

172) Click the **top horizontal edge** of the Extrude-Thin1 feature for Direction1. Edge<1> is displayed in the Pattern Direction box. The Direction arrow points to the right. If required, click the **Reverse Direction** button

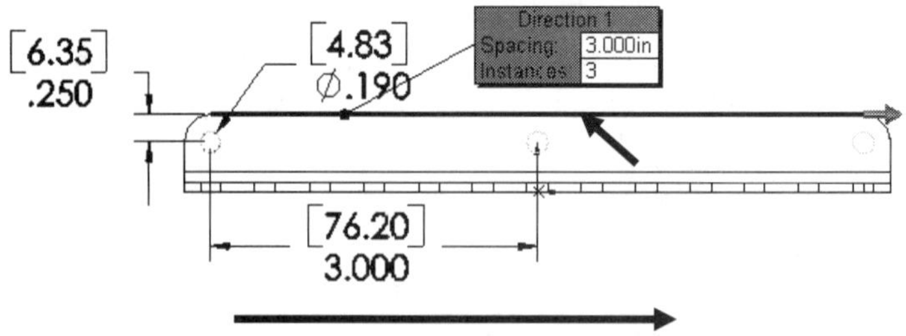

173) Enter **3.000**in, [**76.20**] for Spacing.

174) Enter **3** for Number of Instances.

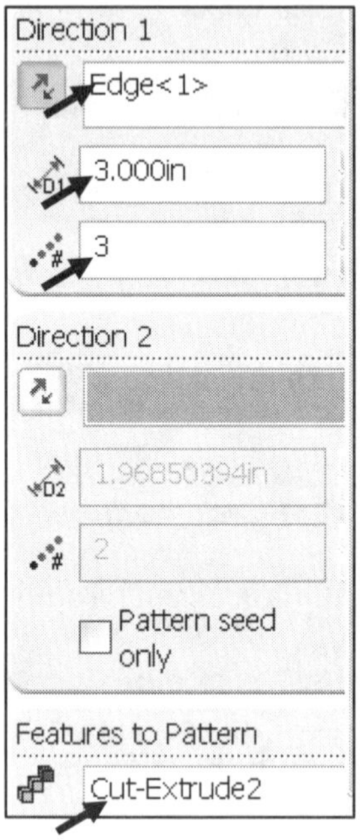

175) Click **OK** from the Linear Pattern PropertyManager. LPattern2 is displayed in the FeatureManager.

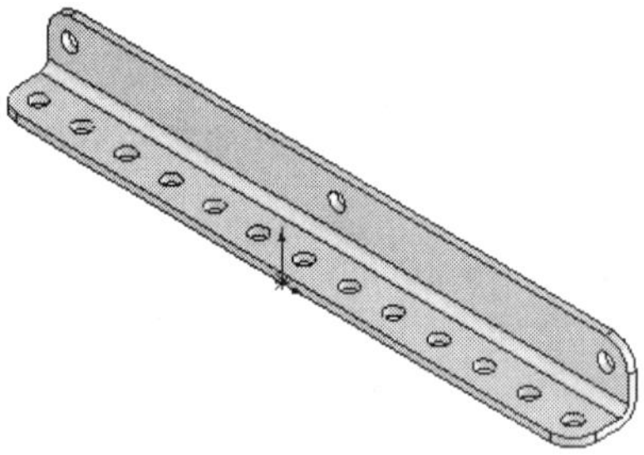

176) Click **Isometric view** .

177) Click **Shaded With Edges** .

Save the ANGLE-13HOLE part.

178) Click **Save** .

Activity: ANGLE-13HOLE Part-Third Extruded Cut

Insert a new sketch for the third Extruded Cut Feature.

179) Select the Sketch plane. Click the **front face** of Extrude-Thin1.

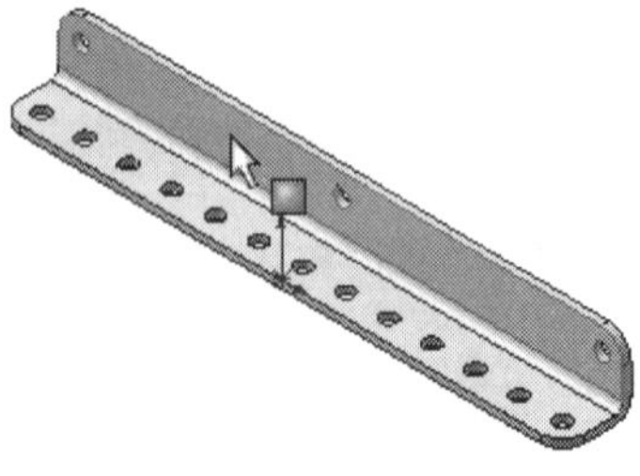

180) Click **Sketch** Sketch from the Control Area.

181) Click **Front view** . Click **Wireframe** .

Sketch a vertical centerline.

182) Click **Centerline** Centerl... from the Sketch toolbar.

183) Click the **Origin**.

184) Click a vertical **position** above the top horizontal line as illustrated.

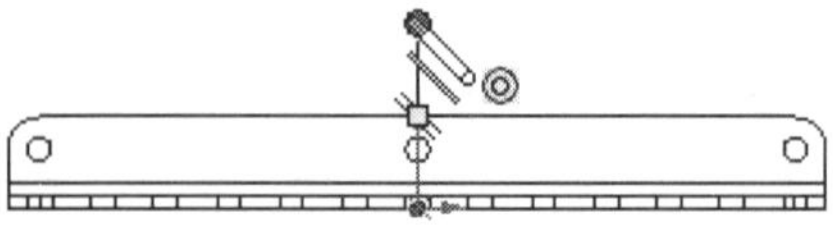

185) Click **Tools**, **Sketch Tools**, **Dynamic Mirror** from the Main menu.

186) Click the **centerline** in the Graphics window.

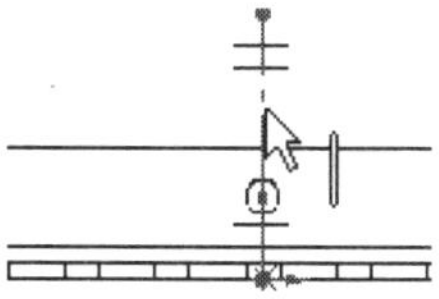

Sketch a rectangle.

187) Click **Rectangle** Rectan... from the Sketch toolbar. Do not align the rectangle first point and second point to the center points of Lpattern1.

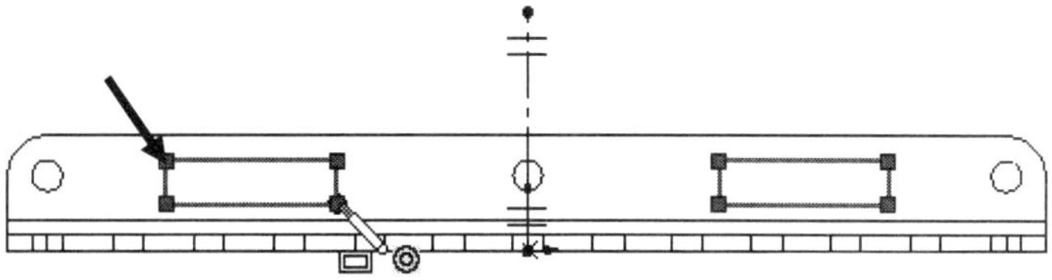

188) Click the **first point** of the rectangle to the left of the Origin.

189) Click the **second point** to create the rectangle diagonally from the first point, to the left of the Origin.

Trim the vertical lines of the rectangle.

190) Click **Trim Entities** Trim from the Sketch toolbar. The Trim PropertyManager is displayed.

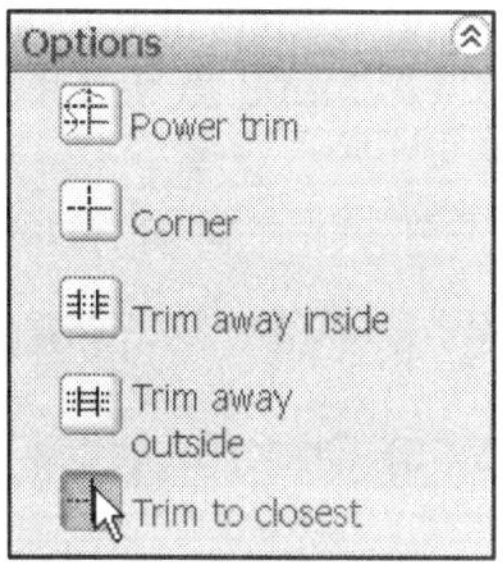

191) Click **Trim to closest** from the Options box.

192) Click the **left vertical line** of the left rectangle as illustrated. The left vertical line is removed.

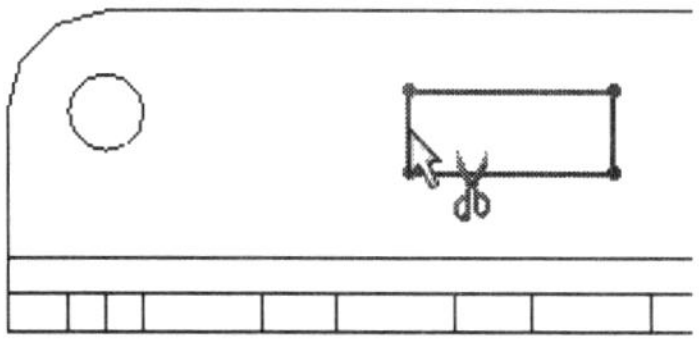

193) Click the **right vertical line** of the left rectangle. The right vertical line is removed.

194) Perform the **same procedure** on the right rectangle as illustrated.

Sketch the left 180° arc on the left side of the centerline.

195) Click **Tangent Arc** Tangent Arc from the Sketch toolbar. The Tangent Arc icon is displayed on the mouse pointer.

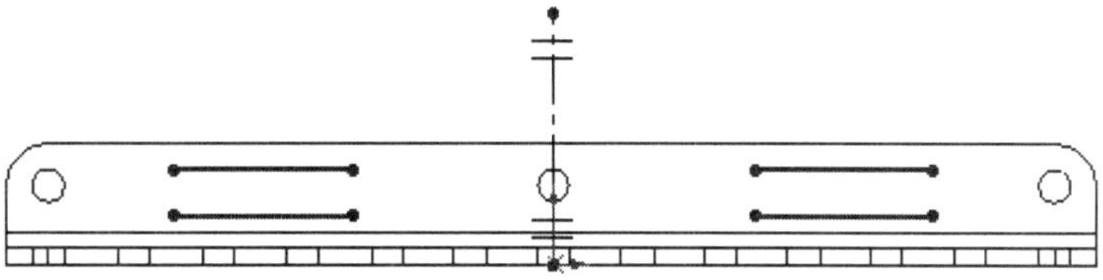

196) Click the **top left endpoint**.

197) Drag the **mouse pointer** to the left and downward.

198) Click the **bottom left endpoint** as illustrated.

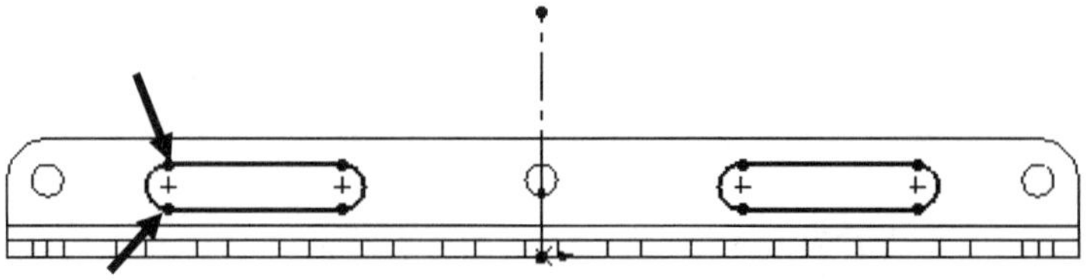

Sketch the right 180° arc on the left side of the centerline.

199) Click the **top right endpoint**.

200) Drag the **mouse pointer** to the right and downward.

201) Click the **bottom right endpoint**.

202) Click **OK**  from the Arc PropertyManager.

203) Click **Tools**, **Sketch Tools**, **Dynamic Mirror** from the Main menu to deactivate.

Add a Concentric relation.

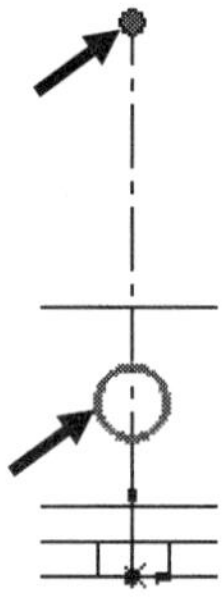

204) Zoom to Area  on the centerline.

205) Click the **top endpoint** of the centerline.

206) Hold the **Ctrl** key down.

207) Click the **circumference** of the circle.

208) Release the **Ctrl** key.

209) Click **Concentric**  from the Add Relations box.

210) Click **OK**  from the Properties PropertyManager.

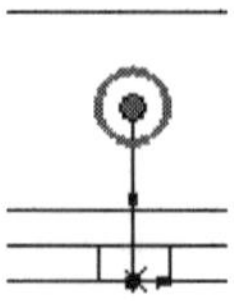

The endpoint of the centerline is positioned in the center of the circle. Note: Right-click Clear Selections to remove selected entities from the Add Relations box.

Add an Equal relation.

211) Click the circumference of the **circle**. Hold the **Ctrl** key down.

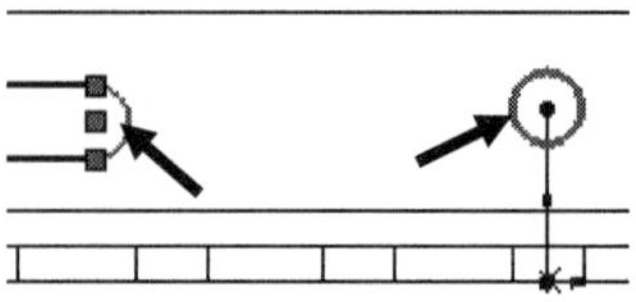

212) Click the **right arc** of the first rectangle. Release the **Ctrl** key.

213) Click **Equal** = from the Add Relations box. The arc radius is equal to the circle radius.

Add a Horizontal relation.

214) Click the **top endpoint** of the centerline.

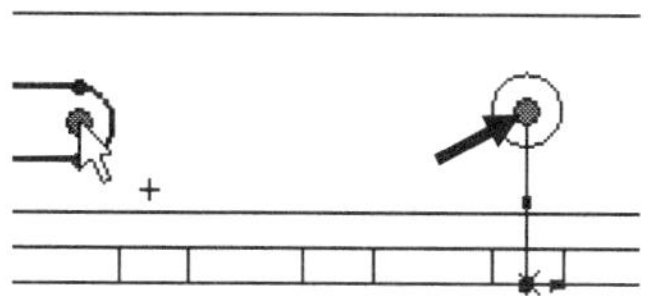

215) Hold the **Ctrl** key down. Click the **center point** of the right arc of the first rectangle. Release the **Ctrl** key.

216) Click **Horizontal** from the Add Relations box.

Add a Tangent relation.

217) Click the **bottom horizontal line** of the first rectangle. Hold the **Ctrl** key down.

218) Click the **first arc tangent**. Release the **Ctrl** key.

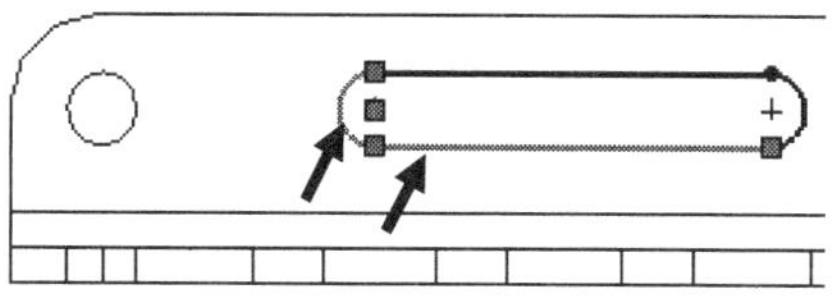

219) Click **Tangent** from the Add Relations box.

220) Perform the same **Tangent relation** procedure on the second rectangle.

221) Click **OK** from the Properties PropertyManager.

The right arc is horizontally aligned to the left arc due to symmetry from the Sketch Mirror tool.

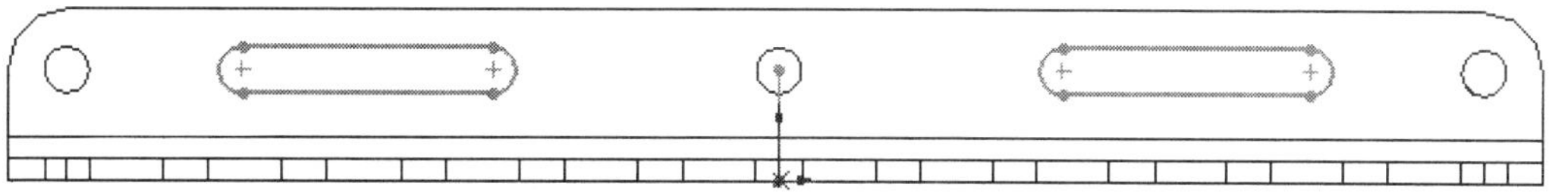

Add a dimension. Dimension the distance between the two slots.

222) Click **Smart Dimension** Smart Dimens... from the Sketch toolbar.

223) Click the **right arc centerpoint** of the left slot.

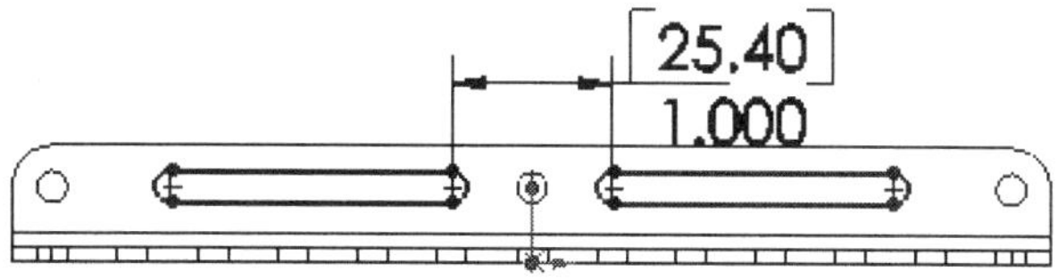

224) Click the **left arc centerpoint** of the right slot. Click a **position** above the top horizontal line.

225) Enter **1.000**in, [**25.40**] in the Modify dialog box.

226) Click the **Green Check mark**.

227) Click the **left center point** of the left arc.

228) Click the **right center point** of the left arc.

229) Click a **position** above the top horizontal line.

230) Enter **2.000**in, [**50.80**] in the Modify dialog box.

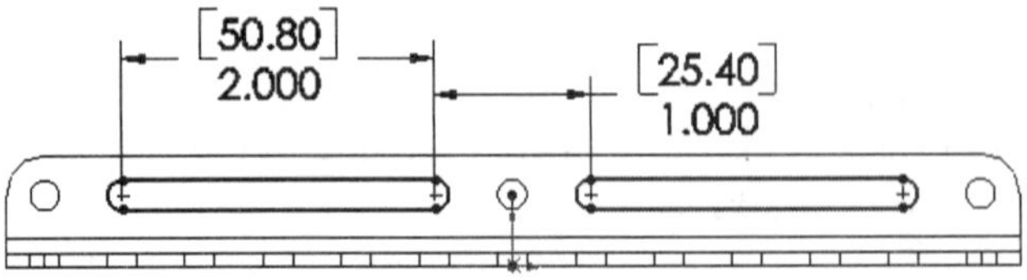

231) Click the **Green Check mark**. The black sketch is fully defined.

232) Click **Isometric view**.

Insert an Extruded Cut Feature.

233) Click **Extruded Cut** Extruded Cut from the Features toolbar. The Cut-Extrude PropertyManager is displayed.

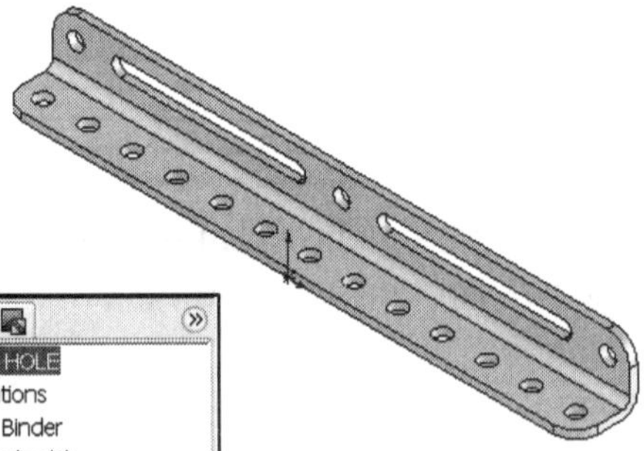

234) Select **Through All** for End Condition in Direction1. The direction arrow points to the right.

235) Click **OK** from the Cut-Extrude PropertyManager. Cut-Extrude3 is displayed in the FeatureManager.

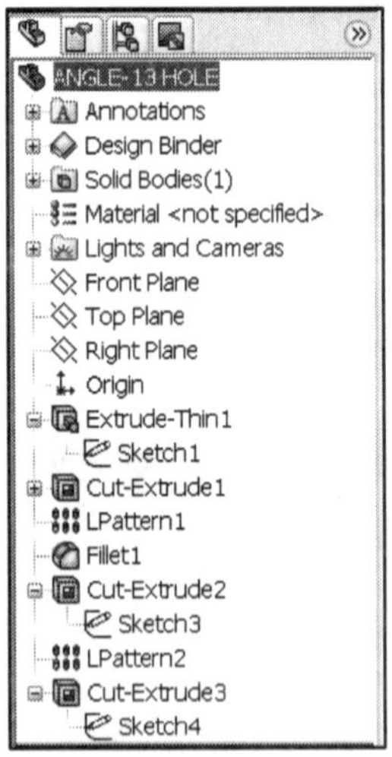

236) Click **Shaded With Edges**.

Save the ANGLE-13HOLE part.

237) Click **Save**. The ANGLE-13HOLE is complete. All Sketches in the FeatureManager should be Fully Defined.

Note: The dimension between the two slots is over-defined if the arc center points are aligned to the center points of the LPattern1 feature.

The mouse pointer displays a blue dashed line when horizontal and vertical sketch references are inferred.

Utilize the Display/Delete Display... Relations Sketch tool to delete unwanted sketch references.

Review the ANGLE-13HOLE Part.

The ANGLE-13HOLE part utilized an open L-Shaped profile sketched on the Right plane. The Extruded Thin feature with the Mid Plane option located the part symmetrical to the Right plane. The first Extruded Cut feature created the first hole sketched on the top face of the Extruded Thin feature.

The first Linear Pattern feature created an array of 13 holes along the bottom horizontal edge. The Fillet feature rounded the four corners. The second Extruded Cut feature created a hole on the Front face. The second Linear Pattern feature created an array of 3 holes along the top horizontal edge. The third Extruded Cut feature created two slot cuts.

Additional details on Extruded Base/Thin, Extruded Cut, Linear Pattern, Fillet, Mirror Entities, Add Relations, Trim Entities, Centerline, Line, Rectangle, Tangent Arc, and Smart Dimensions are available in Help. Keywords: Extrude Boss/Base - Thin, Extruded Cut, Patterns, Fillet, Sketch Entities, Sketch Tools, and Dimensions.

TRAINGLE Part

The TRIANGLE part is a multipurpose supporting plane.

The TRIANGLE is manufactured from .090in, [2.3] aluminum. The TRIANGLE contains numerous features.

Utilize symmetry and Sketch tools to simplify the geometry creation.

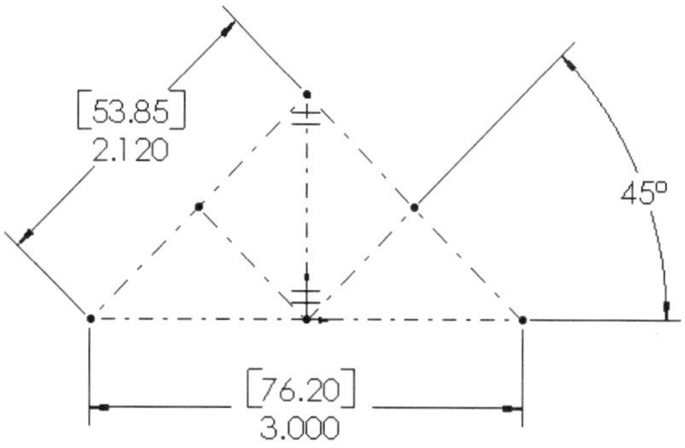

The center points of the slots and holes locate key geometry for the TRIANGLE.

Utilize sketched construction geometry to locate the center points.

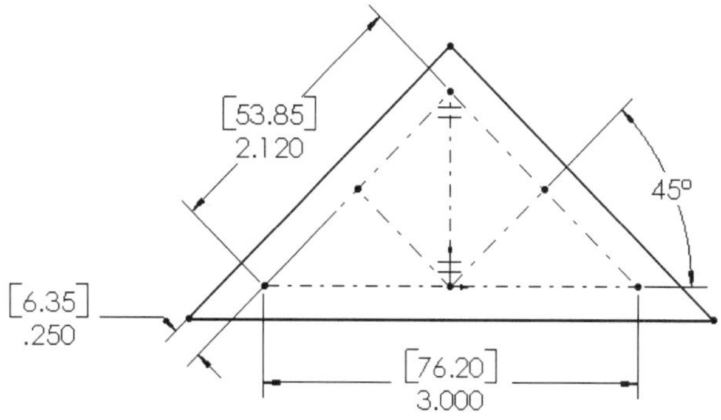

Construction geometry is not calculated in the extruded profile.

Utilize the Sketch Offset tool and Sketch Fillet to create the sketch profile for the Extruded Base feature.

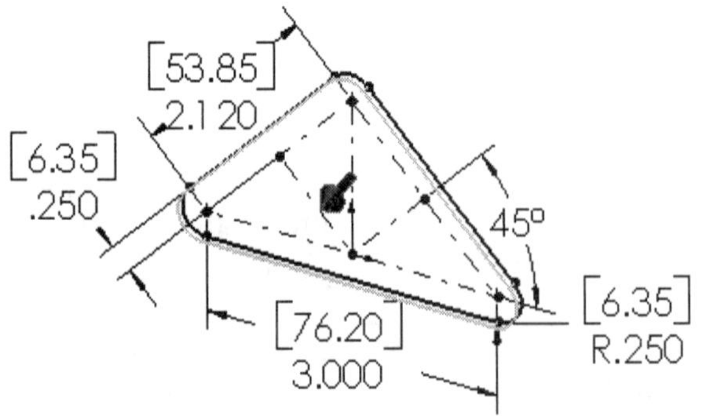

Utilize Sketch Mirror and the Circle Sketch tools to create the Extruded Cut features.

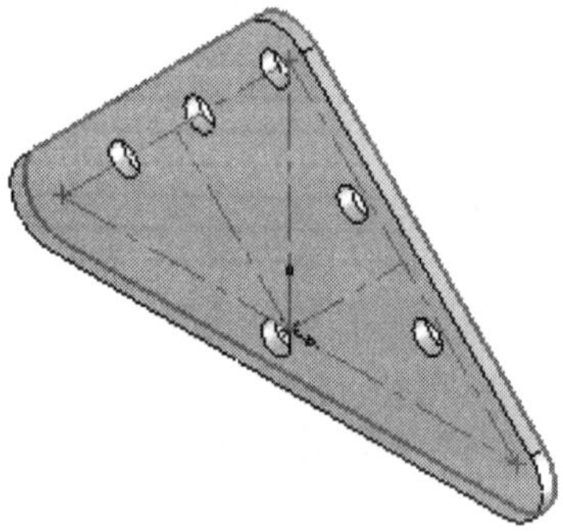

Utilize the Rectangle, Sketch Trim, and the Tangent Arc tool to create the Extruded Cut left bottom slot. Utilize the Mirror feature to create the right bottom slot.

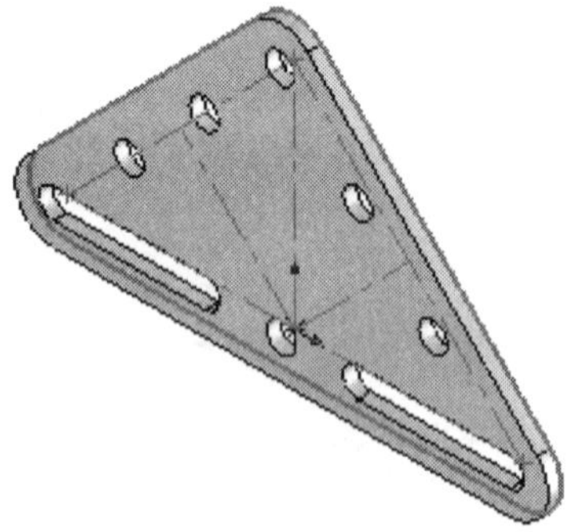

Utilize the Parallelogram and Tangent Arc Sketch tools to create the Extruded Cut feature.

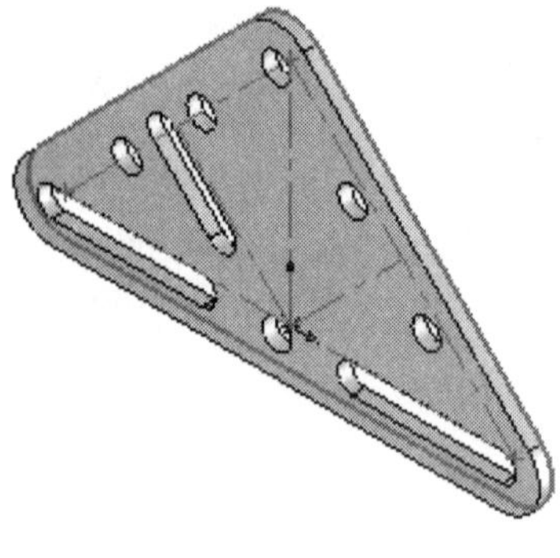

Utilize the Circular Pattern feature to create the three radial slot cuts.

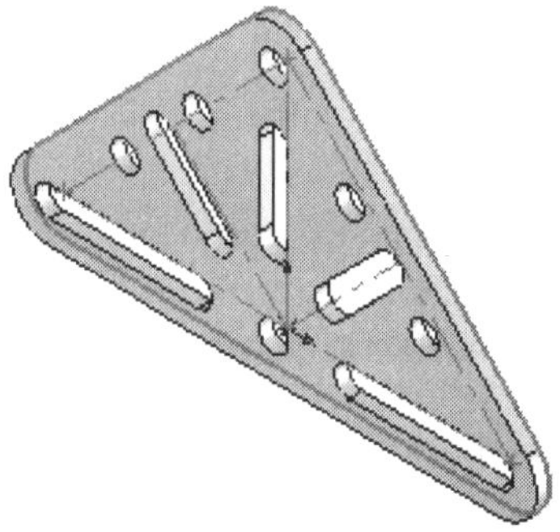

Activity: TRIANGLE Part-Mirror, Offset, and Fillet Sketch Tools

Create a new Part.

238) Click **File**, **New** from the Main menu. The Templates tab is the default tab.

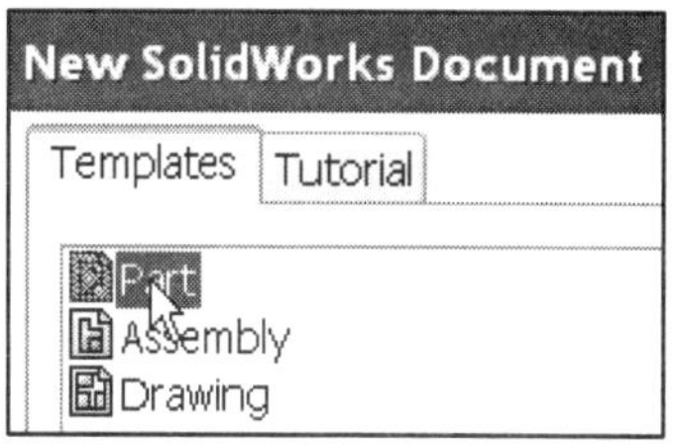

239) Double-click **Part**. The Part FeatureManager is displayed.

Save the Part.

240) Click **File**, **Save As** from the Main menu.

241) Select **SW-TUTORIAL-2007** for the Save in file folder.

242) Enter **TRIANGLE** for File name.

243) Enter **TRIANGLE** for Description.

244) Click **Save**. The TRIANGLE FeatureManager is displayed.

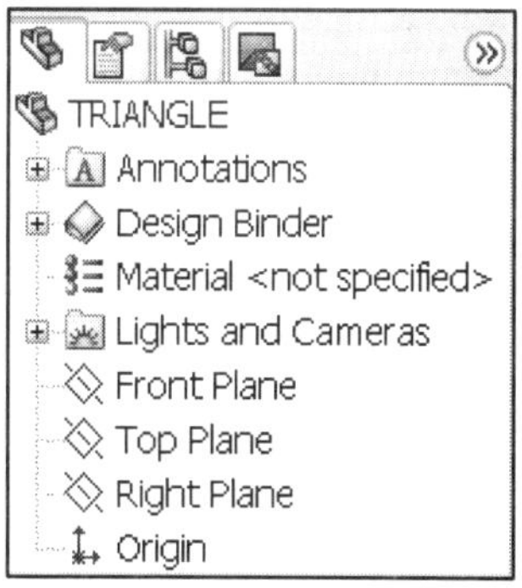

Set the Dimensioning Standard and Part Units.

245) Click **Tools, Options**, **Document Properties** tab from the Main menu.

246) Select **ANSI** from the Dimensioning standard box.

247) Click **Units**.

248) Click **IPS**, **[MMGS]** for Unit system.

249) Select **3**, **[2]** for Length units Decimal places.

250) Select **0**, **[0]** for Angular units Decimal places.

251) Click **OK** to set the document units.

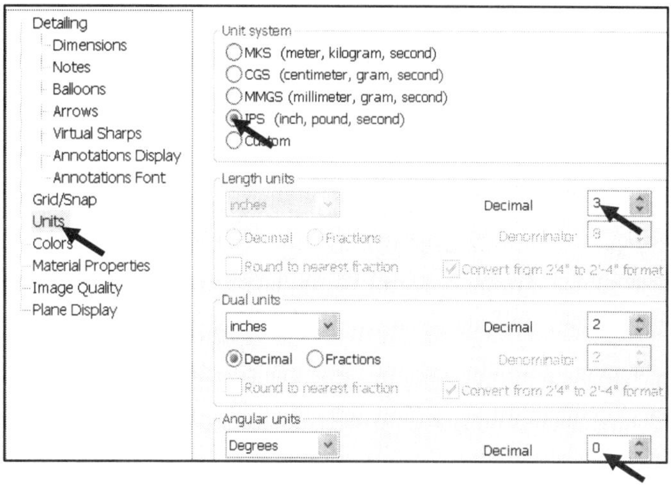

Insert a new Sketch for the Extruded Base feature.

252) Click **Front Plane** from the FeatureManager.

253) Click **Sketch** Sketch from the Control Area.

Sketch a vertical centerline.

254) Click **Centerline** Centerl... from the Sketch toolbar.

255) Click the **Origin**.

256) Click a vertical **position** above the Origin as illustrated.

Sketch a Mirrored profile.

257) Click **Tools**, **Sketch Tools**, **Dynamic Mirror** from the Main menu.

258) Click the **centerline** in the Graphics window.

259) Click **Centerline** Centerl... from the Sketch toolbar.

260) Click the **Origin**.

261) Click a **position** to the right of the Origin to create a horizontal line.

262) Click the **top end point** of the vertical centerline to complete the triangle as illustrated.

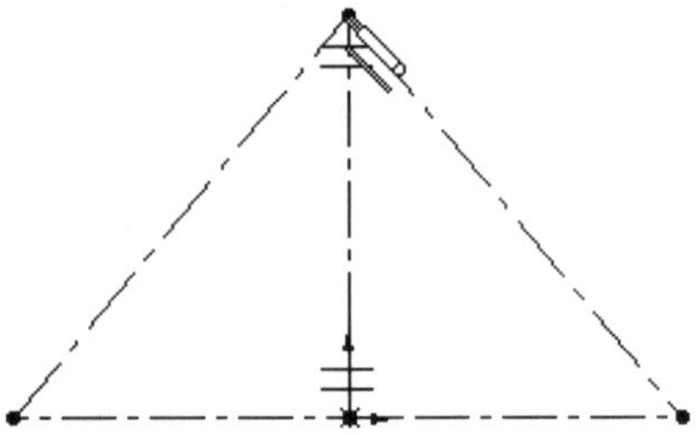

263) Right-click **End Chain** to end the line segment. The Centerline tool is still active.

264) Click the **Origin**.

265) Click a **position** coincident with the right-angled centerline. Do not select the Midpoint.

266) Right-click **End Chain** to end the line segment.

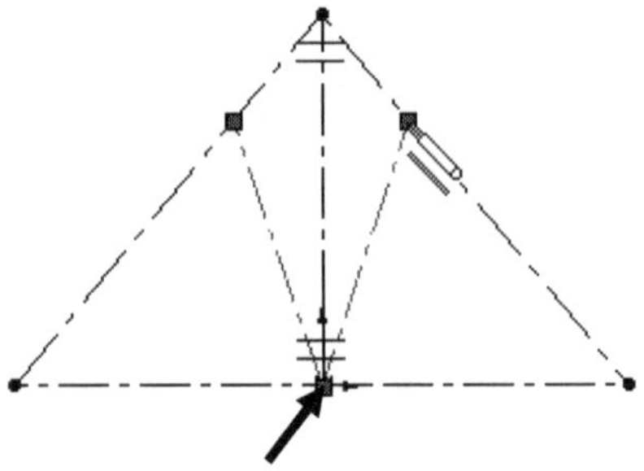

Deactivate the Dynamic Mirror Sketch tool.

267) Click **Tools**, **Sketch Tools**, **Dynamic Mirror** from the Main menu.

Add a dimension.

268) Click **Smart Dimension** Smart Dimens... from the Sketch toolbar.

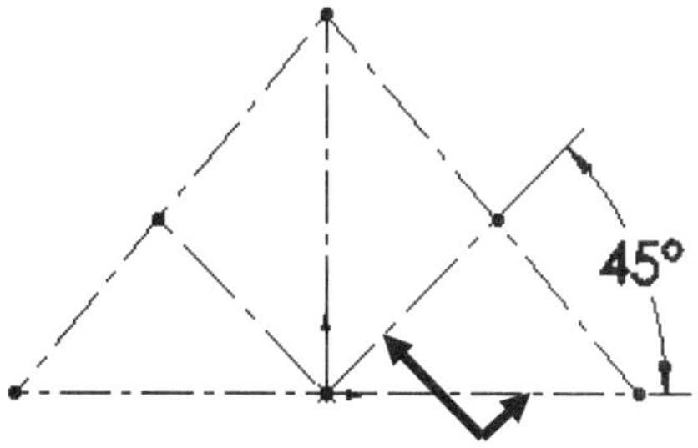

269) Click the **right horizontal** centerline.

270) Click the **inside right** centerline.

271) Click a **position** between the two lines.

272) Enter **45**deg in the Modify dialog box for the angular dimension.

273) Click the **Green Check mark**.

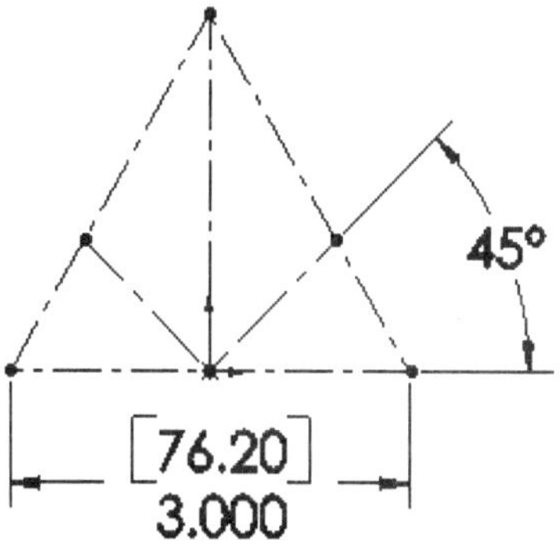

274) Click the **horizontal centerline**.

275) Click a position **below** the centerline.

276) Enter **3.000**in, [**76.20**].

277) Click the **Green Check mark**.

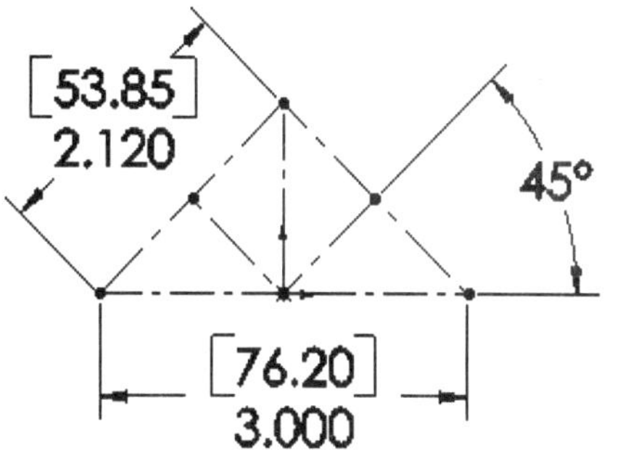

278) Click the **left angled** centerline.

279) Click **position** aligned to the left angled centerline.

280) Enter **2.120**in, [**53.85**].

Offset the sketch

281) Right-click **Select** in the Graphics window.

282) Hold the **Ctrl** key down.

283) Click the **three outside centerlines**; Line2, Line4, and Line5 are displayed in the Selected Entities box.

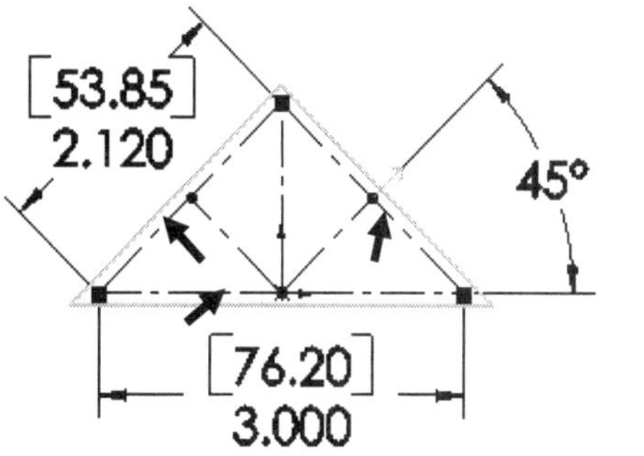

284) Release the **Ctrl** key.

285) Click **Offset Entities** Offset from the Sketch toolbar

286) Enter **.250**in, [**6.35**] for Offset Distance. The yellow Offset direction is outward.

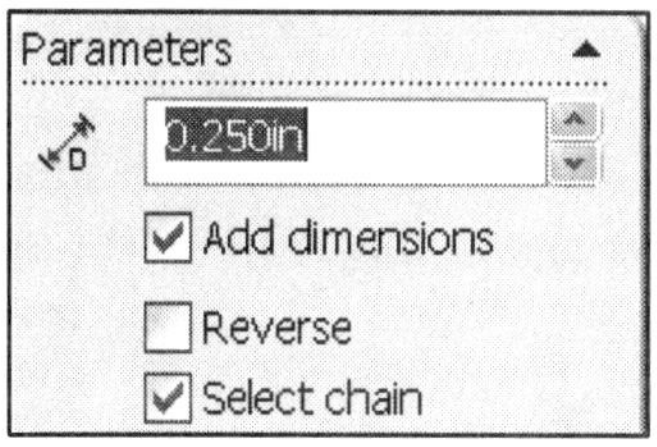

287) Click **OK** from the Offset Entities PropertyManager.

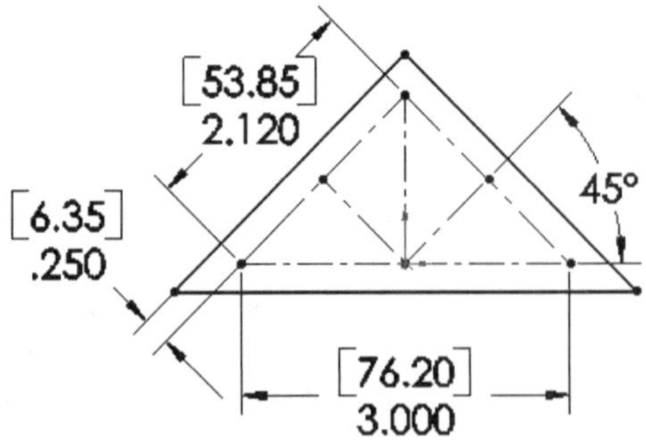

Three profile lines are displayed. The centerlines are on the inside.

Insert the Sketch Fillet.

288) Click **Sketch Fillet** Sketch Fillet from the Sketch toolbar. The Sketch Fillet PropertyManager is displayed.

289) Enter **.250**in, [**6.35**] for Radius.

290) Click the **three outside corner points**.

291) Click **OK** from the Sketch Fillet PropertyManager.

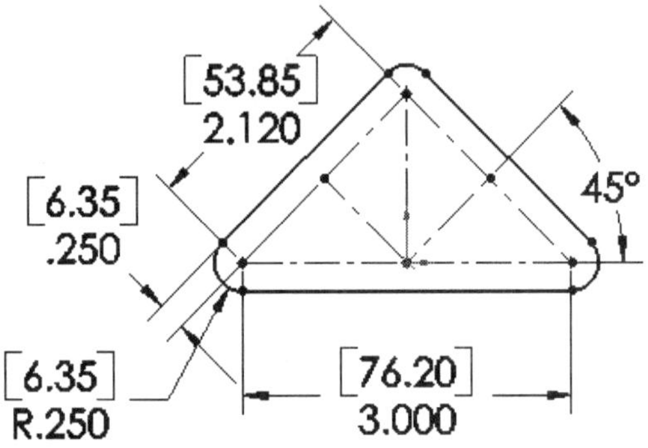

Activity: TRIANGLE Part-Extruded Base Feature

Extrude the Sketch.

292) Click **Extruded Boss/Base** Extruded Boss/B... from the Features toolbar. Blind is the default End Condition in Direction1.

293) Enter **.090**in, [**2.3**] for Depth in Direction 1. The direction arrow points to the left.

294) Click **OK** from the Extrude PropertyManager. Extrude1 is displayed in the FeatureManager.

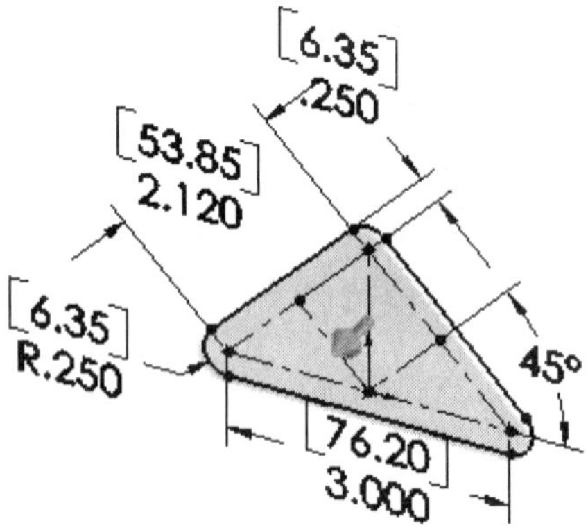

Save the TRIANGLE part.

295) Click **Isometric view**.

296) Click **Save**.

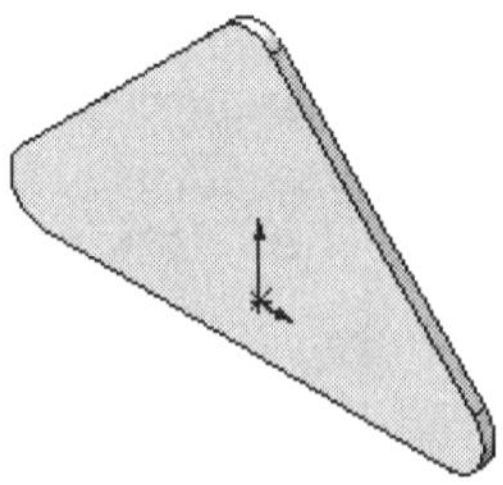

Insert centerlines and add relations to build sketches that will be referenced by multiple features.

Display the sketch.

297) Expand Extrude1 in the FeatureManager.

298) Right-click **Sketch1**.

299) Click **Show**.

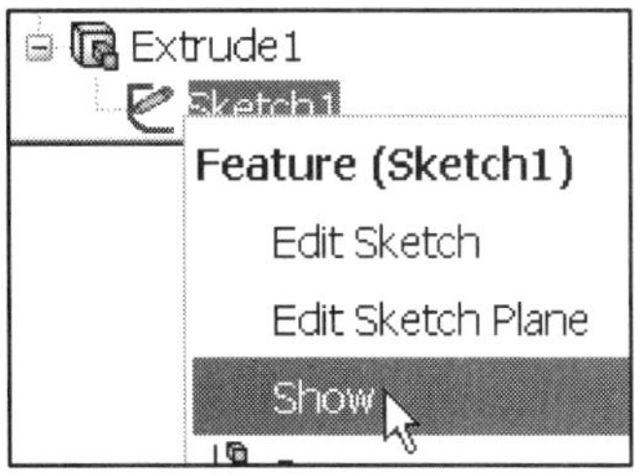

Activity: TRIANGLE Part-First Extruded Cut Feature

Insert a new sketch for the first Extruded Cut.

300) Click the **front face** of Extrude1. This is your Sketch plane.

301) Click **Sketch** Sketch from the Control Area.

302) Click **Front view**.

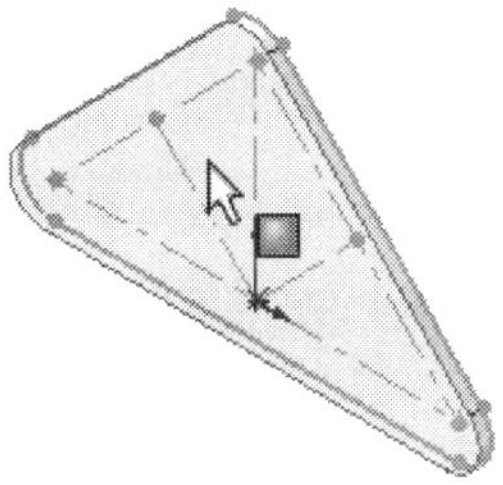

303) Click **Circle** Circle from the Sketch toolbar.

304) Sketch a **circle** centered at the Origin.

305) Sketch a **circle** centered at the endpoint of the vertical centerline as illustrated.

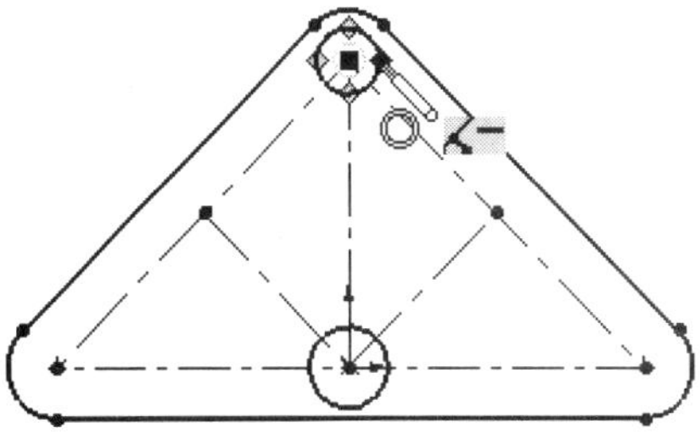

Sketch a vertical centerline.

306) Click **Centerline** Centerl... from the Sketch toolbar.

307) Click the **Origin**.

308) Click the **centerpoint** of the top circle.

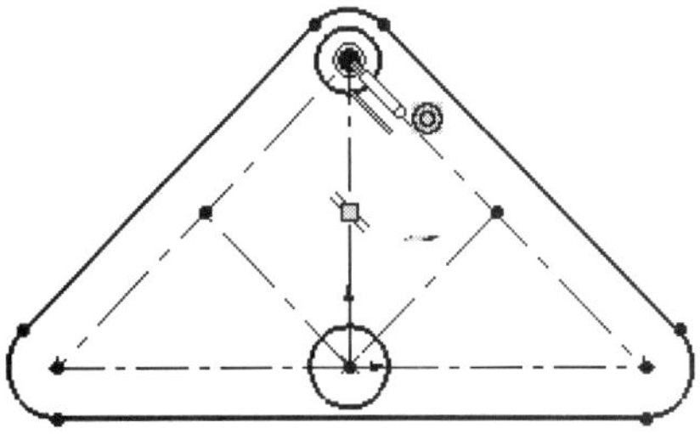

Sketch a Mirrored profile.

309) Click **Tools**, **Sketch Tools**, **Dynamic Mirror** from the Main menu.

310) Click the **centerline** in the Graphics window.

311) Click **Circle** Circle from the Sketch toolbar.

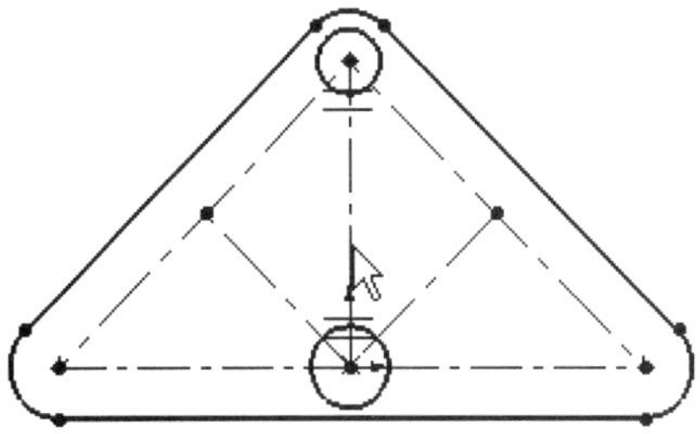

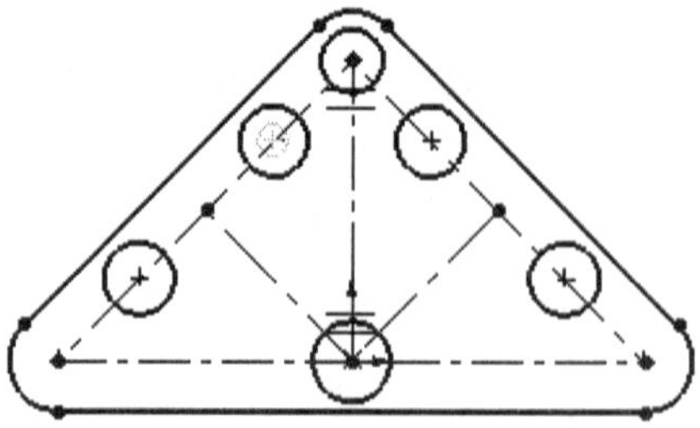

312) Sketch a **circle** on the left side of the centerline, coincident with the left centerline, in the lower half of the triangle.

313) Sketch a **circle** on the left side of the centerline, coincident with the left centerline, in the upper half of the triangle.

314) Click **Tools**, **Sketch Tools**, **Dynamic Mirror** from the Main menu.

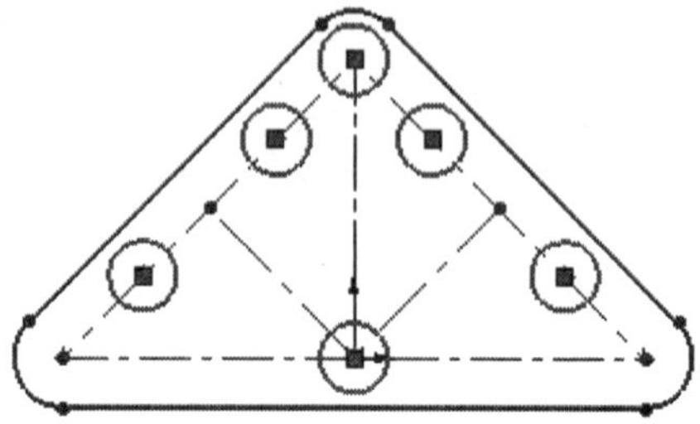

Add an Equal relation.

315) Click a **circle**. Hold the **Ctrl** key down. Click the five other **circles**. Release the **Ctrl** key.

316) Click **Equal** = from the Add Relations box.

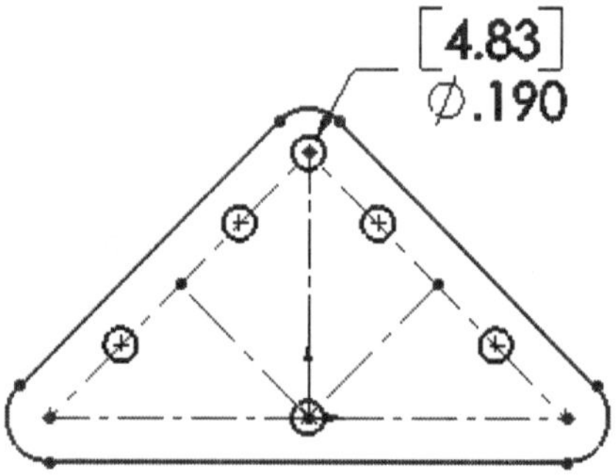

Add a dimension.

317) Click **Smart Dimension** Smart Dimens... from the Sketch toolbar.

318) Click the circumference of the **top circle**.

319) Click a **position** off the TRIANGLE.

320) Enter **.190**in, [**4.83**].

321) Click the **Green Check mark**.

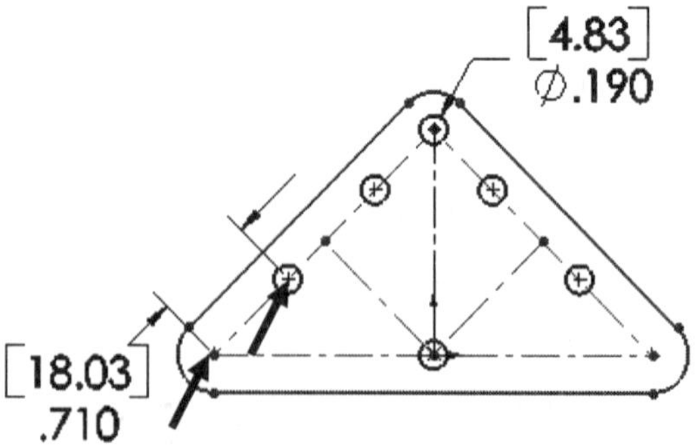

Create the aligned dimensions.

322) Click the bottom **left point**. Click the **center point** of the bottom left circle.

323) Click a **position** aligned to the angled centerline. Enter .**710**in, [**18.03**].

324) Click the **Green Check mark**.

325) Click the bottom **left point**.

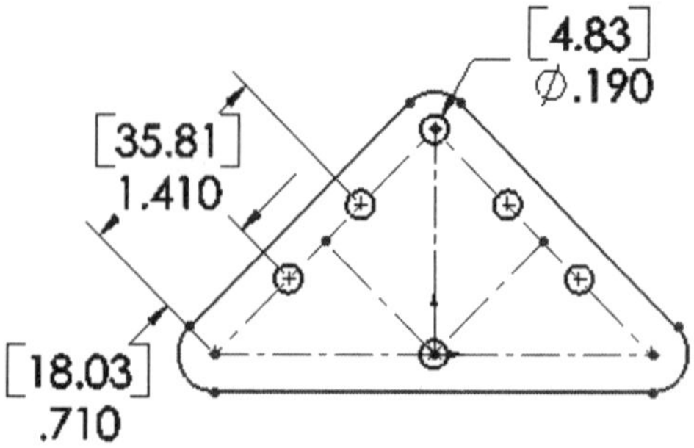

326) Click the **center point** of the top left circle as illustrated. Click a **position** aligned to the angled centerline.

327) Enter **1.410**in, [**35.81**].

328) Click the **Green Check mark**.

Insert an Extruded Cut Feature.

329) Click **Extruded Cut** Extruded Cut from the Features toolbar. The Cut-Extrude PropertyManager is displayed.

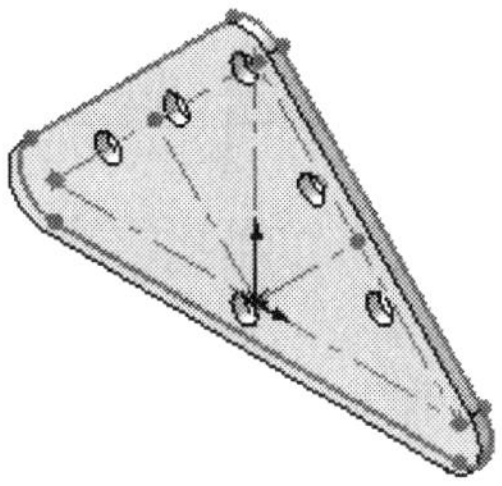

330) Select **Through All** for the End Condition in Direction1.

331) Click **OK** from the Cut-Extrude PropertyManager. Cut-Extrude1 is displayed in the FeatureManager.

332) Click **Isometric view**.

333) Click **Save**.

Activity: TRIANGLE Part-Second Extruded Cut Feature

Insert a new slot sketch for the second Extruded Cut.

334) Click the **front face** of Extrude1 for the Sketch plane.

335) Click **Sketch** Sketch from the Control Area.

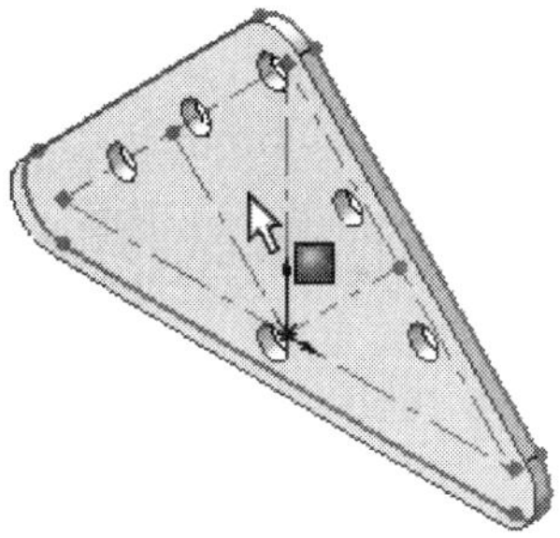

336) Click **Front view**.

337) Click **Rectangle** Rectan... from the Sketch toolbar.

338) Sketch a **rectangle** to the left of the Origin as illustrated.

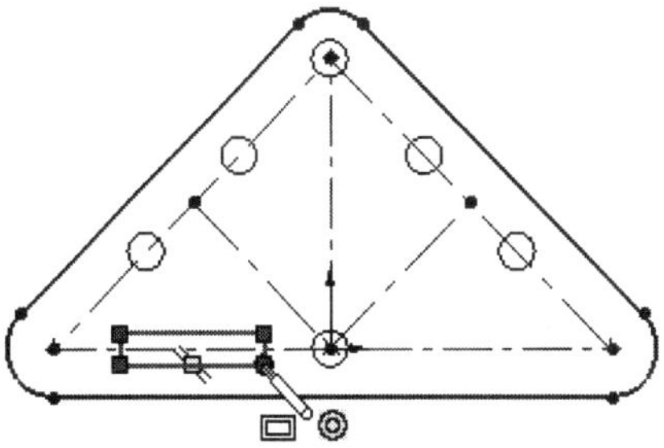

Trim the vertical lines.

339) Click **Trim Entities** Trim from the Sketch toolbar. The Trim PropertyManager is displayed.

340) Click **Trim to closest** in the Options box.

341) Click the **left vertical** line of the rectangle.

342) Click the **right vertical** line of the rectangle.

343) Click **OK** from the Trim PropertyManager.

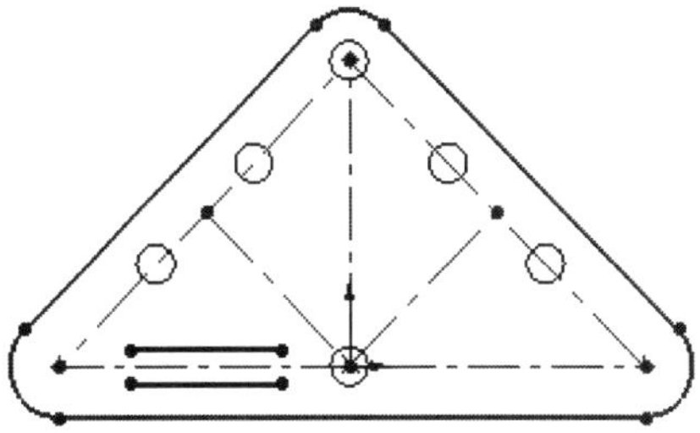

Sketch the Tangent Arcs.

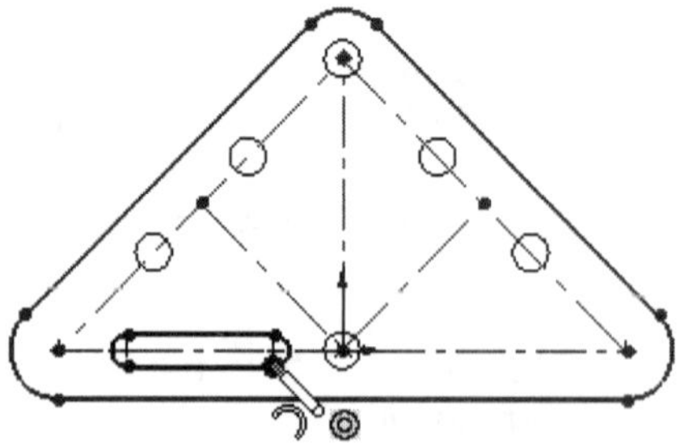

344) Click **Tangent Arc** Tangent Arc from the Sketch toolbar.

345) Sketch a **180º arc** on the left side as illustrated.

346) Sketch a **180º arc** on the right side.

347) Click **OK** from the Arc PropertyManager.

348) Right-click **Select** in the Graphics window.

Add an Equal relation.

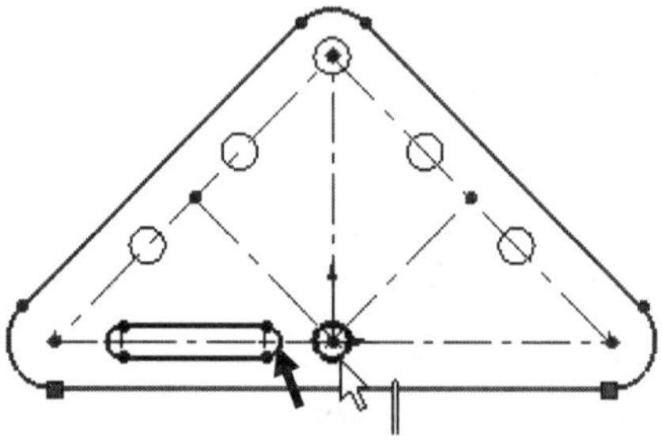

349) Click the **Right arc**. Hold the **Ctrl** key down.

350) Click the **bottom center circle**.

351) Release the **Ctrl** key.

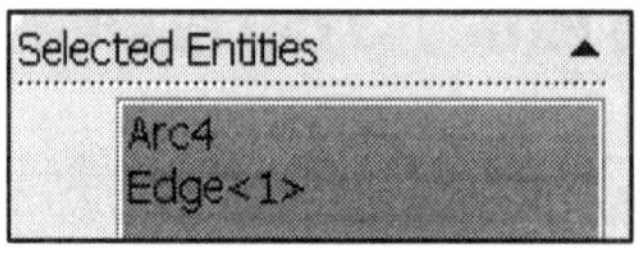

352) Click **Equal** = from the Add Relations box.

353) Click **OK** from the Properties PropertyManager.

Add a Coincident relation.

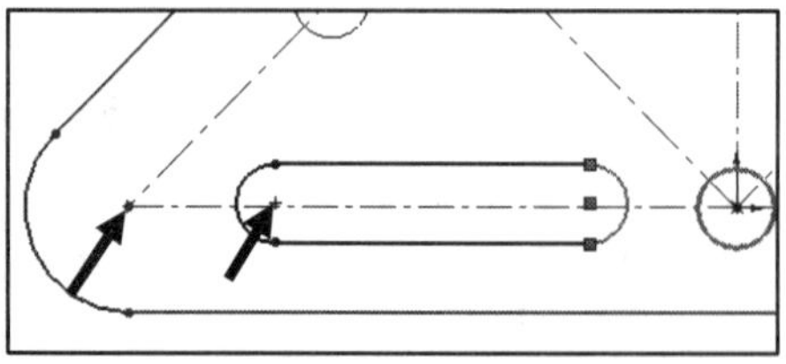

354) Click the **center point** of the left arc.

355) Hold the **Ctrl** key down.

356) Click the **left lower point**. Release the **Ctrl** key.

357) Click **Coincident** from the Add Relations box.

Add a Tangent relation.

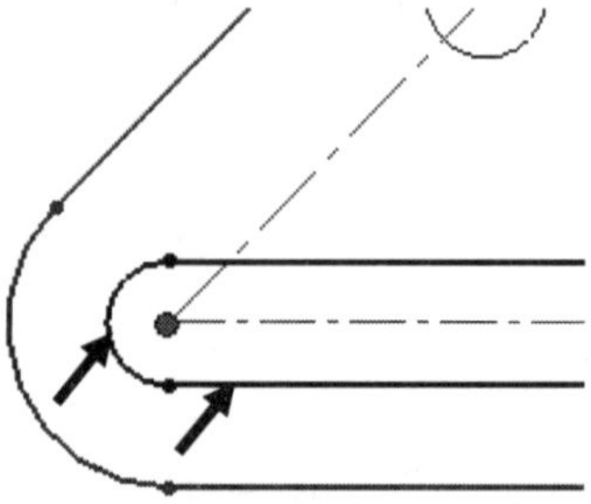

358) Click the **bottom horizontal** line.

359) Hold the **Ctrl** key down.

360) Click the **first arc tangent**.

361) Release the **Ctrl** key.

362) Click **Tangent** from the Add Relations box.

363) Click **OK** from the Properties PropertyManager.

Add a dimension.

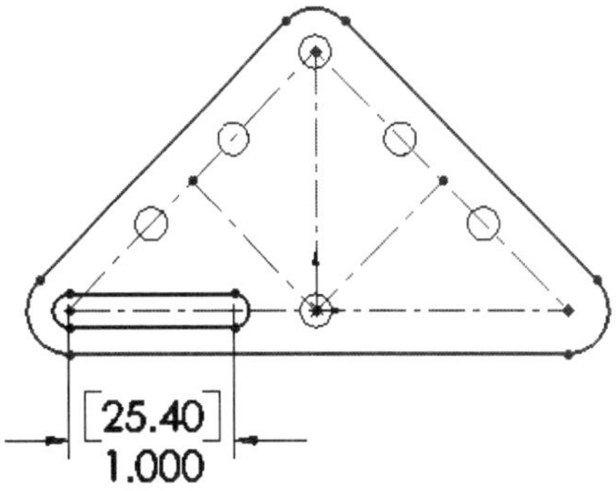

364) Click **Smart Dimension** Smart Dimens... from the Sketch toolbar.

365) Click the **left center point** of the left arc. Click the **right center point** of the right arc.

366) Click a **position** below the horizontal line. Enter **1.000**in, [**25.40**] in the Modify dialog box.

367) Click the **Green Check mark**.

Insert an Extruded Cut Feature.

368) Click **Isometric view**.

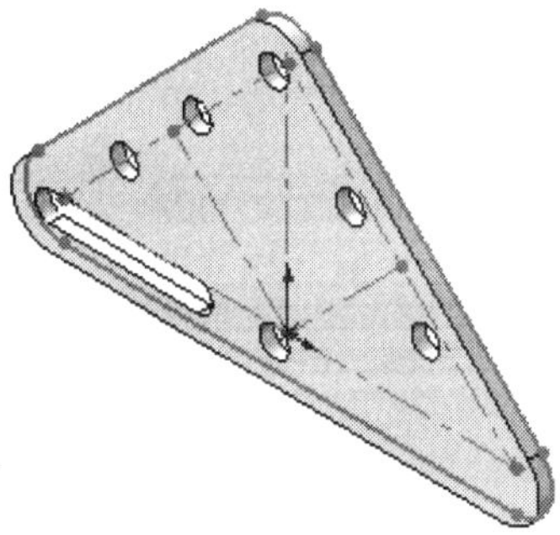

369) Click **Extruded Cut** Extruded Cut from the Features toolbar.

370) Select **Through All** for End Condition in Direction 1.

371) Click **OK** from the Cut-Extrude PropertyManager. Cut-Extrude2 is displayed in the FeatureManager.

372) Click **Save**.

Activity: TRIANGLE Part-Mirror Feature

Mirror the Cut-Extrude2 Feature.

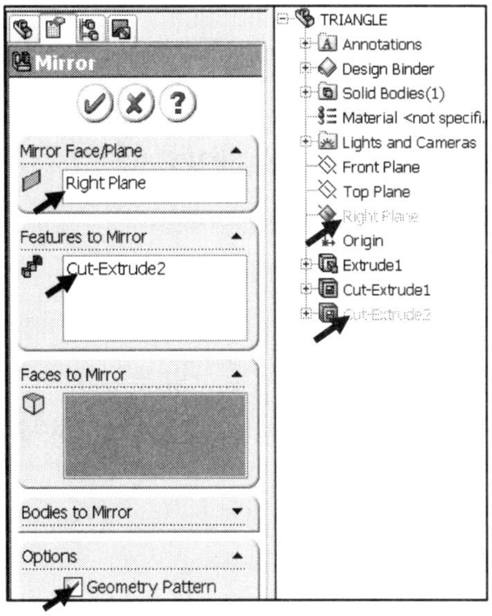

373) Click **Mirror** Mirror from the Features toolbar. The Mirror PropertyManager is displayed. Cut-Extrude2 is displayed in the Feature to Mirror box.

374) Click **Right Plane** from the fly-out TRIANGLE FeatureManager. Right Plane is displayed in the Mirror Face/Plane box.

375) Check the **Geometry Pattern** box.

376) Click **OK** from the Mirror PropertyManager. Mirror1 is displayed in the FeatureManager.

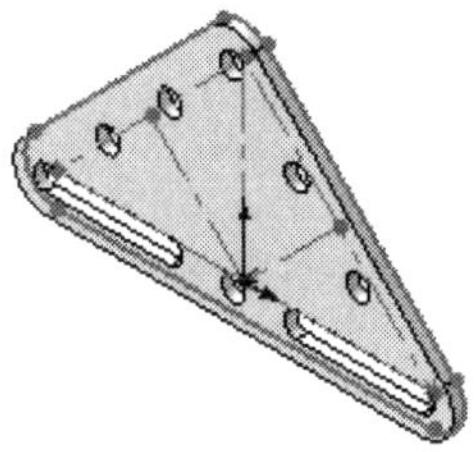

The Rectangle Sketch tool provides 4 lines with 2 horizontal and 2 vertical relations. The Parallelogram Sketch tool provides 4 lines with 2 perpendicular and 1 parallel relations.

Activity: TRIANGLE Part-Third Extruded Cut Feature

Insert a new sketch for the third Extruded Cut.

377) Click the **front face** of Extrude1 for the Sketch plane.

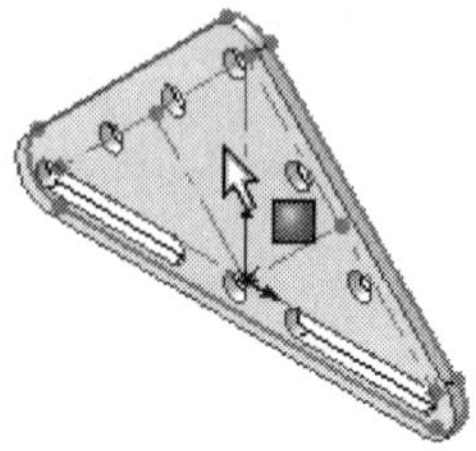

378) Click **Sketch** Sketch from the Control Area.

379) Click **Front view**.

380) Click **Tools**, **Sketch Entities**, **Parallelogram** from the Main menu.

Sketch a Parallelogram.

381) Sketch the first point. Click a **position** coincident with the left angled centerline as illustrated.

382) Sketch the second point. Click a position **approximately** parallel to the inside left centerline. A dashed blue line is displayed.

383) Sketch the third point. Click a **position** above the inside left centerline.

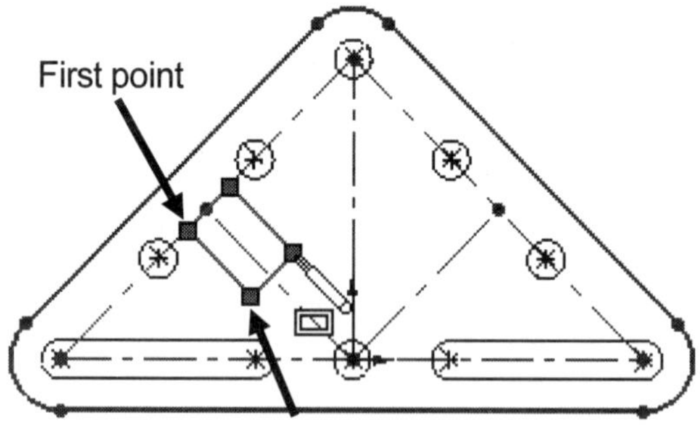

Trim the Parallelogram.

384) Click **Trim Entities** Trim from the Sketch toolbar. The Trim PropertyManager is displayed.

385) Click **Trim to closest** from the Options box.

386) Click the **left short** parallelogram line as illustrated.

387) Click the **right short** parallelogram line.

388) Click **OK** from the Trim PropertyManager.

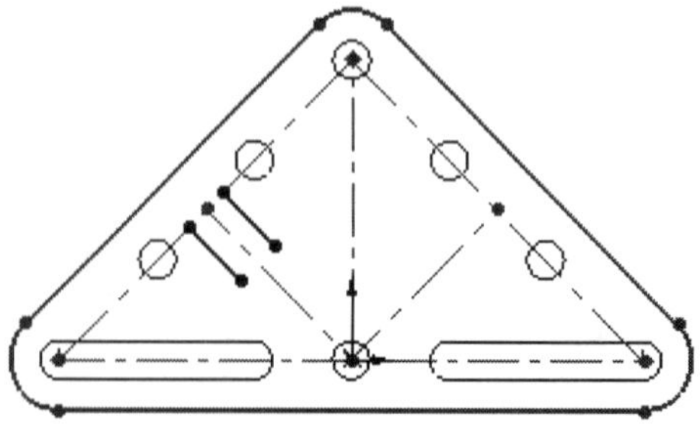

Sketch the Tangent Arcs.

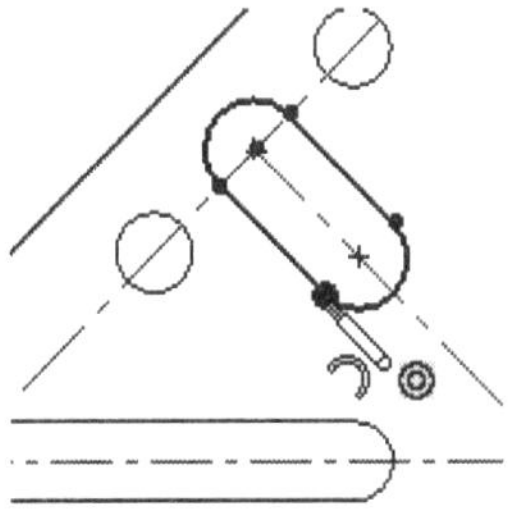

389) Click **Tangent Arc** Tangent Arc from the Sketch toolbar.

390) Sketch a **180° arc** on the left side as illustrated.

391) Sketch a **180° arc** on the right side.

392) Click **OK** from the Arc PropertyManager.

393) Right-click **Select** in the Graphics window.

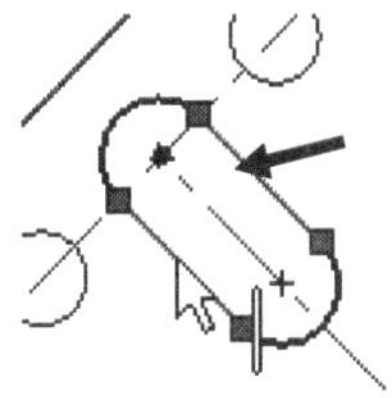

Add an Equal relation.
394) Click the **left parallel line**.

395) Hold the **Ctrl** key down.

396) Click the **right parallel line**. Release the **Ctrl** key.

397) Click **Equal** = from the Add Relations box.

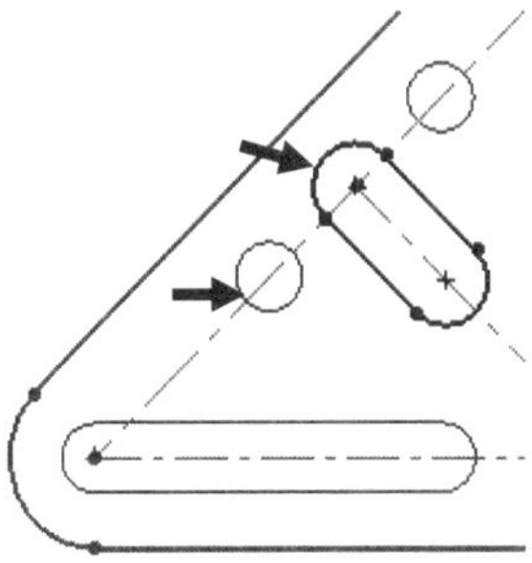

Add an Equal relation.
398) Click the **left arc**. Hold the **Ctrl** key down.

399) Click the **bottom circle**. Release the **Ctrl** key.

400) Click **Equal** = from the Add Relations box.

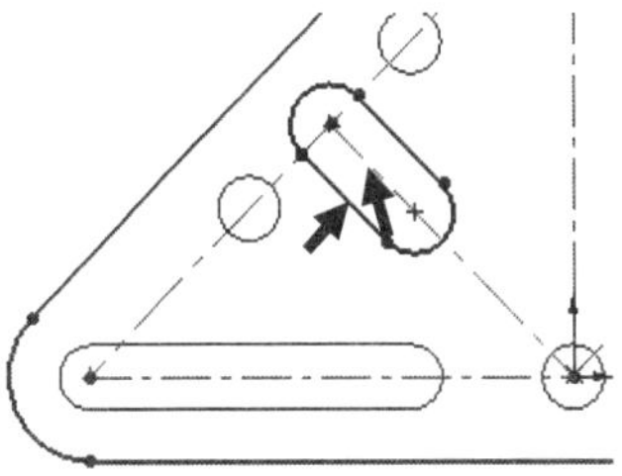

Add a Parallel relation.
401) Click the **lower parallel** line. Hold the **Ctrl** key down.

402) Click the **angular centerline**. Release the **Ctrl** key.

403) Click **Parallel** from the Add Relations box.

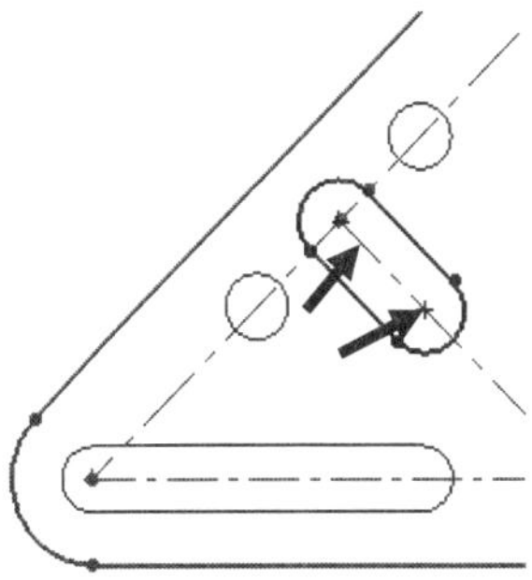

Add a Coincident relation.
404) Click the **arc center** point as illustrated.

405) Hold the **Ctrl** key down.

406) Click the **angular centerline**.

407) Release the **Ctrl** key.

408) Click **Coincident** from the Add Relations box.

409) Click **OK** from the Properties PropertyManager.

Add a Tangent relation.

410) Click the **bottom horizontal line**.

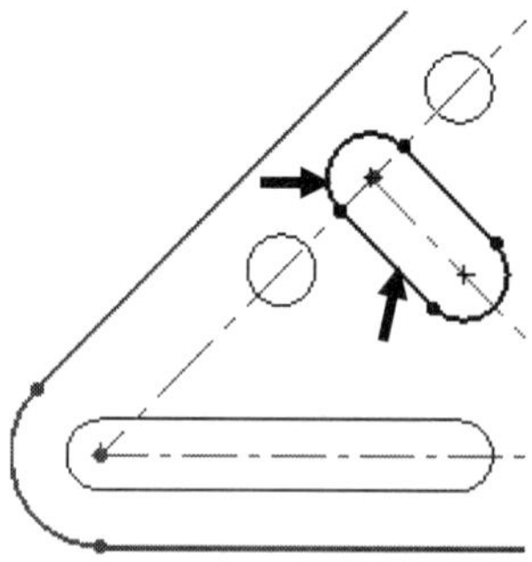

411) Hold the **Ctrl** key down.

412) Click the **first tangent arc**. Release the **Ctrl** key.

413) Click **Tangent** from the Add Relations box.

414) Click **OK** from the Properties PropertyManager.

Add a dimension.

415) Click **Smart Dimension** Smart Dimens... from the Sketch toolbar.

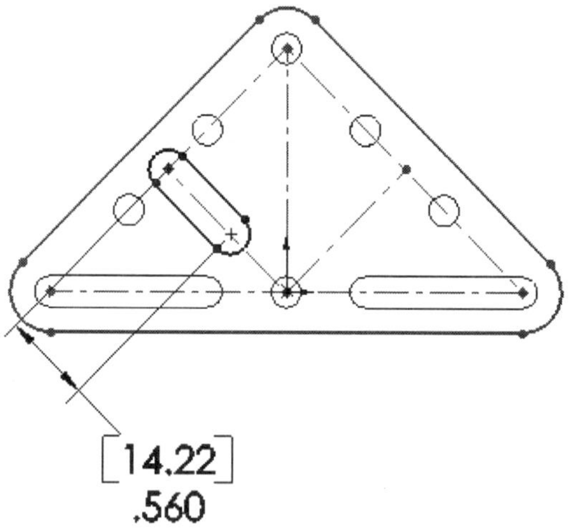

416) Click the **left center point** of the left arc.

417) Click the **right center point** of the right arc.

418) Click a **position** below the horizontal line.

419) Enter **.560**in, [**14.22**] in the Modify dialog box.

420) Click the **Green Check mark**.

Insert an Extruded Cut Feature.

421) Click **Isometric view**.

422) Click **Extruded Cut** Extruded Cut from the Features toolbar. The Cut-Extrude PropertyManager is displayed.

423) Select **Through All** for the End Condition in Direction 1.

424) Click **OK** from the Cut-Extrude PropertyManager. Cut-Extrude3 is displayed in the FeatureManager.

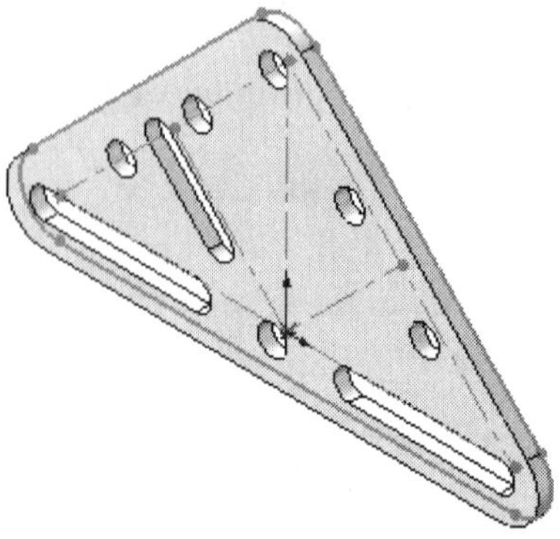

Save the model.

425) Click **Save**.

Display the Temporary Axis.

426) Click **View**; check **Temporary Axes** from the Main menu.

Activity: TRIANGLE Part-Circular Pattern Feature

Insert a Circular Pattern Feature.

427) Click **Circular Pattern** Circular from the Features toolbar. The Circular Pattern PropertyManager is displayed.

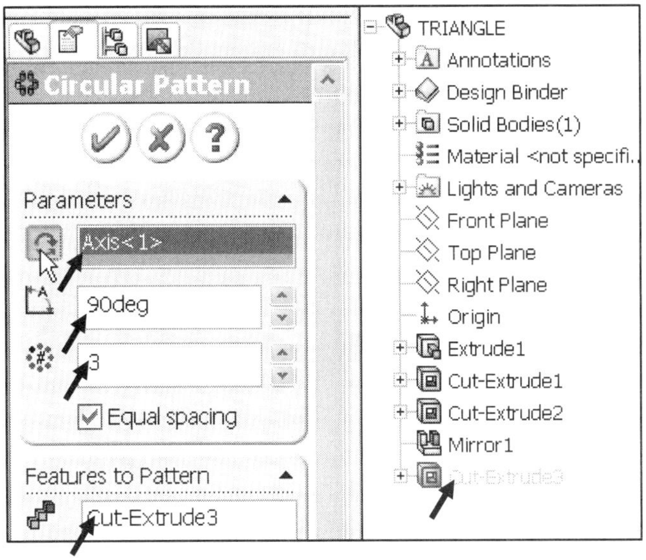

428) Click inside the **Features to Pattern** box.

429) Click **Cut-Extrude3** from the fly-out FeatureManager. Cut-Extrude3 is displayed in the Features to Pattern box.

430) Click inside the **Pattern Axis** box.

431) Click the **Temporary Axis** displayed through the center hole located at the Origin. The Temporary Axis is displayed as Axis <1> in the Pattern Axis box.

432) Enter **90**deg for Angle.

433) Enter **3** for Number of Instances.

434) Check the **Equal spacing** box. If required, click **Reverse Direction**.

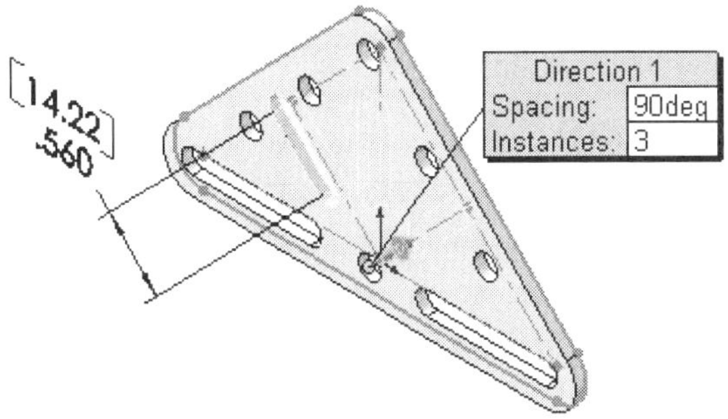

435) Click **OK** from the Circular Pattern PropertyManager. CirPattern1 is displayed in the FeatureManager.

Hide the Sketch.
436) **Expand** Extrude1 from the FeatureManager.

437) Right-click **Sketch1**. Click **Hide**.

Fit the model to the Graphics window.
438) Press the **f** key.

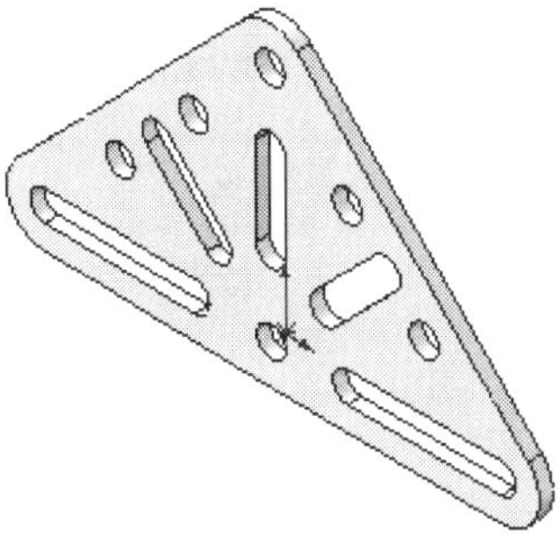

Save the TRIANGLE part.
439) Click **Isometric view**.

440) Click **View**; uncheck **Temporary Axes** from the Main menu

441) Click **Save**. The TRIANGLE part is complete.

Review the TRIANGLE Part.

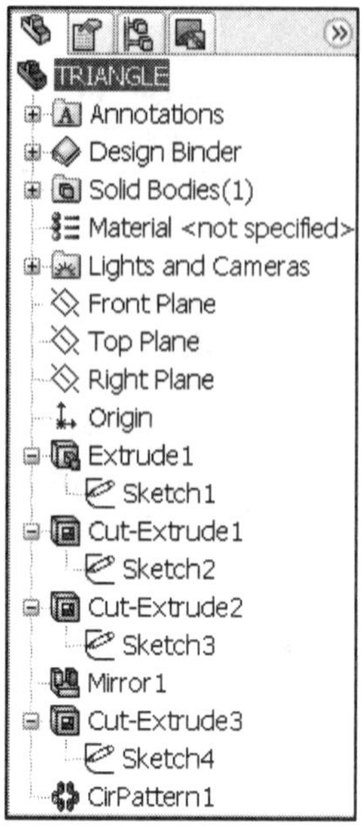

The TRIANGLE part utilized an Extruded Base feature. A triangular shape profile was sketch on the Front plane. Symmetry and construction geometry sketch tools located centerpoints for slots and holes.

The Sketch Fillet tool created rounded corners for the profile. The Sketch Mirror and Circle Sketch tools were utilized to create Extruded Cut features.

The Rectangle, Sketch Trim, and Tangent Arc tools were utilized to create the Extruded Cut left bottom slot. The Mirror feature was utilized to create the right bottom slot.

The Parallelogram and Tangent Arc Sketch tools were utilized to create the Extruded Cut. The Circular Pattern feature created the three radial slot cuts. The following Relations were utilized: Equal, Parallel, Coincident, and Tangent.

Additional details on Rectangle, Circle, Tangent Arc, Parallelogram, Mirror Entities, Sketch Fillet, Offset Entities, Extruded Boss/Base, Extruded Cut, Mirror, and Circular Pattern are available in SolidWorks Help.

SCREW Part

The SCREW part is a simplified model of a 10-24 x 3/8 machine screw. Screws, nuts and washers are classified as fasteners.

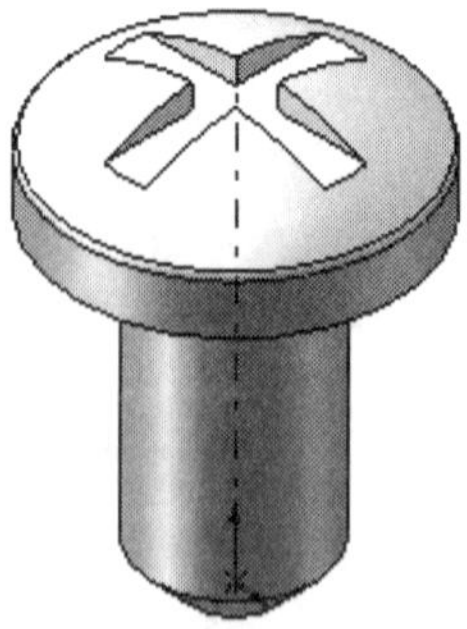

Simplified version

An assembly contains hundreds of fasteners. Utilize simplified versions to conserve model and rebuild time.

Machine screws are described in terms of the following:

- Nominal diameter – Size 10.
- Threads per inch –24.
- Length – 3/8.

Screw diameter, less than ¼ inch, are represented by a size number. Size 10 refers to a diameter of .190 inch. Utilize the SCREW part to fasten components in the FRONT-SUPPORT assembly.

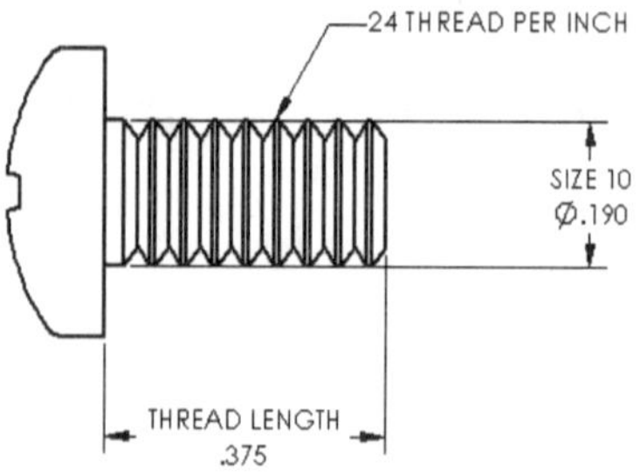

The SCREW part utilizes a Revolved Base feature to add material. The Revolved Boss/Base feature requires a centerline and sketch on a Sketch plane. A Revolved feature require an angle of revolution. The sketch is revolved around the centerline.

Sketch a centerline on the Front sketch plane.

Sketch a closed profile.

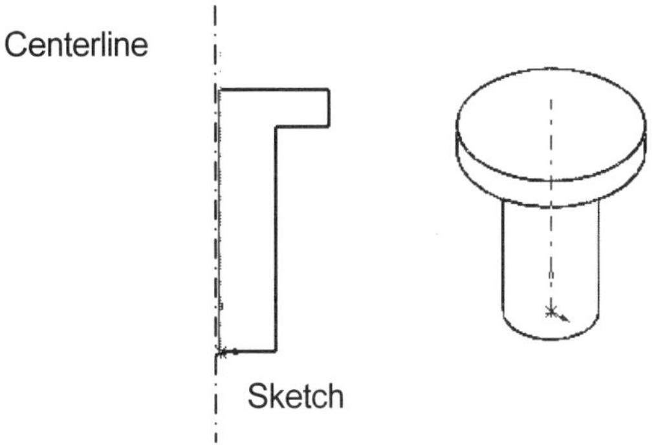

Revolve the sketch 360 degrees.

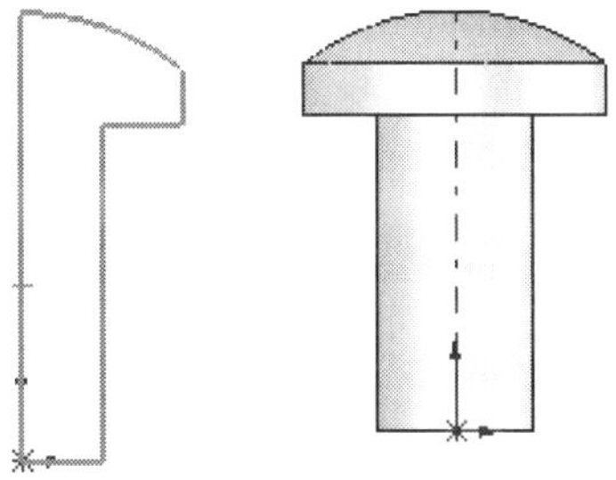

Utilize Edit Sketch to modify the sketch. Utilize the Sketch Trim and Tangent Arc tool to create the new profile.

Utilize an Extruded Cut feature sketched on the Front plane.

Utilize the Circular Pattern feature to create four instances.

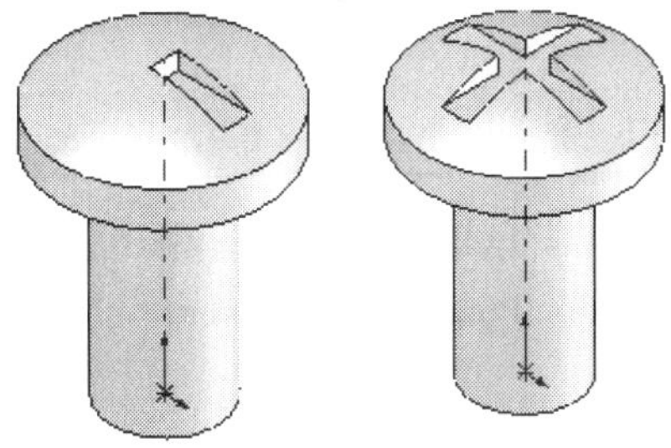

The Fillet feature rounds edges and faces. Utilize the Fillet feature to round the top edge.

The Chamfer feature bevels edges and faces. Utilize a Chamfer feature to bevel the bottom face.

Note: Utilize an M5 machine screw for metric units.

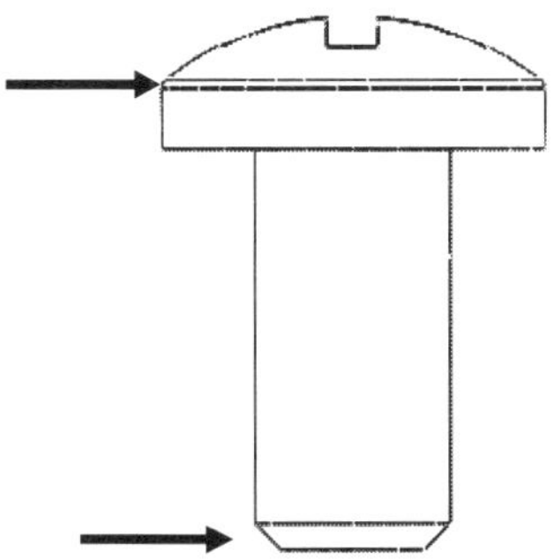

Activity: SCREW Part-Documents Properties

Create a new Part.

442) Click **File**, **New** from the Main menu. The Templates tab is the default tab.

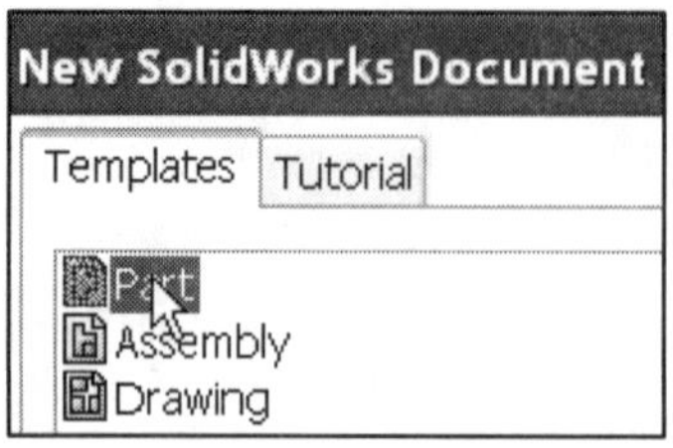

443) Double-click **Part**.

Save the Part.

444) Click **File**, **Save As** from the Main menu.

445) Select **SW-TUTORIAL-2007** for the Save in file folder.

446) Enter **SCREW** for File name.

447) Enter **MACHINE SCREW 10-24x3/8** for Description. Click **Save**. The SCREW FeatureManager is displayed.

Set the Dimensioning standard and part units.

448) Click **Tools**, **Options**, **Documents Properties** tab from the Main menu.

449) Select **ANSI** from the Dimensioning standard box.

450) Click **Units**. Select **IPS**, [**MMGS**] for Unit system.

451) Select **3**, [**2**] for Length units Decimal places. Select **0**, [**0**] for Angular units Decimal places.

452) Click **OK**.

Activity: SCREW Part-Revolved Feature

Insert a Revolved feature sketched on the Front plane. The Front plane is the default Sketch plane.

Insert a new sketch.

453) Click **Front Plane** from the FeatureManager.

454) Click **Sketch** Sketch.

455) Click **Centerline** Centerl... from the Sketch toolbar.

Sketch a vertical centerline.

456) Click the **Origin**.

457) Click a **position** directly above the Origin as illustrated.

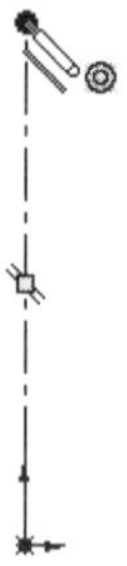

458) Right-click **End Chain** to end the centerline.

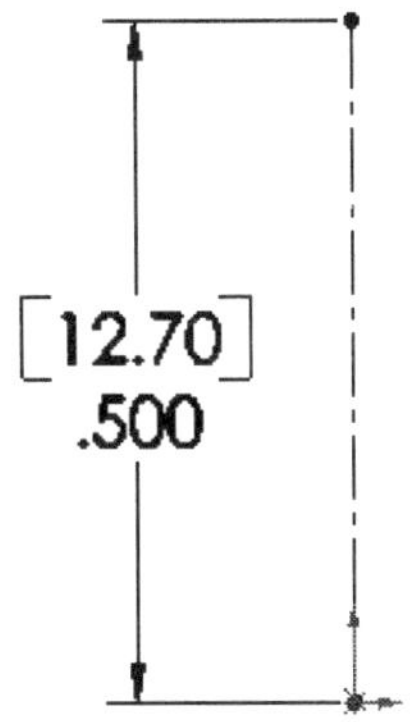

Add a dimension.

459) Click **Smart Dimension** Smart Dimens... from the Sketch toolbar.

460) Click the **centerline**. Click a **position** to the left.

461) Enter **.500**in, [**12.70**]. Click the **Green Check mark**.

Fit the Sketch to the Graphics Window.

462) Press the **f** key.

Sketch the profile.

463) Click **Line** Line from the Sketch toolbar.

Sketch the first horizontal line.

464) Click the **Origin**. Click a **position** to the right of the Origin.

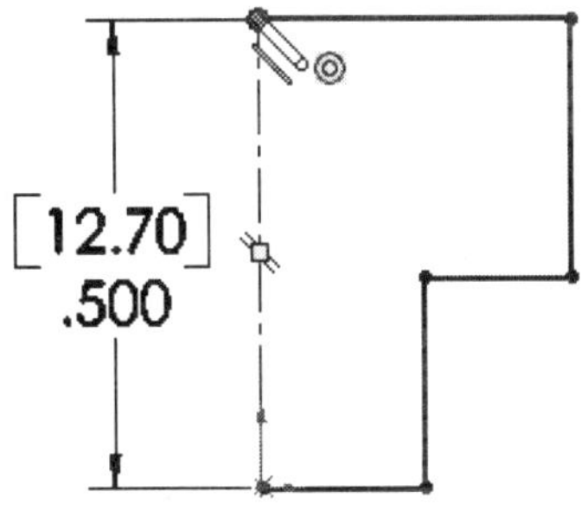

Sketch the first vertical line.

465) Click a position **above** the horizontal line endpoint.

466) Sketch the second **horizontal line**. Sketch the second **vertical line**. The top point of the vertical line is collinear with the top point of the centerline.

467) Sketch the third **horizontal line**. The left endpoint of the horizontal line is coincident with the top point of the centerline. **Double-click** to end the line.

468) Right-click **Select**.

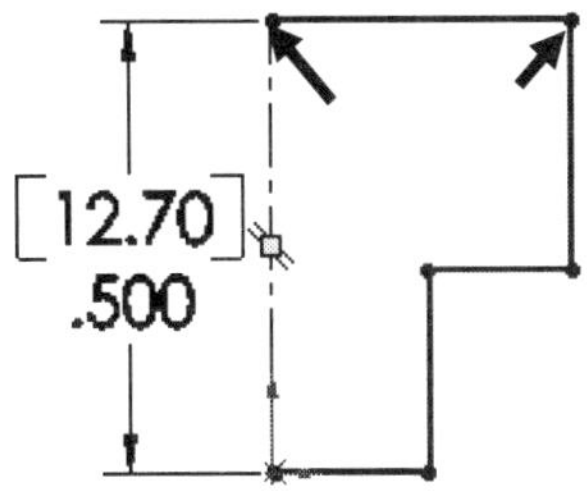

Add a Horizontal relation.

469) Click the **top** most right point. Hold the **Ctrl** key down.

470) Click the **top** most left point. Release the **Ctrl** key.

471) Click **Horizontal** from the Add Relations box.

472) Click **OK** from the Properties PropertyManager.

Add a dimension.

473) Click **Smart Dimension** Smart Dimens... from the Sketch toolbar. Create the first diameter dimension.

474) Click the **centerline**. Click the **first vertical line**.

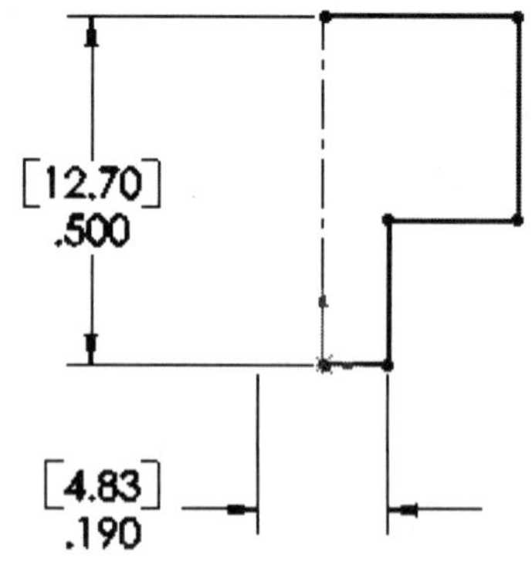

475) Click a **position** to the left of the Origin to create a diameter dimension.

476) Enter **.190**in, [**4.83**]. Click the **Green Check mark**.

A diameter dimension for a Revolved sketch requires a centerline, profile line, and a dimension position to the left of the centerline.

A dimension position directly below the bottom horizontal line creates a radial dimension.

477) Create a diameter dimension. Click the **centerline**.

478) Click the **second vertical line**.

479) Click a **position** to the left of the Origin to create a diameter dimension.

480) Enter **.373**in, [**9.47**].

Create a vertical dimension.
481) Click the **first vertical line**.

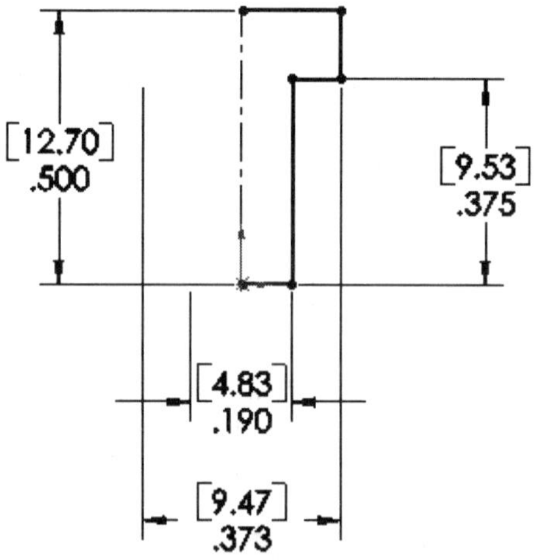

482) Click a **position** to the right of the line.

483) Enter **.375**in, [**9.53**].

Center the dimension text.
484) Click the **.190**in, [**4.83**] dimension.

485) Drag the **text** between the two extension lines.

486) Click the **.373**in, [**9.47**] dimension.

487) Drag the **text** between the two extension lines. If required, click the **green dots** to flip the arrows inside the extension lines.

Select the Centerline for axis of revolution.
488) Right-click **Select**.

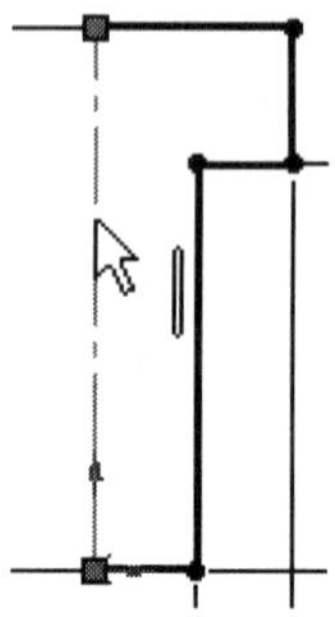

489) Click the **vertical centerline**.

Revolve the sketch.

490) Click **Revolved Boss/Base** Revolved Boss/B... from the Features toolbar. The Revolve PropertyManager is displayed.

491) Click **Yes**.

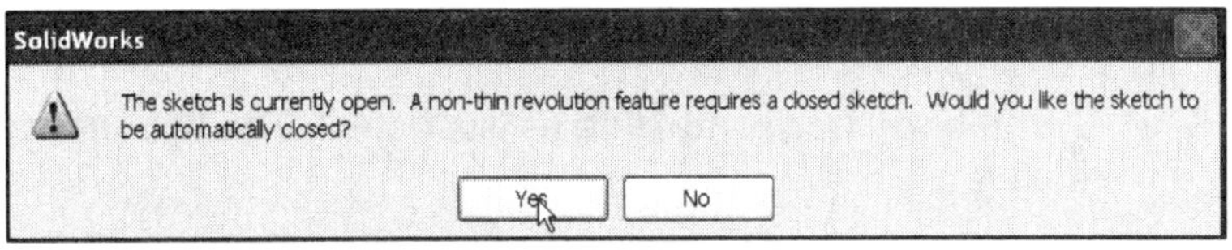

The "Yes" button causes a vertical line to be automatically sketched from the top left point to the Origin. The Graphics window displays the Isometric view and a preview of the Revolved Base feature.

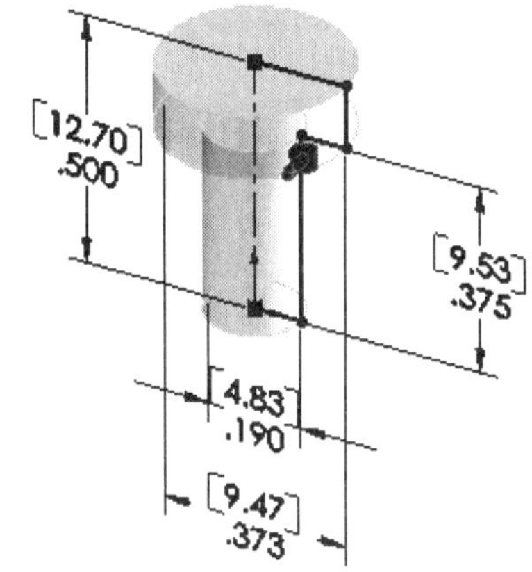

The Revolve PropertyManager displays 360 degrees for the Angle of Revolution.

492) Click **OK** from the Revolve PropertyManager.

The FeatureManager displays the Revolve1 name for the first feature. The Revolved Boss/Base feature requires a centerline, sketch, and an angle of revolution. A solid Revolved Boss/Base feature requires a closed sketch. Draw the sketch on one side of the centerline.

The SCREW requires a rounded profile. Edit the Revolved Base sketch. Insert a Tangent Arc.

Edit the Revolved Base sketch.

493) Right-click **Revolve1** in the FeatureManager.

494) Click **Edit Sketch**.

495) Click **Front view**.

496) Click **Tangent Arc** Tangent Arc from the Sketch toolbar.

497) Click the **top left point**. Drag the **mouse pointer** to the right and downward.

498) Click a **position** collinear with the right vertical line, below the midpoint. The arc is displayed tangent to the top horizontal line.

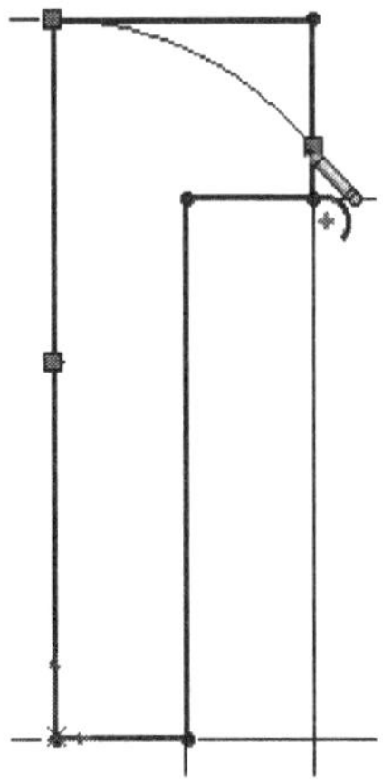

499) Right-click **Select**.

Delete unwanted geometry.

500) Click **Trim Entities** Trim from the Sketch toolbar.

501) Click **Trim to closest** from the Options box.

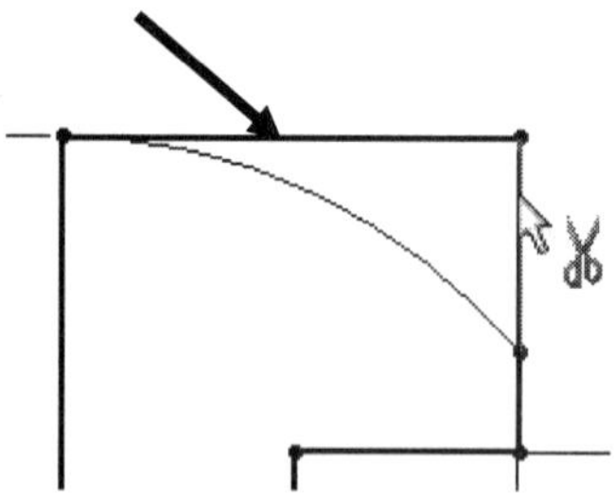

502) Click the **right top vertical line** as illustrated.

503) Click the **top horizontal line** as illustrated. The two lines are removed.

504) Click **OK** from the Trim PropertyManager.

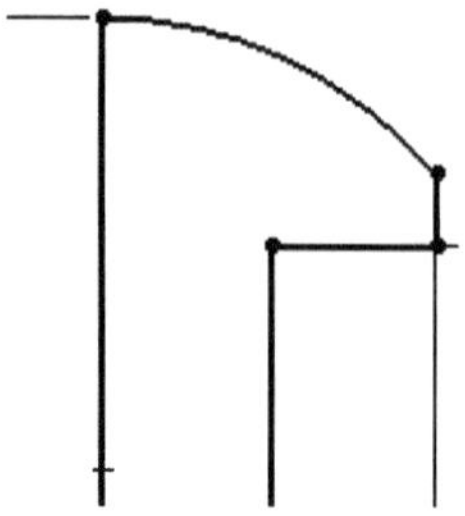

Add a dimension.

505) Click **Smart Dimension** Smart Dimens....

506) Click the **arc**.

507) Click a **position** above the profile.

508) Enter **.304**in, [**7.72**].

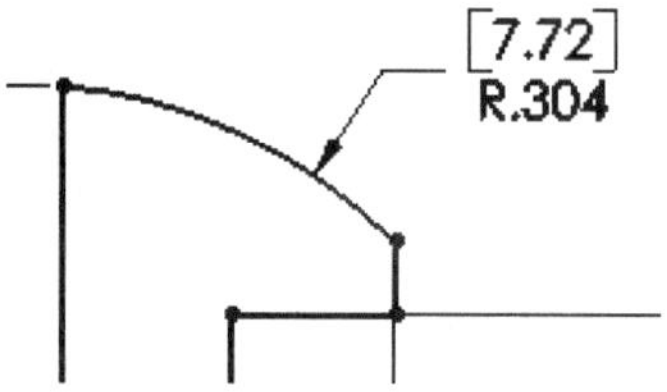

509) Click the **Green Check mark**.

510) Click **Exit Sketch** Exit Sketch.

511) Click **Save**.

The SCREW requires an Extruded Cut feature on the Front plane. Utilize the Convert Entities Sketch tool to extract the Revolved Base top arc edge for the profile of the Extruded Cut.

Activity: SCREW Part-Extruded Cut Feature

Insert a new sketch for the Extruded Cut.

512) Click **Front Plane** from the FeatureManager.

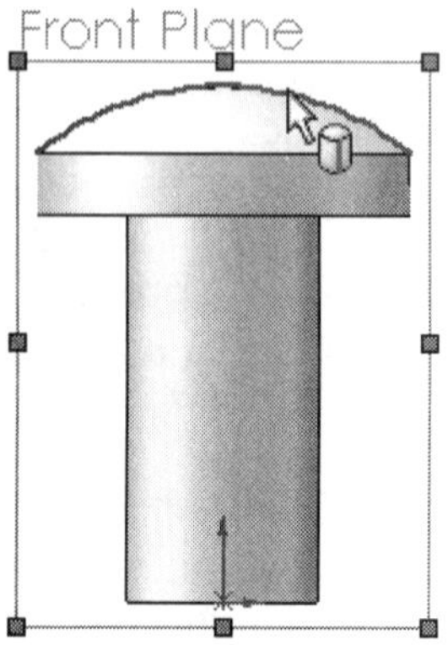

513) Click **Sketch** Sketch from the Control Area.

514) Click **Sketch** Sketch from the Sketch toolbar.

515) Click the **top arc** as illustrated. The mouse pointer displays the silhouette edge icon for feedback.

516) Click **Convert Entities** Convert from the Sketch toolbar.

517) Click **Line** Line from the Sketch toolbar.

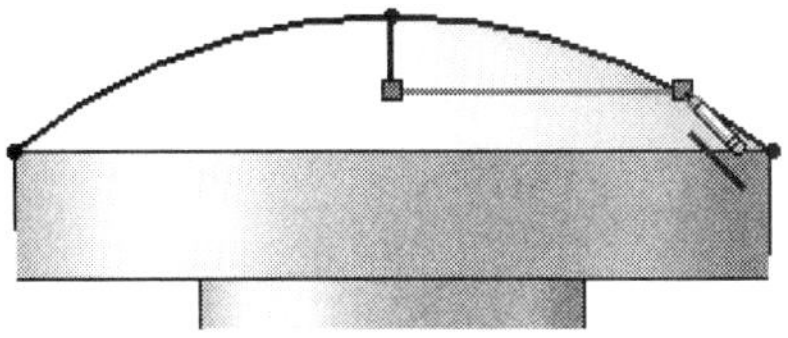

518) Sketch a **vertical line**. The top endpoint of the line is coincident with the arc, vertically aligned to the Origin.

519) Sketch a **horizontal line**. The right end point of the line is coincident with the arc. Do not select the arc midpoint. Right-click **Select**.

520) Click **Isometric view**.

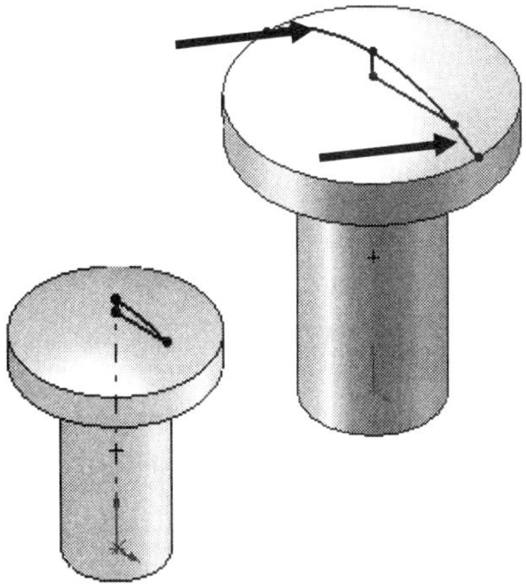

521) Click **Trim Entities** Trim from the Sketch toolbar.

522) Click **Power trim** from the Options box. Click a position to the **left** side of the arc. Drag the mouse pointer to **intersect** the left arc line.

523) Click a position to the **right** side of the right arc. Drag the mouse pointer to **intersect** the right arc line.

524) Click **OK** from the Trim PropertyManager.

Add a dimension.

525) Click **Smart Dimension** Smart Dimens....

526) Click the **vertical line**. Click a **position** to the right of the profile.

527) Enter **.030**in, [**0.76**]. Click the **Green Check mark**.

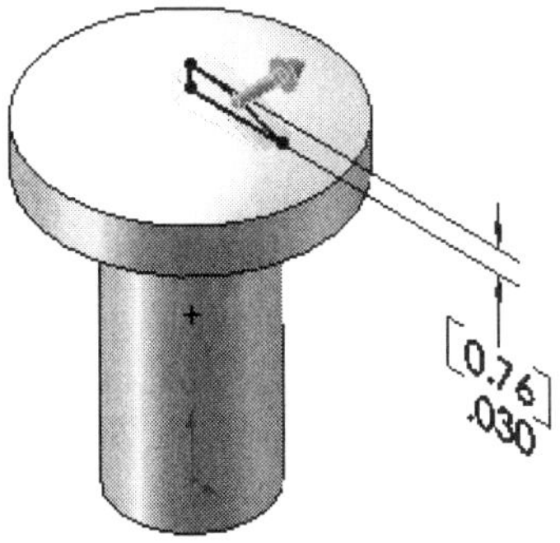

Insert an Extruded Cut Feature.

528) Click **Isometric view**.

529) Click **Extruded Cut** Extruded Cut from the Features toolbar.

530) Select **Mid Plane** for the End Condition in Direction 1.

531) Enter **.050**in, [**1.27**] for Depth.

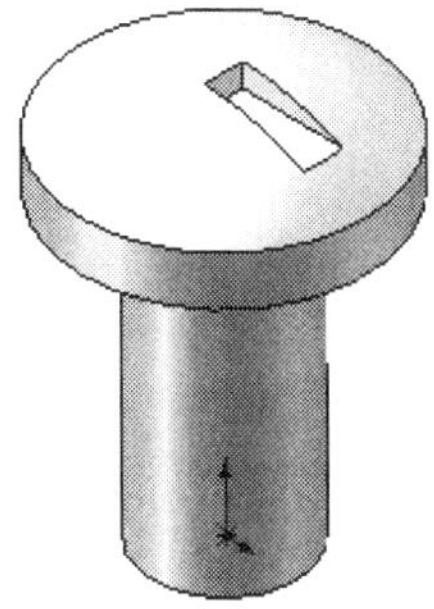

532) Click **OK** from the Cut-Extrude PropertyManager. Cut-Extrude1 is displayed in the FeatureManager.

Note: The first tool you utilized in the Sketch requires different icon selection. Select Sketch Sketch from the Control Area to activate sketch creation entities such as Rectangle, Circle, and Arc.

Select Sketch Sketch from the Sketch toolbar to activate sketch tools such as Mirror Entities, Offset Entities, and Convert Entities.

Activity: SCREW Part-Circular Pattern Feature

Insert the Circular Pattern Feature.

533) Click **View**; check **Temporary Axes** from the Main menu. The Temporary Axis is required for the Circular Pattern feature.

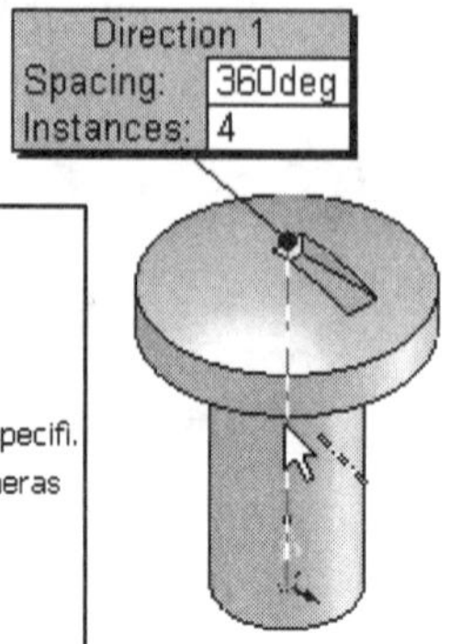

534) Click **Circular Pattern** Circular from the Features toolbar. Cut-Extrude1 is displayed in the Features to Pattern box.

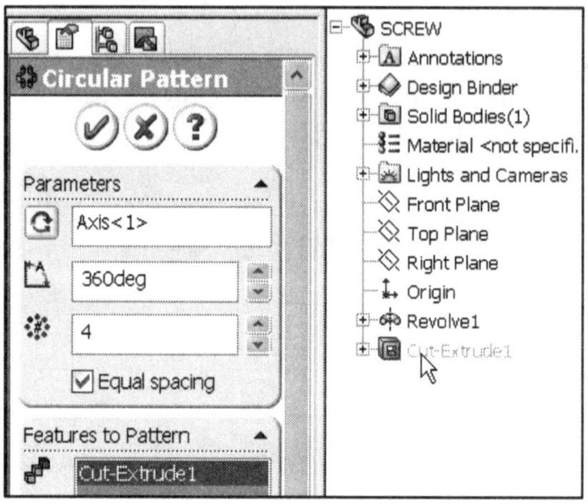

535) Click the **Temporary Axis** in the Graphics window. Axis<1> is displayed in the Pattern Axis box.

536) Enter **360**deg for Angle.

537) Enter **4** for Number of Instances.

538) Check the **Equal spacing** box.

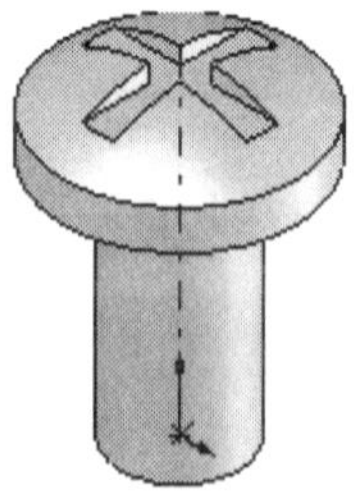

539) Click **OK** from the Circular Pattern PropertyManager. CirPattern1 is displayed in the FeatureManager.

Save the Model.

540) Click **Save**.

Activity: SCREW Part-Fillet Feature

Insert the Fillet feature.

541) Click the **top circular edge** as illustrated.

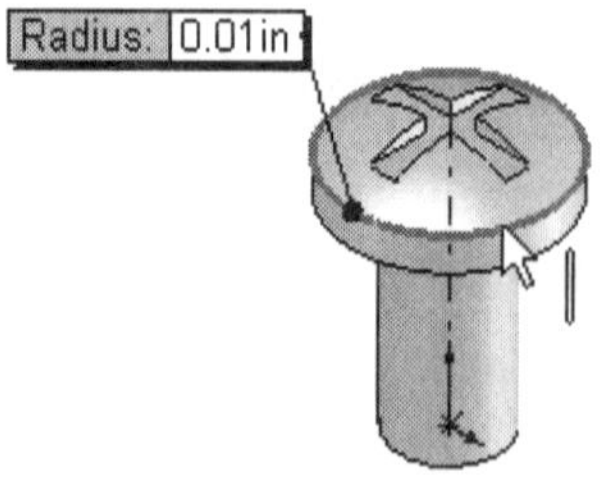

542) Click **Fillet** Fillet from the Features toolbar. Click the Manual tab. Edge<1> is displayed in the Items to Fillet box.

543) Enter **.010**in, [**.25**] for Radius.

544) Click **OK** from the Fillet PropertyManager. Fillet1 is displayed in the FeatureManager.

Activity: SCREW Part-Chamfer Feature

Insert the Chamfer feature.

545) Click the **bottom circular edge**.

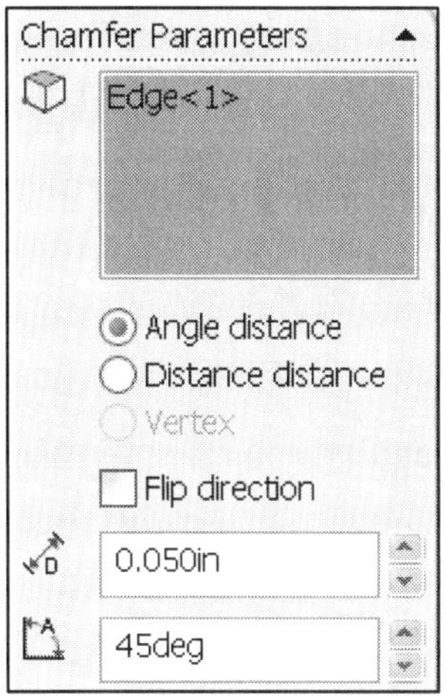

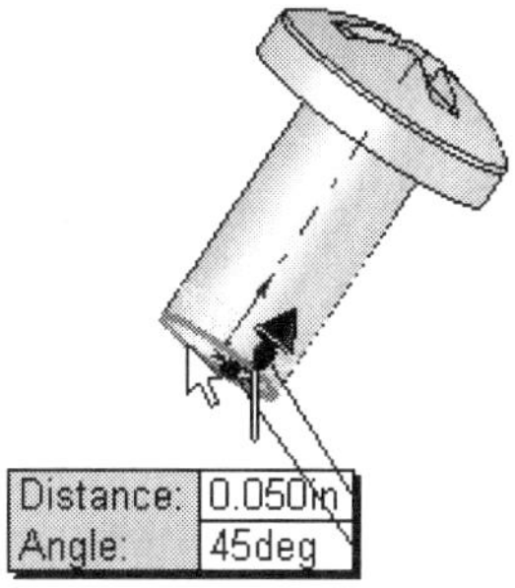

546) Click **Chamfer** Chamfer from the Features toolbar. Edge<1> is displayed in the Items to Chamfer box.

547) Enter **.050**in, [**1.27**] for Distance.

548) Click **OK** from the Chamfer PropertyManager. Chamfer1 is displayed in the FeatureManager.

Simplify the part. Save rebuild time. Suppress features that are not required in the assembly.

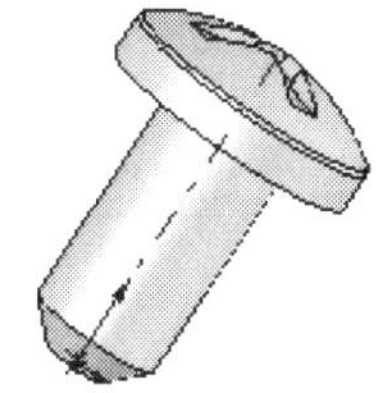

A suppressed feature is not displayed in the Graphics window. A suppressed feature is removed from any rebuild calculations.

Suppress the Fillet and Chamfer feature.

549) Hold the **Ctrl** key down.

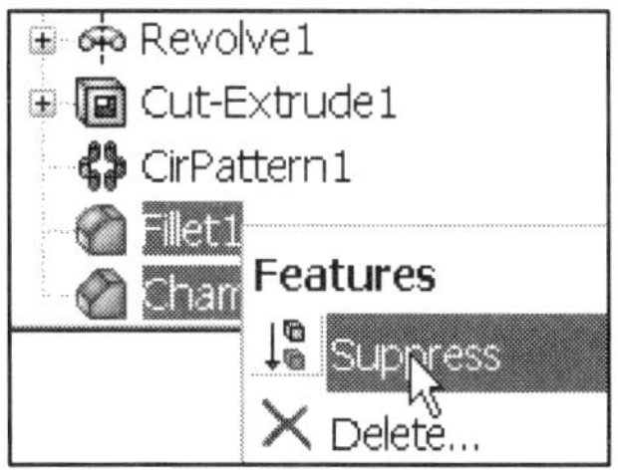

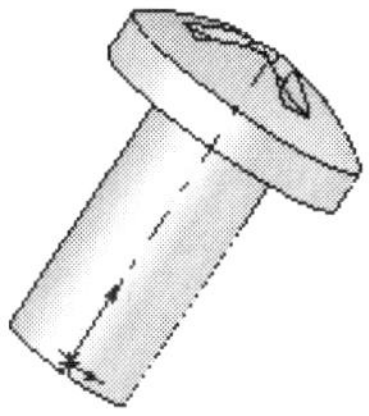

550) Select **Fillet1** and **Chamfer1** from the FeatureManager.

551) Release the **Ctrl** key.

552) Right-click **Suppress** Suppress.

Hide the Temporary Axis.

553) Click **View**; uncheck **Temporary Axes** from the Main menu.

Save the SCREW part.

554) Click **Isometric view** .

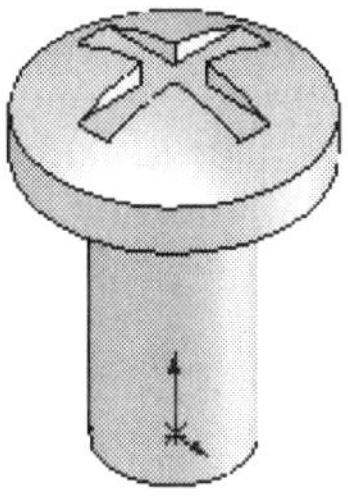

555) Click **Save** .

Close all documents.

556) Click **Window**, **Close All** from the Main menu.

Review the SCREW Part.

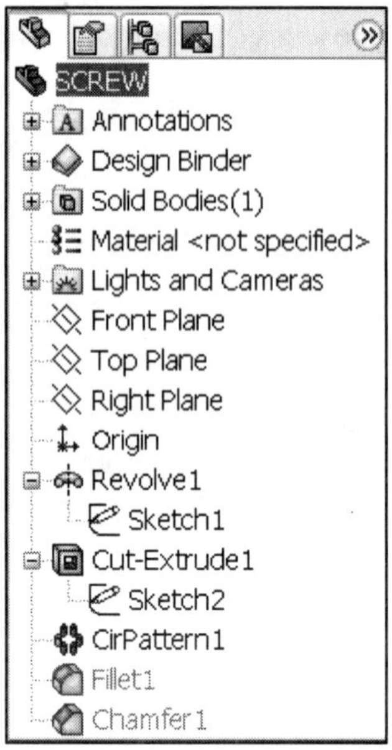

The Revolved Boss/Base feature was utilized to create the SCREW part. The Revolved Boss/Base feature required a centerline sketched on the Front Sketch plane and a closed profile. The sketch was revolved 360 degrees to create the Base feature for the SCREW part.

Edit Sketch was utilized to modify the sketch. The Sketch Trim and Tangent Arc tools created a new profile. The Extruded Cut feature was sketched on the Front plane. The Circular Pattern feature created four instances.

The Fillet feature rounded the top edges. The Chamfer feature beveled the bottom edge. The Fillet and Chamfer are suppressed to save rebuild time in the assembly.

Additional details on Convert Entities, Silhouette Edge, Revolved Boss/Base, Circular Pattern, Fillet, and Chamfer are available in SolidWorks Help. Keywords: Sketch tools, silhouette, features, Pattern, Revolve, Fillet and Chamfer.

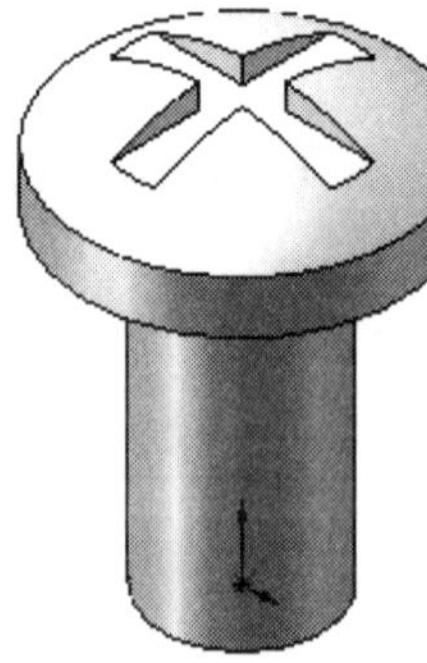

FRONT-SUPPORT Assembly

The FRONT-SUPPORT assembly consists of the following parts:

- ANGLE-13HOLE part.
- TRIANGLE part.
- HEX-STANDOFF part.
- SCREW part.

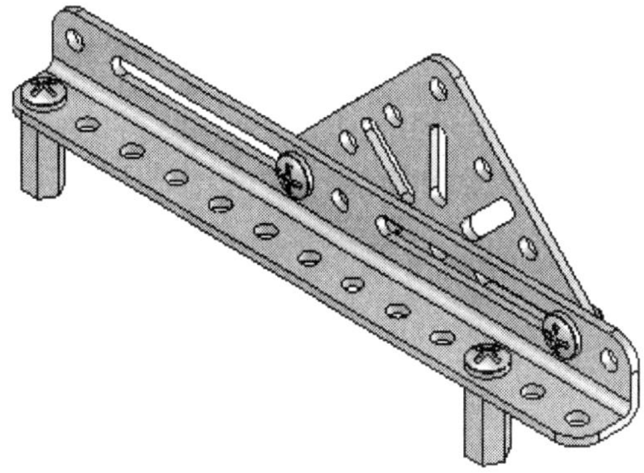

Create the FRONT-SUPPORT assembly. Insert the ANGLE-13HOLE part. The ANGLE-13HOLE part is fixed to the FRONT-SUPPORT Origin. Insert the first HEX-STANDOFF part.

Utilize Concentric and Coincident Mates to assemble the HEX-STANDOFF to the left hole of the ANGLE-13HOLE part. Insert the second HEX-STANDOFF part.

Utilize Concentric and Coincident Mates to assemble the HEX-STANDOFF to the third hole from the right side. Insert the TRIANGLE part. Utilize Concentric, Distance, and Parallel Mates to assemble the TRIANGLE. Utilize Concentric and Coincident Smart Mates to assemble the four SCREWS.

Activity: FRONT-SUPPORT Assembly-Insert ANGLE-13HOLE

Create a new assembly.

557) Click **File**, **New** from the Main menu.

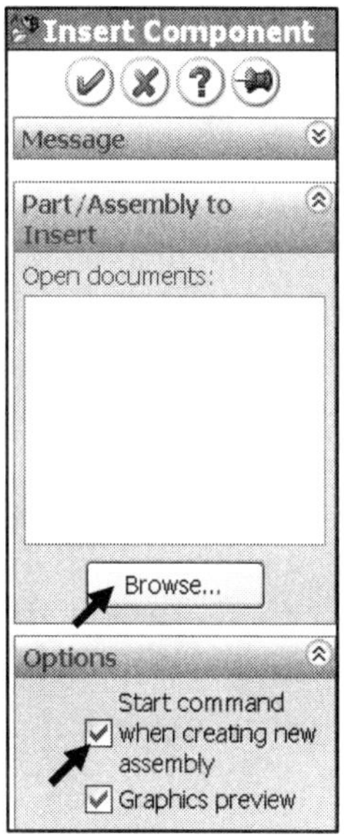

558) Double-click **Assembly** from the Templates tab. The Insert Component PropertyManager is displayed. Note: The Insert Component PropertyManager is displayed if the Start command when creating new assembly box is checked.

559) Click **View**; check **Origins** from the Main menu.

560) Click **Browse**.

561) Select **Part** from the Files of type in the SW-TUTORIAL-2007 folder.

562) Double-click the **ANGLE-13HOLE** part.

563) Drag the **ANGLE-13HOLE** part to the Origin of the Assembly.

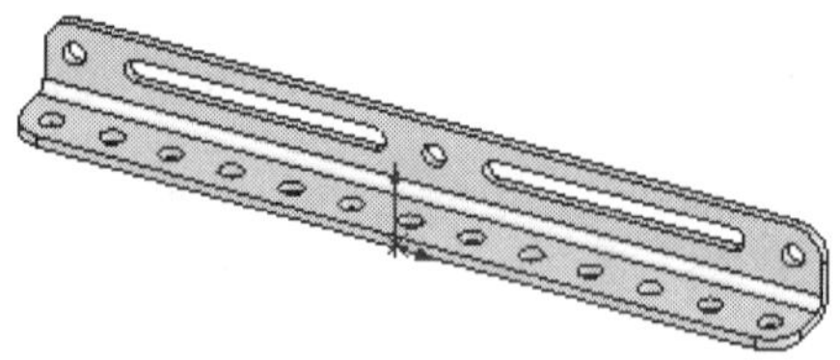

564) Click the **Origin**. The cursor displays the Insert Component Fixed at the Origin feedback symbol.

Save the assembly.

565) Click **File**, **Save As** from the Main menu.

566) Select **SW-TUTORIAL-2007** for the Save in file folder.

567) Enter **FRONT-SUPPORT** for File name.

568) Enter **FRONT SUPPORT ASSEMBLY** for Description.

569) Click **Save**. The FRONT-SUPPORT assembly FeatureManager is displayed.

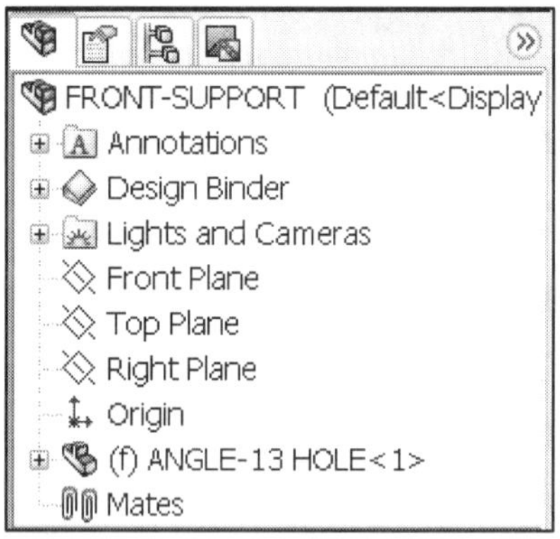

Set the Dimensioning standard and units.

570) Click **Tools**, **Options**, **Document Properties** tab from the Main menu.

571) Select **ANSI** from the Dimensioning standard box.

Set the units.

572) Click **Units**.

573) Select **IPS**, [**MMGS**] for Unit system.

574) Select **3**, [**2**] for Length units Decimal places.

575) Select **0**, [**0**] for Angular units Decimal places.

576) Click **OK**.

The ANGLE-13HOLE name in the FeatureManager displays an (f) symbol. The (f) symbol indicates that the ANGLE-13HOLE part is fixed to the FRONT-SUPPORT assembly Origin. The part cannot move or rotate.

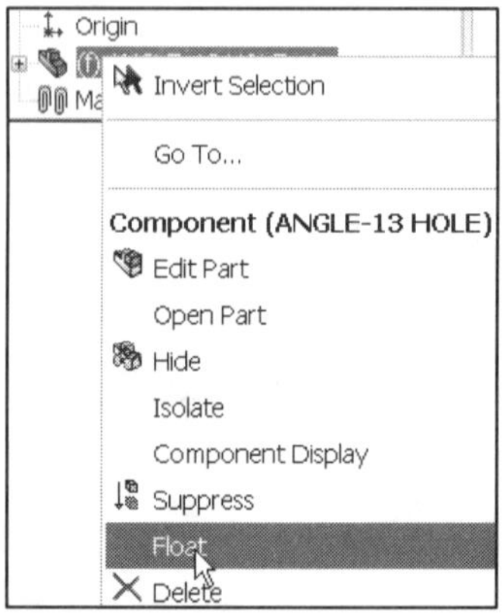

To remove the fixed state, Right-click a component name in the FeatureManager. Click Float. The component is free to move.

Display the Isometric view.

577) Click **Isometric view**.

Save the assembly.

578) Click **Save**.

Activity: FRONT-SUPPORT Assembly-Inset HEX-STANDOFF

Insert the HEX-STANDOFF part.

579) Click **Insert Component** Insert Compo... from the Assembly toolbar. The Insert Component PropertyManager is displayed.

580) Click **Browse**.

581) Select **Part** from the Files of type box.

582) Double-click **HEX-STANDOFF**.

583) Click a **position** near the left top hole.

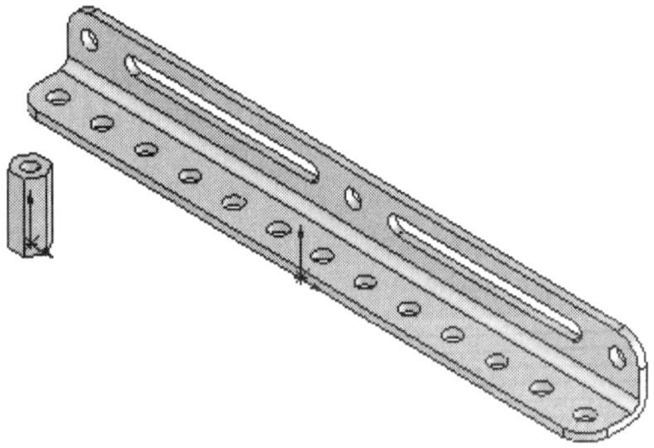

Enlarge the view.

584) Click **Zoom to Area** on the left side to enlarge the view.

Move the component.

585) Click and drag the **HEX-STANDOFF** part below the ANGLE-13HOLE left hole.

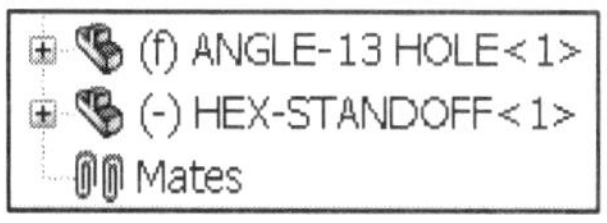

The HEX-STANDOFF name in the FeatureManager displays a (-) Minus sign. The Minus sign indicates that the HEX-STANDOFF part is free to move.

Insert a Concentric Mate.

586) Click **Mate** Mate from the Assembly toolbar. The Mate PropertyManager is displayed.

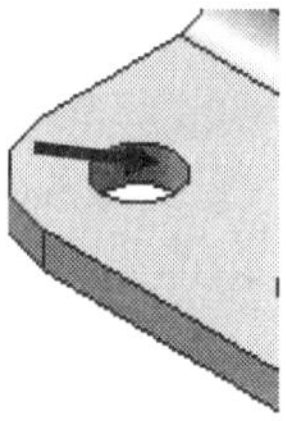

587) Click the **left inside cylindrical hole face** of the ANGLE-13HOLE part.

588) Click inside the **cylindrical hole face** of the HEX-STANDOFF part. The selected faces are displayed in the Mate Selections box. Concentric is selected by default.

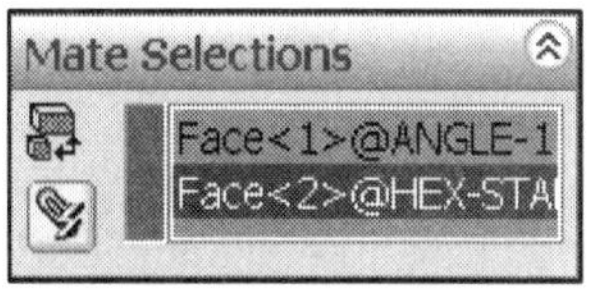

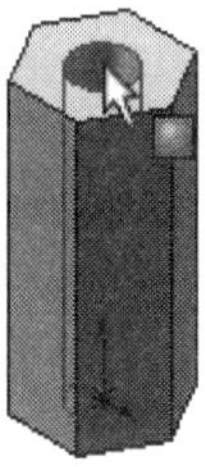

589) Click the **Green Check mark**.

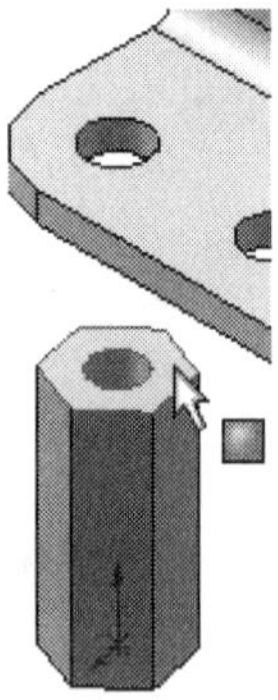

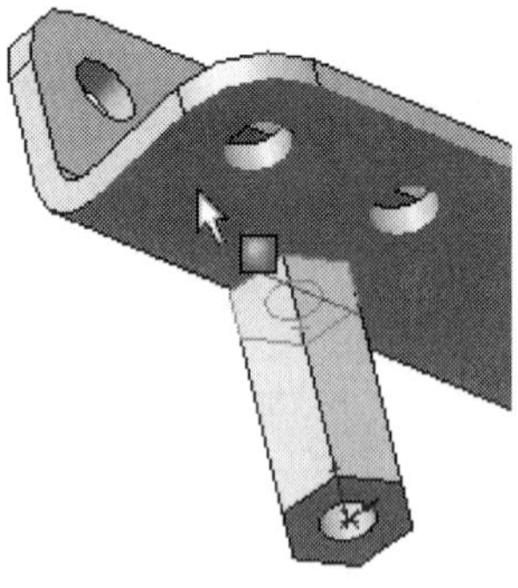

590) Click and drag the **HEX-STANDOFF** below the ANGLE-13HOLE part until the top face is displayed.

Insert a Coincident Mate.

591) Click the **HEX-STANDOFF top face**.

592) Press the **Up Arrow key** approximately 5 times to view the bottom face of the ANGLE-13HOLE part.

593) Click the **ANGLE-13HOLE bottom face**. The selected faces are displayed in the Mate Selections box. Coincident Mate is selected by default.

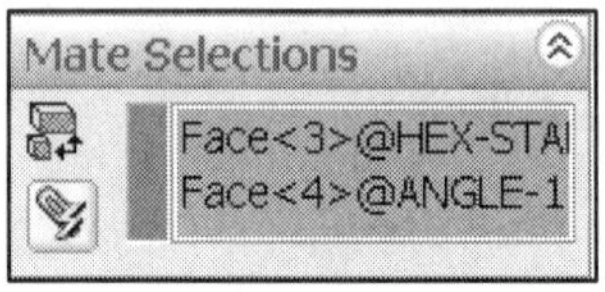

594) Click the **Green Check mark**.

595) Click **Isometric view**.

596) Click and drag the **HEX-STANDOFF**. The HEX-STANDOFF rotates about its axis.

Insert a Parallel Mate.

597) Click **Front view**.

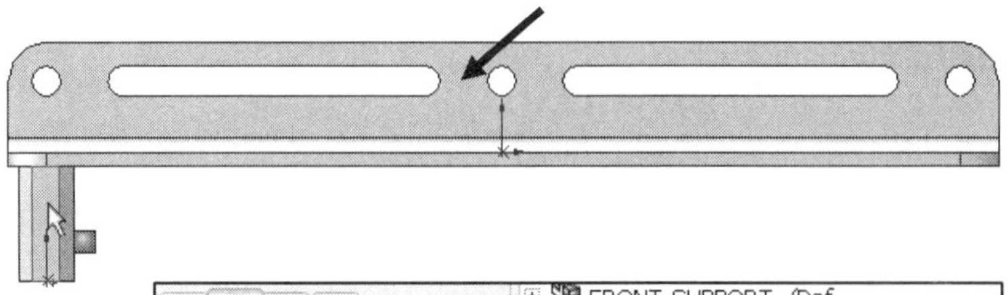

598) Click the **HEX-STANDOFF front face**.

599) Click the **ANGLE-13HOLE front face**. The selected faces are displayed in the Mate Selections box. A Mate message is displayed.

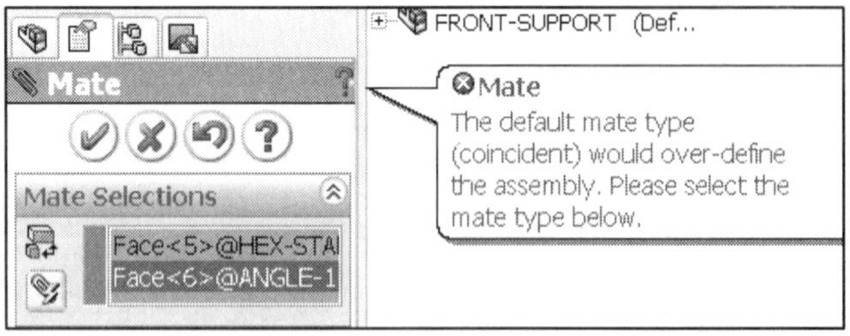

600) Click **Parallel**.

601) Click the **Green Check mark**.

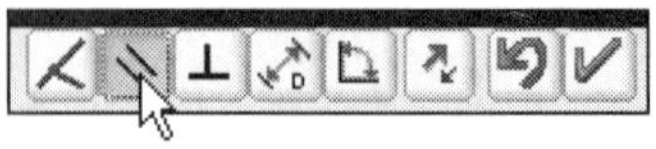

602) Click **OK** from the Mate PropertyManager.

Display the Mates.

603) **Expand** the Mates folder in the FRONT-SUPPORT FeatureManager. Three Mates are displayed between the ANGLE-13HOLE part and the HEX-STANDOFF part. The HEX-STANDOFF part is fully defined.

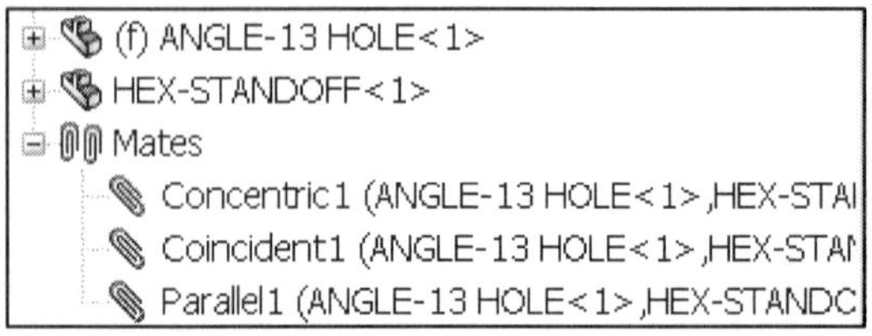

Save the FRONT-SUPPORT assembly.

604) Click **Save** .

Insert the second HEX-STANDOFF part.

605) Hold the **Ctrl** key down.

606) Click and drag the **HEX-STANDOFF<1>** (f) ANGLE-13 HOLE<1> name from the FeatureManager into the FRONT-SUPPORT assembly Graphics window.

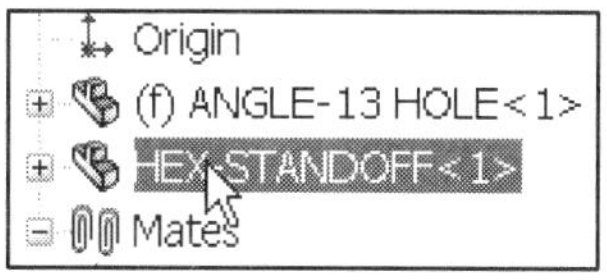

607) Release the **mouse pointer** below the far right hole of the ANGLE-13HOLE part.

608) Release the **Ctrl** key. HEX-STANDOFF<2> is displayed in the Graphics window and listed in the FeatureManager.

Note: The number <2> indicates the second instance or copy of the same component. The instance number increments every time you insert the same component. If you delete a component and then reinsert the component in the same SolidWorks session, the instance number increments by one.

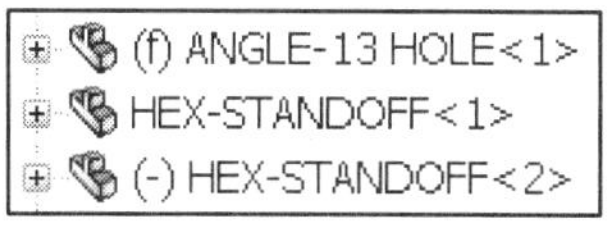

Enlarge the view.

609) Click **Zoom to Area** on the right side to enlarge the view.

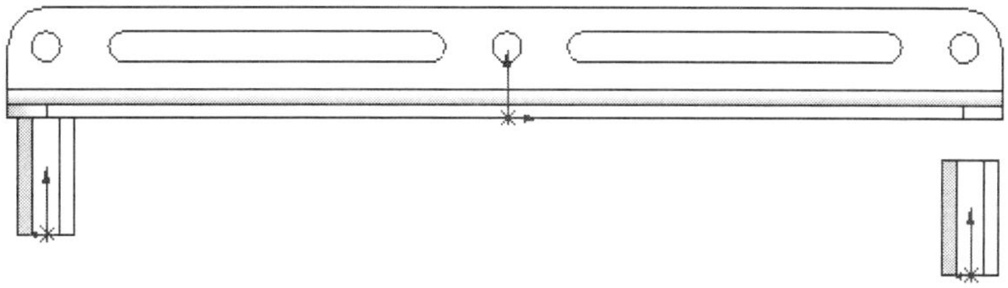

Insert a Concentric Mate.

610) Click **Mate** from the Assembly toolbar. The Mate PropertyManager is displayed.

611) Click the **third hole cylindrical face** from the right ANGLE-13HOLE part.

612) Click inside the **cylindrical hole face** of the second HEX-STANDOFF part. Concentric Mate is selected by default.

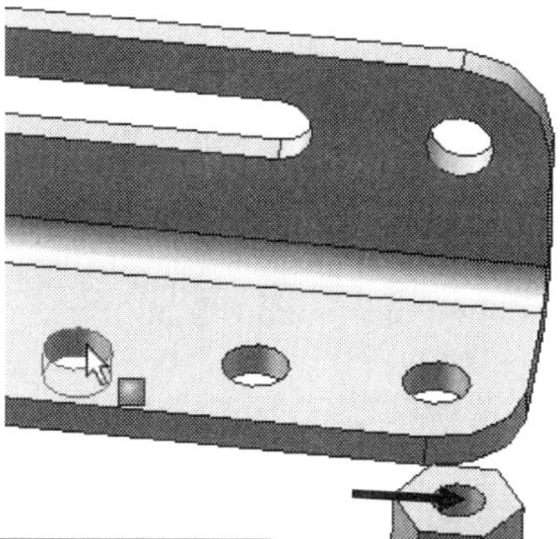

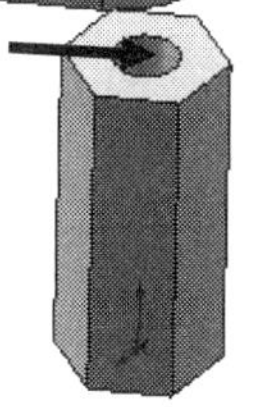

613) Click the **Green Check mark** .

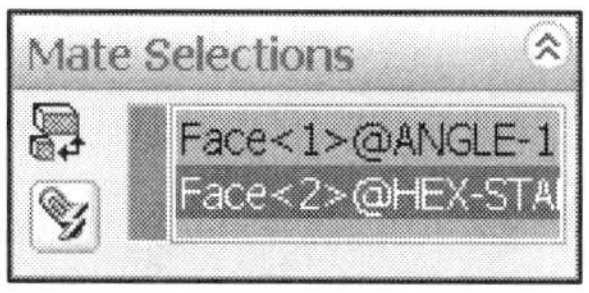

Move the second HEX-STANDOFF part.

614) Click and drag the **HEX-STANDOFF** part below the ANGLE-13HOLE part until its top face is displayed.

Insert a Coincident Mate.

615) Click the **second HEX-STANDOFF** top face.

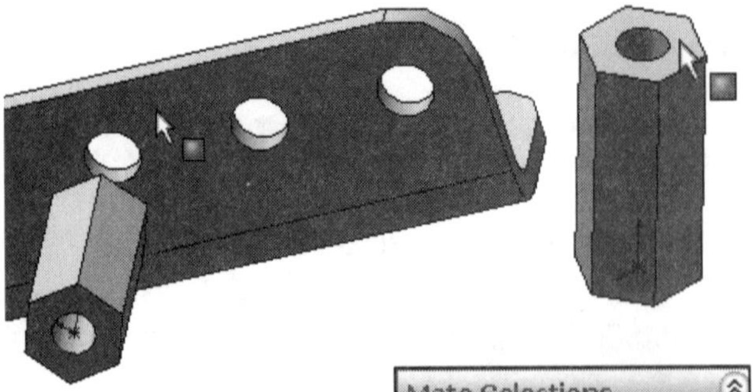

616) Press the **Up Arrow key** approximately 5 times to view the bottom face of the ANGLE-13HOLE part.

617) Click the **ANGLE-13HOLE bottom face**. The selected faces are displayed in the Mate Selections box. Coincident Mate is selected by default.

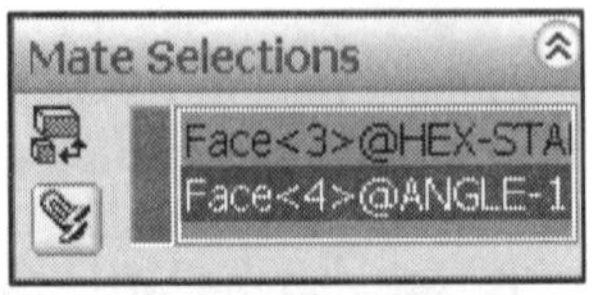

618) Click the **Green Check mark**.

Insert a Parallel Mate.

619) Click **Front view**.

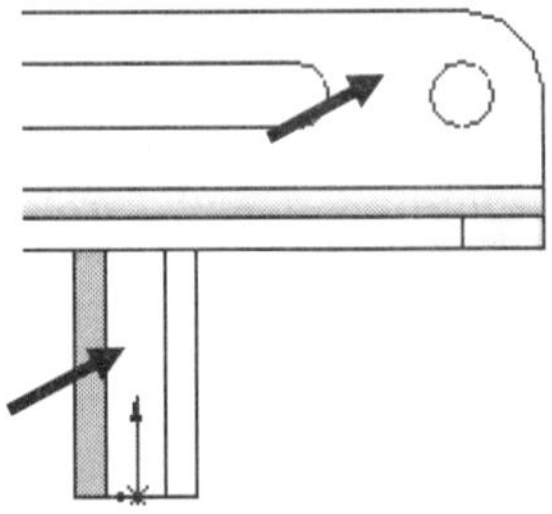

620) Click the **front face** of the second HEX-STANDOFF.

621) Click the **front face** of the ANGLE-13HOLE.

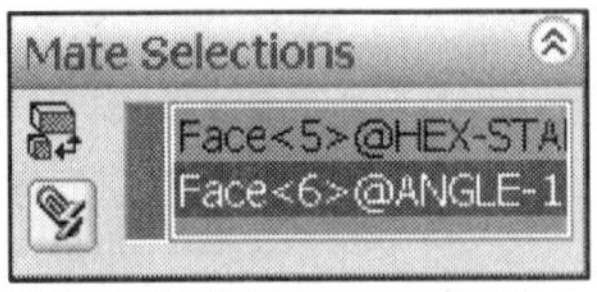

622) Click **Parallel**.

623) Click the **Green Check mark**.

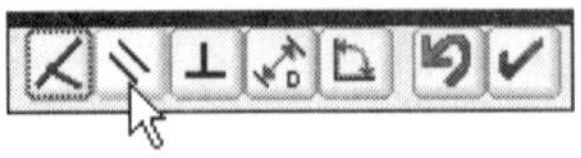

624) Click **OK** from the Mate PropertyManager.

Display the Mates.

625) **Expand** the Mates folder in the FRONT-SUPPORT FeatureManager. Three Mates are displayed between the ANGLE-13HOLE part and the second HEX-STANDOFF part. The second HEX-STANDOFF is fully defined.

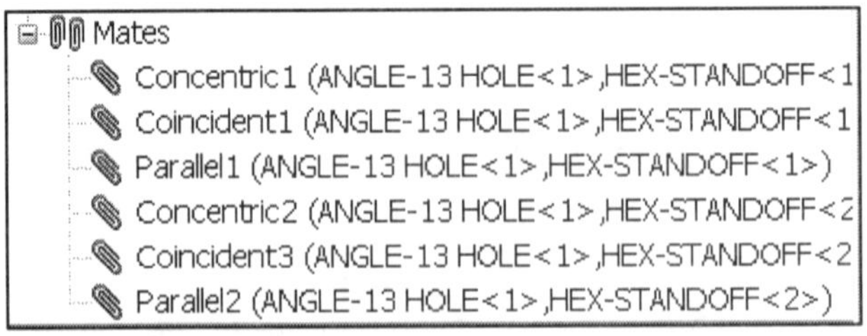

Activity: FRONT-SUPPORT Assembly-Insert the TRIANGLE

Insert the TRIANGLE part.

626) Click **Isometric view**.

627) Click **Insert Component** Insert Compo... from the Assembly toolbar. The Insert Component PropertyManager is displayed.

628) Click **Browse**. Select **Part** from the Files of type box.

629) Double-click **TRIANGLE**.

630) Click a **position** in back of the ANGLE-13HOLE part as illustrated.

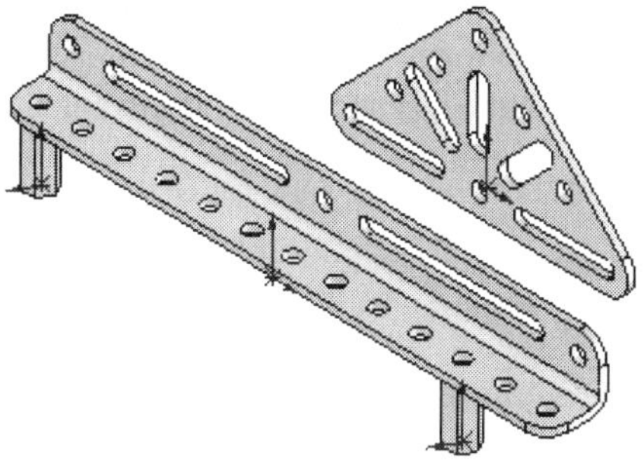

Enlarge the view.

631) Click **Zoom to Area** on the right side of the TRIANGLE and the ANGLE-13HOLE.

Insert a Concentric Mate.

632) Click **Mate** from the Assembly toolbar.

633) Click the **inside right arc face** of the TRAINGLE.

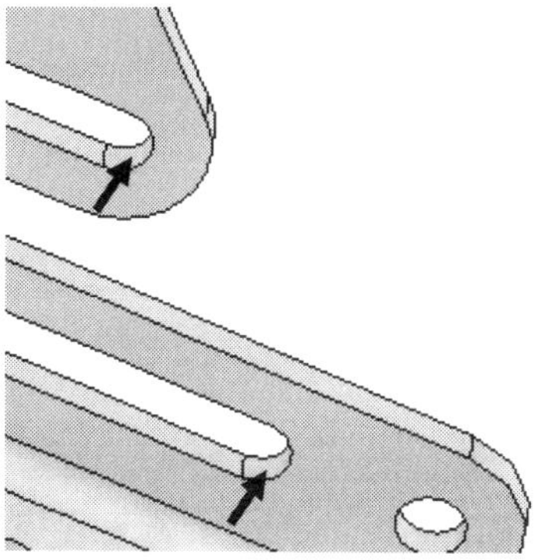

634) Click the **inside right arc face** of the ANGLE-13HOLE slot. Concentric Mate is selected by default. Note: Utilize the Undo button if the Mate is not correct.

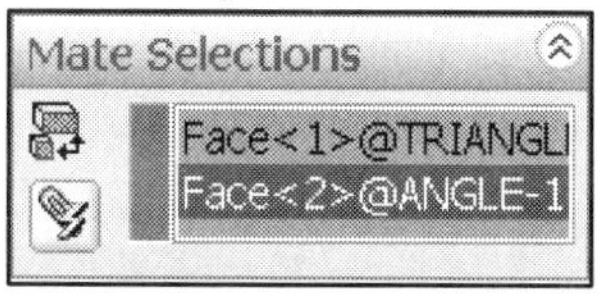

635) Click the **Green Check mark**.

Fit the model to the Graphics window.

636) Press the **f** key.

Insert a Distance Mate.

637) Click the **front face** of the TRIANGLE.

638) Press the **left Arrow key** approximately 5 times to view the back face of the ANGLE-13HOLE part.

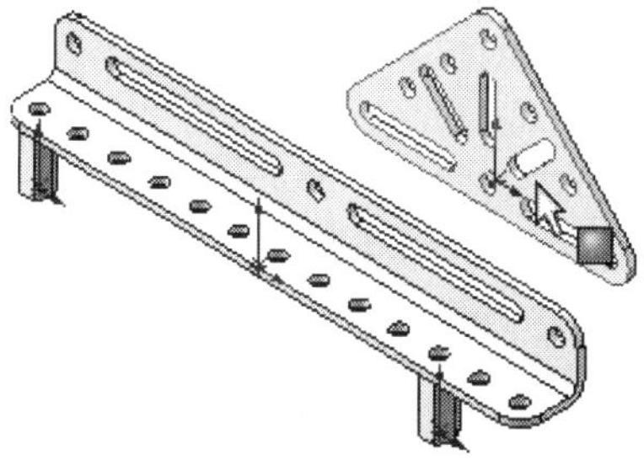

639) Click the **back face** of the ANGLE-13HOLE part.

640) Click **Distance** from the Mate dialog box.

641) Enter **0**.

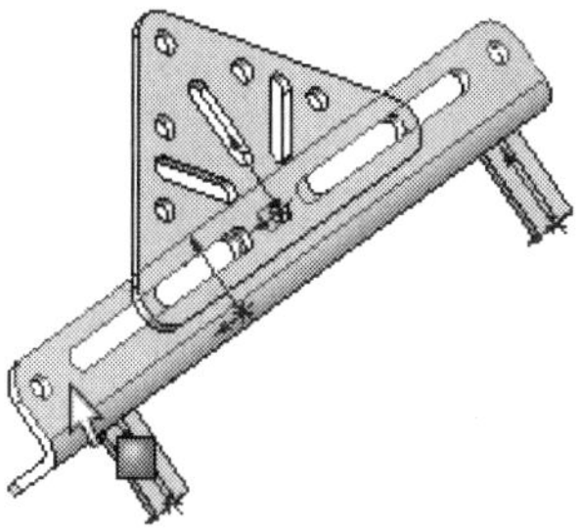

642) Click the **Green Check mark**.

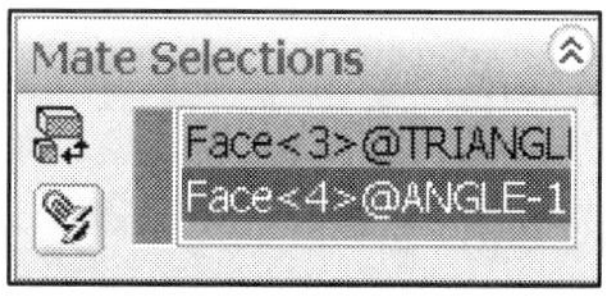

A Distance Mate of 0 provides additional flexibility compared to a Coincident Mate. A Distance Mate value can be modified.

Insert a Parallel Mate.

643) Click **Bottom view**.

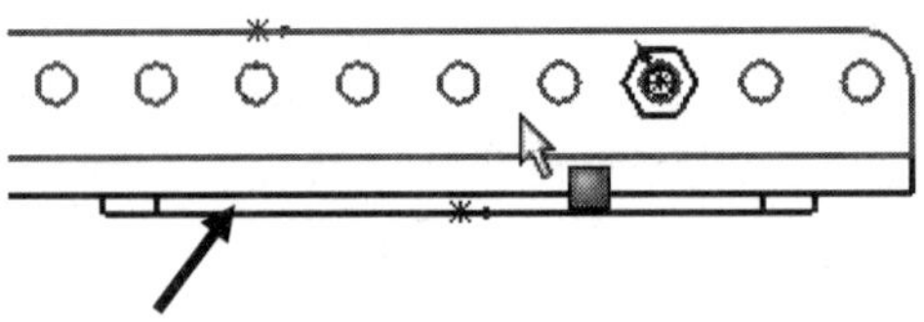

644) Click the **narrow bottom face** of the TRIANGLE.

645) Click the **bottom face** of the ANGLE-13HOLE. The selected faces are displayed in the Mate Selections box. A Mate message is displayed.

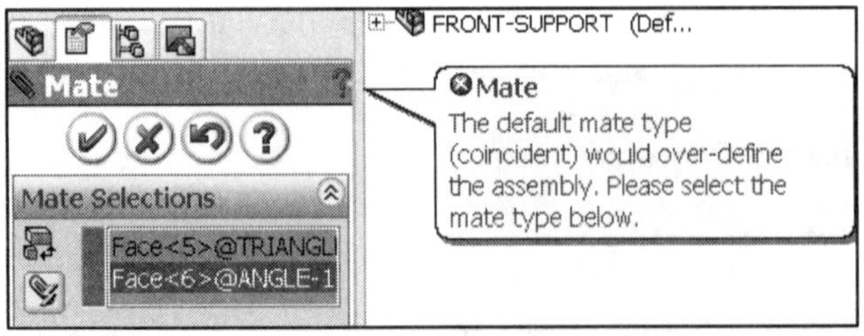

646) Click **Parallel**.

647) Click the **Green Check mark**.

648) Click **OK** from the Mate PropertyManager.

Display the Isometric view.

649) Click **Isometric view**.

Save the FRONT-SUPPORT assembly.

650) Click **Save**.

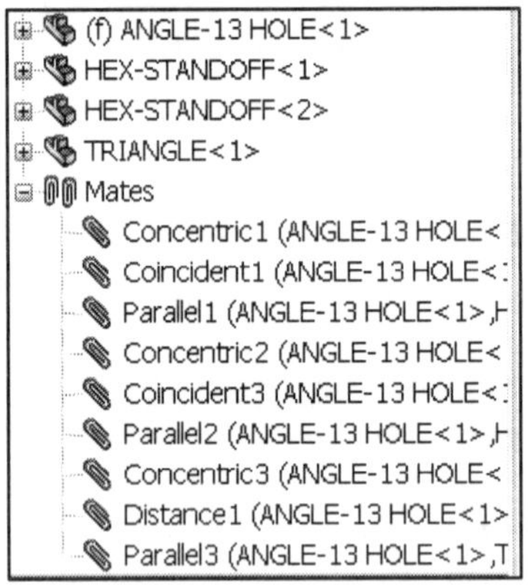

Assemble the four SCREW parts with SmartMates.

A SmartMate is a Mate that automatically occurs when a component is placed into an assembly.

The mouse pointer displays a SmartMate feedback symbol when common geometry and relationships exist between the component and the assembly.

SmartMates are Concentric, Coincident, or Concentric and Coincident.

Smart Mate Combinations:

Mating entities	Type of mate	Pointer
2 linear edges	Coincident	
2 planar faces	Coincident	
2 vertices	Coincident	
2 conical faces, or 2 axes, or 1 conical face and 1 axis	Concentric	
2 circular edges (the edges do not have to be complete circles)	Concentric (conical faces) coincident (adjacent planar faces)	

A Concentric SmartMate assumes that the geometry on the component has the same center as the geometry on an assembled reference.

As the component is dragged into place, the mouse pointer provides feedback such as:

- Concentric .
- Coincident .
- Concentric and Coincident .

The SCREW utilizes the Concentric and Coincident SmartMate. Assemble the first SCREW. The circular edge of the SCREW mates Concentric and Coincident with the circular edge of the right slot of the TRIANGLE.

Activity: FRONT-SUPPORT Assembly-Inset the SCREW

Insert the SCREW part.

651) Click **File**, **Open** from the Main menu.

652) Double-click **SCREW** from the SW-TUTORIAL-2007 folder.

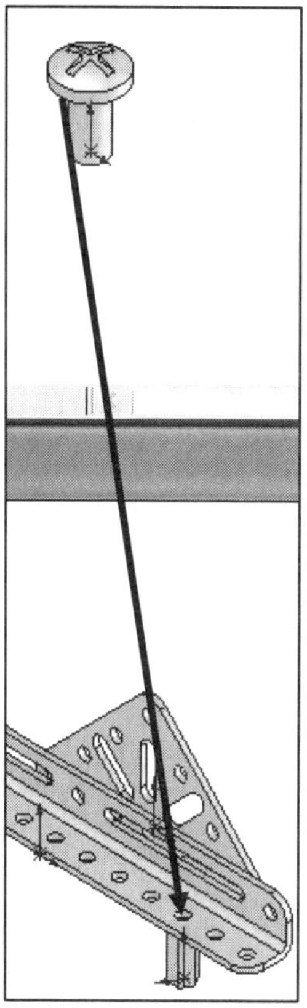

Display the SCREW part and the FRONT-SUPPORT assembly.

653) Click **Window**, **Tile Horizontally** from the Main menu.

654) Zoom in on the right side of the FRONT-SUPPORT assembly. Note: Work between the two tile windows.

Insert the first SCREW.

655) Click and drag the **circular edge** of the SCREW part into the FRONT-SUPPORT assembly Graphic window.

656) Release the mouse pointer on the **top 3rd circular hole edge** of the ANGLE-13HOLE. The mouse pointer displays the Coincident/ Concentric Circular edges feedback symbol.

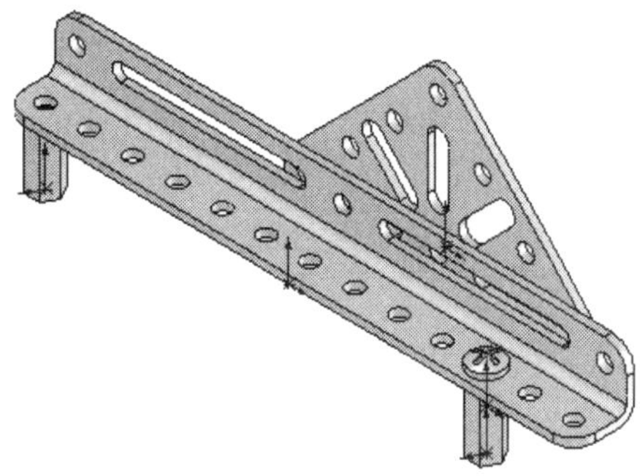

Insert the second SCREW.

657) Zoom in on the right side of the FRONT-SUPPORT assembly.

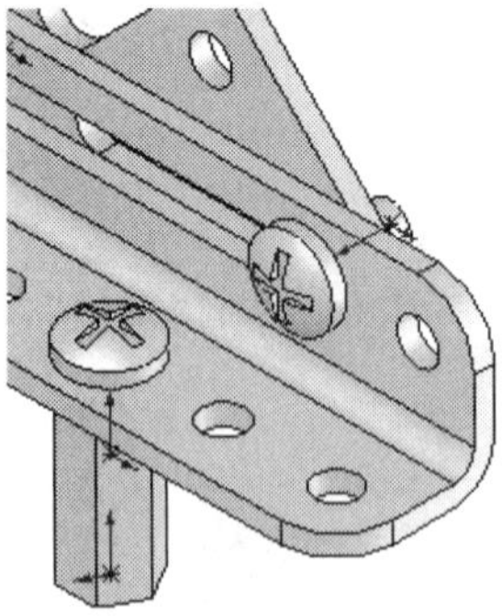

658) Click and drag the **circular edge** of the SCREW part into the FRONT-SUPPORT assembly Graphic window.

659) Release the mouse pointer on the **right arc edge** of the ANGLE-13HOLE. The mouse pointer displays the Coincident/ Concentric Circular edges feedback symbol.

Insert the third SCREW part.

660) Zoom in on the left side of the FRONT-SUPPORT assembly

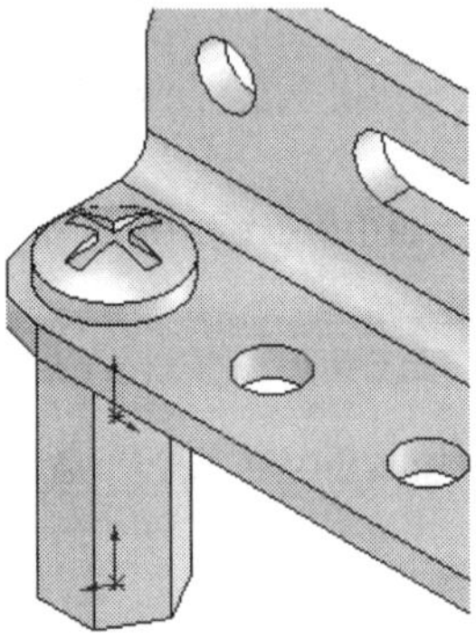

661) Click and drag the **circular edge** of the SCREW part into the FRONT-SUPPORT Assembly Graphic window.

662) Release the mouse pointer on the **left arc edge** of the ANGLE-13HOLE. The mouse pointer displays the Coincident/ Concentric Circular edges feedback symbol.

Insert the forth SCREW part.

663) Zoom in on the bottom circular edge of the ANGLE-13HOLE.

664) Click and drag the **circular edge** of the SCREW part into the FRONT-SUPPORT Assembly Graphic window.

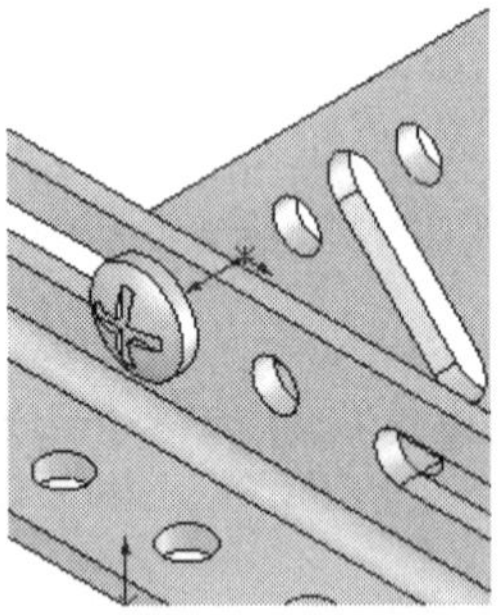

665) Release the mouse pointer on the **bottom circular edge** of the ANGLE-13HOLE. The mouse pointer displays the Coincident/Concentric Circular edges feedback symbol.

666) Close the SCREW part window.

667) Maximize the FRONT-SUPPORT assembly window.

Display the Isometric view.

668) Click **Isometric view**.

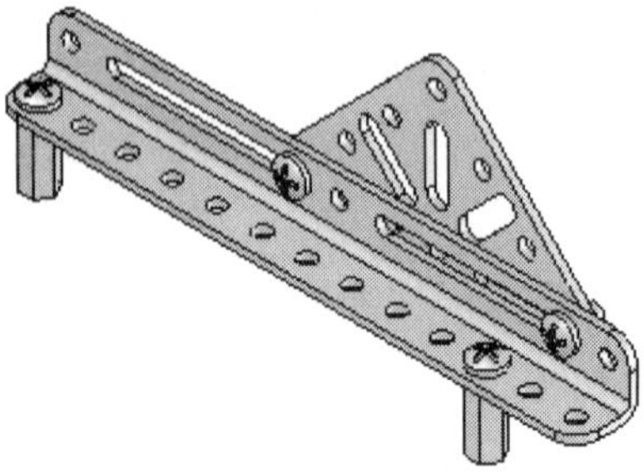

Save the FRONT-SUPPORT assembly.

669) Click **Save** .

Select the Ctrl-Tab keys to quickly alternate between open SolidWorks documents.

Close all parts and assemblies.

670) Click **Windows**, **Close All** from the Main menu.

The FRONT-SUPPORT assembly is complete.

Display the Mates in the FeatureManager to check that the components and the Mate Types correspond to the design intent. Utilize the Edit Feature command to modify mate references.

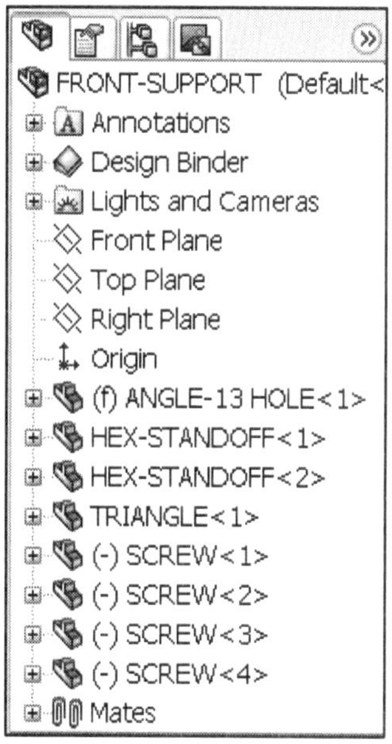

Review the FRONT-SUPPORT Assembly.

The ANGLE-13HOLE part was the first part inserted into the FRONT-SUPPORT assembly. The ANGLE-13HOLE part was fixed to the FRONT-SUPPORT Origin.

Concentric, Coincident and Parallel Mates were utilized to assemble the HEX-STANDOFF to the ANGLE-13HOLE. Concentric, Distance, and Parallel Mates were utilized to assemble the TRIANGLE to the ANGLE-13HOLE. The Concentric/Coincident Smart Mate was utilized to mate the four SCREW parts to the FRONT-SUPPORT assembly.

Project Summary

In this project you created four parts; HEX-STANDOFF, ANGLE-13HOLE, TRIANGLE, and SCREW utilizing the Top, Front, and Right planes. You obtained the knowledge of the following SolidWorks features: Extruded Boss/Base, Extruded Thin, Extruded Cut, Revolved Boss/Base, Hole Wizard, Linear Pattern, Circular Pattern, Fillet, and Chamfer.

You applied Sketch techniques with various Sketch tools: Line, Circle, Rectangle, Centerline, Polygon, Parallelogram, Dynamic Mirror, and Convert Entities.

You also utilized centerlines as construction geometry to reference dimensions and relationships.

You incorporated the four new parts to create the FRONT-SUPPORT assembly. Concentric, Distance, and Parallel Mates were utilized to assemble the TRIANGLE to the ANGLE-13HOLE. The Concentric/Coincident Smart Mate was utilized to mate the four SCREW parts to the FRONT-SUPPORT assembly.

Project Terminology

Utilize SolidWorks Help for additional information on the terms utilized in this project.

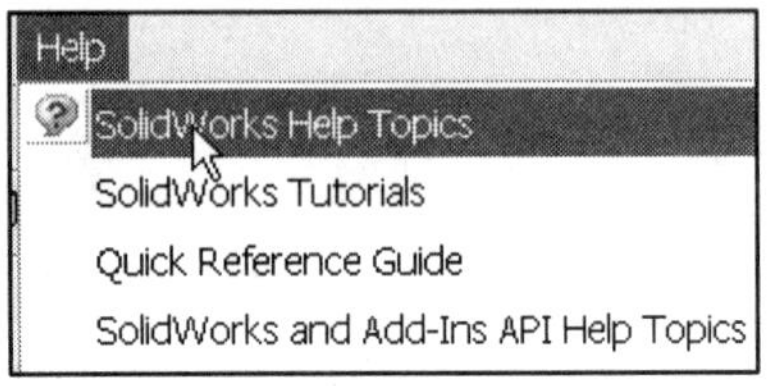

Assembly: An assembly is a document which contains components, features, and other sub-assemblies. When a part is inserted into an assembly it is called a component. Components are Mated together. The filename extension for a SolidWorks assembly file name is .SLDASM.

Component: A part or sub-assembly within an assembly.

Convert Entities: Converts model entities or sketch entities into sketch segments on the current sketch plane.

Features: Features are geometry building blocks. Features add or remove material. Features are created from sketched profiles or from edges and faces of existing geometry.

Mates: A Mate is a geometric relationship between components in an assembly.

Mirror Entities: Sketch tool that mirrors sketch geometry to the opposite side of a sketched centerline

Offset Entities: Insert sketch entities by offsetting faces, edges, curves, construction geometry by a specified distance on the current sketch plane.

Orthographic Projection: Orthographic projection is the process of projecting views onto parallel planes with ⊥ projectors. The default reference planes are the Front, Top and Right side viewing planes.

Part: A part is a single 3D object made up of features. The filename extension for a SolidWorks part file name is .SLDPRT.

Plane: To create a sketch, choose a plane. Planes are flat and infinite. They are represented on the screen with visible edges. The Front, Top, and Right planes were utilized as sketch planes for parts in this project.

Relation: A relation is a geometric constraint between sketch entities or between a sketch entity and a plane, axis, edge, or vertex. Utilize Add Relations to manually connect related geometry.

Sketch: The name to describe a 2D or 3D profile is called a sketch. 2D Sketches are created on flat faces and planes within the model. Typical geometry types are lines, arcs, rectangles, circles, and ellipses.

SmartMates: A SmartMate is a Mate that automatically occurs when a component is placed into an assembly and references geometry between that component and the assembly.

Standard Views: Front, Back, Right, Left, Top, Bottom, and Isometric are the Standard views utilized to orient the model.

Suppress features: A suppress feature is not displayed in the Graphics window. A suppress feature is removed from any rebuild calculations.

Trim Entities: Sketch tool that removes highlighted geometry.

Project Features

View the Multimedia CD in the book to review the features in this project.

Chamfer: A Chamfer feature creates bevels on selected edges and faces.

Circular Pattern: A Circular Pattern feature repeats features or faces about an axis in a circular array. A Circular Pattern requires and axis, number of instances, and the angle of revolution.

Extruded Boss/Base: An Extruded Base feature is the first feature in a part. An Extruded Boss feature occurs after the Extruded Base feature. The Extruded Boss/Base feature adds material by extrusion.

Steps to create an Extruded Boss/Base Feature:

- Select the Sketch plane; Sketch the profile; Add Dimensions and Relations; Select Extruded Boss/Base from the Features toolbar; Select an End Condition and/or options; Enter a depth; Click OK from the Extrude PropertyManager.

Extruded Cut: The Extruded Cut feature removes material from a solid. The Extruded Cut feature performs the opposite function of the Extruded Boss/Base feature. The Extruded Cut feature starts with either a 2D or 3D sketch and removes material by extrusion.

Steps to create an Extruded Cut Feature:

- Select the Sketch plane; Sketch the profile; Add Dimensions and Relations; Select Extruded Cut from the Features toolbar; Select an End Condition and/or options; Enter a depth; Click OK from the Cut-Extrude PropertyManager.

Extruded Thin: The Extruded Thin feature adds material of constant thickness. The Extruded Thin feature requires an open profile.

Fillet: The Fillet feature creates a rounded internal or external face on a part. You can fillet all edges of a face, selected sets of faces, selected edges, or edge loops.

Hole Wizard: The Hole Wizard feature provides the ability to determine the capabilities, available selections, and graphic previews for various hole types. First select a hole type, then determine the appropriate fastener. The fastener dynamically updates the appropriate parameters.

Linear Pattern: A Linear Pattern repeats features or geometry in an array. A Linear Patten requires the number of instances and the spacing between instances.

Steps to create a Linear Pattern Feature:

- Select the features to repeat; Select Linear Pattern from the Feature toolbar; Enter Direction of the pattern; Enter Number of pattern instances in each direction; Enter Distance between pattern instances; Optional: Pattern instances to skip; Click OK from the Linear Pattern PropertyManager.

Mirror: The Mirror feature mirrors features or faces about a selected plane. Select the features to copy and a plane about which to mirror them. If you select a planar face on the model, you mirror the entire model about the selected face.

Revolved Boss/Base: The Revolved Boss/Base feature adds material by revolving one or more profiles around a centerline. Create Revolved boss/bases, Revolved cuts, or Revolved surfaces. The Revolve feature can be a solid, a thin feature, or a surface.

Engineering Journal

Engineers and designers research their customer's requirements and criteria. They utilize mathematics, science, economics and history to calculate additional information about a project.

Engineers adhere to federal regulations and standards to design parts that are safe and reliable. Record the answers to the questions in an engineering journal.

Model Courtesy of
Scott Baugh, CSWP
www.scottjbaugh.com

1. Estimation. The volume of the golf ball is approximated with the model of a sphere. A sphere is a revolved feature. What is the volume of the sphere?

Volume of a sphere is provided by the formula; $V = 4/3\ \pi\ r^3$. Where:

- V is volume.
- r is the radius.

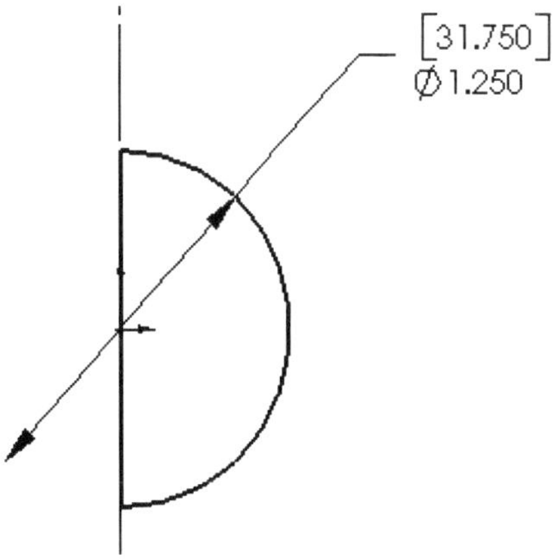

a.) Determine the radius of the sphere in mm and inches.

b.) Calculate the Volume of the sphere in mm^3 and in^3.

c.) The actual volume of the golf ball model is 1.001 in^3. Why does the volume value differ from the calculated volume of the sphere?

2. Sketching.

- Sketch the top view of a Flat Plate. The overall dimensions of the Flat Plate are: 8.688in x 5.688in x 0.090in.

The four corners of the Flat Plate are rounded with a .25in Radius.

A two dimensional array of Ø.190in holes is spaced .500in apart.

The holes are .344in from all four sides.

- Determine the size of the two dimensional array of holes. Determine the total number of holes contained on the Flat Plate. (Note: Sketch Not to Scale).

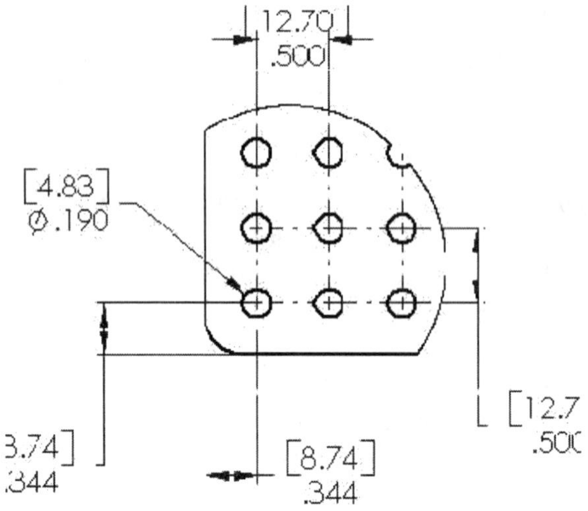

3. Sketching on Planes.

a) Label the Front, Top, and Right planes. Sketch an L-shaped profile on the Front plane.

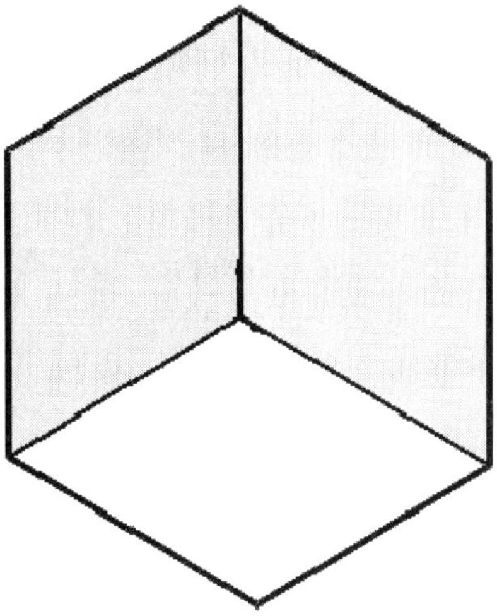

b) Sketch an L-shaped profile on the Top plane. Label the Primary Datum plane.

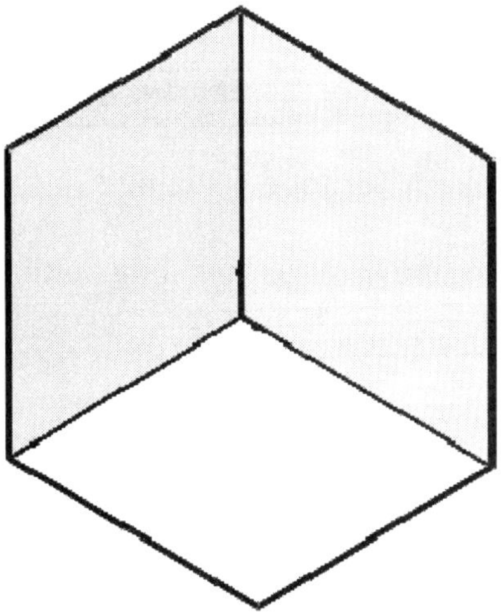

c) Sketch an L-shaped profile on the Right plane. Label the Secondary Datum plane.

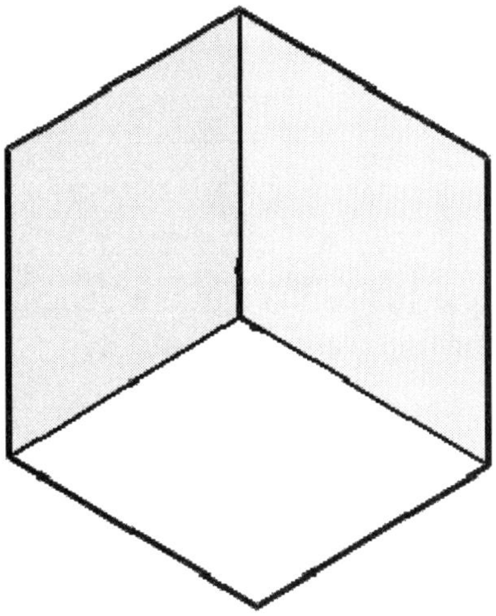

4. Industry Application

Calculating material volume is important when designing parts.

Volume = Width x Height x Depth.

The Extruded Base feature of the Container is 45cm x 20cm x 30cm.

- Estimate the approximate volume of the container in cm^3.

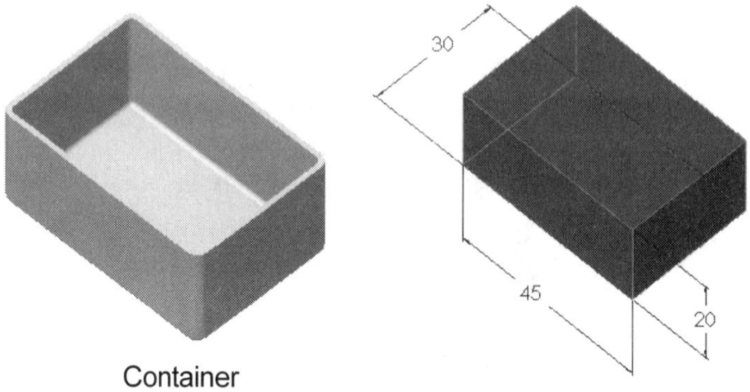

Container

Volume for food containers is commonly provided in liters or gallons.

Examples: 2-liter soda bottle or a gallon of milk.

- Calculate the volume of the container in liters and in gallons.

Given: 1 liter = 1000 cm^3

1 gallon = 3.785 liters.

- Approximately how many liters would the container hold? How many gallons?

The actual volume of the Container is 23 liters. Explain why this value does not equal your first estimated volume.

5. Industry Application

Engineers at Rubbermaid Commercial Products, Winchester, VA, utilize volume to design the tooling required to produce food storage containers.

Courtesy of Rubbermaid Commercial Products
Winchester, Virginia, USA
www.rubbermaidcommercial.com

Rubbermaid was formed in 1920 as the Wooster Rubber Company, a maker of toy balloons. In 1934 the companied introduced the first rubber dustpan to create the house wares business. During WWII rubber could not be utilized in non-military products. Focus shifted to other applications for the US military.

- Utilize the World Wide Web to research the types of parts that were produced during World War II.

In 1957, the Wooster Rubber Company changed its name to Rubbermaid Inc. Rubbermaid Commercial Products was established in 1967 and provides products for the industrial and agricultural markets. Today, Rubbermaid Commercial Products is a division of Newell Rubbermaid Inc.

Rubbermaid Commercial Products designs and manufactures a variety of food preparation, transport, serving and storage products.

Engineers utilize SolidWorks to create the tooling required to produce the 3304 Food Service Box used in schools, restaurants and hotels throughout the world.

The 3304 Food Service box is designed with the following criteria:

- Meet National Sanitation Standards (NSF) for cleaning.
- Food and Drug Administration (FDA) compliant materials.
- Stackable.
- Tight fitting snap-on lids.
- Slide fit into a multi-rack system.

Engineers must be cognizant of the size and shape of the part. They must also understand their customer's requirements.

There are hundreds of different types of plastic materials.

- Utilize the World Wide Web to determine the type of plastic material utilized in food storage containers.

3. Plastics engineers continuously research cost saving during the injection molding process. A new mold is produced for an existing high volume part at a cost of $10,000.

The new mold utilizes less material and requires a shorter cycle time. The factory produces 60 parts per hour and operates 24 hours per day. The manufacturer saves 10 cents per part with the new mold.

- How many days are required to justify the cost of the mold?

- How many parts are produced in this time frame?

Questions

1. Identify the three default Reference planes.

2. True or False. Sketches are created only on the Front plane.

3. Identify the sketch tool required to create a hexagon.

4. Describe the profile required for an Extruded Thin feature.

5. Mirror Entities, Offset Entities, Sketch Fillet, and Trim Entities are located in the ______________ toolbar.

6. List the six principle views in a drawing ___________, ___________, ___________, ___________, ___________, ___________,

7. Identify the type of Geometric Relations that can be added to a Sketch.

8. Describe the difference between a Circular Pattern and a Linear Pattern feature.

9. Describe the difference between a Fillet feature and a Chamfer feature.

10. Identify the function of the Hole Wizard feature.

11. Four 10-24X3/8 Machine Screws are required in the FRONT-SUPPORT assembly. The diameter is _________________. The threads per inch are ____________. The length is _____________.

12. Describe the difference between a Distance Mate and a Coincident Mate.

13. True or False. A fixed component cannot move in an assembly.

14. Describe the procedure to move a component an assembly.

15. Determine the procedure to rotate a component in an assembly. Utilize online Help.

16. Review the Design Intent section in the Introduction. Identify how you incorporated design intent into the parts and assembly.

17. Review the Keyboard Short Cut keys. Identify the Short Cut keys you incorporated into this project.

Exercises

Exercise 2.1a: HEX-NUT Part.

Create a HEX-NUT part using the following dimensions:

- Depth: .125 in, [3.18].
- Inside hole diameter: .190in, [4.83].
- Outside diameter: .375in, [9.53].

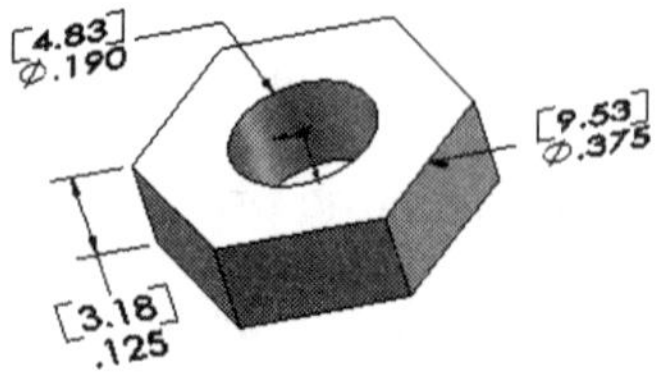

Use the Top plane as the Sketch plane.

Exercise 2.1b: FRONT-SUPPORT-2 Assembly.

Create the FRONT-SUPPORT-2 assembly.

- Name the new assembly FRONT-SUPPORT-2.
- Insert the FRONT-SUPPORT assembly. Fix the FRONT-SUPPORT assembly to the Origin.
- Insert the first HEX-NUT (Exercise 2.1a) into the FRONT-SUPPORT-2 assembly.
- Insert a Concentric Mate.
- Insert a Coincident Mate.
- Insert the second HEX-NUT part.
- Insert a Concentric Mate.
- Insert a Coincident Mate.

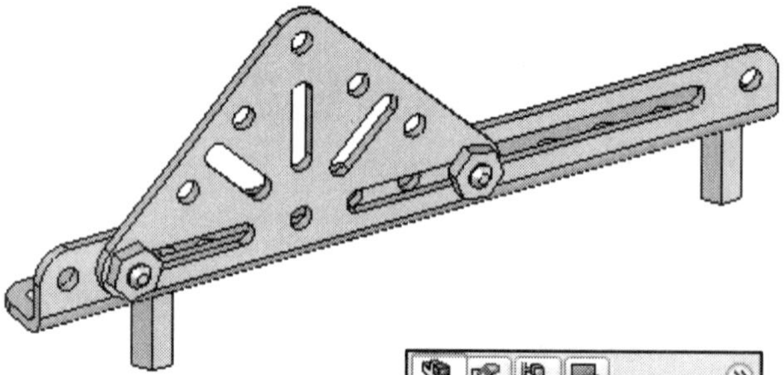

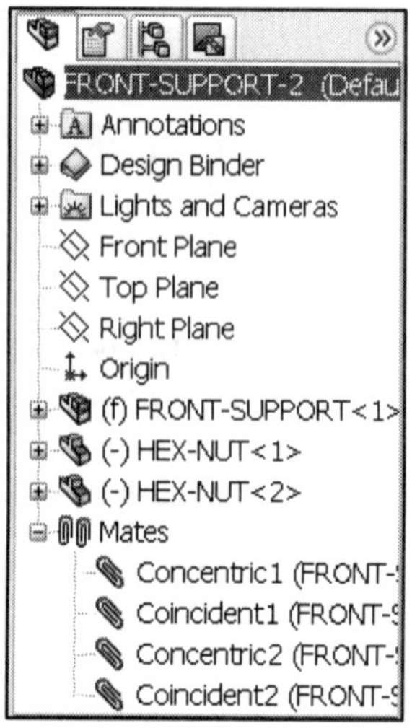

Exercise 2.2a: BALL Part.

Create a Ball part. Utilize the Revolved Base feature.

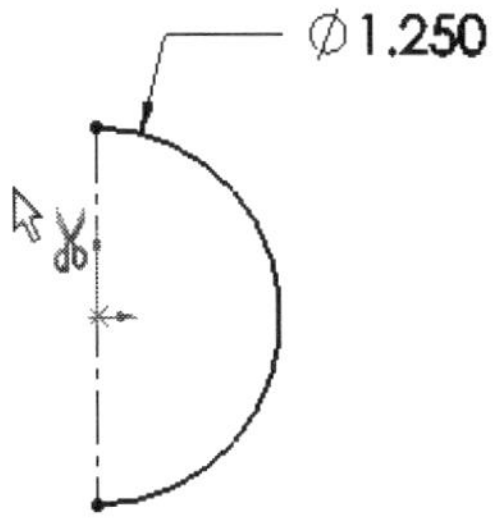

- Create a new part named BALL.
- Use the Front plane as the Sketch plane.
- Sketch a circle with a diameter of 1.250in, [31.75].
- Sketch a vertical centerline coincident with the Origin.
- Use Power Trim to trim the left half of the ball to create an arc.
- Utilize a Revolved Base feature to create the Revolve-Thin1 feature as illustrated in the FeatureManager.

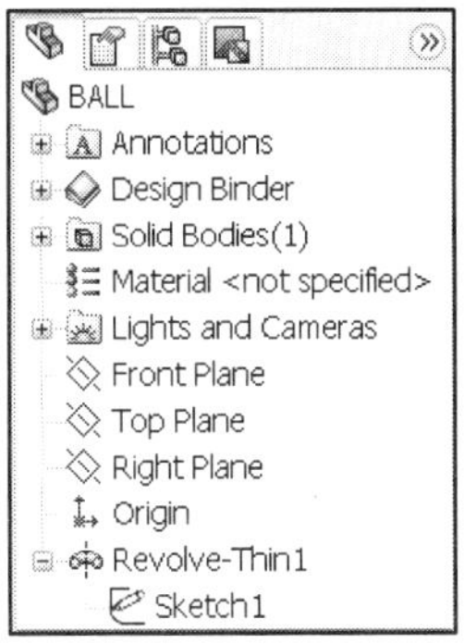

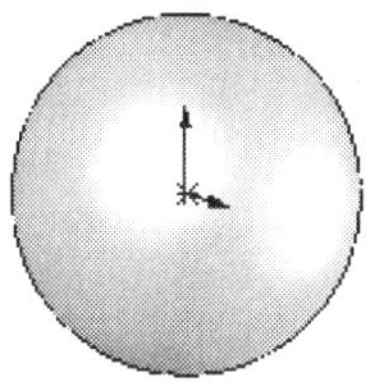

Exercise 2.2b: Mounting-Nut Part.

Create a Mounting-Nut Part using the features displayed in the FeatureManager.

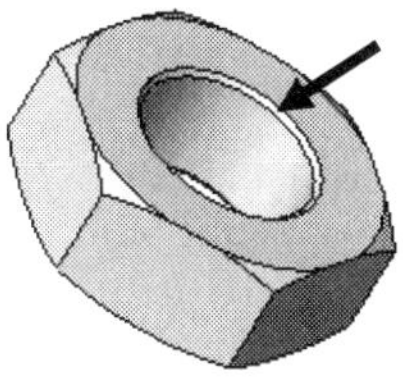

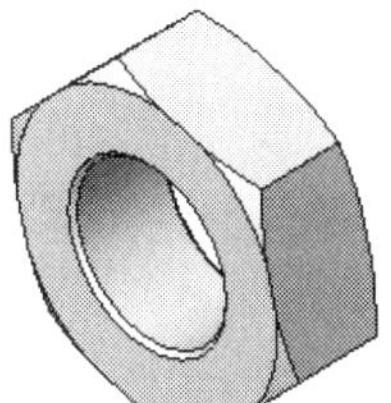

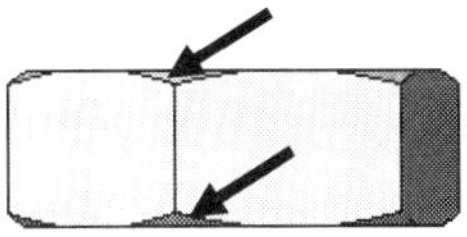

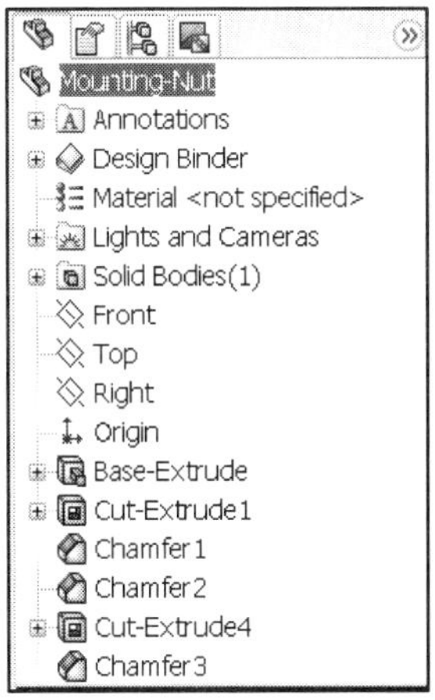

Exercise 2.3: Container Part.

Plastic parts require tapered sides in order to remove the part from the mold. The Draft option in the Extruded Boss/Base feature produces this function.

Courtesy of Rubbermaid Commercial Products
Winchester, Virginia, USA
www.rubbermaidcommercial.com

Injection molded plastic parts require a constant wall thickness. The Shell feature produces a constant wall thickness by removing a selected face.

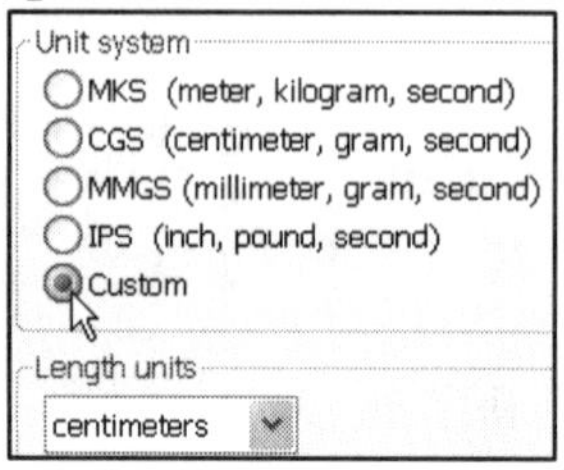

- Create a new part named Container. Units are in centimeters.

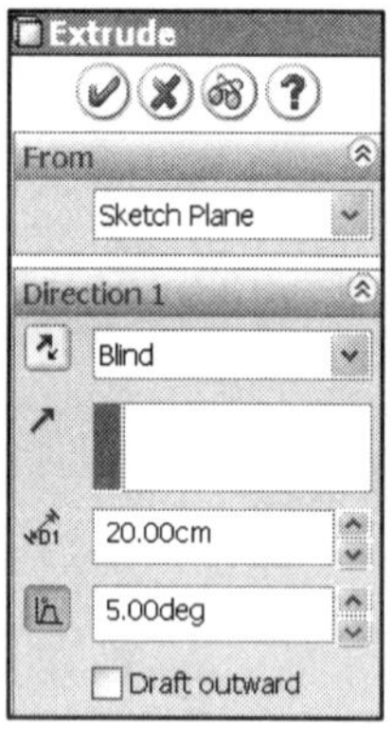

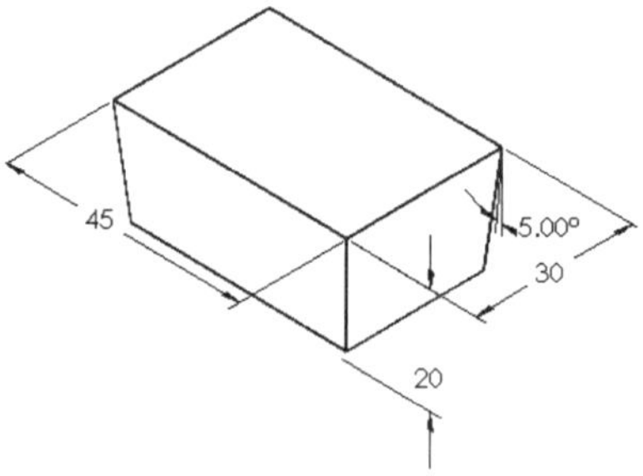

- Utilize the Extruded Boss/Base feature, 45cm x 20cm x 30cm with Draft.
- Enter 5 degrees for the Draft Angle.
- Add Fillets to the four vertical edges and to the bottom face. The Fillet radius is 3cm.

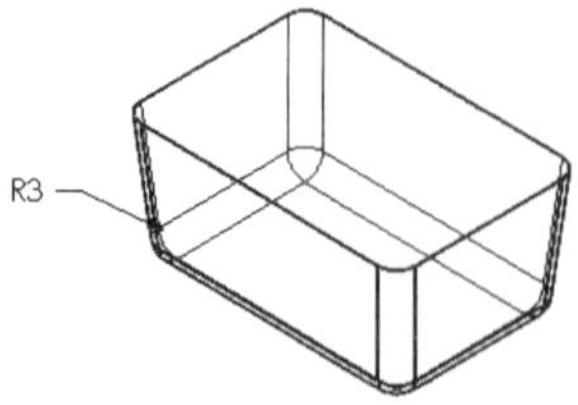

- Utilize the Shell feature on the top face to create a 1cm wall thickness.

SolidWorks contains hundreds of features with multiple options.

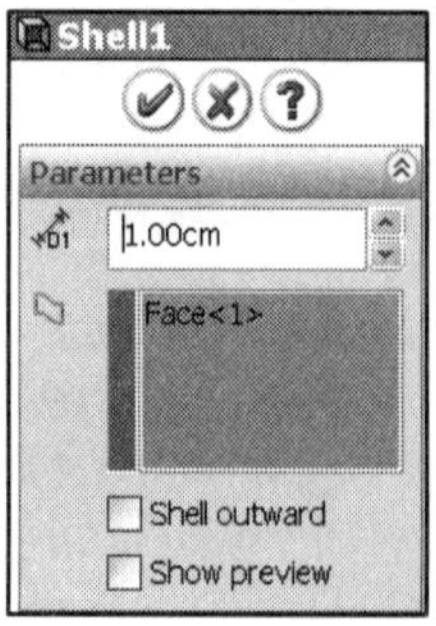

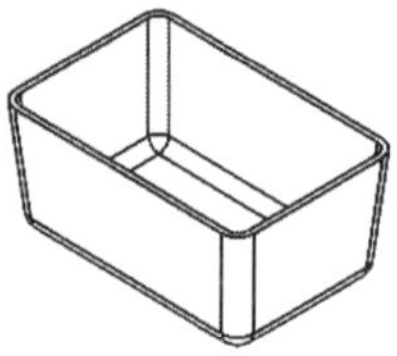

- Utilize Online Help to review new functionality.

Exercise 2.4: AIR RESERVOIR SUPPORT AND PLATE Assembly.

The project team developed a concept sketch of the PNEUMATIC TEST MODULE assembly. Develop the AIR RESERVOIR SUPPORT AND PLATE assembly.

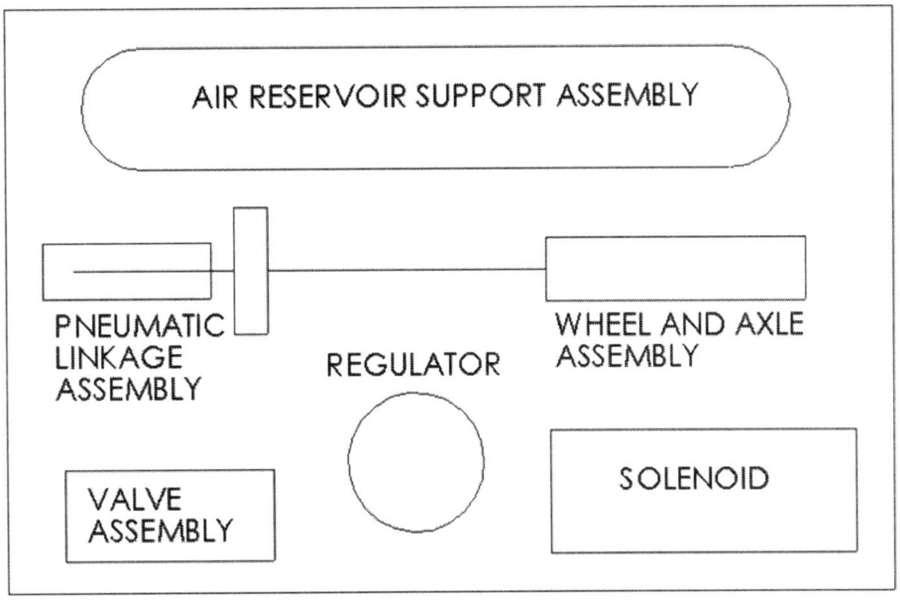

PNEUMATIC TEST MODULE Assembly Layout

Create three new parts:

- FLAT-PLATE.
- IM15-MOUNT.
- ANGLE-BRACKET.

The SMC AIR RESERVOIR is a purchased part. The assembly file is available from the CD in the book.

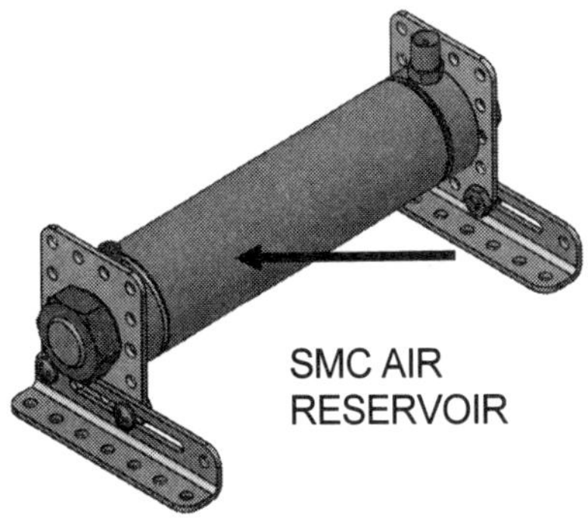

AIR RESERVOIR SUPPORT Assembly
Courtesy of Gears Educational Systems & SMC Corporation of America

- Create a new assembly named AIR RESERVOIR SUPPORT AND PLATE.
- Two M15-MOUNT parts and two ANGLE-BRACKET parts hold the SMC AIR RESERVOIR.
- The ANGLE-BRACKET parts are fastened to the FLAT-PLATE.

Exercise 2.4a: **FLAT-PLATE Part.**

- Create the FLAT-PLATE Part on the Top plane. The FLAT-PLATE is machined from .090, [2.3] aluminum flat stock. The default units are inches.
- Utilize the Top plane for the Sketch plane.
- Locate the Origin at the Midpoint of the left vertical line.

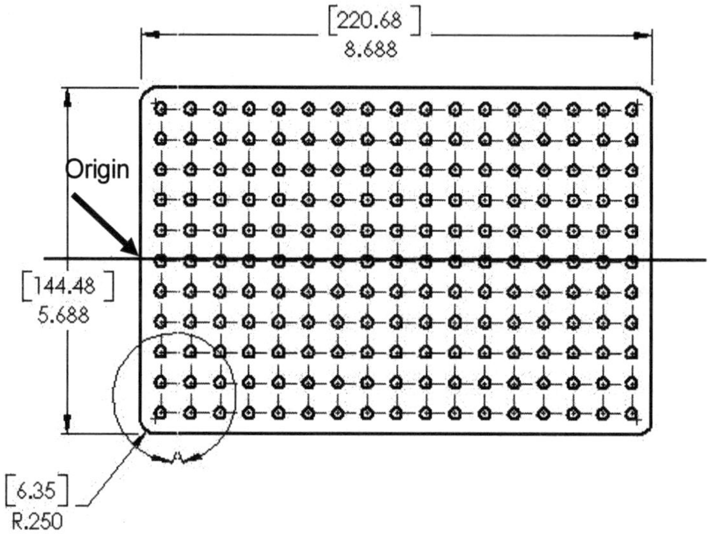

- The 8.688, [220.68mm] x 5.688, [144.48mm] FLAT PLATE contains a Linear Pattern of ∅.190, [4.83mm] Thru holes.
- The Holes are equally spaced, .500, [12.70mm] apart.

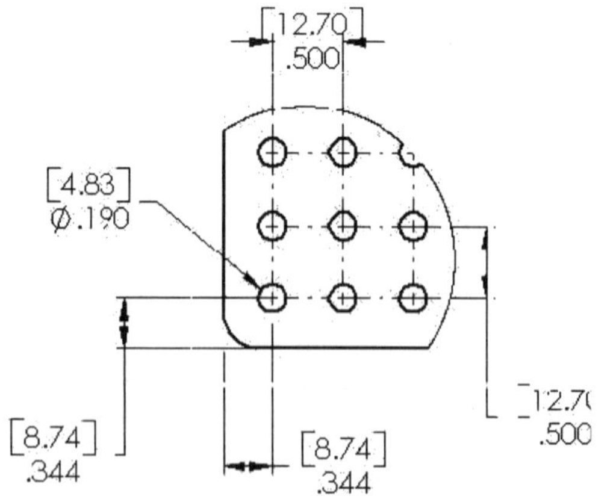

- Determine the maximum number of holes contained in the FLAT-PLATE.

  Maximum # of holes_______________.

- Utilize a Linear Pattern in two Directions to create the holes. Utilize yhe Geometric Pattern Option.

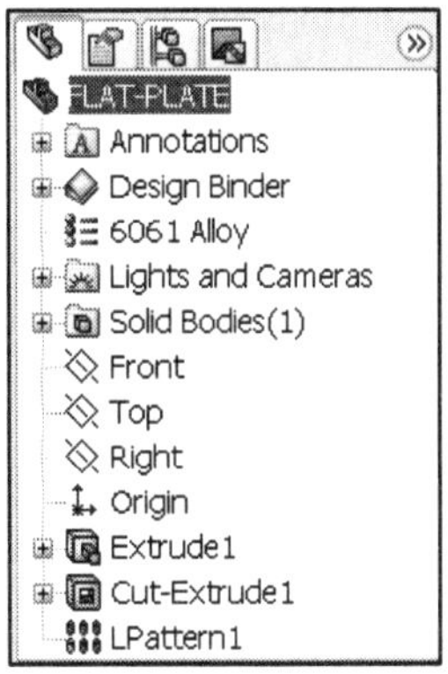

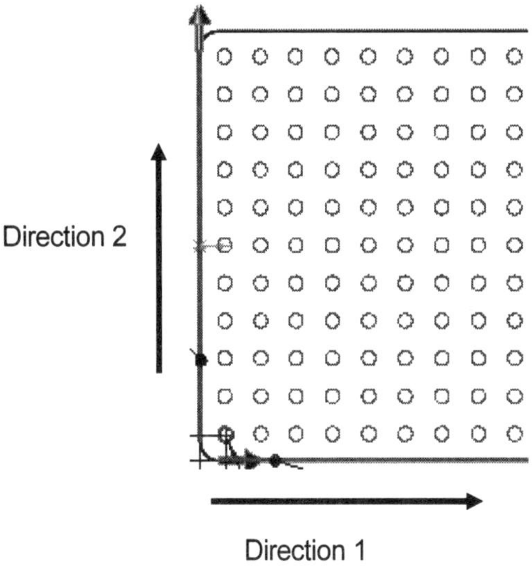

Exercise 2.4b: **IM15-MOUNT Part.**

- Create the IM15-MOUNT Part on the Right plane.

- Center the part on the Origin. Utilize the features in the FeatureManager.

The IM15-MOUNT Part is machined from 0.060, [1.5mm] Stainless Steel flat stock. The default units are inches.

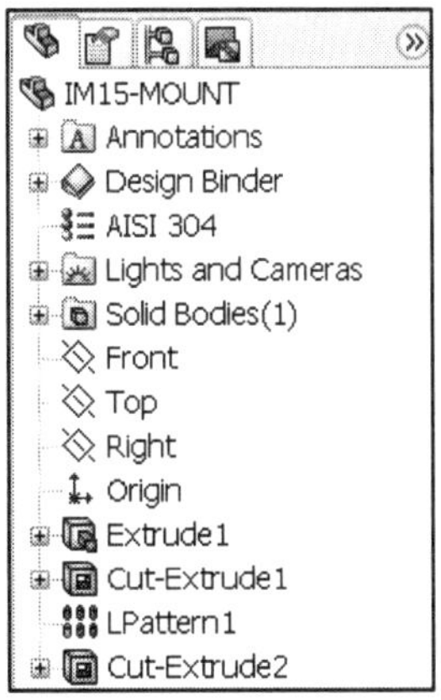

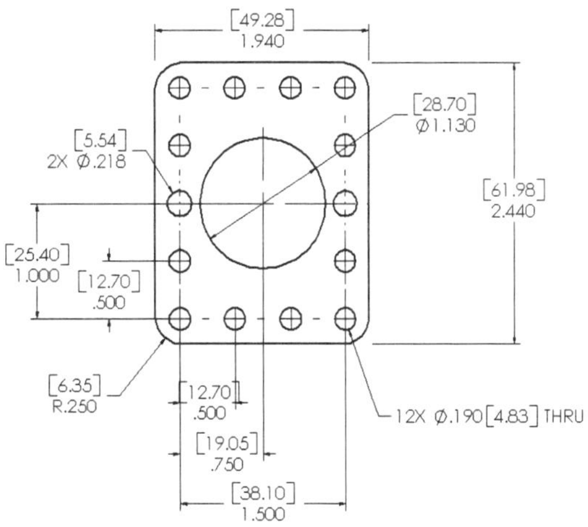

Exercise 2.4c: ANGLE BRACKET Part.

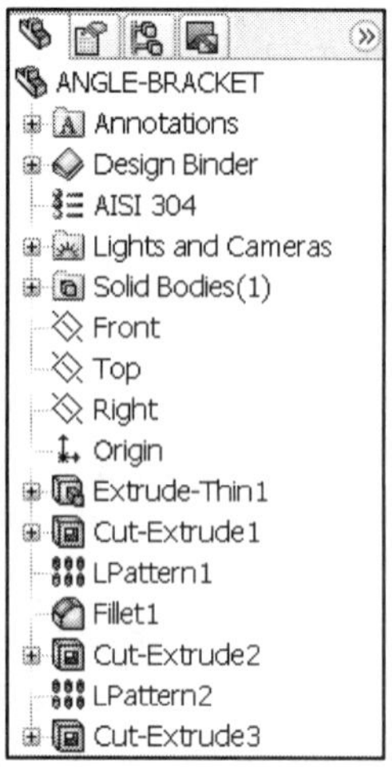

- Create the ANGLE BRACKET Part.
- The Extrude Base feature is sketched with an L-Shaped profile on the Right plane. The ANGLE BRACKET Part is machined from 0.060, [1.5mm] Stainless Steel flat stock. The default units are inches.

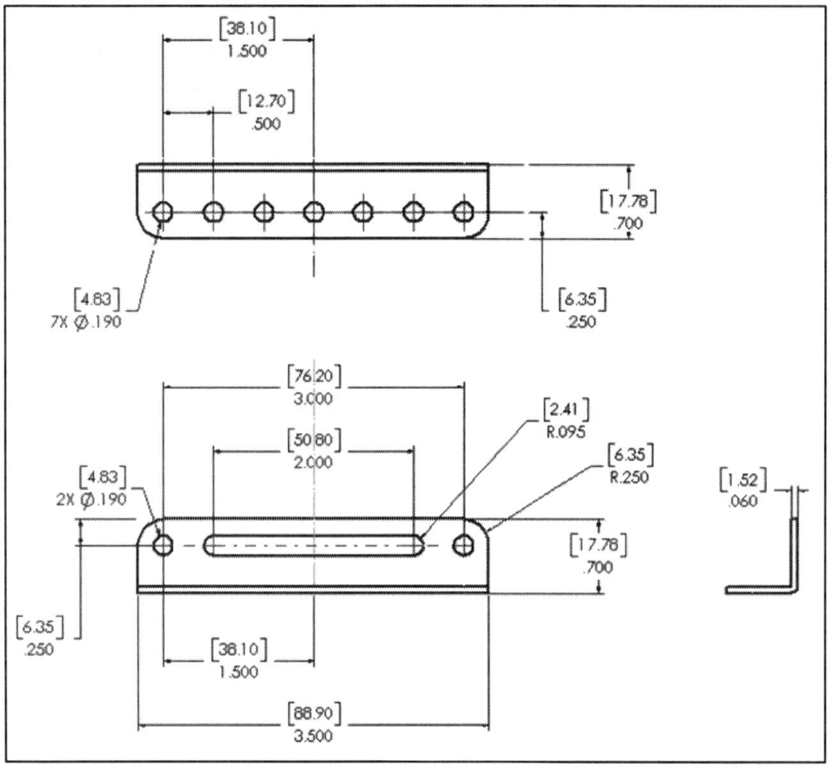

Exercise 2.4d: RESERVOIR Assembly.

The RESERVOIR stores compressed air. Air is pumped through a Schrader Valve into the RESERVOIR.

A Quick Connect Straight Fitting is utilized to supply air to the Pneumatic Test Module Assembly. Quick Connect Fittings allow air tubing to be assembled and disassembled without removing the fitting.

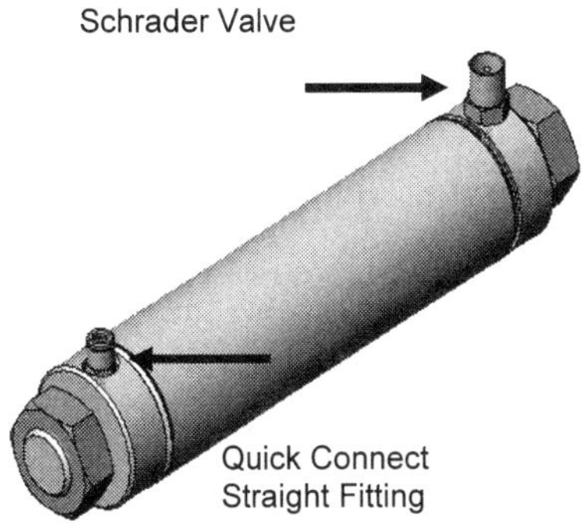

Reservoir and Fittings
Courtesy of SMC Corporation of America and Gears Educational Systems

Copy the Pneumatic Components folder from the CD in the book to the SW-TUTORIAL folder. Open the part, RESERVOIR from the Pneumatics Components folder. The RESERVOIR default units are in millimeters.

Engineers and designers work in metric and english units. Always verify your units for parts and other engineering data. In pneumatic systems, common units for volume, pressure and temperature are defined in the below table.

Magnitude	Metric Unit (m)	English (e)
Mass	kg g	pound ounce
Length	m m mm	foot yard inch
Temperature	°C	°F
Area, Section	m^2 cm^2	sq.ft sq.inch
Volume	m^3 cm^3 dm^3	cu.yard cu.inch cu.ft.
Volume Flow	m^3n / min dm^3n /min (ℓ/min)	scfm scfm
Force	N	pound force (ℓbf.)
Pressure	bar	ℓbf./sq.inch (psi)

Common Metric and English Units

The ISO unit of pressure is the Pa (Pascal). 1Pa = 1N/m.

Exercise 2.4e: AIR RESERVOIR SUPPORT AND PLATE Assembly.

Create the AIR RESERVOIR SUPPORT AND PLATE assembly. Note: There is more than one solution for the Mate types illustrated below.

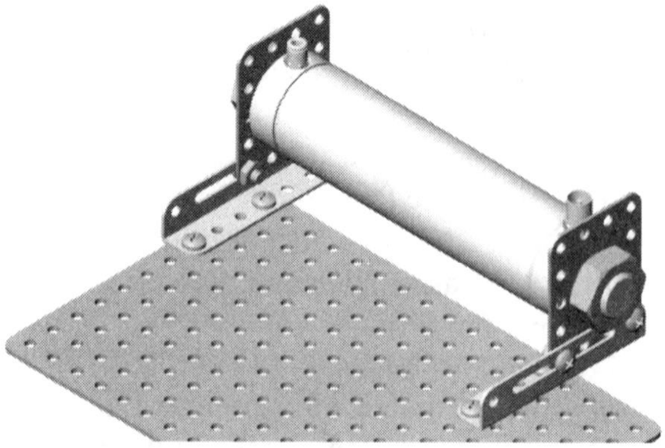

AIR RESERVOIR SUPPORT AND PLATE Assembly
Courtesy of Gears Educational Systems & SMC Corporation of America

The FLAT PLATE is the first component in the AIR RESERVOIR SUPPORT AND PLATE assembly. Insert the FLAT PLATE. The FLAT PLATE is fixed to the Origin.

- Insert the ANGLE BRACKET.
- Mate the ANGLE BRACKET to the FLAT PLATE. The bottom flat face of the ANGLE BRACKET is coincident to the top face of the FLAT PLATE.
- The center hole of the ANGLE BRACKET is concentric to the upper left hole of the FLAT PLATE.
- The first hole of the ANGLE bracket is concentric with the hole in the 8th row, 1st column of the FLAT PLATE.

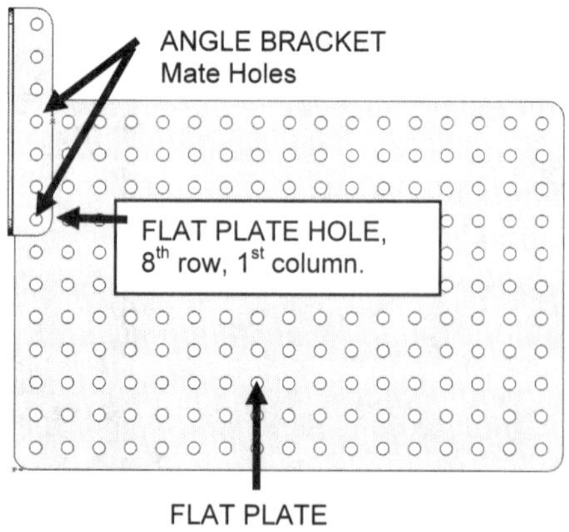

- Insert the IM15-MOUNT.
- Mate the IM15-MOUNT. The IM15-MOUNT flat back face is coincident to the flat inside front face of the ANGLE BRACKET.
- The bottom right hole of the IM15-MOUNT is concentric with the right hole of the ANGLE BRACKET.
- The bottom edge of the IM15-MOUNT is parallel to bottom edge of the ANGLE BRACKET.

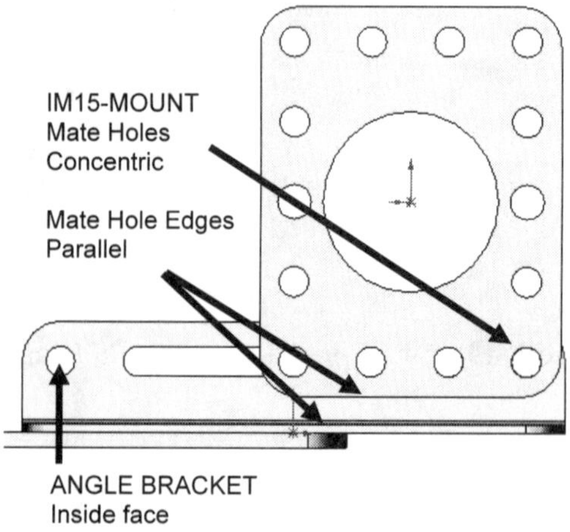

- Insert the Reservoir Assembly.
- Mate the Reservoir Assembly. The conical face of the Reservoir is concentric to the IM15-MOUNT center hole.
- The left end cap of the Reservoir Assembly is coincident to the front face of the IM15-MOUNT.
- The Hex Nut flat face is parallel to the top face of the FLAT PLATE.
- Insert the second ANGLE BRACKET.

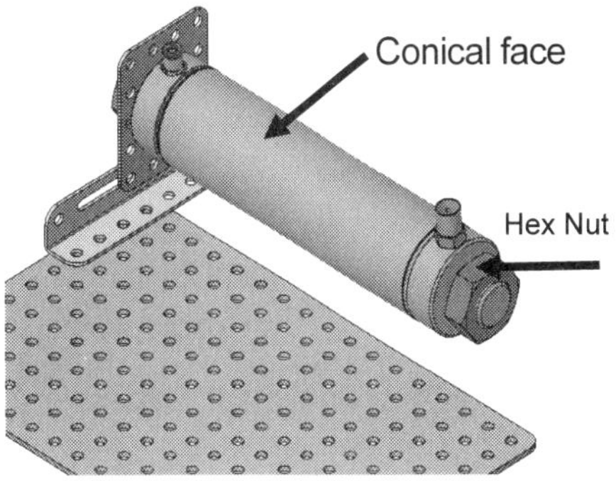

- Mate the ANGLE BRACKET to the FLAT PLATE. The bottom flat face of the ANGLE BRACKET is coincident to the top face of the FLAT PLATE.
- The center hole of the ANGLE BRACKET is concentric with the hole in the 11th row, 13th column of the FLAT PLATE.

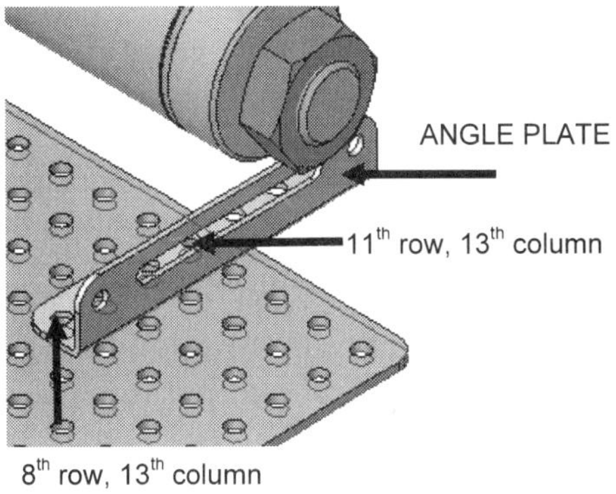

- The first hole of the ANGLE bracket is concentric with the hole in the 8th row, 13th column of the FLAT PLATE.
- Insert the second IM15-MOUNT.
- Mate the IM15-MOUNT to the outside face of the ANGLE BRACKET. The bottom right hole of the IM15-MOUNT is concentric with the right hole of the ANGLE BRACKET.
- The top edge of the IM15-MOUNT is parallel to the top edge of the ANGLE BRACKET.
- Save the assembly. Insert the required SCREWS. The AIR RESERVOIR SUPPORT AND PLATE assembly is complete.

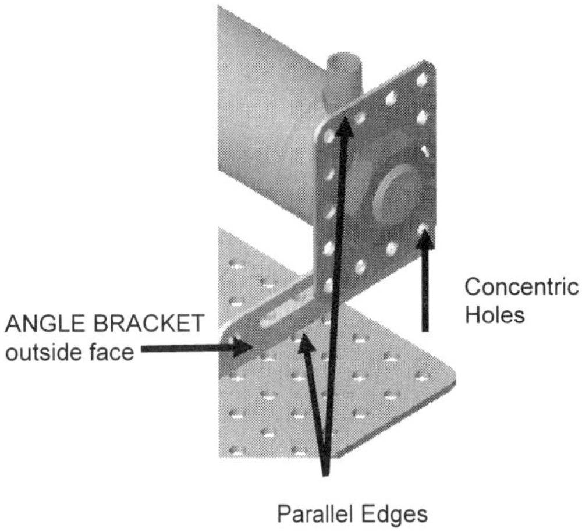

Notes:

Project 3

Fundamentals of Drawing

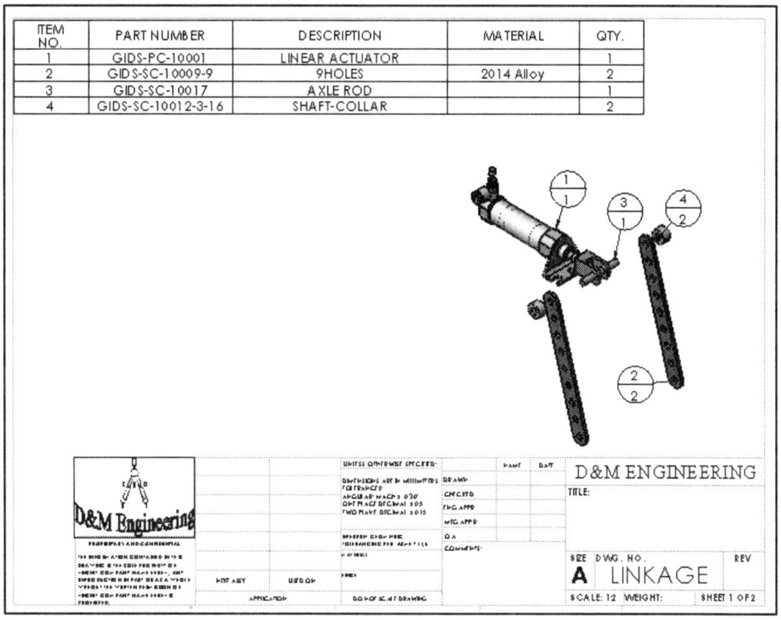

Below are the desired outcomes and usage competencies based on the completion of Project 3.

Desired Outcomes:	**Usage Competencies:**
• CUSTOM-A Sheet Format. • A-ANSI-MM Drawing Template.	• Ability to create a Custom sheet format, Drawing Template, Company logo, and Title block.
• FLATBAR configurations. • FLATBAR drawing.	• An understanding of Standard, Isometric, Detail, Section, and Exploded views. Knowledge to use the View Palette.
• LINKAGE drawing.	• Skills to insert, create, and edit drawing dimensions and annotations.
• FLATBAR-SHAFTCOLLAR assembly.	• Aptitude to create a Design Table.
• A LINKAGE assembly drawing with a Bill of Materials.	• Knowledge to incorporate a Bill of Materials with Custom Properties.

Notes:

[redacted]

Project 3 – Fundamentals of Drawing

Project Objective

Create a FLATBAR drawing with a customized sheet format and a Drawing Template containing a Company logo and Title block.

Obtain an understanding to display the following views with the ability to insert, add, and edit dimensions:

- Standard: Top, Front, and Right.
- Isometric, Detail, and Section.
- Exploded.

Create a LINKAGE assembly drawing with a Bill of Materials. Obtain knowledge to develop and incorporate a Bill of Materials with Custom Properties. Create a FLATBAR-SHAFTCOLLAR assembly.

On the completion of this project, you will be able to:

- Create a customized sheet format.
- Generate a custom Drawing Template.
- Produce a Bill of Materials with Custom Properties.
- Develop various drawing views.
- Reposition views on a drawing.
- Move dimensions in the same view.
- Use Edit Sheet Format and Edit Sheet.
- Modify the dimension scheme.
- Create a Parametric drawing note.
- Link notes in the Title block to SolidWorks properties.
- Generate an Exploded view.
- Create and edit a Design Table.

Project Overview

Generate two drawings in this project:

- A FLATBAR drawing and a LINKAGE assembly drawing.

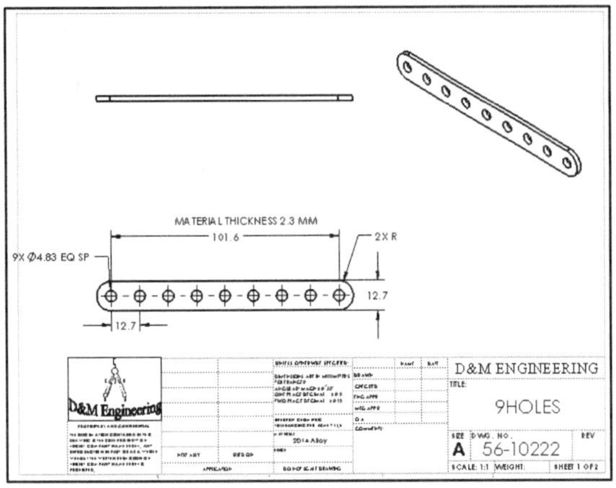

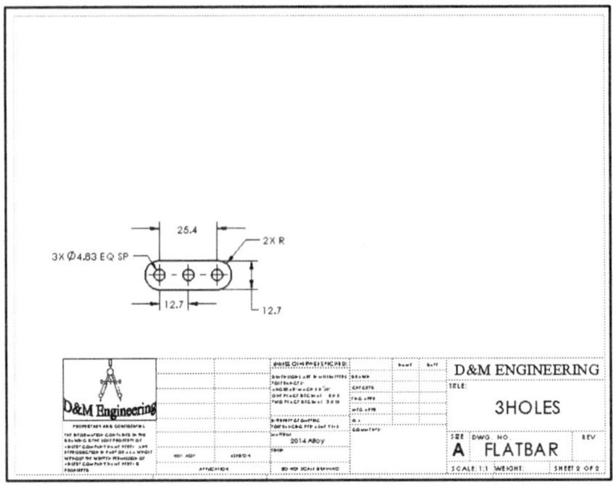

The FLATBAR drawing utilizes a custom Drawing Template and a custom Sheet Format. The FLATBAR drawing contains two sheets:

- Sheet1 contains a Front, Top, and Isometric view with dimensions and a linked Parametric note.
- Sheet2 contains the 3HOLE configuration of the FLATBAR. Configurations are created with a Design Table.

The LINKAGE assembly drawing contains two sheets:

- Sheet1 contains the LINKAGE assembly in an Exploded view with a Bill of Materials.
- Sheet2 contains the AIRCYLINDER assembly with a Section view, Detail view, and a Scale view.

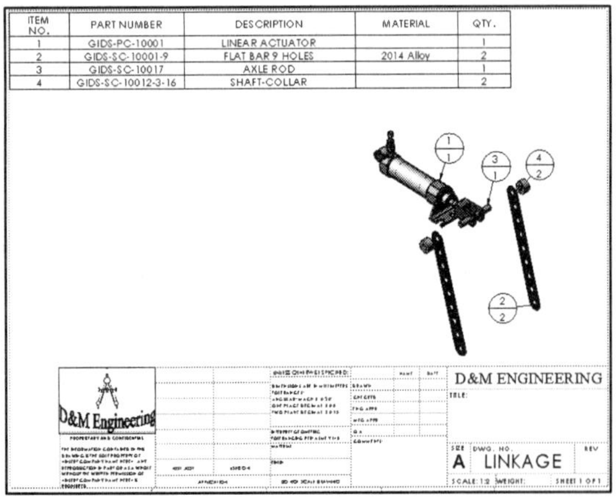

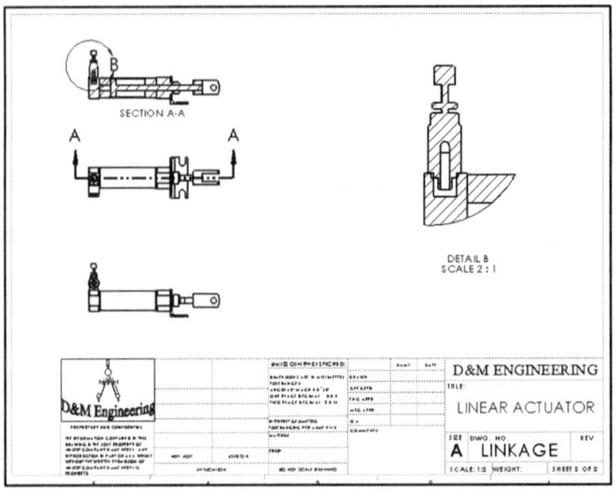

Create the FLATBAR-SHAFTCOLLAR assembly. Utilize a Design Table to create four new configurations of the assembly.

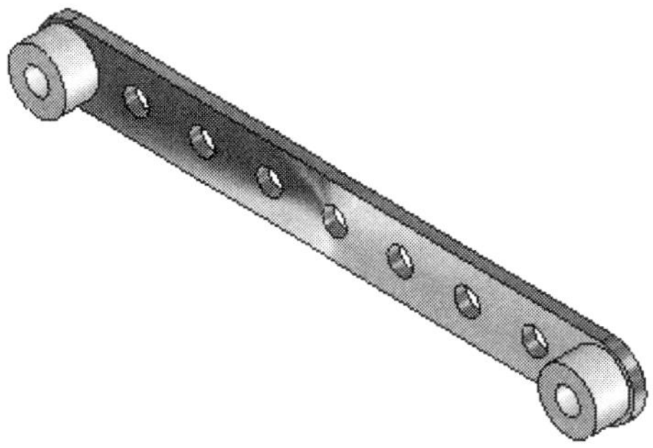

There are two major design modes used to develop a drawing:

- Edit Sheet Format.
- Edit Sheet.

The Edit Sheet Format mode provides the ability to:

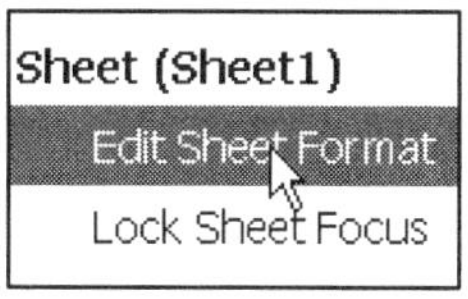

- Change the Title block size and text headings.
- Incorporate a Company logo.
- Add Custom Properties and text.

The Edit Sheet mode provides the ability to:

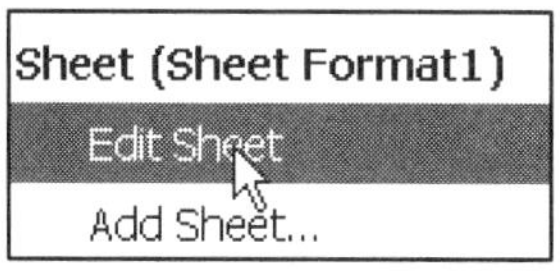

- Add or modify views.
- Add or modify dimensions.
- Add or modify notes.

Drawing Template and Sheet Format

The foundation of a SolidWorks drawing is the Drawing Template. Drawing size, drawing standards, company information, manufacturing and or assembly requirements, units and other properties are defined in the Drawing Template.

The Sheet Format is incorporated into the Drawing Template. The Sheet Format contains the border, Title block information, Revision block information, Company name and or Logo information, Custom Properties, and SolidWorks Properties.

Custom Properties and SolidWorks Properties are shared values between documents. Utilize an A-size Drawing Template with Sheet Format for the FLATBAR drawing and LINKAGE assembly drawing.

Views from the part or assembly are inserted into the SolidWorks Drawing.

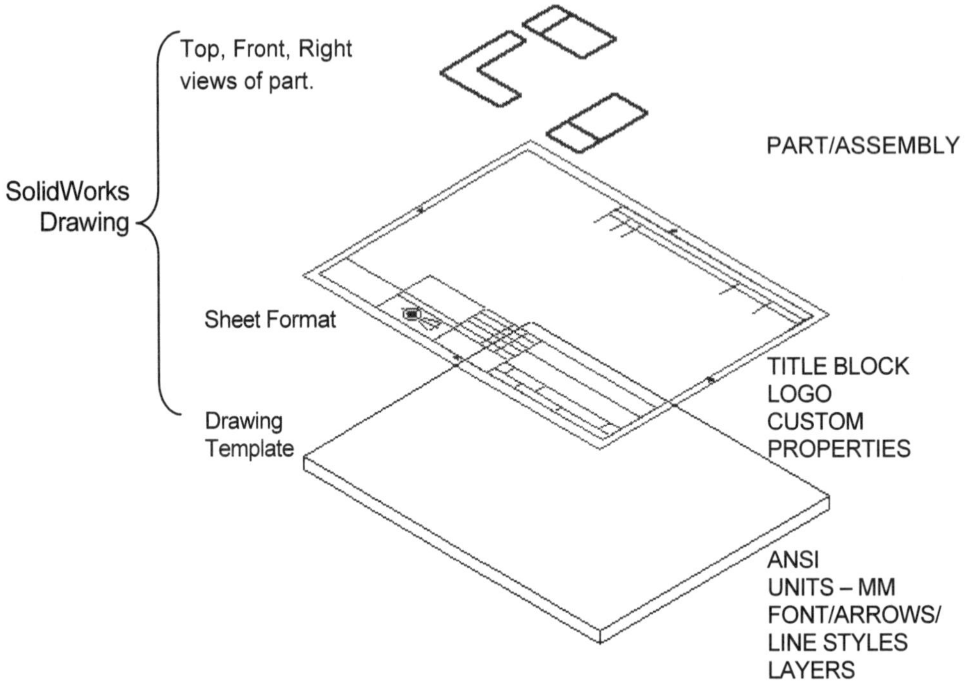

Create Sheet Formats for different parts types. Example: sheet metal parts, plastic parts, and high precision machined parts.

Create Sheet Formats for each category of parts that are manufactured with unique sets of title block notes.

Note: A Third Angle Projection scheme is illustrated in this project.

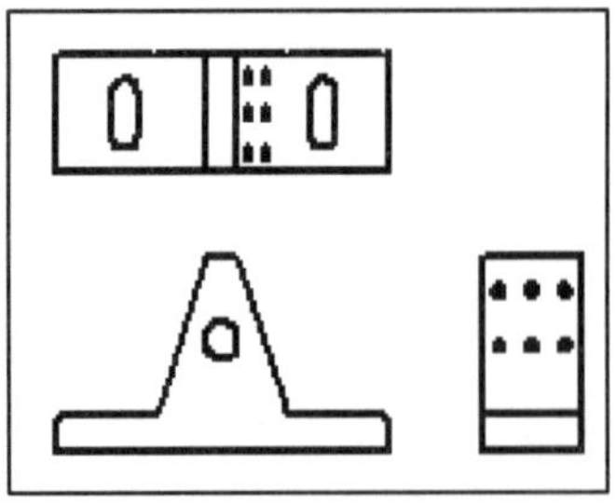
Third Angle Projection

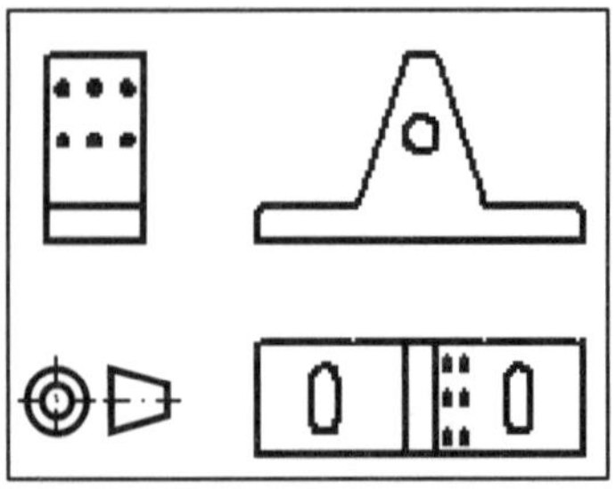
First Angle Projection

For non-ANSI dimension standards, the dimensioning techniques are the same, even if the displayed arrows and text size are different. For printers supporting millimeter paper sizes, select A4-Landscape (297mm × 210mm).

The default Drawing Templates contain predefined Title block Notes linked to Custom Properties and SolidWorks Properties.

Activity: New Drawing

Create a new drawing. Close all parts and drawings.

1) Click **Windows**, **Close All** from the Main menu.

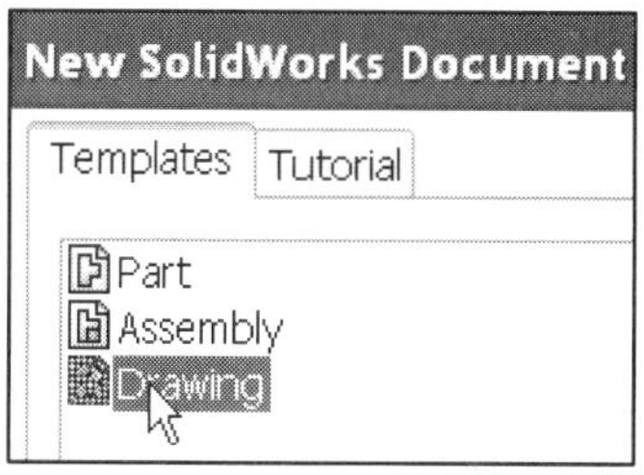

2) Click **File**, **New** from the Main menu.

3) Double-click **Drawing** from the Templates tab.

4) Select **A-Landscape**.

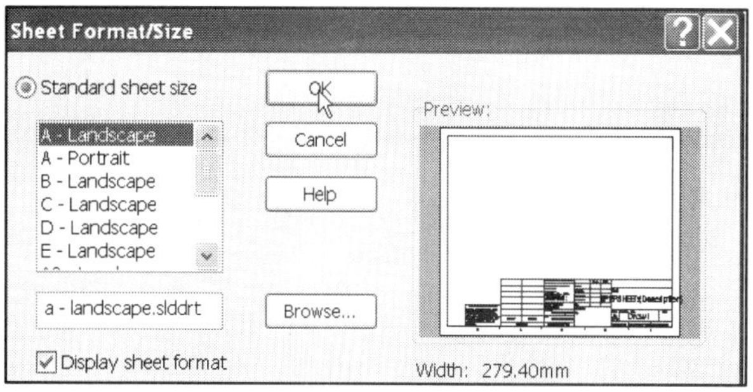

5) Click **OK** from the Sheet Format/Size box.

6) If required, click **Cancel** from the Model View PropertyManager. The Draw FeatureManager is displayed.

A New Drawing invokes the Model View option if the Start Command When Creating New Drawing option is checked.

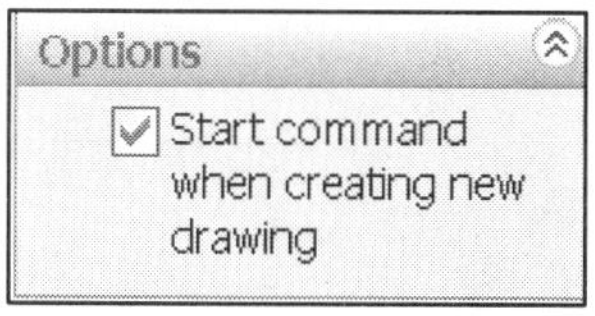

The A-Landscape paper is displayed in a new Graphics window. The sheet border defines the drawing size, 11″ × 8.5″ or (279.4mm × 215.9mm).

The Drawing toolbar is displayed in the CommandManager.

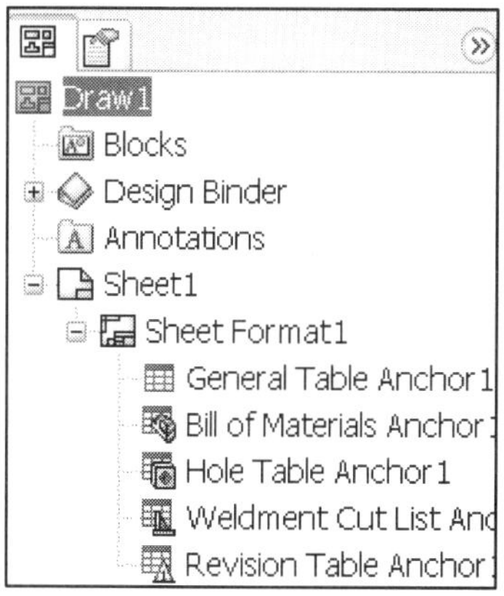

Draw1 is the default drawing name. Sheet1 is the default first sheet name. The Control Area alternates between the Drawings, Sketch, and Annotations toolbars. The Model View PropertyManager is selected by default.

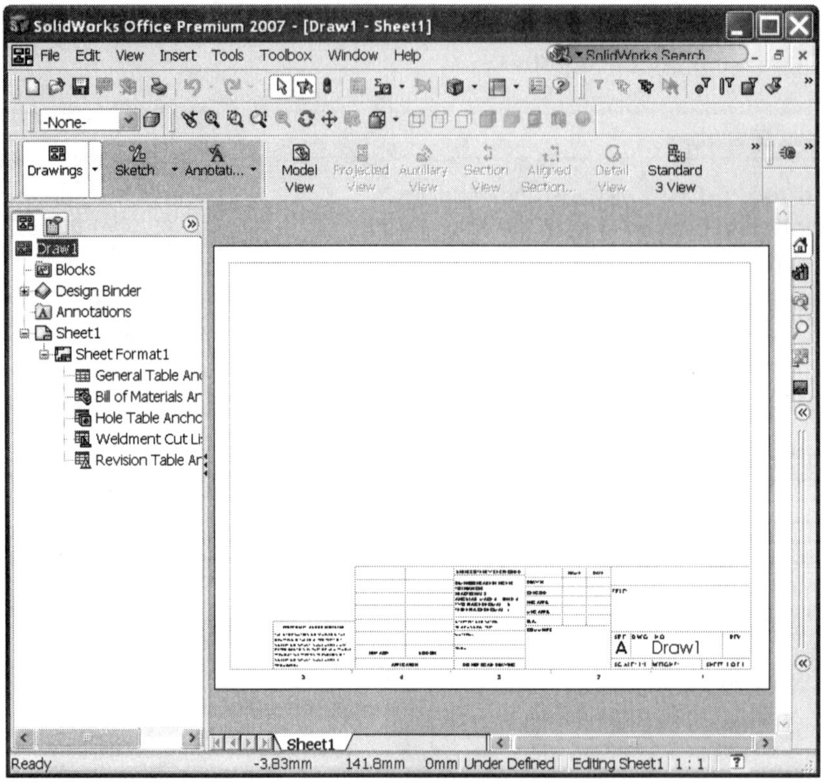

Right-click in the gray area and check the Drawing, Annotation, Sketch, or Dimension/Relations toolbar to display each toolbar. Drag individual toolbars to the borders of the Graphics window. Utilize the CommandManager or individual toolbars.

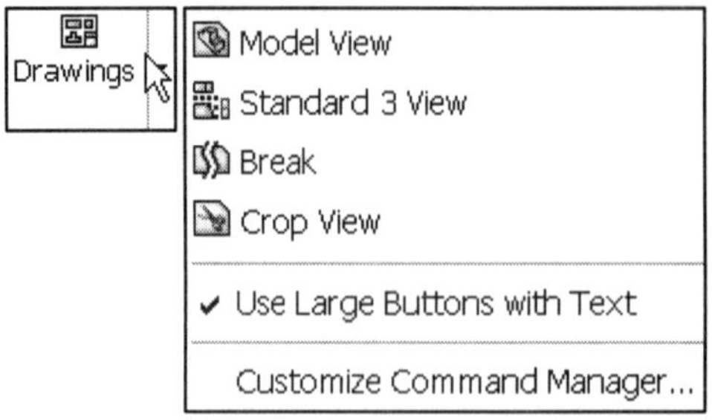

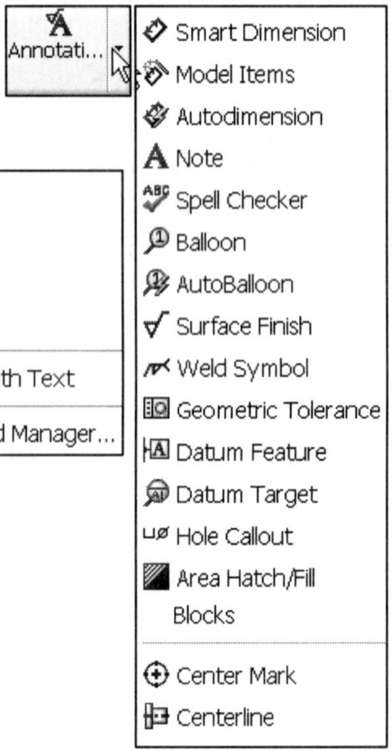

Set the Sheet Properties.

7) Right-click in the **Graphics window**.

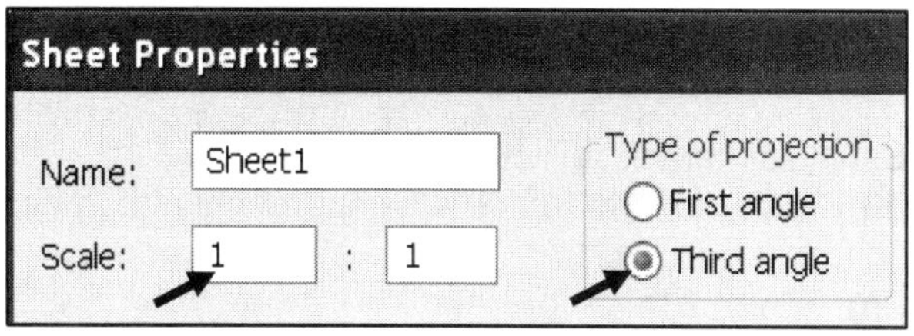

8) Click **Properties**. The Sheet Properties are displayed.

9) Select Sheet Scale **1:1**.

10) Select **Third Angle** for Type of projection.

11) Click **OK** from the Sheet Properties dialog box.

Activity: Drawing-Document Properties

Set Document Properties.

12) Click **Tools**, **Options**, **Document Properties** tab from the Main menu.

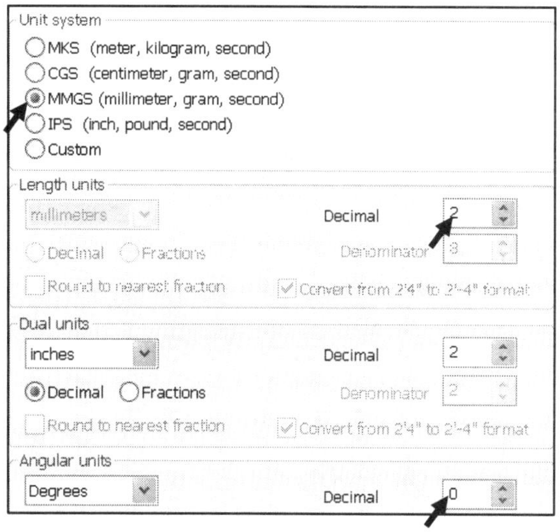

13) Select **ANSI** for Dimensioning standard.

14) Click **Units**. Select **MMGS** for Unit system.

15) Enter **2** for Length units Decimal places.

16) Enter **0** for Angular units Decimal places.

Detailing options provide the ability to address: dimensioning standards, text style, center marks, extension lines, arrow styles, tolerance, and precision.

There are numerous text styles and sizes available in SolidWorks. Companies develop drawing format standards and use specific text height for Metric and English drawings. Numerous engineering drawings use the following format:

- Font: Century Gothic – All capitals.
- Text height: 3mm for drawings up to B Size, 17in. × 22in.
- Text height: 5mm for drawings larger than B Size, 17in × 22in.
- Arrow heads: Solid filled with a 1:3 ratio of arrow width to arrow height.

Set the dimension Font.

17) Click **Annotations Font**.

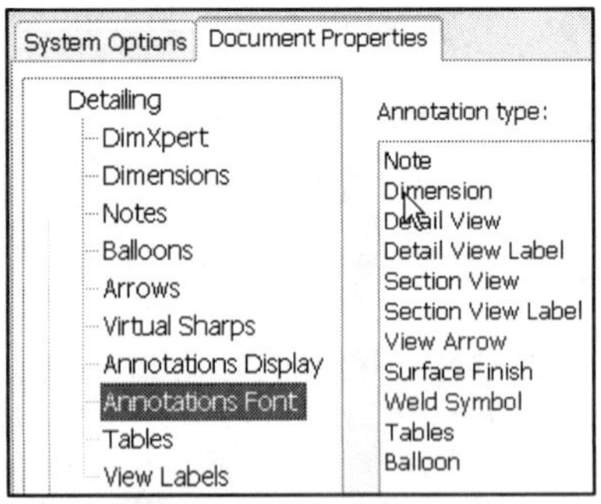

18) Click **Dimension** for Annotation type.

Set the dimension text height.

19) Check **Units** from the Choose Font dialog box.

20) Enter **3.0**mm for Height.

21) Click **OK** from the Choose Font dialog box.

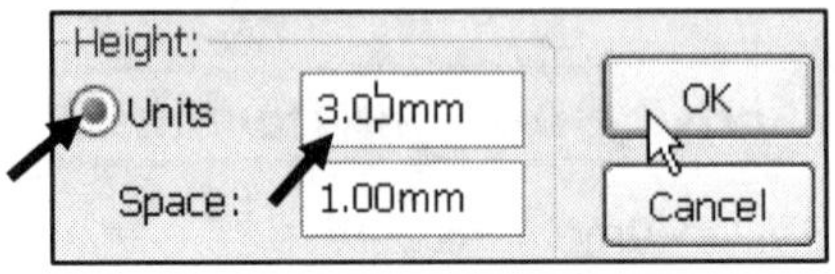

Set the Arrow size.

22) Click **Arrows** on the left side, below the Detailing entry. The Detailing - Arrows dialog box is displayed.

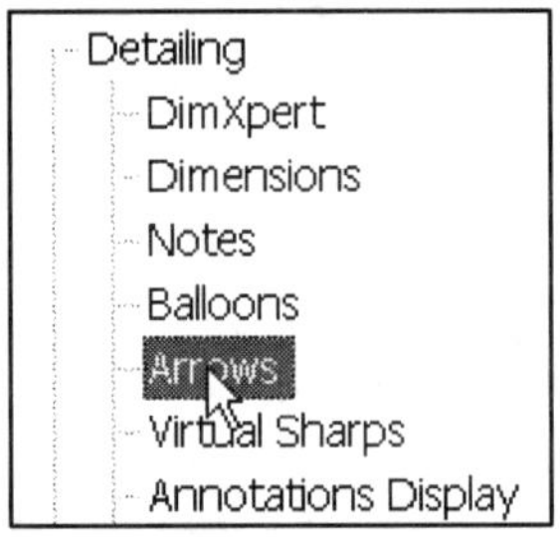

23) Enter **1**mm for arrow Height.

24) Enter **3**mm for arrow Width.

25) Enter **6**mm for arrow Length.

Set Section/View size.

26) Enter **2**mm for arrow Height.

27) Enter **6**mm for arrow Width.

28) Enter **12**mm for arrow Length.

29) Click **OK** from the Document Properties dialog box.

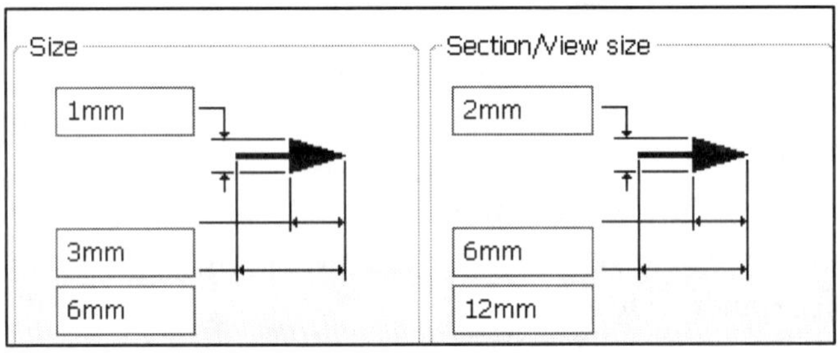

Title Block

The Title block contains text fields linked to System Properties and Custom Properties. System Properties are determined from the SolidWorks documents. Custom Property values are assigned to named variables.

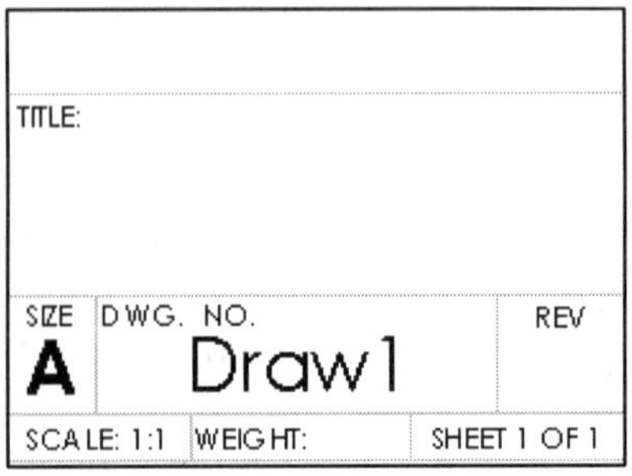

Save time. Utilize System Properties and define Custom Properties in your Sheet Formats.

System Properties Linked to fields in default Sheet Formats:	**Custom Properties of drawings linked to fields in default Sheet Formats:**		**Custom Properties of parts and assemblies linked to fields in default Sheet Formats:**
SW-File Name (in DWG. NO. field):	CompanyName:	EngineeringApproval:	Description (in TITLE field):
SW-Sheet Scale:	CheckedBy:	EngAppDate:	Weight:
SW-Current Sheet:	CheckedDate:	ManufacturingApproval:	Material:
SW-Total Sheets:	DrawnBy:	MfgAppDate:	Finish:
	DrawnDate:	QAApproval:	Revision:
	EngineeringApproval:	QAAppDate:	

The Title block is located in the lower right hand corner of Sheet1.

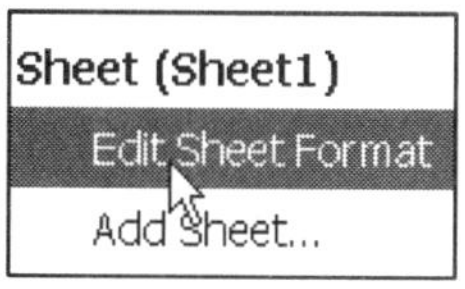

The Drawing contains two modes:

1. Edit Sheet Format.

2. Edit Sheet.

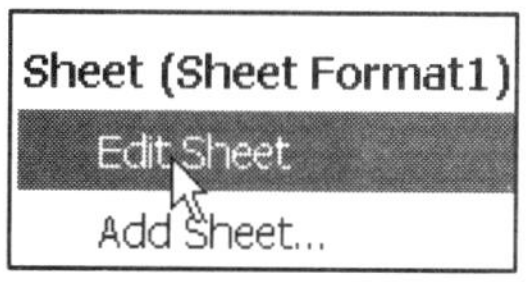

Insert views and dimensions in the Edit Sheet mode. Modify the Sheet Format text, lines or title block information in the Edit Sheet Format mode.

The CompanyName Custom Property is located in the title block above the TITLE box. There is no value defined for CompanyName. A small text box indicates an empty field.

Define a value for the Custom Property CompanyName. Example: D&M ENGINEERING.

Activity: Title Box

Activate the Edit Sheet Format Mode.

30) Right-click in the **Graphics window**.

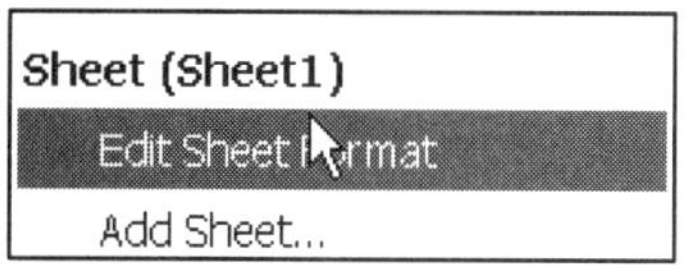

31) Click **Edit Sheet Format**. The Title block lines turn blue.

View the right side of the Title block.

32) Click **Zoom to Area** on the Title block.

33) Click **Zoom to Area** to deactivate.

Define CompanyName Custom Property.

34) Position the **mouse pointer** in the middle of the box above the TITLE box as illustrated.

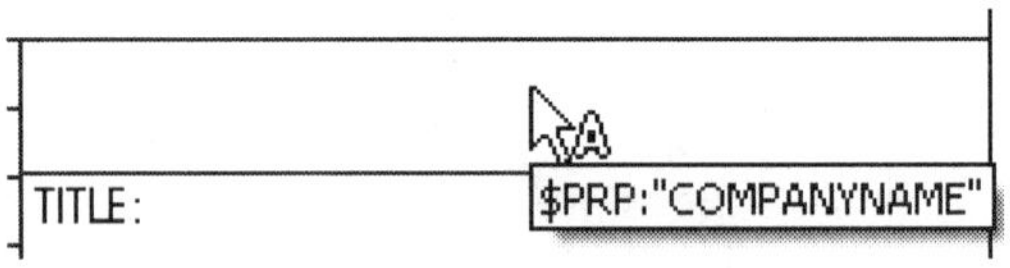

35) Click **File**, **Properties** from the Main menu.

36) Click the **Custom** tab.

37) Click inside the **Property Name box**.

38) Click the **drop down arrow** in the Property Name box.

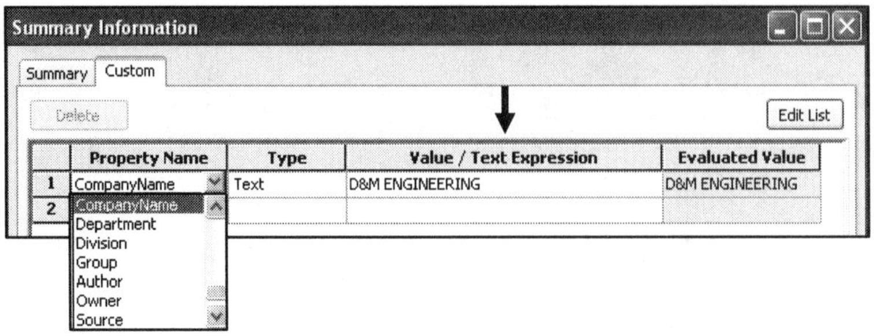

39) Select **CompanyName** from the Property List.

40) Enter **D&M ENGINEERING** (or your company name) in the Value/Text Expression box.

41) Click inside the **Evaluated Value** box. The CompanyName is displayed in the Evaluated Value box. Click **OK**. Move the **mouse pointer** in the center of the block as illustrated. The Custom Property, $PRP: "COMPANYNAME", is displayed in the Title block.

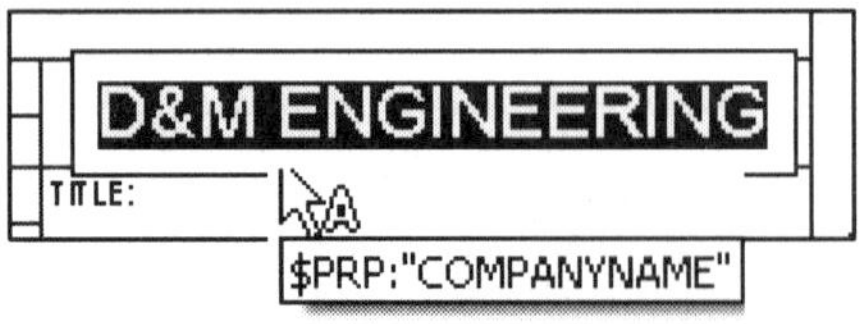

Change the font size.

42) Double-click the **D&M ENGINEERING** text. Click the **drop down arrows** to set the Text Font and Height from the Formatting toolbar.

43) Click the **Style buttons** and **Justification buttons** to modify the selected text.

44) Click **Close** from the Formatting dialog box.

45) Click **OK** from the Note PropertyManager.

Shortcut: Click a position outside the selected text box to save and exit the text.

The Tolerance block is located in the Title block. The Tolerance block provides information to the manufacturer on the minimum and maximum variation for each dimension on the drawing. If a specific tolerance or note is provided on the drawing, the specific tolerance or note will override the information in the Tolerance block.

General tolerance values are based on the design requirements and the manufacturing process.

Create Sheet Formats for different parts types; examples: sheet metal parts, plastic parts, and high precision machined parts. Create Sheet Formats for each category of parts that are manufactured with unique sets of Title block notes.

Modify the Tolerance block in the Sheet Format for ASME Y14.5 machined, millimeter parts. Delete unnecessary text. The FRACTIONAL text refers to inches. The BEND text refers to sheet metal parts. The Three Decimal Place text is not required for this millimeter part.

Modify the Tolerance Note.

46) Click and drag the **horizontal slider bar** to the left until the Tolerance block is displayed.

47) Double-click the text **INTERPRET GEOMETRIC TOLERANCING PER:**

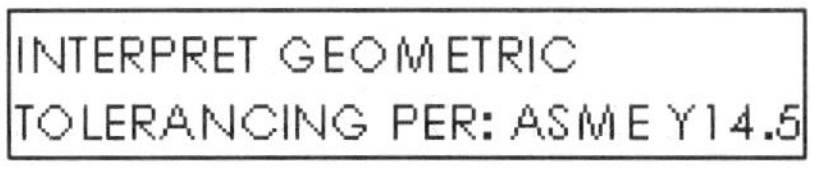

48) Enter **ASME Y14.5**.

49) Click **OK** from the Note PropertyManager.

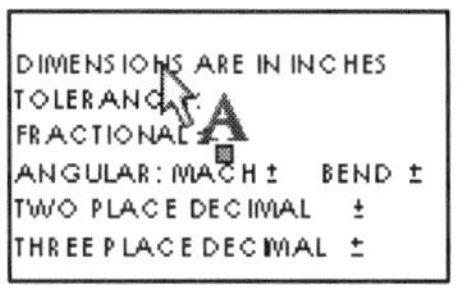

50) Right-click inside the **Tolerance block** text.

51) Click **Properties**. The Properties dialog box is displayed.

52) Delete the text **INCHES**.

53) Enter **MILLIMETERS**.

54) Delete the line **FRACTIONAL <MOD-PM>**.

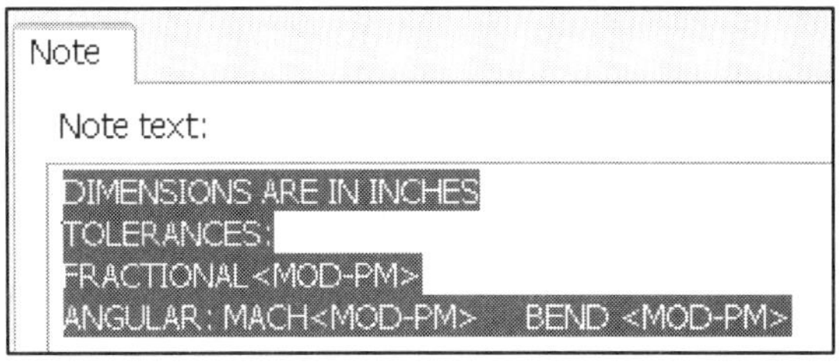

55) Delete the text **BEND <MOD-PM>**.

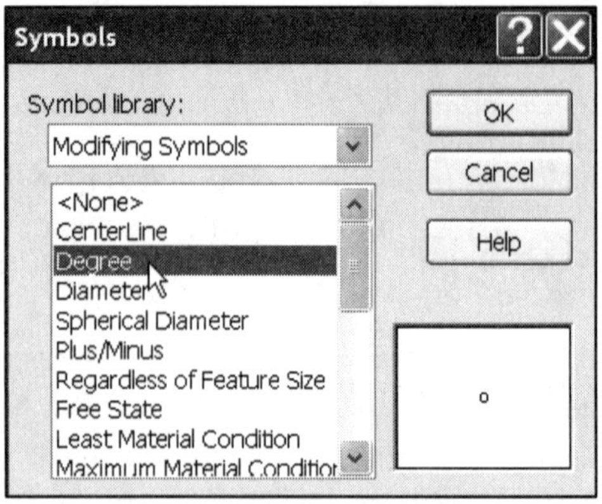

56) Click a **position** at the end of the ANGULAR: MACH<MOD-PM> line.

57) Enter **0**. Click the **Add Symbol** button.

58) Select **Degree** from the Symbols dialog box.

59) Click **OK**. Enter **30'** for minutes of a degree.

Modify the TWO and THREE PLACE DECIMAL LINES.

60) Delete the **TWO** and **THREE PLACE DECIMAL lines**.

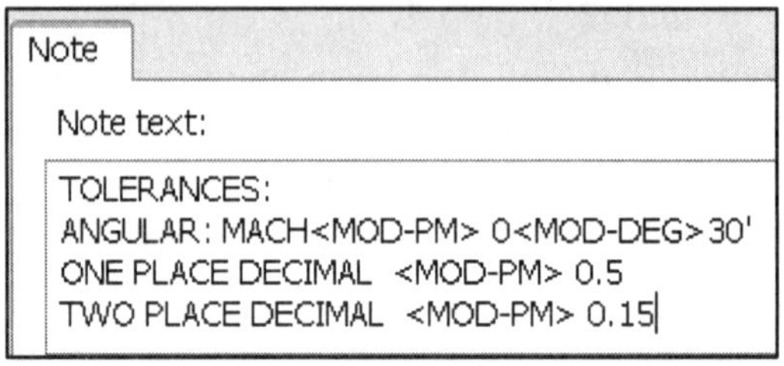

61) Enter **ONE PLACE DECIMAL <MOD-PM> 0.5.**

62) Enter **TWO PLACE DECIMAL <MOD-PM> 0.15**.

63) Click **OK** from the Properties dialog box.

64) Click **OK** from the Note PropertyManager.

Fit the Drawing to the Graphics window.

65) Press the **f** key.

Save Draw1.

66) Click **Save**. Accept the default name.

67) Click **Save** from the Save As box.

Note: Draw1 is the default drawing file name. This name is temporary. In the next activity, invoke Microsoft Word. Always save before selecting another software application.

Various symbols are available through the Symbol button in the Text dialog box. The ± symbol is located in the Modify Symbols list. The ± symbol is displayed as <MOD-PM>. The degree symbol ° is displayed as <MOD-DEG>.

Interpretation of tolerances is as follows:

- The angular dimension 110° is machined between 109.5° and 110.5°.
- The dimension 2.5 is machined between 2.0 and 3.0.
- The dimension 2.05 is machined between 1.90 and 2.20.

Company Logo

A Company logo is normally located in the Title block. Create a Company logo. Copy a picture file from Microsoft ClipArt using Microsoft Word. Paste the logo into the SolidWorks drawing. Note: The following logo example was created in Microsoft Word XP using the COMPASS.wmf. You can utilize any ClipArt picture, scanned image, or bitmap for a logo in this activity. Note: The following procedure uses MS Office 2003.

Activity: Drawing Logo

Create a New Microsoft Word Document.

68) Click **Start** from the Microsoft desktop.

69) Click **All Programs**.

70) Click **Microsoft Office Word 2003**.

71) Click **File**, **New** from the Standard toolbar in MS Word.

72) Click **Insert, Picture, ClipArt** from the Main menu. The Insert Clip Art menu is displayed.

73) In the Search text enter **compass**. Note: Enter any name for Clip Art to Search For. If you do not have the Clip Art loaded on your system, click **Clips Online** to obtain additional Clip Art. Follow the provided directions to select and download.

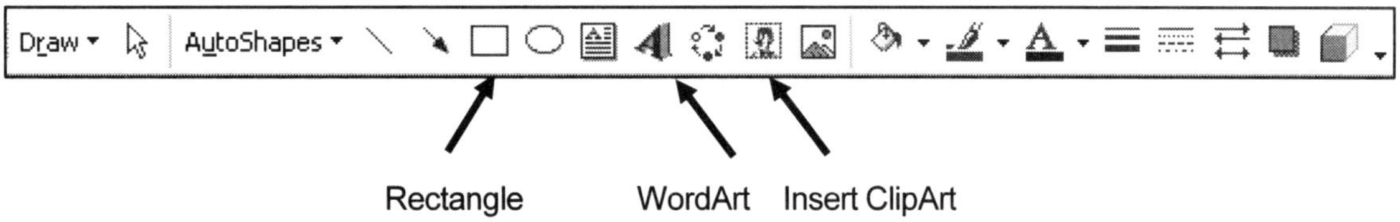

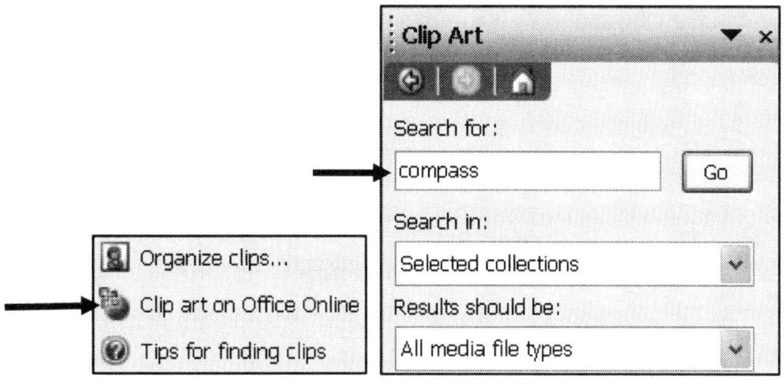

Locate the picture file.

74) Click **Go**. Locate the **Compass.wmf** file. **Double-click** the file. The picture is displayed in the Word document.

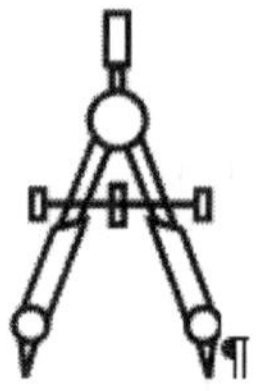

Redefine the picture layout.

75) Click the **picture**.

76) Right-click **Format Picture**. The Format Picture dialog box is displayed.

Display the drag handles.

77) Click the **Layout** tab. Click **Square**.

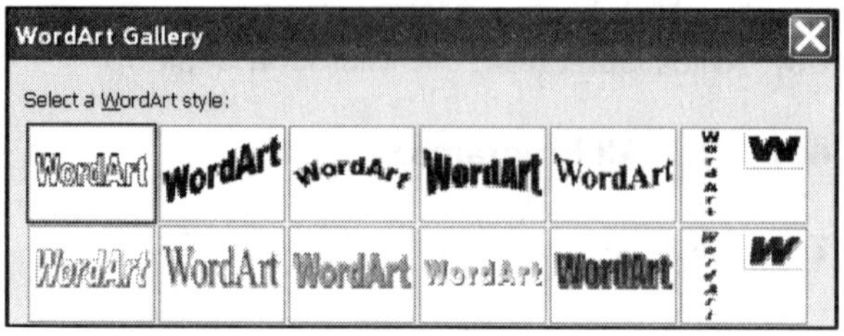

78) Click **OK** from the Format Picture dialog box.

Add text to the logo picture.

79) Click the **picture**. Click **Insert WordArt** from the Draw toolbar. The Word Art Gallery dialog box is displayed.

80) Click a **WordArt** style. Click **OK**.

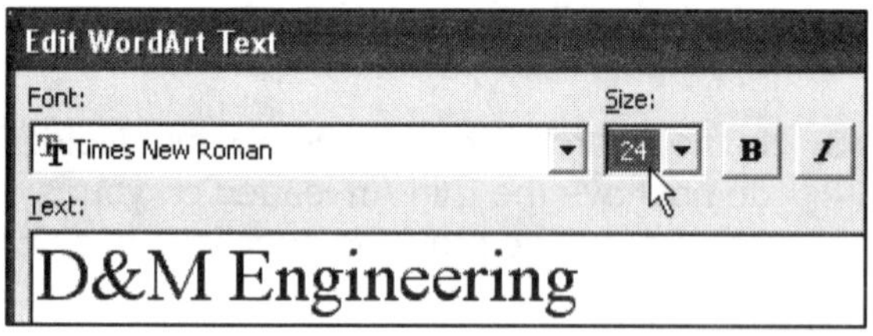

81) Enter **D&M Engineering** in the text box.

82) Click **24** from the Size drop down list.

83) Click **OK** from the Edit WordArt Text dialog box.

84) Click the **Word Art text**. A Word Art toolbar is displayed.

85) Click **Text Wrapping**. Click **Square**.

86) Click and drag the **Word Art text** under the Compass picture.

87) Size the **Word Art text** by dragging the picture handles.

Group the Word Art text and the picture to create the logo.

88) Click on the **Word Art text**. Hold the **Ctrl** key down.

89) Click the **compass** picture. Release the **Ctrl** key. Right-click and select **Grouping**.

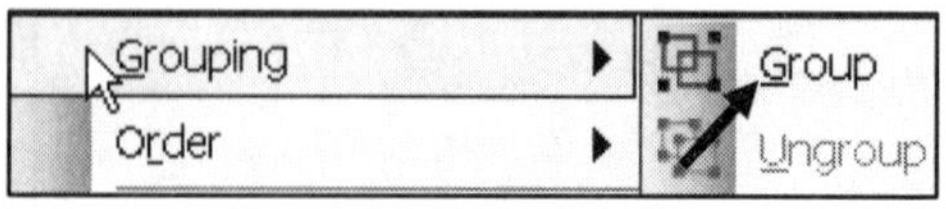

90) Click **Group**. The Word Art text and the picture are grouped. The logo is created.

Copy the new logo.

91) Click **Copy** from the Standards toolbar.

92) The logo is placed into the Clipboard. **Minimize** the Microsoft Word Graphics window.

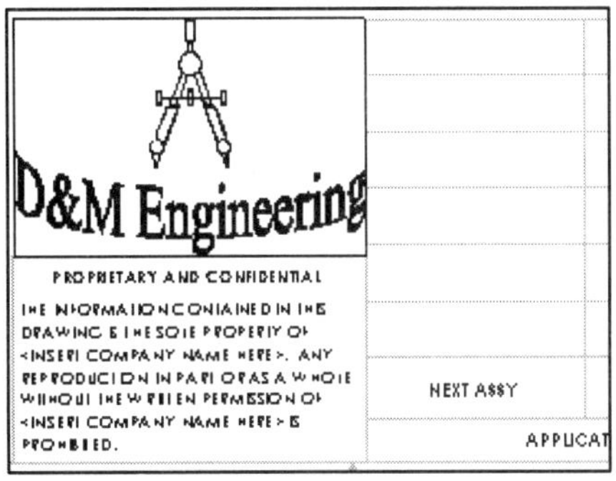

Return to the SolidWorks Title block.

93) Click a **position** on the left side of the Title block in the SolidWorks Graphics window. **Zoom out** if required.

Paste the logo.

94) Click **Edit**, **Paste** from the Main menu.

95) **Move** and **Size** the logo to the SolidWorks Title block by dragging the picture handles.

Return to Edit Sheet mode.

96) Right-click in the **Graphics window**.

97) Click **Edit Sheet**. The Title block is displayed in black/gray.

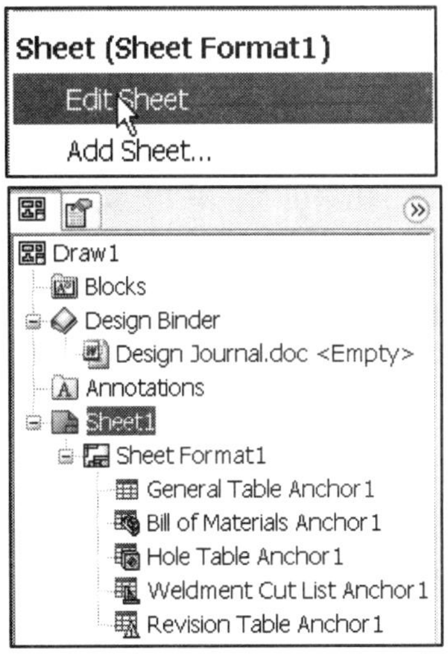

Fit the Sheet Format to the Graphics window.

98) Press the **f** key.

Draw1 displays Editing Sheet1 in the Status bar. The Title block is displayed in black when in Edit Sheet mode.

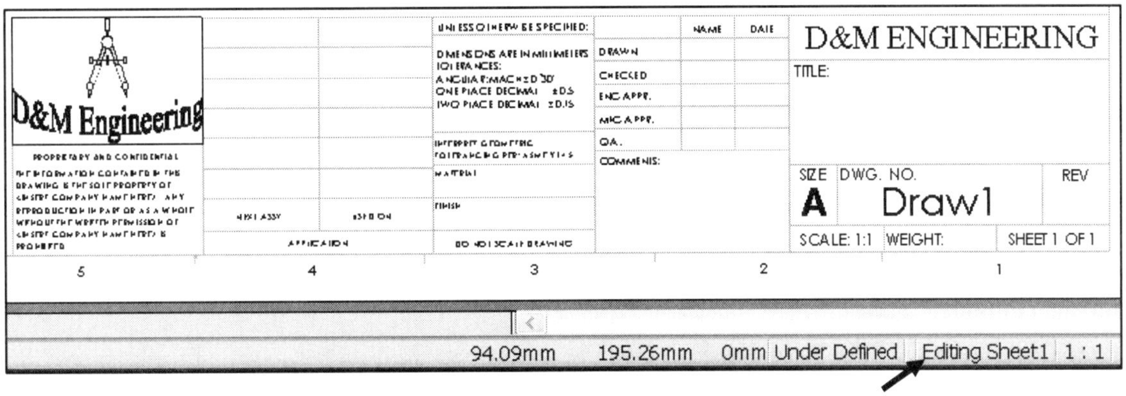

Save Sheet Format and Save As Drawing Template

Save the drawing document in the Graphics window in two forms: Sheet Format and Drawing Template. Save the Sheet Format as a custom Sheet Format named CUSTOM-A. Use the CUSTOM-A Sheet Format for the drawings in this project. The Sheet format file extension is .slddrt.

The Drawing Template can be displayed with or without the Sheet Format. Combine the Sheet Format with the Drawing Template to create a custom Drawing Template named A-ANSI-MM. Utilize the File, Save As option to save a Drawing Template. The Drawing Template file extension is .drwdot.

Always select the Save as type option first, then select the Save in folder to avoid saving in default SolidWorks installation directories.

The System Options, File Locations, Document Templates option is only valid for the current session of SolidWorks in some network locations. Set the File Locations option in order to view the MY-TEMPLATES tab in the New Document dialog box.

Activity: Save Sheet Format and Save As Drawing Template

Save the Sheet Format.

99) Click **File**, **Save Sheet Format** from the Main menu. The Save Sheet Format dialog box appears.

100) Click **drop down arrow** from the Save Sheet Format dialog box.

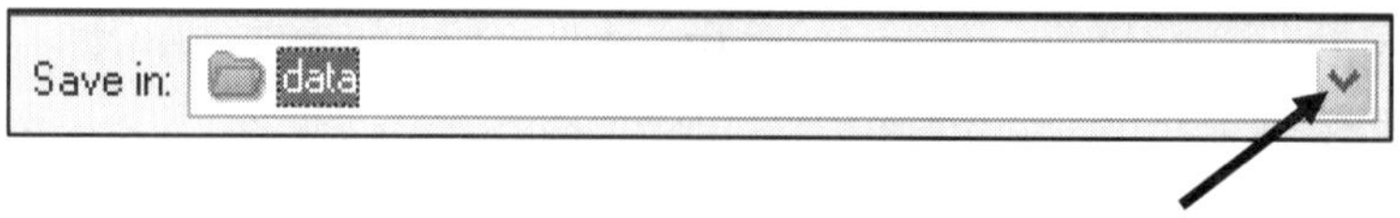

The default Sheet Format folder is called data. Do not select the data folder. The file extension for Sheet Format is .slddrt.

101) Select **SW-TUTORIAL-2007** for the Save in folder.

102) Enter **CUSTOM-A** for File name.

103) Click **Save** from the Save Sheet Format dialog box.

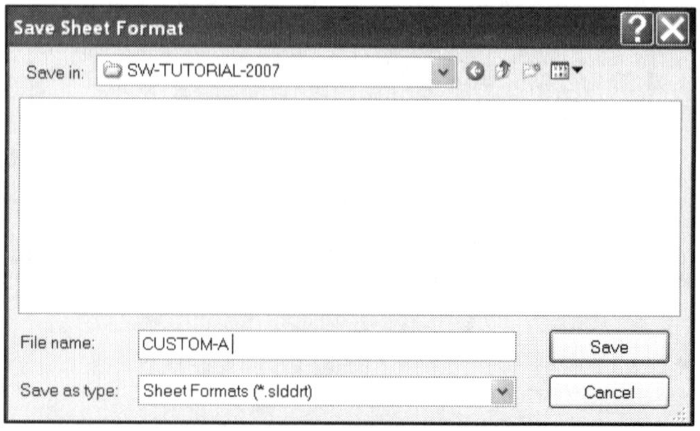

Save the Drawing Template.

104) Click **File**, **Save As** from the Main menu. Click **Drawing Templates (*.drwdot)** from the Save as type box.

105) Select **SW-TUTORIAL-2007** for the Save in folder.

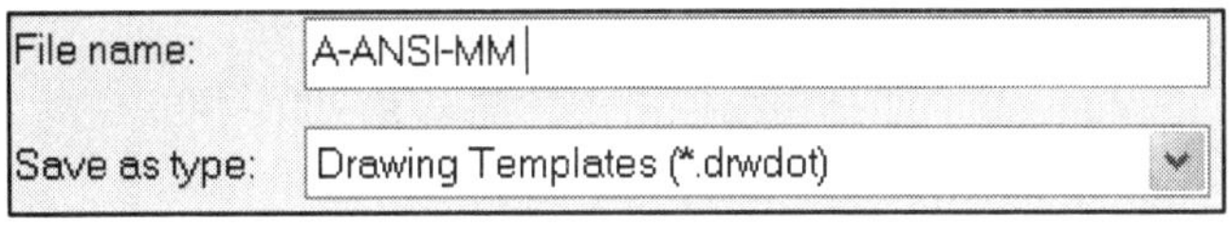

106) Enter **A-ANSI-MM** for File name.

107) Click **Save**.

108) Click **Rebuild** from the Standard menu.

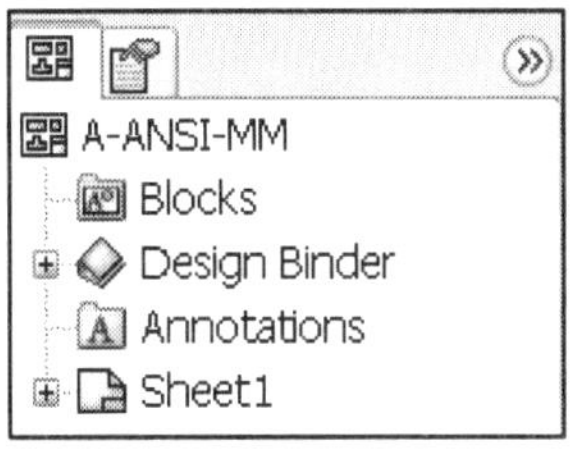

The A-ANSI-MM.drwdot drawing template is displayed in the Graphics window. Add the SW-TUTORIAL-2007 folder to the File Locations Document Template System Option.

Set System Options - File Locations.

109) Click **Tools**, **Options**, **File Locations** from the Main menu.

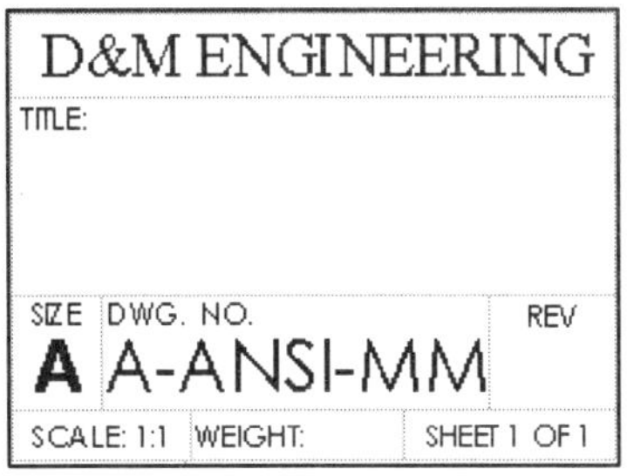

110) Click **Add**.

111) Select the **SW-TUTORIAL-2007** folder.

112) Click **OK** from the Browse for Folder menu.

113) Click **OK** to exit System Options.

Close all files.

114) Click **Windows**, **Close All** from the Main menu.

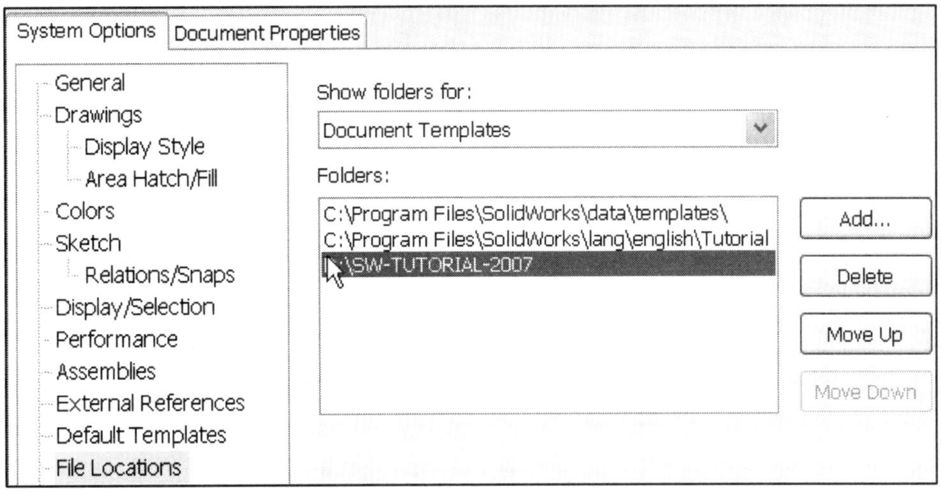

Open a new Drawing.

115) Click **File**, **New** from the Main menu.

116) Select the **SW-TUTORIAL-2007** tab.

117) Double-click the **A-ANSI-MM** Drawing Template.

118) If required, click **Cancel** from the Model View PropertyManager. Draw2 is displayed in the Graphics window.

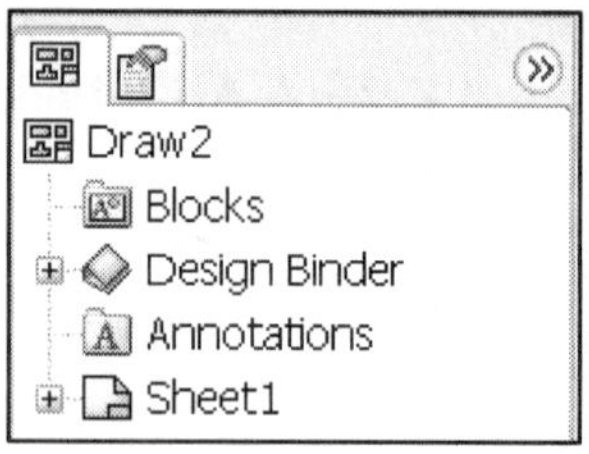

Close all files.

119) Click **Windows**, **Close All** from the Main menu.

The Draw2-Sheet1 drawing is displayed in the Graphics window. You have successfully created a new drawing Template with a Custom sheet format.

Combine customize Drawing Templates and Sheet Formats to match your company's drawing standards. Save the empty Drawing Template and Sheet Format separately to reuse information.

Additional details on Drawing Templates, Sheet Format and Custom Properties are available in SolidWorks Help Topics. Keywords: Documents (templates, properties) Sheet Formats (new, new drawings, note text), Properties (drawing sheets), Customize Drawing Sheet Formats.

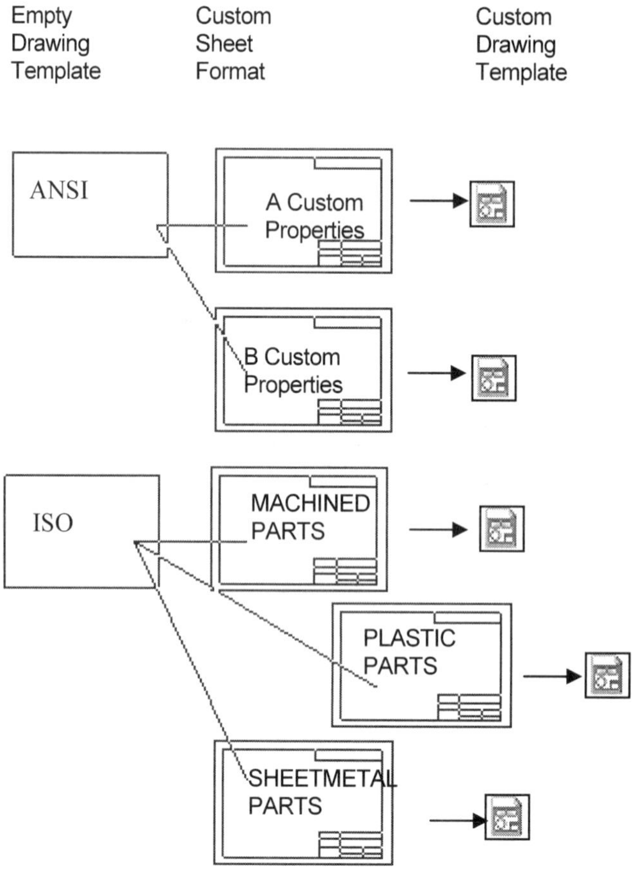

Review Drawing Templates.

The Custom Drawing Template was created from the default Drawing Template. You modified Sheet Properties and Document Properties to control the Sheet size, Scale, Annotations and Dimensions.

The Sheet Format contained a Title block and Custom Property information. You inserted a Company Logo and modified the Title block.

The Save Sheet Format option was utilized to save the CUSTOM-A.slddrt Sheet Format. The File, Save As option was utilized to save the A-ANSI-MM.drwdot Template.

The Sheet Format and Drawing Template were saved in the SW-TUTORIAL-2007 folder.

FLATBAR Drawing

A drawing contains part views, geometric dimensioning and tolerances, notes and other related design information. When a part is modified, the drawing automatically updates. When a dimension in the drawing is modified, the part is automatically updated.

Create the FLATBAR drawing from the FLATBAR part. Display the Front, Top, Right, and Isometric views. Utilize the Model View command in the Drawings toolbar.

Insert dimensions from the part. Utilize Insert Model Items from the Annotation toolbar. Insert and modify dimensions and notes.

Insert a Parametric note that links the dimension text to part depth. Utilize a user defined Part Number. Define the part material with the Material Editor. Add Custom Properties for Material and Number.

Activity: FLATBAR Drawing-Open the FLATBAR Part

Open the FLATBAR part.

120) Click **File**, **Open** from the Main menu.

121) Select the **SW-TUTORIAL-2007** folder.

122) Select **Part** for Files of type.

123) Double-click **FLATBAR**. The FLATBAR FeatureManager is displayed.

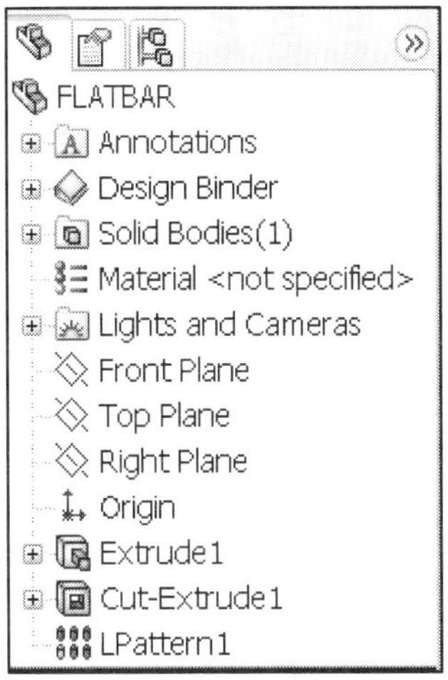

Create a new drawing.

124) Click **File**, **New** from the Main menu.

125) Select the **SW-TUTORIAL-2007** tab.

126) Double-click **A-ANSI-MM**.

The Model View PropertyManager is displayed if the Start command when creating new drawing box is check. The FLATBAR part icon is displayed in the Open documents box. Drawing view names are based on the part view orientation. The Front view is the first view inserted into the drawing. The Top view and Right view are projected from the Front view.

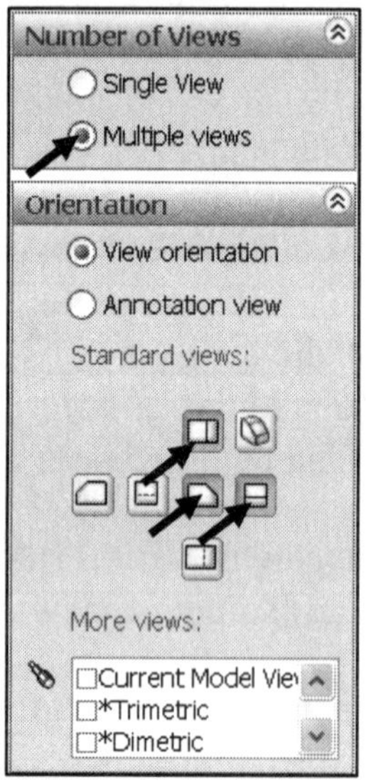

Insert the Front, Top, and Right view.

127) Click **Next** from the Model View PropertyManager.

128) Click **Multiple views**. Click **View orientation**.

129) Click ***Front**, ***Top** and ***Right** view. Note: If the *Isometric view is highlighted, deactivate.

130) Click **OK** from the Model View PropertyManager. The three views are displayed on Sheet1

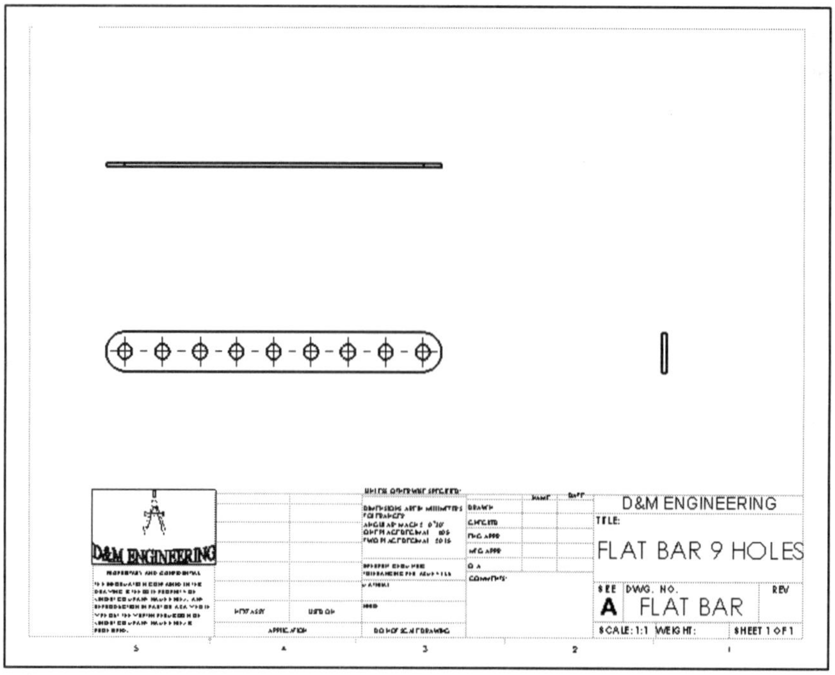

Note: A part cannot be inserted into a drawing when the Edit Sheet Format is selected. You are required to be in the Edit Sheet mode.

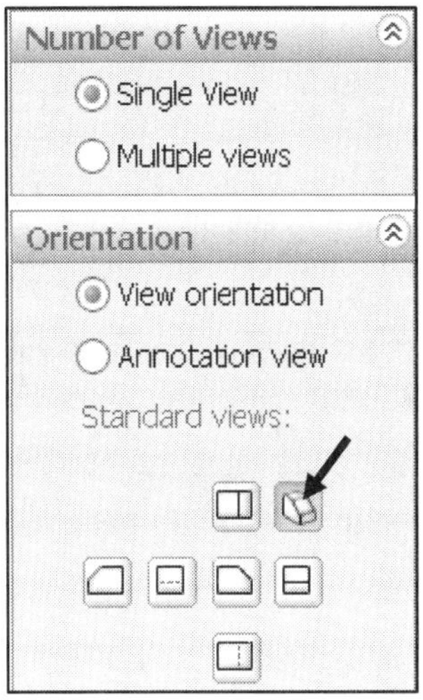

Insert an Isometric view.

131) Click **Model View** Model View from the Drawings toolbar.

132) Click **Next**.

133) Click **Single View**. View orientation is selected by default. *Isometric view is selected by default. The Isometric view is placed on the mouse pointer. Click a **position** in the upper right corner of Sheet1.

134) Click **OK** from the Drawing View4 PropertyManager.

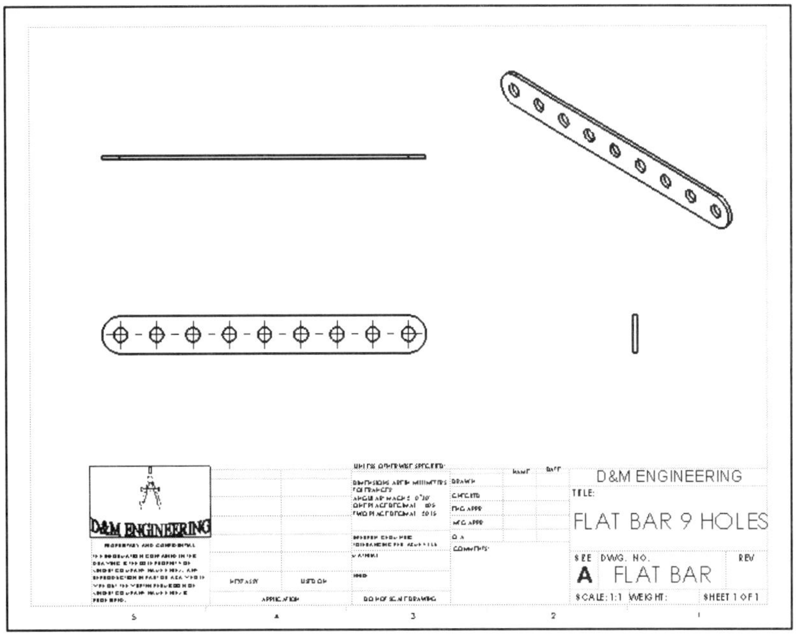

The View Palette is new for 2007. Click the View Palette icon in the Task Pane. Click the drop down arrow to view an open part or click the Browse button to locate a part. Click and drag the desired view/views into the active drawing sheet.

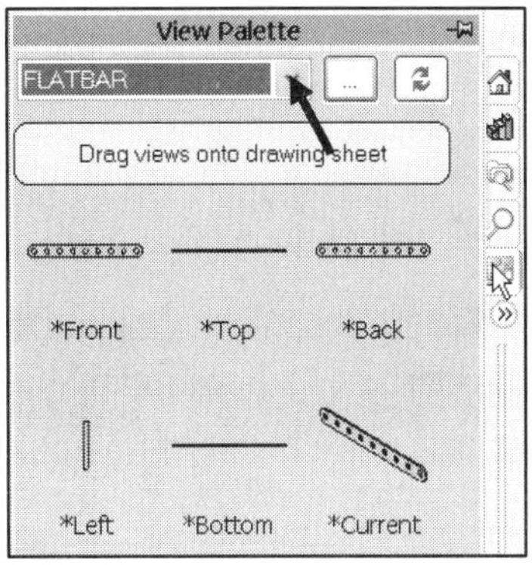

Modify the Sheet Scale.

135) Right-click a **position** inside the Sheet1 boundary.

136) Click **Properties** Properties... .

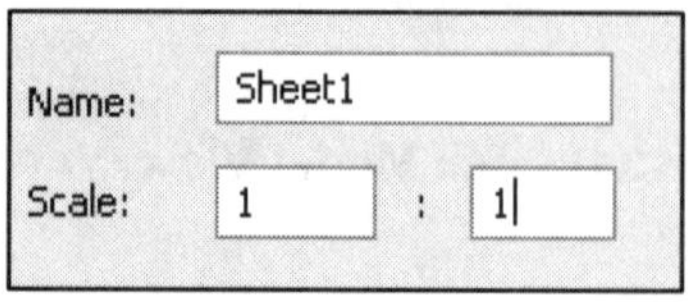

137) Enter **1:1** for Sheet Scale. Click **OK** from the Sheet Properties dialog box.

Hide the Origins.

138) If required, click **View**; uncheck **Origins** from the Main menu.

Save the Drawing.

139) Click **File**, **Save As** from the Main menu.

140) Enter **FLATBAR** in the SW-TUTORIAL-2007 folder. Click **Save**.

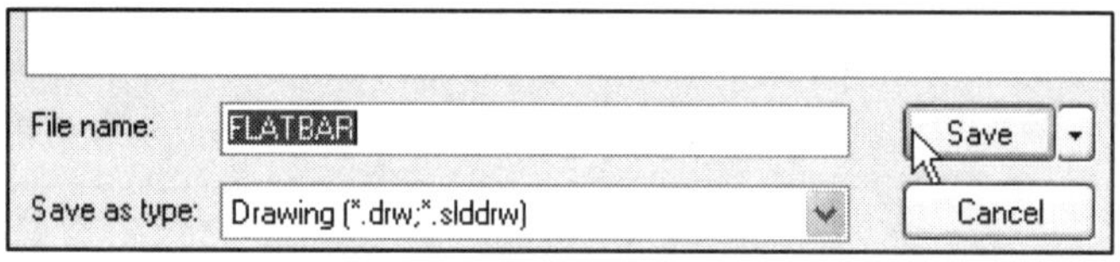

141) Click **Rebuild** from the Standard menu.

142) Click **Save** .

Text in the Title block is linked to the Filename and Description created in the part. The DWG. NO. text box utilizes the Property, $PRP:"SW-File Name" passed from the FLATBAR part to the FLATBAR drawing. The Title text box utilizes the Property, $PRPSHEET: "Description".

The filename FLATBAR is displayed in the DWG. NO. box. The Description FLATBAR 9 HOLE is displayed in the Title box. The FLATBAR drawing contains three Principle Views (Standard Views): Front, Top, Right, and an Isometric View. You created the views with the Model View option. Drawing views are inserted as follows:

- Utilize the Model View option.
- Click and drag a part into the drawing or select the Standard 3 Views option.
- Predefine views in a custom Drawing Template.

The mouse pointer provides feedback in both the Drawing Sheet and Drawing View modes. The mouse pointer displays the Drawing Sheet icon when the Sheet properties and commands are executed.

The mouse pointer displays the Drawing View icon when the View properties and commands are executed.

View the mouse pointer for feedback to select Sheet, View, Component and Edge properties in the Drawing.

- Sheet Properties display properties of the selected sheet.

  Right-click in the sheet boundary.

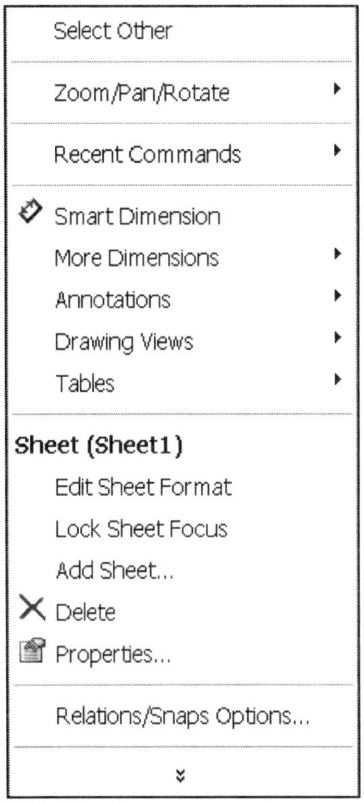

- View Properties display properties of the selected view. Right-click on the view boundary.

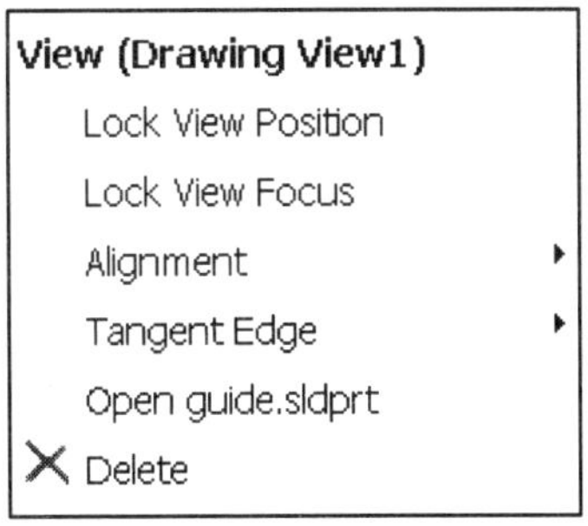

- Component Properties display properties of the selected component. Right-click on the face of the component.

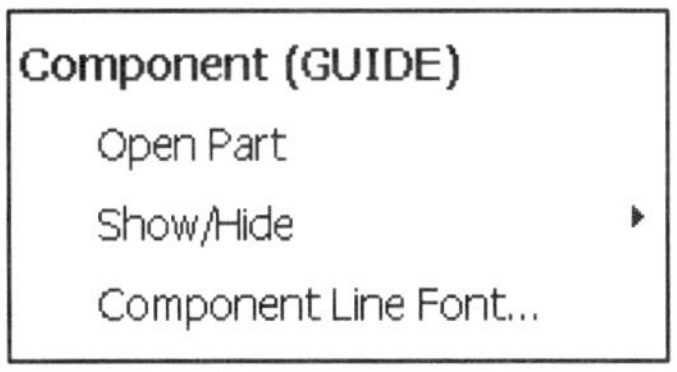

- Edge Properties display properties of the geometry.

  Right-click on an edge.

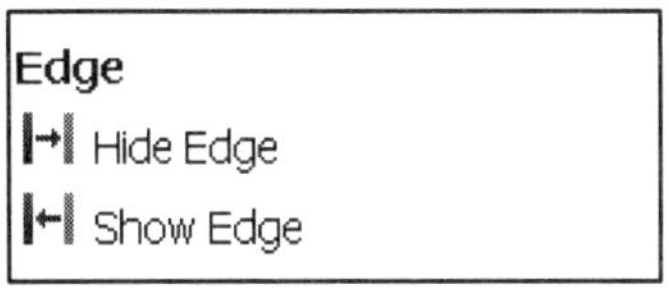

The Drawing views are complete. Move the views to allow for ample spacing for the dimensions and notes. Zoom In on narrow view boundary boxes if required.

Move Views

Reposition the view on a drawing. Provide approximately 25mm - 50mm between each view for dimension placement.

Activity: FLATBAR Drawing-Position Views

Position the views.

143) Click inside the view boundary of **Drawing View1** (Front). The mouse pointer displays the Drawing View icon.

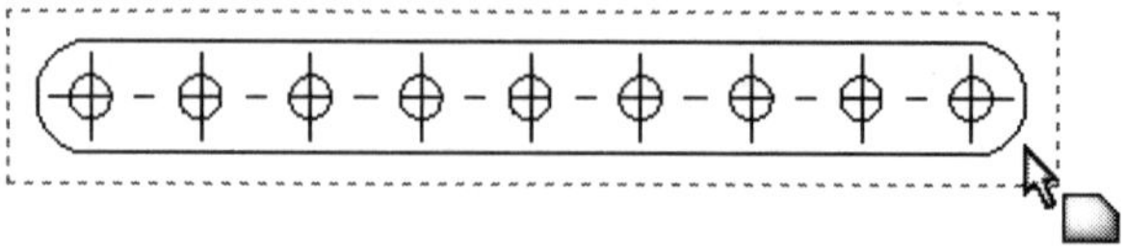

144) Position the **mouse pointer** on the edge of the view boundary until the Drawing View icon is displayed.

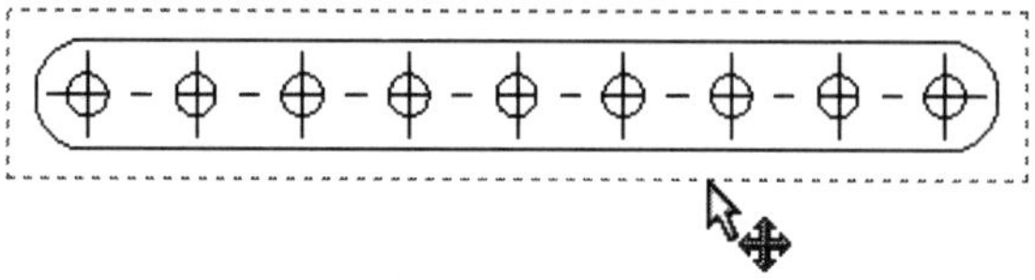

145) Drag **Drawing View1** in an upward vertical direction. The Top and Right views move aligned to Drawing View1 (Front).

146) Press **Shift + Z** key to Zoom in on Sheet1.

147) Move the **Right view** in a right to left direction.

148) Click the **Right view** boundary.

149) Position the **mouse pointer** on the edge of the view until the Drawing Move View icon is displayed.

150) Drag the **Right view** in a right to left direction towards the Front view.

Move the Top view in a downward vertical direction.

151) Click the **Top view**, "Drawing View3" boundary.

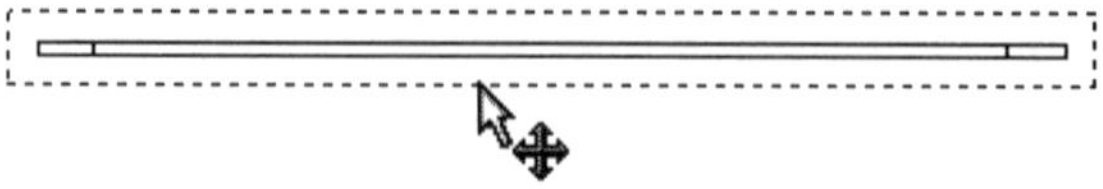

152) Drag the **Top view** in a downward direction towards Drawing View1.

153) Press the **f** key to fit Sheet1 to the Graphics window.

Detail Drawing

The design intent of this project is to work with dimensions inserted from parts and to incorporate them into the drawings. Explore methods to move, hide and recreate dimensions to adhere to a drawing standard.

There are other solutions to the dimensioning schemes illustrated in this project. Detail drawings require dimensions, annotations, tolerance, materials, Engineering Change Orders, authorization, etc. to release the part to manufacturing and other notes prior to production.

Review a hypothetical "worse case" drawing situation. You just inserted dimensions from a part into a drawing. The dimensions, extensions lines and arrows are not in the correct locations. How can you address the position of these details? Answer: Dimension to an ASME Y14.5M standard.

No.	Situation:
1	Extension line crosses dimension line. Dimensions not evenly spaced.
2	Largest dimension placed closest to profile.
3	Leader lines overlapping.
4	Extension line crossing arrowhead.
5	Arrow gap too large.
6	Dimension pointing to feature in another view. Missing dimension – inserted into Detail view (not shown).
7	Dimension text over centerline, too close to profile.
8	Dimension from other view – leader line too long.
9	Dimension inside section lines.
10	No visible gap.
11	Arrows overlapping text.
12	Incorrect decimal display with whole number (millimeter), no specified tolerance.

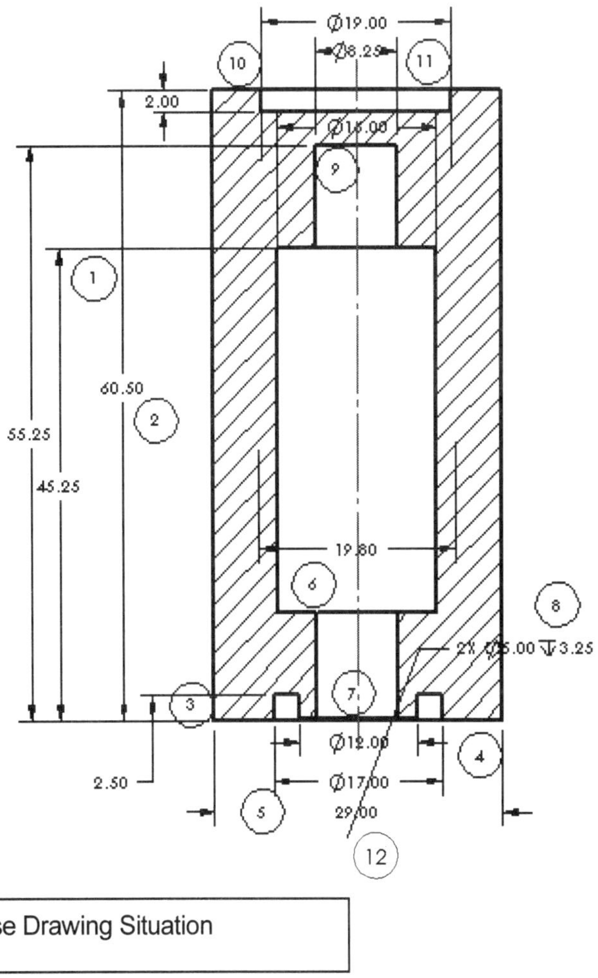

Worse Case Drawing Situation

The ASME Y14.5M standard defines an engineering drawing standard. Review the twelve changes made to the drawing to meet the standard.

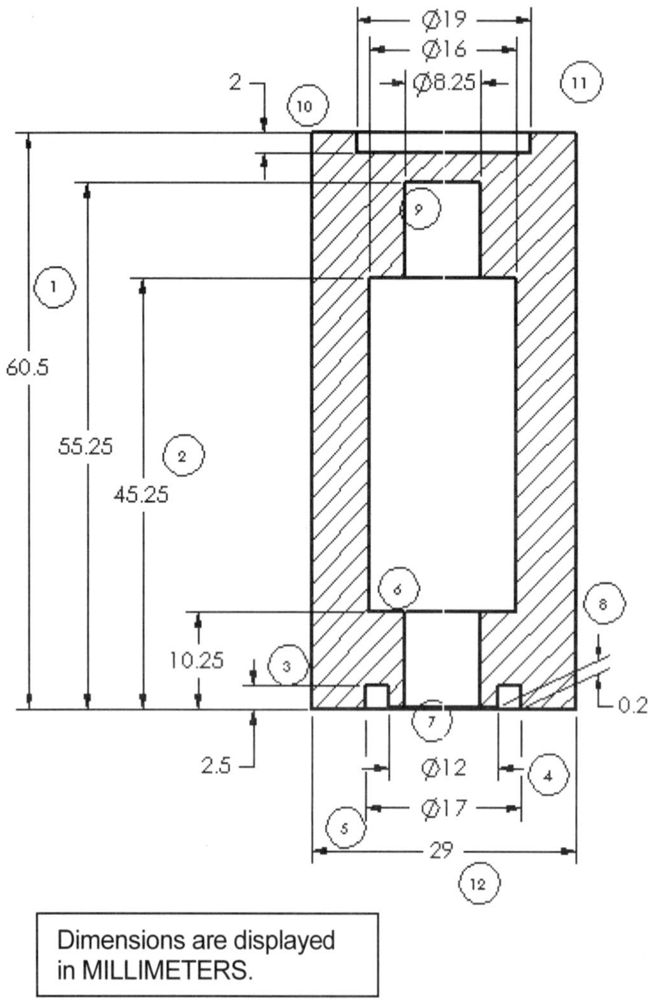

No.	Preferred Application of the Dimensions:
1	Extension lines do not cross unless situation is unavoidable. Stagger dimension text.
2	Largest dimension placed farthest from profile. Dimensions are evenly spaced and grouped.
3	Arrow heads do not overlap.
4	Break extension lines that cross close to arrowhead.
5	Flip arrows to the inside.
6	Move dimensions to the view that displays the outline of the feature. Insure that all dimensions are accounted for.
7	Move text off of reference geometry (centerline).
8	Drag dimensions into their correct view boundary. Create reference dimensions if required. Slant extension lines to clearly illustrate feature.
9	Locate dimensions outside off section lines.
10	Create a visible gap between extension lines and profile lines.
11	Arrows do not overlap the text.
12	Whole numbers displayed with no zero and no decimal point (millimeter).

Apply these dimension practices to the FLATBAR and other drawings in this project.

A Detailed Drawing is used to manufacture a part. A mistake on a drawing can cost your company substantial loss in revenue. The mistake could result in a customer liability lawsuit.

Dimension and annotate your parts clearly to avoid common problems and mistakes.

Dimensions and Annotations

Dimensions and annotations are inserted from the part. The annotations are not in the correct location. Additional dimensions and annotations are required.
Dimensions and annotations are inserted by selecting individual features, views or the entire sheet. Select the entire sheet. Insert Model Items command from the Annotations toolbar.

Activity: FLATBAR Drawing-Dimensions and Annotations

Insert dimensions.

154) Click **Sheet1** in the center of the drawing. The mouse pointer displays the Sheet icon. Click **Annotations** Annotati... from the CommandManager.

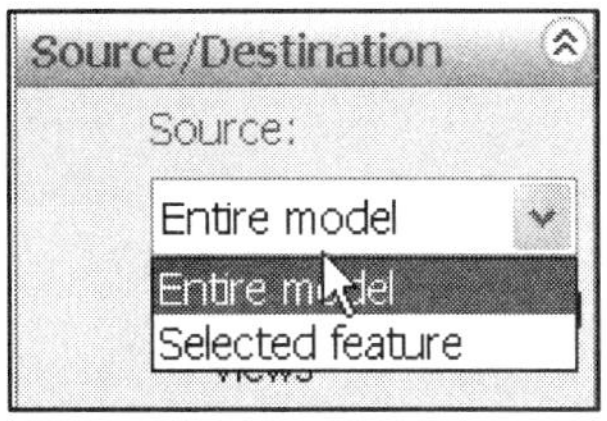

155) Click **Model Items** Model Items from the Annotations toolbar. The Model Items PropertyManager is displayed. The Import items into all views option is checked.

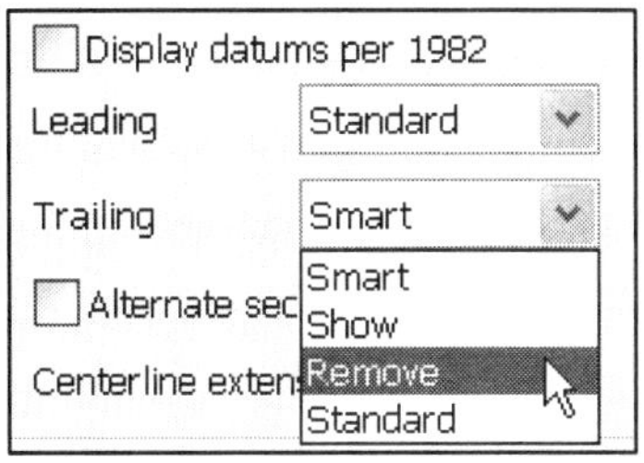

156) Select **Entire model** from the Source box.

157) Click **OK** from the Model Items PropertyManager.

Remove Trailing zeroes.

158) Click **Tools**, **Options**, **Document Properties** tab from the Main menu.

159) Select **Remove** for the Trailing zeroes drop down list.

160) Click **OK**.

Note: Dimensions are inserted into the drawing. The dimensions are not in the correct location with respect to the profile lines. Move them later in the project.

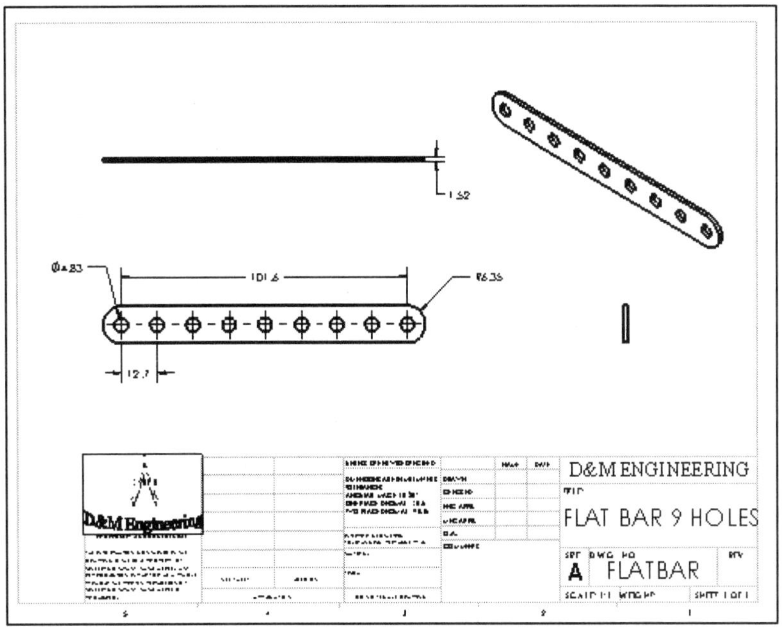

The dimensions and text in the next section have been enlarged for visibility. Drawing dimension location is dependent on:

- Feature dimension creation.
- Selected drawing views.

Move dimensions within the same view. Use the mouse pointer to drag dimensions and leader lines to a new location. Leader lines reference the size of the profile. A gap must exist between the profile lines and the leader lines. Shorten the leader lines to maintain a drawing standard. Use the green Arrow buttons to flip the dimension arrows.

Plan ahead for general drawing notes. Notes provide relative part or assembly information. Example: Material type, material finish, special manufacturing procedure or considerations, preferred supplier, etc.

Below are a few helpful guidelines to create general drawing notes:

- Use capitol letters.
- Use left text justification.
- Font size should be the same as the dimension text.

Create parametric notes by selecting dimensions in the drawing. Example: Specify the material thickness of the FLATBAR as a note in the drawing. If the thickness is modified, the corresponding note is also modified.

Hide superfluous feature dimensions. Do not delete feature dimensions. Recall hidden dimension with the View, Show Annotations command. Move redundant, dependent views outside the sheet boundary.

Move the linear dimensions in Drawing View1, (Front).

161) Click the vertical dimension text **101.6**. The dimension text turns green. Drag the **dimension text** downward. Click the horizontal dimension **12.7**.

162) Drag the **text** approximately 10mm's from the profile. The smallest linear dimensions are closest to the profile.

163) Click the radial dimension **R6.35**. Drag the **text** diagonally off the profile if required.

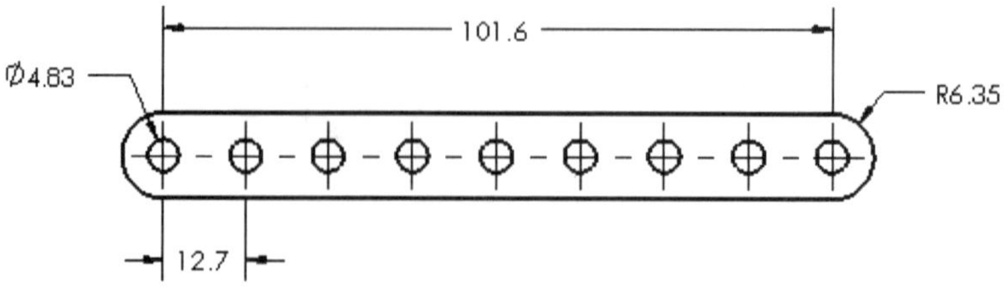

Modify dimension text.

164) Click the diameter dimension **4.83**. It turns green

165) Click inside the **Dimension Text** box.

166) Enter **9X** before <MOD-DIAM>. Enter **EQ SP** after <DIM>.

167) Click **OK** from the Dimension PropertyManager.

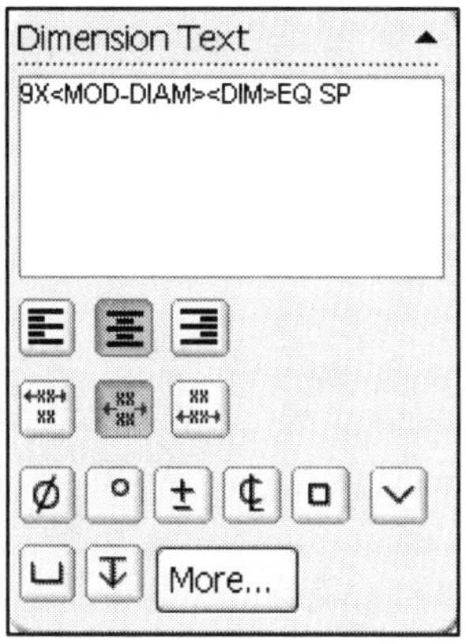

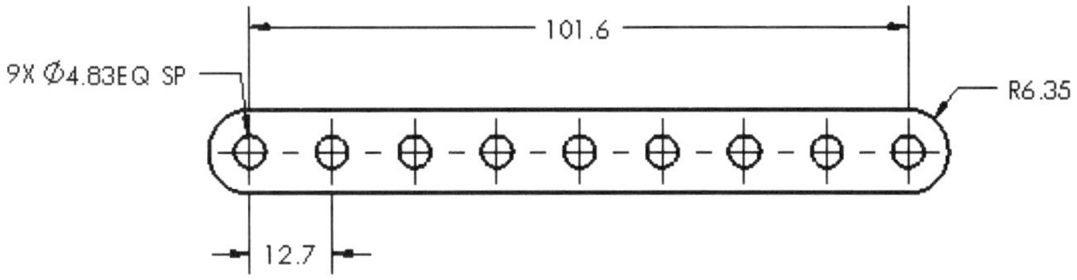

Inserted dimensions can be moved from one drawing view to another. Hold the Shift key down. Click and drag the dimension text from one view into the other view boundary. Release the Shift key.

Modify the Precision of the Material Thickness.

168) Click the depth dimension text **1.52** in Drawing View3. Select **.1** from the Tolerance/Precision box.

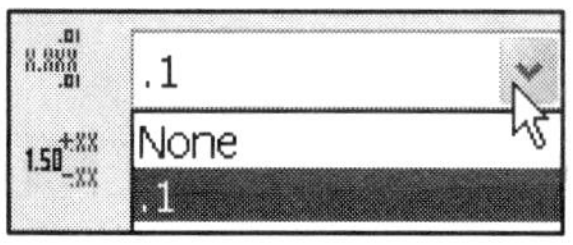

169) Click **OK** from the Dimension PropertyManager. The text displays 1.5.

Add a Parametric note.

170) Click **Note** from the Annotations toolbar. Click a **position** above Drawing View1 (Front view).

171) Enter **MATERIAL THICKNESS**. Click the depth dimension text **1.5** in Drawing View3 (Top view). The variable name for the dimension is displayed in the text box.

172) Enter **MM**.

173) Click **OK** from the Note PropertyManager.

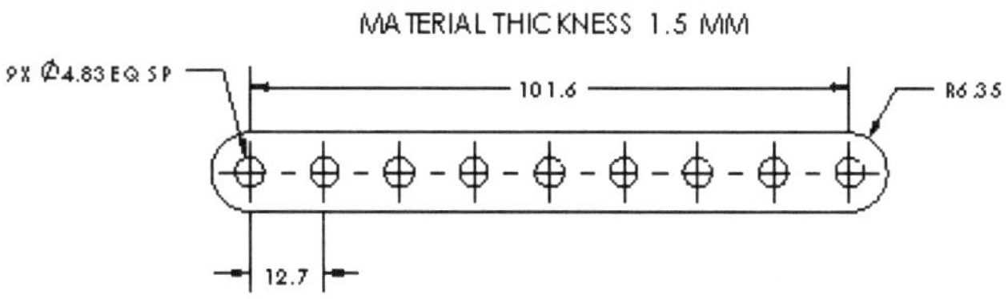

Hide superfluous dimensions.

174) Right-click the **1.5** dimension text in the Top view.

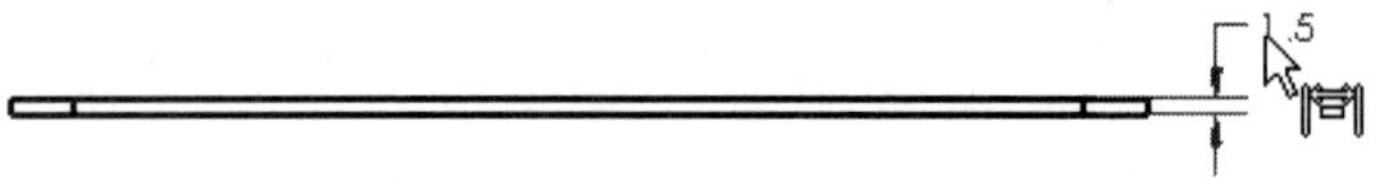

175) Click **Hide**.

Hide the Right view.

176) Right-click the **Right view** boundary. Click **Hide**. The Right view is not displayed in the Graphics window.

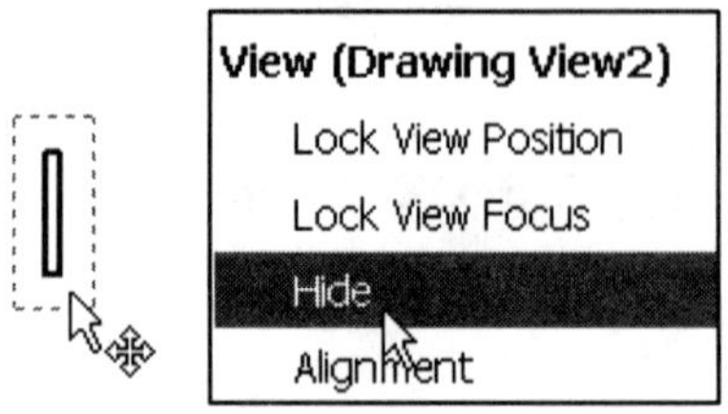

177) Click **OK** from the Drawing View2 PropertyManager.

Fit the Model to the drawing.

178) Press the **f** key.

Save the drawing.

179) Click **Save**.

Locate the Top view off of Sheet1.

180) Click and drag the **Top view boundary** off of the Sheet1 boundary as illustrated.

Views and notes outside the sheet boundary do not print. The Parametric note is controlled through the FLATBAR part Extrude1 depth. Modify the depth to update the note.

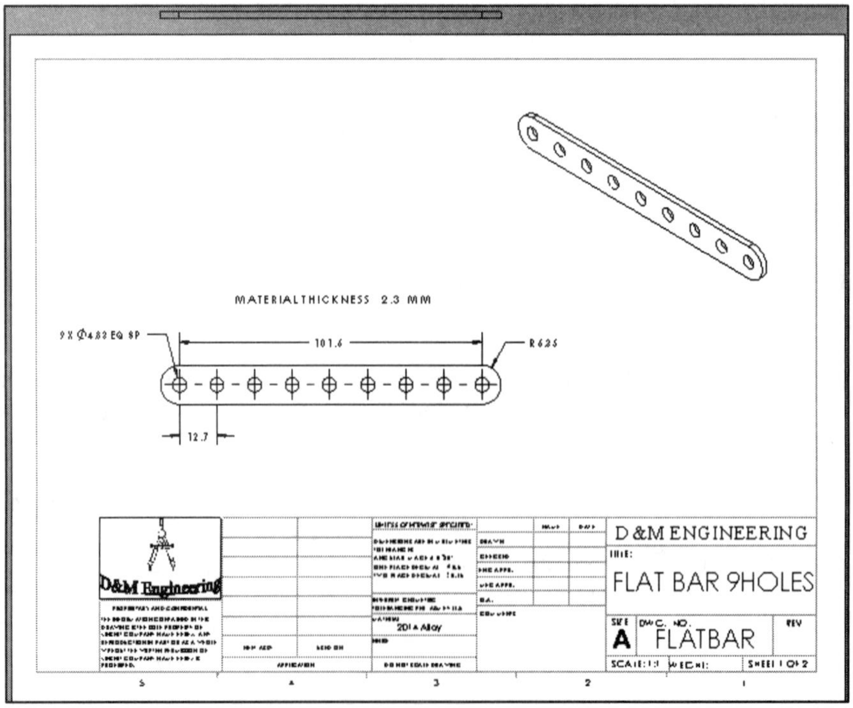

Open the FLATBAR part.

181) Right-click inside the **Drawing View1** boundary.

182) Click **Open flatbar.sldprt**. The FLATBAR part opens.

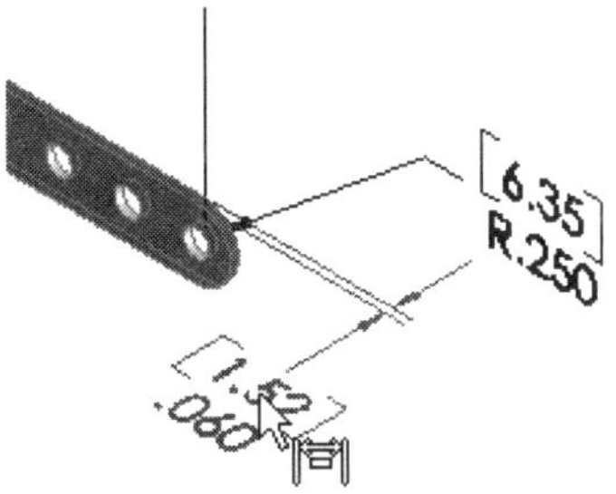

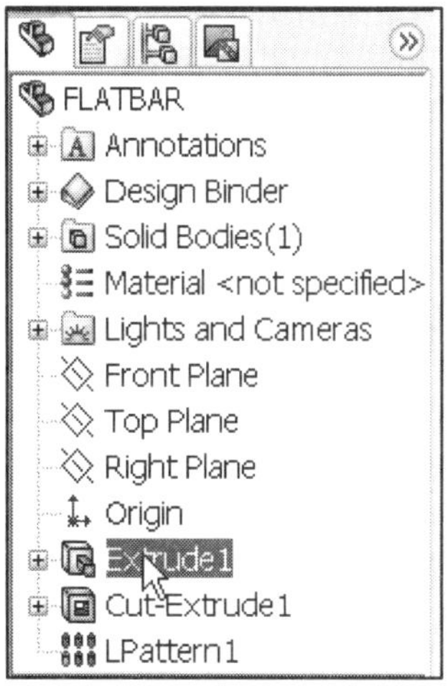

Modify the Extrude1 depth dimension.

183) Double click **Extrude1** from the FeatureManager.

184) Double-click **1.52**in.

185) Enter **2.3MM**. Note: You need to enter MM.

186) Click **Rebuild**.

187) Click the **Green Check mark**.

Return to the drawing.

188) Click **Window**, **FLATBAR – Sheet1** from the Main menu. The Parametric note is updated to reflect the dimension change in the part.

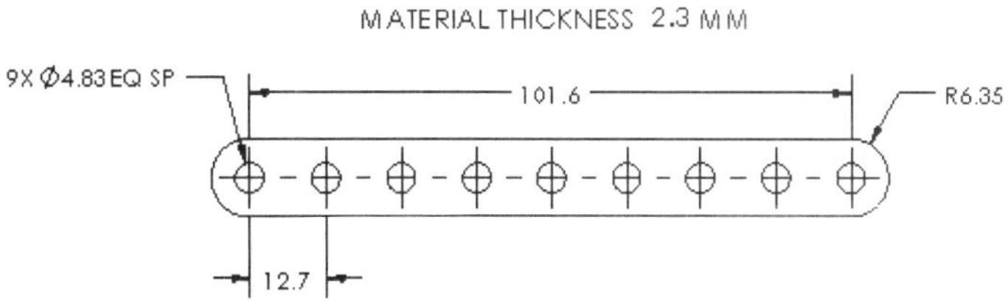

The FLATBAR drawing references the FLATBAR part. Do not delete the part or move the part location. Work between multiple documents:

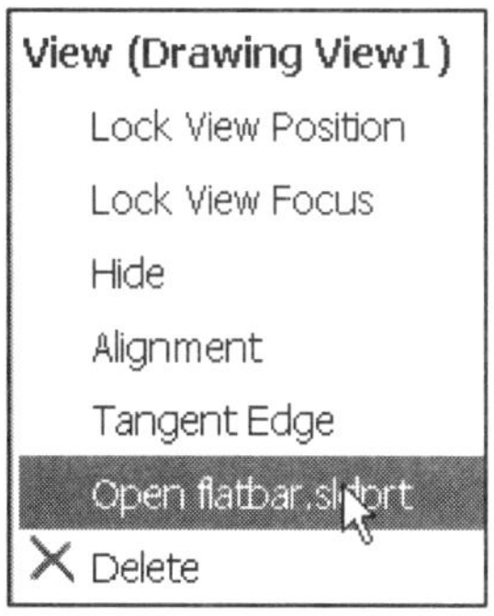

- Press Ctrl-Tab to toggle between open SolidWorks documents.
- Right-click inside the Drawing view boundary. Select Open Part. Example: Open flatbar.sldprt.
- Right-click the part icon in the FeatureManager. Select Open Drawing.

Commands are accessed through the Toolbars and Menus. Commands are also accessed with a Right-click in the Graphics window and FeatureManager.

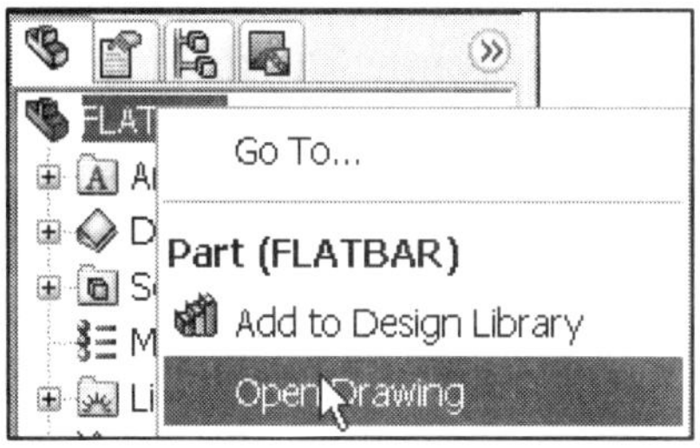

A majority of FLATBAR drawing dimensions are inserted from the FLATBAR part. An overall dimension is required to dimension the slot shape profile. Add a dimension in the drawing.

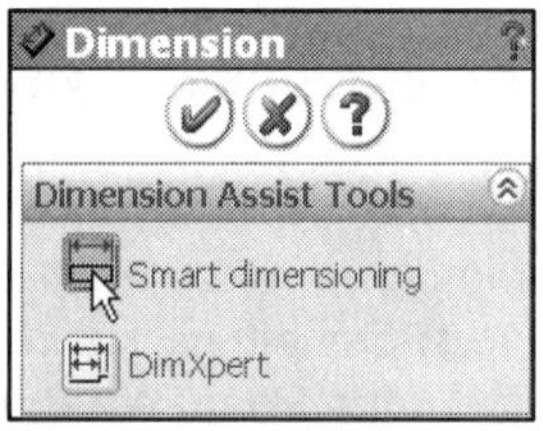

Add a dimension to Drawing View1.

189) Click **Smart Dimension** Smart Dimens.... Click the **Smart dimensioning** icon.

190) Click the **top horizontal line** of the FLATBAR.

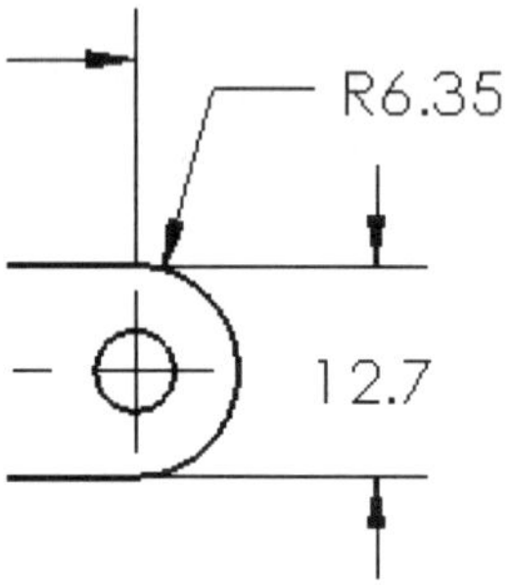

191) Click the **bottom horizontal line** of the FLATBAR.

192) Click a **position** to the right of Drawing View1 (Front).

Modify the Radius text.

193) Click the **R6.36** dimension text.

194) Delete **R<DIM>** in the Dimension text box.

195) Click **Yes** to confirm dimension override.

196) Enter **2X R** for Dimension text. Do not enter the radius value.

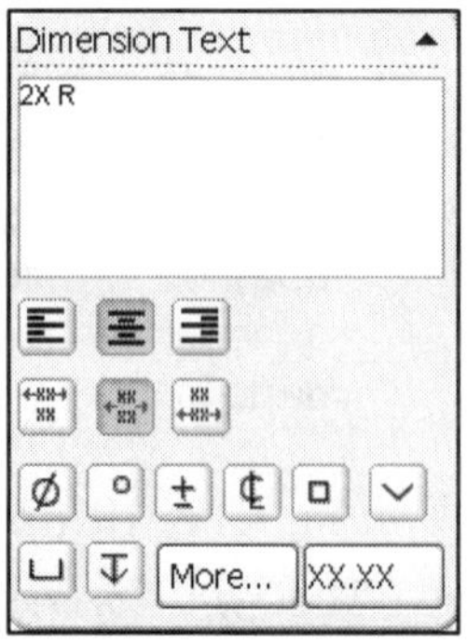

197) Click **OK** from the Dimension PropertyManager.

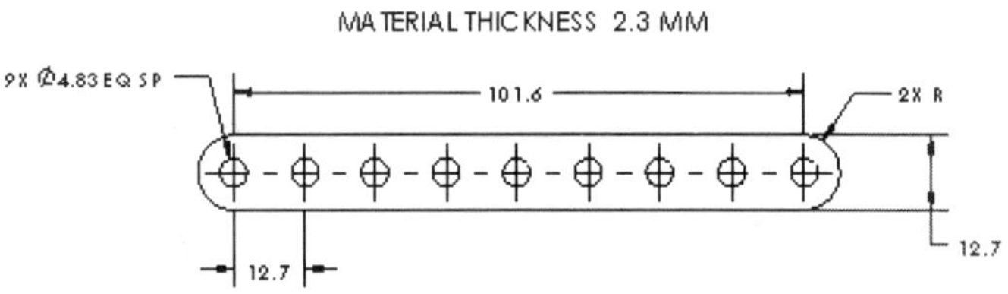

Save the FLATBAR drawing.

198) Click **Save**. Click **Yes** to the updates.

Part Number and Document Properties

Engineers manage the parts they create and modify. Each part requires a Part Number and Part Name. A part number is a numeric representation of the part. Each part has a unique number. Each drawing has a unique number. Drawings incorporate numerous part numbers or assembly numbers.

There are software applications that incorporate unique part numbers to create and perform:

- Bill of Materials.
- Manufacturing procedures.
- Cost analysis.
- Inventory control / Just in Time, JIT.

You are required to procure the part and drawing numbers from the documentation control manager. Utilize the following prefix codes to categories created parts and drawings. The part name, part number and drawing numbers are as follows:

Category:	Prefix:	Part Name:	Part Number:	Drawing Number:
Machined Parts	56-	FLATEPLATE AXLE SHAFT-COLLAR	GIDS-SC-10001-9 GIDS-SC-10017 GIDS-SC-10012-3-16	56-10222 56-10223 56-10224
Purchased Parts	99-	AIRCYLINDER	99-FBM8x1.25	999-101-8
Assemblies	10-	LINKAGE ASM	GIDS-SC-1000	10-10123

Link notes in the Title block to SolidWorks Properties. Properties are variables shared between documents and applications.

The machined parts are manufactured from Aluminum. Specify the Material Property in the part. Link the Material Property to the drawing title block. Create a part number that is utilized in the Bill of Materials. Create additional notes in the title block to complete the drawing.

Activity: FLATBAR Drawing-Part Number and Document Properties

Return to the FLATEBAR part.

199) Right-click in the **Drawing View1** boundary.

200) Click **Open flabar.sldprt**.

201) Right-click **Material** in the FeatureManager.

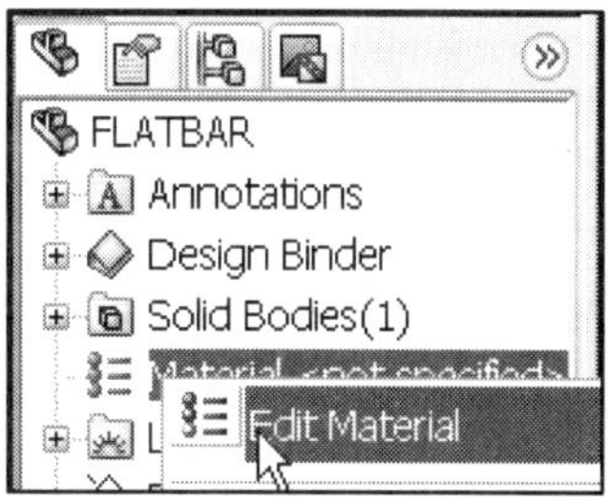

202) Click **Edit Material**.

203) **Expand** Aluminum Alloys.

204) Select **2014** Alloy.

205) Click **OK** from the Materials Editor PropertyManager.

206) Click **Rebuild** from the Standard menu.

Save the FLATBAR.

207) Click **Save**.

Define the part number property for the BOM.

208) Click the FLATBAR **ConfigurationManager** tab.

209) Right-click **Default**.

210) Click **Properties**.

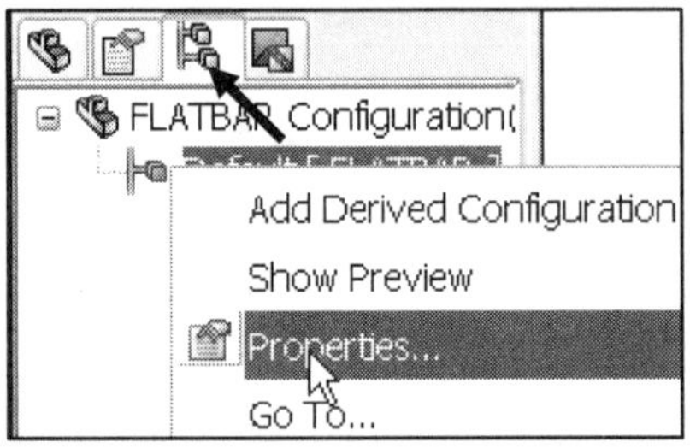

211) Click **User Specified Name** from the drop down box under Document Name.

212) Enter **GIDS-SC-10001-9** in the Part number text box.

Define a material property.

213) Click the **Custom Properties** button.

214) Click inside the **Property Name** box.

215) Click the **down arrow**.

216) Select **Material** from the Property Name list.

217) Click inside the **Value / Text Expression** box.

218) Click the **down arrow**.

219) Select **Material**.

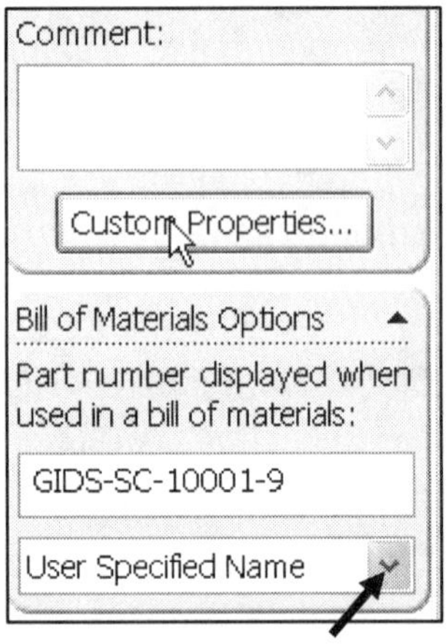

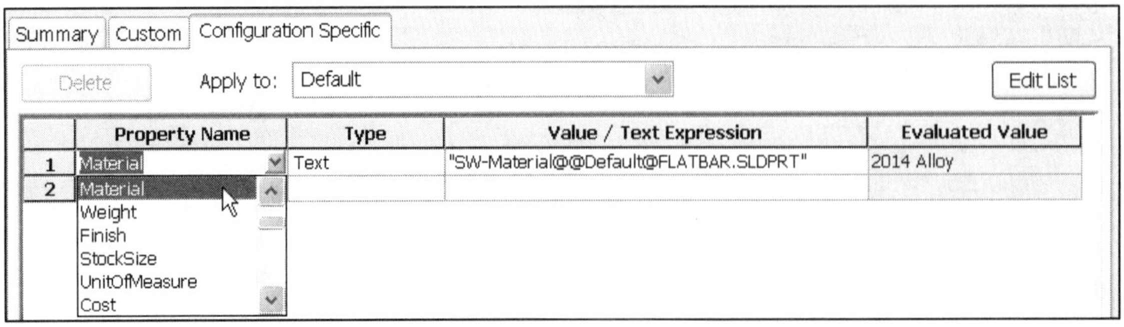

Define the Number Property.

220) Click inside the **second Property Name** box. Click the **down arrow**.

221) Select **Number** from the Name list.

222) Click inside the **Value / Text Expression** box.

223) Enter **56-10222** for Drawing Number.

224) Click **OK** from the Summary Information box.

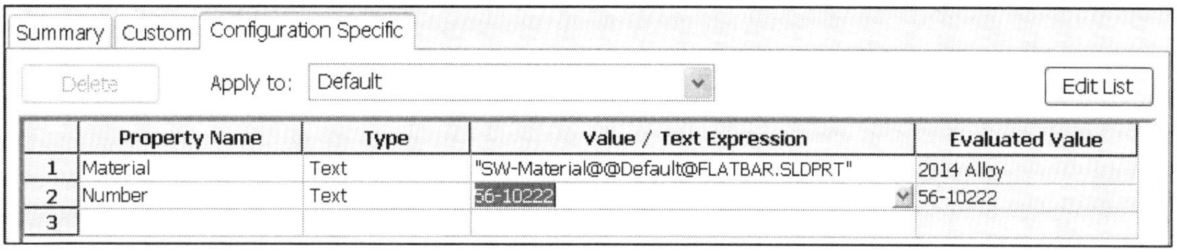

225) Click **OK** from the Configuration Properties PropertyManager.

226) Click the FLATBAR **FeatureManager** tab.

Save the FLATBAR part.

227) Click **Save**.

Return to the drawing.

228) Click **Windows**, **FLATBAR** - **Sheet1** from the Main menu.

The Material Property is inserted into the Title block.

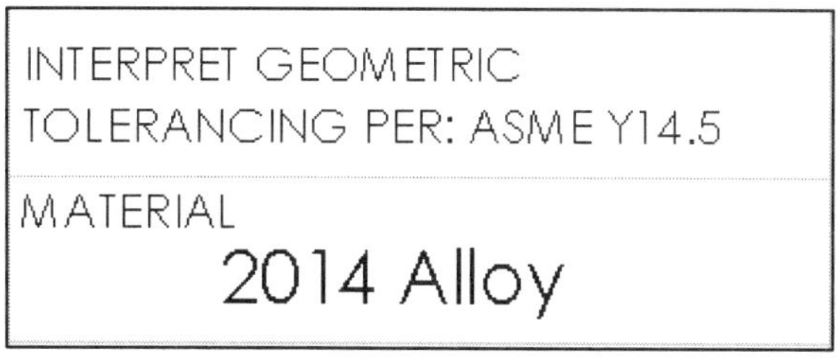

Activity: FLATBAR Drawing-Linked Note

Create a Linked Note.

229) Right-click in **Sheet1**.

230) Click **Edit Sheet Format**. **Zoom in** on the lower right corner of the drawing.

231) Double-click on the DWG. NO. text **FLATBAR**.

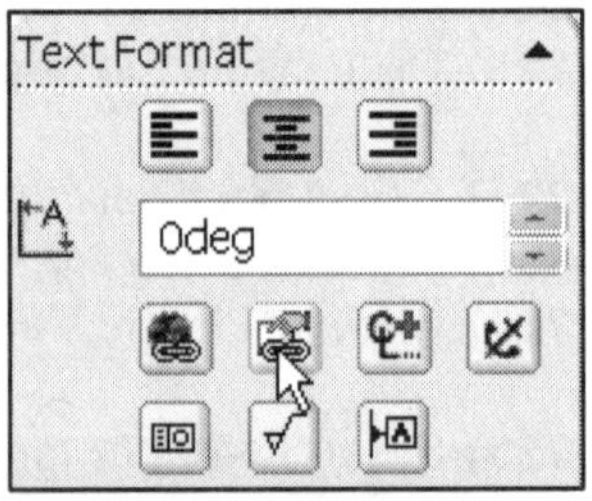

232) Click **Link to Property** from the Text Format box.

233) Select **Model in view specified in sheet properties**.

234) Select **Number** from the Link to Property drop down list.

235) Click **OK** from the Link to Property box.

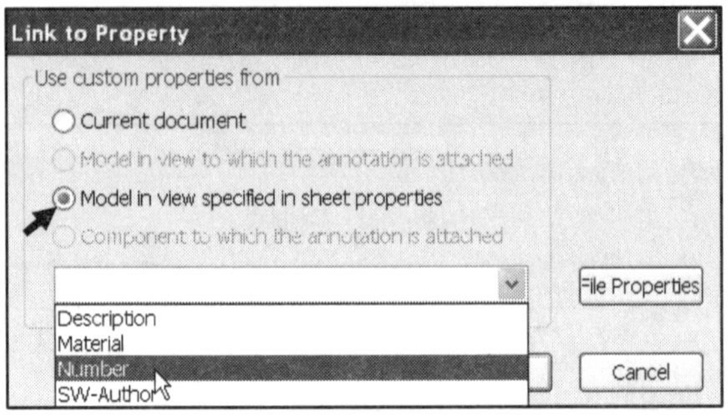

236) Click **OK** from the Note PropertyManager.

Return to the drawing sheet.

237) Right-click a **position** in the Graphics window.

238) Click **Edit Sheet**.

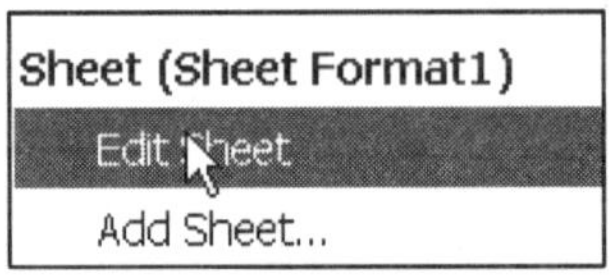

Save the FLATBAR drawing.

239) Click **Save**.

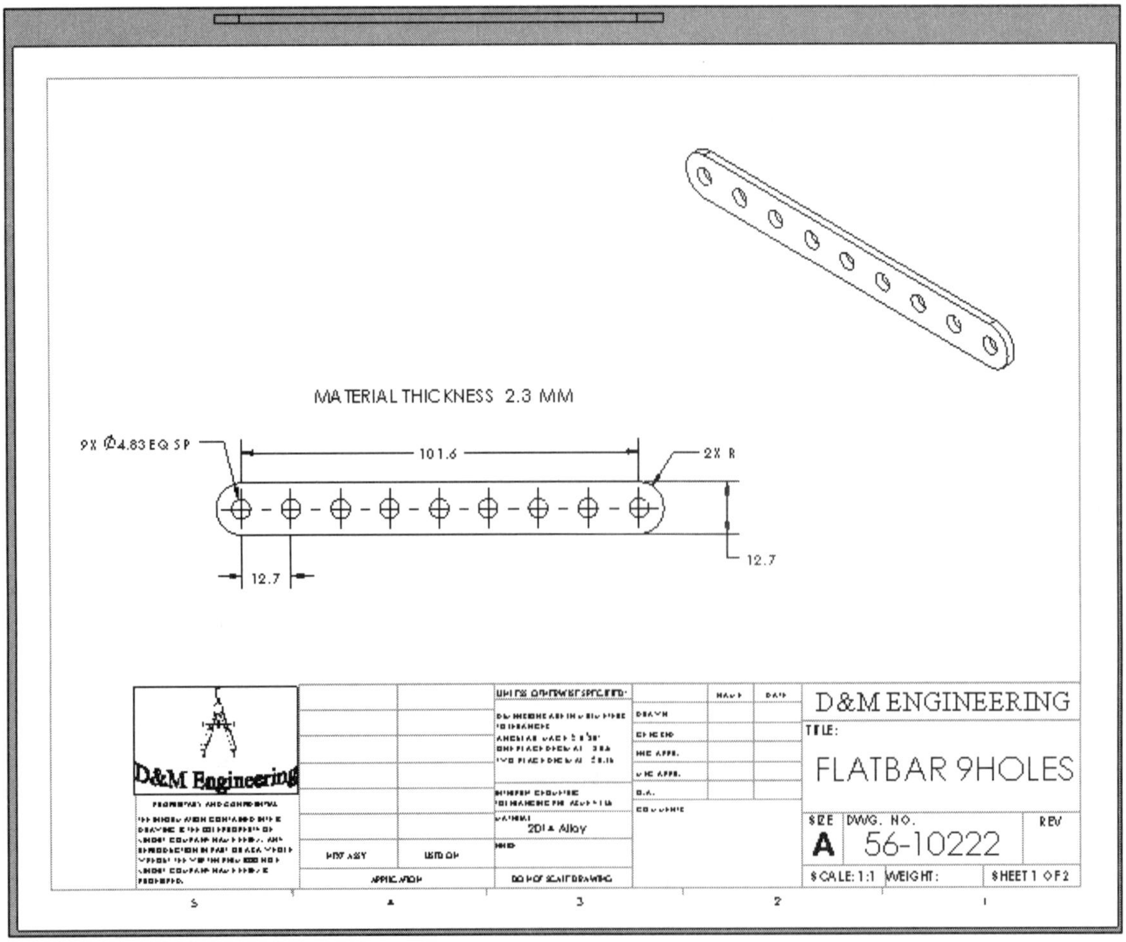

Custom Properties such as Revision and Drawn By are created in the project exercises.

Additional details on Drawing Views, New Drawing, Details, Dimensions, Dimensions and Annotations are available in SolidWorks Help.

Keywords: Drawing Views (overview), Drawing Views (model), Move (drawing views), Dimensions (circles, extension lines, inserting into drawings, move, parenthesis), Annotations (Note, Hole Callout, Centerline, Centermark), Notes (linked to properties, in sheet formats, parametric).

Review the FLATBAR Drawing.

You created the FLATBAR drawing with the A-ANSI-MM Drawing Template. The FLATBAR drawing utilized the FLATBAR part in the Model View PropertyManager.

The Model View PropertyManager allowed new views to be inserted with a View Orientation. You selected Front, Top, Right, and Isometric to position the FLATBAR views. You moved the views by dragging the green view boundary.

You inserted part dimensions and annotations into the drawing with the Insert Model Items command. Dimensions were moved to new positions. Leader lines and dimension text were repositioned. Annotations were edited to reflect the dimension standard.

You created a parametric note that referenced part dimensions in the drawing text. Aluminum 2014 was assigned in the FLATBAR part. The Material Custom Property and Number Custom Property were assigned in the FLATBAR part and referenced in the drawing Title block.

Know inch/mm decimal display. The ASME Y14.5 standard states:

- For millimeter dimensions < 1, display the leading zero. Remove trailing zeros.
- For inch dimensions < 1, delete the leading zero. The dimension is displayed with the same number of decimal places as its tolerance.

Note: The FLATBAR drawing linked Title block notes to Custom Properties in the drawing and in the part. The additional drawings in this project utilize drawing numbers linked to the model file name. The Title of the drawing utilizes a Note.

LINKAGE Assembly Drawing – Sheet1

The LINKAGE assembly drawing Sheet 1 utilizes the LINKAGE assembly. Add an Exploded view and a Bill of Materials to the drawing.

Create an Exploded view in the LINKAGE assembly. The Bill of Materials reflects the components of the LINKAGE assembly. Create a drawing with a Bill of Materials. Perform the following steps:

- Create a new drawing with the custom A-ANSI-MM size Drawing Template with the CUSTOM-A sheet format.
- Create and display the Exploded view of the LINKAGE assembly.
- Insert the Exploded view of the assembly into the drawing.
- Insert a Bill of Materials.
- Label each component with Balloon text.

Activity: LINKAGE Assembly Drawing-Sheet1

Close all parts and drawings.
240) Click **Windows**, **Close All** from the Main menu.

Create a new drawing.
241) Click **File**, **New** from the Main menu.

242) Double-click **A-ANSI-MM** from the SW-TUTORIAL-2007 folder. The Model View PropertyManager is displayed.

Open the LINKAGE assembly.
243) Click **Browse**.

244) Select **Assembly** for Files of type in the SW-TUTORIAL-2007 folder.

245) Double-click **LINKAGE**.

246) Click **Single View**.

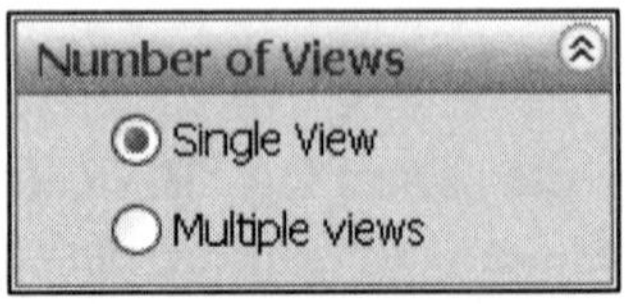

247) Click ***Isometric view**.

248) Select **Shaded With Edges**.

249) Check **Use custom scale**.

250) Select **User Defined** from the drop down arrow.

251) Enter **2:3** for Scale.

252) Click a **position** on the right side of Sheet1 as illustrated.

253) Click **OK** from the Drawing View1 PropertyManager.

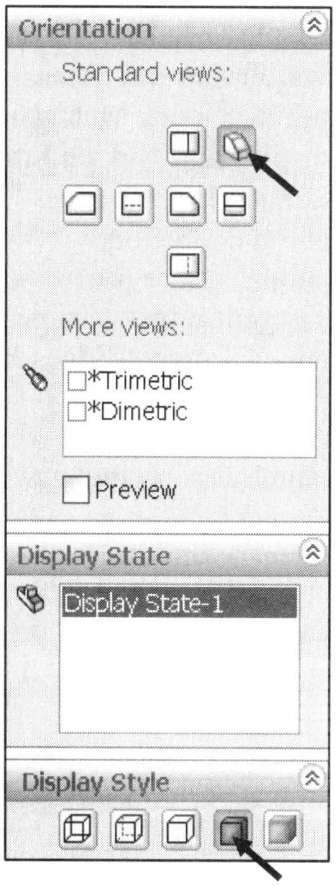

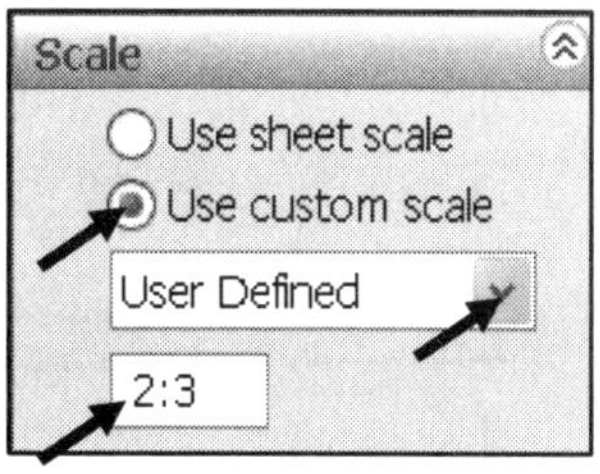

Save the LINKAGE assembly drawing.

254) Accept the default file name. Click **Save**.

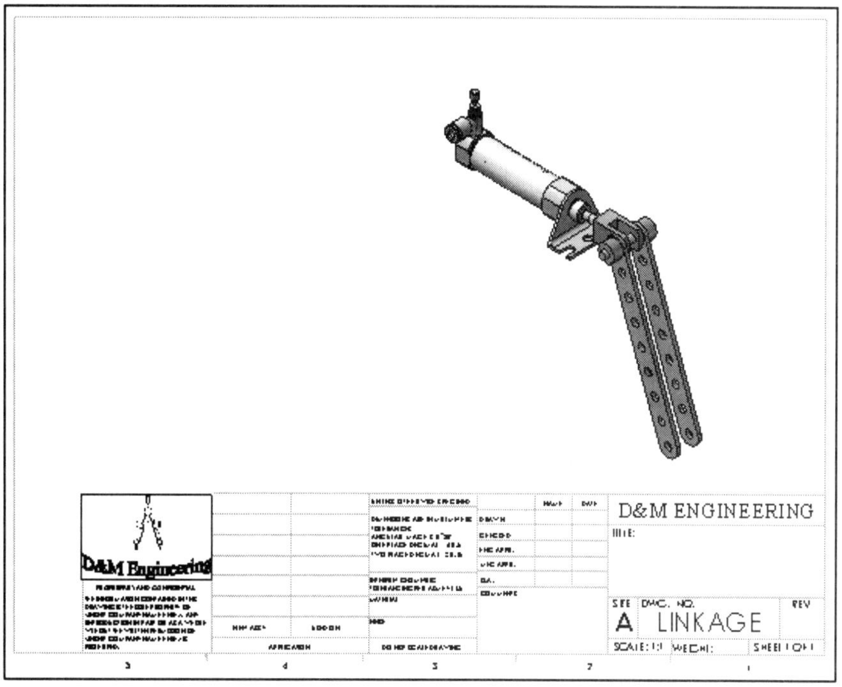

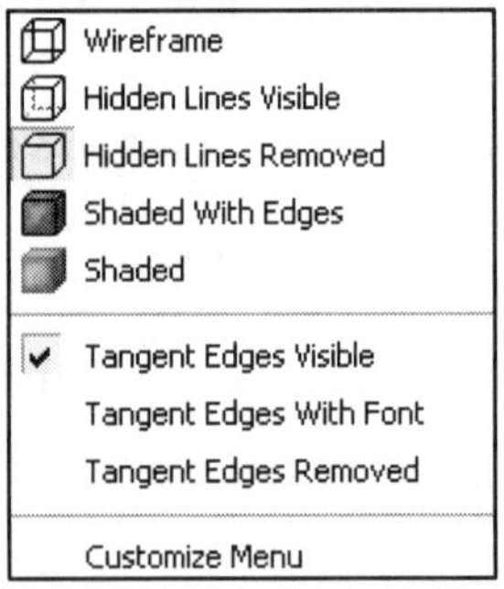

Display Modes for a Drawing View are similar to a part. Wireframe and Shaded Display Modes provide the best graphic performance. Mechanical details require Hidden Lines Visible display and Hidden Lines Removed display. Select Shaded/Hidden Lines Removed to display Auxiliary Views to avoid confusion.

Tangent Edges Visible provides clarity for the start of a Fillet edge. Tangent Edges Removed provides the best graphic performance.

Right-click in the view boundary to access the Tangent Edge options.

Utilize the Lightweight Drawing option to improve performance for large assemblies.

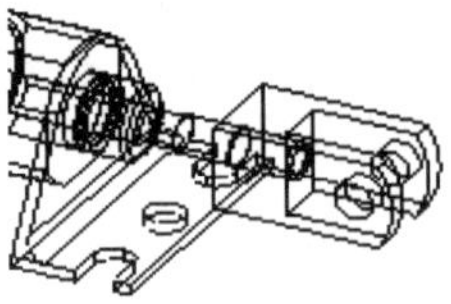
Wireframe

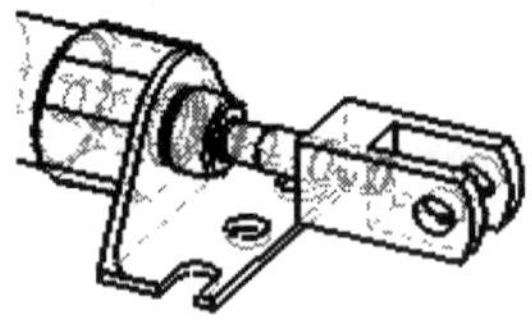
Hidden Lines Visible

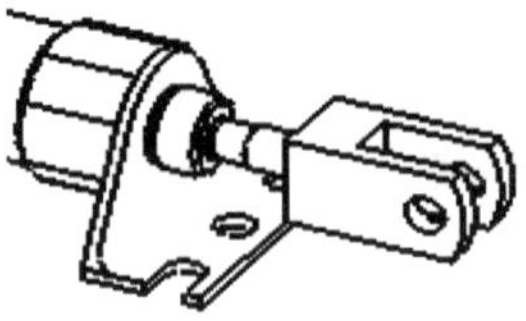
Hidden Lines Removed

Shaded

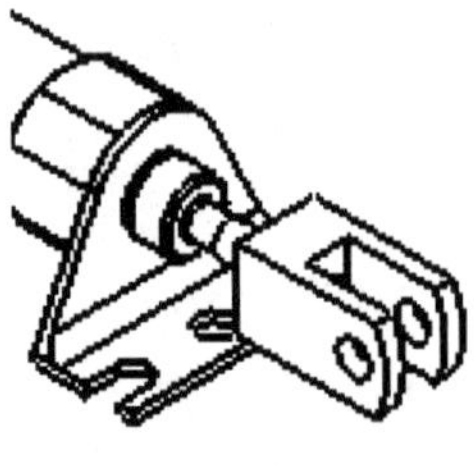
Tangent Edges Visible

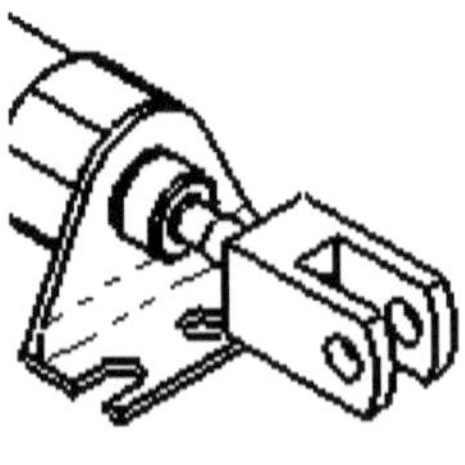
Tangent Edges With Font

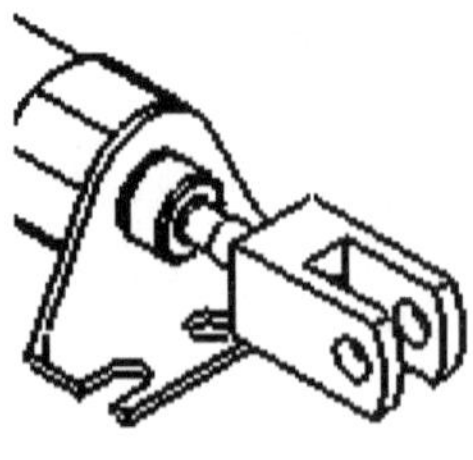
Tangent Edges Removed

To address Tangent lines views:

- Right-click in a Drawing view.
- Click Tangent Edge.
- Click a Tangent Edge view option.

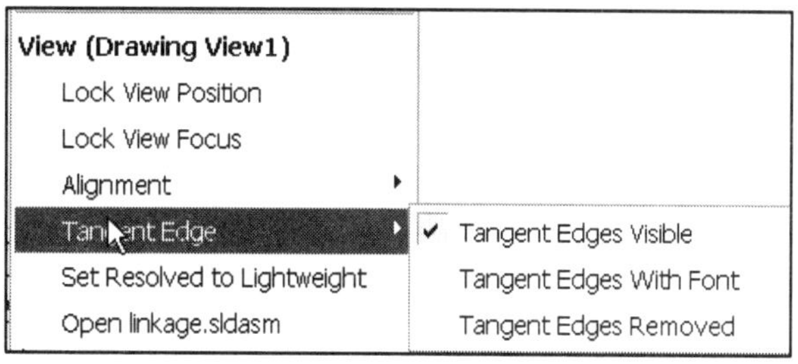

Return to the LINKAGE assembly.

255) Right-click in the **Isometric view**.

256) Click **Open linkage.sldasm**.

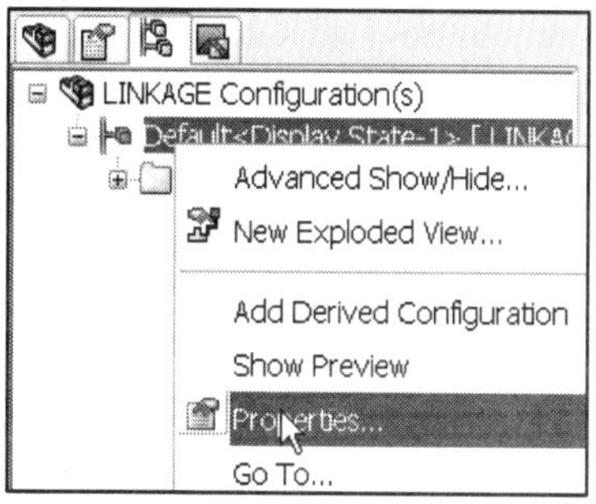

257) Click the **ConfigurationManager** tab.

258) Right-click **Default [LINKAGE]**.

259) Click **Properties** Properties... .

260) Select **User Specified Name** from the Part number displayed when used in Bill of Materials.

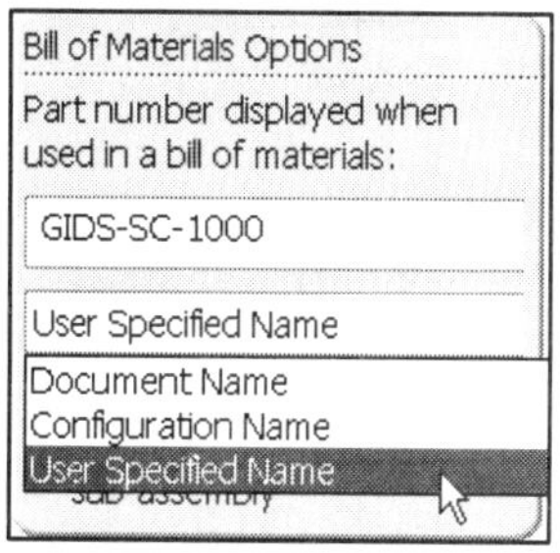

261) Enter **GIDS-SC-1000** in the Part Number text box.

262) Click **OK** from the Configuration Properties PropertyManager.

263) Click the LINKAGE **FeatureManager** tab.

264) Click **Save**.

Exploded View

The Exploded View illustrates how to assemble the components in an assembly. Create an Exploded View with four steps. Click and drag components in the Graphics window.

The Manipulator icon indicates the direction to explode. Select an alternate component edge for the Explode direction. Drag the component in the Graphics window or enter an exact value in the Explode distance box.

Manipulate the top-level components in the assembly. Access the Explode view option as follows:

- Right-click the configuration name in the ConfigurationManager.
- Select the Exploded View tool in the Assembly toolbar.
- Select Insert, Exploded View from the Main menu.

Activity: LINKAGE Assembly Drawing-Exploded View

Insert an Exploded view.

265) Click the **ConfigurationManager** tab.

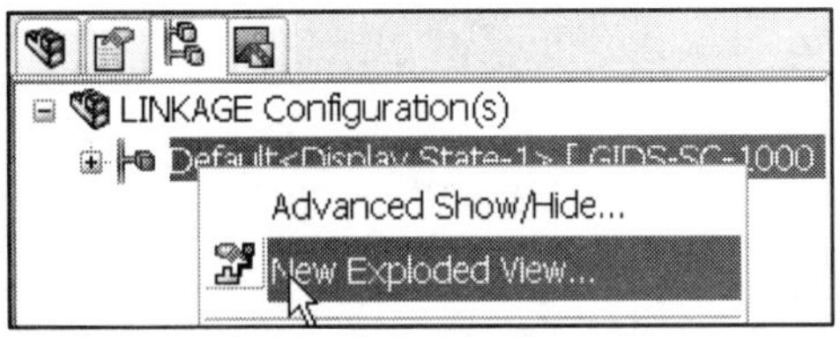

266) Right-click **Default [GIDS-SC-1000]**.

267) Click **New Exploded view** New Exploded View.... The Explode PropertyManager is displayed.

Create Explode Step 1. Use the distance box option.

268) Click the right **SHAFT-COLLAR** as illustrated.

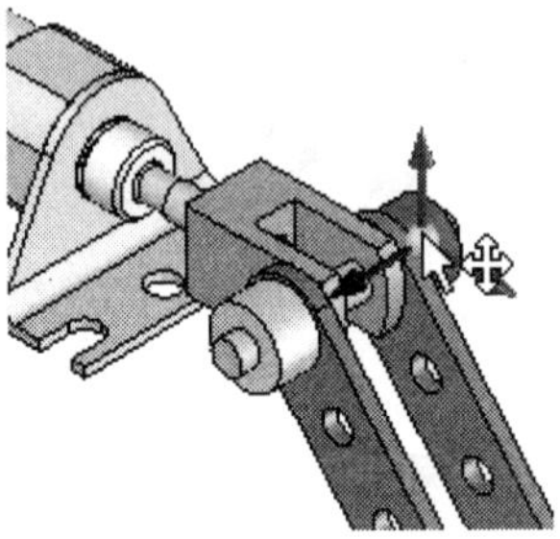

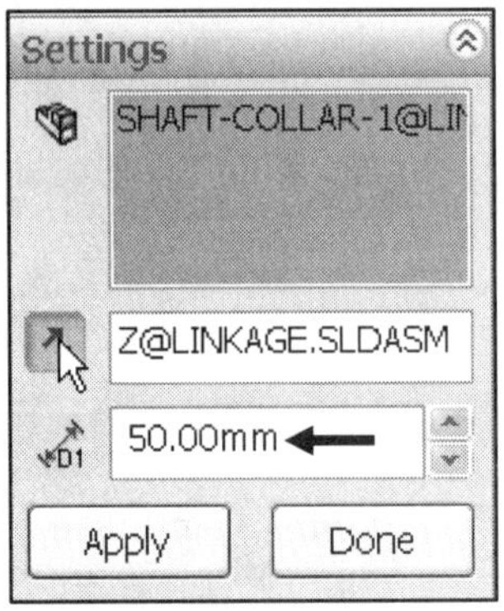

269) Enter **50**mm in the Explode distance box.

270) Click **Apply**. If required, click the **Reverse direction** button. The SHAFT-COLLAR moves 50mms to the right.

271) Click **Done**. Explode Step1 is created.

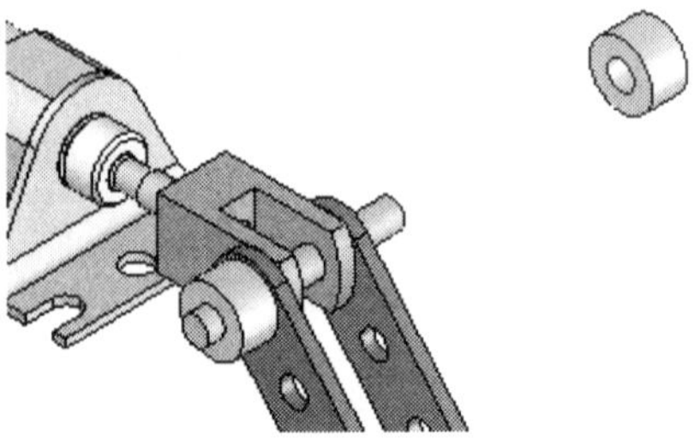

Create Explode Step 2. Use the Manipulator icon.

272) Click the **left SHAFT-COLLAR** in the Graphics window as illustrated.

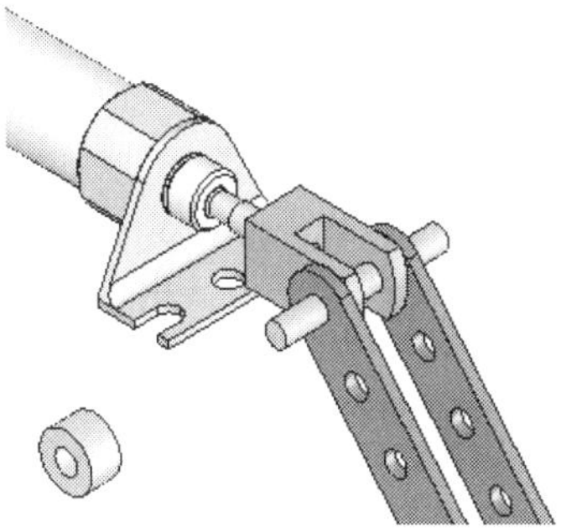

273) Drag the blue **Manipulator icon** to the left of the assembly approximately 50mms.

274) Click **inside** the Graphics window. Explode Step2 is created.

Create Explode Step 3.

275) Click the **right FLATBAR** in the Graphics window as illustrated.

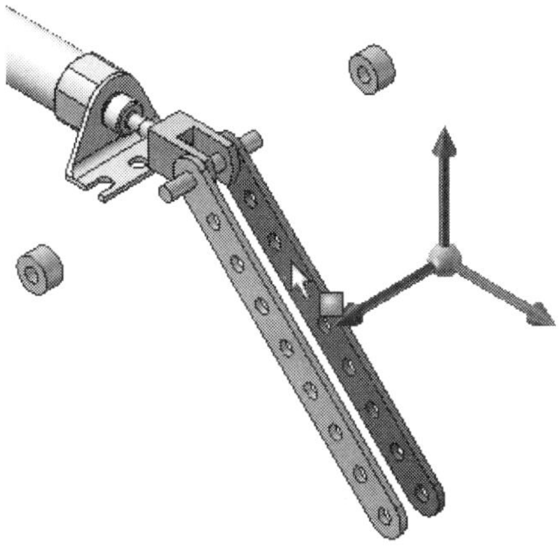

276) Drag the blue **Manipulator icon** to the right of the assembly. Explode Step3 is created.

Create Explode Step 4.

277) Click the **left FLATBAR** in the Graphics window.

278) Drag the blue **Manipulator icon** to the left of the assembly. Explode Step4 is created.

279) Click **inside** the Graphics window.

280) **Expand** each Explode Step to review.

281) Click **OK** from the Explode PropertyManager.

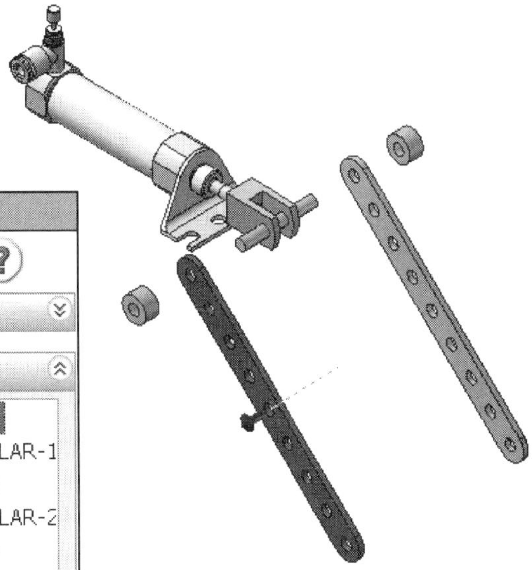

Save the LINKAGE part in the Exploded State.

282) Click **Save**.

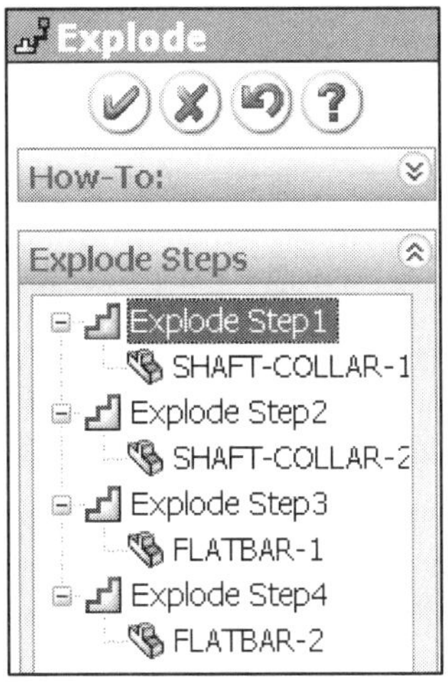

Activity: LINKAGE Assembly Drawing-Animation

Animate the Exploded view.

283) Expand Default [GIDS-SC-1000].

284) Right-click **ExplView1** in the ConfigurationManager.

285) Click **Animate collapse** to play the animation.

286) Click **Stop** from the Animation Controller.

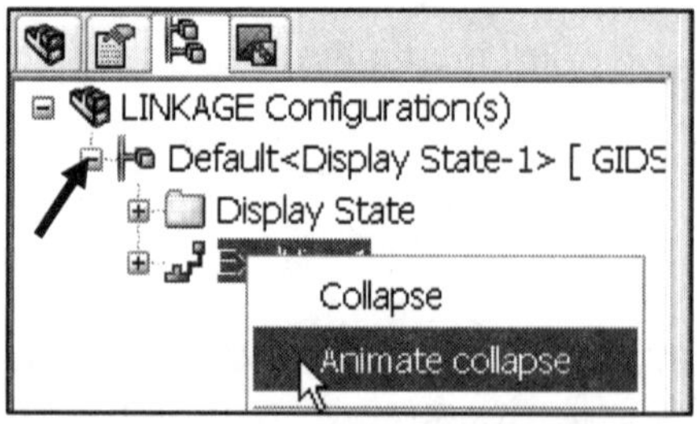

Return the Exploded view in its collapsed state.

287) Click **Close** from the Animation Controller.

288) Click the LINKAGE **FeatureManager** tab.

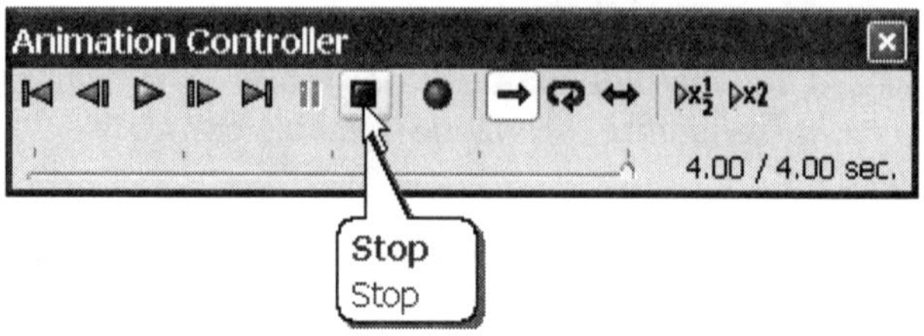

Open the LINKAGE drawing.

289) Click **Window, LINKAGE – SHEET1** from the Main menu.

Display the Exploded view in the drawing.

290) Right-click in the **Isometric view**.

291) Click **Properties**.

292) Check **Show in exploded state**.

293) Click **OK** from the Drawing Views Properties box.

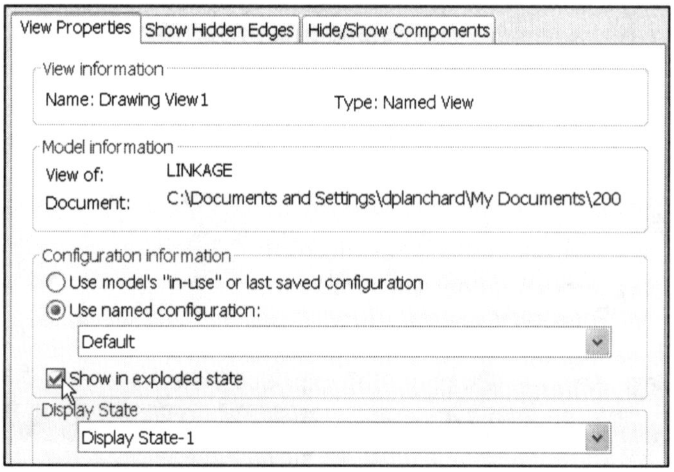

294) Click **OK** from the Drawing View1 PropertyManager.

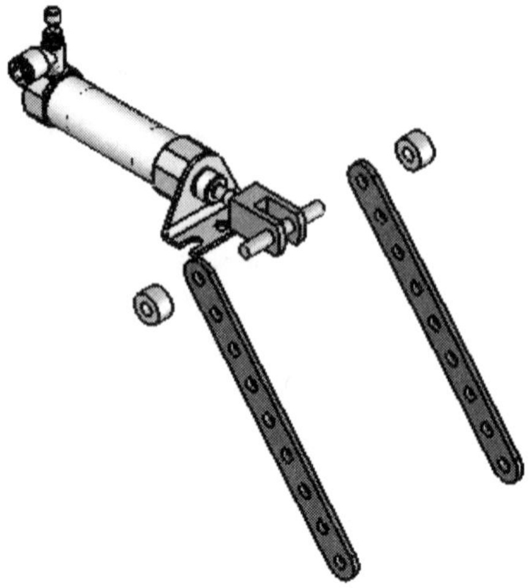

Bill of Materials

A Bill of Materials (BOM) is a table inserted into a drawing to keep a record of the parts used in an assembly. The default BOM template contains the Item Number, Quantity, Part No. and Description. The default Item number is determined by the order in which the component is inserted into the assembly. Quantity is the number of instances of a part or assembly.

Part No. is determined by the following: file name, default and the User Defined option, Part number used by the Bill of Materials. Description is determined by the description entered when the document is saved.

Activity: LINKAGE Assembly Drawing-Bill of Materials

Create a Bill of Materials.

295) Click in the **Isometric view**.

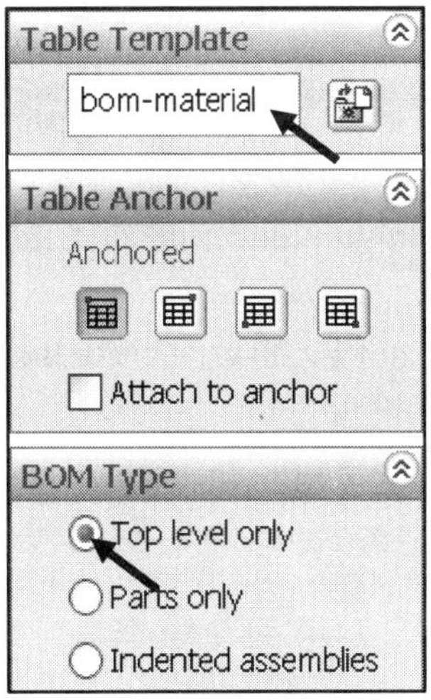

296) Click **Insert**, **Tables**, **Bill of Materials** from the Main menu. The Bill of Materials PropertyManager is displayed.

297) Select **bom-material** for Table Template.

298) Select **Top Level only** for BOM Type.

299) Click **OK** from the Bill of Materials PropertyManager.

300) Double-click a position in the **upper left corner** of the Sheet1.

ITEM NO.	PART NUMBER	DESCRIPTION	MATERIAL	QTY.
1	GIDS-PC-10001	LINEAR ACTUATOR		1
2	AXLE	AXLE ROD		1
3	GIDS-SC-10001-9	FLAT BAR 9 HOLES	2014 Alloy	2
4	SHAFT-COLLAR	SHAFT-COLLAR		2

The Bill of Materials requires some editing. The AXLE and SHAFT-COLLAR PART NUMBER values are not defined. The current part file name determines the PART NUMBER value. The current part description determines the DESCRIPTION values. Redefine the PART NUMBER for the Bill of Materials. Note: You will also resize the LINKAGE assembly.

Modify the AXLE Part number.

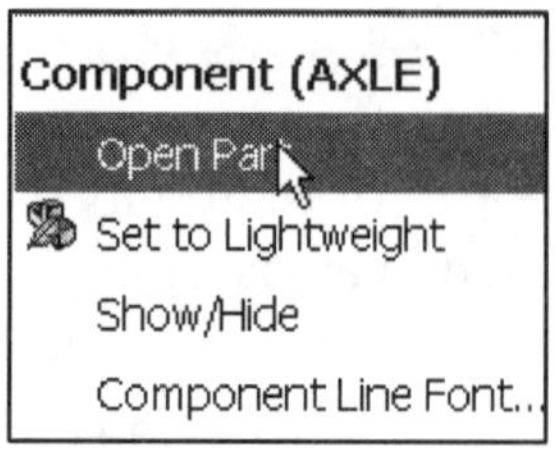

301) Right-click the **AXLE** part in the LINKAGE drawing. Click **Open Part**. The AXLE FeatureManager is displayed.

302) Click the AXLE **ConfigurationManager** tab.

303) Right-click **Default** [**AXLE**] in the ConfigurationManager.

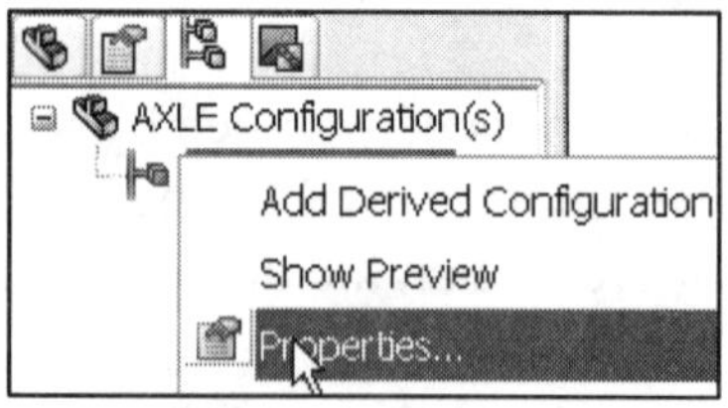

304) Click **Properties**.

305) Select **User Specified Name** from the Configuration Properties dialog box.

306) Enter **GIDS-SC-10017** for the Part Number to be utilized in the Bill of Materials.

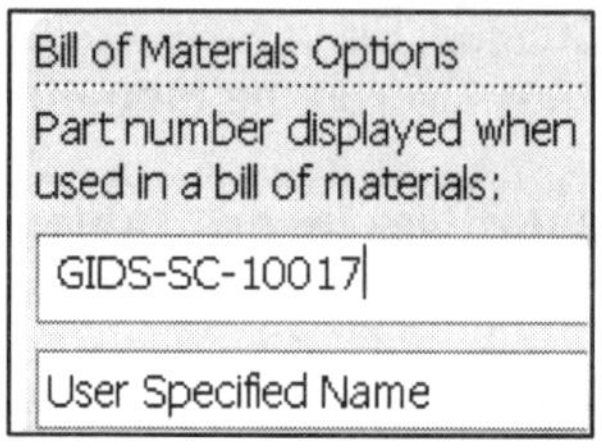

307) Click **OK** from the Configuration Properties PropertyManager. **Return** to the FeatureManager.

308) Click **Save**.

Return to the LINKAGE drawing.

309) Click **Window**, **LINKAGE - Sheet1** from the Main menu.

Modify the SHAFT-COLLAR PART NUMBER.

310) Right-click the left **SHAFT-COLLAR** part in the LINKAGE drawing.

311) Click **Open Part**. The SHAFT-COLLAR FeatureManager is displayed.

312) Click the SHAFT-COLLAR **ConfigurationManager** tab.

313) Right-click **Default** [**SHAFT-COLLAR**] from the ConfigurationManager.

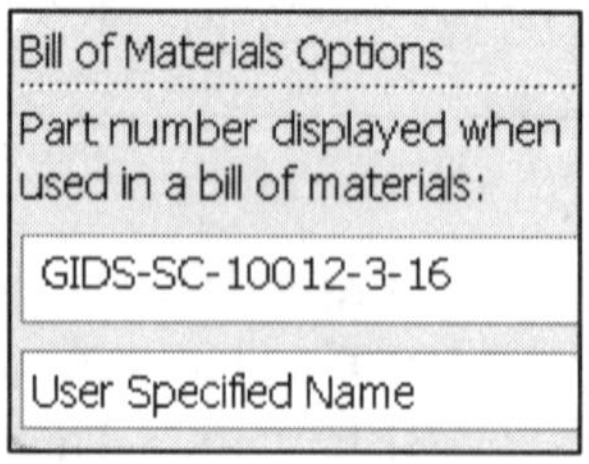

314) Click **Properties**. Select the **User Specified Name** from the Configuration Properties box.

315) Enter **GIDS-SC-10012-3-16** for the Part Number in the Bill of Materials.

316) Click **OK** from the Configuration Properties PropertyManager. **Return** to the FeatureManager.

317) Click **Save**.

Return to the LINKAGE assembly drawing.

318) Click **Window**, **LINKAGE - Sheet1** from the Main menu.

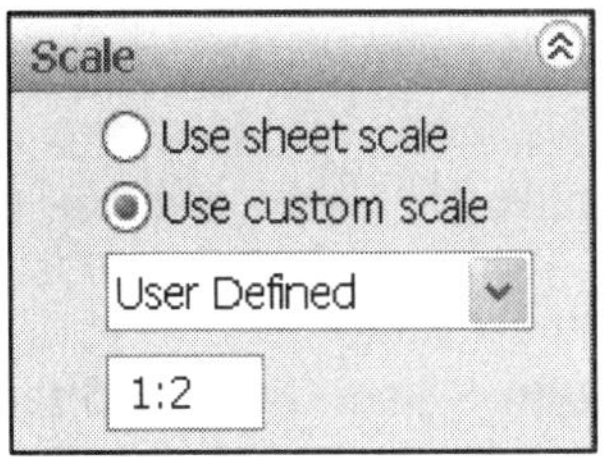

Modify the LINKAGE assembly scale.

319) Click inside the **Isometric view**. Enter **1:2** for Scale.

320) Click **OK** from the Drawing View1 PropertyManager.

321) Click **Rebuild**. Click **Save**.

ITEM NO.	PART NUMBER	DESCRIPTION	MATERIAL	QTY.
1	GIDS-PC-10001	LINEAR ACTUATOR		1
2	GIDS-SC-10017	AXLE ROD		1
3	GIDS-SC-100001-9	FLAT BAR 9 HOLES	2014 Alloy	2
4	GIDS-SC-10012-3-16	SHAFT-COLLAR		2

Note: As an exercise, complete the Bill of Materials. Label each component with a unique item number. The item number is placed inside a circle. The circle is called Balloon text. List each item in a Bill of Materials table. Utilize Auto Balloon to apply Balloon text to all BOM components.

The Circle Split Line option contains the Item Number and Quantity. Item number is determined by the order listed in the assembly FeatureManager. Quantity lists the number of instances in the assembly.

Activity: LINKAGE Assembly Drawing-Automatic Balloons

Insert the Automatic Balloons.

322) Click inside the **Isometric view** boundary of the LINKAGE.

323) Click **Auto Balloons** AutoBal... from the Annotations toolbar. The Auto Balloon PropertyManager is displayed. Accept the Square default Balloon Layout.

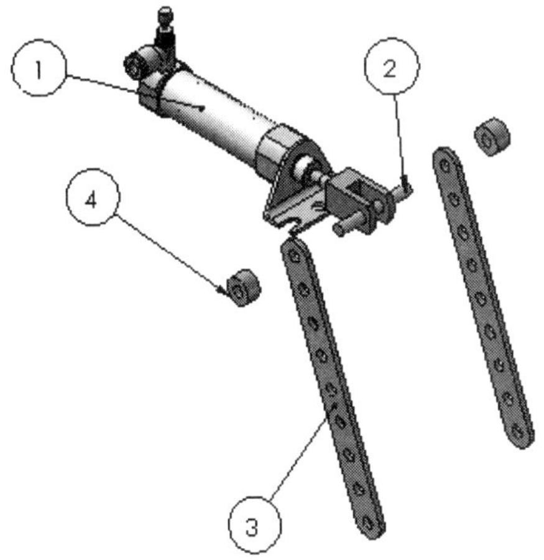

324) Click **OK** from the Auto Balloon PropertyManager.

Reposition the Balloon text.

325) Click and drag each **Balloon** to the desired position.

326) Click and drag the **Balloon arrowhead** to reposition the arrow on a component edge.

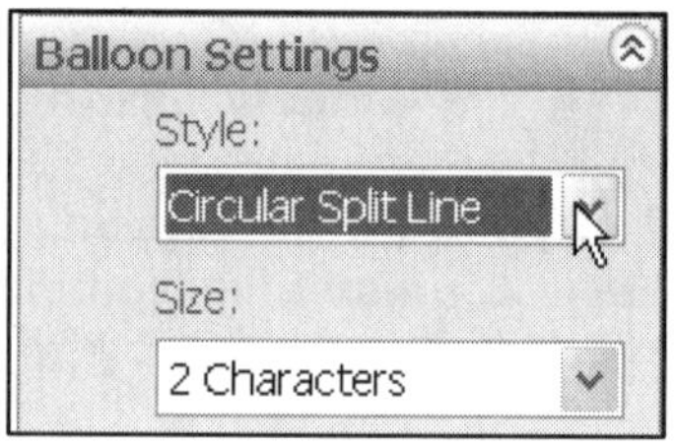

327) Click **OK** from the Balloon PropertyManager.

Display Item Number/Quantity.

328) Ctrl-Select the **four Balloon text**. The Balloon PropertyManager is displayed.

329) Select **Circular Split Line** for Style.

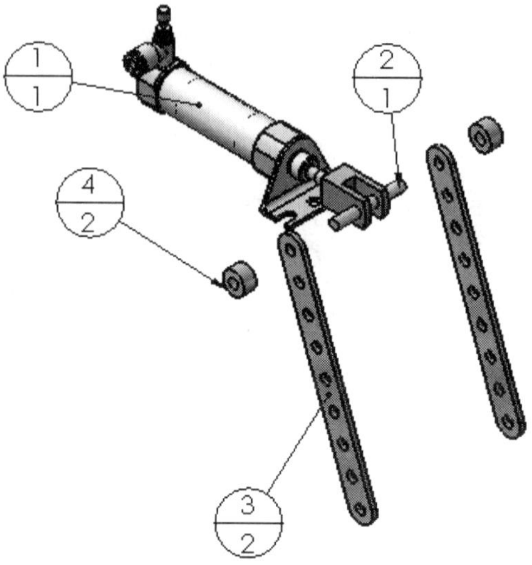

330) Click **OK** from the Balloon PropertyManager.

Save the LINKAGE assembly drawing.

331) Click **Save**.

Select the BOM table in the drawing and Right-click Properties to modify entries and display table parameters.

LINKAGE Assembly Drawing – Sheet2

A drawing consists of one or more sheets. Utilize the Model View command in the Drawings toolbar to insert the AIRCYLINDER assembly. The LINKAGE drawing Sheet2 displays the Front view and Top view of the AIRCYLINDER assembly.

Insert a Section View to display the internal features of the AIRCYLINDER. Insert a Detail View to display an enlarged area of the AIRCYLINDER.

Activity: LINKAGE Assembly Drawing-Sheet2

Add Sheet2.

332) Right-click in the Graphics window.

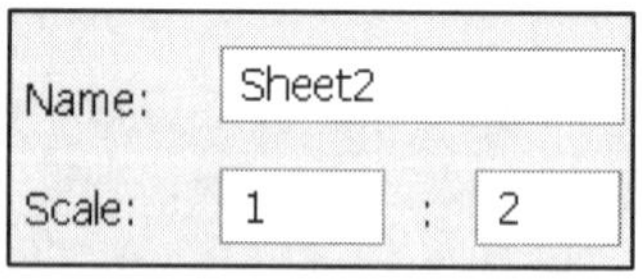

333) Click **Add Sheet**. Sheet2 is displayed. **Right-click** in Sheet2.

334) Click **Properties**.

335) Enter **1:2** for Scale.

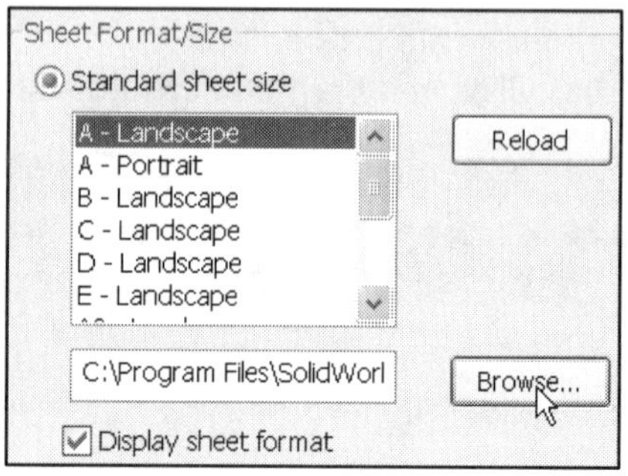

Select the CUSTOM-A Sheet Format.

336) Click **Browse** from the Sheet Properties box.

337) Select **SW-TUTORIAL-2007** for Look in folder.

338) Double-click **CUSTOM-A**.

339) Click **OK** from the Sheet Properties box. Sheet 2 of 2 is displayed in the Graphics window.

Insert the AIRCYLINDER assembly.

340) Click **Model View** from the Drawings toolbar. The Model View PropertyManager is displayed.

341) Click **Browse**. Double-click the **AIRCYLINDER** assembly from the SW-TUTORIAL-2007 folder.

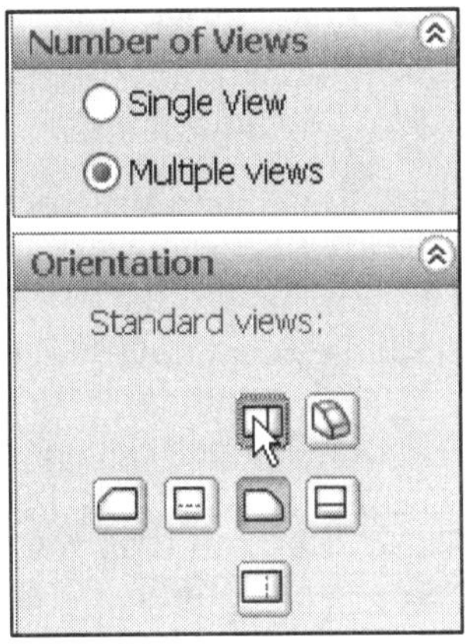

342) Click **Multiple views**.

343) Click ***Top view**. Note: Front view is selected by default. Both views should be active.

344) Click **OK** from the Model View PropertyManager.

Save Sheet2.

345) Click **Save**.

Modify the Title Name font size.

346) **Right-click** in the Graphics window.

347) Click **Edit Sheet Format**.

348) Double-click on the Title: **LINEAR ACTUATOR**.

349) Resize the text to the Title block. Enter **5mm** for text height.

350) Click in the **Graphics window**.

351) **Right-click** in the Graphics window.

352) Click **Edit Sheet**.

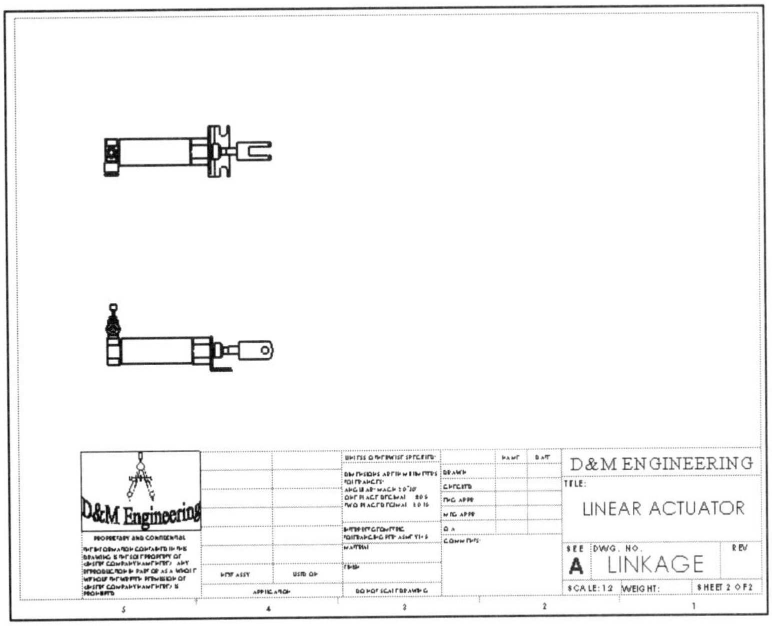

Section Views display the interior features. Define a cutting plane with a sketched line in a view perpendicular to the Section View. Create a full Section View by sketching a section line in the Top view. Detailed views enlarge an area of an existing view. Specify location, shape and scale. Create a Detail View from a Section View at a 2:1 scale.

Activity: LINKAGE Assembly Drawing-Sheet2 Section View

Add a Section View to the drawing.

353) Click the **Drawing View3** boundary.

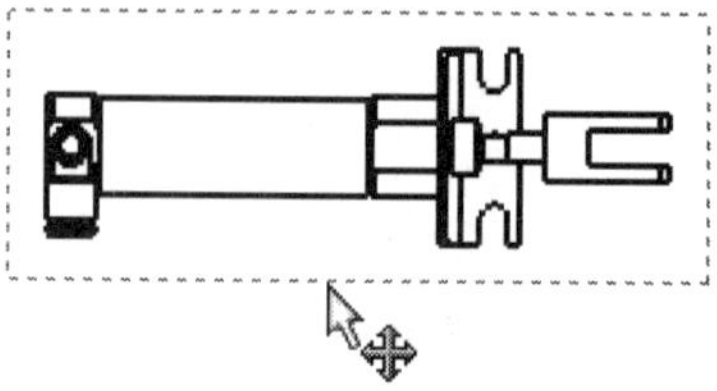

354) Click **Section View** Section View from the Drawing toolbar. The Section View PropertyManager is displayed.

355) Sketch a section line through the **midpoints** of the view boundary. The Section line extends beyond the left and right profile lines.

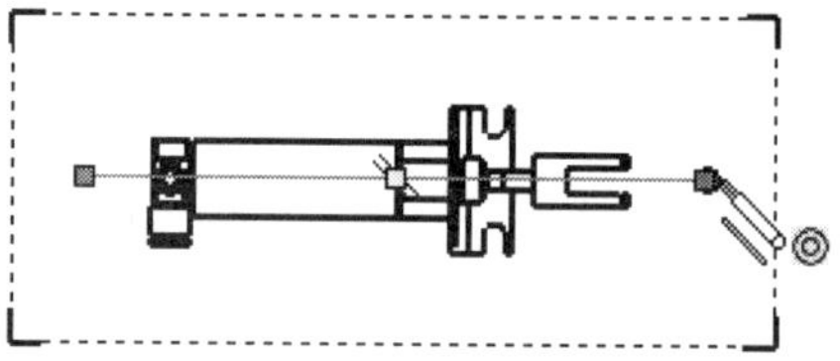

Position Section View A-A.

356) Click **OK** from the Section View dialog box.

357) Click a **location** above the Top view. The section arrows point upwards. If required, check the **Flip direction** box.

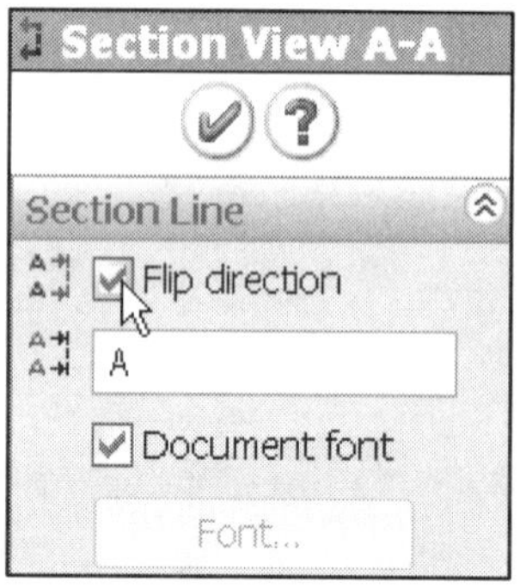

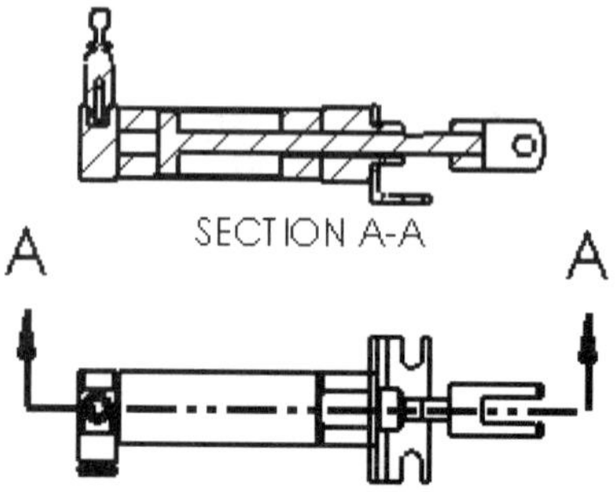

358) Click **OK** from the Section View PropertyManager.

Fit the drawing to the Graphics window.

359) Press the **f** key.

Activity: LINKAGE Assembly Drawing-Sheet2 Detail View

Add a Detail View to the drawing.

360) Click inside the **Section View** boundary. The Section View A-A PropertyManager is displayed.

361) Click **Zoom to Selection** to enlarge the view.

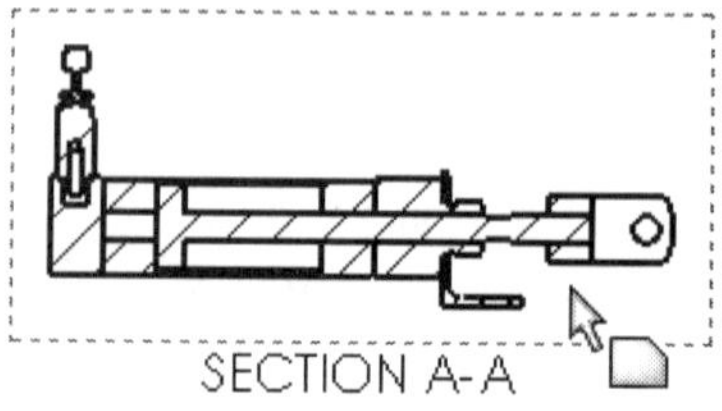

362) Click **Detail View** from the Drawing toolbar. The Circle Sketch tool is selected.

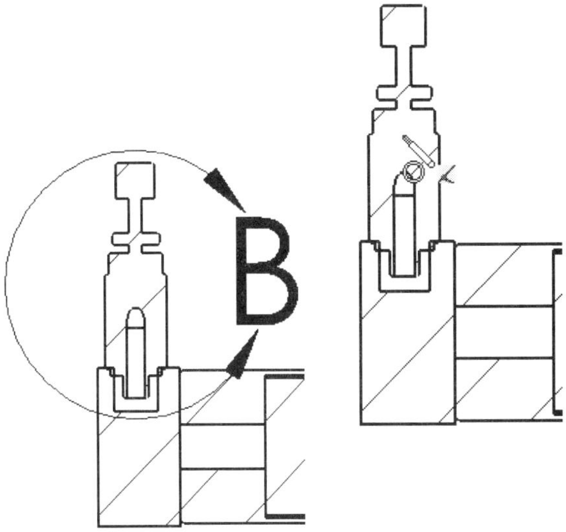

363) Click the **center** of the air fitting on the left side in the Section View as illustrated.

364) Sketch a **Circle** to encompass the air fitting.

365) If required, enter **B** for Detail View Name in the Label text box.

Position Detail View B.

366) Press the **f** key.

367) Click a **location** on Sheet2 to the right of the SECTION View.

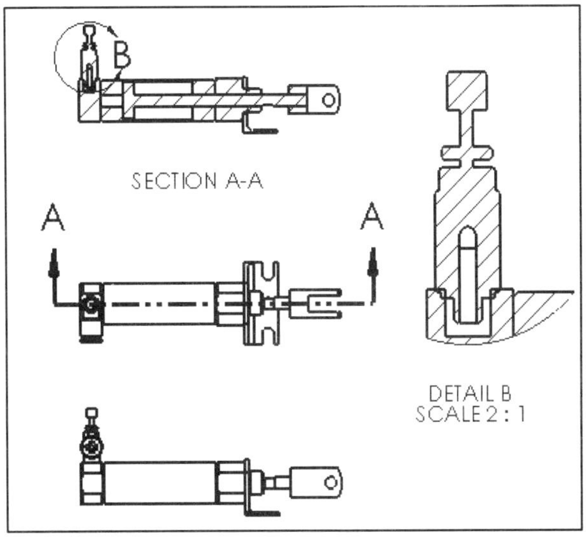

368) Enter **2:1** for Scale.

369) Click **OK** from the Detail View B PropertyManager.

Select a view boundary before creating Projected Views, Section Views or Detail Views. The view boundary is displayed in green.

Move views if required.

370) Click and drag the **view boundary** to allow for approximately 1 inch, [25mm] spacing between views.

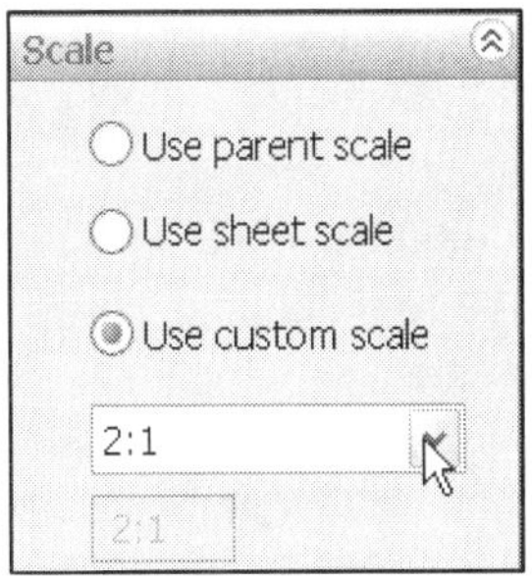

Save the LINKAGE assembly drawing.

371) Click **Save**.

Close all parts and assemblies.

372) Click **Window**, **Close All** from the Main menu.

Additional details on Exploded View, Notes, Properties, Bill of Materials, Balloons, Section View and Detail View are available in SolidWorks Help. Keywords: Exploded, Notes, Properties (configurations), Bill of Materials, Balloons, Auto Balloon, Section, and Detail.

Review the LINKAGE Assembly Drawing.

The LINKAGE Assembly drawing consisted of two sheets. Sheet1 contained an Exploded view. The Exploded view was created in the LINKAGE assembly.

The Bill of Materials listed the Item Number, Part Number, Description, Material and Quantity of components in the assembly. Balloons were inserted to label top level components in the LINKAGE assembly. You developed Custom Properties in the part and utilized the Properties in the drawing and Bill of Materials.

Sheet2 contained the Front view, Top view, Section view, and Detail view of the AIRCYLINDER assembly.

Design Tables

A Design Table is a spreadsheet used to create multiple configurations in a part or assembly. The Design Table controls the dimensions and parameters in the part. Utilize the Design Table to modify the overall length and number of holes in each FLATBAR.

Create three configurations of the FLATBAR:

- 3HOLE.
- 5HOLE.
- 7HOLE.

Utilize the Design Table to control the Part Number and Description in the Bill of Materials. Insert the custom parameter $PRP@DESCRIPTION into the Design Table. Insert the system parameter $PARTNUMBER into the Design Table.

Activity: FLATBAR Part-Design Table

Open the FLATBAR part.

373) Click **File**, **Open** from the Main menu.

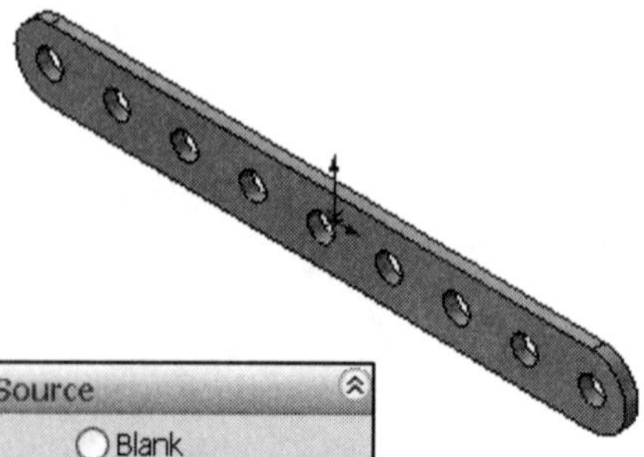

374) Double-click the **FLATBAR** part from the SW-TUTORIAL-2007 folder. The FLATBAR FeatureManager is displayed.

Insert a Design Table.

375) Click **Insert**, **Design Table** from the Main menu. The Auto-create option is selected.

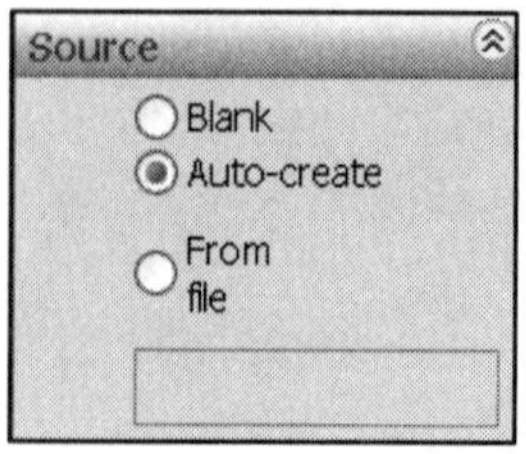

376) Click **OK** from the Design Table PropertyManager.

Select the input dimension.

377) Hold the **Ctrl** key down.

378) Click the **D1@Sketch1**, **D2@Sketch1**, **D1@Extude1**, **D1@Sketch2**, **D3@LPattern1** and **D1@LPattern1** from the Dimensions box.

379) Release the **Ctrl key**.

380) Click **OK** from the Dimensions dialog box.

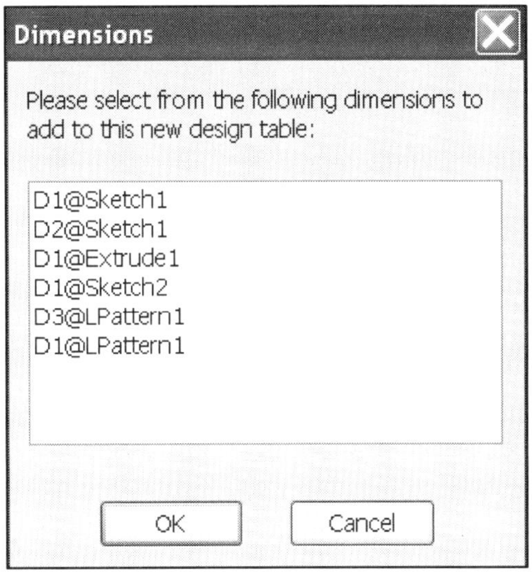

Note: The dimension variable name will be different if sketches or features were deleted.

The input dimension names and default values are automatically entered into the Design Table. The Design Table displays the Primary Units of the Part. Example: Inches. The value Default is entered in Cell A3.

The values for the FLATBAR are entered in Cells B3 through G9. The FLATBAR length is controlled in Column B. The Number of Holes is controlled in Column G.

Enter the three configuration names.

381) Click **Cell A4**.

382) Enter **3HOLE**.

383) Click **Cell A5**.

384) Enter **5HOLE**.

385) Click **Cell A6**.

386) Enter **7HOLE**.

387) Click Cell **D3**.

388) Enter **0.09** to round off the Thickness value.

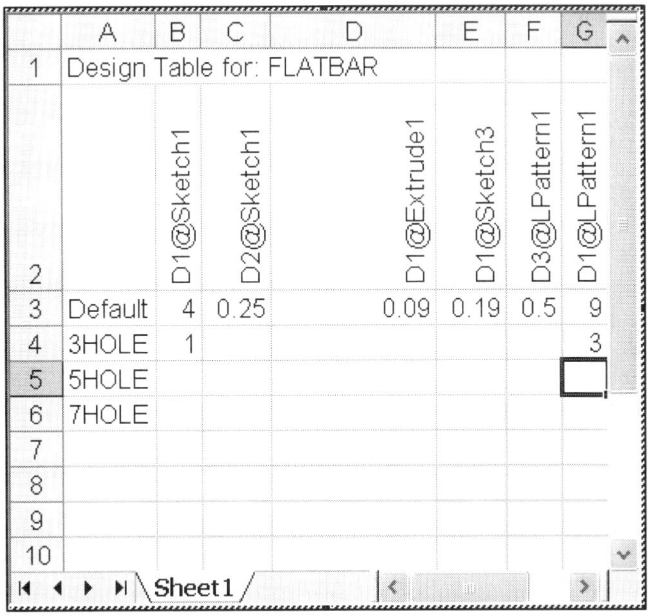

Enter the dimension values for the 3HOLE configuration.

389) Click **Cell B4**. Enter **1**.

390) Click **Cell G4**. Enter **3**.

Enter the dimension values for the 5HOLE configuration.

391) Click **Cell B5**.

392) Enter **2**.

393) Click **Cell G5**.

394) Enter **5**.

	A	B	C	D	E	F	G
1	Design Table for: FLATBAR						
2		D1@Sketch1	D2@Sketch1	D1@Extrude1	D1@Sketch3	D3@LPattern1	D1@LPattern1
3	Default	4	0.25	0.09	0.19	0.5	9
4	3HOLE	1					3
5	5HOLE	2					5
6	7HOLE	3					7

Enter the dimension values for the 7HOLE configuration.

395) Click **Cell B6**.

396) Enter **3**.

397) Click **Cell G6**.

398) Enter **7**.

Build the three configurations.

399) Click a **position** outside the EXCEL Design Table in the Graphics window.

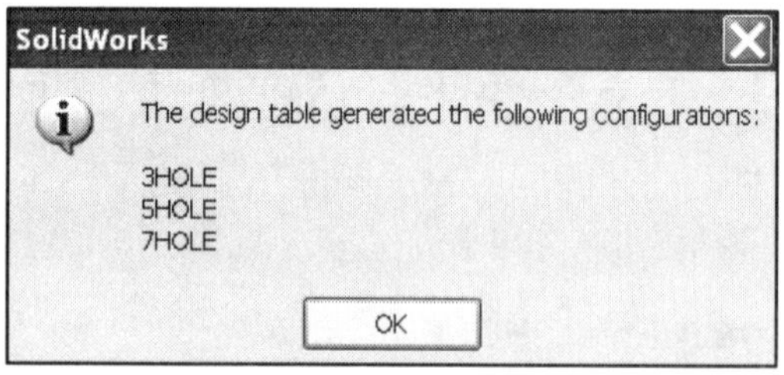

400) Click **OK** to generate the configurations. The Design Table icon is displayed in the FLATBAR FeatureManager.

Display the configurations.

401) Click the **ConfigurationManager** tab.

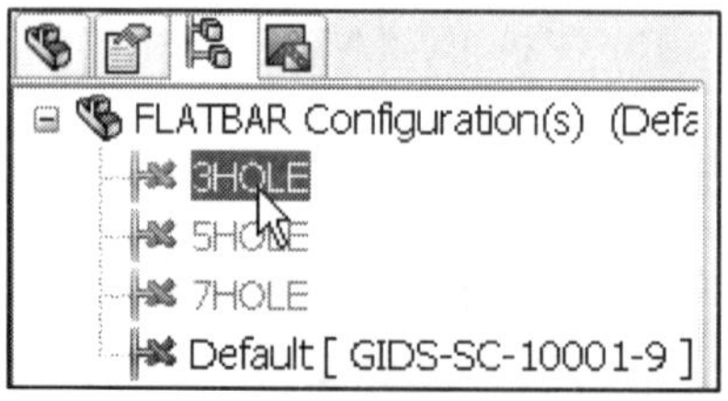

402) Double-click **3HOLE**.

403) Double-click **5HOLE**.

404) Double-click **7HOLE**.

405) Double-click **Default**.

Return to the FeatureManager.

406) Click the **FeatureManager** tab.

407) Click **Save**.

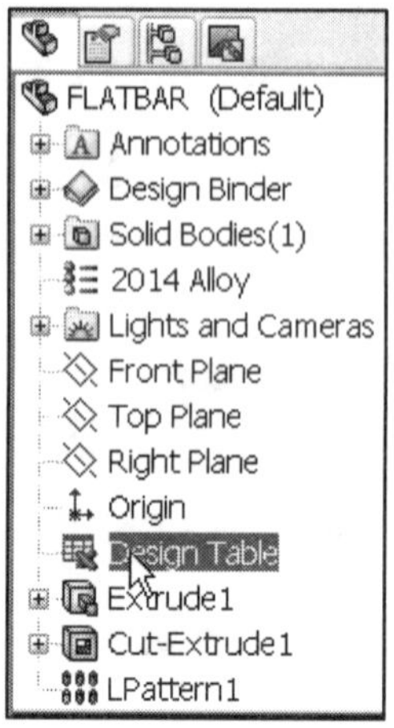

Edit the Design Table.

408) Right-click **Design Table** in the FeatureManager.

409) Click **Edit Table**.

410) Click **Cancel** from the Add Rows and Columns dialog box.

Columns C through F are filled with the default FLATBAR values.

Enter parameters for DESCRIPTION and PARTNUMBER. Custom Properties begin with the prefix, "$PRP@". SolidWorks Properties begin with the prefix, "$".

	A	B	C	D	E	F
1	Design Table for: FLATBAR					
2		D1@Sketch1	D2@Sketch1	D1@Extrude1	D1@Sketch2	D3@LPattern1
3	Default	4	0.25	0.09	0.19	0.5
4	3HOLE	1	0.25	0.09	0.19	0.5
5	5HOLE	2	0.25	0.09	0.19	0.5
6	7HOLE	3	0.25	0.09	0.19	0.5
7						
8						
9						
10						

Sheet1

Enter DESCRIPTION custom Property.

411) Double-click **Cell H2**.

412) Enter **$PRP@DESCRIPTION**.

413) Click **Cell H3**. Enter **9HOLES**.

414) Click **Cell H4**. Enter **3HOLES**.

415) Click **Cell H5**. Enter **5HOLES**.

416) Click **Cell H6**. Enter **7HOLES**.

F	G	H
D3@LPattern1	D1@LPattern1	$PRP@DESCRIPTION
0.5	9	9HOLES
0.5	3	3HOLES
0.5	5	5HOLES
0.5	7	7HOLES

Enter the PARTNUMBER Property.

417) Double-click **Cell I2**.

418) Enter **$PARTNUMBER**.

419) Click **Cell I3**.

420) Enter **GIDS-SC-10009-9**.

421) Click **Cell I4**.

422) Enter **GIDS-SC-10009-3**.

423) Click **Cell I5**.

424) Enter **GIDS-SC-10009-5**.

425) Click **Cell I6**.

426) Enter **GIDS-SC-10009-7**.

E	F	G	H	I	J
D1@Sketch3	D3@LPattern1	D1@LPattern1	$PRP@DESCRIPTION	$PARTNUMBER	
0.19	0.5	9	9HOLES	GIDS-SC-10009-9	
0.19	0.5	3	3HOLES	GIDS-SC-10009-3	
0.19	0.5	5	5HOLES	GIDS-SC-10009-5	
0.19	0.5	7	7HOLES	GIDS-SC-10009-7	

427) Click a **position** in the Graphics window to update the Design Table.

Activity: FLATBAR Drawing-Sheet2

Select configurations in the drawing. The Properties option in the Drawing view displays a list of configuration names.

Open the FLATBAR drawing.

428) Click **File**, **Open** from the Main menu.

429) Select Files of type: **Drawing (#drw,*slddrw)**.

430) Double-click **FLATBAR** from the SW-TUTORIAL-2007 folder. The FLATBAR drawing is displayed.

Copy the Front view.

431) Click inside the FLATBAR **Front view** boundary.

432) Press **Ctrl C**. **Right-click** in the Graphics window.

433) Click **Add Sheet**. Sheet2 is displayed. Right-click **Properties**.

434) Click **Browse** from the Sheet Properties dialog box.

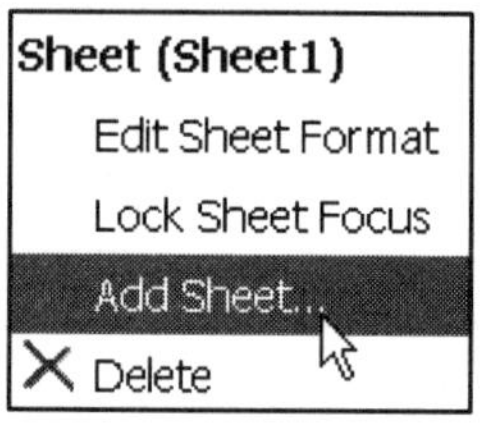

435) Double-click **CUSTOM-A** Sheet Format from the SW-TUTORIAL-2007 folder.

436) Click **OK** from the Sheet Properties box.

Paste the Front view from Sheet1.

437) Click a **position** inside the Sheet2 boundary.

438) Press **Ctrl V**. The Front view is displayed.

Display the 3HOLE FLATBAR configuration on Sheet2.

439) Right-click inside the **Front** view boundary.

440) Click **Properties**.

441) Select **3HOLE** from the Use named configuration list.

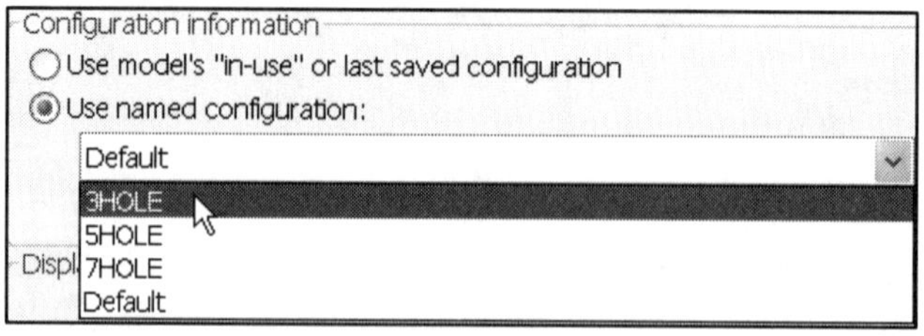

442) Click **OK** from the Drawing View Properties dialog box. The 3HOLE FLATBAR configuration is displayed.

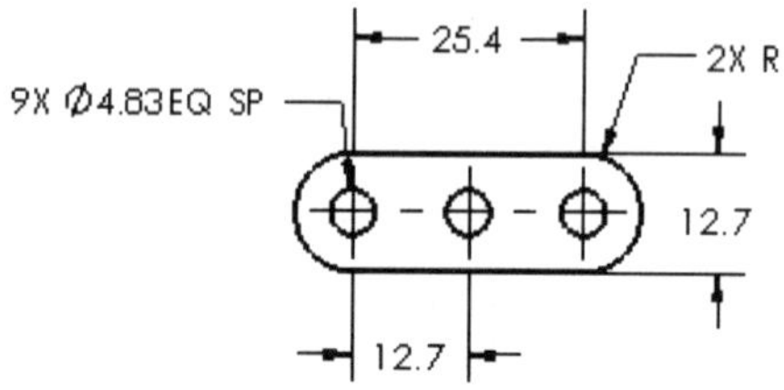

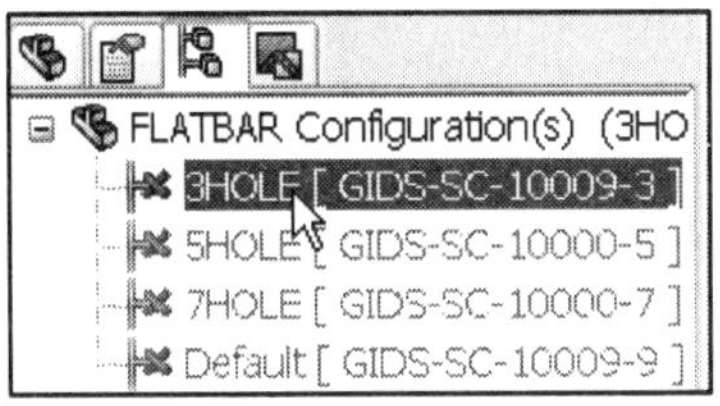

443) Right-click inside the **Drawing View boundary**.

444) Click **Open flatbar.sldprt**. The FLATBAR (3HOLE) FeatureManager is displayed. Click the **ConfigurationManager** tab.

445) Double-click the **3HOLE** configuration.

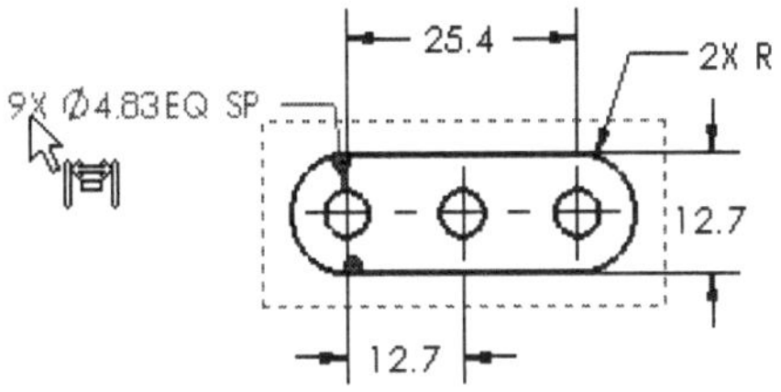

Return to the FLATBAR Drawing Sheet2.

446) Click **Window**, **FLATBAR – Sheet2** from the Main menu.

447) Click on the **9X** dimension text. Replace the 9X dimension text with **3X**.

448) Click **OK** from the Dimension PropertyManager.

Save the FLATBAR Sheet2 drawing.

449) Click **Save**.

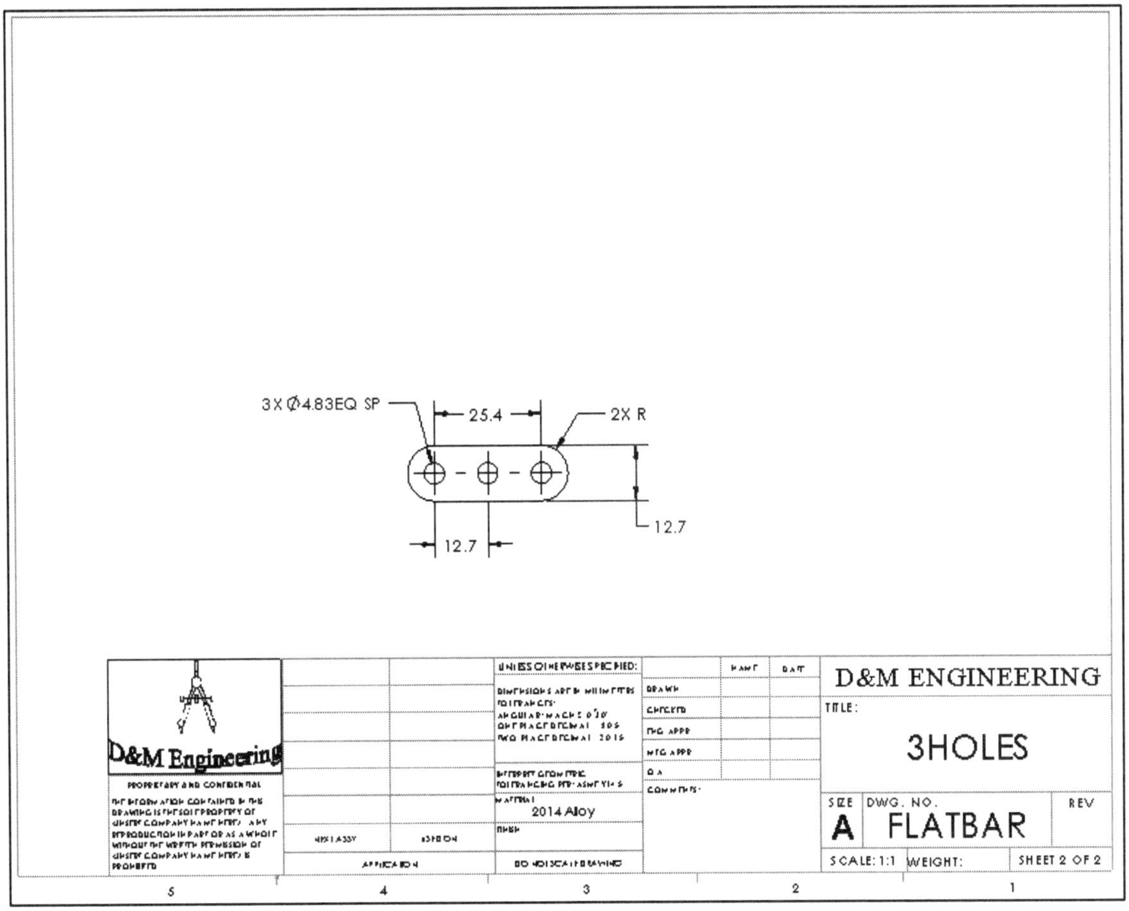

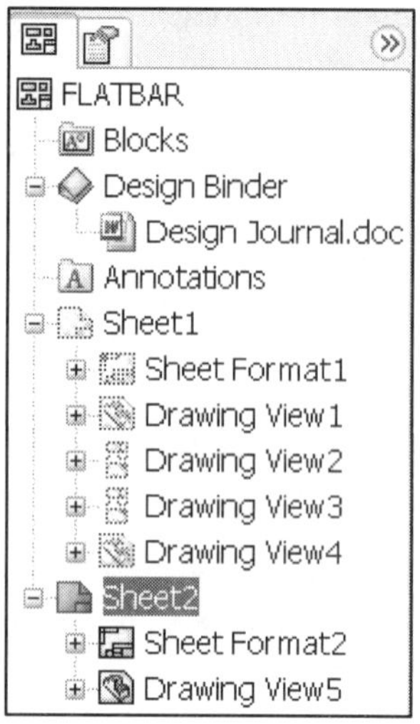

The 5HOLE and 7HOLE configurations are explored as an exercise. Combine the FLATBAR configurations with the SHAFT-COLLAR part to create three different assemblies. Select configuration in the assembly. The Properties in the FeatureManager option displays a list of configuration names.

The FLATBAR-SHAFTCOLLAR assembly contains a FLATBAR fixed to the assembly Origin and a SHAFTCOLLAR mated to the FLATBAR left hole. The default configuration utilizes a FLATBAR-9HOLE part.

Design Tables exist in the assembly. Utilize a Design Table to control part configurations, 3HOLE, 5HOLE, and 7HOLE. Utilize the Design Table to Control Suppress/Resolve state of a component in an assembly. Insert the parameter $STATE into the Design Table.

Activity: FLATBAR-SHAFTCOLLAR Assembly

Return to the Default FLATBAR configuration.

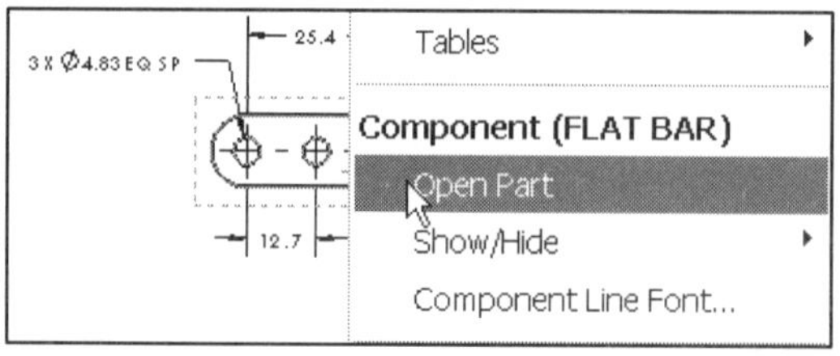

450) Right-click on the **3HOLE FLATBAR**. Click **Open Part**.

451) Click the **ConfigurationManager** tab. Double-click the **Default** configuration. Click the **FeatureManager** tab. The FLATBAR (Default) FeatureManager is displayed.

452) Click **Save**.

Create the FLATBAR-SHAFTCOLLAR assembly.

453) Click **File**, **New** from the Main menu. Double-click **Assembly** from the Templates tab. The Insert Component PropertyManager is displayed.

454) Click **View**; check **Origins** from the Main menu. Click **Browse** from the Insert Component PropertyManager. Double-click **FLATBAR** part from the SW-TUTORIAL-2007 folder.

455) Click the assembly **Origin**. The FLATBAR is fixed to the Origin.

Save the FLATBAR-SHAFTCOLLAR assembly.

456) Click **Save**.

457) Enter **FLATBAR-SHAFTCOLLAR** for Assembly name. Click **Save**.

Insert the SHAFTCOLLAR part.

458) Click **Insert Component** Insert Compo... from the Assembly toolbar. The Insert Component PropertyManager is displayed.

459) Click **BROWSE**.

460) Double-click the **SHAFT-COLLAR** part.

461) Click a **position** to the left of the FLATBAR as illustrated in the Graphics window.

Fit the Model to the Graphics window.
462) Press the **f** key.

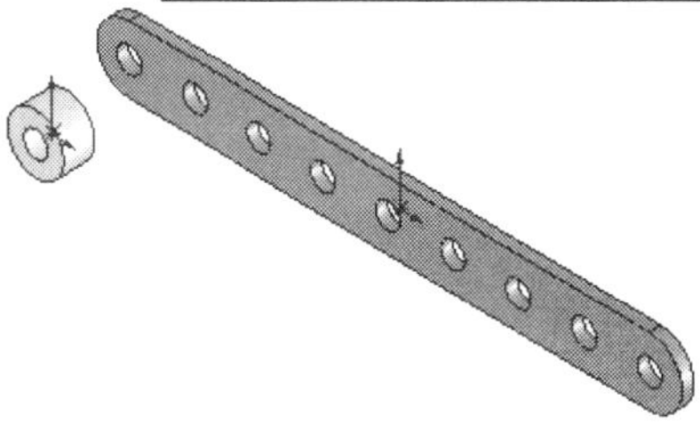

463) Click **Save**.

Mate the SHAFTCOLLAR.

464) Click **Mate** Mate from the Assembly toolbar. The Mate PropertyManager is displayed.

Create a Concentric Mate.
465) Click the **left hole face** of the FLATBAR.

466) Click the outside **cylindrical face** of the SHAFT-COLLAR. The selected faces are displayed in the Mate Selections box. Concentric is selected by default.

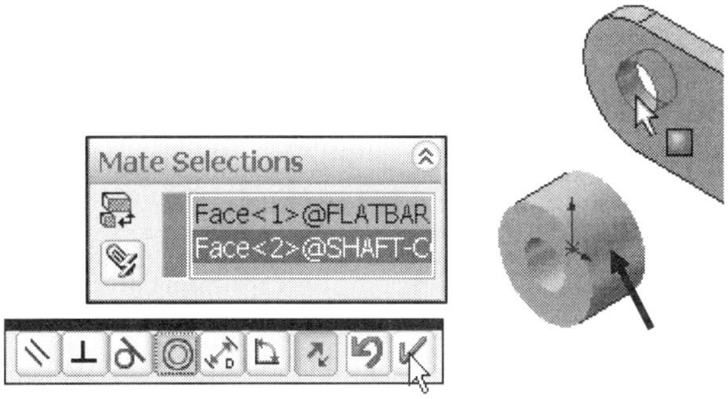

467) Click the **Green Check mark**.

Create a Coincident Mate.
468) Click the **back flat face** of the SHAFT-COLLAR.

469) Click the **front face** of the FLATBAR as illustrated. Coincident is selected by default.

470) Click the **Green Check mark**.

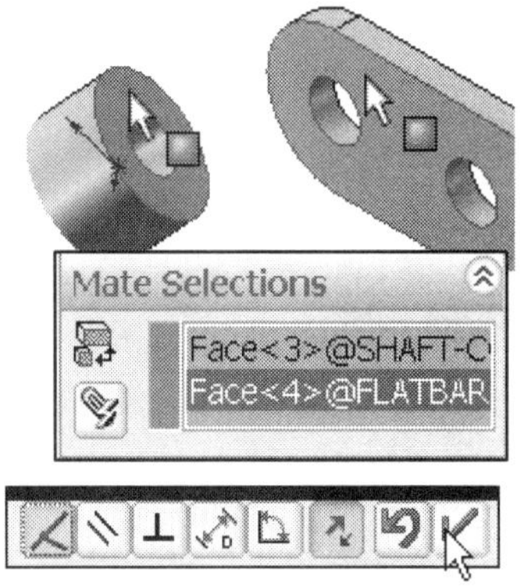

471) Click **OK** from the Mate PropertyManager.

Insert and Mate the second SHAFT-COLLAR to the right hole.

472) Click **Insert Component** Insert Compo... from the Assembly toolbar. The Insert Component PropertyManager is displayed.

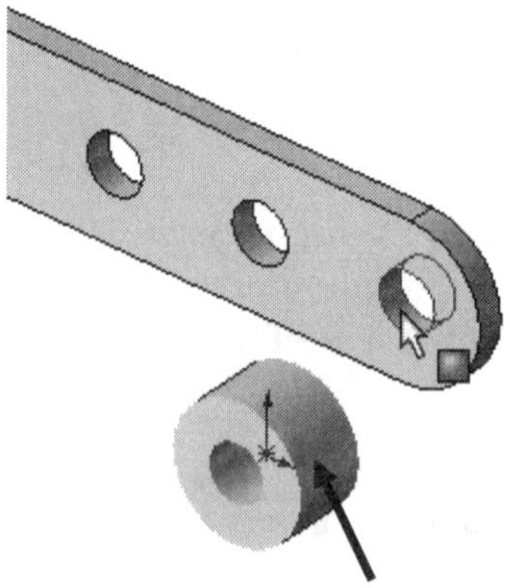

473) Click **BROWSE**.

474) Double-click the **SHAFT-COLLAR** part.

475) Click a **position** to the right of the FLATBAR as illustrated.

Mate the Second SHAFTCOLLAR.

476) Click **Mate** Mate from the Assembly toolbar. The Mate PropertyManager is displayed.

Create a Concentric Mate.

477) Click the **right hole face** of the FLATBAR.

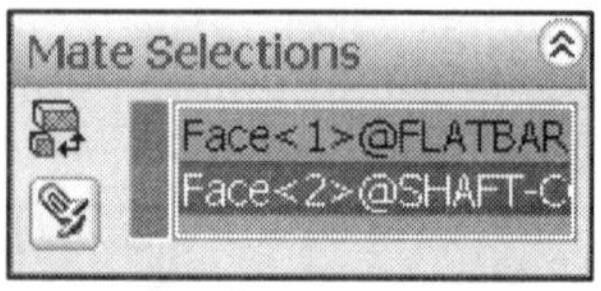

478) Click the **cylindrical face** of the SHAFT-COLLAR. Concentric is selected by default.

479) Click the **Green Check mark**.

Create a Coincident Mate.

480) Click the **back flat face** of the SHAFT-COLLAR.

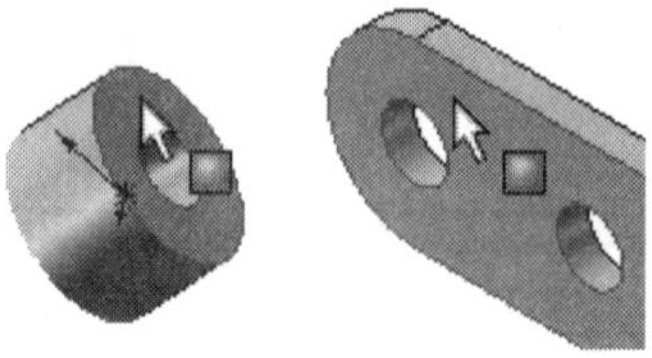

481) Click the **front face** of the FLATBAR. Coincident is selected by default.

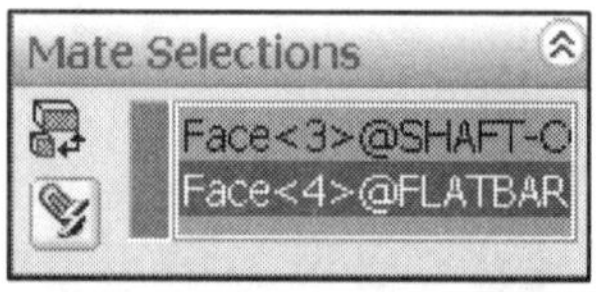

482) Click the **Green Check mark**.

483) Click **OK** from the Mate PropertyManager.

Save the FLATBAR-SHAFTCOLLAR assembly.

484) Click **Save**.

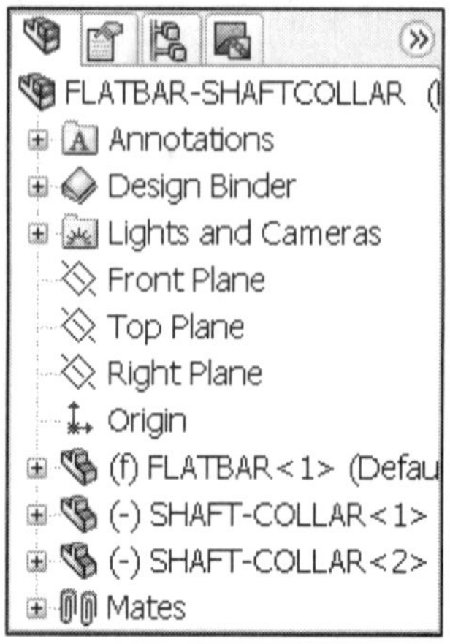

The FLATBAR-SHAFTCOLLAR FeatureManager displays the Default configuration of the FLATBAR in parenthesis, FLATBAR<1> (Default).

The Instance Number, <1> indicates the first instance of the FLATBAR. Note: Your instance number will be different, if you delete the FLATBAR and then reinsert into the assembly. The exact Instance Number is required for the Design Table.

Create a Design Table that contains three new configurations. Each configuration utilizes a different FLATBAR configuration. Control the Suppress/Resolve State of the second SHAFT-COLLAR.

Insert a Design Table.

485) Click **Insert**, **Design Table** from the Main menu. The Auto-create option is selected by default.

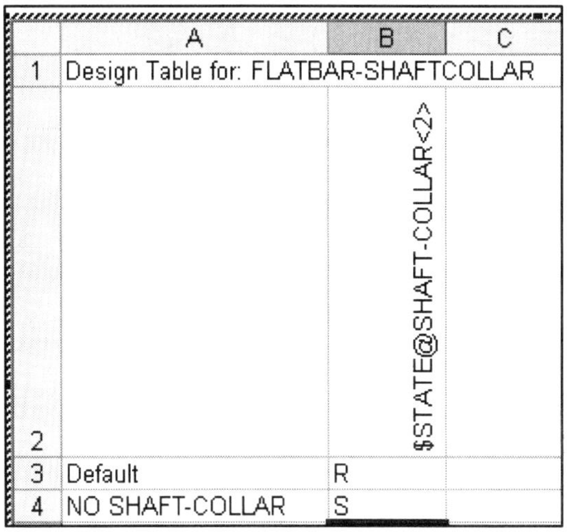

486) Click **OK** from the Design Table PropertyManager.

Enter the Design Table values.

487) Default is displayed in Cell A3. Click **Cell A4**. Enter **NO SHAFT-COLLAR**.

488) Double-click **CELL B2**.

489) Enter **$STATE@SHAFT-COLLAR<2>**. Click **Cell B3**.

490) Enter **R** for Resolved.

491) Click **Cell B4**.

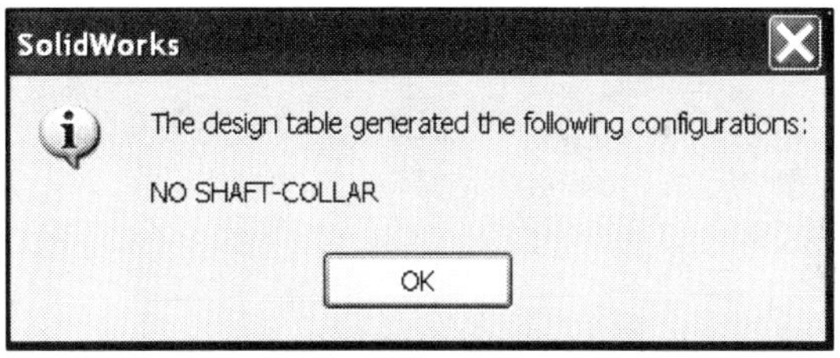

492) Enter **S** for Suppressed.

493) Click a **position** outside the Design Table.

494) Click **OK** to display the NO SHAFT-COLLAR configuration.

Display the configurations.

495) Click the **ConfigurationManager** tab.

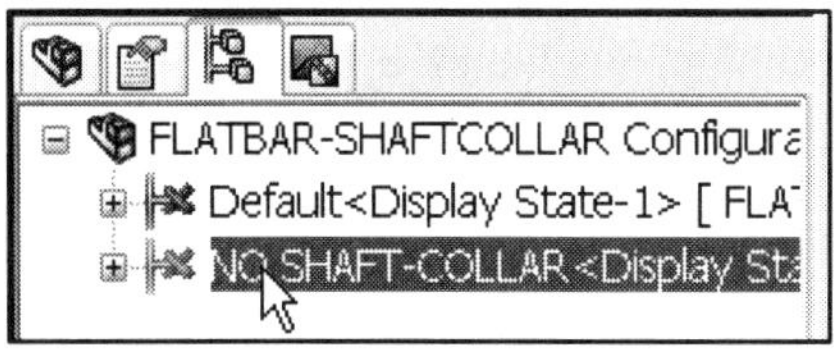

496) Double-click the **NO SHAFT-COLLAR** configuration. The second SHAFT-COLLAR is suppressed in the Graphics window.

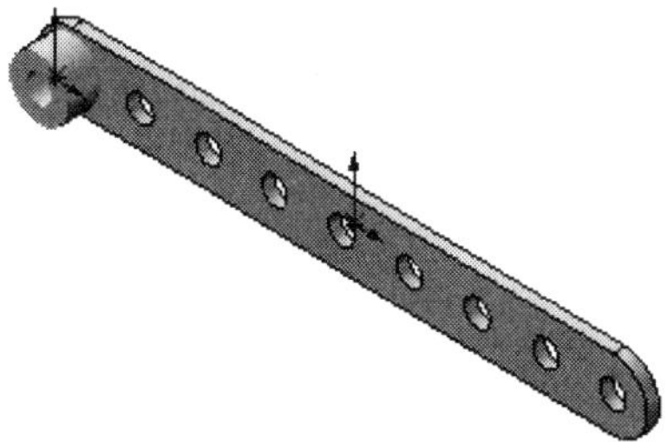

497) Double-click the **Default** configuration. The second SHAFT-COLLAR is resolved. Both SHAFT-COLLARs are displayed in the Graphics window.

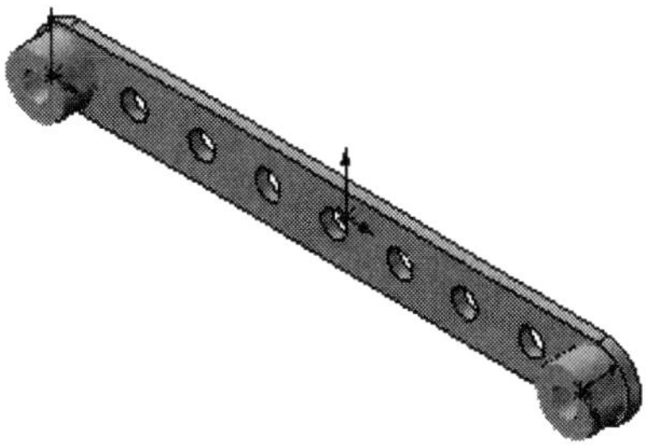

Insert FLATBAR configurations.

498) Click the **Assembly FeatureManager** tab.

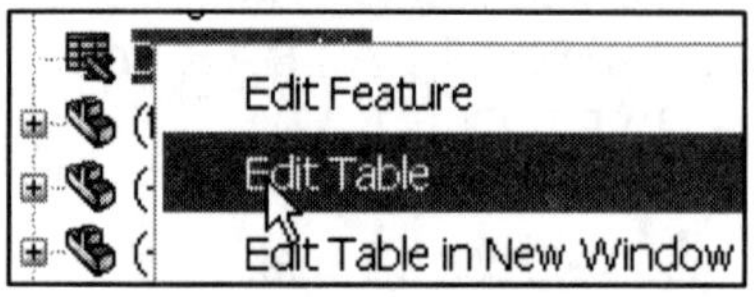

499) Right-click **Design Table**.

500) Click **Edit Table**.

501) Click **Cancel** from the Add Rows and Columns dialog box.

Enter Configuration names.

502) Click **Cell A5**. Enter **3HOLE FLATBAR**.

503) Click **Cell A6**. Enter **5HOLE FLATBAR**.

504) Click **Cell A7**. Enter **7HOLE FLATBAR**.

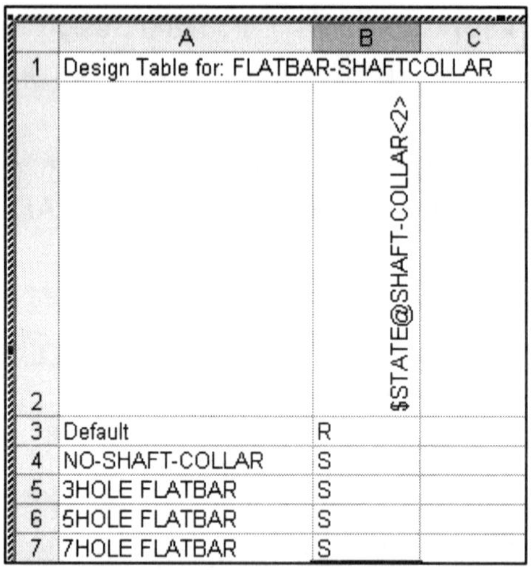

	A	B	C
1	Design Table for: FLATBAR-SHAFTCOLLAR		
2		$STATE@SHAFT-COLLAR<2>	
3	Default	R	
4	NO-SHAFT-COLLAR	S	
5	3HOLE FLATBAR	S	
6	5HOLE FLATBAR	S	
7	7HOLE FLATBAR	S	

Enter STATE values.

505) Click **Cell B5**. Enter **S** for Suppress.

506) Click Cell **B6**. Enter **S**.

507) Click **Cell B7**. Enter **S**.

Enter Design Table values.

508) Double-click **Cell C2**.

509) Enter **$CONFIGURATION@FLATBAR<1>**.

510) Click **Cell C5**.

511) Enter **3HOLE**.

512) Click **Cell C6**.

513) Enter **5HOLE**.

514) Click **Cell C7**.

515) Enter **7HOLE**.

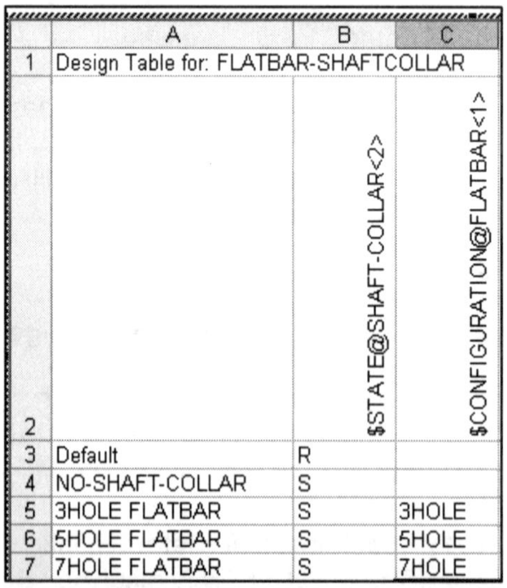

	A	B	C
1	Design Table for: FLATBAR-SHAFTCOLLAR		
2		$STATE@SHAFT-COLLAR<2>	$CONFIGURATION@FLATBAR<1>
3	Default	R	
4	NO-SHAFT-COLLAR	S	
5	3HOLE FLATBAR	S	3HOLE
6	5HOLE FLATBAR	S	5HOLE
7	7HOLE FLATBAR	S	7HOLE

516) Click a **position** in the Graphics window to exit.

517) Click **OK** to create the three configurations.

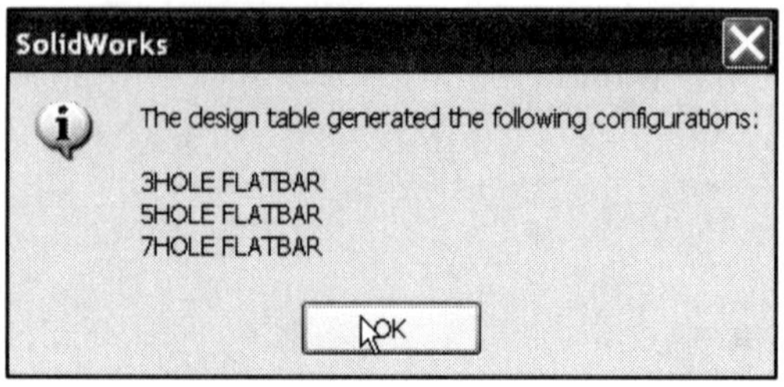

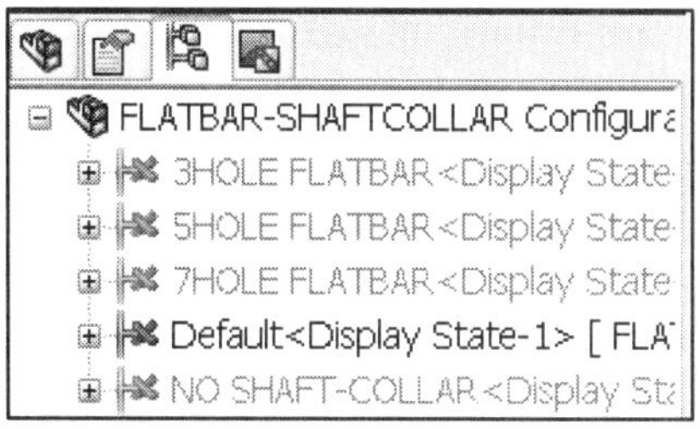

Display the configurations.

518) Click the **ConfigurationManager** tab.

519) Double-click the **3HOLE FLATBAR** configuration.

520) Double-click the **5HOLE FLATBAR** configuration.

521) Double-click the **7HOLE FLATBAR** configuration.

522) Double-click the **Default** configuration.

523) Click the **Assembly FeatureManager** tab.

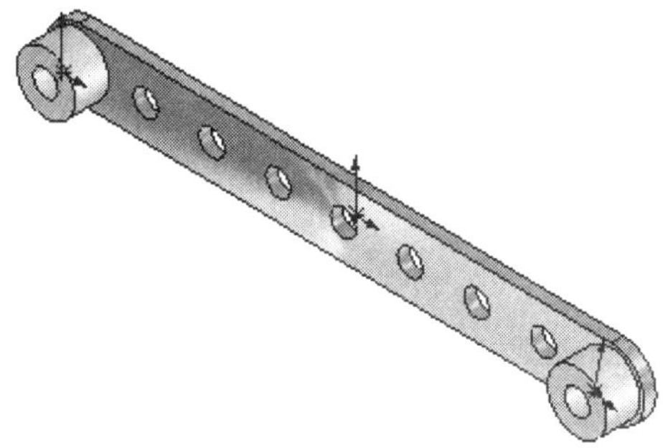

Save the FLATBAR-SHAFTCOLLAR assembly.

524) Click **Isometric view**.

525) Click **Save**.

Close all documents.

526) Click **Windows**, **Close All** from the Main menu.

Configurations are displayed in the Component PropertyManager. Access named configurations through the assembly FeatureManager, Properties option.

The complete list of configurations is displayed in the Open dialog box.

Always return to the Default configuration in the assembly. Control the individual configuration through properties of a view in a drawing and properties of a component in the assembly.

To modify configuration specific notes or dimensions in an assembly drawing, the configuration in the assembly must be the active configuration.

Additional details on Design Tables and Configurations are available in SolidWorks Help.

Project Summary

You created two drawings: the FLATBAR drawing and the LINKAGE assembly drawing. The drawings contained Standard views, a Detail View, a Section View, and an Isometric view.

The drawings utilized a Custom sheet format and a Custom Drawing Template. The sheet format contained the Company logo and Title block information.

The FLATBAR drawing consisted of two Sheets: Sheet1 and Sheet2. You obtained an understanding of displaying views with the ability to insert, add, and modify dimensions. You used two major design modes in the drawings: Edit Sheet Format and Edit Sheet.

The LINKAGE assembly drawing contained two sheets. Sheet1 contained an Exploded view and a Bill of Materials. The Properties for the Bill of Materials were developed in each part and assembly. Sheet2 utilized a Detail View and a Section View of the AIRCYLINDER assembly.

You created three configurations of the FLATBAR part with a Design Table. The Design Table controlled parameters and dimensions of the FLATBAR part. You utilized these three configurations in the FLATBAR-SHAFTCOLLAR assembly.

Drawings are an integral part of the design process. Part, assemblies, and drawings all work together. From your initial design concepts, you created parts and drawings that fulfilled the design requirements of your customer.

Additional SolidWorks examples are provided in the text **Drawing and Detailing with SolidWorks**, Planchard & Planchard, SDC Publications.

Project Terminology

Bill of Materials (BOM): A BOM is a EXCEL table in a drawing that lists the item, quantity, part number and description of the components in an assembly. Balloon labels are placed on items in the drawing that correspond to the number in the table. A BOM template controls additional information such as Material or Cost.

Center marks: Represents two perpendicular intersecting centerlines.

Design Table: A Design Table is a spreadsheet used to create multiple configurations in a part or assembly. The Design Table controls the dimensions and parameters in the part.

Detailed view: Detailed views enlarge an area of an existing view. Specify location, shape, and scale.

Drawing file name: Drawing file names end with a .slddrw suffix.

Drawing Layers: Contain dimensions, annotations, and geometry.

Drawing Template: The foundation of a SolidWorks drawing is the Drawing Template. Drawing size, drawing standards, company information, manufacturing and or assembly requirements, units and other properties are defined in the Drawing Template. In this project, the Drawing Template contained the drawing Size and Document Properties.

Edit Sheet Format Mode: Provides the ability to:

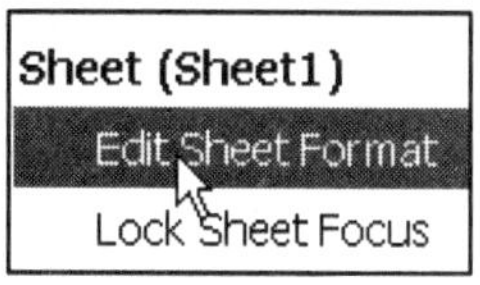

- Change the Title block size and text headings.
- Incorporate a Company logo.
- Add a drawing, design or company text.

Remember: A part cannot be inserted into a drawing when the Edit Sheet Format mode is selected.

Edit Sheet Mode: Provides the ability to:

- Add or modify views.
- Add or modify dimensions.
- Add or modify text.

General Notes: Below are a few helpful guidelines to create general drawing notes:

- Use capitol letters.
- Use left text justification.
- Font size should be the same as the dimension text.

Hole Callout: The Hole Callout function creates additional notes required to dimension the holes.

Hole centerlines: Are composed of alternating long and short dash lines. The lines identify the center of a circle, axes or other cylindrical geometry.

Insert Model Items: The command utilized to insert part dimensions and annotations into drawing views. Located on the Annotation toolbar.

Leader lines: Reference the size of the profile. A gap must exist between the profile lines and the leader lines.

ModelView: The command utilized to insert named views into a drawing. The ModelView tool is located on the Drawing toolbar.

Notes: Notes can be used to add text with leaders or as a stand-alone text string. If an edge, face or vertex is selected prior to adding the note, a leader is created to that location.

Part file name: Part file names end with a .sldprt suffix. Note: A drawing or part file can have the same prefix. A drawing or part file cannot have the same suffix. Example: Drawing file name: FLATBAR.slddrw. Part file name: FLATBAR.sldprt

Section View: Section Views display the interior features. Define a cutting plane with a sketched line in a view perpendicular to the Section View.

Sheet Format: The Sheet Format is incorporated into the Drawing Template. The Sheet Format contains the border, title block information, revision block information, company name and or logo information, Custom Properties and SolidWorks Properties. In this project the Sheet Format contained the title block information.

Title block: Contains vital part or assembly information. Each company can have a unique version of a title block.

View Appearance: There are two important factors that affect the appearance of views:

1. Whether the view is shown wireframe, hidden lines removed, or hidden lines visible.

2. How tangent edges on entities such as fillets are displayed.

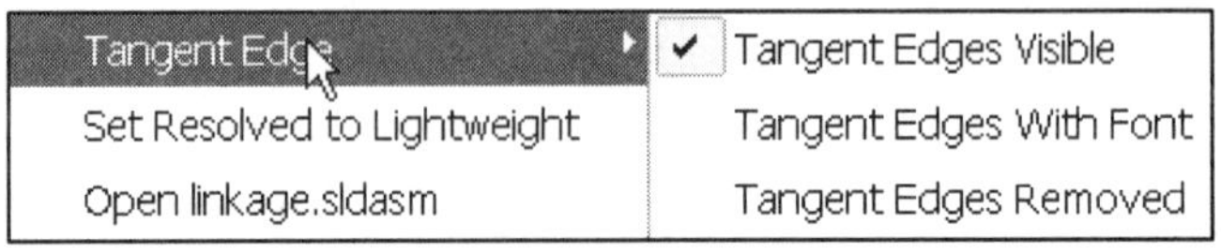

Questions

1. Describe a Bill of Materials and its contents.

2. Name the two major design modes used to develop a drawing in SolidWorks.

3. True or False. Units, Dimensioning Standards, Arrow size, Font size are modified in Tools, Options, Document Properties option.

4. How do you save a sheet format?

5. Identify seven components that are commonly found in a title block.

6. Describe the procedure to insert an Isometric view to the drawing?

7. In SolidWorks, drawing file names end with a ______ suffix. Part file names end with a ______ suffix.

8. True or False. In SolidWorks, if a part is modified, the drawing is updated with a Rebuild command.

9. True or False. In SolidWorks, when a dimension in the drawing is modified, the part is updated with a Rebuild command.

10. Name three guidelines to create General Notes on a drawing.

11. True or False. Most engineering drawings use the following font: Times New Roman – All small letters.

12. What are Leader lines? Provide an example.

13. Describe the key differences between a Detailed View and a Section View on a drawing.

14. Identify the procedure to create an Exploded View.

15. Describe the purpose of a Design Table in a part and in an assembly.

16. Review the Design Intent section in the Introduction. Identify how you incorporated design intent into the drawing.

17. Identify how you incorporate design intent into configurations with a Design Table.

18. Review the Keyboard Short Cut keys in the Appendix. Identify the Short Cut keys you incorporated into this project.

19. Discuss why a part designed in inch units would utilize a drawing detailed in millimeter units.

Exercises

Exercise 3.1: FLATBAR – 3 HOLE Drawing.

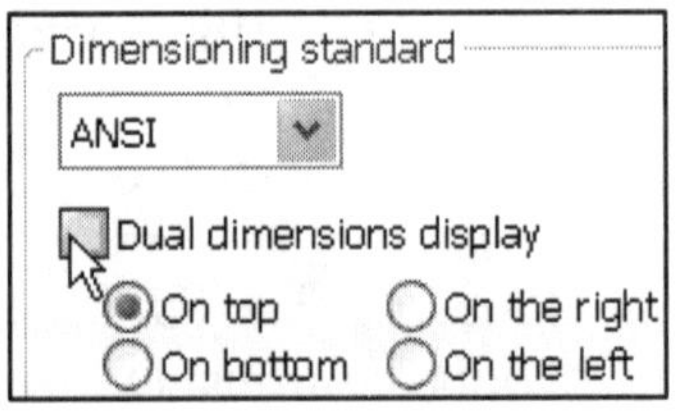

Note: Dimensions are enlarged for clarity. Utilize inch, millimeter, or dual dimensioning.

- Create the FLAT BAR – 3HOLE Drawing.
- Insert a Shaded Isometric view.

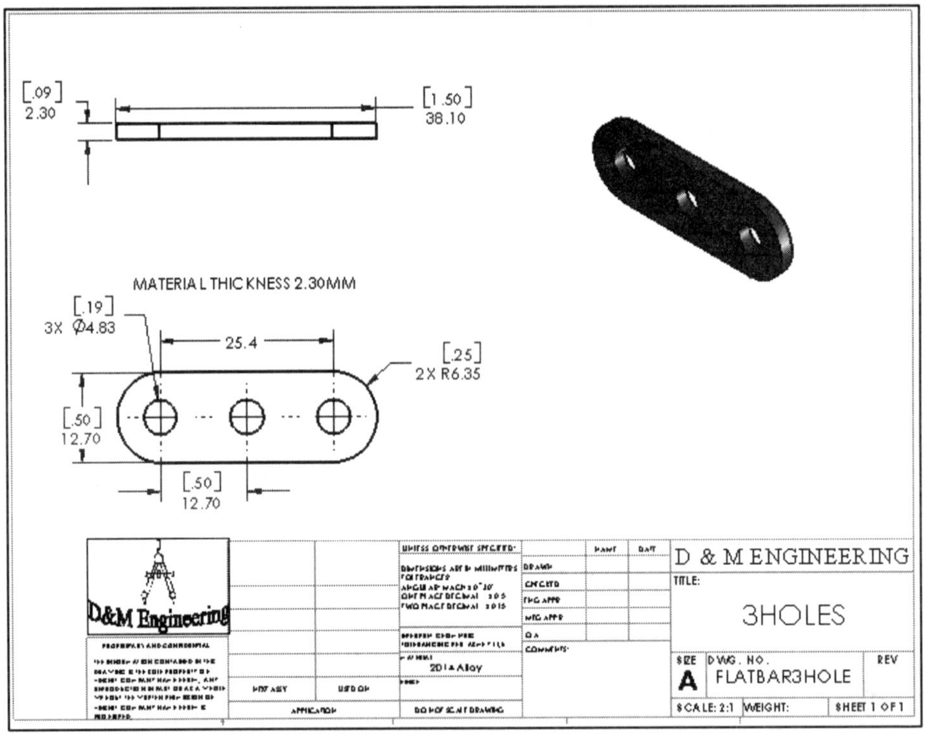

- Insert a Front and Top view.
- Insert dimensions from the part.
- Modify the hole dimension to include three holes.
- Add a Parametric Note for MATERIAL THICKNESS.
- Utilize the Material Editor. Enter Aluminum Alloy 2014.

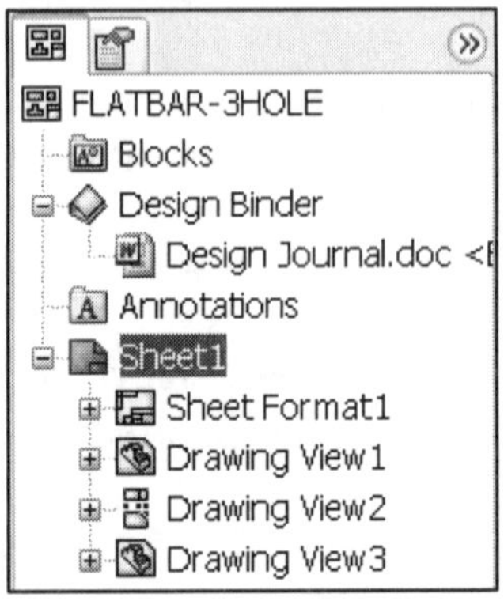

Exercise 3.2: **AXLE Drawing**.

Create the AXLE Drawing.

- Insert a Front, Top, and Shaded Isometric view. Fit the part to the drawing.
- Insert dimensions from the part.
- Add a centerline in the Top view.

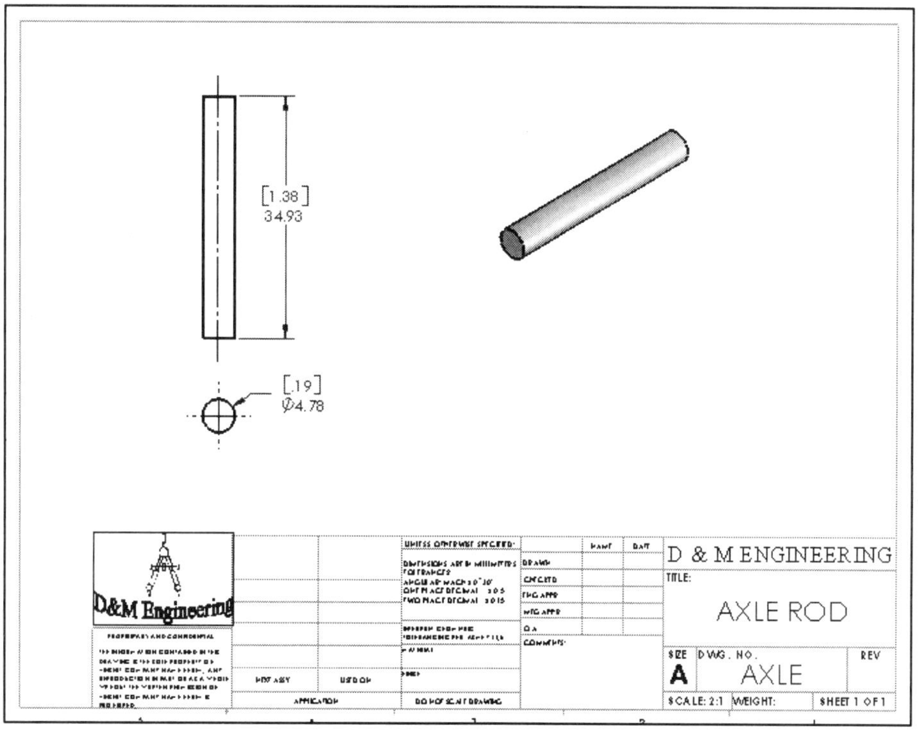

- Utilize the Material Editor. The Material is Aluminum Alloy 2014.
- Utilize Tools, Mass Properties to calculate the volume and mass of the AXLE part.

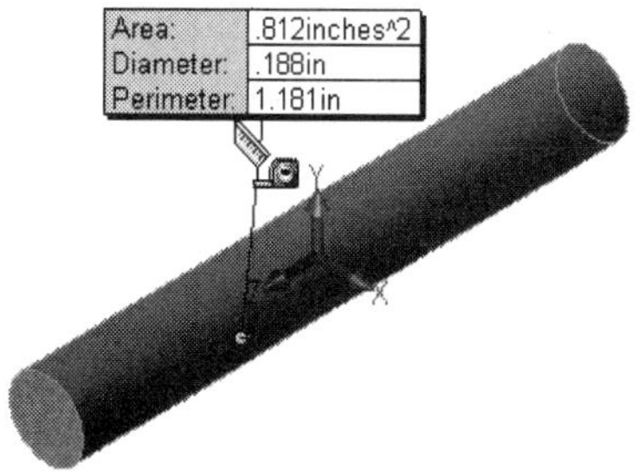

Exercise 3.3: SHAFT COLLAR Drawing.

Create the SHAFT COLLAR Drawing.

- Insert a Front, Top, and Shaded Isometric view. Add a 4:1 scale to the Isometric view.
- Insert and add dimensions as illustrated. Add a centerline to the Isometric view. .

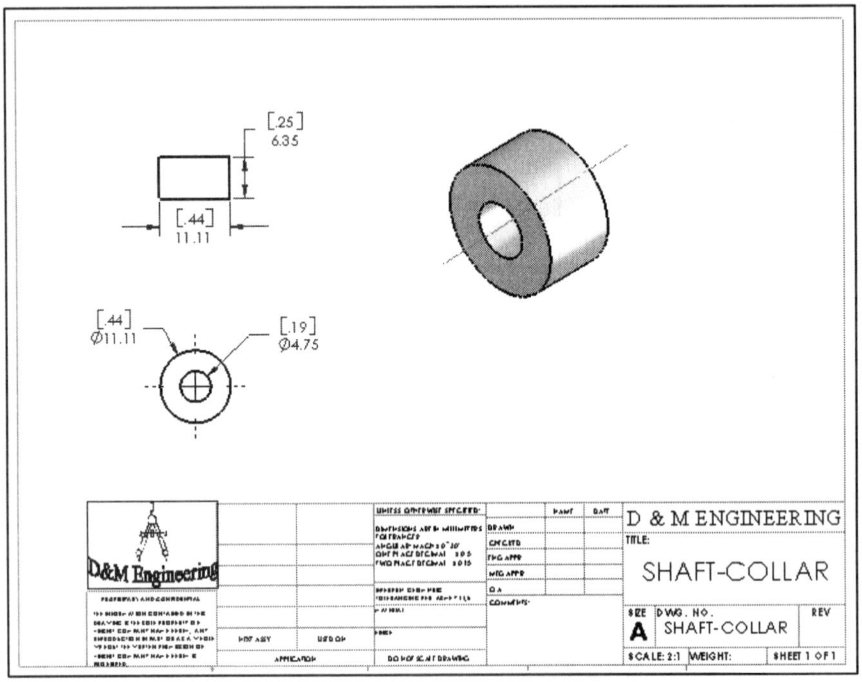

Exercise 3.4: 3LINKS Assembly.

- Utilize three different FLATBAR configurations and a SHAFT-COLLAR configuration.
- Create an assembly drawing for the 3LINKS Assembly. Insert a Bill of Materials.

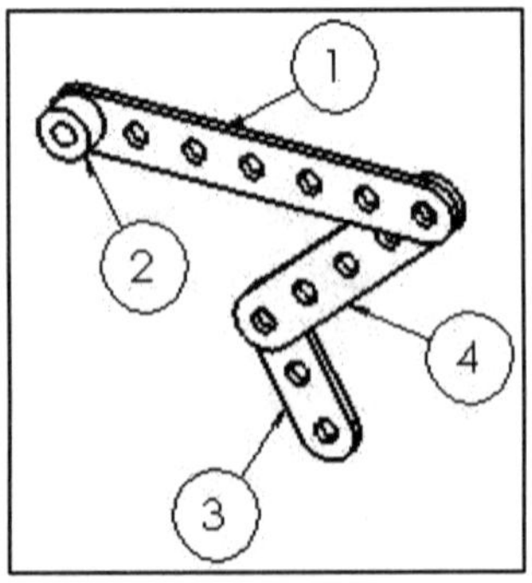

ITEM NO.	PART NUMBER:	DESCRIPTION:	QTY:
1	GIDS-SC-10009-7	FLATBAR-7HOLES	1
2	GIDS-CS-10012-3-16	SHAFT-COLLAR	1
3	GIDS-SC-10009-3	FLATBAR-3HOLES	1
4	GIDS-SC-10009-5	FLATBAR-5HOLES	1

Exercise 3.5: SHAFT-COLLAR Drawing: Design Tables.

Utilize a Design Table to create three configurations of the SHAFT-COLLAR:

- Small.
- Medium.
- Large.

	A	B	C	D
1	Design Table for: SHAFT-COLLAR			
2		D1@Sketch1	D1@Extrude1	D1@Sketch2
3	Default	0.4375	0.25	0.1875
4	Small	0.5	0.25	0.25
5	Medium	0.75	0.375	0.25
6	Large	1	0.5	0.5

Note: The dimension variable name will be different if sketches or features were deleted.

- Add a Sheet to the SHAFT-COLLAR drawing.
- Insert three different configurations: Small, Medium, and Large as illustrated.

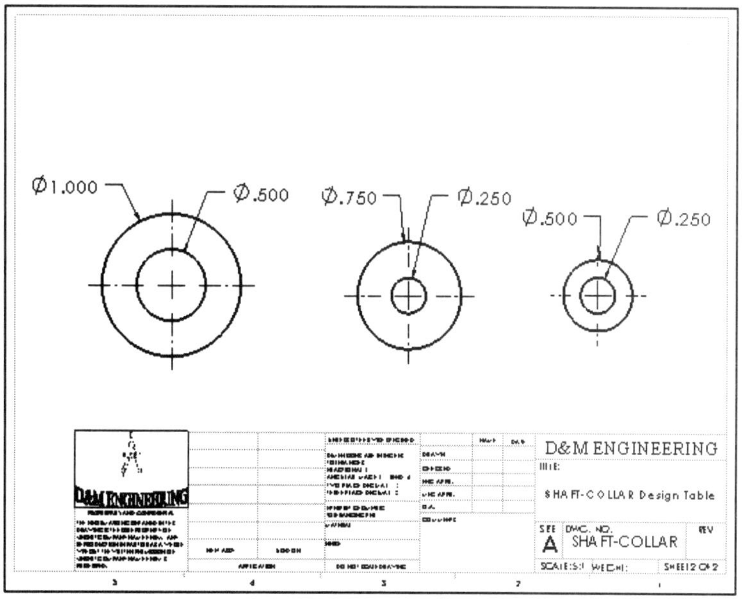

Exercise 3.6: Create a 5HOLE FLATBAR Drawing.

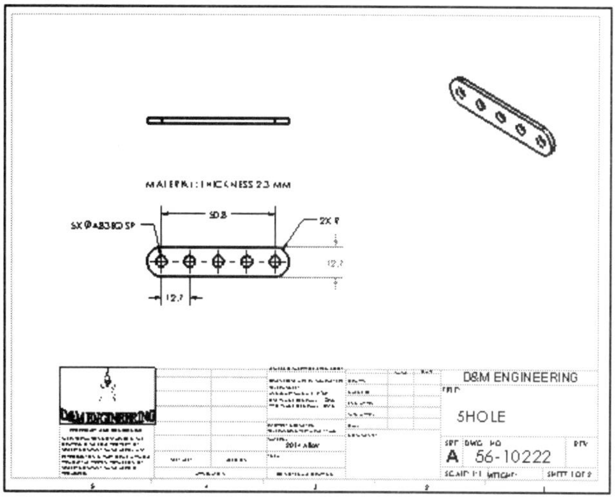

Exercise 3.7: LINKAGE-2 Drawing.

- Create a new drawing named, LINKAGE-2.
- Insert an Isometric view, shaded view of the LINKAGE-2 Assembly created in the Project 1 exercises.

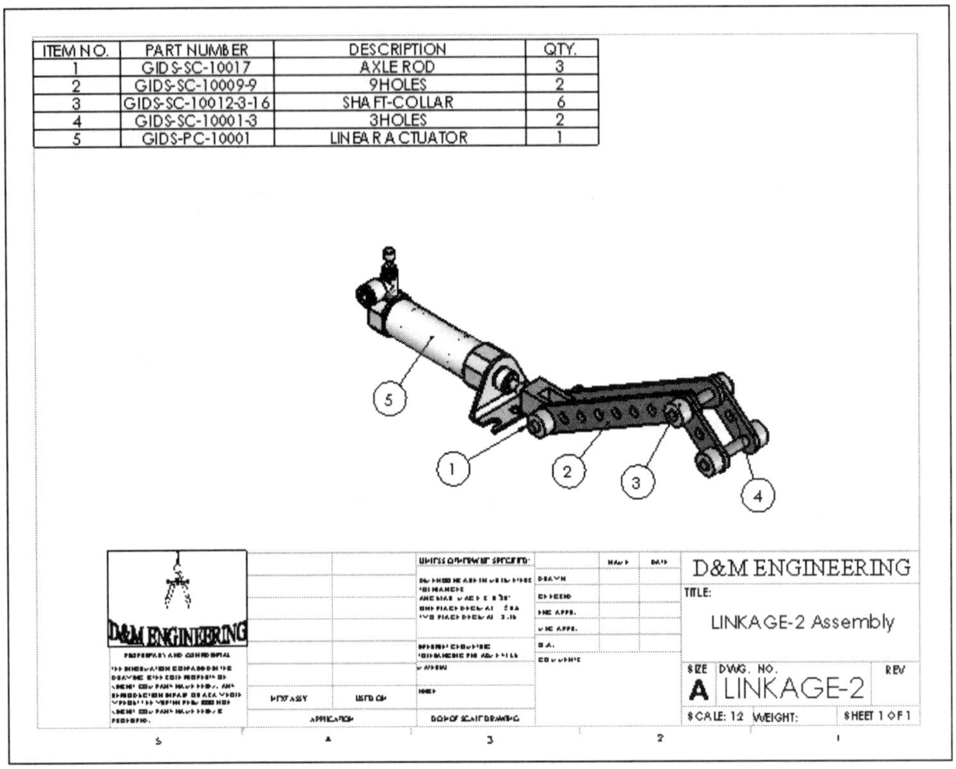

- Define the PART NO. Property and the DESCRIPTION Property for the AXLE, FLATBAR- 9HOLE, FLATBAR – 3HOLE and SHAFT COLLAR.
- Save the LINKAGE-2 assembly to update the properties. Return to the LINKAGE-2 Drawing. Insert a Bill of Materials with Auto Balloons.

Exercise 3.8: **eDrawing Exercise**.

Create an eDrawing of the LINKAGE-2 drawing. A SolidWorks eDrawing is a compressed document that does not require the corresponding part or assembly. SolidWorks eDrawing is animated to display multiple views and dimensions. Review the eDrawing On-line Help for additional functionality.

- Select Tools, Add-Ins, eDrawings 2007 from the Main memu.
- Click Publish eDrawing  from the eDrawing toolbar.
- Click the Play  button.
- Click the Stop  button.
- Save the LINKAGE eDrawing.

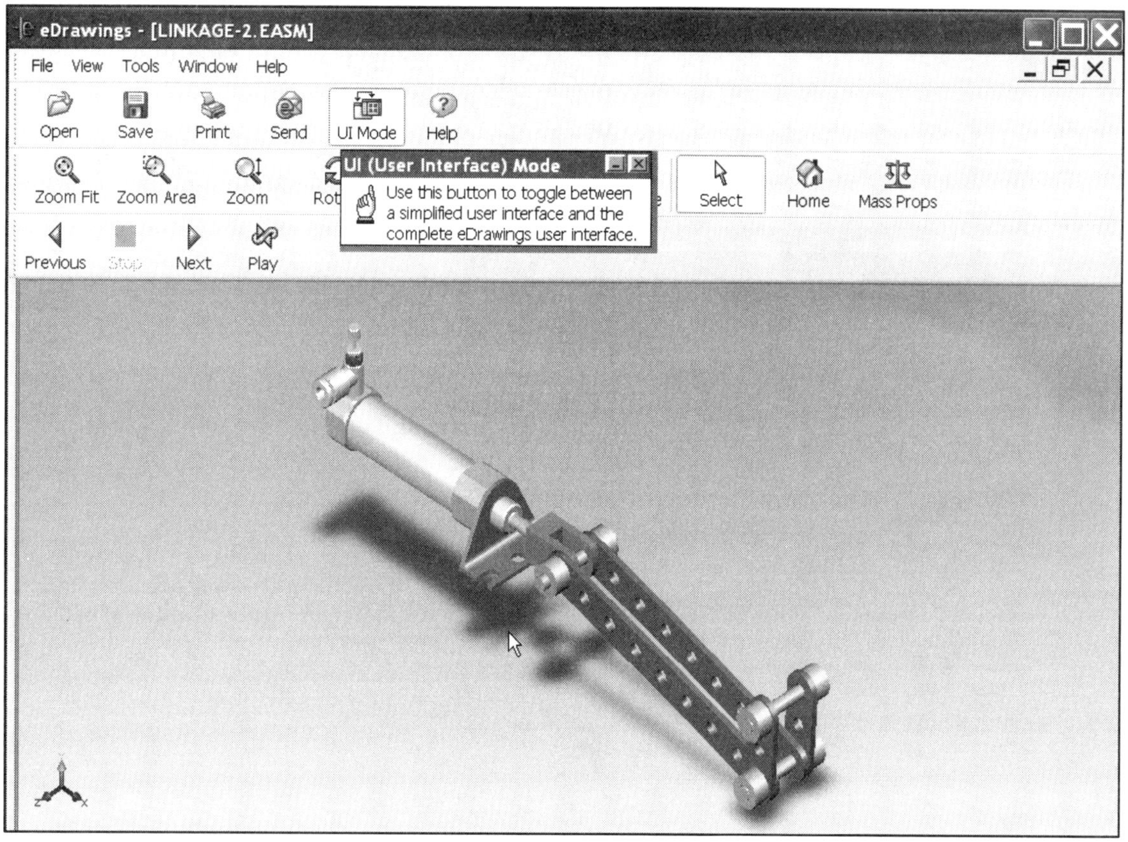

Exercise 3-9: Industry Collaborative Exercise.

Engineers create drawings for a new design. There are part drawings, assembly drawings, inspection drawings and many others.

Utilize the World Wide Web to identify how companies utilize engineering drawings.

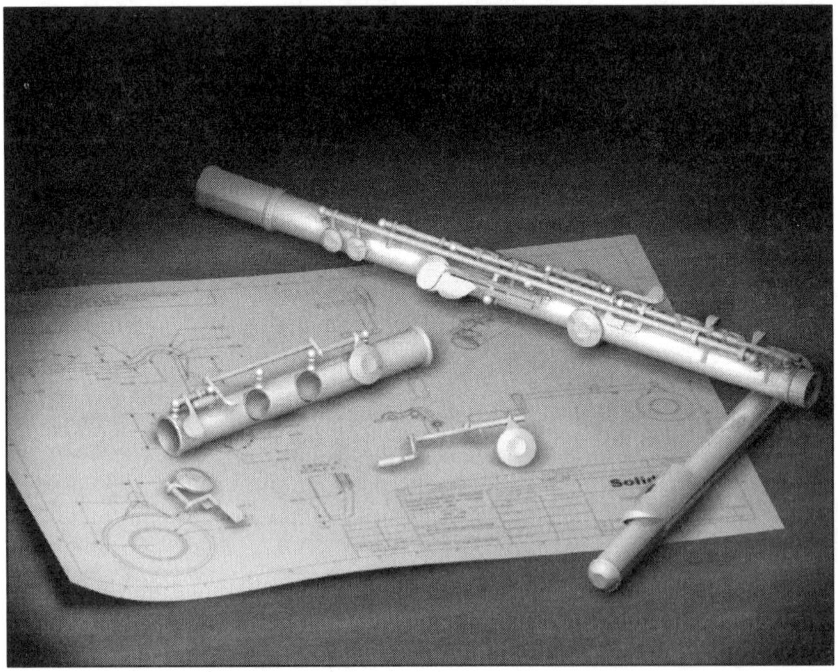

Armstrong Model 104 Flute
Model Courtesy of United Musical Instruments USA, Inc.
Elkhart, IN
PhotoWorks
Courtesy of SolidWorks Corporation.

Project 4

PNEUMATIC-TEST-MODULE Assembly

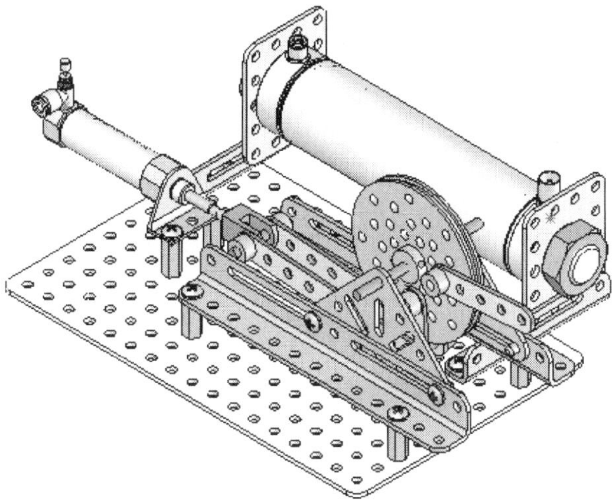

Below are the desired outcomes and usage competencies based on the completion of Project 4.

Desired Outcomes:	**Usage Competencies**:
• Six Parts: ○ WEIGHT. ○ HOOK. ○ WHEEL. ○ HEX-ADAPTER. ○ AXLE-3000. ○ SHAFTCOLLAR-500.	• Apply the following model features: Loft, Sweep, Sweep Cut, Revolved Cut, Dome, and Circular Pattern. • Reuse geometry. • Modify existing parts to create new parts with the Save as copy command.
• Five Assemblies: ○ WHEEL-AND-AXLE. ○ WHEEL-FLATBAR. ○ 3HOLE-SHAFTCOLLAR. ○ 5HOLE-SHAFTCOLLAR. ○ PNEUMATIC-TEST-MODULE.	• Reuse geometry. • Modify existing assemblies to create new assemblies. • Utilize Derived Component Pattern, Local Component Pattern, Mirror Component, and Replace assembly options. • Provide an understanding of working with multiple documents in an assembly.

Notes:

Project 4 – PNEUMATIC-TEST-MODULE Assembly

Project Objective

Obtain an understanding to create new complex parts that utilize the Loft feature and Sweep feature. Attain the ability to reuse geometry by modifying existing parts and to create new parts. Knowledge of the following SolidWorks features: Loft, Sweep, Sweep Cut, Revolved Cut, Dome, and Circular Pattern.

Create six individual parts:

- WEIGHT.
- HOOK.
- WHEEL.
- HEX-ADAPTER.
- AXLE-3000.
- SHAFTCOLLAR-500.

Develop a working understanding with multiple documents in an assembly. Build on sound assembly modeling techniques that utilize symmetry, component patterns, and mirrored components.

Create five assemblies:

- 3HOLE-SHAFTCOLLAR assembly.
- 5HOLE-SHAFTCOLLAR assembly.
- WHEEL-FLATBAR assembly.
- WHEEL-AND-AXLE assembly.
- PNEUMATIC-TEST-MODULE assembly.

On the completion of this project, you will be able to:

- Create new parts and copy parts with the Save as copy command to reuse similar geometry.
- Utilize construction geometry in a sketch.

- Understand various Assembly techniques.
- Create new assemblies and copy assemblies to reuse similar parts.
- Apply the following SolidWorks features:
  - Loft and Sweep.
  - Sweep Cut and Revolved Cut.
  - Dome and Circular Pattern.

Project Overview

Six additional parts are required for the final PNEUMATIC-TEST-MODULE assembly. Each part explores various modeling techniques.

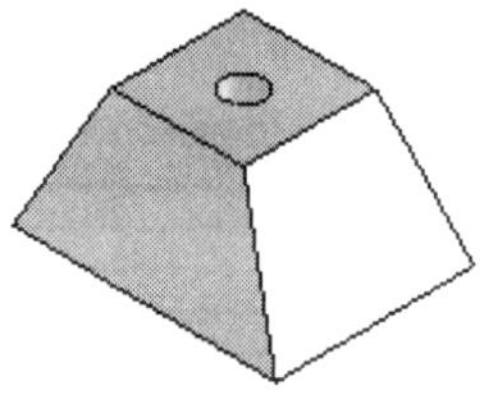

Create three new parts in this project:

- WEIGHT.
- HOOK.
- WHEEL.

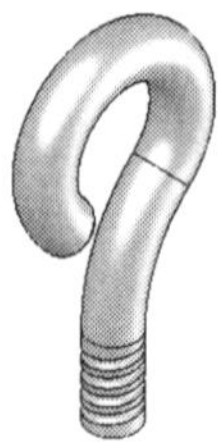

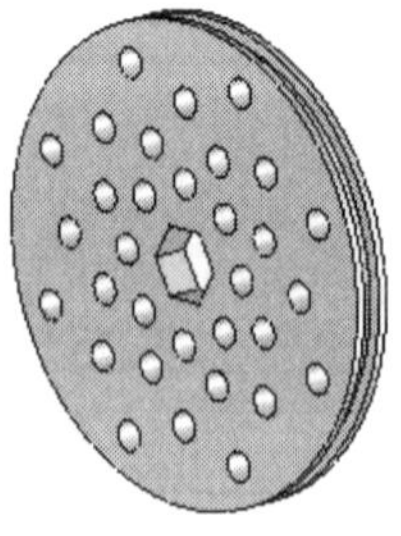

Note: The WEIGHT and HOOK are used in the Project exercises.

Utilize Save as copy and modify existing parts that were created in the previous Projects to create three additional parts for the PNEUMATIC-TEST-MODULE assembly.

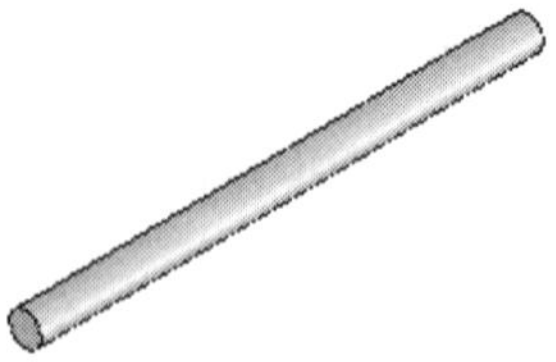

- HEX-ADAPTER.
- AXLE-3000.
- SHAFTCOLLAR-500.

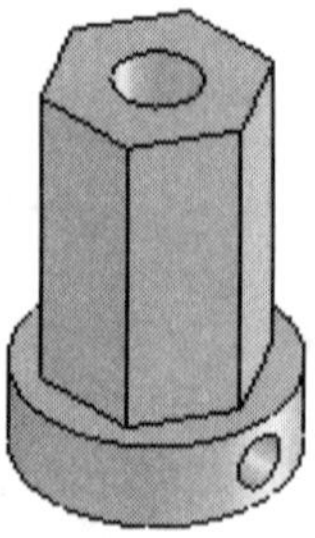

The HEX-ADAPTER part utilizes modified geometry from the HEX-STANDOFF part.

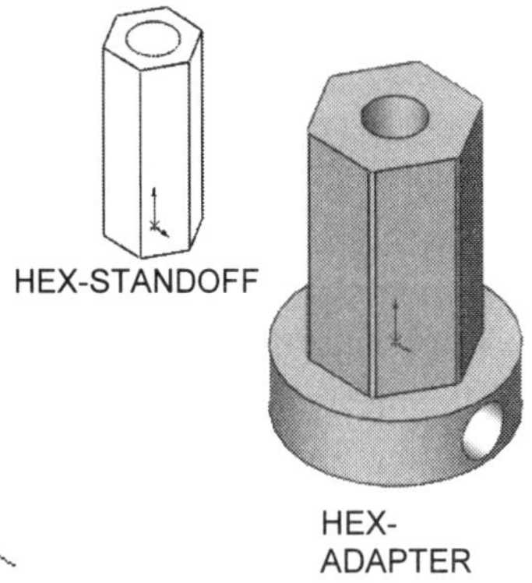

The AXLE3000 part utilizes modified geometry from the AXLE part.

The SHAFTCOLLAR-500 part utilizes modified geometry from the SHAFT-COLLAR part.

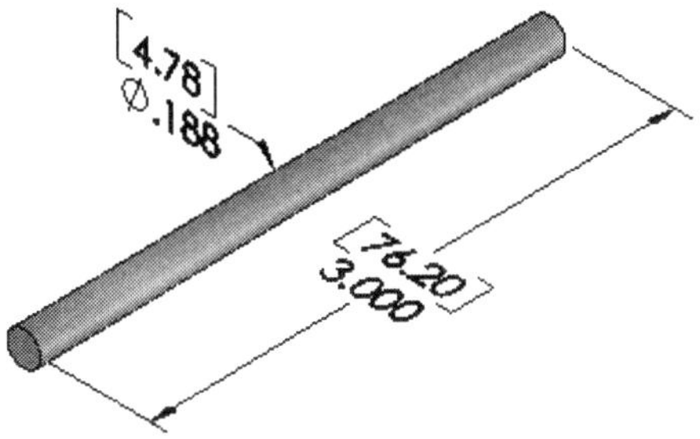

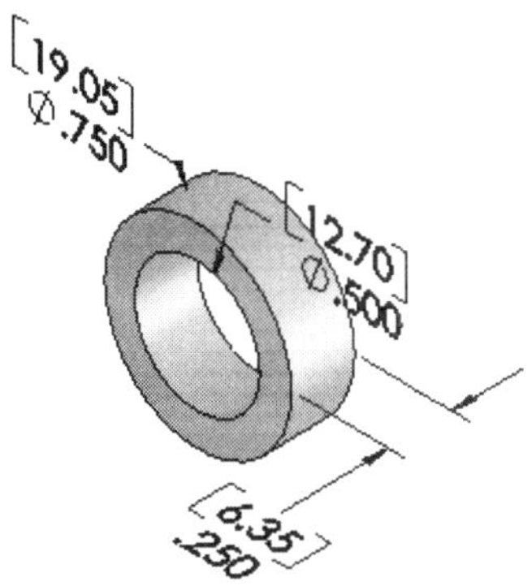

Create the 3HOLE-SHAFTCOLLAR assembly.

Utilize the 3HOLE-SHAFTCOLLAR assembly to create the 5HOLE-SHAFTCOLLAR assembly.

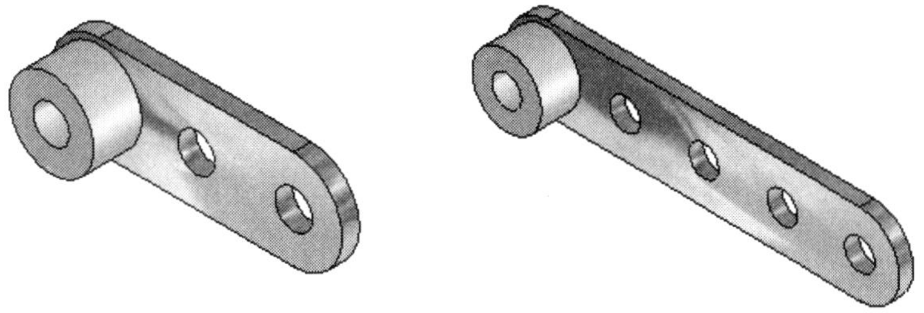

The WHEEL-FLATBAR assembly contains the following items:

- 3HOLE-SHAFTCOLLAR assembly.
- 5HOLE-SHAFTCOLLAR assembly.
- WHEEL part.

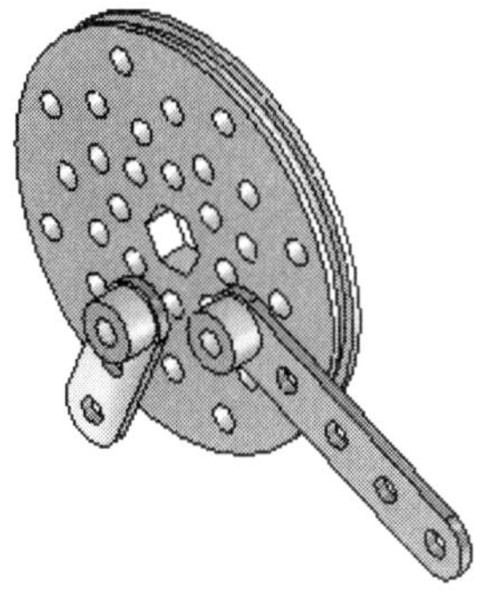

The WHEEL-AND-AXLE assembly contains the following items:

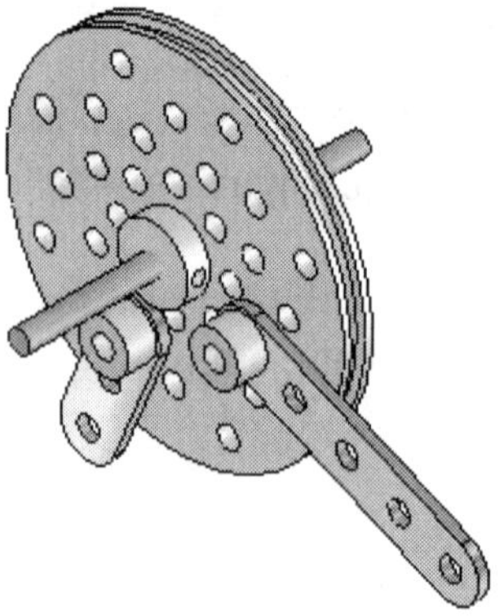

- WHEEL-FLATBAR assembly.
- AXLE3000 part.
- SHAFTCOLLAR-500 part.
- HEX-ADAPTER part.

Combine the created new assemblies and parts to develop the top level PNEUMATIC-TEST-MODULE assembly. Add additional pneumatic components in the Project exercises.

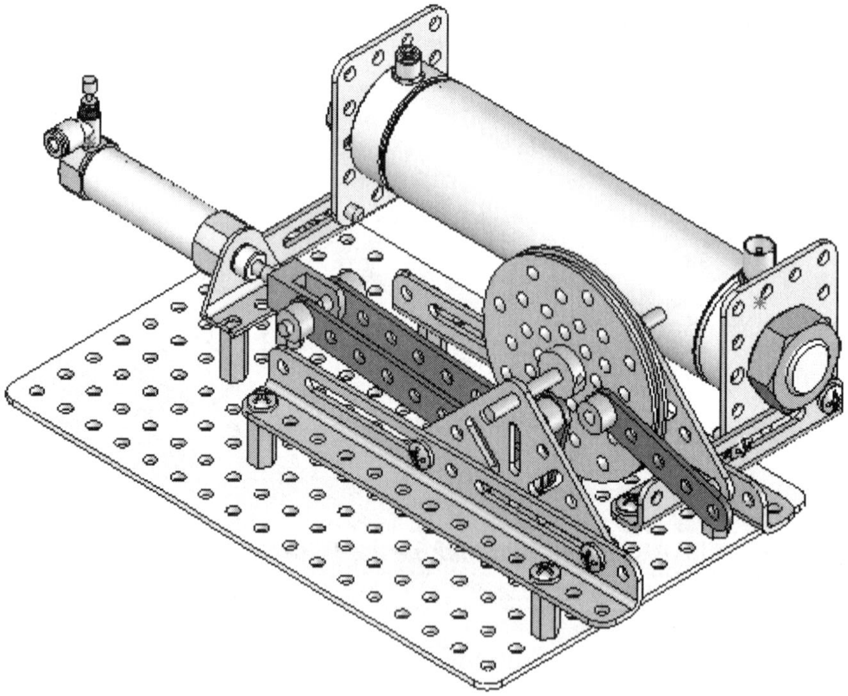

WEIGHT Part

The WEIGHT part is a machined part. Utilize the Loft feature. Create a Loft by blending two or more profiles. Each profile is sketched on a separate plane.

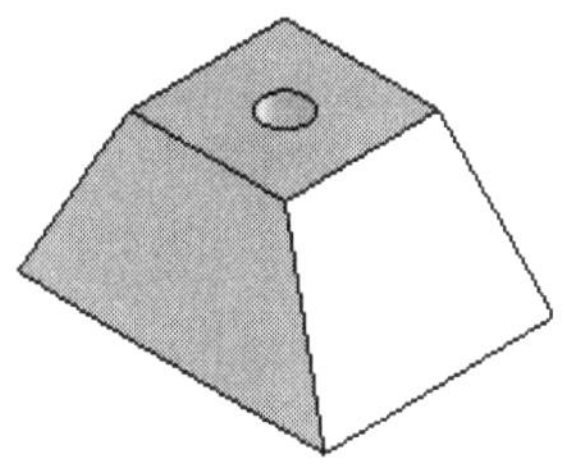

Create Plane1 offset from to the Top plane.

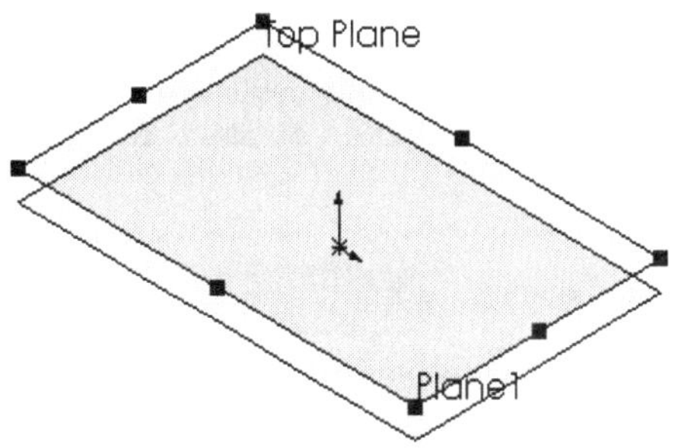

Sketch a rectangle for the first profile on the Top plane. Sketch a square for the second profile on Plane1.

Select the corner of each profile to create the Loft feature.

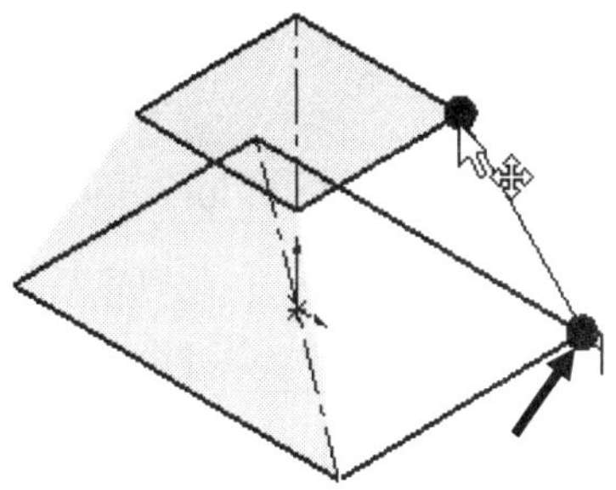

Utilize an Extruded Cut Feature with the Through All End Condition option to create a hole centered on the top face of the Loft feature.

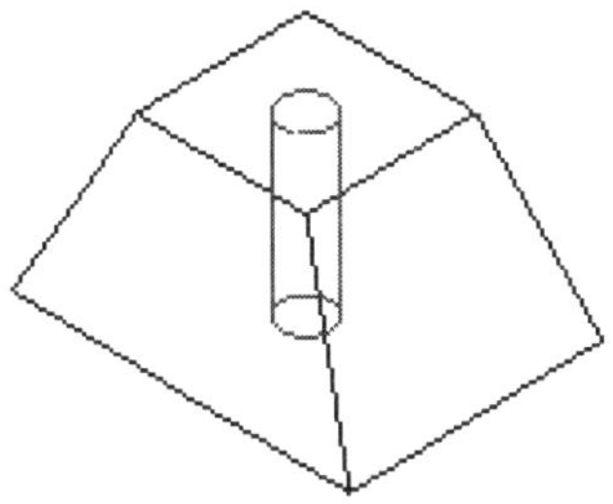

All parts in this project utilize a custom part template. Create the custom part template from the default part template. Save the custom part template in the SW-TUTORIAL-2007 folder.

Activity: WEIGHT Part

Create a new part template.

1) Click **File**, **New** from the Main menu.

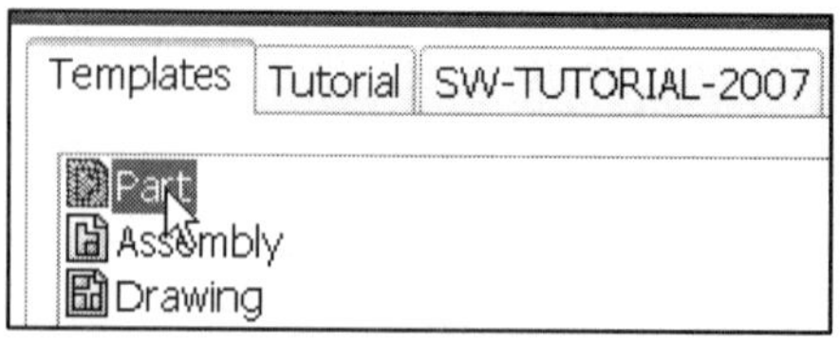

2) Double-click **Part** from the Templates tab. The Part FeatureManager is displayed.

Set the Dimensioning standard.

3) Click **Tools**, **Options**, **Document Properties** tab from the Main menu.

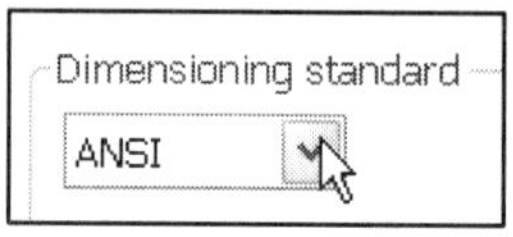

4) Select **ANSI** from the Dimensioning standard box.

Set the units.

5) Click **Units**.

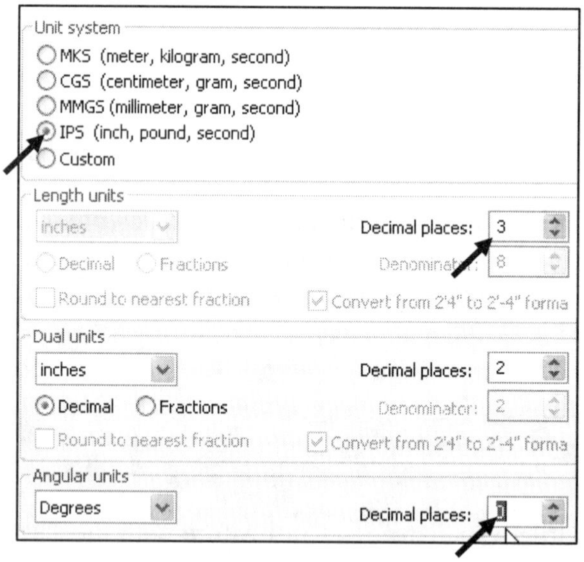

6) Select **IPS**, [**MMGS**] for Unit system.

7) Select **3**, [2] for Linear units Decimal places.

8) Select **0**, [0] for Angular units Decimal places.

9) Click **OK** to set the document units.

Save the part template.

10) Click **File**, **Save As** from the Main menu.

11) Select **Part Templates (*.prtdot)** for Save as type.

12) Select **SW-TUTORIAL-2007** for Save in folder.

13) Enter **PART-ANSI-IN**, [PART-ANSI-MM] for File name.

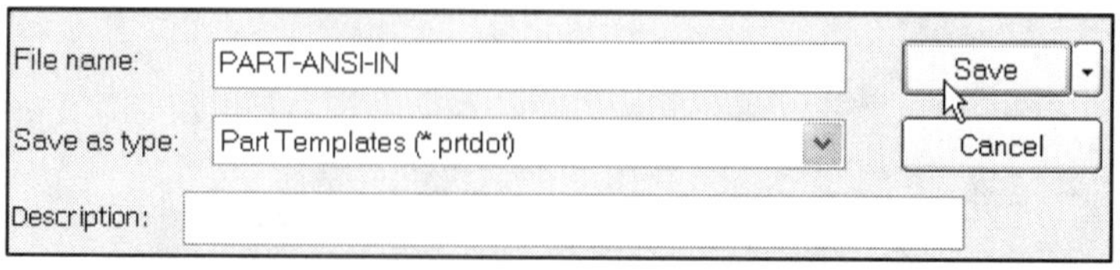

14) Click **Save**.

15) Click **File**, **Close** from the Main menu.

Create the new part.

16) Click **File**, **New** from the Main menu.

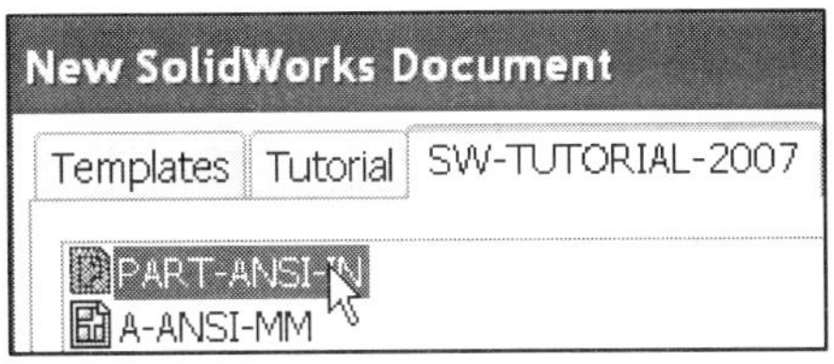

17) Click the **SW-TUTORIAL-2007** tab.

18) Double-click **PART-ANSI-IN**, [PART-ANSI-MM]. The Part FeatureManager is displayed.

Save the part.

19) Click **File**, **Save As** from the Main menu.

20) Select the **SW-TUTORIAL-2007** folder.

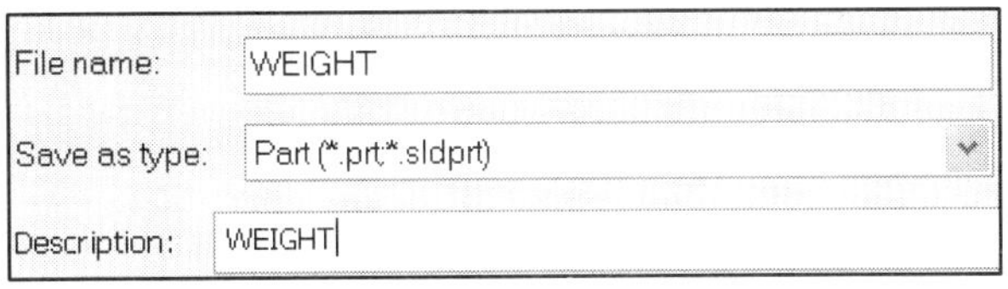

21) Enter **WEIGHT** for File name.

22) Enter **WEIGHT** for Description.

23) Click **Save**.

Insert Plane1.

24) Click Isometric view.

25) Right-click **Top Plane** from the FeatureManager.

26) Click **Show**.

27) Hold the **Ctrl** key down.

28) Click the **boundary** of the Top Plane as illustrated.

29) Drag the **mouse pointer** upward.

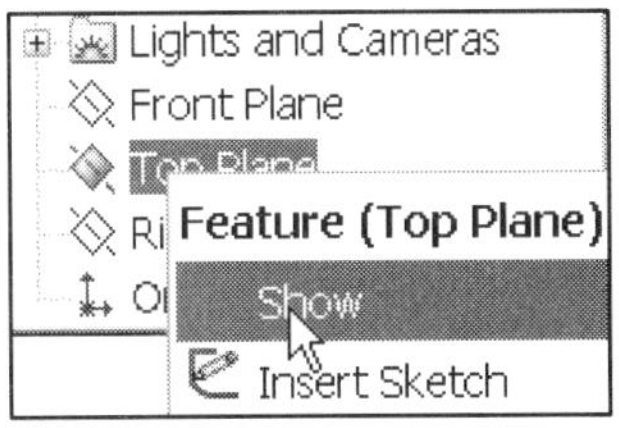

30) Release the **mouse pointer**.

31) Release the **Ctrl** key. The Plane PropertyManager is displayed. Top Plane is displayed in the Selections box.

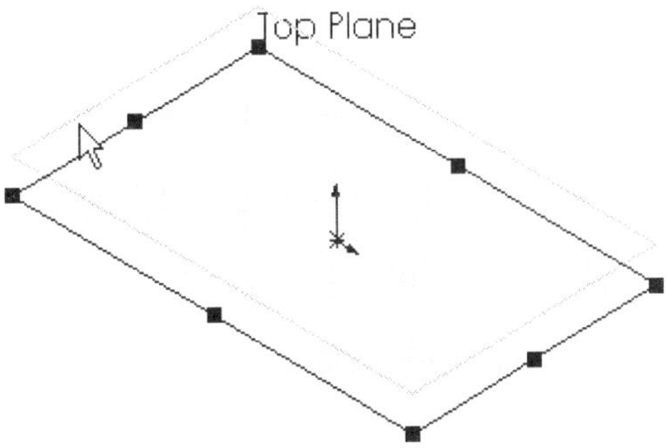

32) Enter **.500**in, [**12.70**] for Distance.

33) Click **OK** from the Plane PropertyManager.

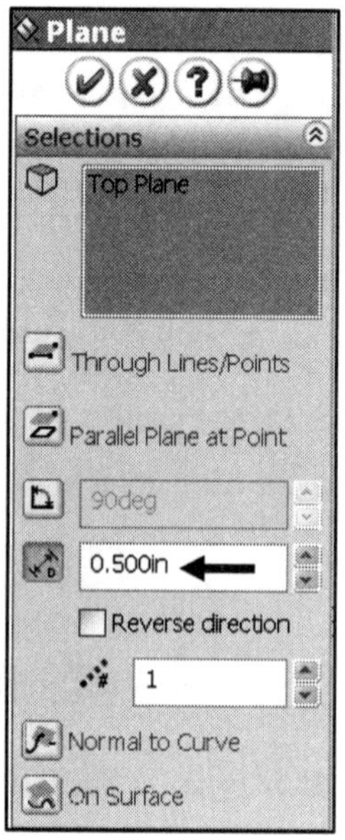

Plane1 is displayed in the Graphics window and is listed in the FeatureManager. Plane1 is offset from the Top plane.

The Loft requires two sketches. Sketch1 is a rectangle sketched on the Top plane centered about the Origin. Sketch2 is a square sketched on Plane1 centered about the Origin.

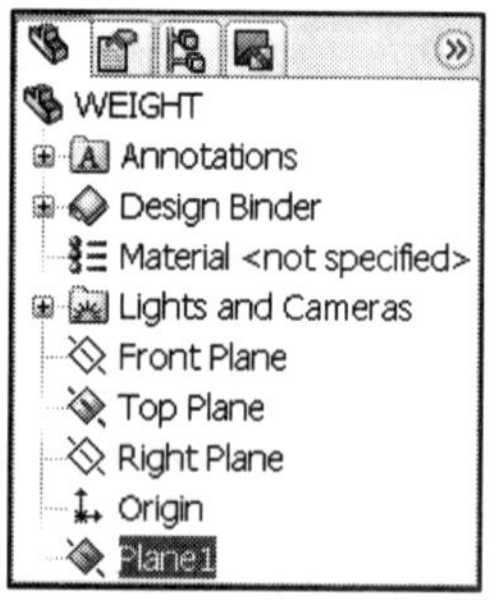

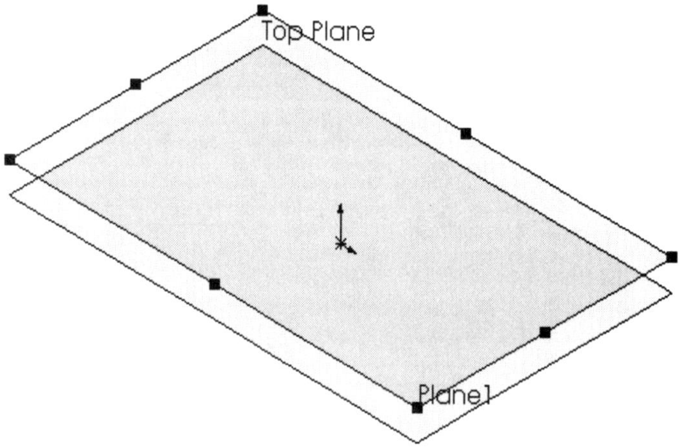

Create Sketch1.

34) Click **Top Plane** from the FeatureManager.

35) Click **Sketch** Sketch in the Control Area.

36) Click **Rectangle** Rectan... from the Sketch toolbar.

37) Sketch a **Rectangle** centered about the Origin as illustrated.

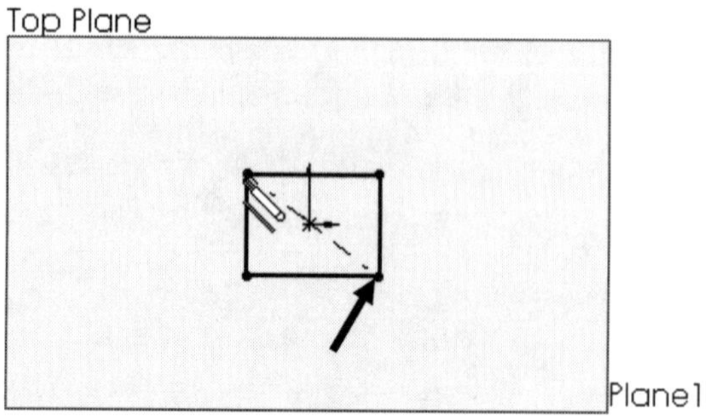

38) Click **Centerline** Centerl... from the Sketch toolbar. Click the **lower right point**.

39) Click the upper left point.

40) Click **Centerline** Centerl... to deactivate the centerline tool.

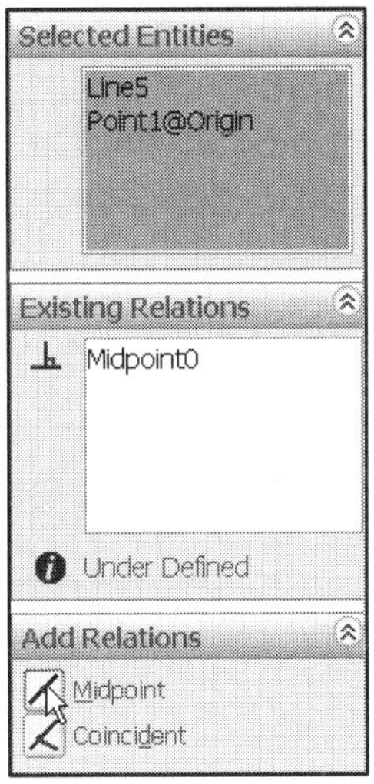

Add a Midpoint relation between the Origin and the centerline.

41) Click the **centerline** from the Graphics window.

42) Hold the **Ctrl** key down. Click the **Origin**.

43) Release the **Ctrl** key. The selected entities are displayed in the Selected Entities box.

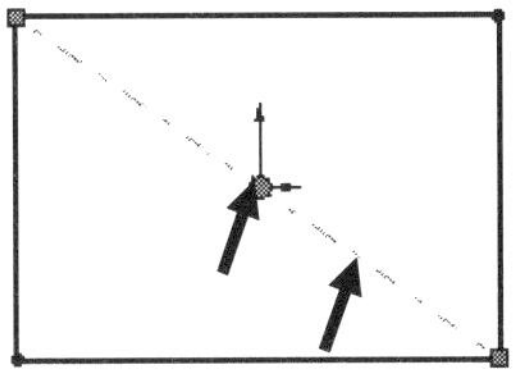

44) Click **Midpoint** from the Add Relations box. Midpoint0 is displayed.

45) Click **OK** from the Properties PropertyManager.

Add dimensions.

46) Click **Smart Dimension** Smart Dimens... from the Sketch toolbar.

47) Click the **top horizontal** line.

48) Click a **position** above the line.

49) Enter **1.000**in, [25.40].

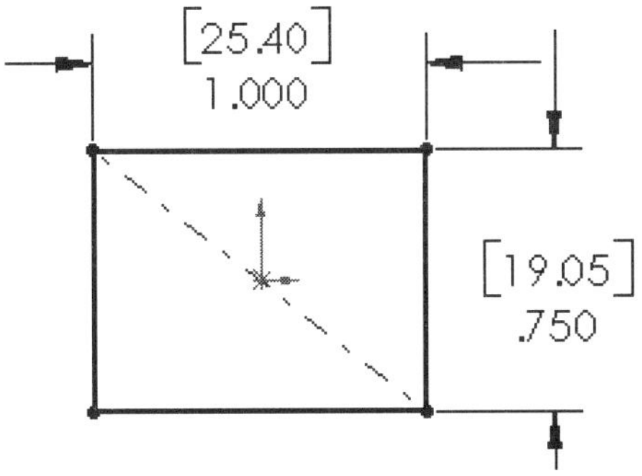

50) Click the Green Check mark.

51) Click the **right vertical** line.

52) Click a **position** to the right.

53) Enter **.750**in, [19.05].

54) Click the Green Check mark.

Close Sketch1.

55) Click **Exit Sketch** Exit Sketch from the Sketch toolbar. The sketch is fully defined and is displayed in black.

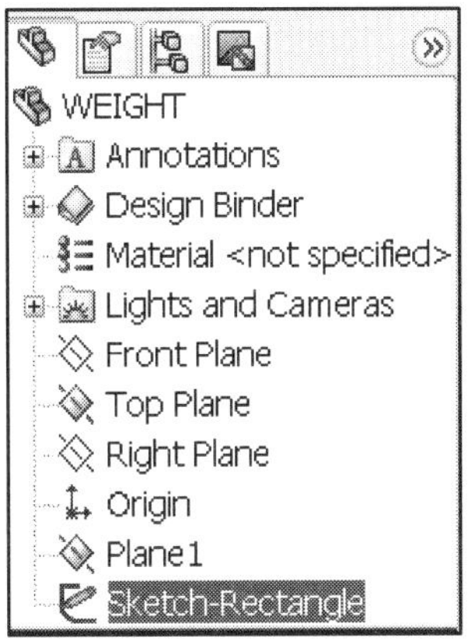

Rename Sketch1.

56) Click **Sketch1** from the FeatureManager.

57) Enter **Sketch-Rectangle** for name.

Save the part

58) Click **Save**.

Display the Isometric View.

59) Click Isometric view.

Create Sketch2.

60) Click **Plane1** from the FeatureManager.

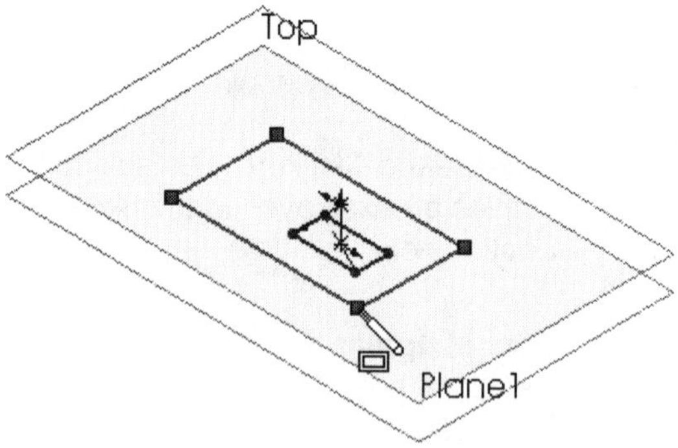

61) Click **Rectangle** Rectan... from the Sketch toolbar.

62) Sketch a **Rectangle** centered about the Origin as illustrated.

63) Click **Centerline** Centerl... from the Sketch toolbar.

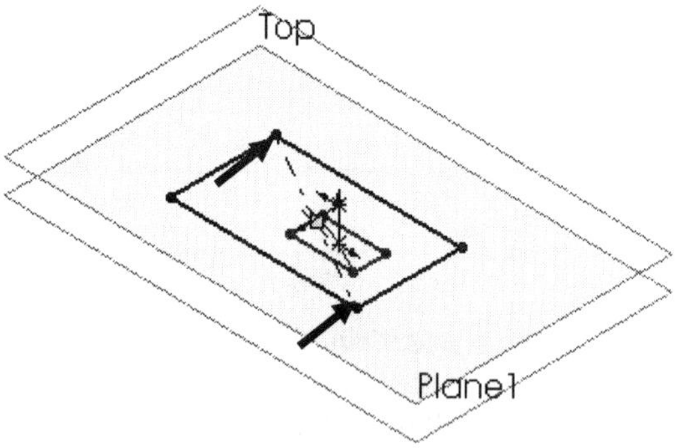

64) Click the lower right point.

65) Click the **upper left point** as illustrated.

66) Right-click **Select**.

Add a Midpoint relation between the Origin and the centerline.

67) Click the **Origin**. Hold the **Ctrl** key down.

68) Click the **centerline**. Release the **Ctrl** key.

69) Click **Midpoint** from the Add Relations box.

Add an Equal relation between the left vertical line and the top horizontal line.

70) Click the **left vertical line** of the rectangle.

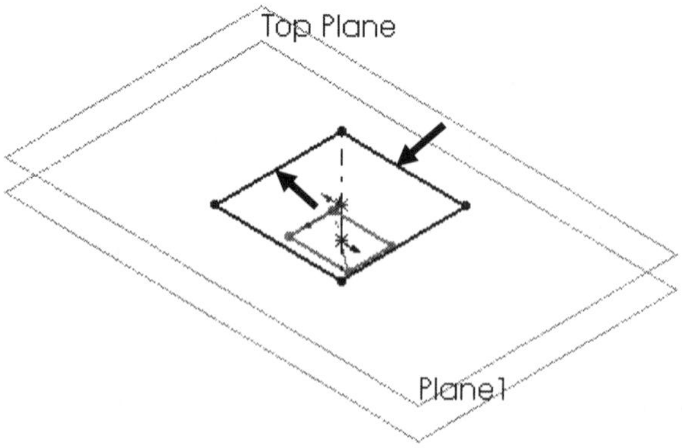

71) Hold the **Ctrl** key down. Click the **top horizontal line** of the rectangle. Release the **Ctrl** key.

72) Click **Equal** = from the Add Relations box.

73) Click **OK** from the Properties PropertyManager.

Add a dimension.

74) Click **Smart Dimension** from the Sketch toolbar.

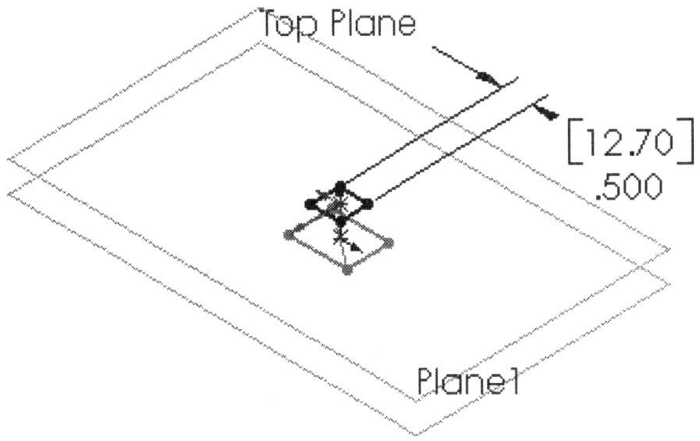

75) Click the **top horizontal** line.

76) Click a **position** above the line.

77) Enter **.500**in, [**12.70**].

78) Click the Green Check mark.

Close Sketch2.

79) Click **Exit Sketch**.

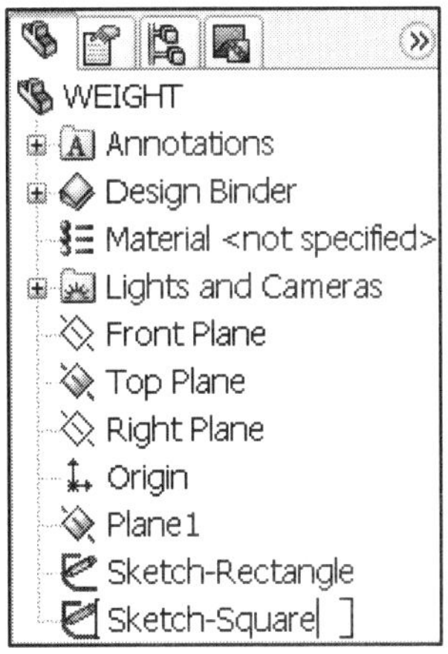

Rename Sketch2.

80) Click **Sketch2** from the FeatureManager.

81) Enter **Sketch-Square** for name.

Save the WEIGHT part.

82) Click **Save**.

Loft features are comprised of multiple sketches. Name sketches for clarity.

Activity: WEIGHT Part-Loft Feature

Insert a Loft feature.

83) Click **Loft** from the Features toolbar. The Loft PropertyManager is displayed.

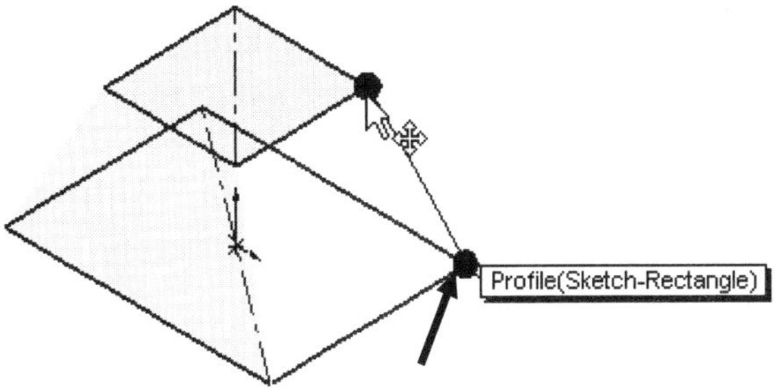

84) Click the **back right corner** of Sketch-Rectangle as illustrated.

85) If required, click the **back right corner** of Sketch-Square. Sketch-Rectangle and Sketch-Square are displayed in the Profiles box.

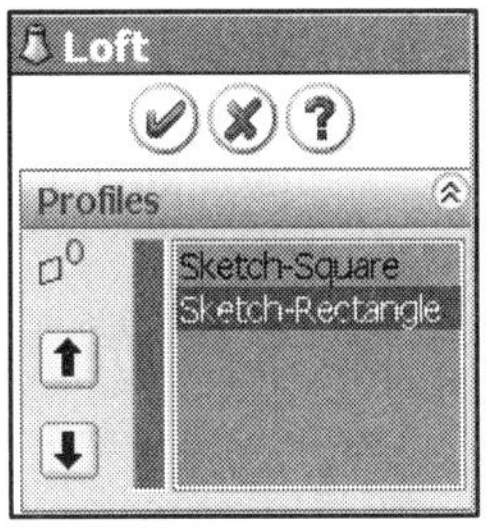

86) Click **OK** from the Loft PropertyManager. Loft1 is displayed in the FeatureManager.

87) **Expand** Loft1 in the FeatureManager. Sketch-Rectangle and Sketch-Square are the two sketches that contain the Loft feature.

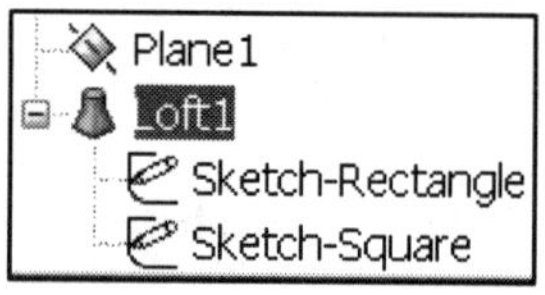

88) **Zoom in** on the Loft1 feature.

Activity: WEIGHT Part-Extruded Cut Feature

Insert a new sketch for the Extruded Cut.

89) Click the **top square face** of the Loft1 feature for the Sketch plane.

90) Click **Sketch** Sketch from the Sketch toolbar.

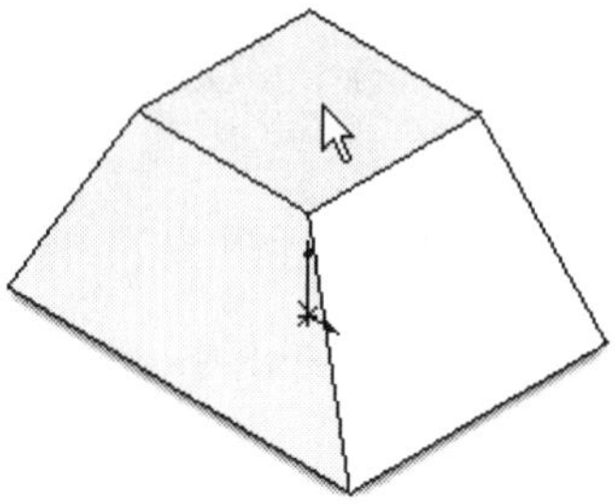

91) Click **Circle** Circle from the Sketch toolbar.

92) Click the **Origin**.

93) Click a **position** to the right of the Origin as illustrated.

Add a dimension.

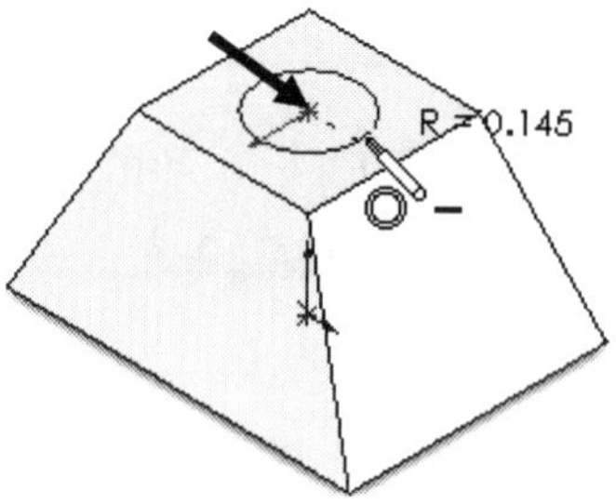

94) Click **Smart Dimension** Smart Dimens... from the Sketch toolbar.

95) Click the **circumference** of the circle.

96) Click a **position** in the Graphics window above the circle to locate the dimension.

97) Enter **.150**in, [**3.81**] in the Modify box.

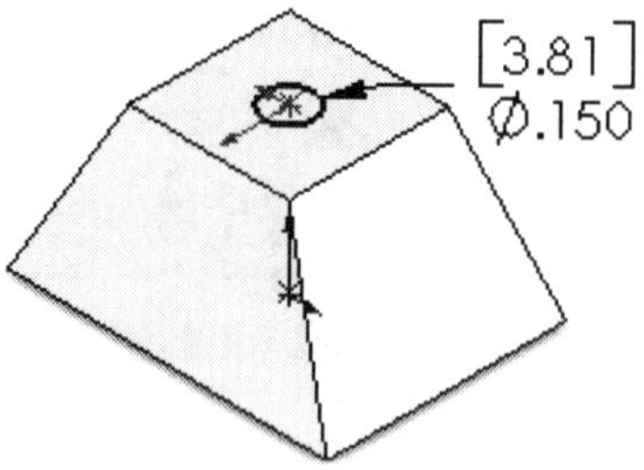

Insert an Extruded Cut feature.

98) Click **Extruded Cut** Extruded Cut from the Features toolbar. The Cut-Extrude PropertyManager is displayed.

99) Select **Through All** for End Condition in Direction 1. The direction arrow points downward.

100) Click **OK** from the Cut-Extrude PropertyManager. Cut-Extrude1 is displayed in the FeatureManager.

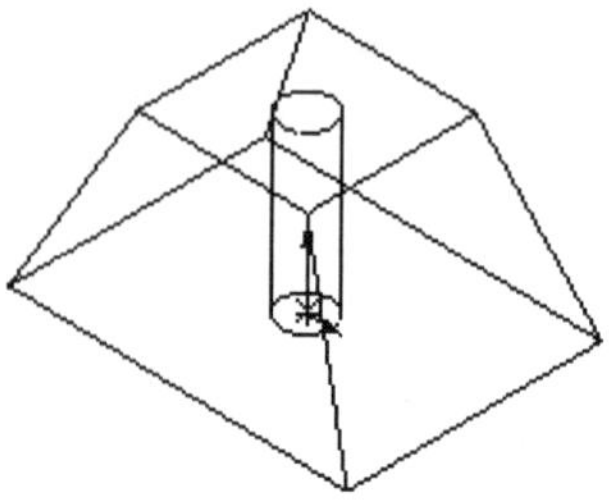

101) Click Wireframe.

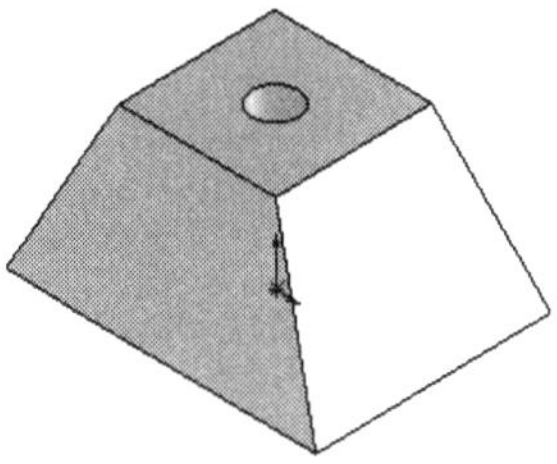

Rename the Cut Extrude1 feature.

102) Click **Cut-Extrude1** from the FeatureManager.

103) Enter **Hole-for-Hook** for name.

Save the WEIGHT part.

104) Click Isometric view.

105) Click Shaded With Edges.

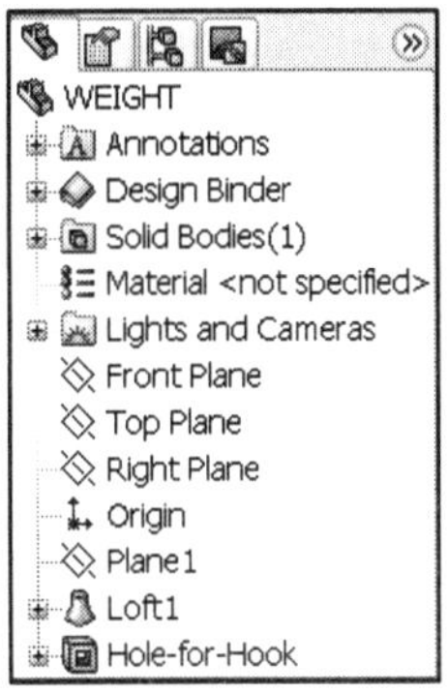

106) Right-click **Top Plane** from the FeatureManager.

107) Click **Hide**.

108) Right-click **Plane1** from the FeatureManager.

109) Click **Hide**.

110) Click **Save**. The WEIGHT part is complete.

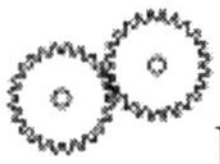

Review the WEIGHT Part.

The WEIGHT part was created with the Loft feature. The Loft feature required two planes: Top plane and Plane1. Profiles were sketched on each plane. Profiles were selected to create the Loft feature.

An Extruded Cut feature with the Through All option was utilized to create a center hole in the WEIGHT. The hole will be utilized to attach the HOOK part in the Project exercises.

HOOK Part

The HOOK part fastens to the WEIGHT part. The HOOK is created with a Sweep feature.

A Sweep feature adds material by moving a profile along a path. A simple Sweep feature requires two sketches. The first sketch is called the path. The second sketch is called the profile.

The profile and path are sketched on perpendicular planes. Create the Hook part with a simple Sweep feature.

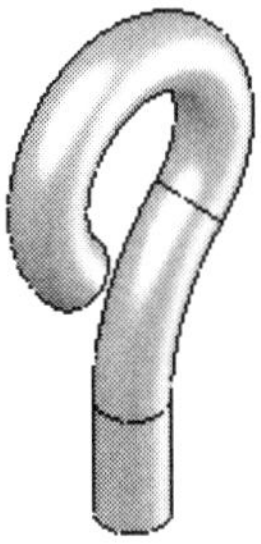

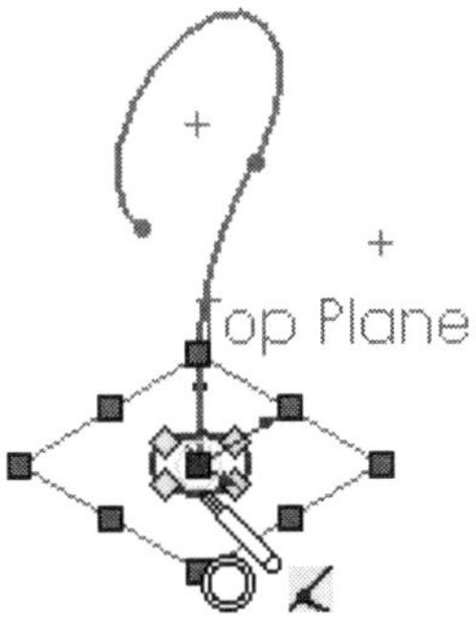

The Sweep feature uses:

- A path sketched on the Right plane.
- A profile sketched on the Top plane.

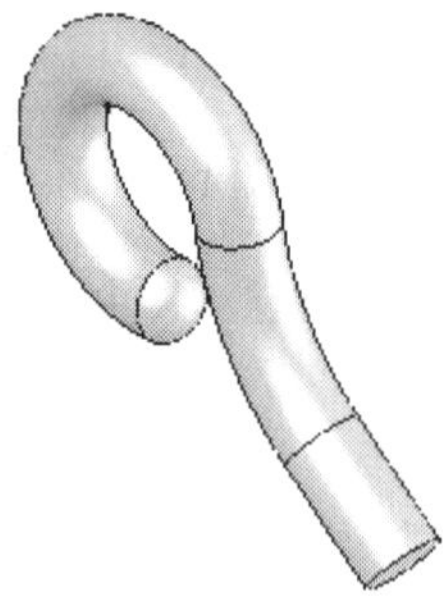

Utilize a Dome feature to create a spherical feature on a circular face.

A Sweep Cut feature removes material. Utilize a Sweep Cut feature to create the Thread for the HOOK part.

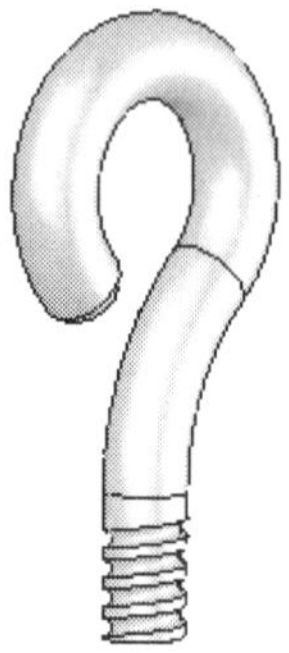

Activity: HOOK Part

Create the new part.

111) Click **File**, **New** from the Main menu.

112) Select the **SW-TUTORIAL-2007** tab.

113) Double-click **PART-ANSI-IN**, [PART-ANSI-MM].

Save the part.

114) Click **Save**.

115) Select the **SW-TUTORIAL-2007** folder.

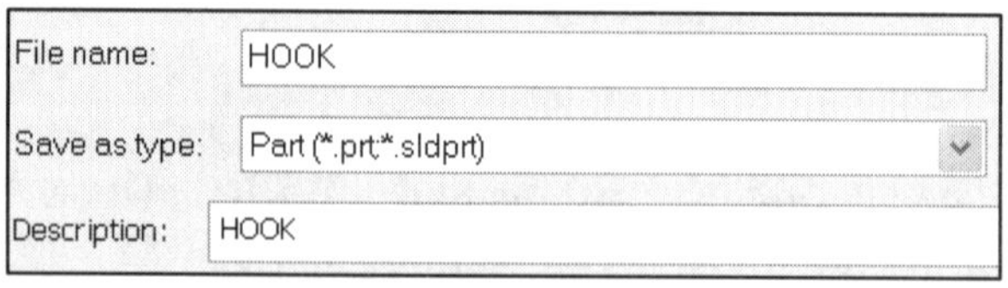

116) Enter **HOOK** for File name.

117) Enter **HOOK** for Description.

118) Click **Save**. The HOOK FeatureManager is displayed.

The Sweep feature requires two sketches. Sketch1 is the Sweep Path sketched on the Right plane. Sketch2 is the Sweep Profile sketched on the Top plane.

Sketch the Sweep Path.

119) Click **Right Plane** from the FeatureManager.

120) Click **Line** Line from the Sketch toolbar. The Insert Line PropertyManager is displayed.

121) Sketch a **vertical line** from the Origin as illustrated.

Add a dimension.

122) Click **Smart Dimension** Smart Dimens... from the Sketch toolbar.

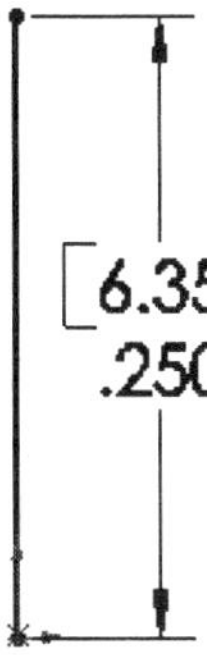

123) Click the **vertical line**.

124) Click a **position** to the right.

125) Enter **.250**in, [**6.35**].

126) Click the Green Check mark.

127) Press the **f** key to fit the Graphics window.

Create the arc.

128) Click **Centerpoint Arc** Center... Arc from the Sketch toolbar.

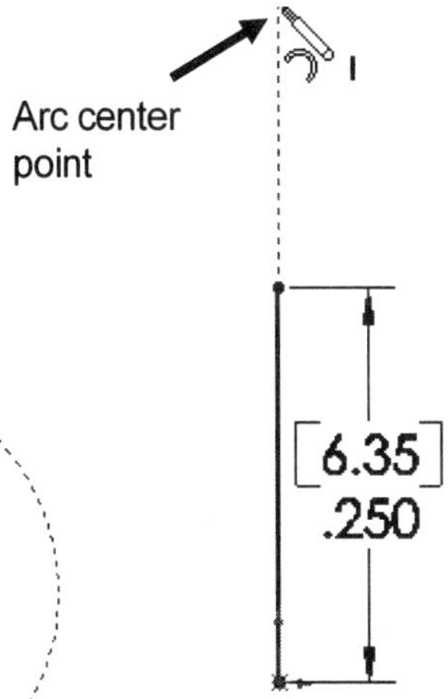

129) Click the **arc center point** vertically aligned to the Origin.

130) Click the **arc start point** as illustrated.

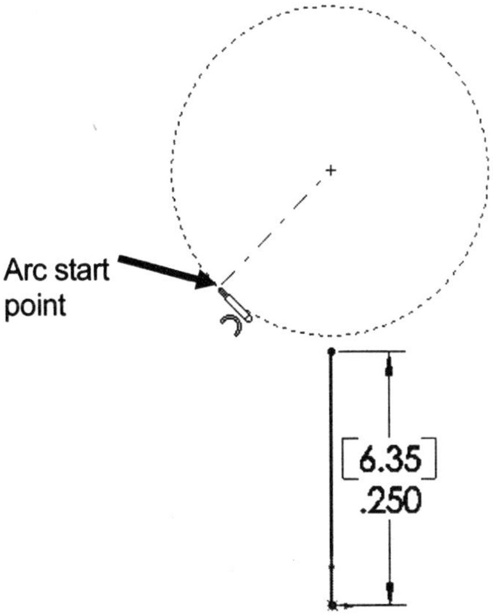

131) Drag the **mouse pointer** counter-clockwise approximately 260°.

132) Release the mouse pointer **horizontally aligned** to the arc start point.

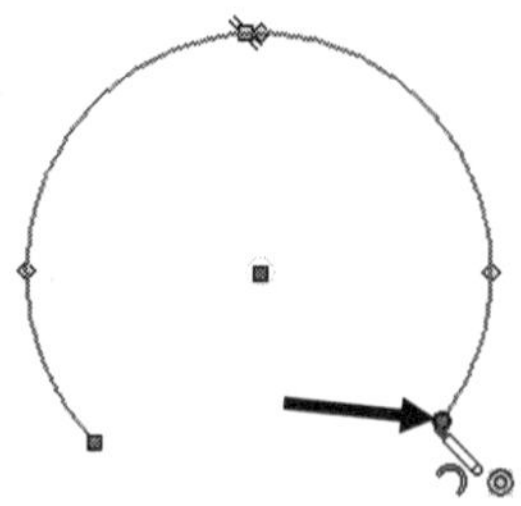

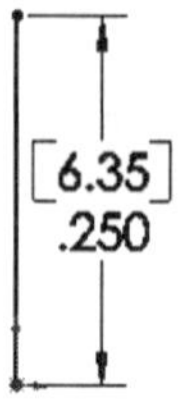

133) Click **3 Point Arc** 3 Point Arc from the Sketch toolbar. The Arc PropertyManager is displayed.

134) Click the vertical line endpoint.

135) Click the Centerpoint arc endpoint.

136) Drag and pull the center of the **3 Point Arc downwards**.

137) Click the center of the **Centerpoint arc line** as illustrated.

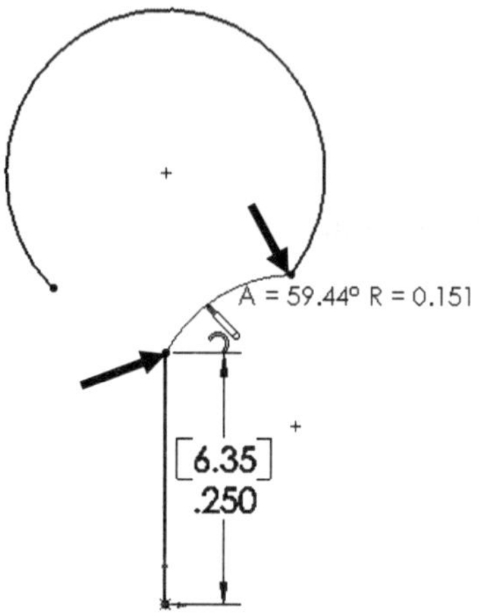

138) Click **OK** from the Arc PropertyManager.

139) Click **3 Point Arc** 3 Point Arc from the Sketch toolbar.

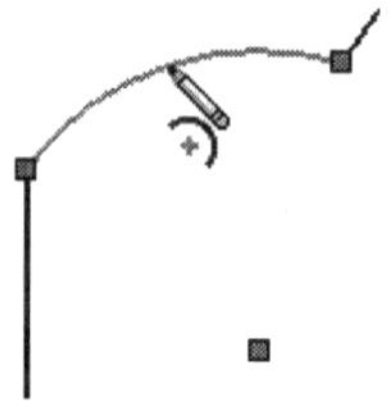
Correct shape

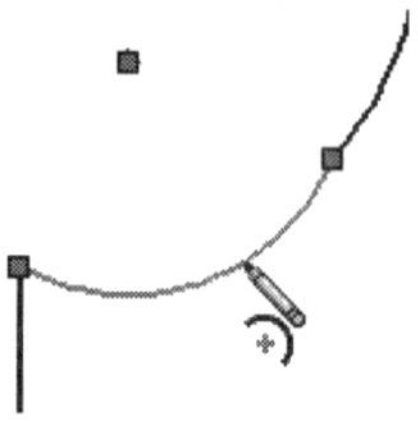
Incorrect shape

It is important to draw the correct shape with the 3 Point Arc tool as illustrated.

Add a Vertical relation between the Origin and the center point of the arc.

140) Click the **Origin**.

141) Hold the **Ctrl** key down.

142) Click the **center point** of the Center point arc.

143) Release the **Ctrl** key.

144) Click **Vertical** | from the Add Relations box.

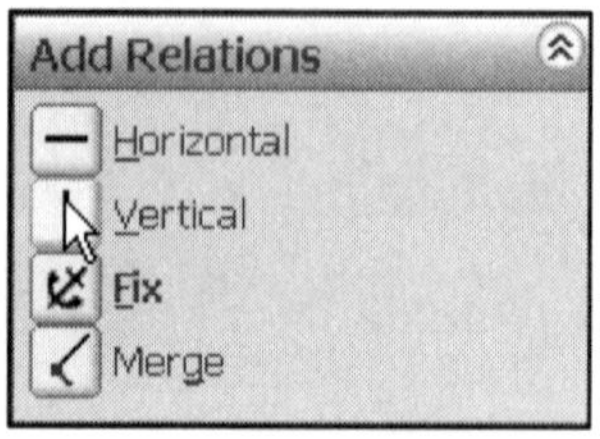

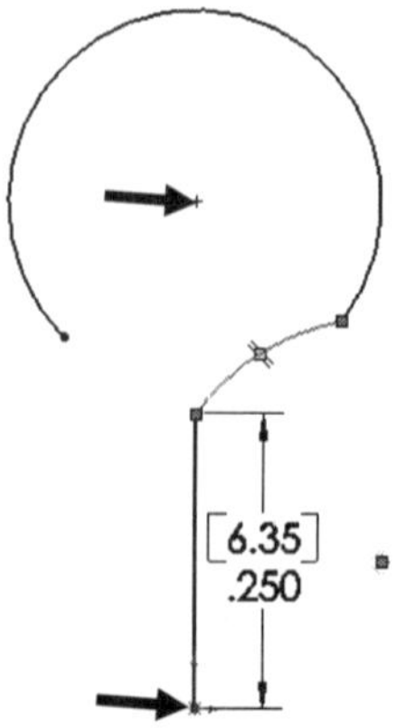

Add a Horizontal relation.

145) Click the **start point** of the Center point arc.

146) Hold the **Ctrl** key down.

147) Click the **end point** of the Center point arc.

148) Release the **Ctrl** key.

149) Click **Horizontal** from the Add Relations box.

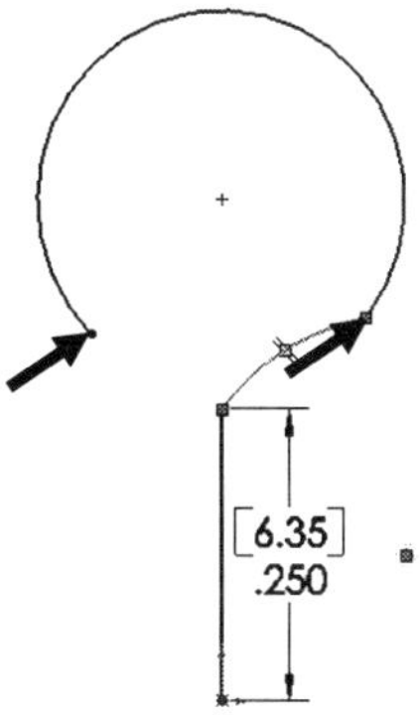

Add a Tangent relation.

150) Click the **vertical line**. Hold the **Ctrl** key down.

151) Click the **3 Point Arc**. Release the **Ctrl** key.

152) Click **Tangent** from the Add Relations box.

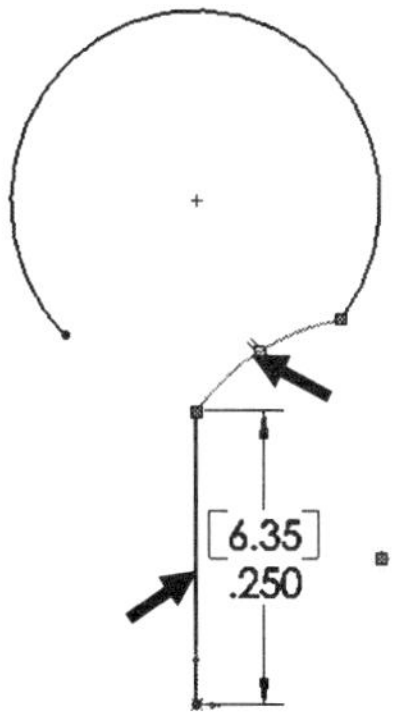

Add a second Tangent relation.

153) Click the **3 Point Arc**. Hold the **Ctrl** key down.

154) Click the Center point arc.

155) Release the **Ctrl** key.

156) Click **Tangent** from the Add Relations box.

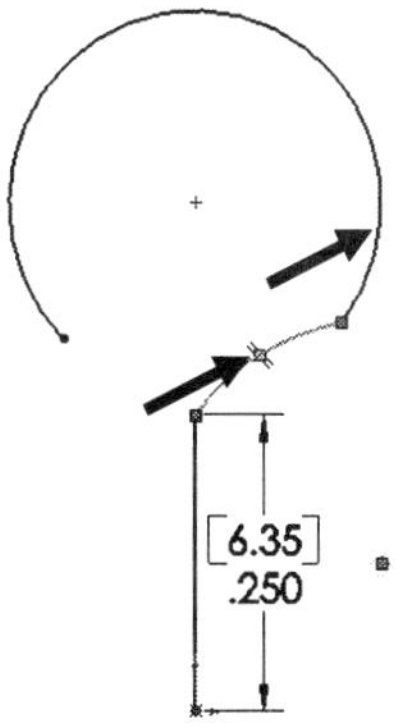

Add dimensions.

157) Click **Smart Dimension** Smart Dimens... from the Sketch toolbar.

158) Click the **3 Point Arc**.

159) Click a **position** to the left.

160) Enter **.500**in, [**12.70**].

161) Click the Green Check mark.

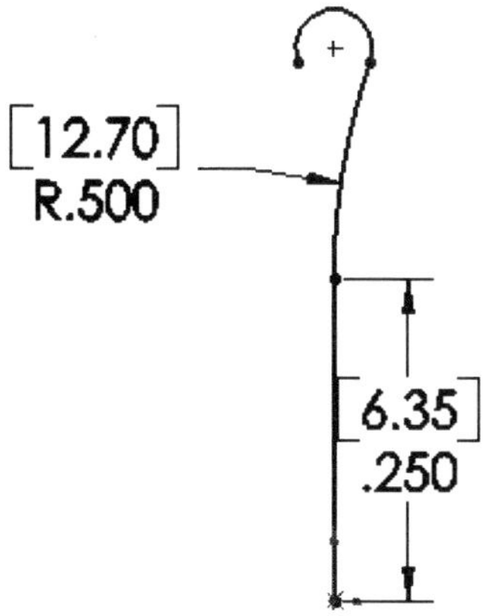

Dimension the overall length of the sketch.

162) Click the **top of the arc**.

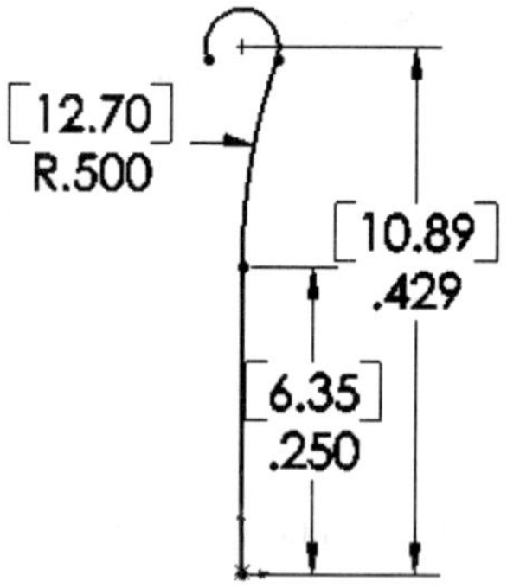

163) Click the **Origin**.

164) Click a **position** to the right of the profile. Accept the default dimension.

165) Click the Green Check mark.

166) Right-click **Properties** on the dimension text.

Modify the Arc condition.

167) Click the First arc condition: **Max**.

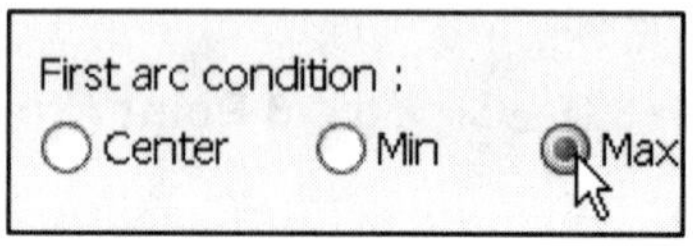

168) Click **OK** from the Dimension Properties box.

Modify the overall length.

169) Double-click the default **dimension**.

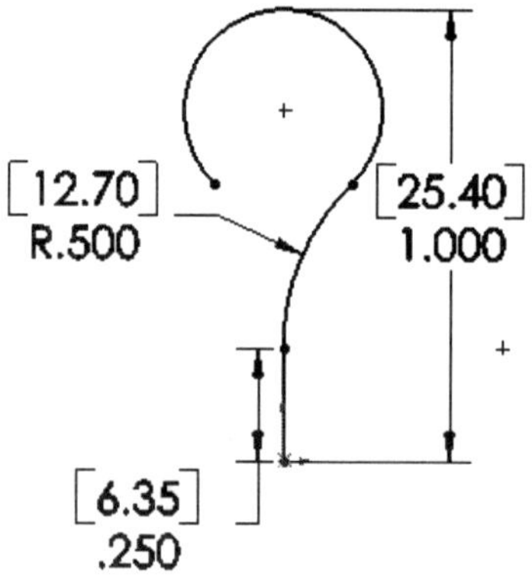

170) Enter **1.000**in, [**25.40**].

171) Click the Green Check mark.

Fit the model to the Graphics window.

172) Press the **f** key. Move the **dimensions** to the correct location.

By default, the Dimension tool utilizes the center point of an arc or circle. Select the circle profile during dimensioning. Utilize Properties to modify the arc condition to Minimum or Maximum.

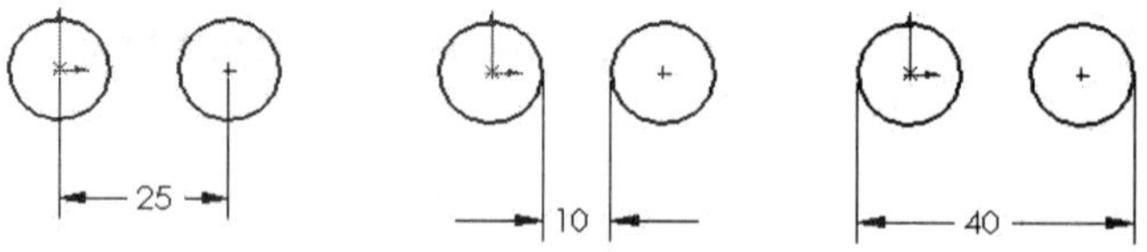

Center point Minimum Maximum
Arc Conditions

Close the Sketch.

173) Click Exit Sketch.

174) Rename Sketch1 to Sketch-Path.

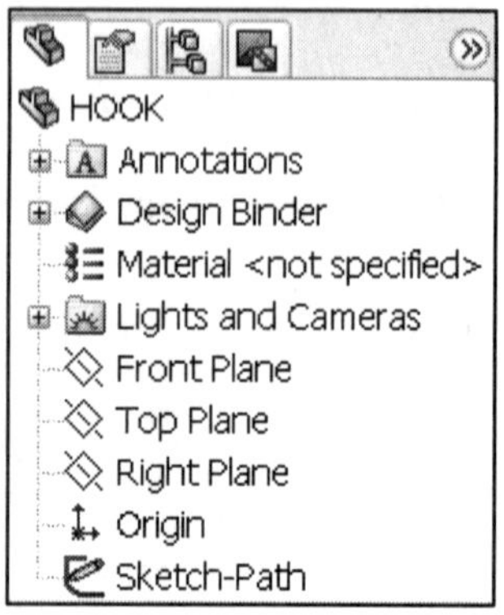

Save the HOOK.

175) Click **Save**.

Activity: HOOK Part-Sweep Profile

Create the Sweep profile (cross section).

176) Click Isometric view.

177) Click **Top Plane** from the FeatureManager.

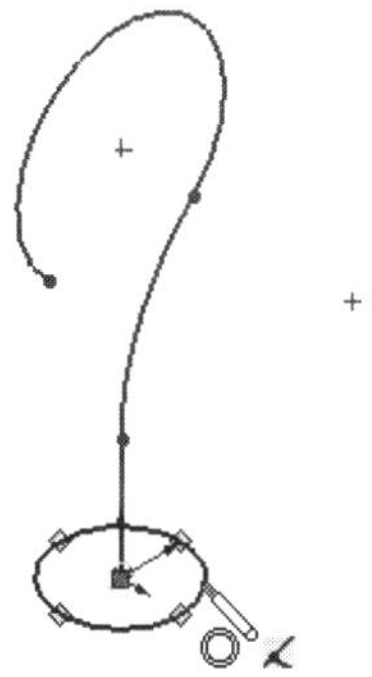

178) Click **Circle** Circle from the Sketch toolbar.

179) Click the **Origin**. Click a **position** to the right of the Origin.

Add a dimension.

180) Click **Smart Dimension** Smart Dimens... from the Sketch toolbar.

181) Click the **circumference** of the small circle.

182) Click a **position** diagonally to the right.

183) Enter **.150**in, [**3.81**].

184) Click the Green Check mark.

185) Click **OK** from the Dimension PropertyManager.

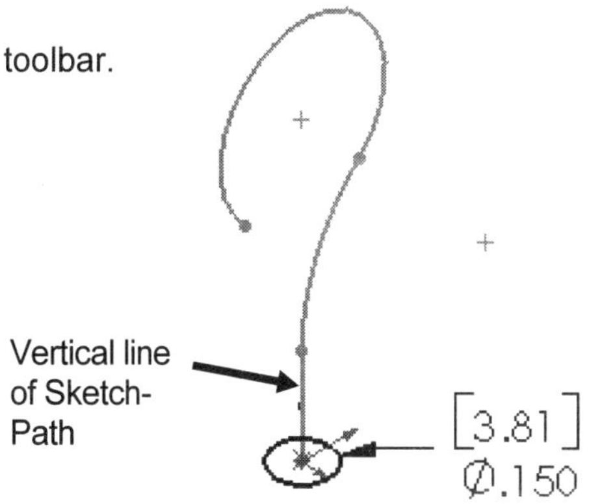

The Pierce geometric relation positions the center of the cross section on the sketched path. The center point of the small circle pierces the sketch-path (vertical line).

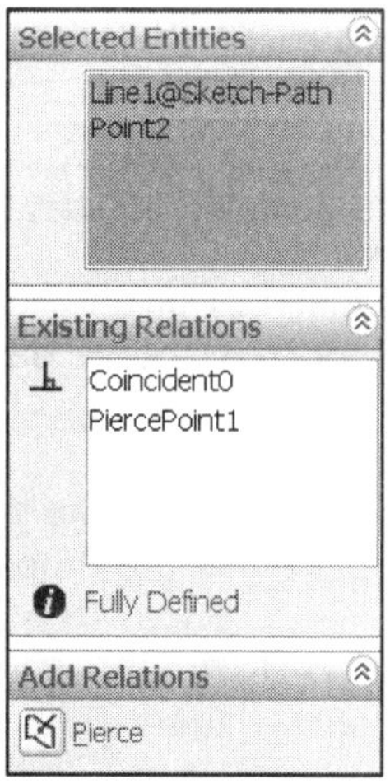

Add a Pierce relation.

186) Click the **Origin**. Hold the **Ctrl** key down.

187) Click the **vertical line** of the Sketch-Path.

188) Release the **Ctrl** key.

189) Click **Pierce** from the Add Relations box.

190) Click **OK** from the Properties PropertyManager

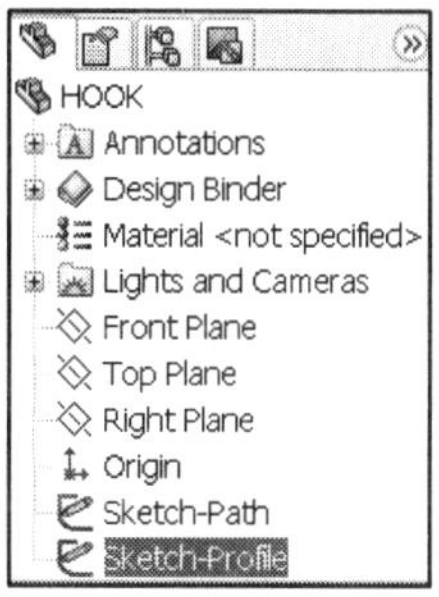

Close the sketch.

191) Click Exit Sketch Exit Sketch.

192) Rename Sketch2 to Sketch-Profile.

Save the part.

193) Click **Save**.

Activity: HOOK Part-Sweep Feature

Insert a Sweep feature.

194) Click **Sweep** Swept Boss/B... from the Features toolbar. The Sweep PropertyManager is displayed. Sketch-Profile is displayed in the Profile box.

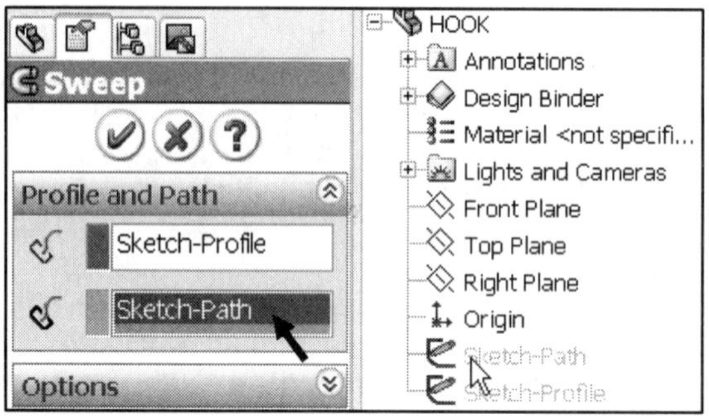

195) Click inside the **Path** box.

196) Click **Sketch-Path** from the fly-out FeatureManager. Sketch-Path is displayed in the Path box.

197) Click **OK** from the Sweep PropertyManager. Sweep1 is displayed in the FeatureManager.

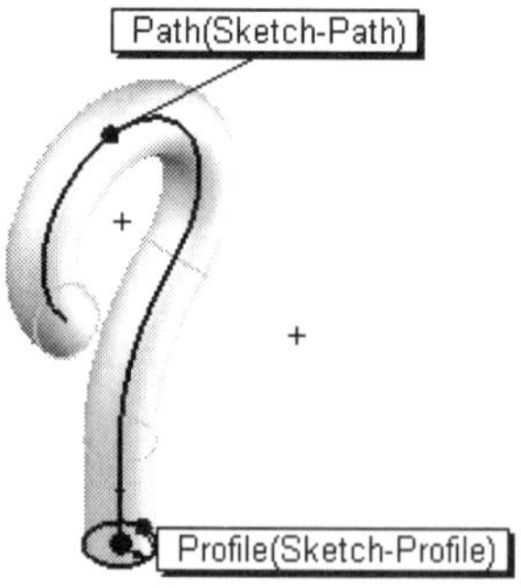

Save the HOOK part.

198) Click **Save**.

Sketch the path, then sketch the profile or cross section for the Sweep feature. Pierce the profile at the start of the path trajectory.

Activity: HOOK Part-Dome Feature

Insert a Dome feature.

199) Click the **flat face** of the Sweep1 feature in the Graphics window as illustrated.

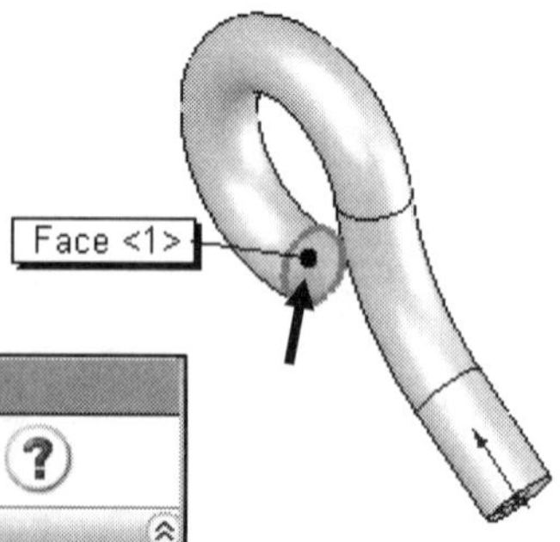

200) Click **Insert**, **Features**, **Dome** from the Main menu. The Dome PropertyManager is displayed.
Face<1> is displayed in the Parameters box.

201) Enter **.050**in, [**1.27**] for Distance.

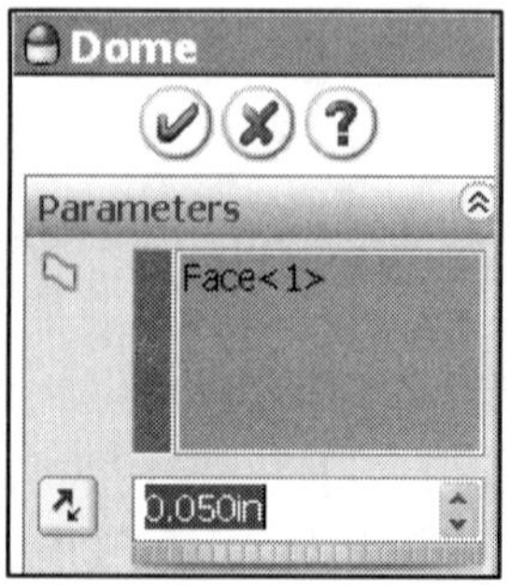

202) Click **OK** from the Dome PropertyManager. Dome1 is displayed in the FeatureManager.

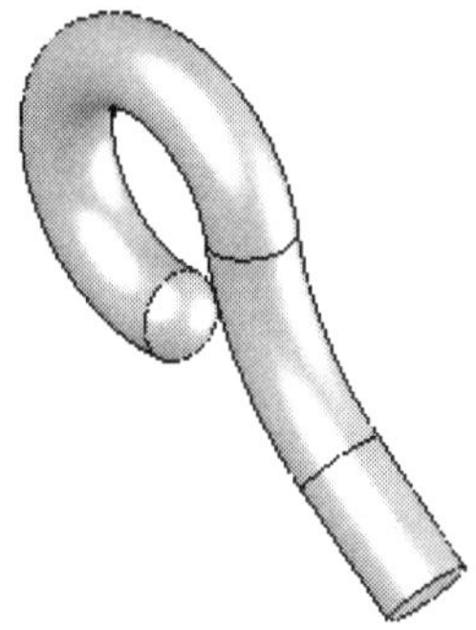

The HOOK requires threads. Use the Sweep feature to create the required threads. The thread requires a spiral path. The path is called the Threadpath. The thread requires a sketched profile. The circular cross section is called the Threadprofile.

There are numerous steps required to create a thread. The thread is not flush with the bottom face. Use an offset plane to start the thread. Create a new offset Sketch plane, ThreadPlane. Use the below steps to create the thread: Note: Steps on threads for plastic parts, springs, and coils.

- Create a new plane for the thread.
- Create the spiral path.
- Create a large cross section circular profile to improve visibility.
- Pierce the cross section circular profile to the spiral path.
- Dimension the circular profile.
- Create a Sweep feature.

Activity: HOOK Part-Threads with Sweep Cut Feature

Create the Offset Reference Plane.

203) Click the **bottom circular** face of Sweep1.

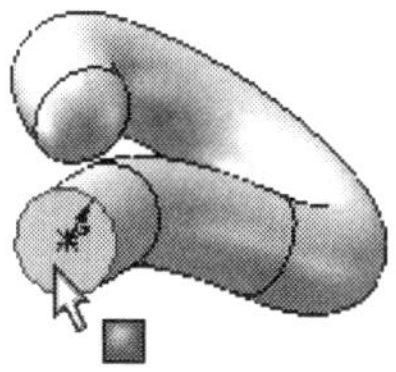

204) Click **Insert**, **Reference Geometry**, **Plane** from the Main menu. The Plane PropertyManager is displayed. Face<1> is displayed in the Selections box.

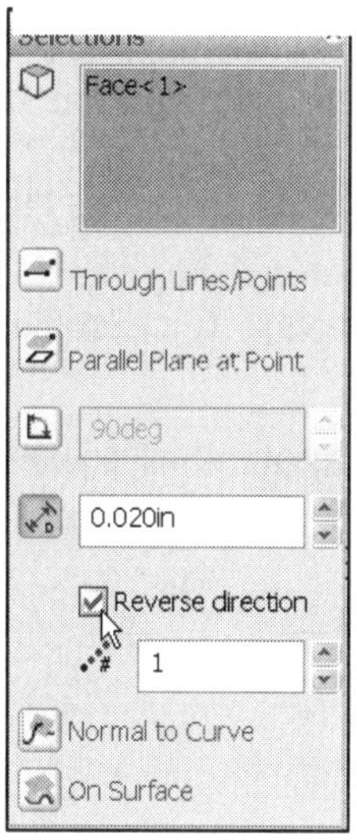

205) Enter **.020**in, [**0.51**] for Distance.

206) Check the **Reverse direction** box. Plane1 is located above the Top plane.

207) Click **OK** from the Plane PropertyManager. Plane1 is displayed in the FeatureManager.

208) Rename Plane1 to Threadplane.

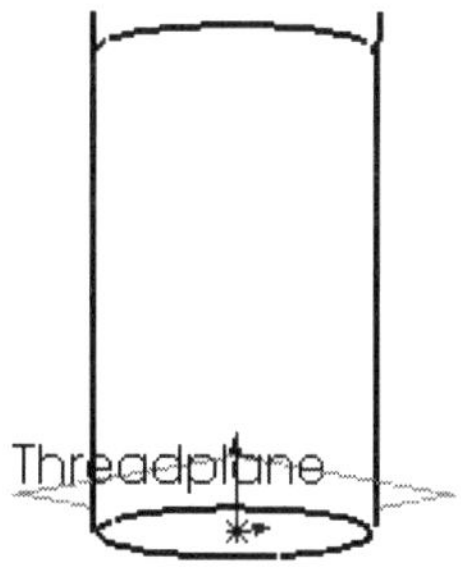

209) Click **Rebuild** from the Standard menu.

Display the Isometric view.

210) Click Isometric view.

211) Click Hidden Lines Removed.

Create the Thread path.

212) **Rotate** and **Zoom to Area** on the bottom of Sweep1.

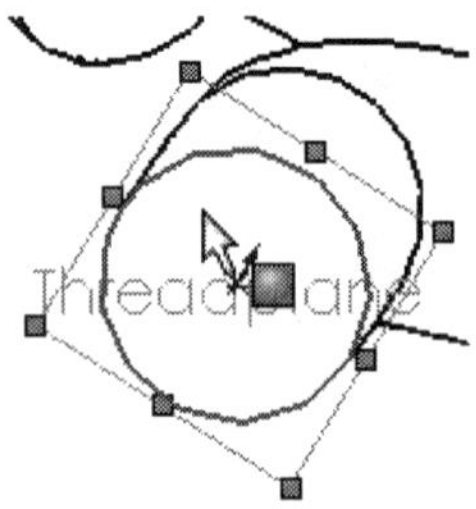

213) Click **Threadplane** from the FeatureManager.

214) Click **Sketch** Sketch from the Sketch toolbar.

215) Click the **bottom** of Sweep1.

216) Click **Convert Entities** Convert from the Sketch toolbar.

Create the Thread Path.

217) Click **Insert**, **Curve**, **Helix/Spiral** from the Main menu. The Helix/Spiral PropertyManager is displayed.

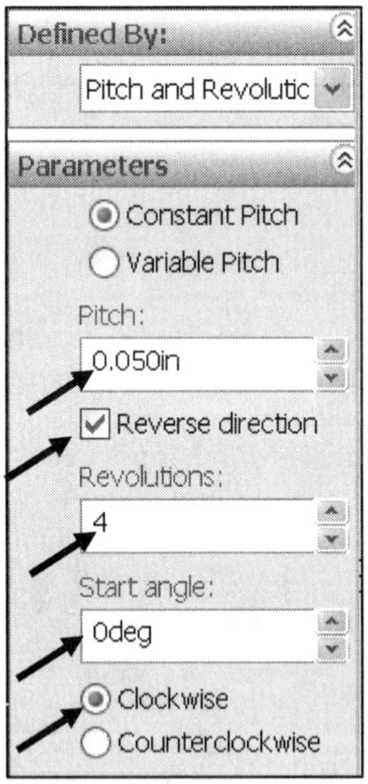

218) Enter **.050**in, [**1.27**] for Pitch.

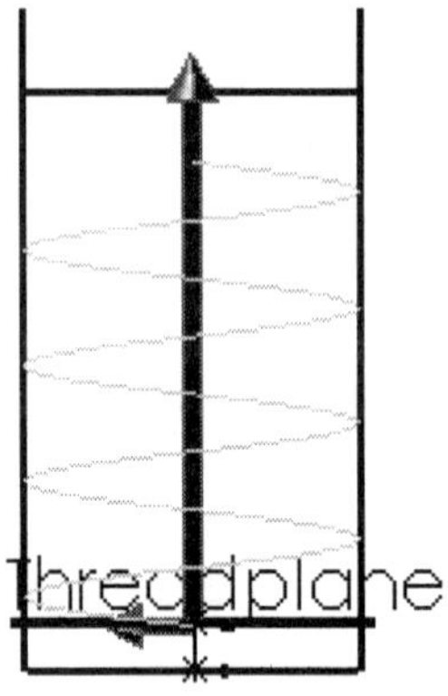

219) Check the **Reverse direction** box.

220) Enter **4** for Revolutions.

221) Enter **0**deg for the Start angle.

222) Click the **Clockwise** box.

223) Click **OK** from the Helix/Spiral PropertyManager. Helix/Sprial1 is displayed in the FeatureManager.

224) Rename Helix/Sprial1 to Threadpath.

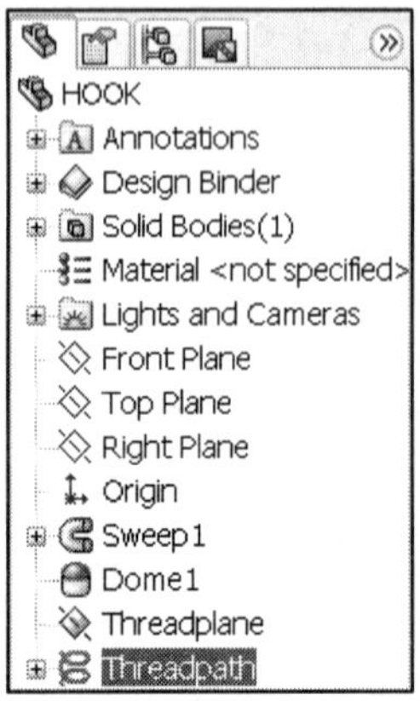

225) Click Isometric view.

226) Click **Save**.

Create the Thread Profile, (cross section).

227) Click **Right Plane** from the FeatureManager.

228) Click **Sketch** Sketch.

229) Click **Right view**.

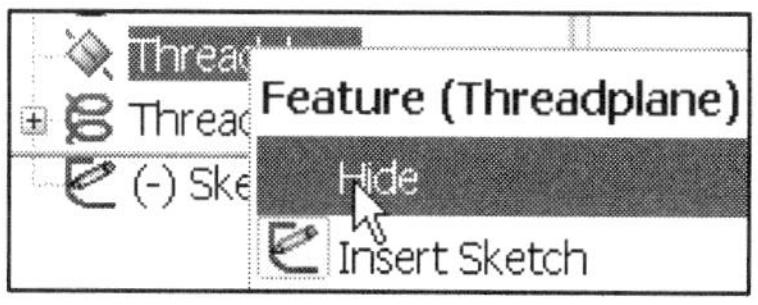

230) Right-click **Threadplane** from the FeatureManager.

231) Click **Hide**.

232) Click **Circle** Circle from the Sketch toolbar.

233) Sketch a **circle** to the right of the profile as illustrated.

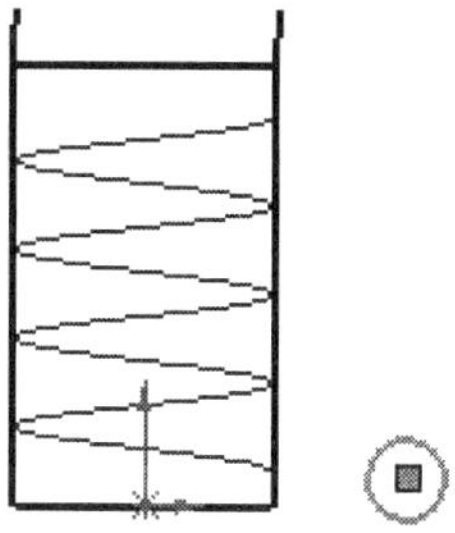

234) Click **Circle** Circle from the Sketch toolbar to deactivate.

Add a Pierce relation.

235) Click the **Threadpath** at the start of the helical curve.

236) Hold the **Ctrl** key down.

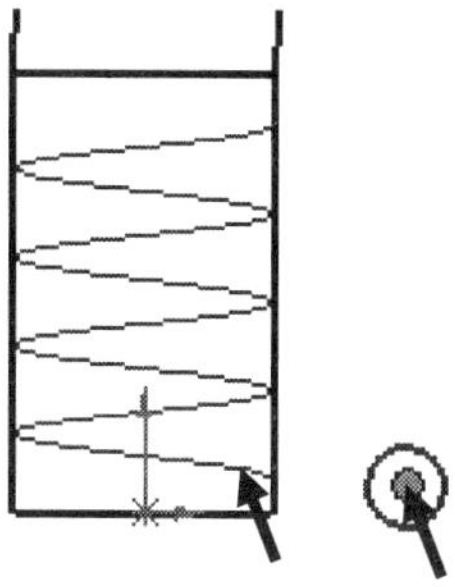

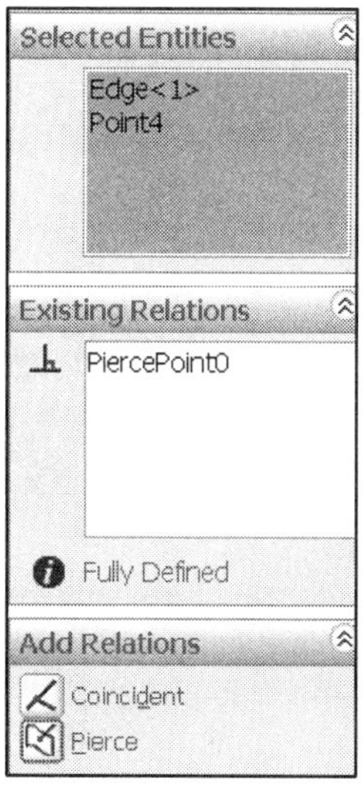

237) Click the **center point** of the circle.

238) Release the **Ctrl** key.

239) Click **Pierce** from the Add Relations box.

240) Click **OK** from the Properties PropertyManager.

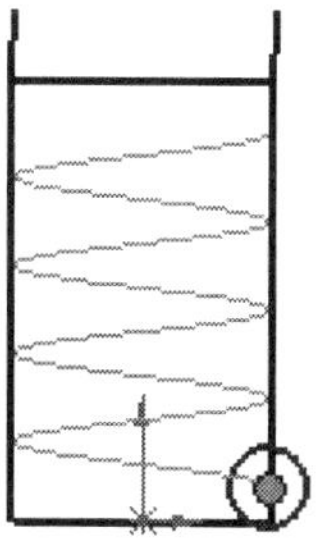

241) Add a dimension.

242) Click **Smart Dimension** Smart Dimens... from the Sketch toolbar.

243) Click the **circumference**.

244) Click a **position** off the profile.

245) Enter **.030**in, [**0.76**].

246) Click the **Green Check mark**.

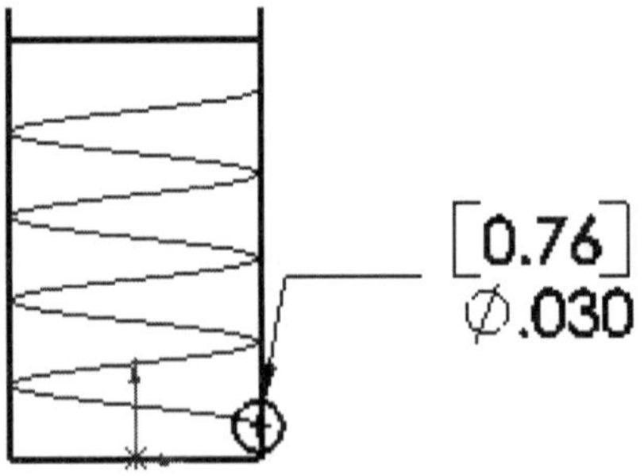

Close the Sketch.

247) Click **Exit Sketch** Exit Sketch.

248) Click Isometric view.

249) Rename Sketch4 to Threadprofile.

Insert the Sweep Cut feature.

250) Click **Insert**, **Cut**, **Sweep** from the Main menu. The Cut-Sweep PropertyManager is displayed. Threadprofile is displayed in the Profile box.

251) Click inside the **Path** box.

252) Click **Threadpath** from the fly-out FeatureManager. Threadpath is displayed in the Path box.

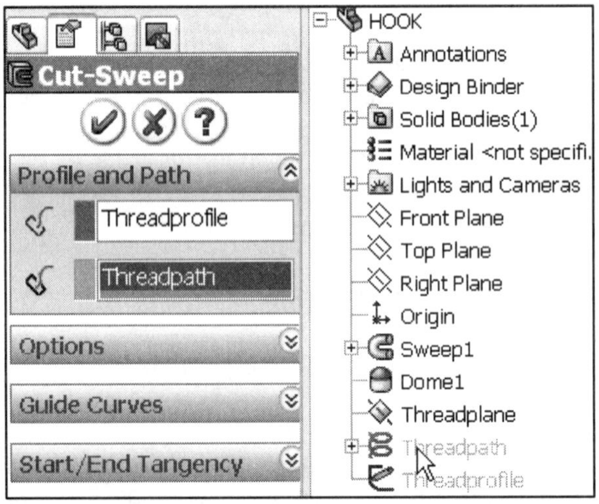

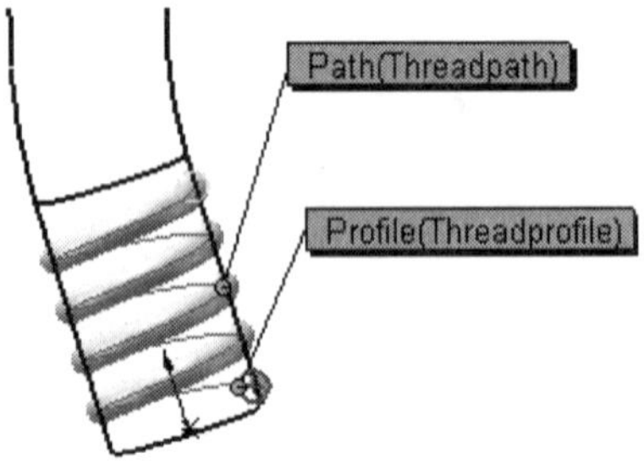

253) Click **OK** from the Cut-Sweep PropertyManager. Cut-Sweep1 is displayed in the FeatureManager.

254) Rename Cut-Sweep1 to Thread.

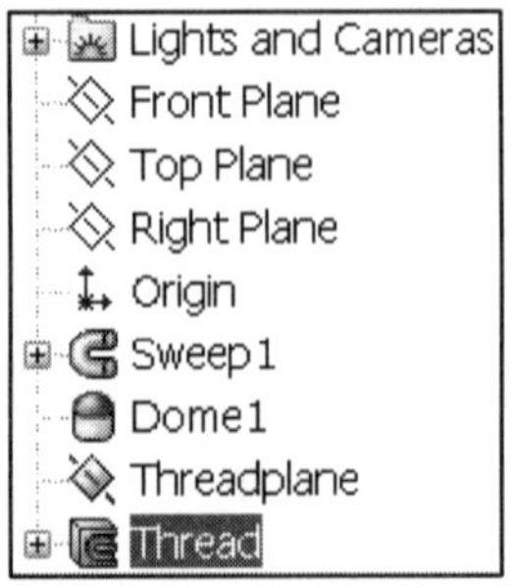

Save the HOOK part.

255) Click Shaded With Edges.

256) Click **Save**. The HOOK part is complete.

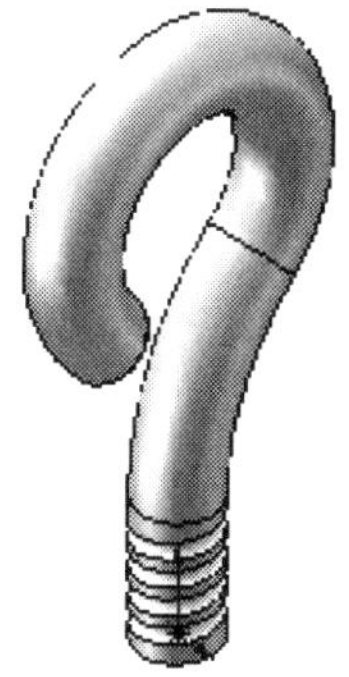

The Sweep Cut feature is one of several features not on the Features toolbar. Utilize Insert, Feature to select other Feature tools. Utilize Tools, Customize, Command, Features to modify the Feature toolbar.

Review the HOOK Part.

The HOOK part was created with a simple Sweep feature. A Sweep feature added material by moving a profile along a path. A Sweep feature required two sketches. The first sketch was called the path. The path was sketched on the Right plane. The second sketch was called profile. The profile was sketched on the Top plane. The path and profile were sketched on perpendicular planes. The path was swept along the profile to create the Sweep feature.

The Dome feature created a spherical face on the end of the Sweep.

A Sweep Cut feature removed material to create the thread. The thread required a spiral path and a circular profile. The path was created on a reference plane, parallel to the Top plane. The path utilized a Helical Curve. The thread required a sketched profile. This circular cross section was sketched perpendicular to the Front plane. The thread profile was pierced to the thread path.

Additional details on Loft, Sweep, Relations, Pierce and Reference planes are available in SolidWorks Help.

WHEEL Part

The WHEEL part is a machined part.

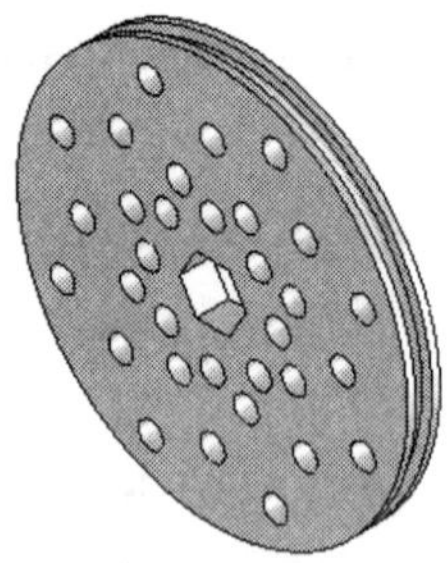

Create the WHEEL part with the Extruded Base feature. Utilize the Mid Plane option to center the WHEEL on the Front plane.

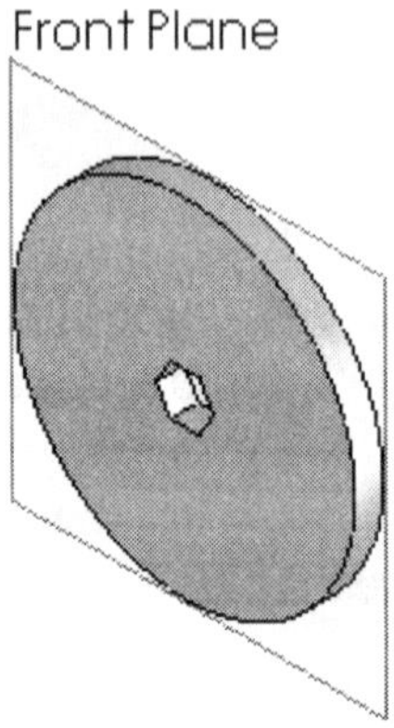

Utilize a Revolved Cut feature to remove material from the WHEEL and to create a groove for a belt.

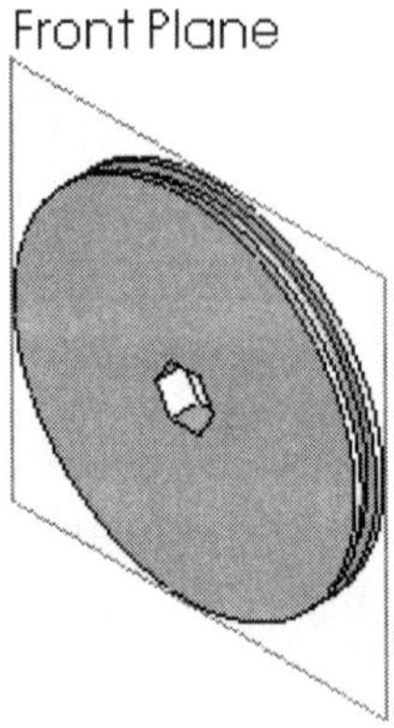

The WHEEL contains a complex pattern of holes.

Simplify the geometry by dividing the four holes into two Extruded Cut features.

The first Extruded Cut feature contains two small circles sketched on two bolt circles. The bolt circles utilize construction geometry.

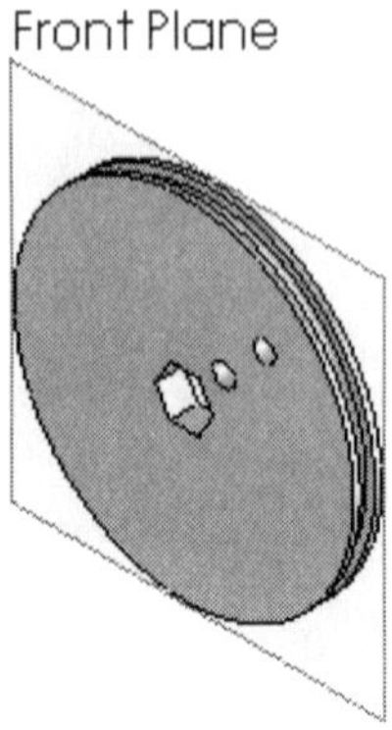

The second Extruded Cut feature utilizes two small circles sketched on two bolt circles. The bolt circles utilize construction geometry.

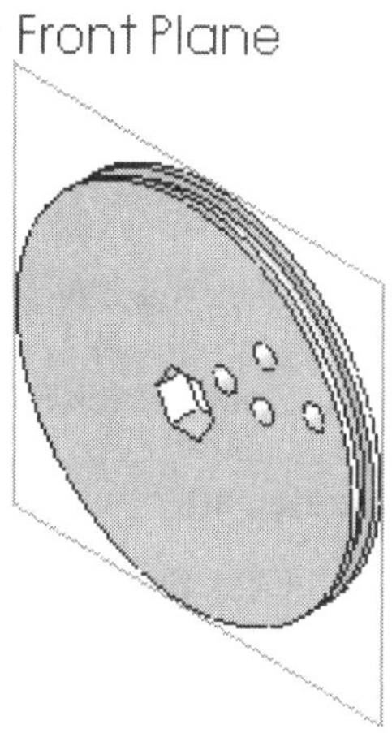

Utilize a Circular Pattern Feature. The two Extruded Cut features are contained in one Circular Pattern. Revolve the Extruded Cut features about the Temporary Axis located at the center of the Hexagon.

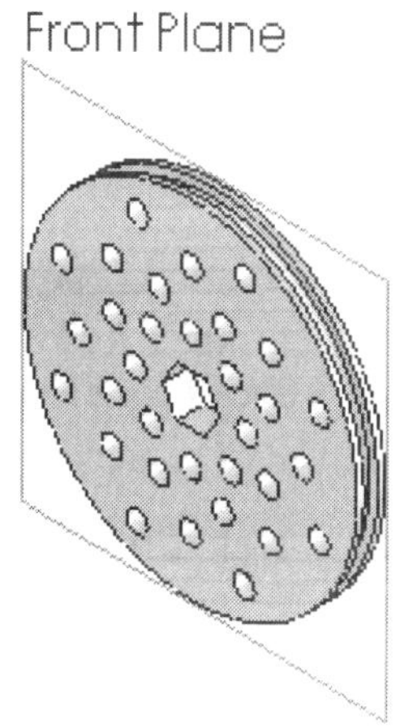

Create a Reference Axis. The Reference Axis is utilized in the WHEEL-AXLE assembly.

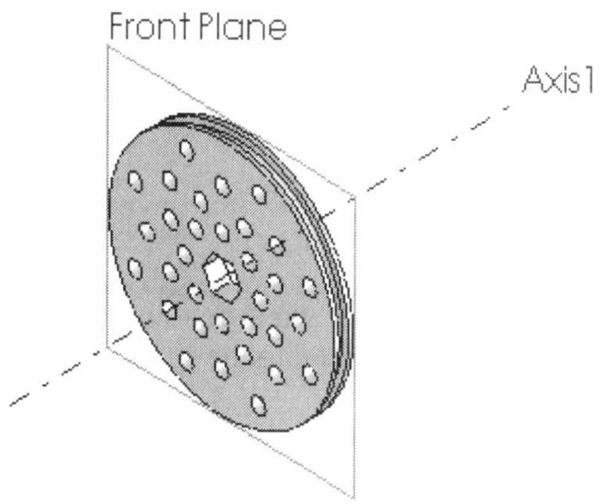

Activity: WHEEL Part

Create the new part.

257) Click **File**, **New** from the Main menu.

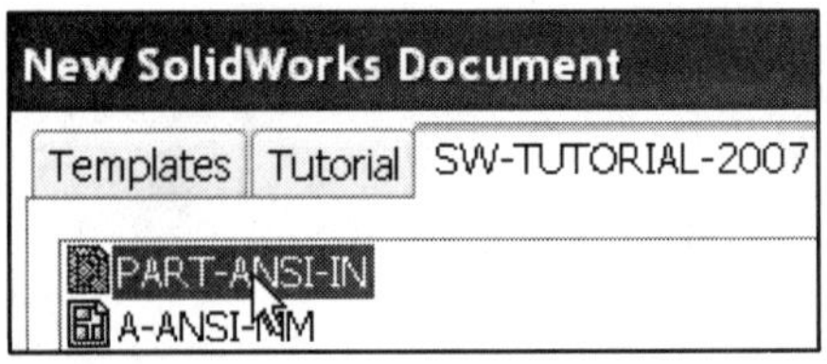

258) Click the **SW-TUTORIAL-2007** tab.

259) Double-click **PART-ANSI-IN**, [PART-ANSI-MM].

Save the part.

260) Click **Save**.

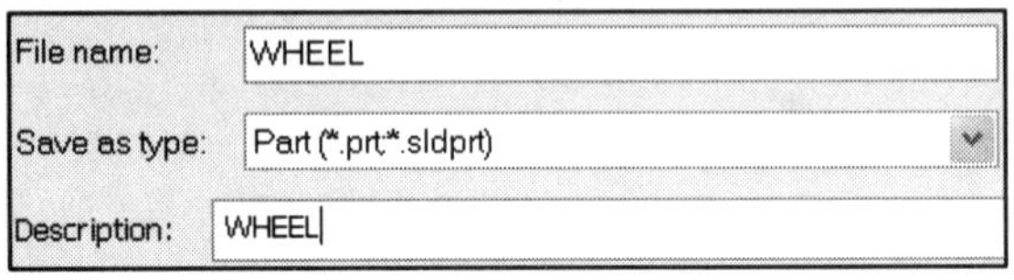

261) Select the **SW-TUTORIAL-2007** folder.

262) Enter **WHEEL** for File name.

263) Enter **WHEEL** for Description.

264) Click **Save**. The WHEEL FeatureManager is displayed.

Insert the sketch for the Extruded Base feature.

265) Click **Front Plane** from the FeatureManager.

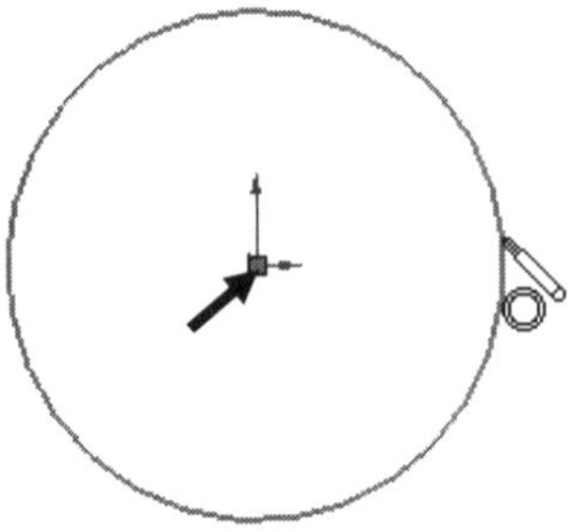

266) Click **Circle** Circle from the Sketch toolbar.

267) Click the **Origin**.

268) Click a **position** to the right of the Origin.

Insert a polygon.

269) Click **Tools**, **Sketch Entities**, **Polygon** from the Main menu. The Polygon PropertyManager is displayed.

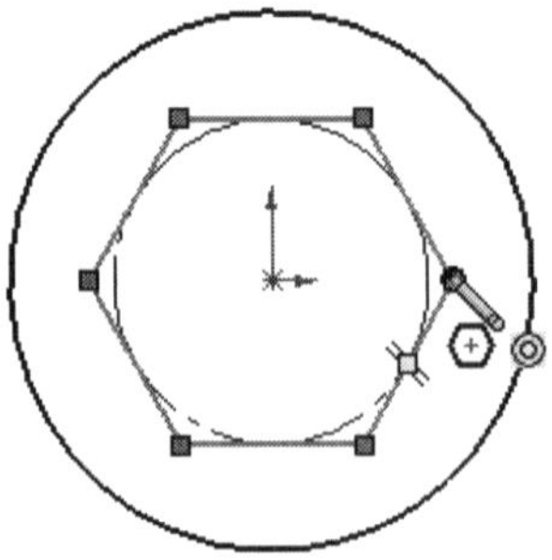

270) Click the **Origin**.

271) Drag and click the **mouse pointer** horizontally to the right of the Origin to create the hexagon as illustrated.

272) Click **OK** from the Polygon PropertyManager.

273) Right-click **Select** in the Graphics window.

Add a Horizontal relation.

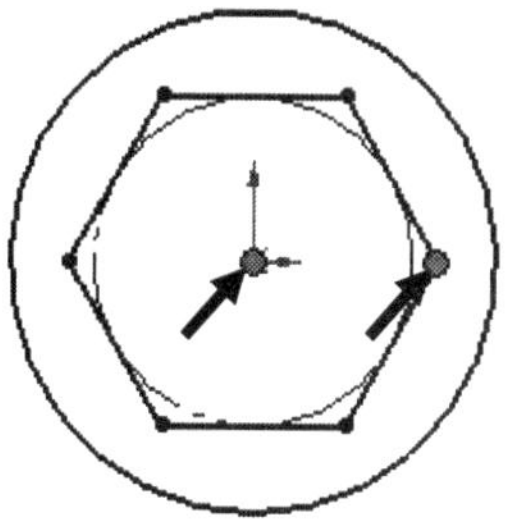

274) Click the **Origin**.

275) Hold the **Ctrl** key down.

276) Click the **right point** of the hexagon.

277) Release the **Ctrl** key.

278) Click **Horizontal** from the Add Relations box.

279) Click **OK** from the Properties PropertyManager.

Add dimensions.

280) Click **Smart Dimension** Smart Dimens... from the Sketch toolbar.

281) Click the **circumference** of the large circle.

282) Click a **position** above the circle.

283) Enter **3.000**in, [**76.20**].

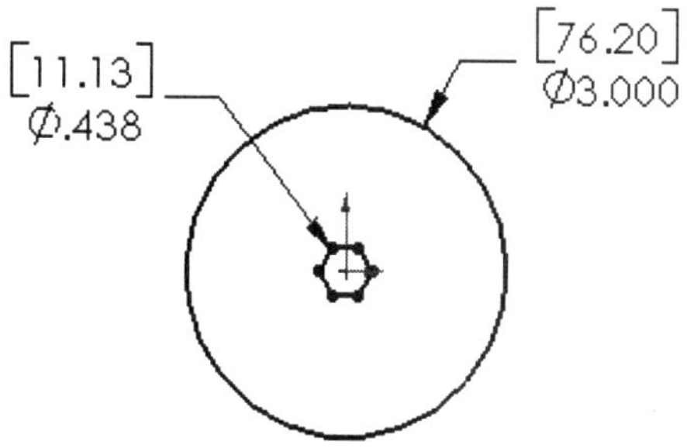

284) Click the Green Check mark.

285) Click the **circumference** of the inscribed circle for the Hexagon.

286) Click a **position** above the Hexagon.

287) Enter **.438**in, [**11.13**].

288) Click the Green Check mark.

Activity: WHEEL Part-Extruded Base Feature

Insert an Extruded Base feature.

289) Click **Extruded Boss/Base** Extruded Boss/B... from the Features toolbar. The Extrude PropertyManager is displayed.

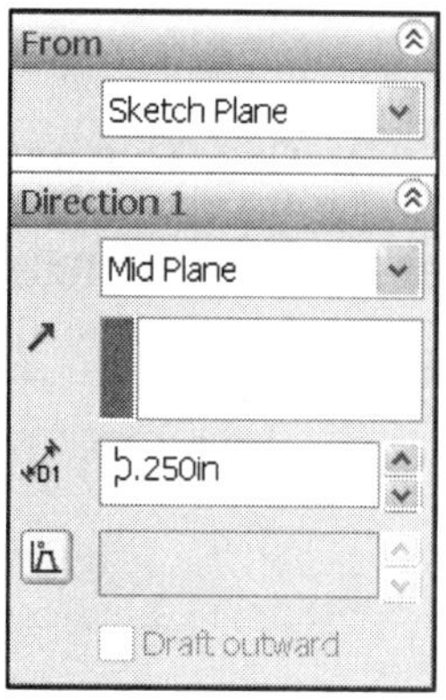

290) Select **Mid Plane** for End Condition in Direction 1.

291) Enter **.250**in, [**6.35**] for Depth.

292) Click **OK** from the Extrude PropertyManager. Extrude1 is displayed in the FeatureManager.

Fit the model to the Graphics window.

293) Press the **f** key.

Save the WHEEL part.

294) Click **Save**.

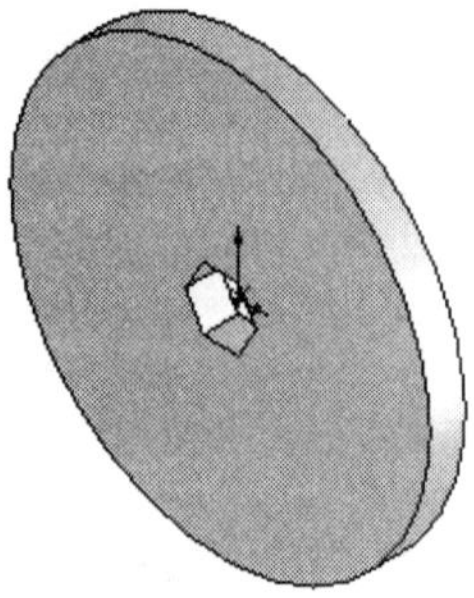

Activity: WHEEL Part-Revolved Cut Feature

Insert a new sketch for the Revolved Cut feature.

295) Click **Right Plane** from the FeatureManager.

296) Click **Sketch** Sketch.

297) Click Right view.

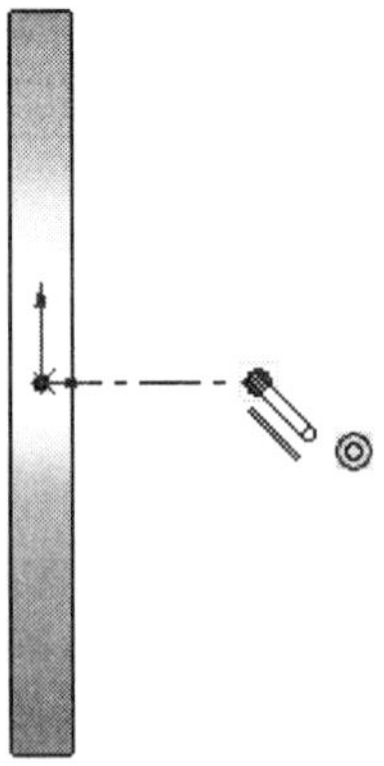

Sketch the axis of revolution.

298) Click **Centerline** Centerl... from the Sketch toolbar.

299) Click the **Origin**.

300) Click a **position** horizontally to the right of the Origin.

301) Click **Zoom to Area** on the top edge.

Sketch the profile.

302) Click **Line** Line from the Sketch toolbar.

303) Click the **top horizontal edge** of Extrude1.

304) Click a **position** directly below the first point.

305) Click **Tangent Arc** Tangent Arc from the Sketch toolbar.

306) Sketch a **180° arc** as illustrated.

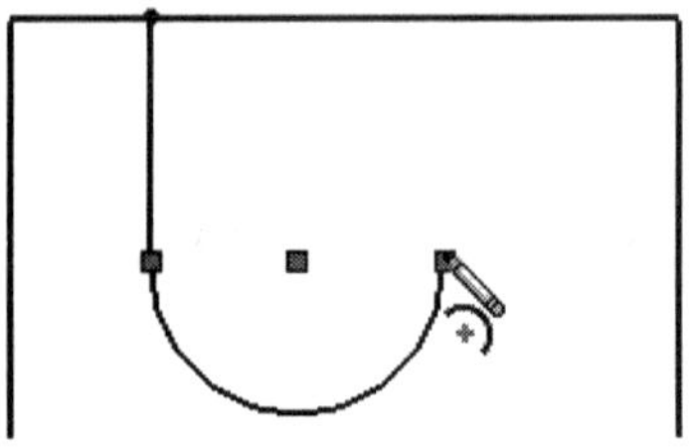

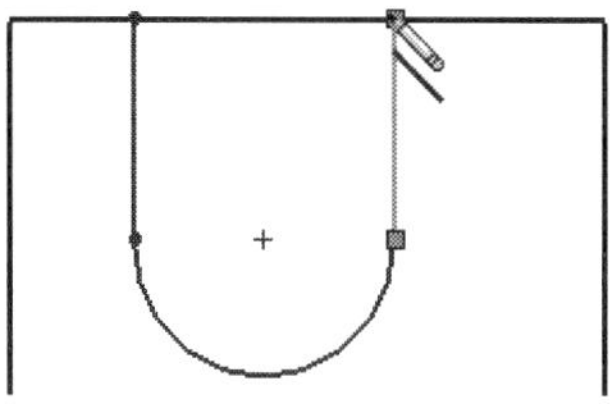

307) Click **Line** Line from the Sketch toolbar.

308) Sketch the second **vertical line**. The end point of the line is coincident with the top horizontal edge of Extrude1.

309) Sketch a **horizontal line** collinear with the top edge to close the profile.

Add a Vertical relation.

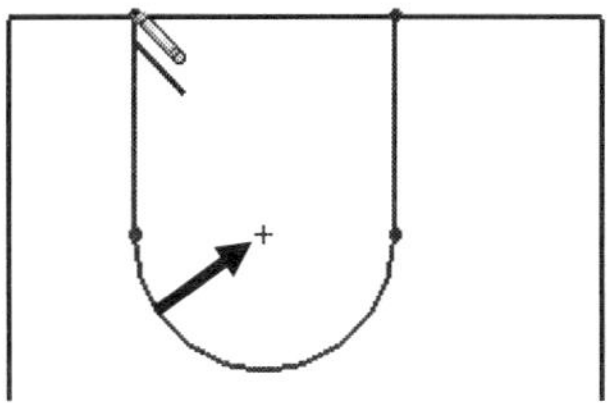

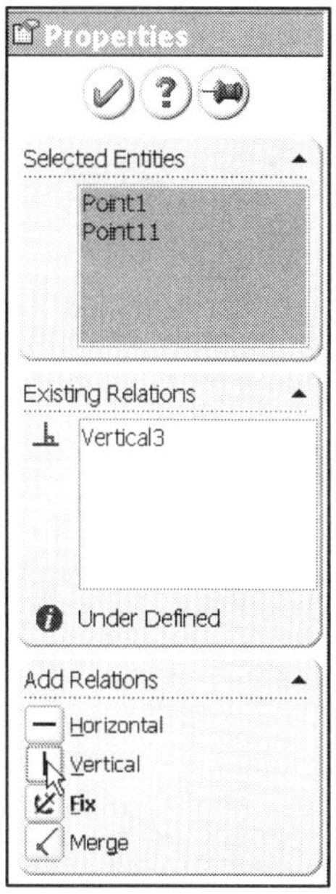

310) Right-click **Select** in the Graphics window.

311) Click the **Origin** from the FeatureManager.

312) Hold the **Ctrl** key down.

313) Click the **center point** of the arc.

314) Release the **Ctrl** key.

315) Click **Vertical** from the Add Relations box.

Add a Collinear relation.

316) Click the **horizontal line**. Hold the **Ctrl** key down.

317) Click the horizontal silhouette edge.

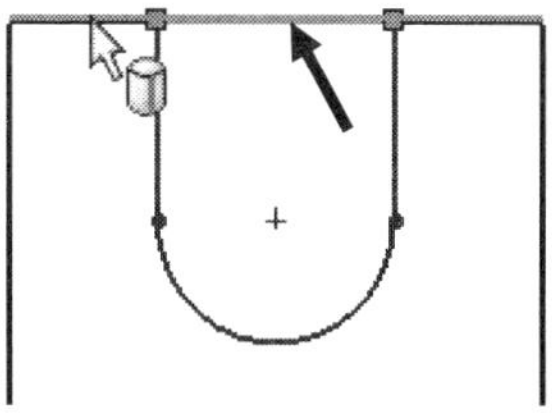

318) Release the **Ctrl** key. Click **Collinear** from the Add Relations box.

Add an Equal relation.

319) Click the **left vertical** line. Hold the **Ctrl** key down. Click the **right vertical** line.

320) Release the **Ctrl** key. Click **Equal** from the Add Relations box.

Add dimensions.

321) Click **Smart Dimension** Smart Dimens... from the Sketch toolbar.

322) Click the **arc**. Click a position to the **left** of the profile. Enter **.063**in, [**1.60**].

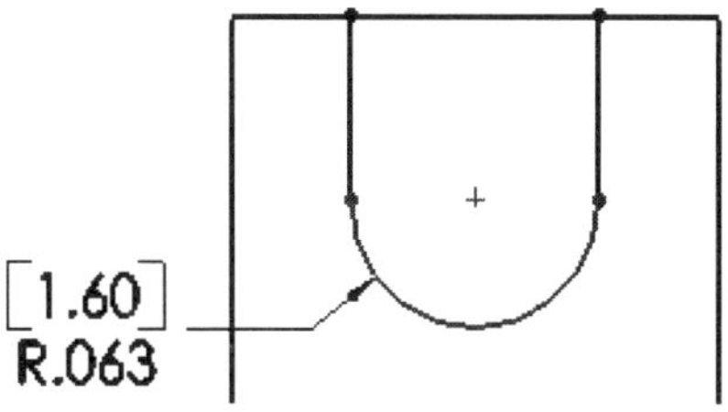

323) Click the Green Check mark.

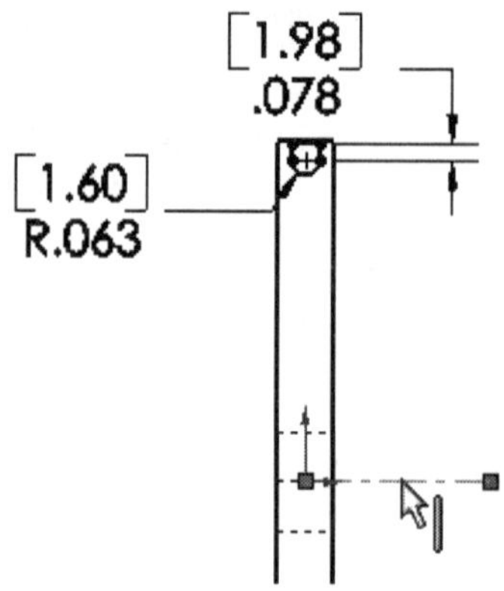

324) Click the right vertical line.

325) Click a position to the **right** of the profile.

326) Enter **.078**in, [**1.98**].

327) Click the Green Check mark.

Fit the Model to the Graphics window.
328) Press the **f** key.

Select the axis of revolution.
329) Right-click **Select** in the Graphics window.

Activity: WHEEL Part-Revolved Cut Feature

Insert a Revolved Cut feature.
330) Click the **centerline** in the Graphics window.

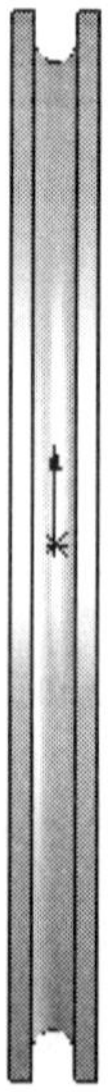

331) Click **Revolved Cut** Revolved Cut from the Features toolbar. The Cut-Revolve PropertyManager is displayed. The Cut-Revolve PropertyManager displays 360 degrees for the Angle of Revolution.

332) Click **OK** from the Cut-Revolve PropertyManager. Cut-Revolve1 is displayed in the FeatureManager.

Save the WHEEL part.
333) Click **Save**.

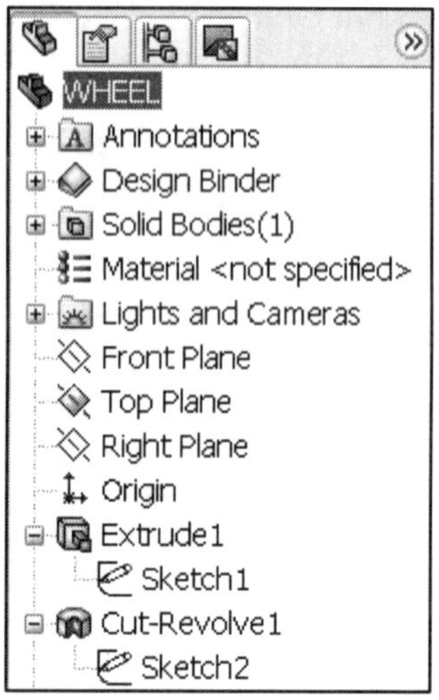

Four bolt circles, spaced 0.5in, [12.7] apart locate the 8 - ∅.190, [4.83] holes. Simplify the situation. Utilize two Extruded Cut features on each bolt circle.

Position the first Extruded Cut feature hole on the first bolt circle and third bolt circle. Position the second Extruded Cut feature hole on the second bolt circle and forth bolt circle.

Activity: WHEEL Part- First Extruded Cut Feature

Display the Top Plane.

334) Right-click **Top Plane** from the FeatureManager.

335) Click **Show**.

336) Click **Front view**.

337) Click Hidden Lines Visible.

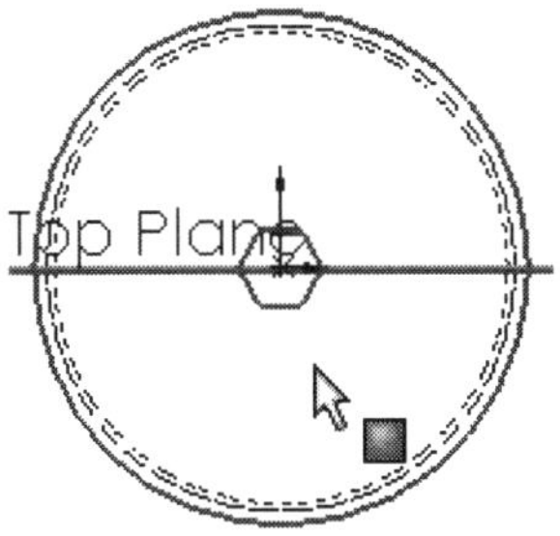

Insert a new sketch for the first Extruded Cut feature.

338) Click the Extrude1 **front face** as illustrated.

339) Click **Sketch** Sketch.

Create the first construction bolt circle.

340) Click **Circle** Circle from the Sketch toolbar. The Circle PropertyManager is displayed.

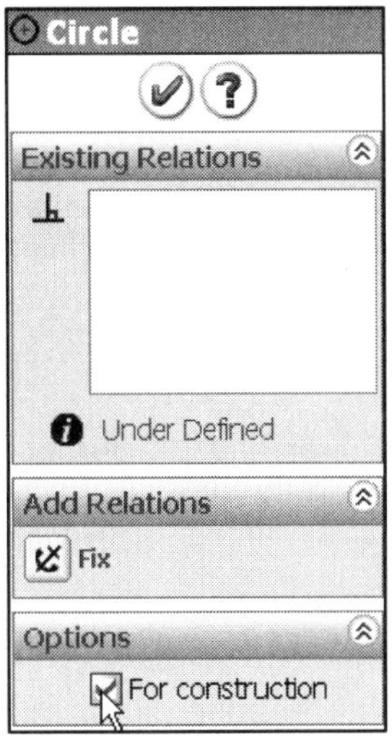

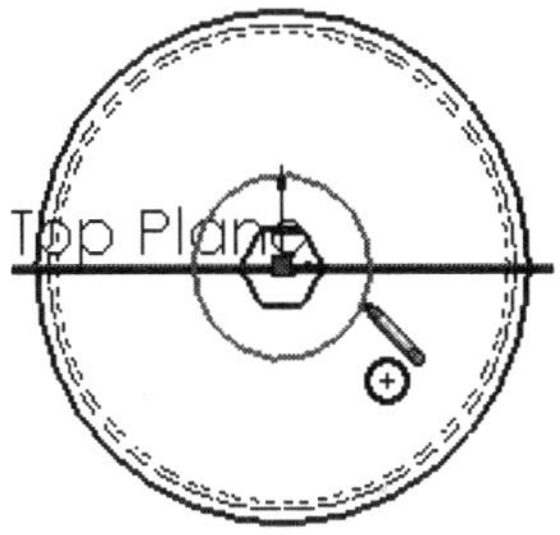

341) Click the **Origin**.

342) Click a **position** to the right of the hexagon.

343) Check the For construction box.

Create the second construction bolt circle.

344) Click the **Origin**.

345) Click a **position** to the right of the first construction bolt circle.

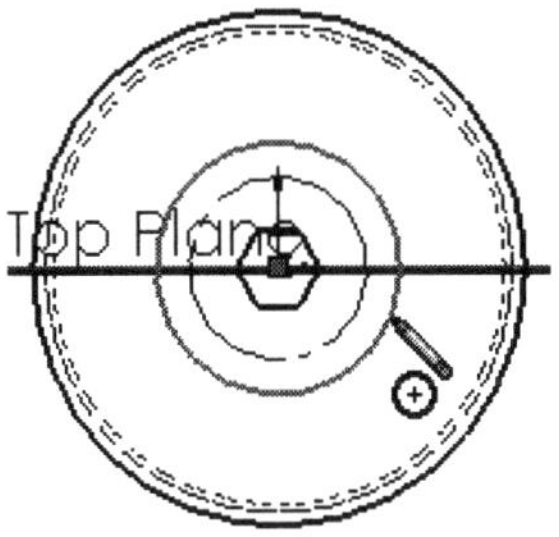

346) Check the **For construction** box. The two bolt circles are displayed with construction line style.

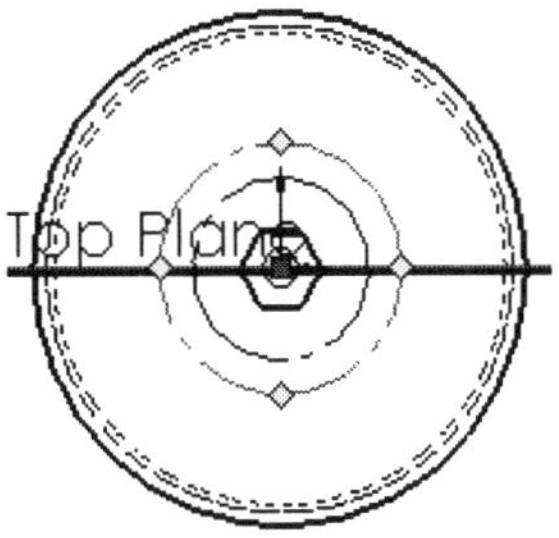

Insert a centerline.

347) Click Hidden Lines Removed.

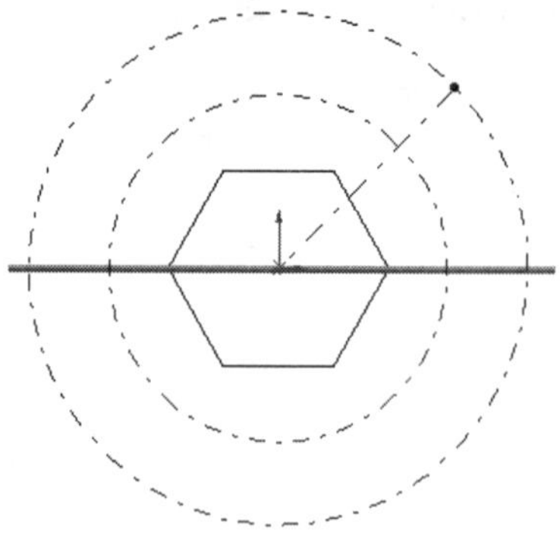

348) Click **Centerline** Centerl... from the Sketch toolbar.

349) Sketch a **45° centerline** from the Origin to the second bolt circle as illustrated.

Sketch the two circle profiles.

350) Click **Circle** Circle from the Sketch toolbar.

351) Sketch a **circle** at the intersection of the centerline and the first bolt circle.

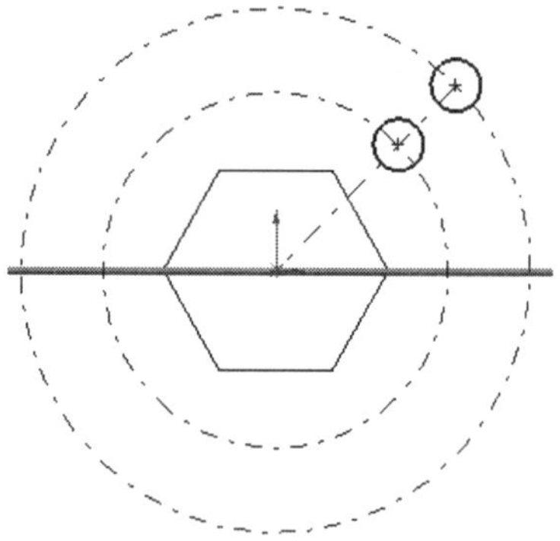

352) Sketch a **circle** at the intersection of the centerline and the second bolt circle.

353) Right-click **Select**.

Note: An intersection relation is created between three entities: the center point of the small circle, the centerline and the bolt circle.

Add an Equal relation.

354) Click the **first circle**.

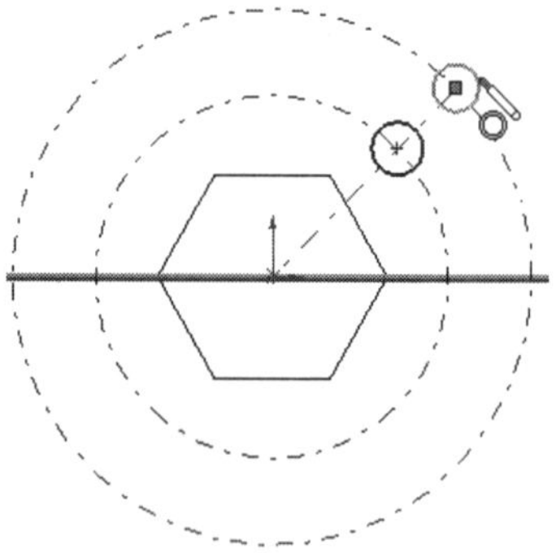

355) Hold the **Ctrl** key down.

356) Click the **second circle**.

357) Release the **Ctrl** key.

358) Click **Equal** = from the Add Relations box.

Add dimensions.

359) Click **Smart Dimension** Smart Dimens... from the Sketch toolbar.

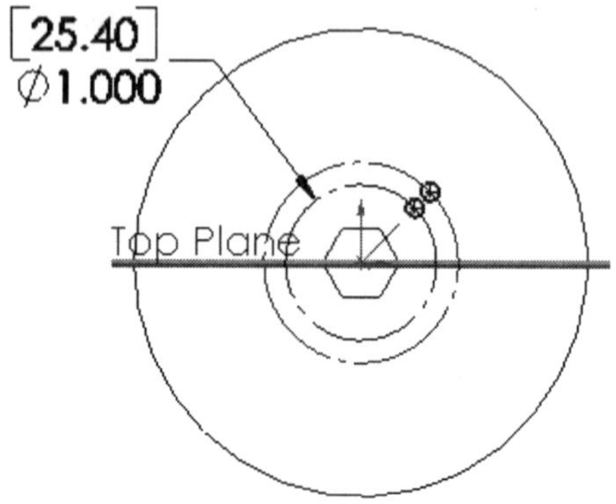

360) Click the first construction circle.

361) Click a **position** above the profile.

362) Enter **1.000**in, [**25.4**].

363) Click the Green Check mark.

364) Click the second construction circle.

365) Click a **position** above the profile.

366) Enter **2.000**in, [**50.80**].

367) Click the **Green Check mark** ✔.

368) Click the **second small circle**. Click a **position** above the profile.

369) Enter **.190**in, [**4.83**].

370) Click the Green Check mark ✔.

371) Click **Top Plane** from the fly-out FeatureManager.

372) Click the **45° centerline**. Click a **position** between the two lines.

373) Enter **45**deg for angle.

374) Click the Green Check mark ✔.

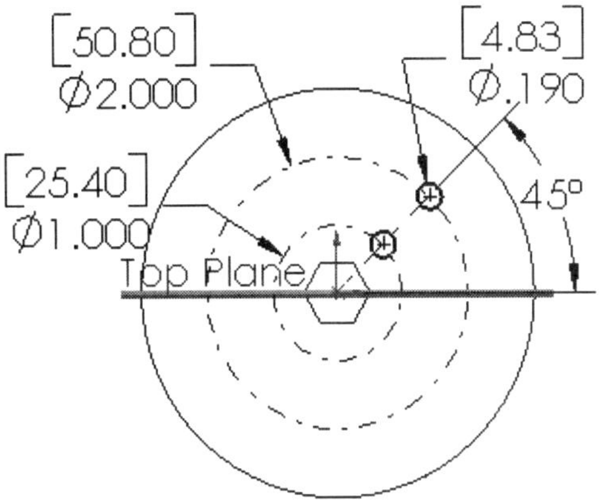

Note: If the sketch is not fully defined, you may need to add an Intersection relation between the center point of the small circle, the centerline, and the bolt circle.

Insert an Extruded Cut feature.

375) Click **Extruded Cut** Extruded Cut from the Features toolbar. The Cut-Extrude PropertyManager is displayed.

376) Select **Through All** for the End Condition in Direction 1.

377) Click **OK** from the Cut-Extrude PropertyManager.

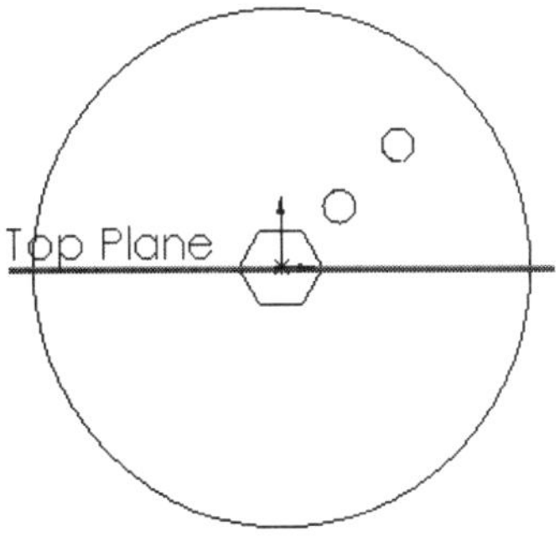

Activity: WHEEL Part- Second Extruded Cut Feature

Insert a new sketch for the second Extruded Cut feature.

378) Click the **Extrude1** front face.

379) Click **Sketch** Sketch.

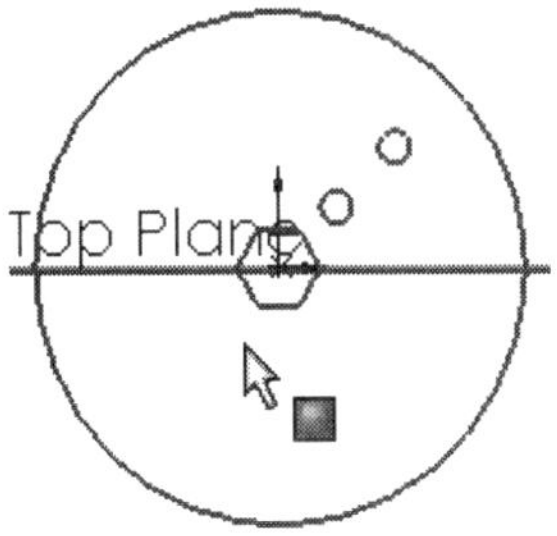

Sketch two additional construction line bolt circles, 1.500in, [38.10] and 2.500in, [63.50]. Create the first construction bolt circle.

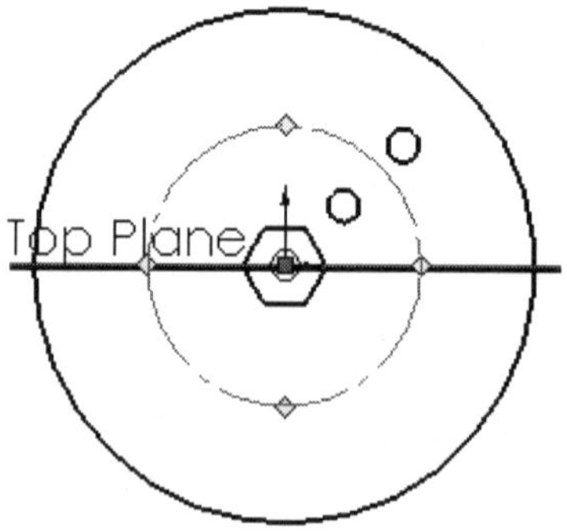

380) Click **Circle** Circle from the Sketch toolbar.

381) Click the **Origin**.

382) Click a **position** between the two small circles.

383) Check the For construction box.

Create the second additional construction bolt circle.

384) Click the **Origin**.

385) Click a **position** to the right of the large construction bolt circle as illustrated.

386) Check the **For construction** box from the Circle PropertyManager. The two bolt circles are displayed with the two construction lines.

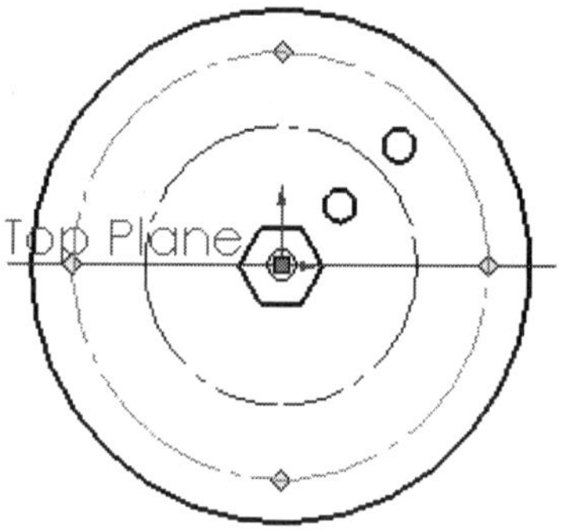

Insert a centerline.

387) Click **Centerline** Centerl... from the Sketch toolbar.

388) Sketch a **22.5° centerline** to the right from the Origin to the second bolt circle as illustrated.

389) Select **.1** from the Primary Unit Precision box.

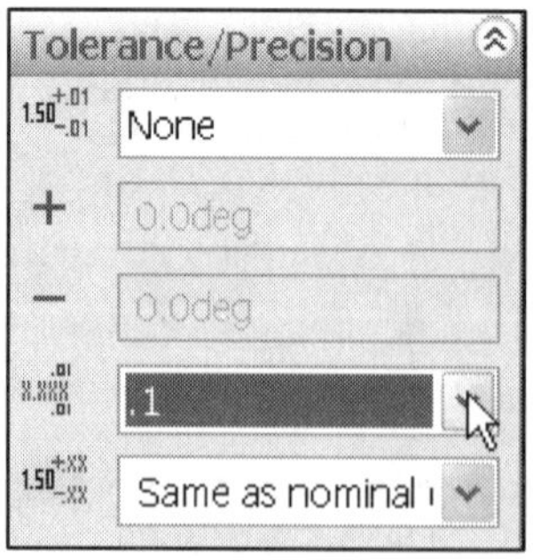

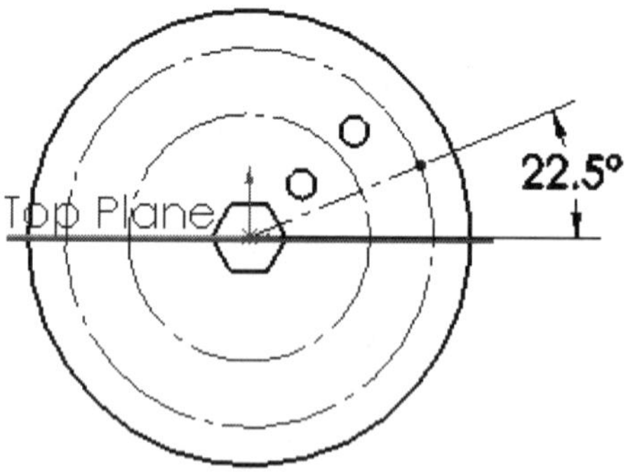

Sketch the two circle profiles.

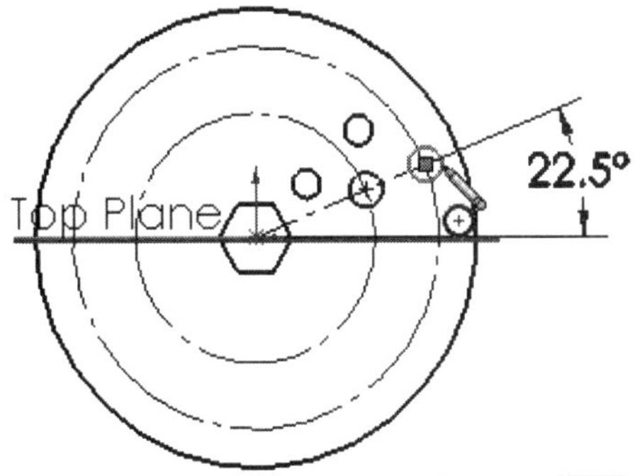

390) Click **Circle** Circle from the Sketch toolbar.

391) Sketch a **circle** at the intersection of the centerline and the first bolt circle.

392) Sketch a **circle** at the intersection of the centerline and the second bolt circle.

393) Right-click **Select**.

Add an Equal relation.

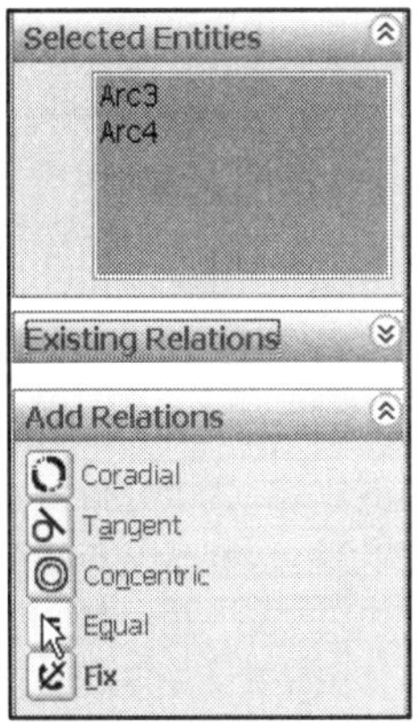

394) Click the **first circle**. Hold the **Ctrl** key down.

395) Click the **second circle**. Release the **Ctrl** key.

396) Click **Equal** = from the Add Relations box.

Add dimensions.

397) Click **Smart Dimension** Smart Dimens... from the Sketch toolbar.

398) Click the first construction circle.

399) Click a **position** above the profile.

400) Enter **1.500**in, [**38.10**].

401) Click the second construction circle.

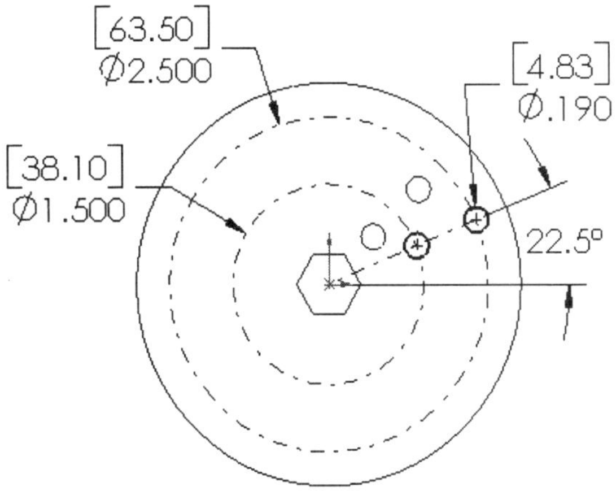

402) Click a **position** above the profile.

403) Enter **2.500**in, [**63.50**].

404) Click the **small circle**.

405) Click a **position** above the profile.

406) Enter **.190**in, [**4.83**].

Note: If the sketch is not fully defined, you may need to add an Intersection relation between the center point of the small circle, the centerline, and the bolt circle.

Insert an Extruded Cut feature.

407) Click **Extruded Cut** Extruded Cut from the Features toolbar. The Cut-Extrude PropertyManager is displayed.

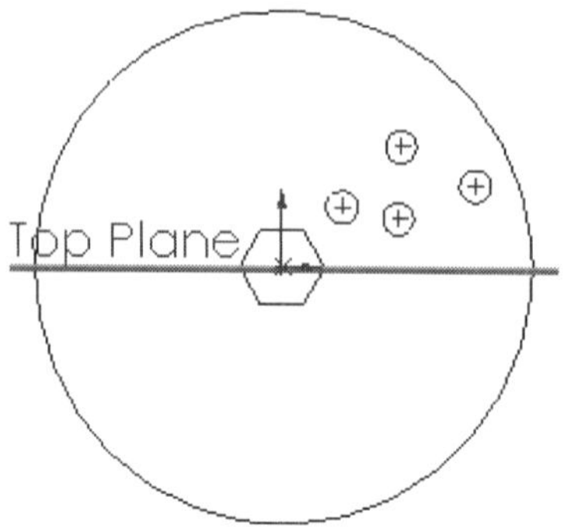

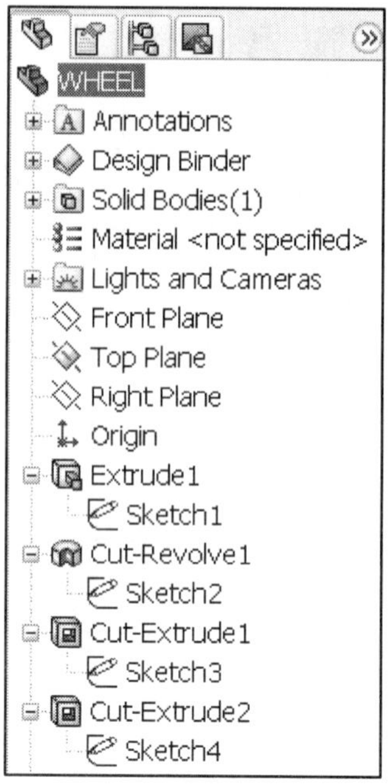

408) Select **Through All** for End Condition in Direction 1.

409) Click **OK** from the Cut-Extrude PropertyManager. Cut-Exturde2 is displayed in the FeatureManager.

410) Click **Save**.

View the Temporary Axes.

411) Click **View**; check **Temporary Axes** from the Main menu.

Activity: WHEEL Part-Circular Pattern Feature

Insert a Circular Pattern.

412) Click Isometric view.

413) Click Shaded With Edges.

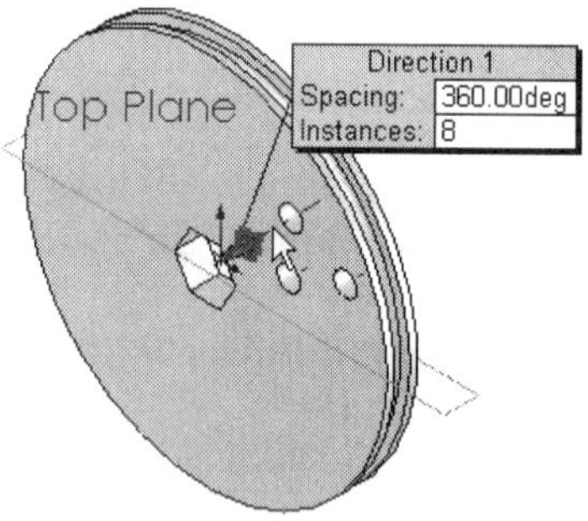

414) Click **Circular Pattern** Circular Pattern from the Features toolbar. The Circular Pattern PropertyManager is displayed.

415) Click the **Temporary Axis** in the Graphics window at the center of the Hexagon. Axis<1> is displayed in the Pattern Axis box.

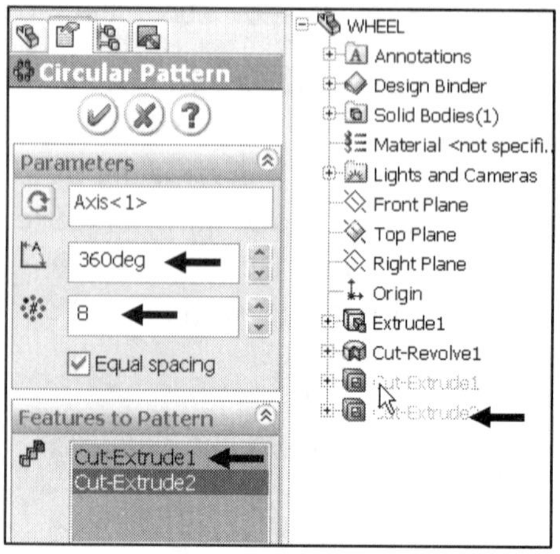

416) Enter **360**deg for Angle.

417) Enter **8** for Number of Instances.

418) Click inside the **Features to Pattern** box.

419) Click **Cut-Extrude1** and **Cut-Extrude2** from the fly-out FeatureManager. Cut-Extrude1 and Cut-Extrude2 are displayed in the Features to Pattern box.

420) Check the **Geometry pattern** box.

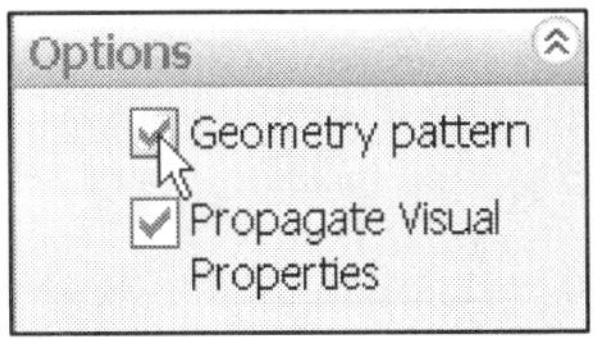

421) Click **OK** from the Circular Pattern PropertyManager. CirPattern1 is displayed in the FeatureManager.

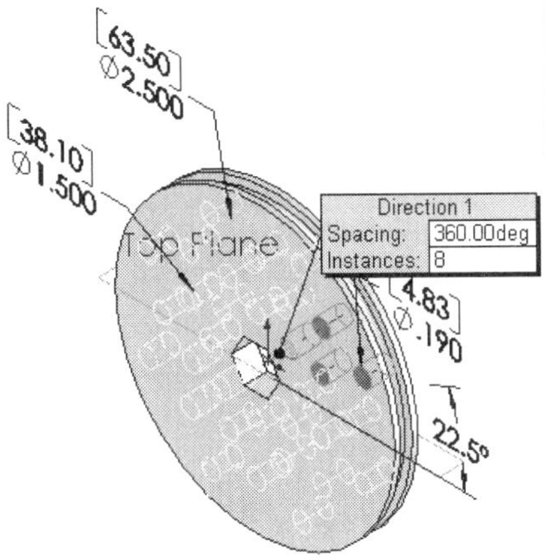

Save the WHEEL part.

422) Click **Save**.

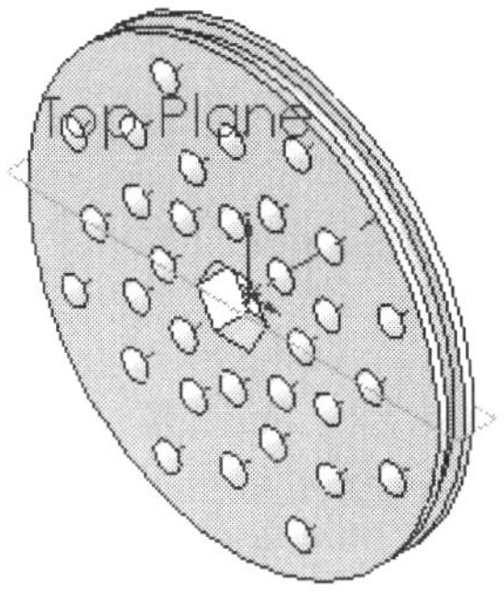

Utilize a Reference Axis to locate the WHEEL in the PNEUMATIC-TEST-MODULE assembly. The Reference Axis is located in the FeatureManager and Graphics window. The Reference Axis is a construction axis defined between two planes.

Insert a reference axis.

423) Click **Insert**, **Reference Geometry**, **Axis** from the Main menu. The Axis PropertyManager is displayed.

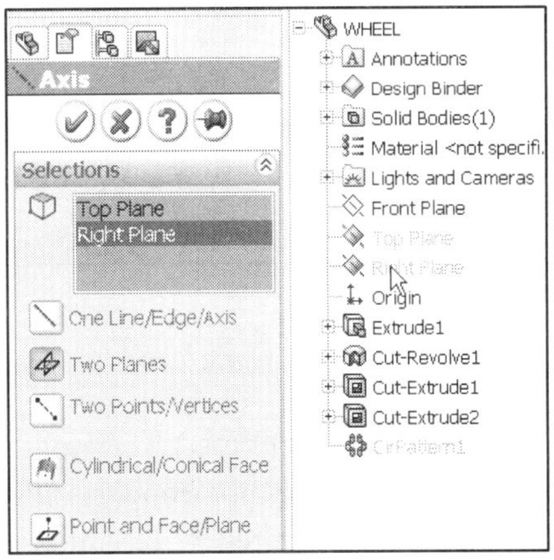

424) Click **Top Plane** from the fly-out FeatureManager.

425) Click **Right Plane** from the fly-out FeatureManager. The selected planes are displayed in the Selections box.

426) Click **OK** from the Axis PropertyManager. Axis1 is displayed in the FeatureManager.

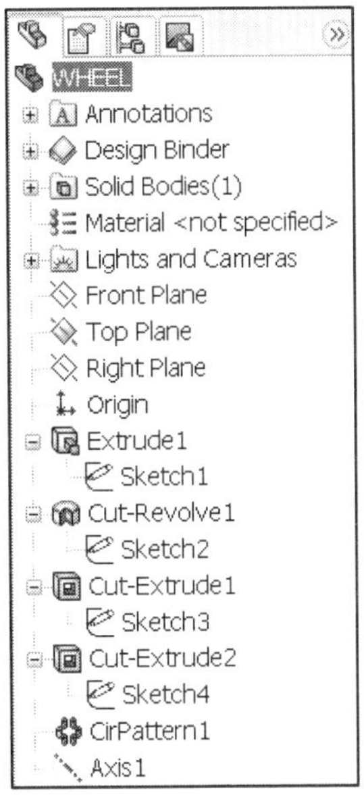

Axis1 is positioned through the Hex Cut centered at the Origin.

427) Click and drag the **Axis1 handles** outward to extend the length on both sides as illustrated.

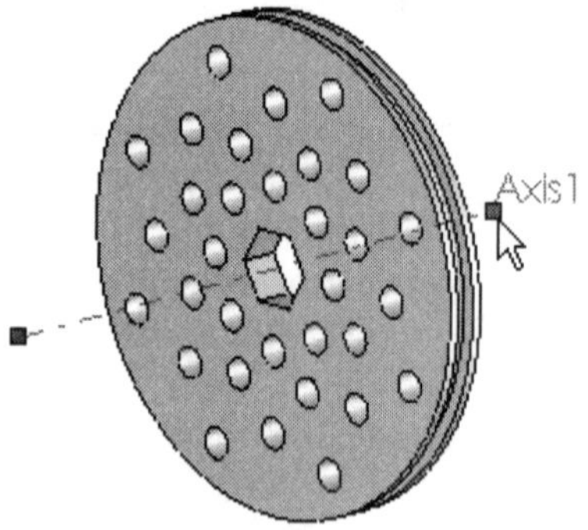

Save the WHEEL part.

428) Click Isometric view.

429) Click **Save**.

The Geometry pattern option in the Circular Pattern PropertyManager and the Linear Pattern PropertyManager saves rebuild time. The End Conditions are not recalculated. For extruded parts, utilize the Geometry pattern option.

Sketched lines, arcs or circles are modified from profile geometry to construction geometry. Select the geometry in the sketch. Check the For construction box option.

Review the WHEEL Part.

The WHEEL part was created with the Extruded Base feature. You sketched a circular sketch on the Front plane and extruded the sketch with the Mid Plane option.

A Revolved Cut feature removed material from the WHEEL and created the groove. The Revolved Cut feature utilized an arc sketched on the Right plane. A sketched centerline was required to create the Revolved Cut feature.

The WHEEL contained a complex pattern of holes. The first Extruded Cut feature contained two small circles sketched on two bolt circles. The bolt circles utilized construction geometry. Geometric relationships and dimensions were used in the sketch. The second Extruded Cut feature utilized two small circles sketched on two bolt circles.

The two Extruded Cut features were contained in one Circular Pattern and revolved about the Temporary Axis. The Reference Axis was created with two perpendicular planes. Utilize the Reference Axis, Axis1 in the WHEEL-AXLE assembly.

Additional details on Reference Geometry, Planes, Axes, Circular Pattern, and Geometry pattern are available in SolidWorks Help.

Modify Parts

Conserve design time and cost. Modify existing parts and assemblies to create new parts and assemblies. Utilize the Save as copy option to avoid updating the existing assemblies with new file names.

The HEX-STANDOFF part was created in Project 2. The HEX-ADAPTER is required to fasten the WHEEL to the AXLE. Start with the HEX-STANDOFF part.

Utilize Save As and enter the HEX-ADAPTER for the new file name. Important: Check the Save as copy check box. The HEX-ADAPTER is the new part name. Open the HEX-ADAPTER. Modify the dimensions of the Extruded Base feature.

Utilize Edit Definition to modify the Hole Wizard Tap Hole to a Standard Hole. Insert an Extruded Boss feature to create the head of the HEX-ADAPTER.

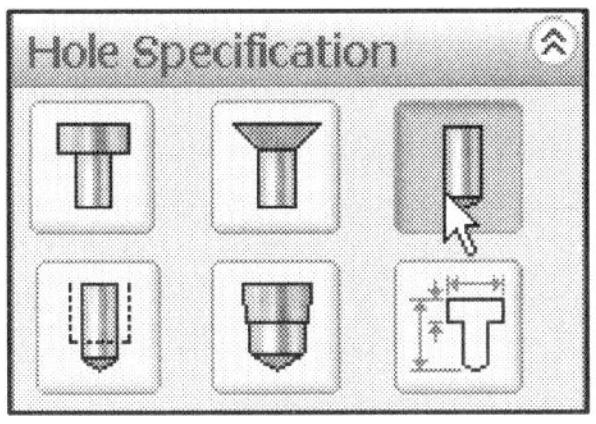

Insert an Extruded Cut feature. Sketch a circle on the Right plane. Extrude the circle in Direction1 and Direction2 with the Through All End Condition option.

Feature order determines the internal geometry of the Hole. If the Hole feature is created before the Extrude2-Head feature, the Through All End Condition will extend through the Extrude1 feature.

If the Hole feature is created after the Extrude2-Head feature, the Through All End Condition will extend through the Extrude1 feature and the Extrude2-Head feature.

Modify feature order by dragging feature names in the FeatureManager. Utilize the Save as copy option to create the AXLE3000 part from the AXLE part.

Utilize the Save as copy option to create the SHAFTCOLLAR-500 part from the SHAFT-COLLAR part. Save the HEX-STANDOFF as the HEX-ADAPTER part.

Activity: HEX-ADAPTER Part

Create the HEX-ADAPTER.

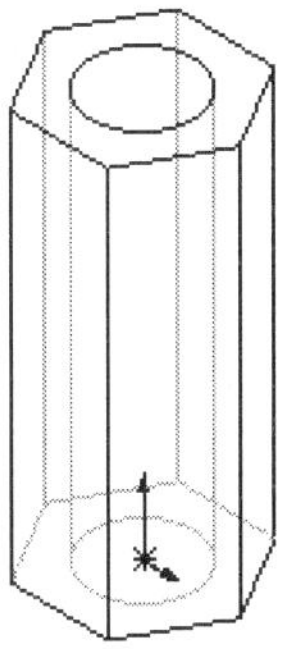

430) Click **File**, **Open** from the Main menu.

431) Select **Part** for Files of type from the SW-TUTORIAL-2007 folder.

432) Double-click **HEX-STANDOFF**. The HEX-STANDOFF FeatureManager is displayed.

433) Click **File**, **Save As** from the Main menu.

434) Select the **SW-TUTORIAL-2007** folder.

435) Enter **HEX-ADAPTER** for File name.

436) Enter **HEX-ADAPTER** for Description.

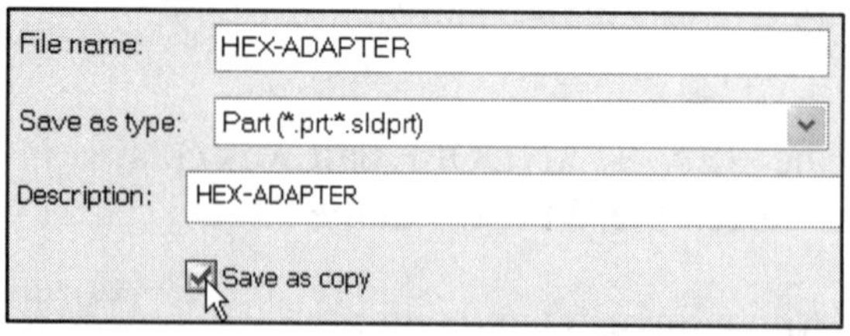

437) Check the **Save as copy** box.

438) Click **Save**.

439) Click **File**, **Close** from the Main menu.

Open the HEX-ADAPTER.

440) Click **File**, **Open** from the Main menu.

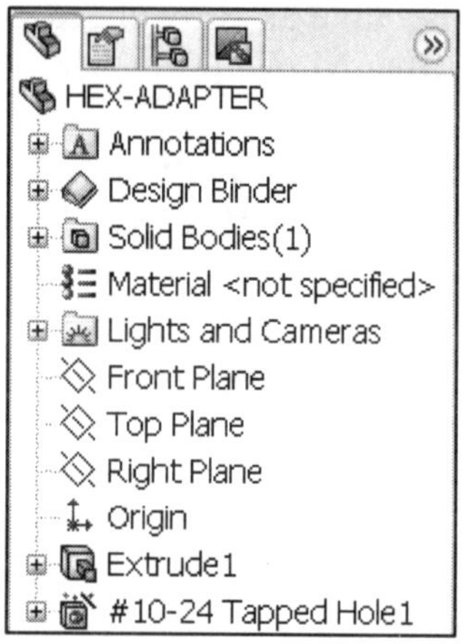

441) Double-click **HEX-ADAPTER** from the SW-TUTORIAL-2007 folder. The HEX-ADAPTER FeatureManager is displayed.

Modify the Extrude1 dimensions.

442) Double-click **Extrude1** from the FeatureManager.

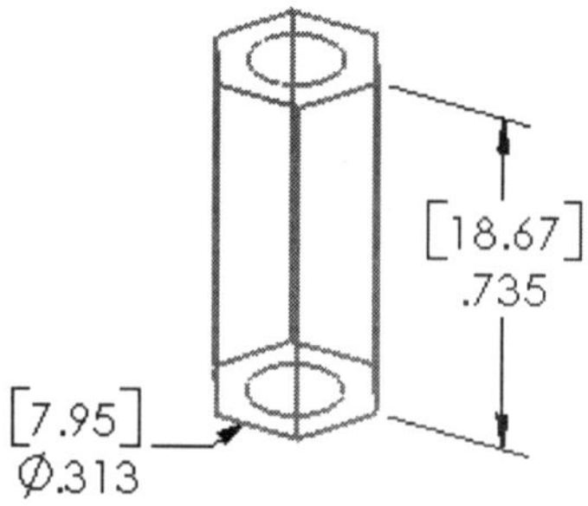

443) Double-click **.735**in, [**18.67**].

444) Enter **.700**in, [**17.78**] for depth.

445) Double-click **.313**in, [**7.95**].

446) Enter **.438**in, [**11.13**] for diameter.

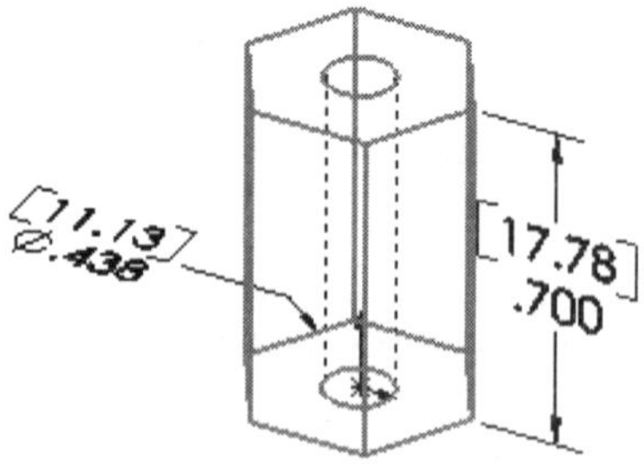

447) Click **Rebuild** from the Standard menu.

Modify the #10-24 Tapped Hole1 feature.

448) Right-click **#10-24 Tapped Hole1** from the FeatureManager.

449) Click **Edit Feature**. The Hole Specification PropertyManager is displayed.

450) Click the **Type** tab.

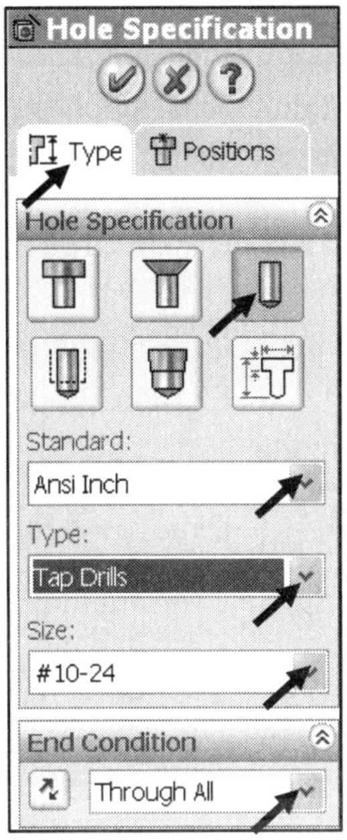

451) Select the **Hole** tab from the Hole Specification box.

452) Select **Ansi Inch** for Standard.

453) Select **Tap Drills** for Type.

454) Select **#10-24** for Size.

455) Select **Through All** for End Condition.

456) Click **OK** from the Hole Specification PropertyManager. The Tap Hole is modified.

Insert a Sketch for the Extruded Boss feature.

457) Press the **Up Arrow key** approximately four times.

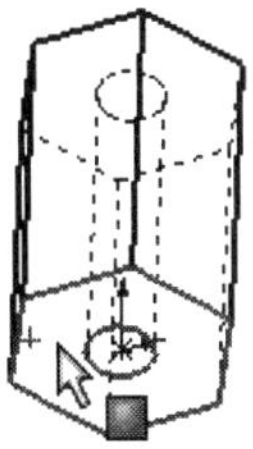

458) Click the **bottom hexagonal face** of the Extrude1 feature as illustrated.

459) Click **Sketch** Sketch from the Sketch toolbar.

460) Click the **Bottom view**.

461) Click **Circle** Circle from the Sketch toolbar.

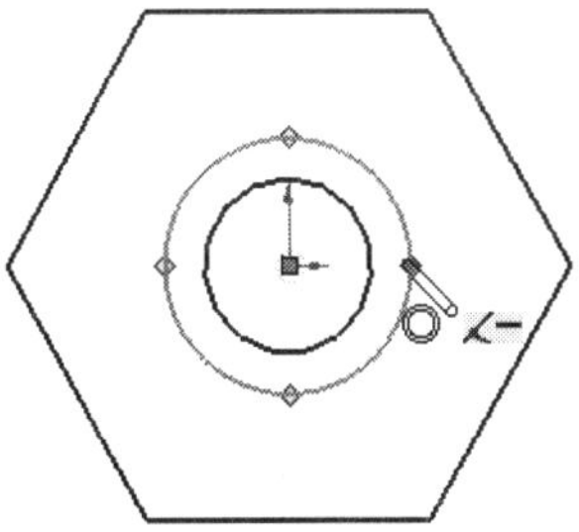

462) Click the **Origin**.

463) Click a **position** in the Graphics window to the right of the Origin.

Add a dimension.

464) Click **Smart Dimension** Smart Dimens.. from the Sketch toolbar.

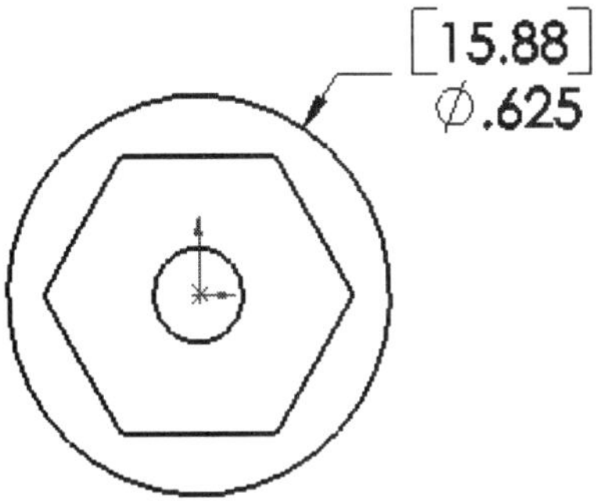

465) Click the circumference of the **circle**.

466) Click a **position** above the circle to locate the dimension.

467) Enter **.625**in, [**15.88**] in the Modify dialog box.

468) Press the **f** key to fit the model to the Graphics window.

Activity: HEX-ADAPTER Part-Extruded Boss Feature

Extrude the sketch to create the Extruded Boss feature.

469) Click Isometric view.

470) Click **Extruded Boss/Base** Extruded Boss/B... from the Features toolbar. The Extrude PropertyManager is displayed.

471) Enter **.200**in, [**6.35**] for Depth. The Direction arrow points downward. Flip the **Direction arrow** if required.

472) Click **OK** from the Extrude PropertyManager. Extrude2 is displayed in the FeatureManager.

473) Rename Extrude2 to Extrude2-Head.

474) Click **Save**.

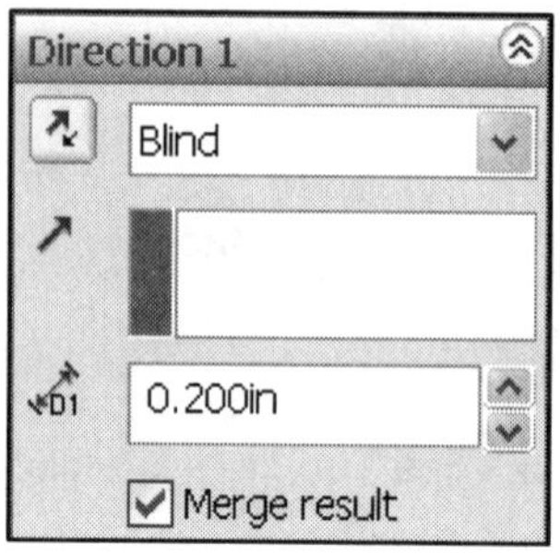

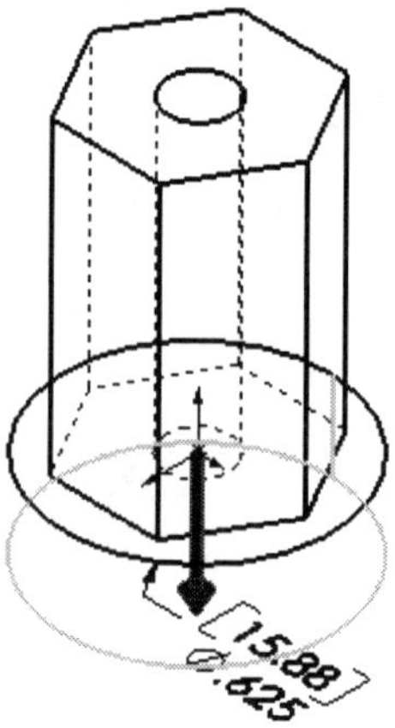

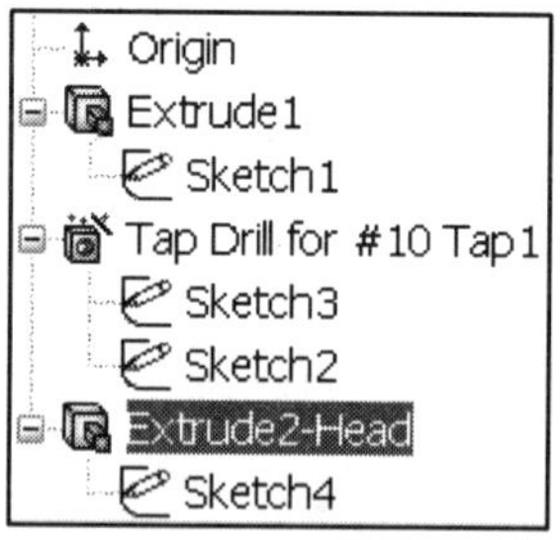

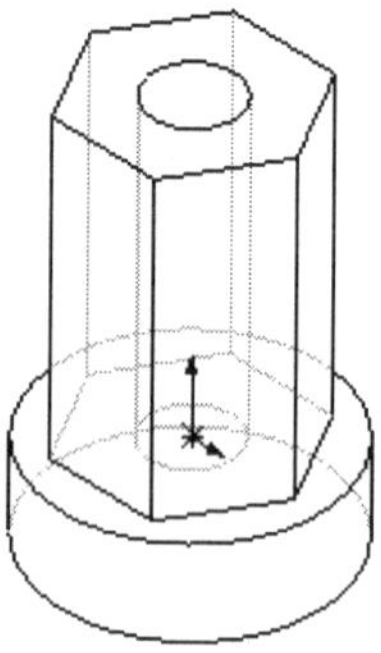

Activity: HEX-ADAPTER Part-Extruded Cut Feature

Insert a new sketch for the Extruded Cut on the Right Plane.

475) Click **Right Plane** from the FeatureManager.

476) Click **Sketch** Sketch.

477) Click **Right view**.

478) Click **Circle** Circle from the Sketch toolbar.

479) Sketch a **circle** below the Origin. The center point is vertically aligned to the Origin as illustrated. If required, add a Vertical relation between the center point of the circle and the Origin.

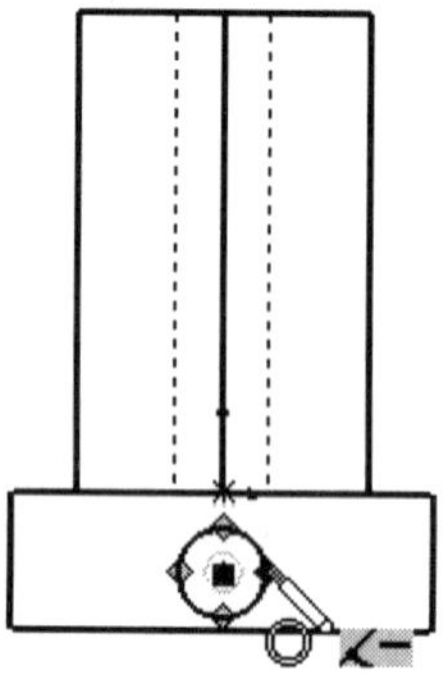

Add dimensions.

480) Click **Smart Dimension** Smart Dimens.. from the Sketch toolbar.

481) Click the **middle horizontal edge**. Click the **center point** of the circle. Click a **position** to the right of the profile.

482) Enter **.100**in, [**2.54**].

483) Click the Green Check mark.

484) Click the circumference of the **circle**. Click a **position** below the profile.

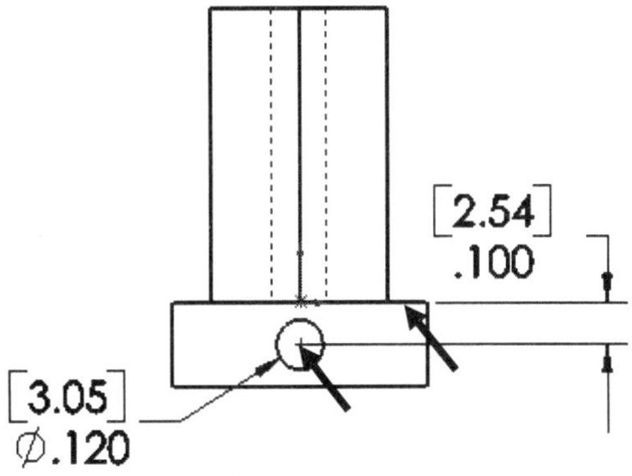

485) Enter .**120**in, [**3.95**].

486) Click the Green Check mark.

Insert an Extruded Cut feature.

487) Click **Extruded Cut** Extruded Cut from the Features toolbar. The Cut-Extrude PropertyManager is displayed.

488) Select **Through All** for End Condition in Direction 1.

489) Check the **Direction 2** box.

490) Select **Through All** for End Condition in Direction 2.

491) Click **OK** from the Cut-Extrude PropertyManager. Cut-Extrude1 is displayed in the FeatureManager.

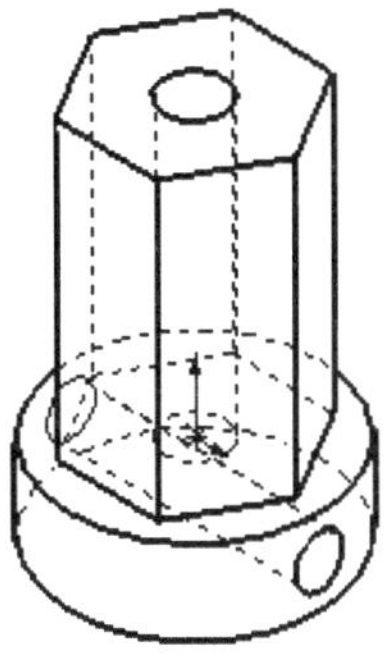

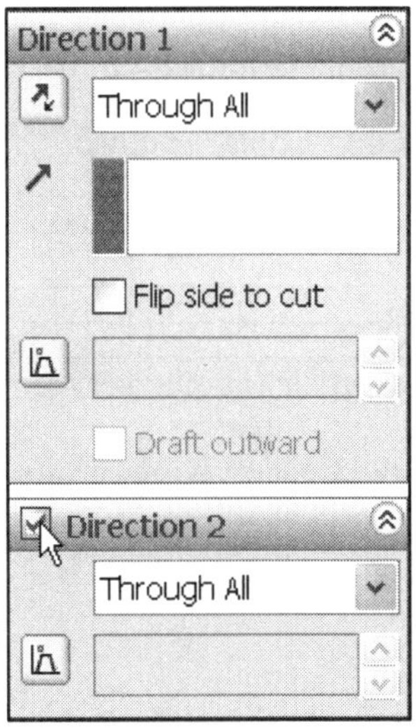

492) Click Isometric view.

493) Rename Cut-Extrude1 to Cut-Extrude1-SetScrew.

Save the HEX-ADAPTER part.

494) Click **Save**.

The Through All End Condition is required to penetrate both the Extrude1 and Extrude2 features. Reorder features in the FeatureManager. Position the Extrude2 feature before the Tap Drill for # 10 Tap 1 feature in the FeatureManager.

Reorder Extrude2.

495) Click **Extrude2-Head** from the FeatureManager.

496) Drag the **Extrude2-Head** text upward.

497) Click a **position** below Extrude1. The Through All End Condition option for the Tap Drill for # 10 Tap 1 feature creates a hole through both Extrude1 and Extrude2.

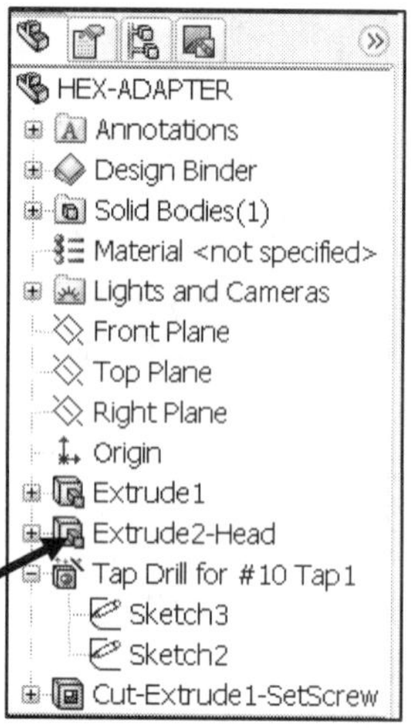

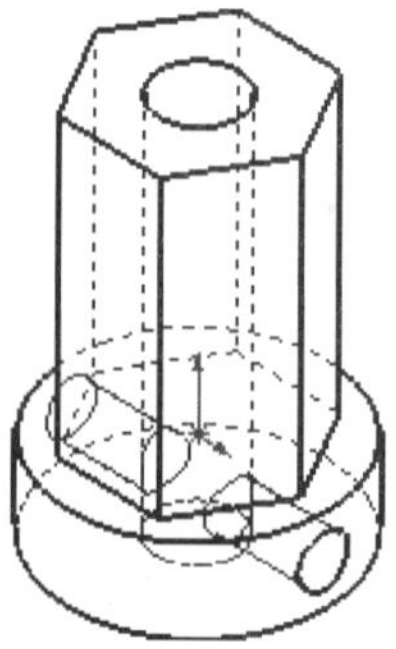

Display the section view.

498) Click **Front Plane** from the FeatureManager.

499) Click **Section** from the View toolbar. The Section View PropertyManager is displayed.

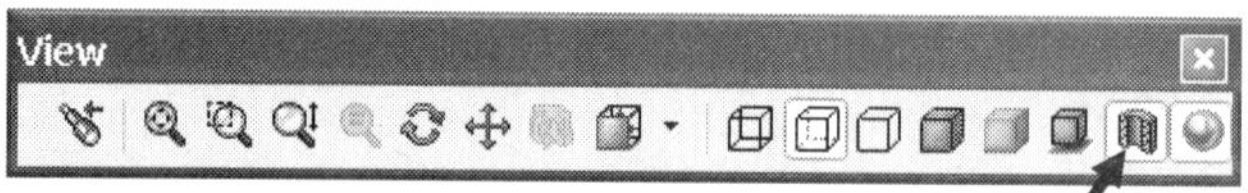

500) Click **OK** from the Section View PropertyManager.

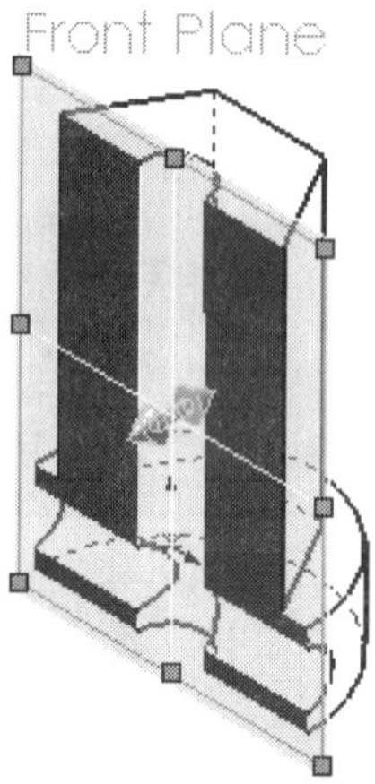

Display the full view.

501) Click **Section** from the View toolbar.

502) Click Shaded With Edges.

Save the HEX-ADAPTER.

503) Click **Save**.

Close all documents.

504) Click **Windows**, **Close All** from the Main menu.

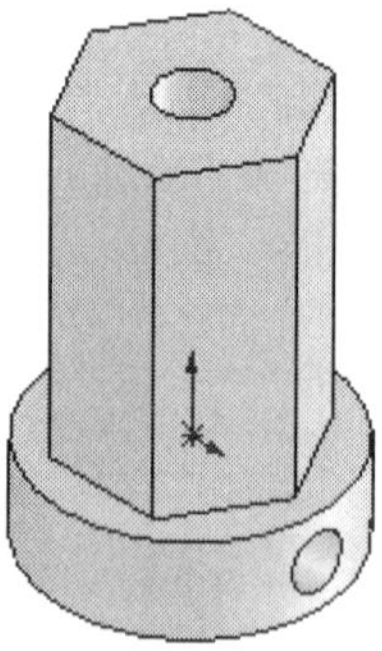

Utilize the Save as copy option and work on the copied version of the document before making any changes to the original. Keep the original document in tact.

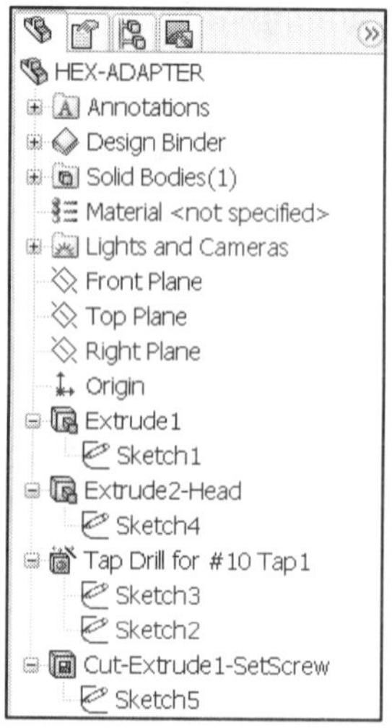

Review the HEX-ADAPTER Part.

The HEX-ADAPTER part was created by utilizing the Save as copy command with the HEX-STANDOFF part. The Extruded Base feature dimensions were modified. Edit Definition was utilized to modify the Hole type from the Hole Wizard feature.

An Extruded Boss feature added material. An Extruded Cut feature, sketched on the Right plane with the Through All End Condition for both Direction1 and Direction2, created a hole through the Extruded Boss. Reordering features in the FeatureManager modified the Hole. Utilizing existing geometry saved time with the Save as copy command. The original part and its references to other assemblies are not affected with the Save as copy command.

You require additional work before completing the PNEUMATIC-TEST-MODULE assembly. The AXLE and SHAFT-COLLAR were created in Project 1. Utilize the Save as copy command to save the parts.

Additional details on Save (Save as copy), Reorder (features), Section View PropertyManager are available in SolidWorks Help.

Utilize Design Table configurations for the AXLE part and SHAFT-COLLAR part developed in Project 3.

Note: The AXLE-3000 part and SHAFT-COLLAR-500 part utilize the Save as copy option in the next section. Utilize the Save as copy components or the configurations developed with Design Tables in Project 3 for the WHEEL-AXLE assembly.

Activity: AXLE-3000 Part

Create the AXLE-3000 part from the AXLE part.

505) Click **File**, **Open** from the Main menu.

506) Double-click **AXLE** from the SW-TUTORIAL-2007 folder. The AXLE FeatureManager is displayed.

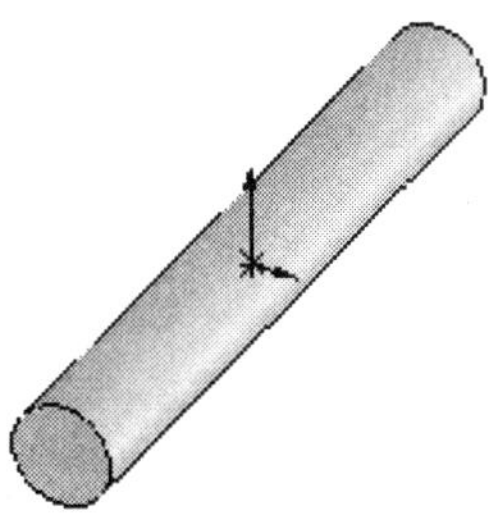

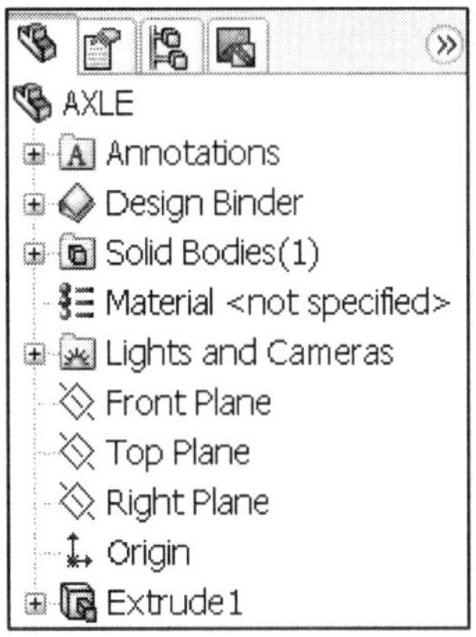

507) Click **File**, **Save As** from the Main menu.

508) Select the **SW-TUTORIAL-2007** folder.

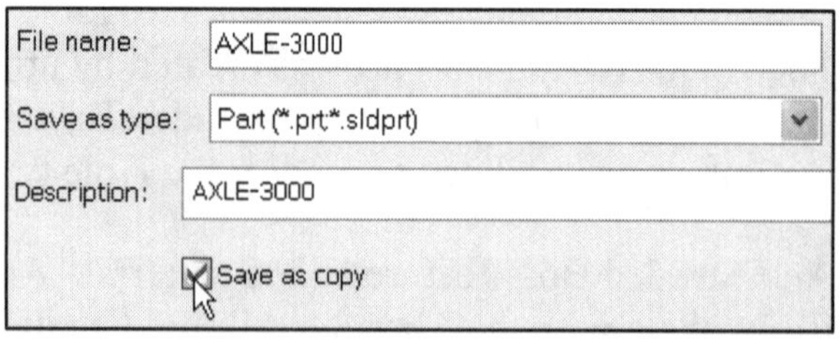

509) Enter **AXLE-3000** for File name.

510) Enter **AXLE-3000** for Description.

511) Click **Save as copy** check box.

512) Click **Save**.

Close the AXLE part

513) Click **File**, **Close** from the Main menu.

Open AXLE-3000 part.

514) Click **File**, **Open** from the Main menu.

515) Double-click **AXLE-3000** from the SW-TUTORIAL-2007 folder. The AXLE-3000 FeatureManager is displayed.

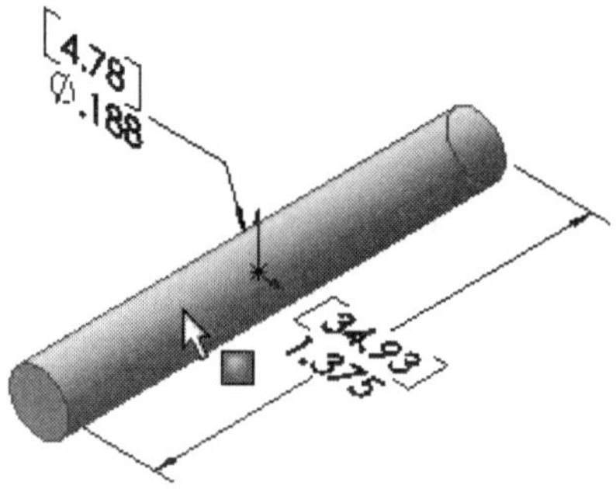

Modify the depth dimension.

516) Double-click the **cylindrical face** in the Graphics window.

517) Double-click **1.375**in, [**34.93**].

518) Enter **3.000**in, [**76.20**].

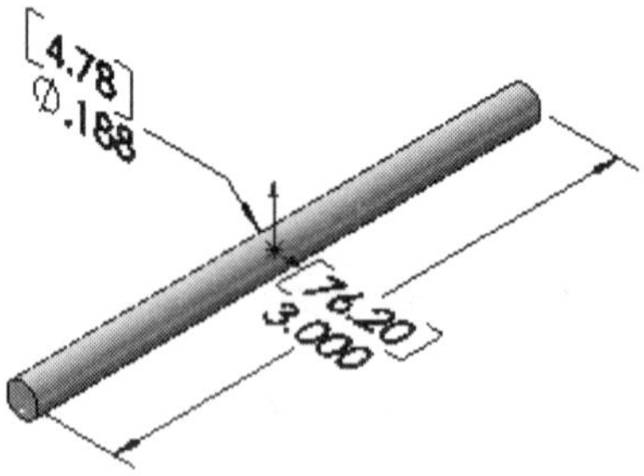

519) Click the Green Check mark.

520) Click **Rebuild** from the Standard menu.

Fit the model to the Graphics window.

521) Press the **f** key.

Save the AXLE-3000 part.

522) Click **Save**.

Activity: SHAFTCOLLAR-500 Part

Create the SHAFTCOLLAR-500 part.

523) Click **File**, **Open** from the Main menu.

524) Double-click **SHAFT-COLLAR** from the SW-TUTORIAL-2007 folder.

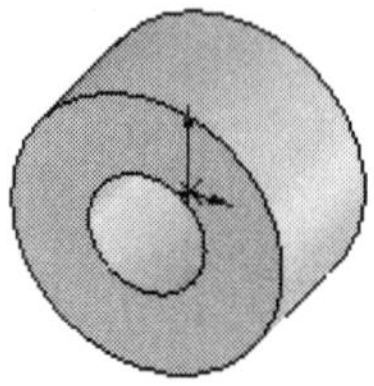

525) Click **File**, **Save As** from the Main menu.

526) Enter **SHAFT-COLLAR-500** for File name.

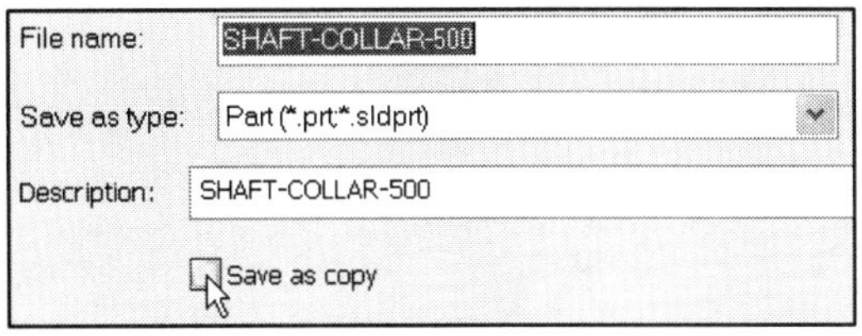

527) Enter **SHAFT-COLLAR-500** for Description.

528) Click **Save as copy** check box.

529) Click **Save**.

Close the SHAFT-COLLAR part.

530) Click **File**, **Close** from the Main menu.

Open the SHAFT-COLLAR 500 part.

531) Click **File**, **Open** from the Main menu.

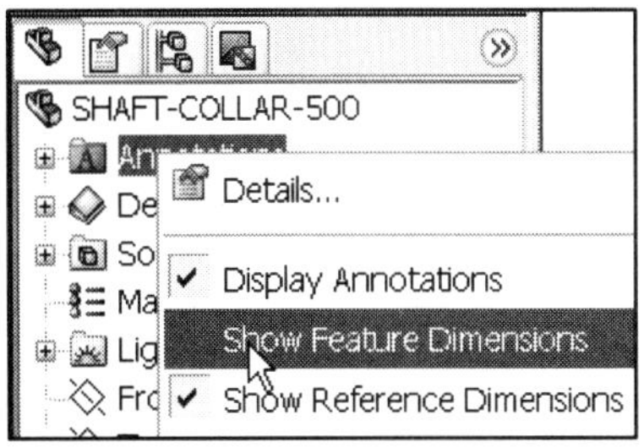

532) Double-click **SHAFT-COLLAR-500** from the SW-TUTORIAL-2007 folder.

Modify the diameter dimensions.

533) Right-click **Annotations** in the FeatureManager.

534) Check Show Feature Dimensions.

535) Double-click **.438**in, [**11.11**].

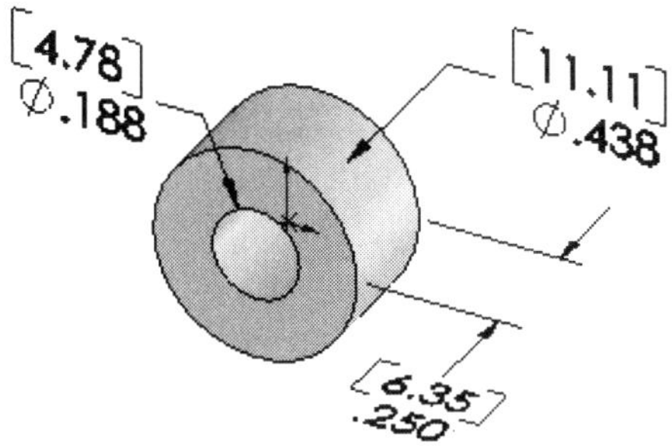

536) Enter **.750**in, [**19.05**] for outside diameter.

537) Click the Green Check mark.

538) Double-click **.188**in, [**4.78**].

539) Enter **.500**in, [**12.70**] for inside diameter.

540) Click the Green Check mark.

541) Click **Rebuild** from the Standard menu.

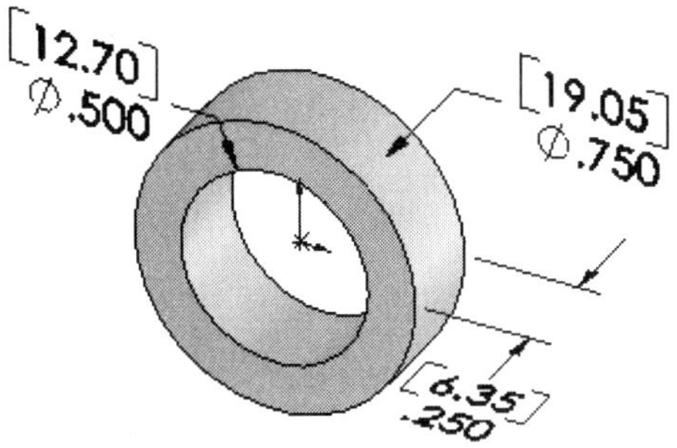

542) Right-click **Annotations** in the FeatureManager.

543) Uncheck Show Feature Dimensions.

Fit the Model to the Graphics window.

544) Press the **f** key.

Save the SHAFT-COLLAR-500 part.

545) Click **Save** .

Close All documents.

546) Click **Windows**, **Close All** from the Main menu.

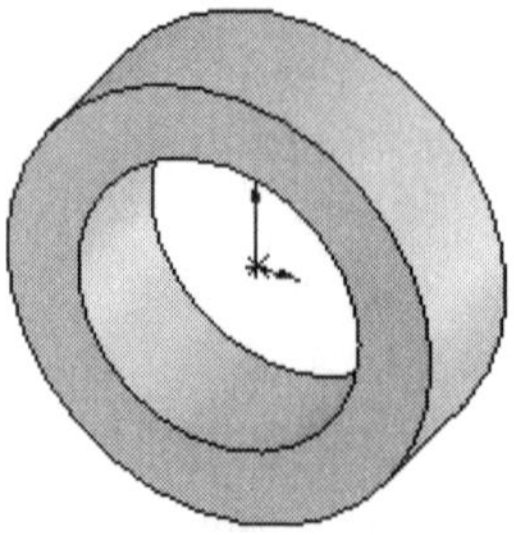

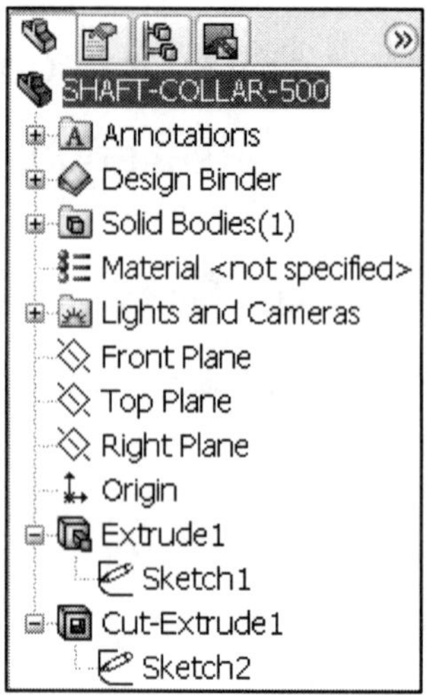

Assembly Techniques

Assembly modeling requires practice and time. Below are a few helpful techniques to address Mating. These techniques are utilized throughout the development of the PNEUMATIC-TEST-MODULE assembly and sub-assemblies.

Mating Techniques:
• Plan your assembly and sub-assemblies in an assembly layout diagram. Group components together to form smaller sub-assemblies.
• Utilize symmetry in an assembly. Utilize Mirror Component and Component Pattern to create multiple instances (copies) of components. Reuse similar components with Save as copy and configurations.
• Use the Zoom and Rotate commands to select the geometry in the Mate process. Zoom to select the correct face.
• Apply various colors to features and components to improve display.
• Activate Temporary Axes and Show Planes when required for Mates, otherwise Hide All Types from the View menu.
• Select Reference planes from the FeatureManager for complex components. Expand the FeatureManager to view the correct plane.
• Remove display complexity. Hide components when visibility is not required.
• Suppress components when Mates are not required. Group fasteners at the bottom of the FeatureManager. Suppress fasteners and their assembly patterns to save rebuild time and file size.
• Utilize Section views to select internal geometry.
• Use the Move Component and Rotate Component commands before Mating. Position the component in the correct orientation.
• Create additional flexibility in a Mate. Distance Mates are modified in configurations and animations. Rename Mates in the FeatureManager.
• Verify the position of the components. Use Top, Front, Right, and Section views.

PNEUMATIC TEST MODULE Layout

The PNEUMATIC TEST MODULE assembly is comprised of four major sub-assemblies:

- LINKAGE assembly.
- RESERVOIR assembly.
- FRONT-SUPPORT assembly.
- WHEEL-AND-AXLE assembly.

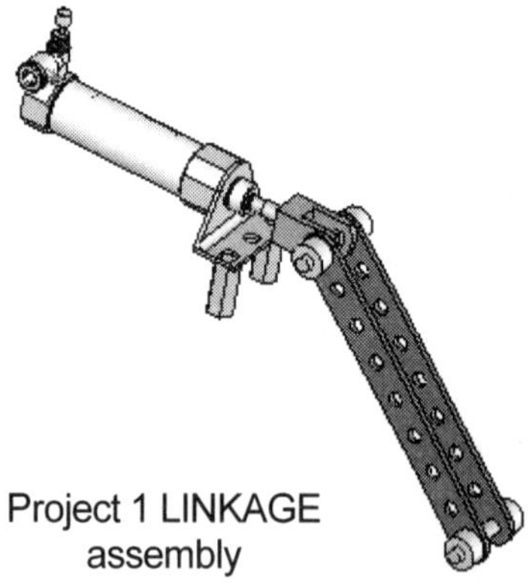

Project 1 LINKAGE assembly

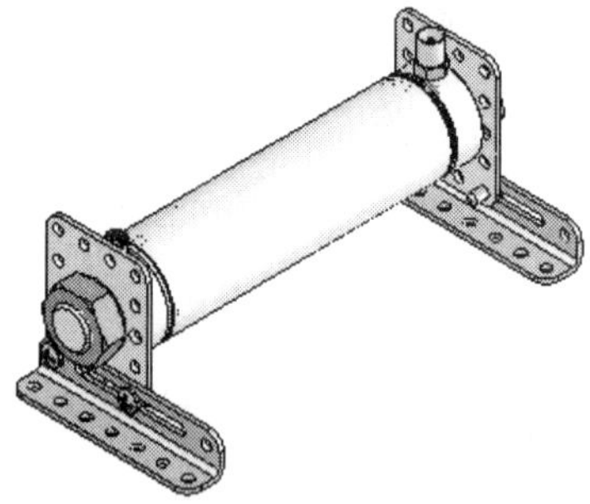

Project 2 AIR RESERVOIR assembly

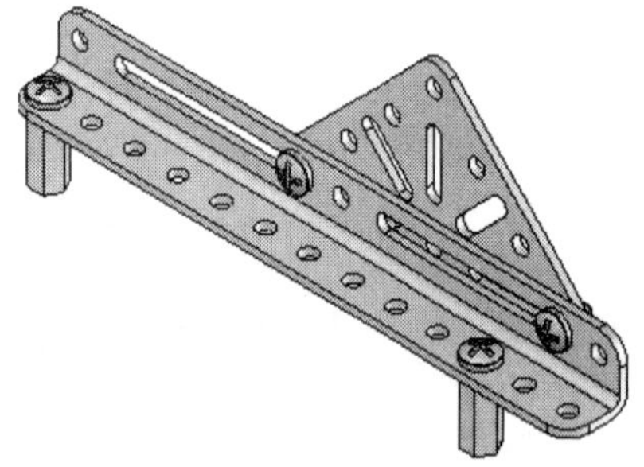

Project 2 FRONT SUPPORT assembly

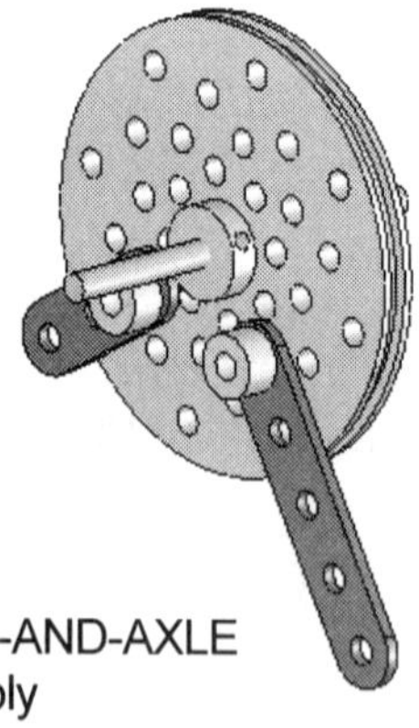

Project 4 WHEEL-AND-AXLE assembly

There are over one hundred components in the PNEUMATIC TEST MODULE assembly. Complex assemblies require planning. The Assembly Layout diagram provides organization for a complex assembly by listing sub-assemblies and parts.

Review the Assembly Layout diagram for the PNEUMATIC TEST MODULE assembly.

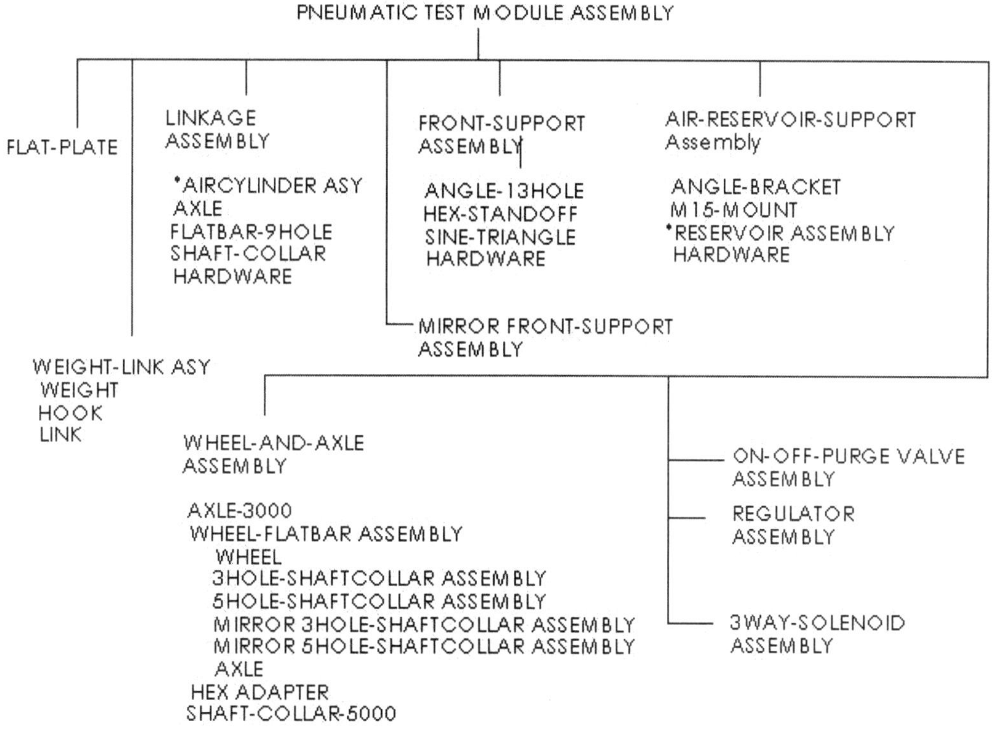

Physical space on the FLAT-PLATE is at a premium. Determine the requirements for hardware and placement after the mechanical components are assembled to the FLAT-PLATE part. The FLAT-PLATE part was created in the Project 1 exercises.

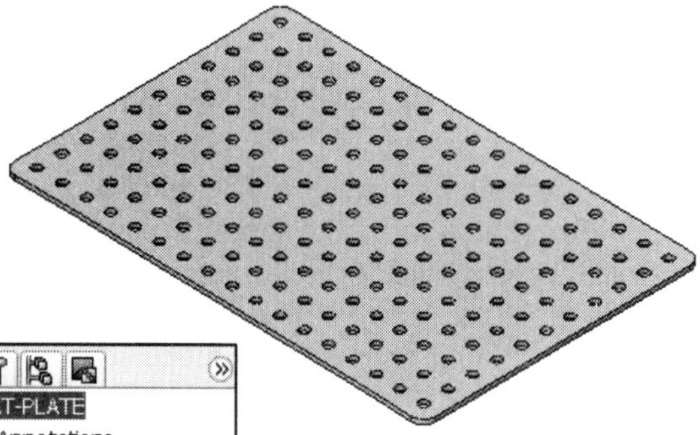

The LINKAGE assembly, FRONT-SUPPORT assembly and the AIR-RESERVOIR SUPPORT assembly were created in Project 1 and Project 2. The ON-OFF-PURGE VALVE assembly, REGULATOR assembly and the 3WAY SOLENOID VALVE assembly require additional hardware and are addressed in the Project exercises.

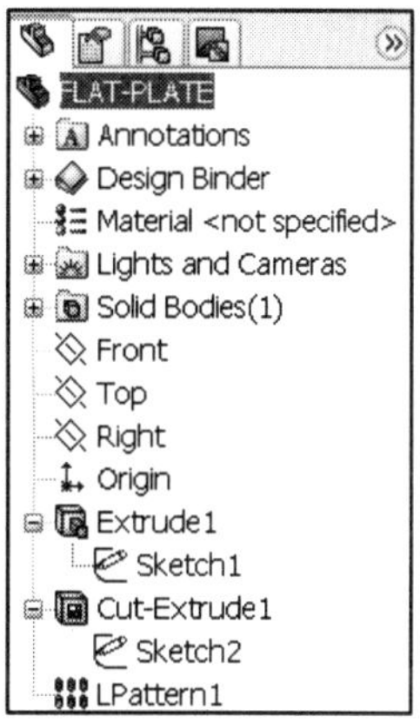

The WHEEL-FLATBAR assembly consists of the following:

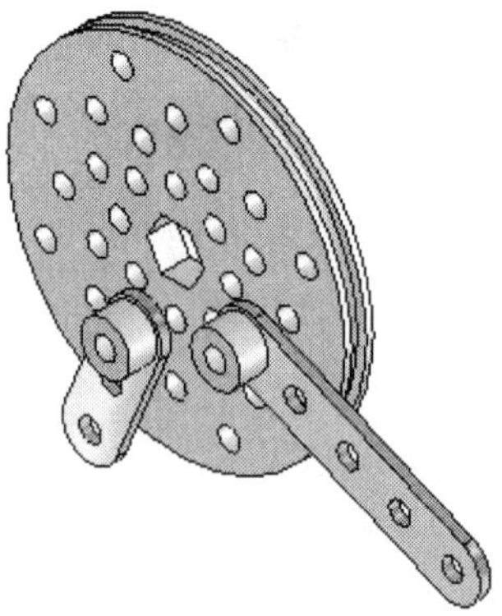

- WHEEL part.
- 3HOLE-SHAFTCOLLAR assembly.
- 5HOLE-SHAFTCOLLAR assembly.

FLATBAR Sub-assemblies

There are two similar sub-assemblies contained in the WHEEL-FLATBAR assembly:

- 3HOLE-SHAFTCOLLAR assembly.
- 5HOLE-SHAFTCOLLAR assembly.

Create the 3HOLE-SHAFTCOLLAR assembly. Utilize parts and mating techniques developed in Project 1. Utilize the Save as copy command and create the 5HOLE-SHAFTCOLLAR assembly.

Combine the 3HOLE-SHAFTCOLLAR assembly, 5HOLE-SHAFTCOLLAR assembly and the WHEEL part to create the WHEEL-FLATBAR assembly. The FLATBAR-3HOLE and FLATBAR 5HOLE parts were created in Exercise 1.1 and Exercise 1.2.

Activity: 3HOLE-SHAFTCOLLAR Assembly

Create the 3HOLE-SHAFTCOLLAR assembly.

547) Click **File**, **New** from the Main menu.

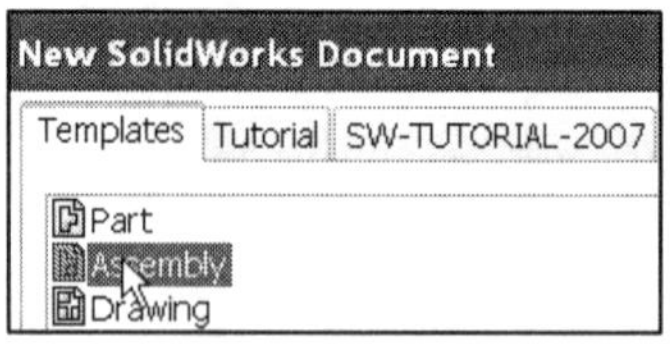

548) Double-click **Assembly** from the Templates tab. The Insert Component PropertyManager is displayed.

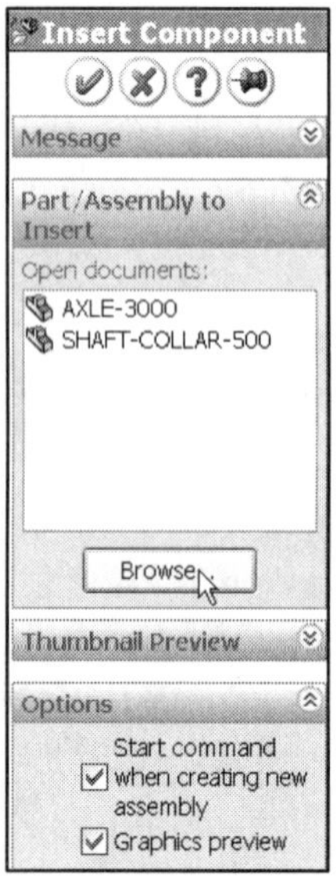

549) Click **View**; check **Origins** from the Main menu.

550) Click **Browse**.

551) Select **Part** for Files of type in the SW-TUTORIAL-2007 folder.

552) Double-click **FLATBAR-3HOLE**. The FLATBAR-3HOLE part was created in the Project 1 exercises. If you did not create this part, follow the below procedures; otherwise, skip to step 582.

553) Click **File**, **Open** from the Main menu.

554) Double-click **FLATBAR** from the SW-TUTORIAL-2007 folder.

555) Click **File**, **Save As** from the Main menu.

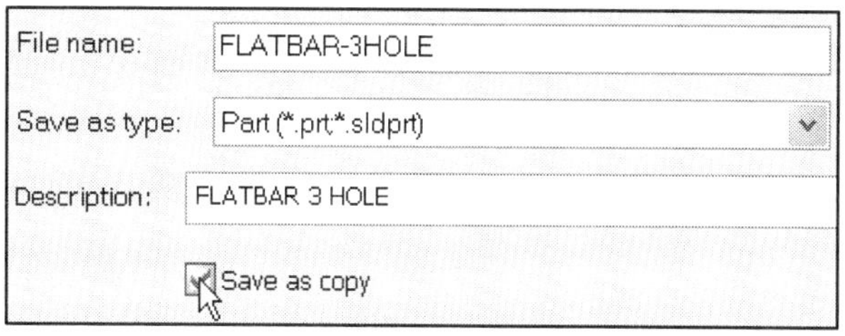

556) Select the **SW-TUTORIAL-2007** folder.

557) Enter **FLATBAR-3HOLE** for File name.

558) Enter **FLATBAR-3HOLE** for Description.

559) Click the **Save as copy** check box.

560) Click **Save**.

561) Click **File**, **Open** from the Main menu.

562) Double-click **FLATBAR-3HOLE** from the SW-TUTORIAL-2007 folder.

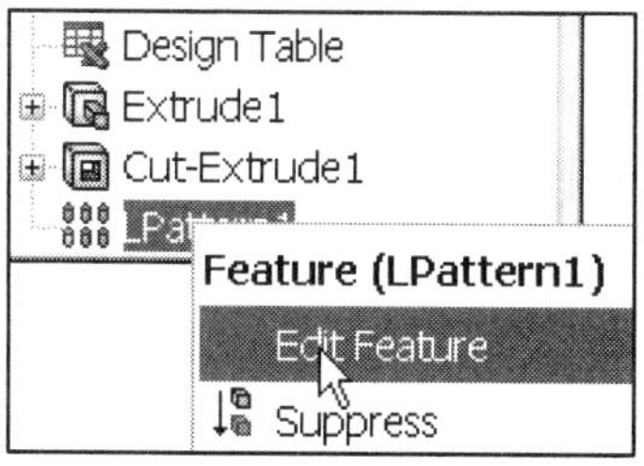

563) Right-click **LPATTERN1** from the FeatureManager.

564) Click **Edit Feature**. The LPattern1 PropertyManager is displayed.

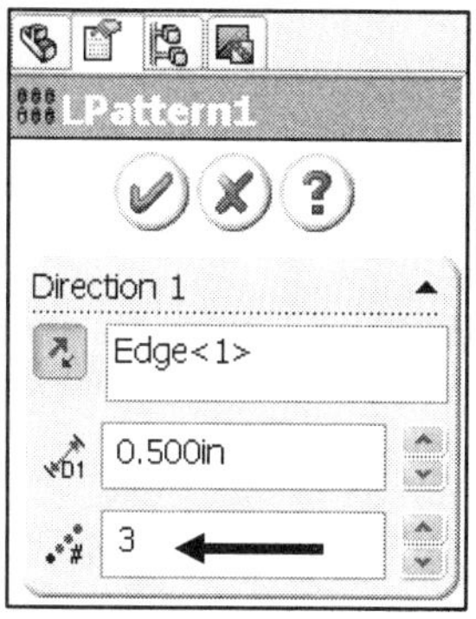

565) Enter **3** in the Number of Instances.

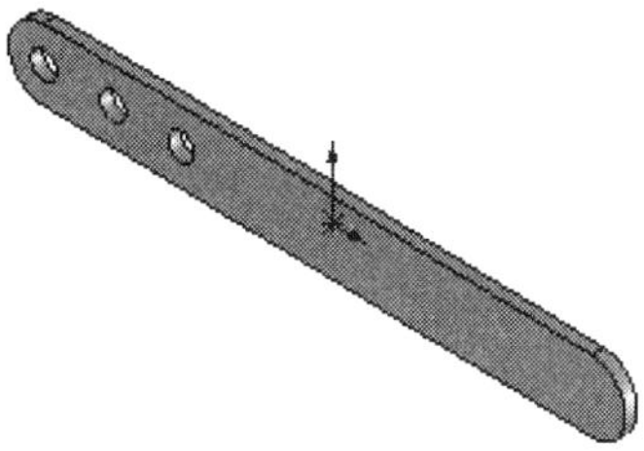

566) Click **OK** from the LPattern1 PropertyManager.

567) Double-click **Extrude1** from the FeatureManager.

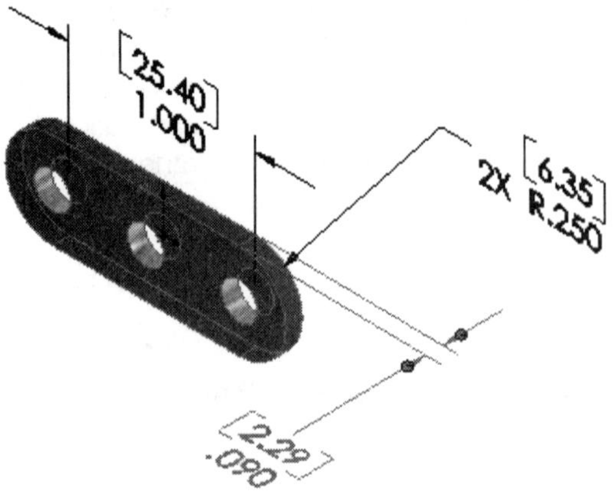

568) Double-click the **4.000**in, [**101.60**] dimension.

569) Enter **1.000**in, [**25.4**].

570) Click **Rebuild** from the Modify dialog box.

571) Click the Green Check mark.

572) Double-click **Cut-Extrude1** from the fly-out FeatureManager.

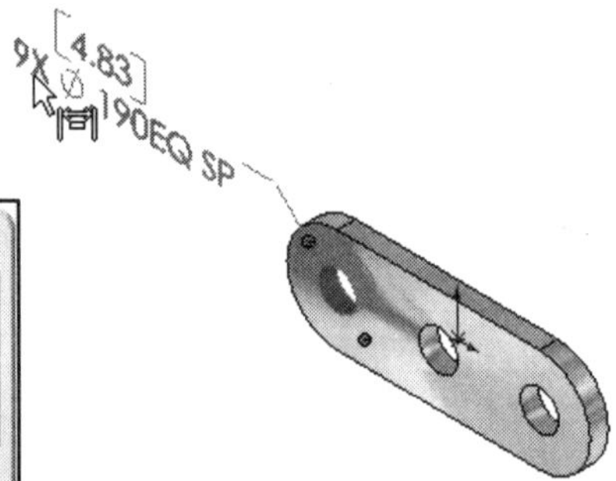

573) Click the **9X** dimension text in the Graphics window.

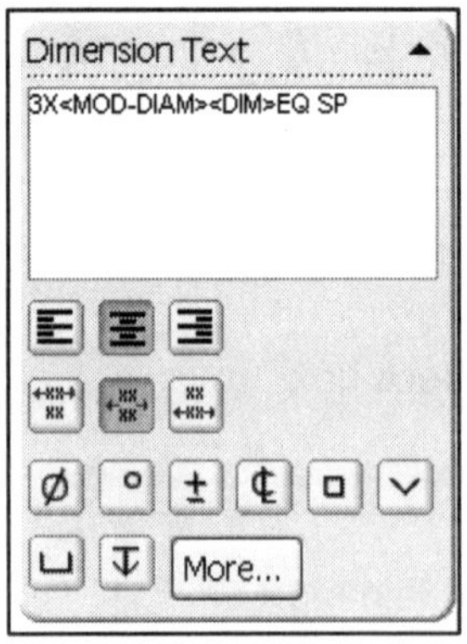

574) Delete the **9X** text in the Dimension Text box.

575) Enter **3X** in the Dimension Text box.

576) Click **OK** from the Dimension PropertyManager.

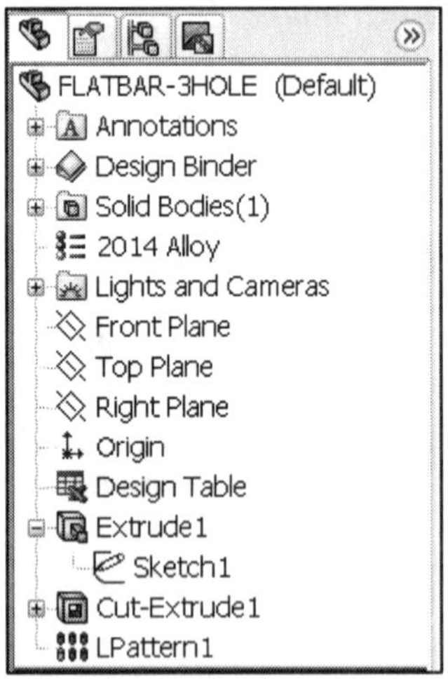

577) Click **Save**.

578) Click **File**, **New** from the Main menu.

579) Double-click **Assembly** from the Templates tab. The Insert Component PropertyManager is displayed.

580) Click **View**; check **Origins** from the Main menu.

581) Double-click **FLATBAR-3HOLE**.

582) Click the assembly **Origin**. The FLATBAR-3HOLE is fixed to the Origin.

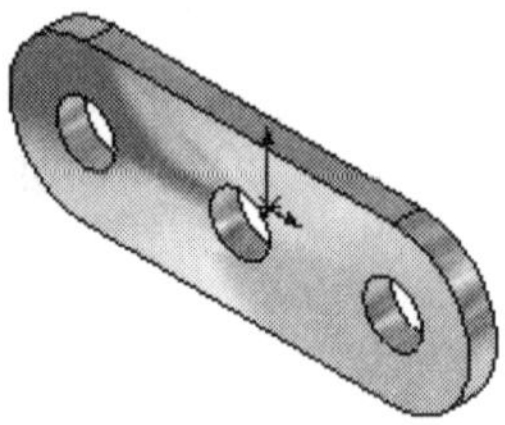

Save the assembly.

583) Click **File**, **Save As** from the Main menu.

584) Enter **3HOLE-SHAFTCOLLAR** for File name.

585) Enter **3HOLE-SHAFTCOLLAR** for Description.

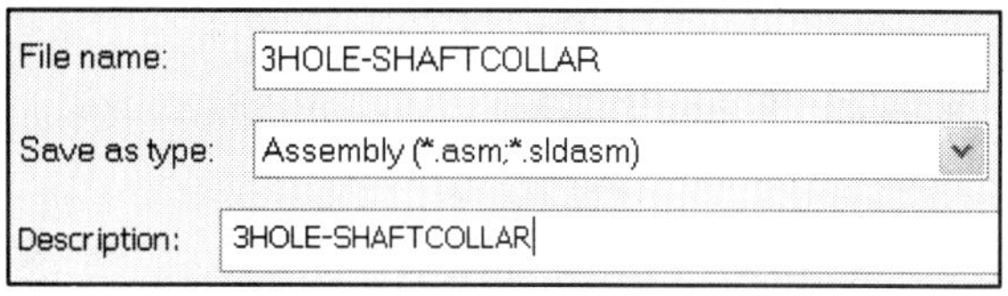

586) Click **Save**.

Save the 3HOLE-SHAFTCOLLAR assembly.

587) Click **Save**.

Utilize a Concentric and Coincident SmartMate between the SHAFT-COLLAR and the FLATBAR-3HOLE.

Open the **SHAFT-COLLAR** part.

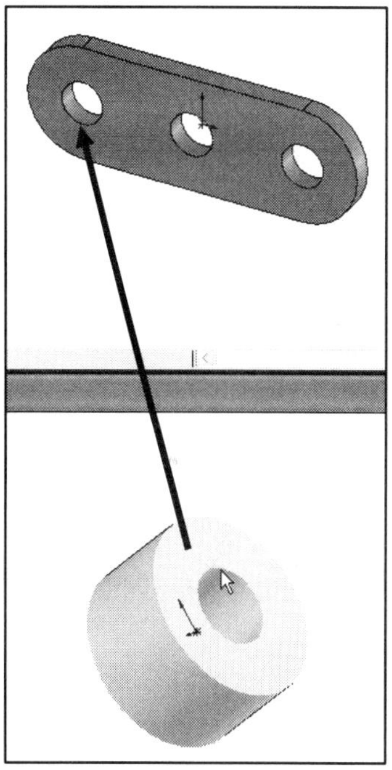

588) Click **File**, **Open** from the Main menu.

589) Double-click **SHAFT-COLLAR** from the SW-TUTORIAL-2007 folder. SHAFT-COLLAR is the current document name.

590) Press the **Left Arrow** key approximately 5 times to rotate the SHAFT-COLLAR to view the back circular edge.

591) Click **Window**, **Tile Horizontally** from the Main menu.

592) Drag the **back circular edge** of the SHAFT-COLLAR to the left circular hole edge of the FLATBAR-3HOLE. The mouse pointer displays the Concentric/Coincident icon.

Save the 3HOLE-SHAFTCOLLAR assembly.

593) Click **Close** on the SHAFT-COLLAR window.

594) **Maximize** the 3HOLE-SHAFTCOLLAR assembly.

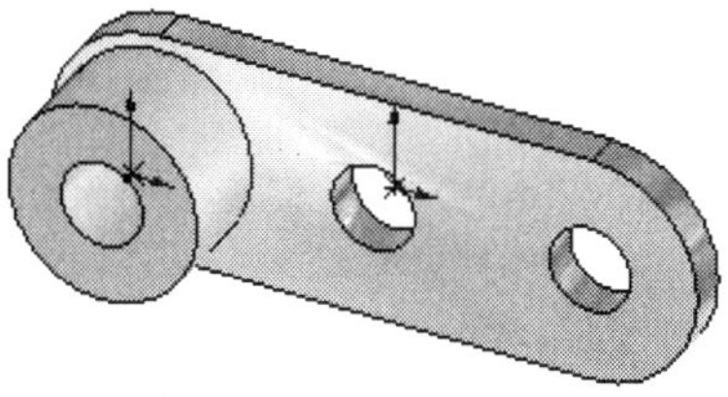

595) Press the **f** key to fit the Model to the Graphics window.

596) Click **Save**.

Create the 5HOLE-SHAFTCOLLAR assembly. Utilize the Save as command with the Save as copy option. Recover from Mate errors.

Save the 3HOLE-SHAFTCOLLAR assembly as the 5HOLE-SHAFTCOLLAR assembly.

597) Click **File**, **Save As** from the Main menu.

598) Check Save as copy.

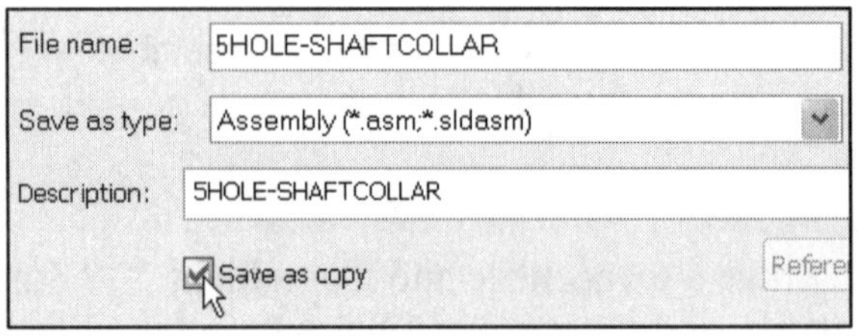

599) Enter **5HOLE-SHAFTCOLLAR** for File name.

600) Enter **5HOLE-SHAFTCOLLAR** for Description.

601) Click **Save**. Click **File**, **Close** from the Main menu.

Open the new assembly.

602) Click **File**, **Open** from the Main menu.

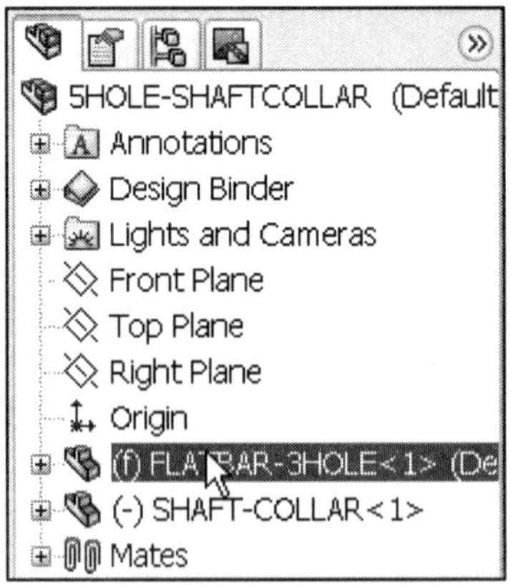

603) Select **Assembly** for Files of type.

604) Double-click **5HOLE-SHAFTCOLLAR**. The 5HOLE-SHAFTCOLLAR FeatureManager is displayed.

605) Right-click **FLATBAR-3HOLE** from the FeatureManager.

606) Click **Replace Components**. The Replace PropertyManager is displayed.

607) Click **Browse** from the Replace PropertyManager.

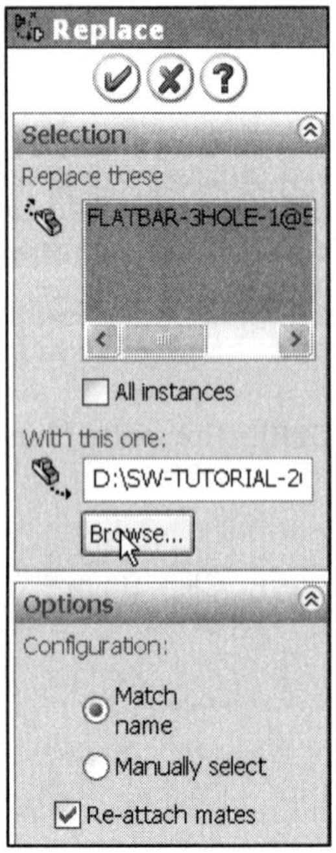

608) Double-click **FLATBAR-5HOLE**. Note: The FLATBAR-5HOLE part was created in the Project 1 exercises.

609) Check Re-attach mates.

610) Click **OK**  from the Replace PropertyManager. The Mate Entities PropertyManager is displayed. There are two red Mate error marks displayed in the Mate Entities box.

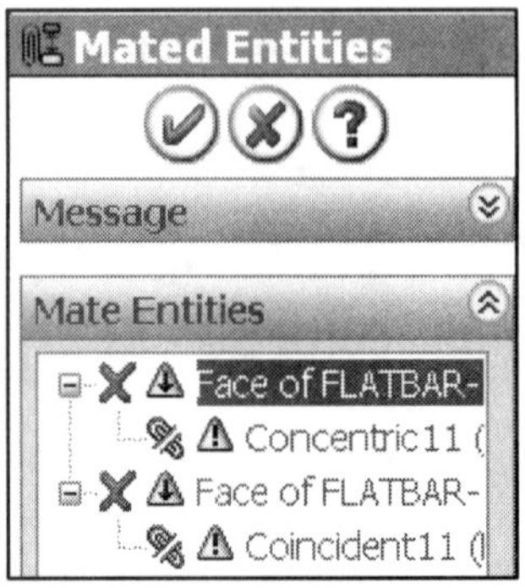

611) The What's Wrong dialog box is displayed. Recover from the Mate errors. Click **Close** from the What's Wrong dialog box.

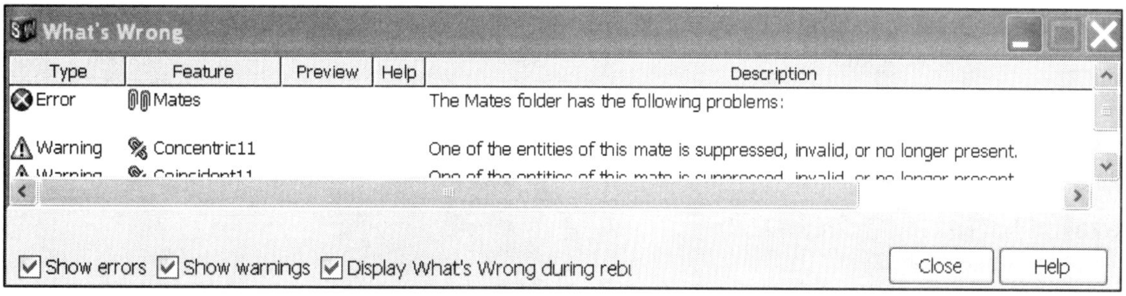

612) Click **OK** from the Mated Entities PropertyManager.

613) Click **Close**.

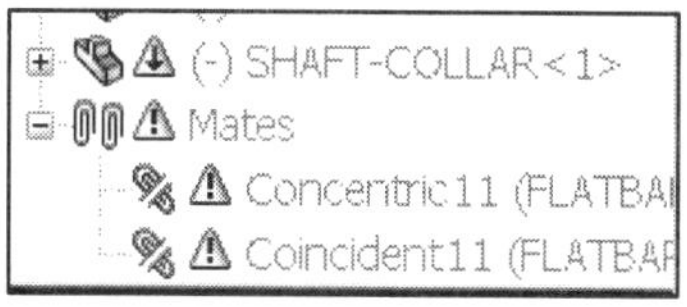

Recover from the Mate errors.

614) **Expand** the Mates folder from the FeatureManager.

615) Right-click the first mate, **Concentric 11**, from the Mates folder.

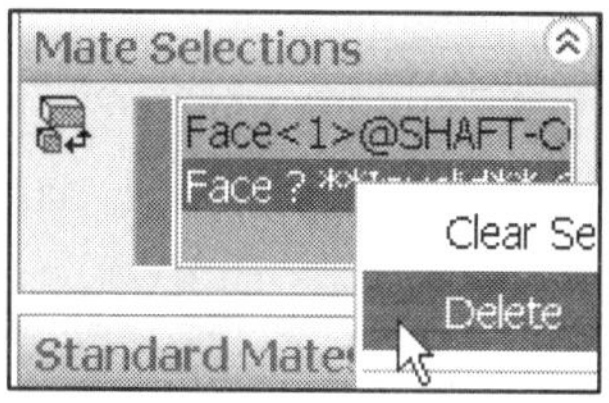

616) Click **Edit Feature**. The Mate PropertyManager is displayed.

617) Right-click the Mate **Face** error in the Mate Selections box as illustrated.

618) Click **Delete**.

619) Click the **inside face** of the left hole of the FLATBAR as illustrated. Concentric is selected by default.

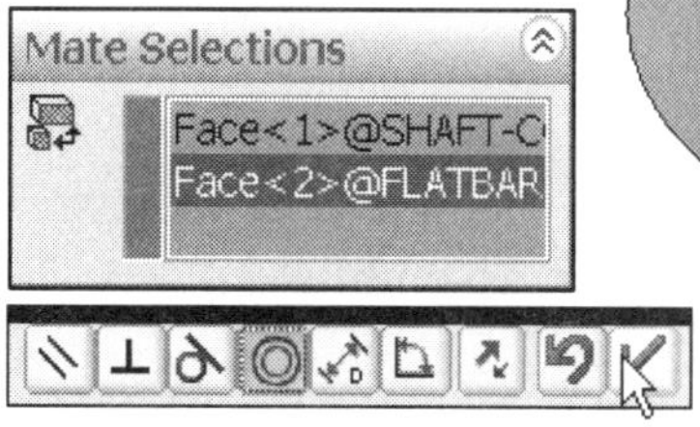

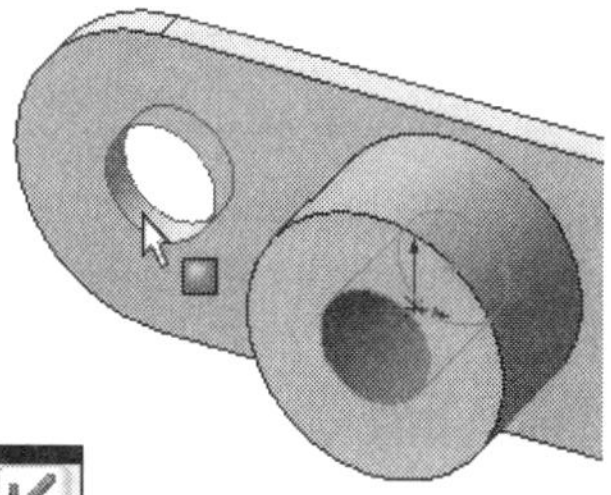

620) Click the Green Check mark.

621) Click **OK** from the Mate PropertyManager.

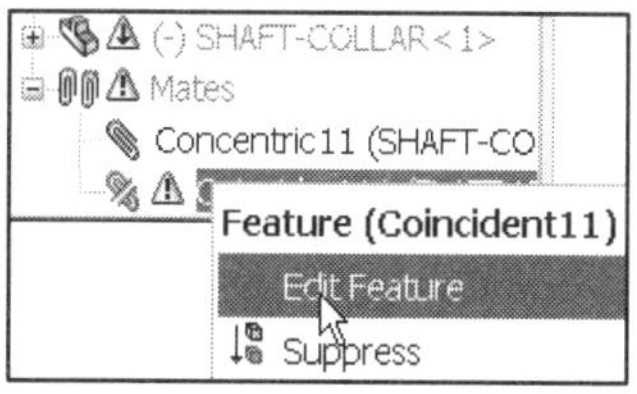

622) Right-click the second mate, **Coincident11,** from the Mates folder.

623) Click **Edit Feature**. The Mate PropertyManager is displayed.

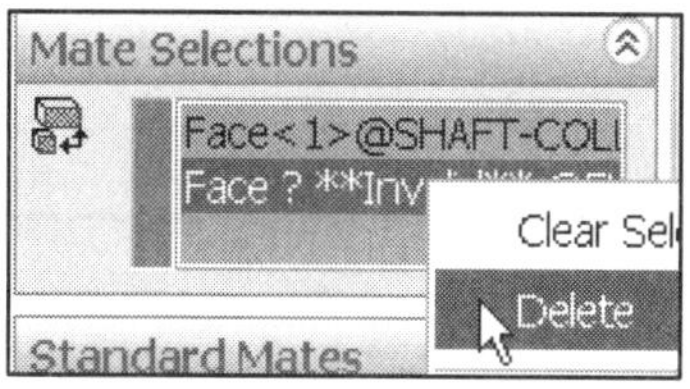

624) Right-click the Mate **Face** error in the Mate Selections box as illustrated.

625) Click **Delete**.

626) Click the **front face** of the FLATBAR as illustrated. The selected faces are displayed in the Mate Selections box. Coincident is selected by default.

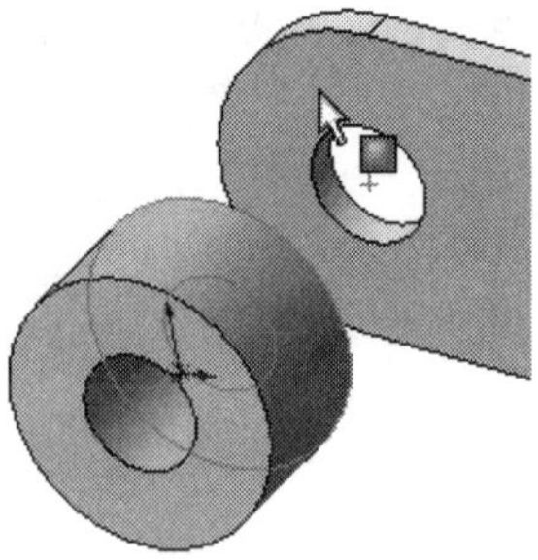

627) Click the Green Check mark.

628) Click **OK** from the Mate PropertyManager.

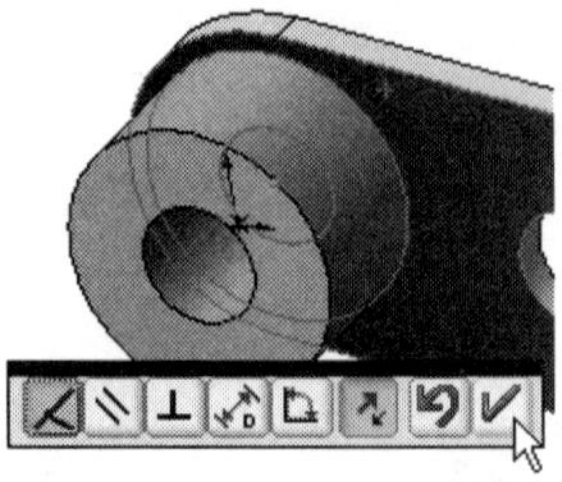

629) **Expand** the Mate folder from the FeatureManager. View the corrected Mates.

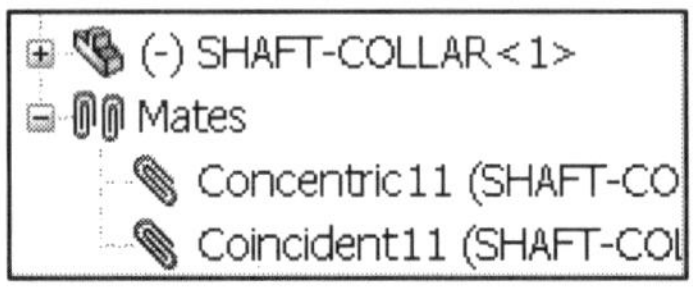

The Mate Entities box will list red X's if the faces, edges or planes are not valid. Expand the Mate Entities and select new references in the Graphics window to redefine the mates.

The FLATBAR-3HOLE is replaced with the FLATBAR-5HOLE part. The Mates are updated.

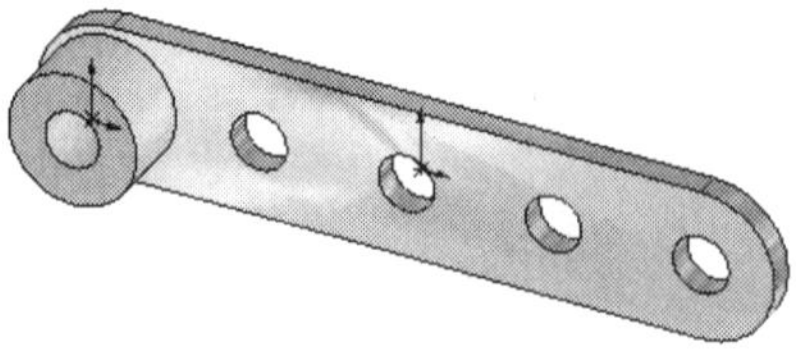

Fit the model to the Graphics window.

630) Press the **f** key.

Save the 5HOLE-SHAFTCOLLAR assembly.

631) Click Isometric view.

632) Click **Save**.

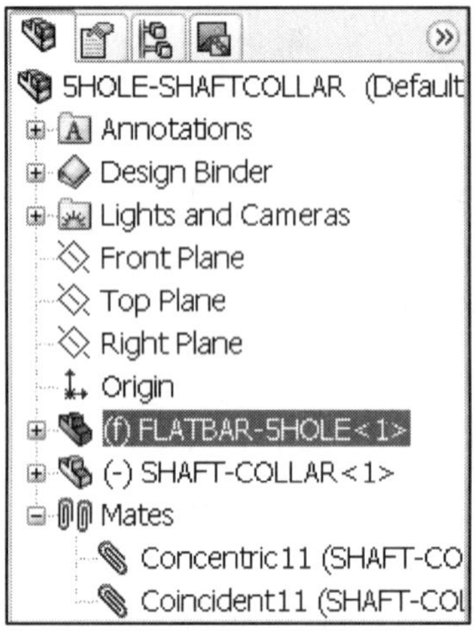

Incorporate symmetry into the assembly. Divide large assemblies into smaller sub-assemblies.

Note: The Multimedia CD illustrates the FLATBAR configurations created in Project 2 to create the FLATBAR-3HOLE and FLATBAR-5HOLE assemblies.

Utilize Design Tables to create multiple configurations of assemblies.

WHEEL-FLATBAR Assembly

The WHEEL-FLATBAR assembly consists of the following components:

- 3HOLE-SHAFTCOLLAR assembly.
- 5HOLE-SHAFTCOLLAR assembly.
- WHEEL part.

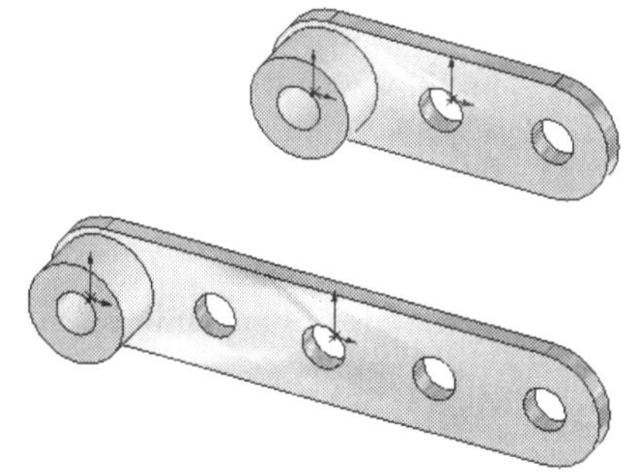

Create the WHEEL-FLATBAR assembly. Mate the 3HOLE-SHAFTCOLLAR assembly 67.5 degrees counterclockwise from the Top plane.

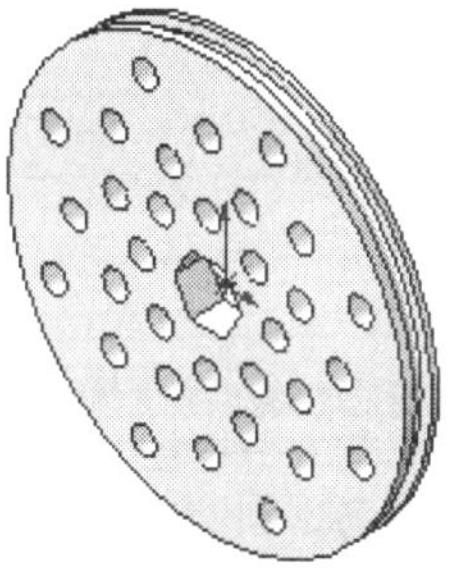

The 3HOLE-SHAFTCOLLAR assembly is concentric with holes on the second and forth bolt circle.

Mate the 5HOLE-SHAFTCOLLAR assembly 22.5 degrees clockwise from the Top plane.

The 5HOLE-SHAFTCOLLAR assembly is concentric with holes on the second and forth bolt circle.

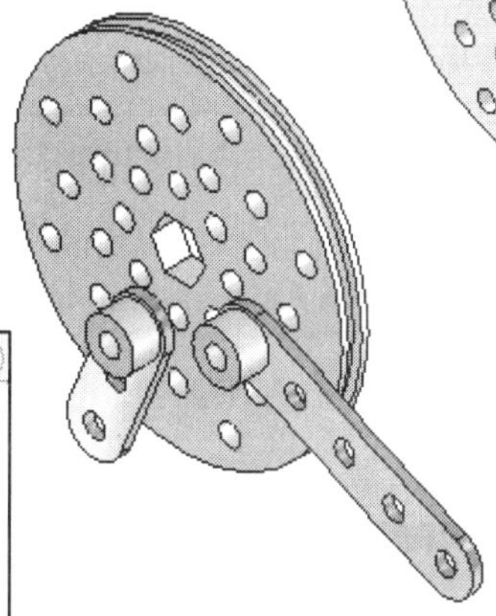

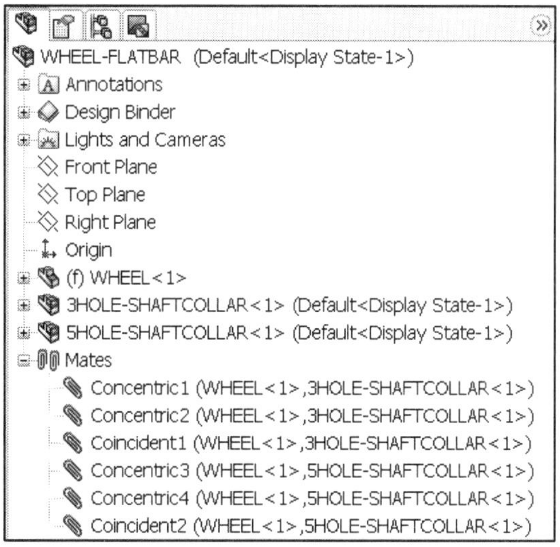

Activity: WHEEL-FLATBAR Assembly

Create the WHEEL-FLATBAR assembly.

633) Click **File**, **New** from the Main menu.

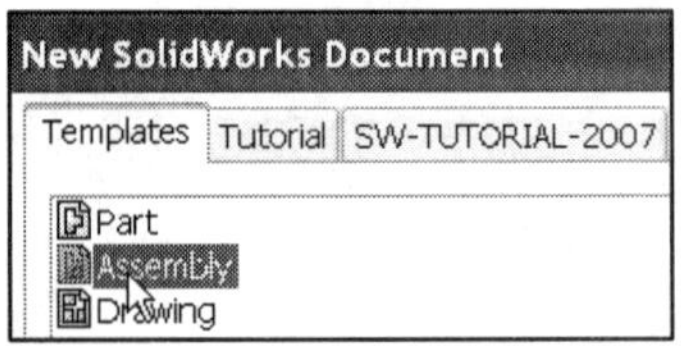

634) Double-click **Assembly** from the Templates tab. The Insert Component PropertyManager is displayed.

635) Click **View**; click **Origins** from the Main menu.

Insert the WHEEL.

636) Click **Browse** from the Insert Component PropertyManager.

637) Select **Part** for Files of type from the SW-TUTORIAL-2007 folder.

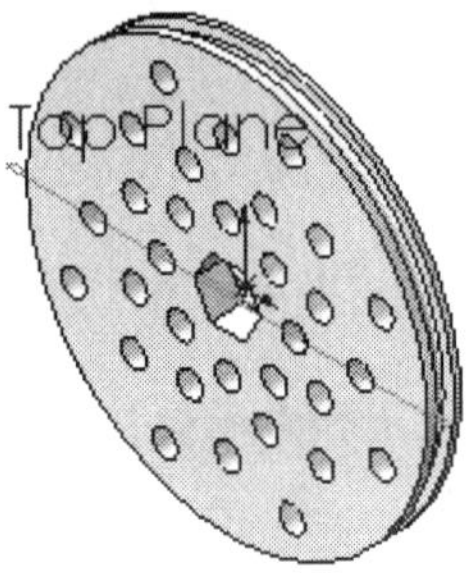

638) Double-click **WHEEL**.

639) Click the **Origin**. The WHEEL part is fixed to the assembly Origin.

640) Click **View**; uncheck **Temporary Axes** from the Main menu.

641) Click **View**; uncheck **Axes** from the Main menu.

Save the assembly.

642) Click **File**, **Save As** from the Main menu.

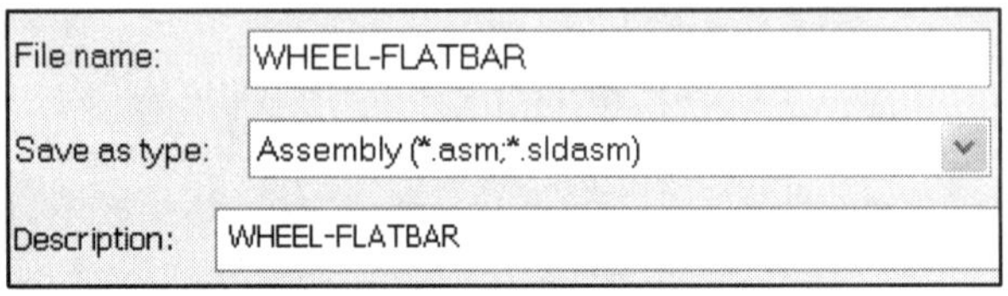

643) Enter **WHEEL-FLATBAR** for File name.

644) Enter **WHEEL-FLATBAR** for Description.

645) Click **Save**.

Display the Top plane in the Front view.

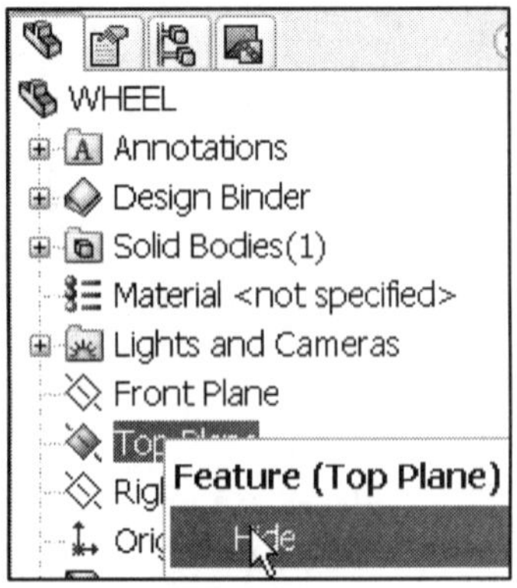

646) Click Front view.

647) Right-click **Top Plane** from the FeatureManager.

648) Click **Hide**.

Locate the first set of holes from the Right plane (-Y-axis). Left Hole1 and Left Hole2 are positioned on the second and forth bolt circle, 22.5° from the Right plane. As an exercise, utilize Tools, Measure. Select Left Hole1. The x, y, z coordinates, -.287, -.693, .125 are displayed.

$\tan^{-1}(-.287/.693) = 22.5°$

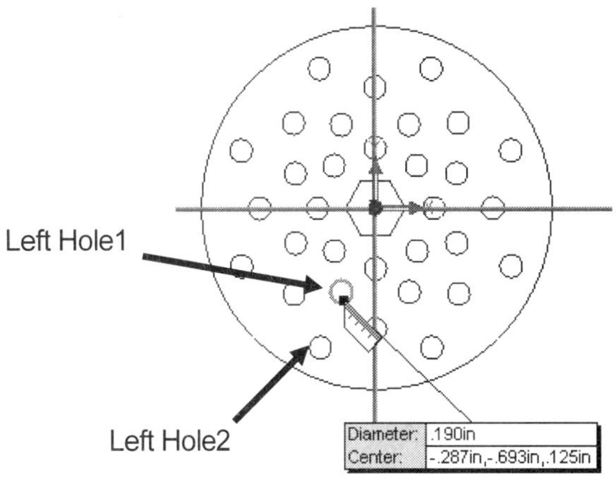

As an exercise, utilize Tools, Measure to determine the center-to-center distance between the Left Hole1 and Left Hole2. The center-to-center distance is .500in.

Insert two Concentric Mates between Left Hole1 and Left Hole2 and the 3HOLE-SHAFTCOLLAR assembly holes. The FLATBAR-3HOLE center-to-center distance is also .500in.

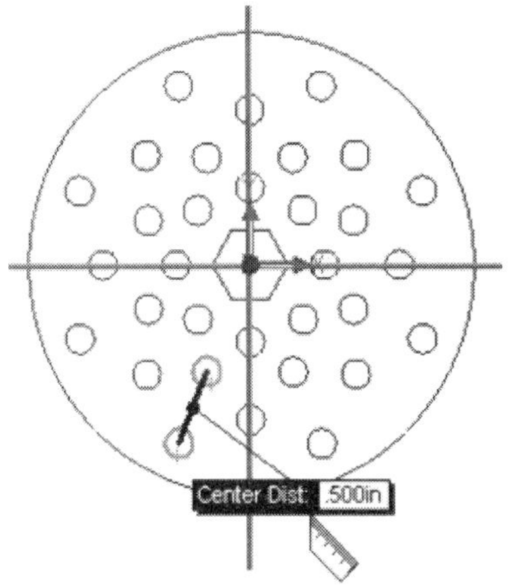

To determine tolerance issues, utilize two Concentric Mates between components with mating cylindrical geometry. If the mating components center-to-center distance is not exact, a Mate error is displayed on the second Concentric Mate.

Insert a Coincident Mate between the back face of the 3HOLE-SHAFTCOLLAR assembly and the front face of the WHEEL.

Right Hole1 and Right Hole2 are 22.5° from the Top plane.

Insert two Concentric Mates between Right Hole1 and Right Hole2 and the 5HOLE-SHAFTCOLLAR assembly holes.

Insert a Coincident Mate between the back face of the 5HOLE-SHAFTCOLLAR assembly and the front face of the WHEEL.

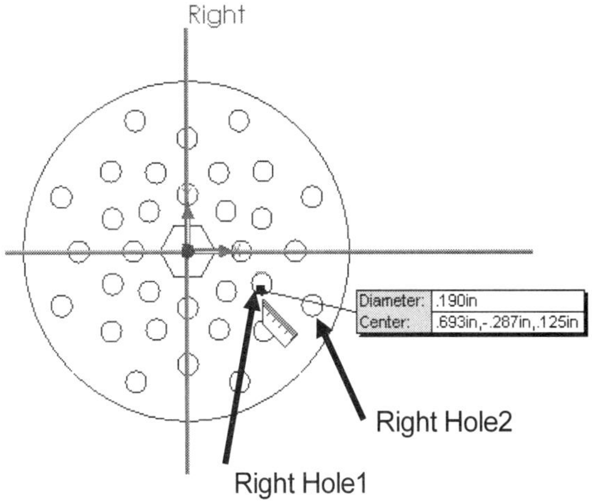

Activity: WHEEL-FLATBAR Assembly-Insert 3HOLE-SHAFT-COLLAR Assembly

Insert the 3HOLE-SHAFT-COLLAR assembly.

649) Click Isometric view.

650) Click **Insert Component** Insert Compo... from the Assembly toolbar.

651) Click **Browse**.

652) Select **Assembly** for Files of type from the SW-TUTORIAL-2007 folder.

653) Double-click the **3HOLE-SHAFTCOLLAR** assembly.

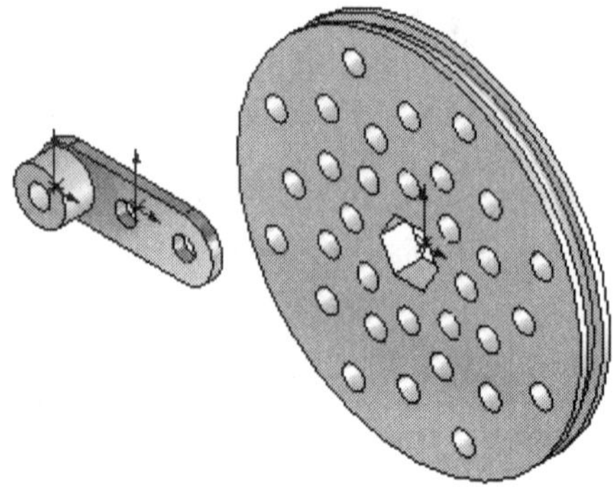

654) Click a **position** to the left of the WHEEL as illustrated.

Move and rotate the 3HOLE-SHAFTCOLLAR component.

655) Click the front face of the **3HOLE-SHAFTCOLLAR**.

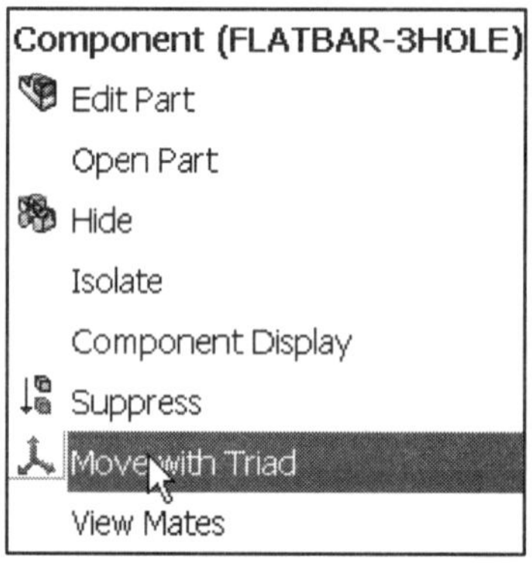

656) Right-click **Move with Triad**.

657) Hold the **left mouse button** down on the X-axis (red).

658) Drag the **component** to the left.

659) Hold the **right mouse button** down on the Z-axis (blue).

660) Drag the **component** and rotate it about the Z-axis.

661) **Position** the component until the SHAFT-COLLAR part is approximately in front of the WHEEL Left Hole1.

662) Release the right mouse button.

663) Click a **position** in the Graphics window to deselect the face.

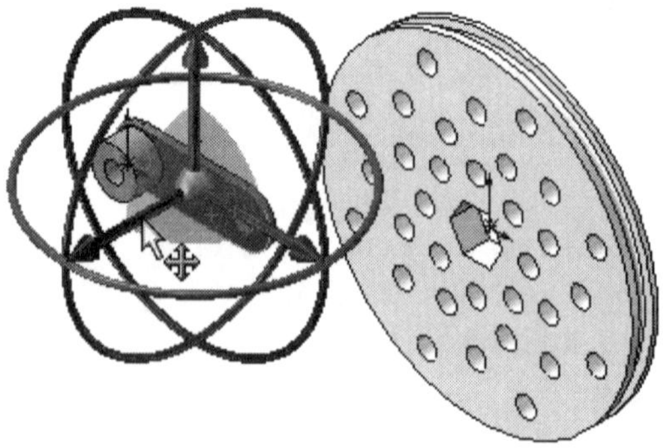

Insert Mates.

664) Click **Mate** from the Assembly toolbar. The Mate PropertyManager is displayed.

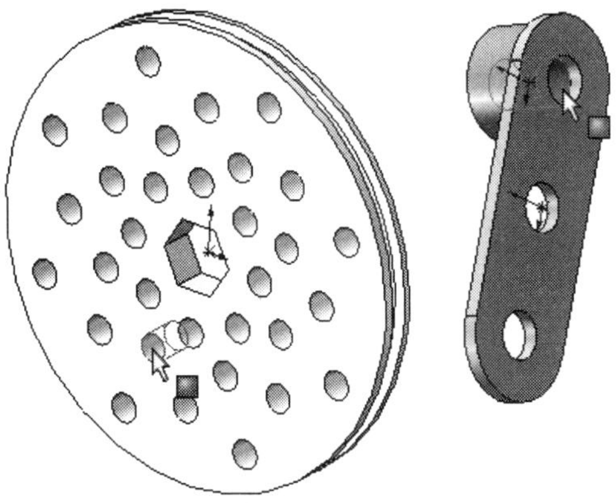

Create a Concentric Mate.

665) Click the **back top inside cylindrical face** of the SHAFT-COLLAR.

666) Click the **WHEEL Left Hole1** cylindrical face as illustrated. Concentric is selected by default. The selected faces are displayed in the Mate Selections box.

667) Click the Green Check mark.

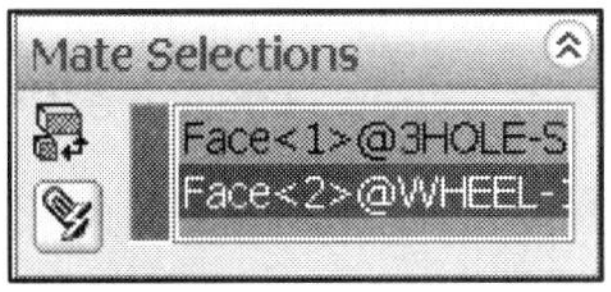

Insert a second Concentric Mate.

668) Click the back middle inside cylindrical face of the SHAFT-COLLAR.

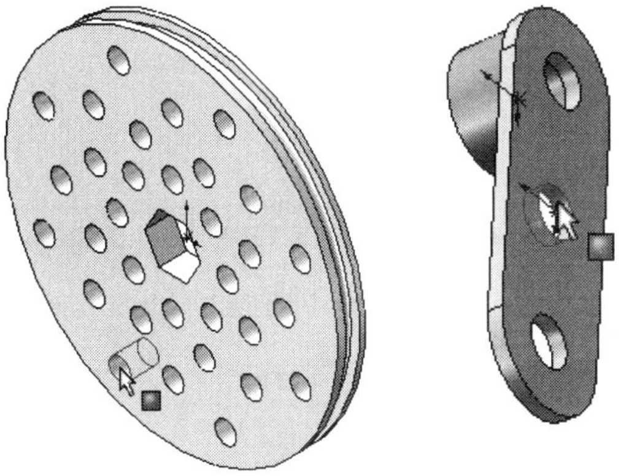

669) Click the **WHEEL Left Hole2** cylindrical face as illustrated. Concentric is selected by default. The selected faces are displayed in the Mate Selections box.

670) Click the Green Check mark.

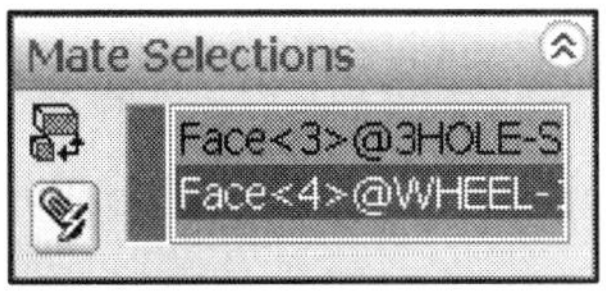

Insert a Coincident Mate.

671) Click the FLATBAR-3HOLE back face.

672) Click the front face of the **WHEEL**. Coincident is selected by default.

673) Click the Green Check mark.

674) Click **OK** from the Mate PropertyManager.

675) Click Front view.

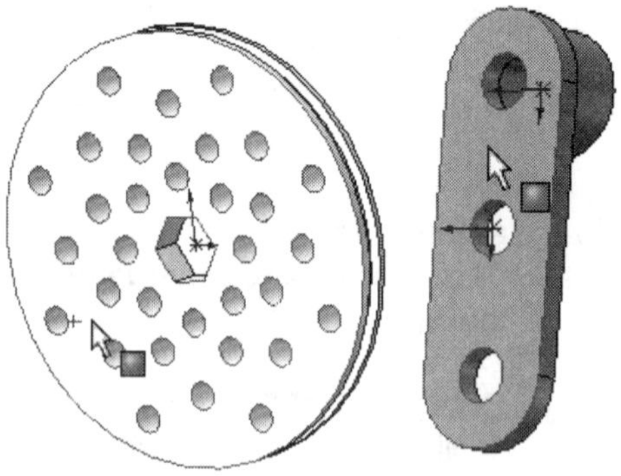

Save the WHEEL-FLATBAR assembly.

676) Click **Save**.

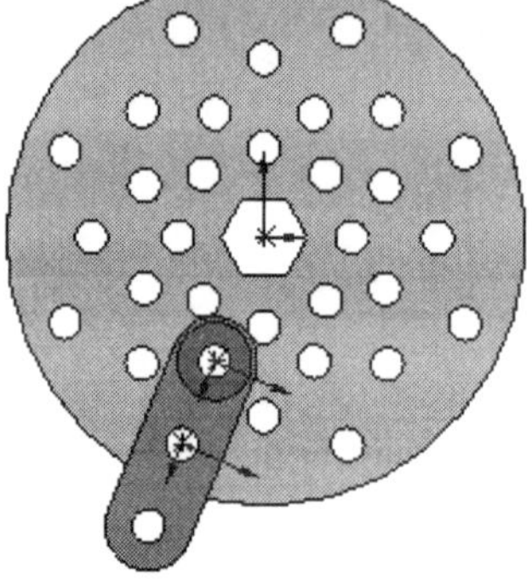

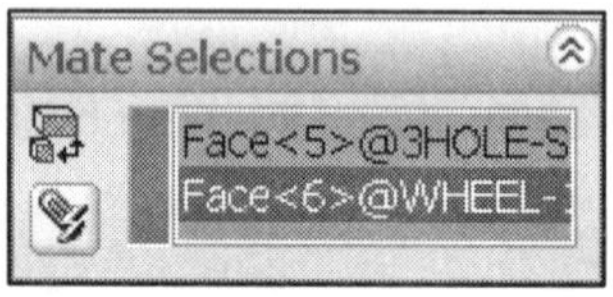

Activity: WHEEL-FLATBAR Assembly-Insert 5HOLE-SHAFTCOLLAR Assembly

Insert the 5HOLE-SHAFTCOLLAR assembly.

677) Click **Insert Component** Insert Compo... from the Assembly toolbar.

678) Click **Browse**.

679) Double-click the **5HOLE-SHAFTCOLLAR** assembly from the SW-TUTORIAL-2007 folder.

680) Click a **position** to the right of the WHEEL.

Move the 5HOLE-SHAFTCOLLAR component.

681) Click the 5HOLE-SHAFTCOLLAR front face.

682) Right-click **Move with Triad**.

683) Hole the **left mouse button** down on the X-axis (red). Drag the **component** to the right.

684) Click **Isometric view**. Click **inside** the Graphics window.

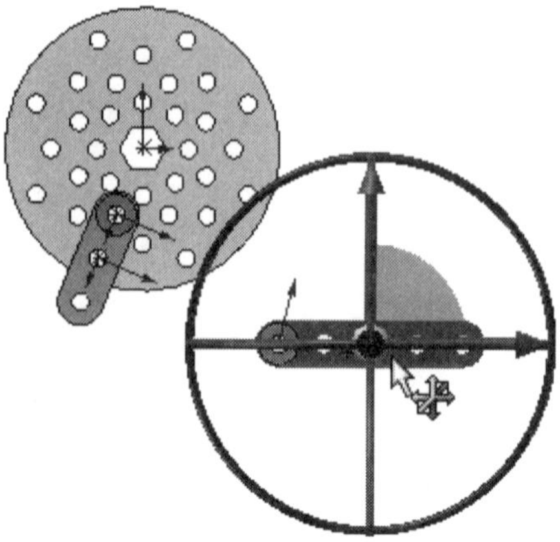

Mate the 5HOLE-SHAFTCOLLAR assembly.

685) Click **Mate** Mate from the Assembly toolbar. The Mate PropertyManager is displayed.

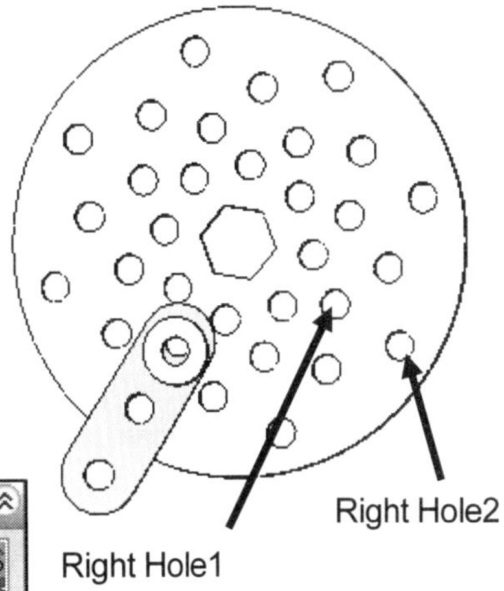

Insert a Concentric Mate.

686) Click the **back inside cylindrical face** of the first hole on the FLATBAR-5HOLE assembly.

687) Click the **WHEEL Right Hole1** cylindrical face. Concentric is selected by default.

688) Click the Green Check mark.

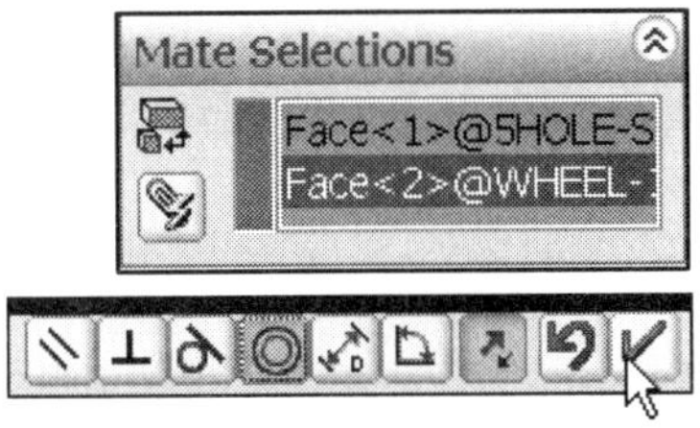

Insert a Concentric Mate.

689) Click the **back inside cylindrical** face of the second hole on the FLATBAR-5HOLE assembly.

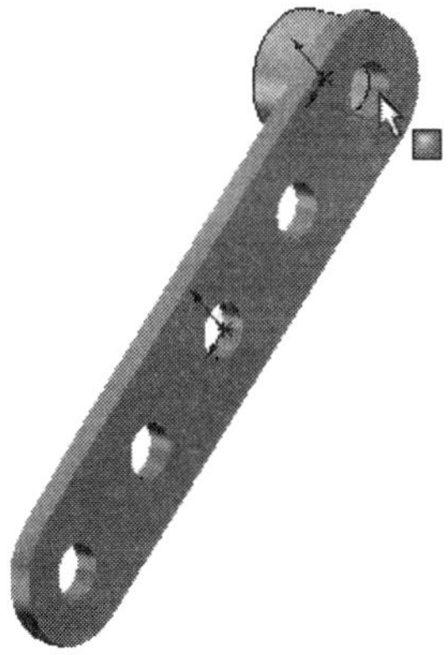

690) Click the **WHEEL Right Hole2** cylindrical face. Concentric is selected by default.

691) Click the Green Check mark.

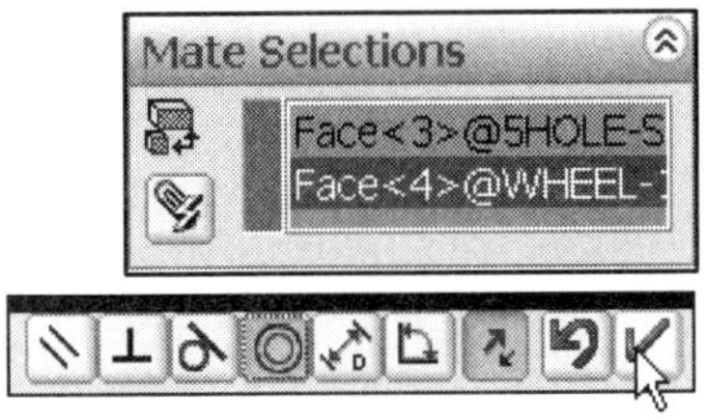

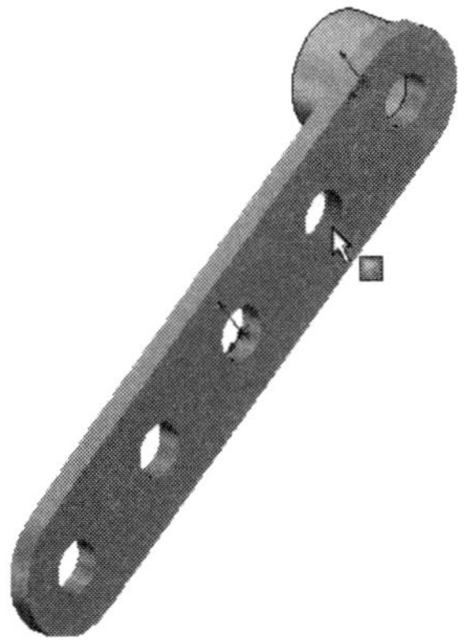

Insert a Coincident Mate.

692) Click the **back face** of the FLATBAR-5HOLE.

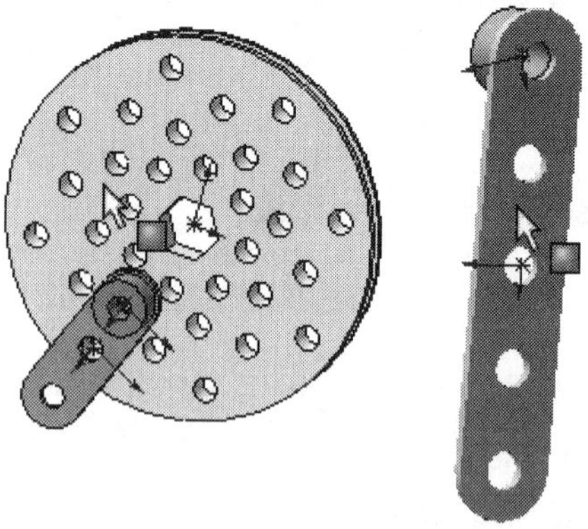

693) Click the **front face** of the WHEEL. Coincident is the selected by default.

694) Click the Green Check mark.

695) Click **OK** from the Mate PropertyManager.

696) Click **View**; uncheck **Origin** from the Main menu.

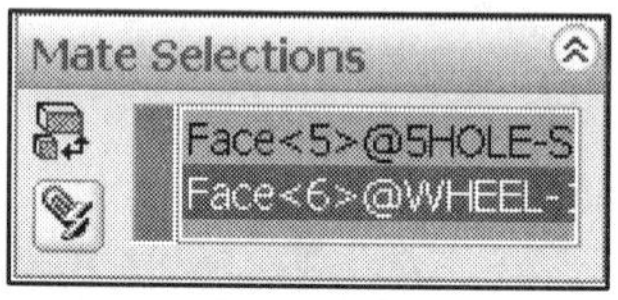

Measure the angle between the 3HOLE-SHAFTCOLLAR assembly and the 5HOLE-SHAFTCOLLAR assembly.

697) Click **Front view**.

698) Click **Tools**, **Measure** Measure... from the Main menu. The Measure dialog box is displayed.

699) Select the **two inside edges** of the FLATBAR assemblies.

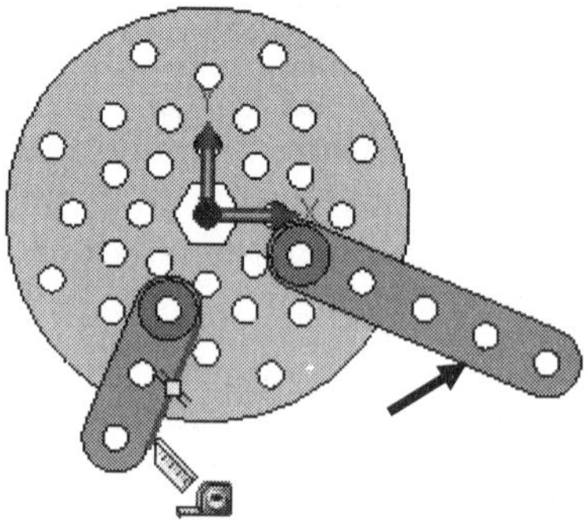

700) If required, click the **Show XYZ Measurements button**. The items are perpendicular.

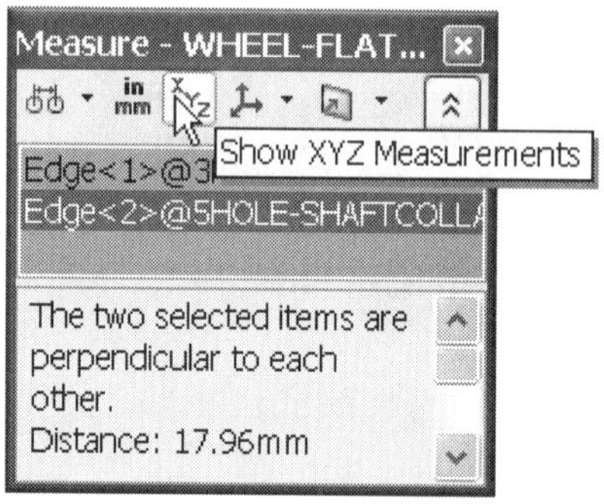

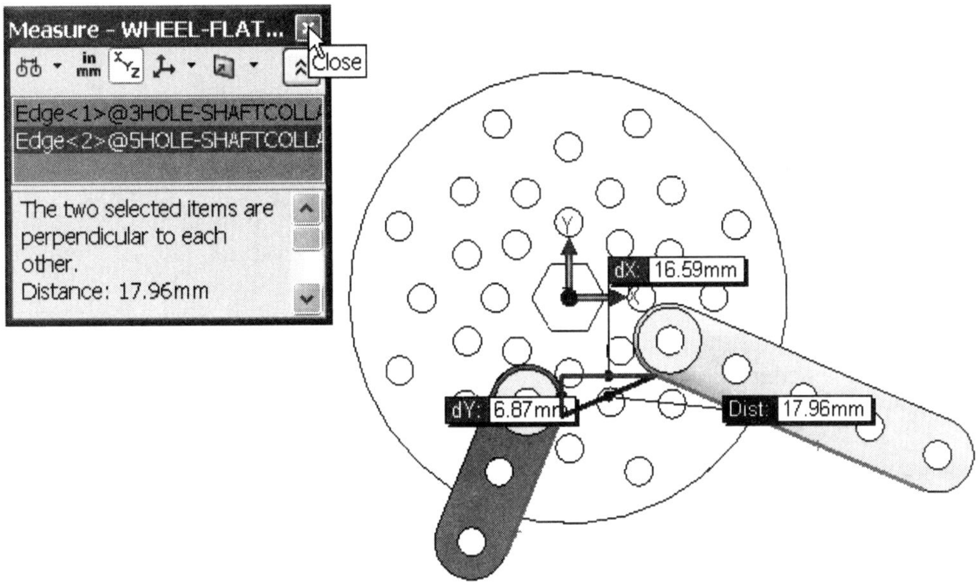

701) Click **Close** from the Measure dialog box.

Fit the Model to the Graphics window.

702) Press the **f** key.

703) Click Isometric view.

Save the WHEEL-FLATBAR assembly.

704) Click **Save**.

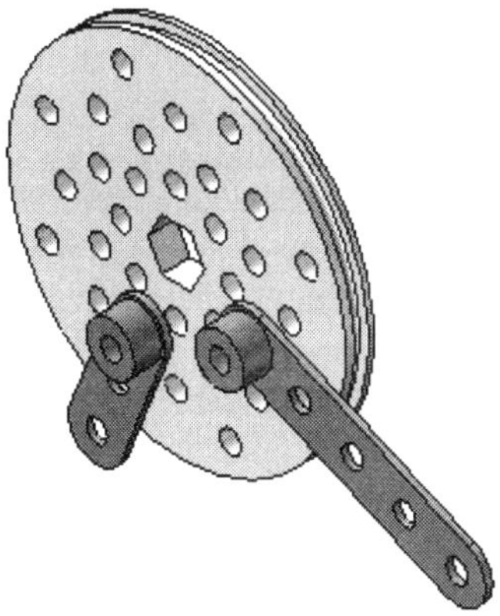

WHEEL-AND-AXLE Assembly

The WHEEL-AND-AXLE assembly contains the following items:

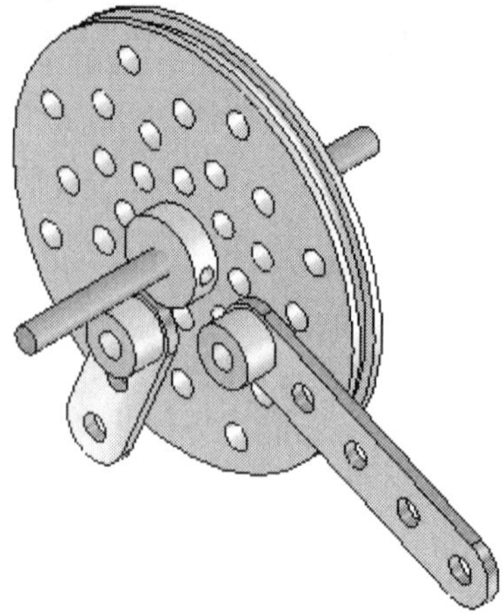

- WHEEL-FLATBAR assembly.
- AXLE3000 part.
- SHAFTCOLLAR-500 part.
- HEX-ADAPTER part.

Create the WHEEL-AND-AXLE assembly. The AXLE-3000 part is the first component in the assembly. A part or assembly inserted into a new assembly is called a component. The WHEEL-FLATBAR assembly rotates about the AXLE part.

Combine the created new assemblies and parts to develop the top level PNEUMATIC-TEST-MODULE assembly.

Activity: WHEEL-AND-AXLE Assembly

Create the WHEEL-AND-AXLE assembly.

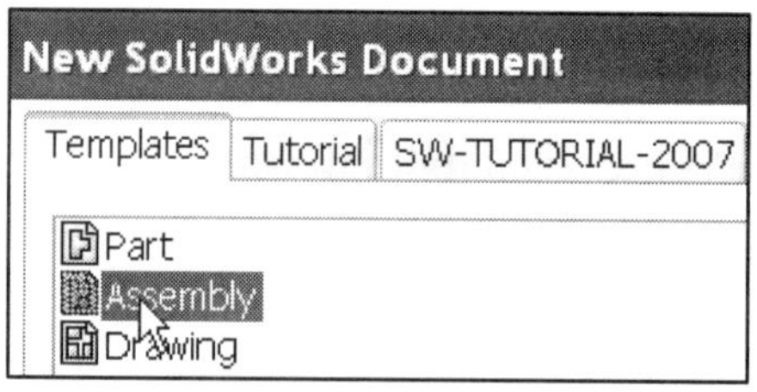

705) Click **File**, **New** from the Main menu.

706) Double-click the **Assembly** Templates tab. The Insert Component PropertyManager is displayed.

Insert the AXLE-3000 part.

707) Click **View**; check **Origins** from the Main menu.

708) Click **Browse**.

709) Select **Part** for Files of type from the SW-TUTORIAL-2007 folder.

710) Double-click **AXLE-3000**.

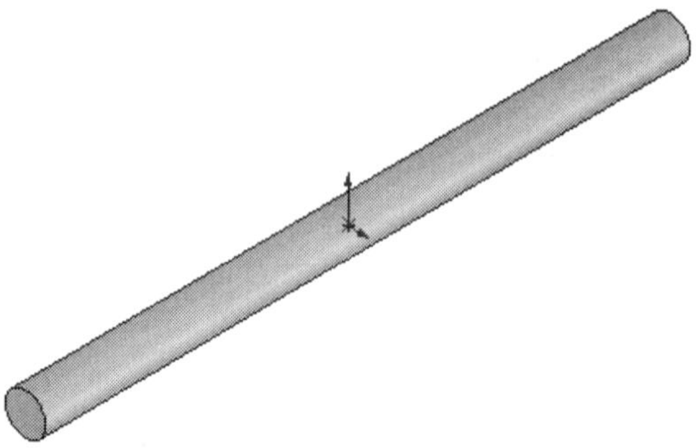

711) Click the **Origin**. The AXLE-3000 part is fixed to the assembly Origin.

Save the assembly.

712) Click **File**, **Save As** from the Main menu.

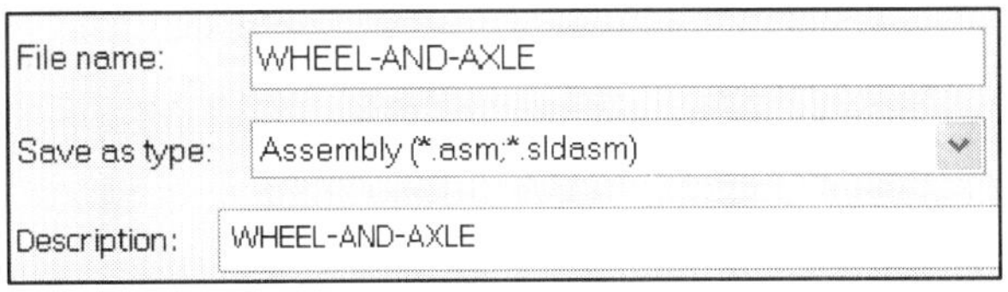

713) Enter **WHEEL-AND-AXLE** for File name in the SW-TUTORIAL-2007 folder.

714) Enter **WHEEL-AND-AXLE** for Description.

715) Click **Save**.

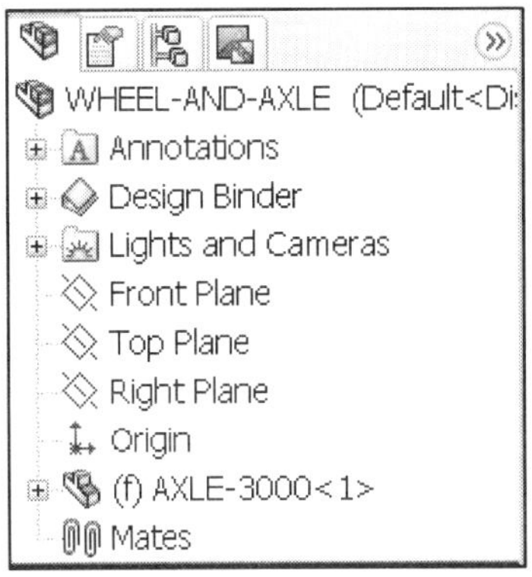

Insert a Coincident Mate between the Axis of the AXLE3000 and the Axis of the WHEEL. Insert a Coincident Mate between the Front plane of the AXLE3000 and the Front plane of the WHEEL. The WHEEL-FLATBAR assembly rotates about the AXLE3000 axis.

Display the Temporary Axes.

716) Click **View**; check **Temporary Axes** from the Main menu.

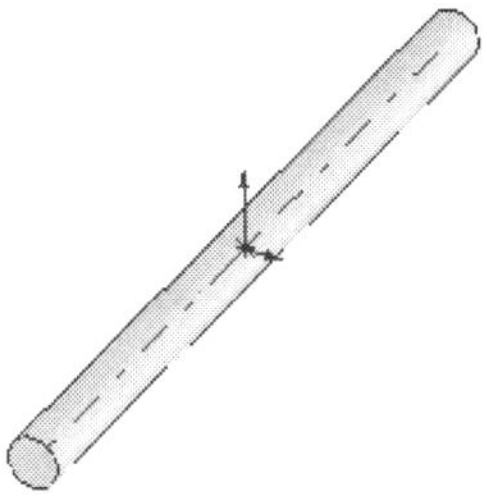

Insert the WHEEL-FLATBAR assembly.

717) Click **Insert Component** Insert Compo.... The Insert Components PropertyManager is displayed.

718) Click **Browse**.

719) Double-click the **WHEEL-FLATBAR** assembly from the SW-TUTORIAL-2007 folder.

720) Click a **position** to the right of AXLE3000.

View Reference WHEEL Axis.

721) Click **View**; check **Axes** from the Main menu.

722) Click **View**; uncheck **Origins** from the Main menu.

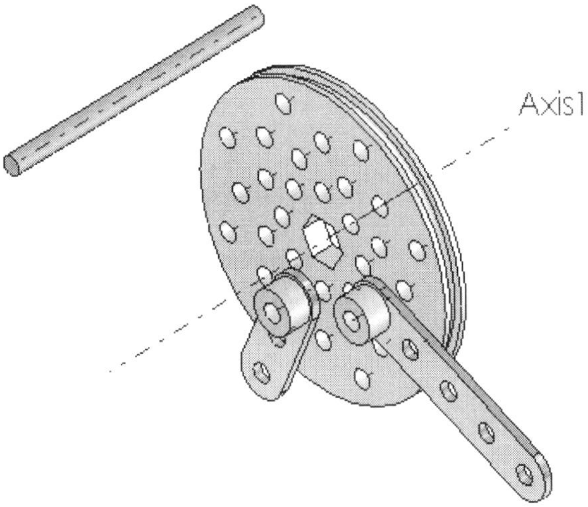

Insert a Coincident Mate.

723) Click **Mate** Mate from the Assembly toolbar. The Mate PropertyManager is displayed.

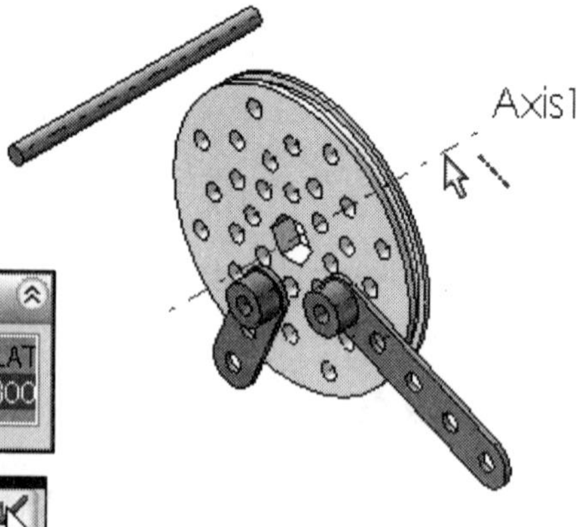

724) Click **Axis1** in the Graphics window.

725) Click the **AXLE3000 Temporary Axis**. Coincident is selected by default.

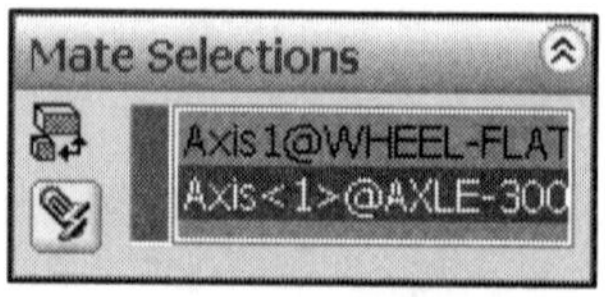

726) Click the Green Check mark.

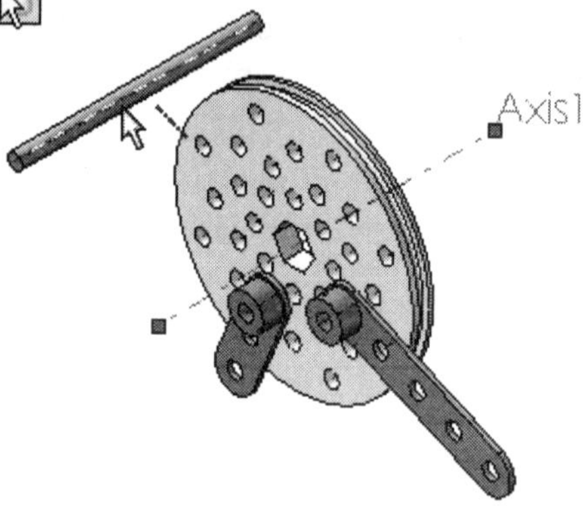

Insert a Coincident Mate.

727) **Expand** WHEEL-AND-AXLE from the fly-out FeatureManager.

728) **Expand** AXLE-3000 from the fly-out FeatureManager.

729) Click **Front Plane** of AXLE-3000<1>.

730) **Expand** WHEEL from the fly-out FeatureManager.

731) Click **Front Plane** of the WHEEL. Coincident is selected by default.

732) Click the Green Check mark.

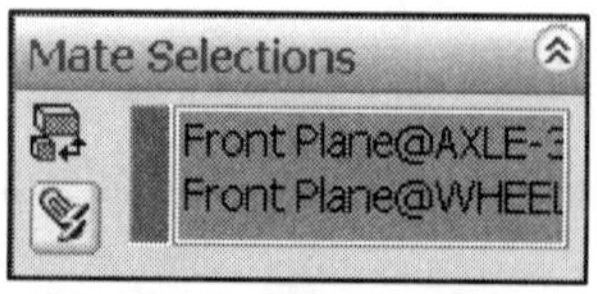

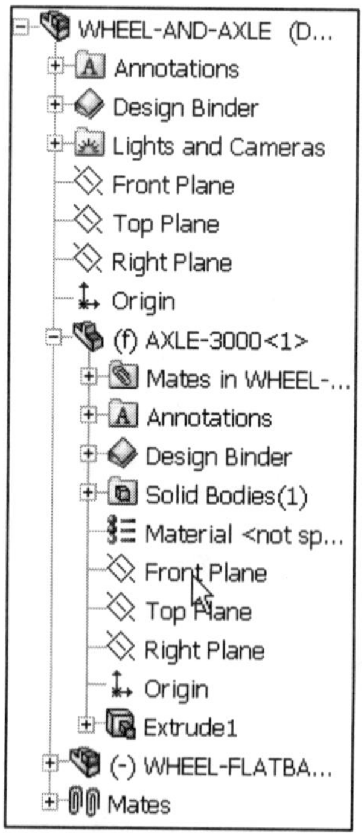

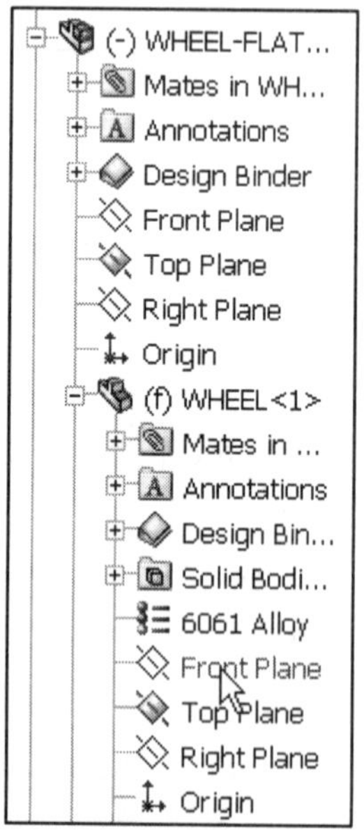

733) Click **OK** from the Mate PropertyManager.

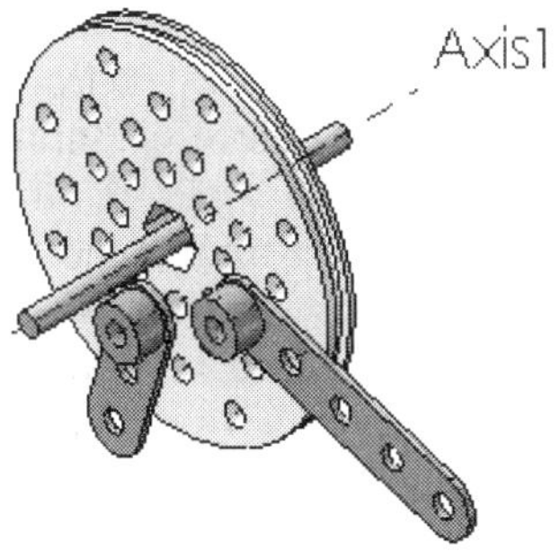

Rotate the WHEEL-FLATBAR assembly about AXLE3000.

734) Click the **WHEEL** in the Graphics window.

735) Click and drag the **WHEEL** around AXLE3000.

Save the WHEEL-AND-AXLE assembly.

736) Click **Save**.

Activity: WHEEL-AND-AXLE Assembly-Insert the HEX-ADAPTER Part

Insert the HEX-ADAPTER part.

737) Click **Insert Component** Insert Compo... from the Assembly toolbar. The Insert Component PropertyManager is displayed.

738) Click **Browse**.

739) Select **Part** for Files of type in the SW-TUTORIAL-2007 folder.

740) Double-click **HEX-ADAPTER**.

741) Click a **position** to the left of the WHEEL as illustrated.

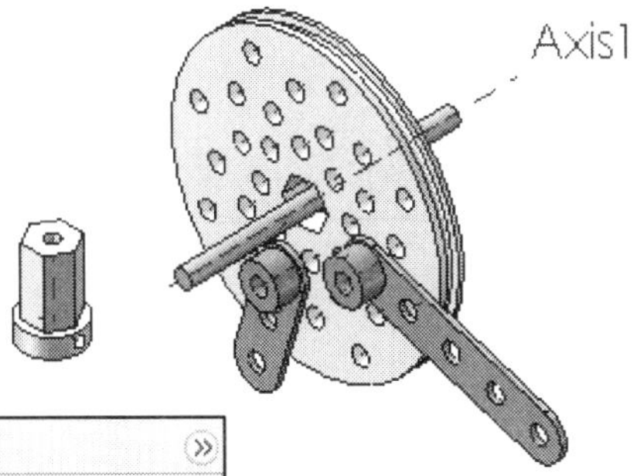

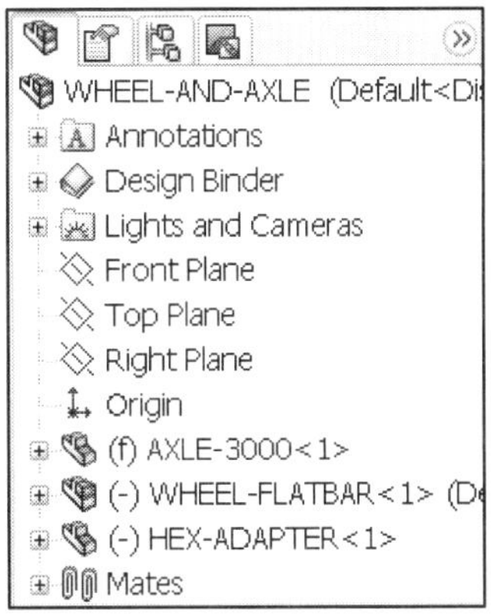

Insert a Concentric Mate.
Mate the HEX-ADAPTER.

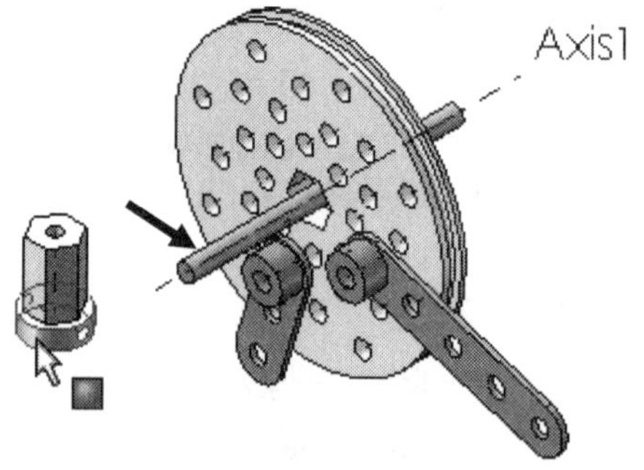

742) Click **Mate** Mate from the Assembly toolbar. The Mate PropertyManager is displayed.

743) Click the **HEX-ADAPTER** cylindrical face in the Graphics window.

744) Click the **AXLE3000** cylindrical face in the Graphics window. Concentric is selected by default. The selected faces are displayed in the Mate Selections box.

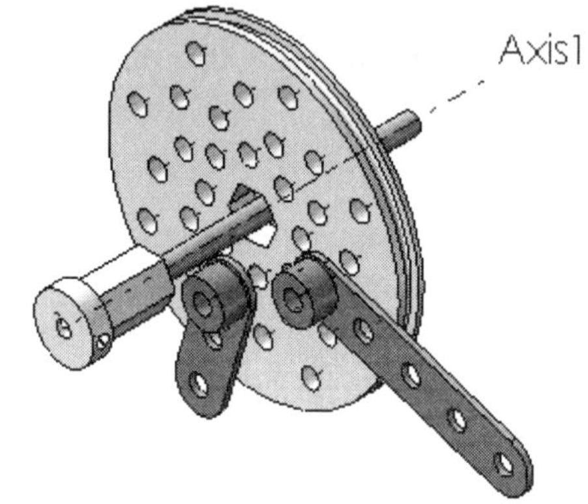

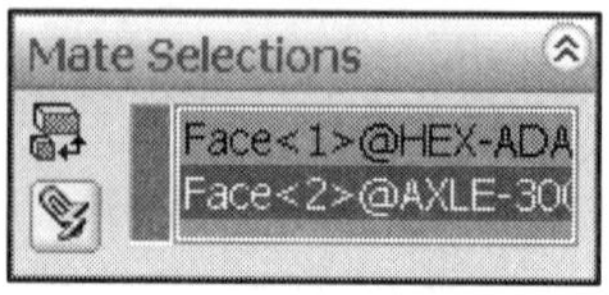

745) Click **Aligned** from the Concentric1 PropertyManager to flip the HEX-ADAPTER, if required.

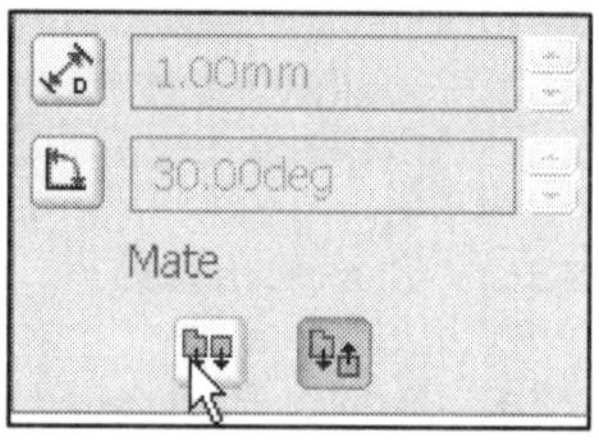

746) Click **OK** from the Concentric PropertyManager.

Insert a Coincident Mate.

747) Click the **front face** of the WHEEL.

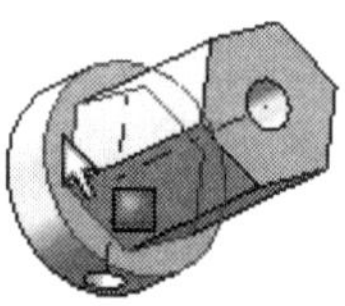

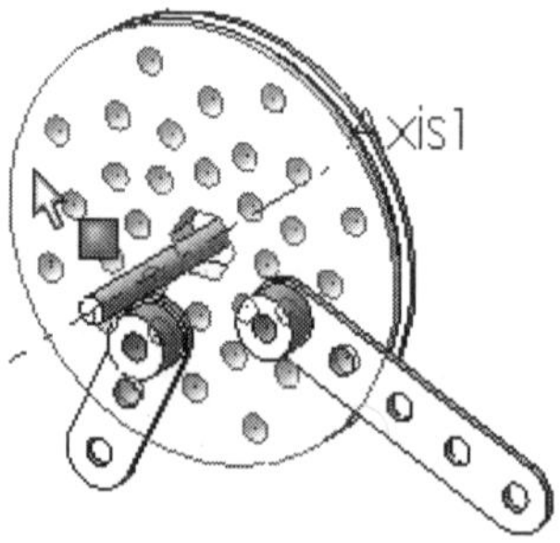

748) Press the **Left Arrow key** to rotate the model.

749) Click the **flat back circular face** of the HEX-ADAPTER as illustrated. Coincident is selected by default.

750) Click the Green Check mark.

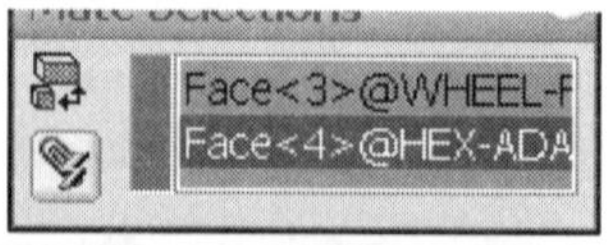

Insert a Parallel Mate.

751) **Rotate** the WHEEL-AND-AXLE assembly to view the back bottom edge of the HEX-ADAPTER.

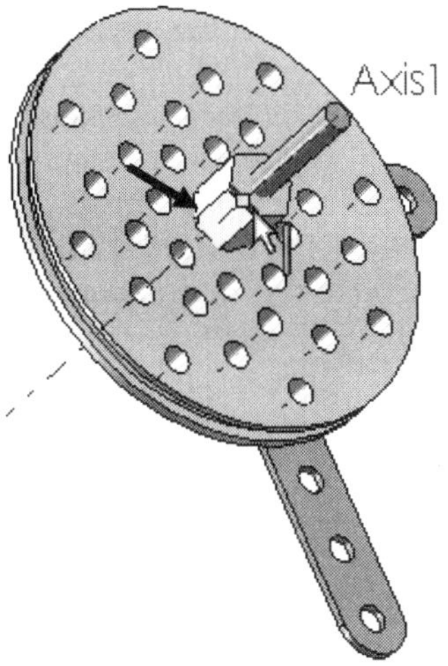

752) **Zoom to Area** on the back bottom edge of the HEX-ADAPTER.

753) Click the **back bottom edge** of the WHEEL.

754) Click the **top edge** of the HEX-ADAPTER. The selected edges are displayed in the Mate Selections box.

755) Click **Parallel**.

756) Click the Green Check mark.

757) Click **OK** from the Mate PropertyManager.

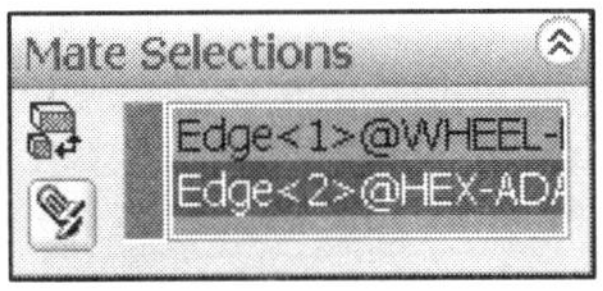

Fit the Model to the Graphics window.

758) Press the **f** key.

759) Click Isometric view.

Save the WHEEL-AND-AXLE assembly.

760) Click **Save**.

Activity: WHEEL-AND-AXLE Assembly-Insert SHAFTCOLLAR-500 Part

Insert the SHAFTCOLLAR-500 part.

761) Click **Insert Component** Insert Compo... from the Assembly toolbar. The Insert Component PropertyManager is displayed.

762) Click **Browse**.

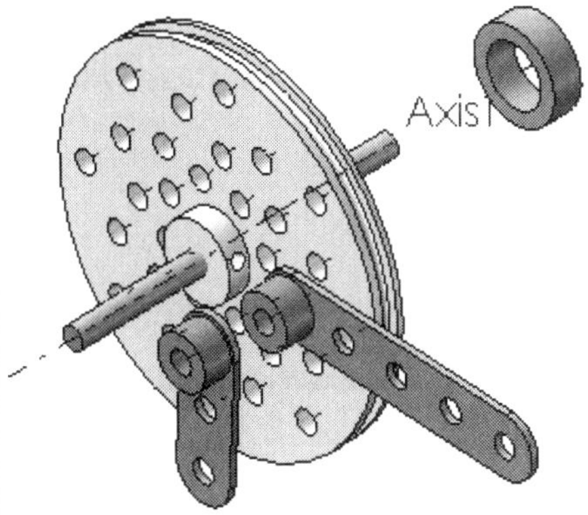

763) Select **Part** for Files of type from the SW-TUTORIAL-2007 folder.

764) Double-click **SHAFTCOLLAR-500**.

765) Click a **position** behind the WHEEL-AND-AXLE assembly as illustrated.

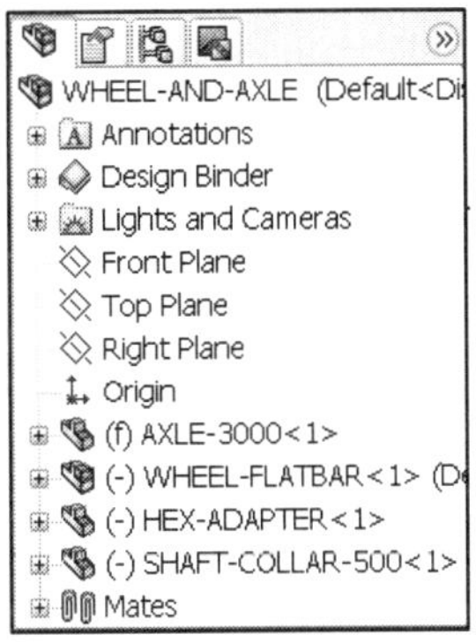

Insert a Concentric Mate.

766) Click **View**; uncheck **Temporary Axes**.

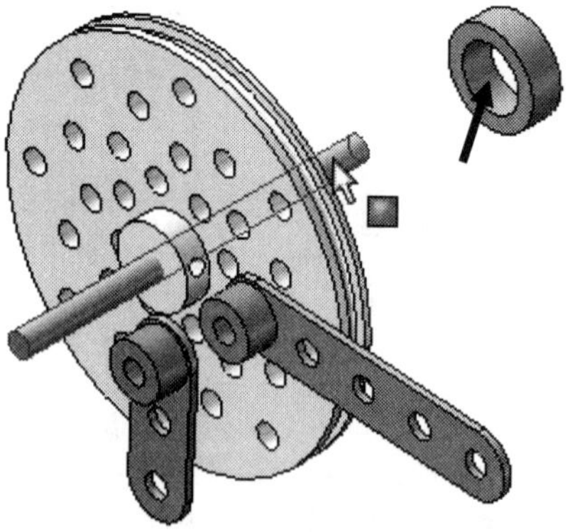

767) Click **View**; uncheck **Axes**.

768) Click **Mate** from the Assembly toolbar. The Mate PropertyManager is displayed.

769) Click the **front inside cylindrical face** of the SHAFTCOLLAR-500 part.

770) Click the **cylindrical face** of the AXLE3000 part. Concentric is selected by default.

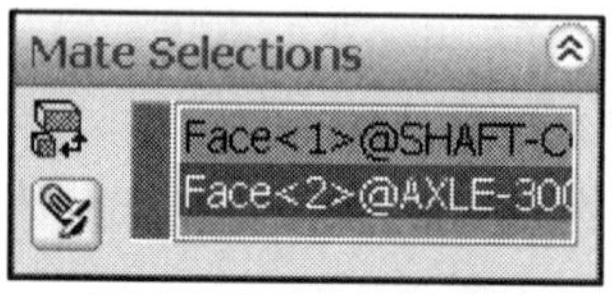

771) Click the Green Check mark.

Insert a Coincident Mate.

772) Click the **front face** of SHAFTCOLLAR-500 part.

773) Click the **back face** of the WHEEL. Coincident is selected by default.

774) Click the **Green Check mark**.

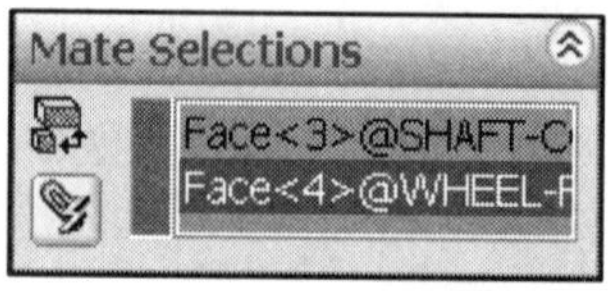

775) Click **OK** from the Mate PropertyManager.

Display an Isometric view.

776) Click Isometric view.

Save the WHEEL-AND-AXLE assembly.

777) Click **Save**.

Close all files.

778) Click **Windows**, **Close All** from the Main menu.

Determine the static and dynamic behavior of mates in each sub-assembly before creating the top level assembly.

Review the WHEEL-AND-AXLE Assembly.

You combined the WHEEL-FLATBAR sub assembly, the AXLE-3000 part, the HEX-ADAPTER part and the SHAFTCOLLAR-500 part to create the WHEEL-AND-AXLE assembly.

The WHEEL-FLATBAR sub-assembly rotated about the AXLE-3000 part. The WHEEL-FLATBAR assembly combined the 3HOLE-SHAFTCOLLAR assembly and the 5HOLE-SHAFTCOLLAR assembly. The 5HOLE-SHAFTCOLLAR assembly was created from the 3HOLE-SHAFTCOLLAR assembly by replacing the FLATBAR component and recovering from two Mate errors. Additional components are added to the WHEEL-AND-AXLE assembly in the project exercises.

Additional details on Save (Save as copy), Save (assemblies) are available in SolidWorks Help.

PNEUMATIC-TEST-MODULE Assembly

Create the PNEUMATIC-TEST-MODULE assembly. The first component is the FLAT-PLATE. The FLAT-PLATE is fixed to the Origin. The FLAT-PLATE part was created in Exercise 2.4a and supports the other components.

Modify the LINKAGE assembly. Insert the HEX-STANDOFF part. Insert the LINKAGE assembly into the PNEUMATIC-TEST-MODULE assembly.

Insert the AIR-RESERVOIR-SUPPORT assembly. Utilize a Derived Component Pattern and Local Component Pattern. Insert the FRONT-SUPPORT assembly. Utilize Mirror Component to create a mirrored version of the FRONT-SUPPORT assembly.

Insert the WHEEL-AND-AXLE assembly. Utilize Component Properties and create a Flexible State Mate. Utilize Configuration Manager to select the Flexible configuration for the AIRCYLINDER assembly. Note: Work between multiple part and sub-assembly documents to create the final assembly. Illustrations indicate the active document.

Activity: PNEUMATIC-TEST-MODULE Assembly

Create the PNEUMATIC-TEST-MODULE assembly.

779) Click **File**, **New** from the Main menu.

780) Double-click **Assembly** from the Templates tab.

Insert the FLAT-PLATE part.

781) Click **View**; check **Origins** from the Main menu.

782) Click **Browse**.

783) Select **Part** for Files of type from the SW-TUTORIAL-2007 folder.

784) Double-click **FLAT-PLATE**. Note: FLAT-PLATE was created in a Project exercise.

785) Click the **Origin**.

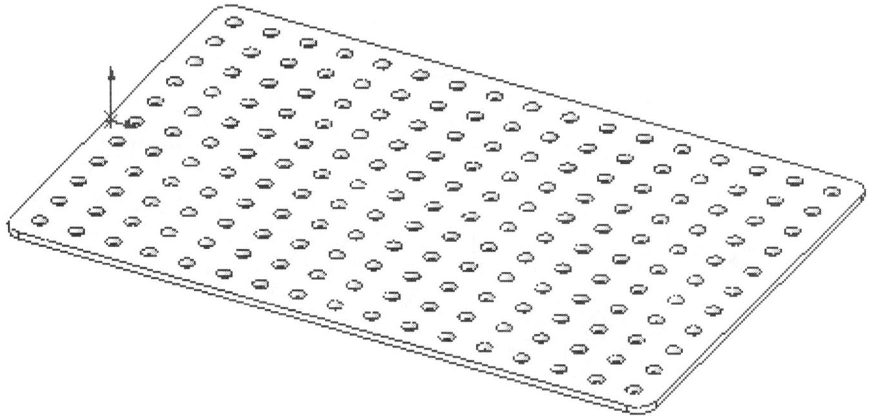

Save the assembly.

786) Click **File**, **Save As** from the Main menu.

787) Enter **PNEUMATIC-TEST-MODULE** for File name.

788) Enter **PNEUMATIC-TEST-MODULE** for Description.

789) Click **Save**.

Display the Front Plane.

790) Right-click **Front Plane** from the FeatureManager.

791) Click **Show**.

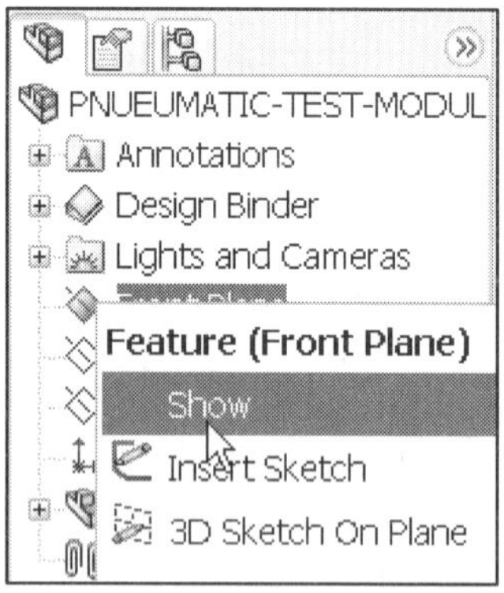

Activity: Modify the LINKAGE Assembly

Modify the LINKAGE assembly created in Project 1.

792) Click **File**, **Open** from the Main menu.

793) Select **Assembly** for Files of type from the SW-TUTORIAL-2007 folder.

794) Double-click **LINKAGE**.

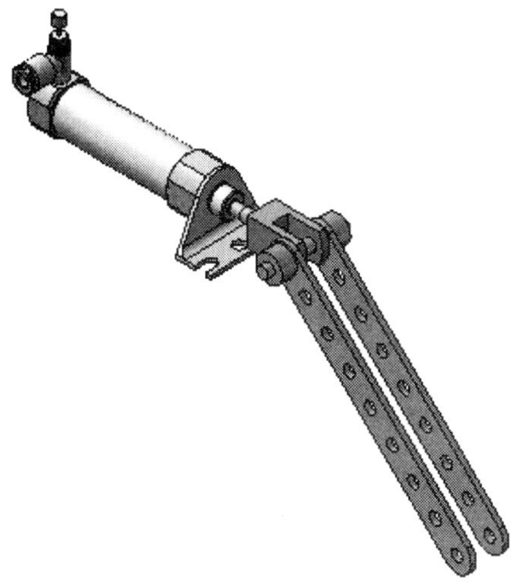

Insert the HEX-STANDOFF part into the LINKAGE assembly.

795) Click **Insert Component** Insert Compo... from the Assembly toolbar. The Insert Component PropertyManager is displayed.

796) Click **Browse**.

797) Select **Parts** for Files of type from the SW-TUTORIAL-2007 folder.

798) Double-click **HEX-STANDOFF**.

799) Click a **position** to the left of the half Slot Cut as illustrated.

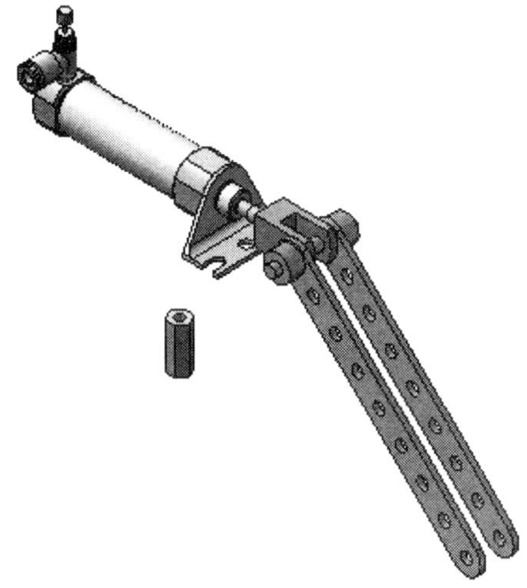

View the Temporary Axes.

800) Click **View**; check **Temporary Axes** from the Main menu.

801) Click **View**; check **Axes** from the Main menu.

Insert a Coincident Mate.

802) Click **Mate** Mate from the Assembly toolbar. The Mate PropertyManager is displayed.

803) Click the **HEX-STANDOFF** tapped hole Temporary Axis.

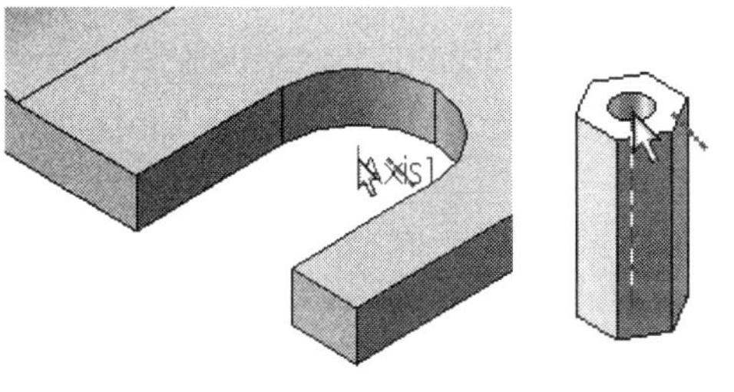

804) Click the **half Slot Cut Axis1**. The selected entities are displayed in the Mate Selections box. Coincident is selected by default.

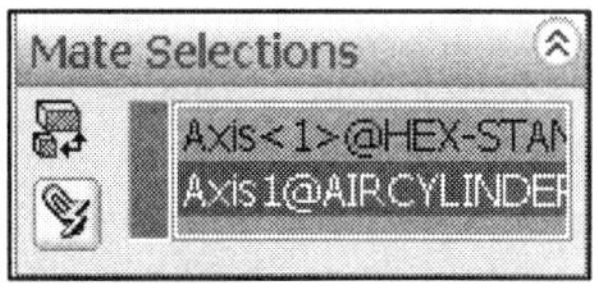

805) Click the Green Check mark.

Insert a Coincident Mate.

806) Click the **HEX-STANDOFF** top face.

807) Click the **BRACKET bottom face**. Coincident is selected by default. The selected faces are displayed in the Mate Selections box.

808) Click the Green Check mark.

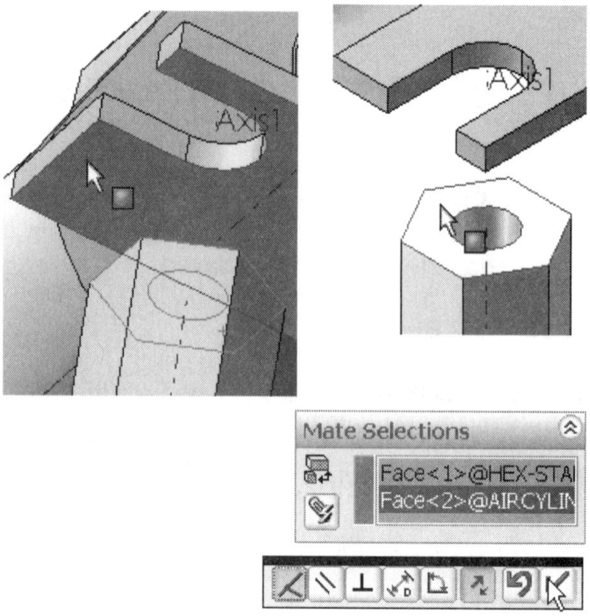

Insert a Parallel Mate.

809) Click the HEX-STANDOFF front face.

810) Click the **BRACKET front face**. The selected faces are displayed in the Mate Selections box.

811) Click Parallel.

812) Click the Green Check mark.

813) Click **OK** from the Mate PropertyManager.

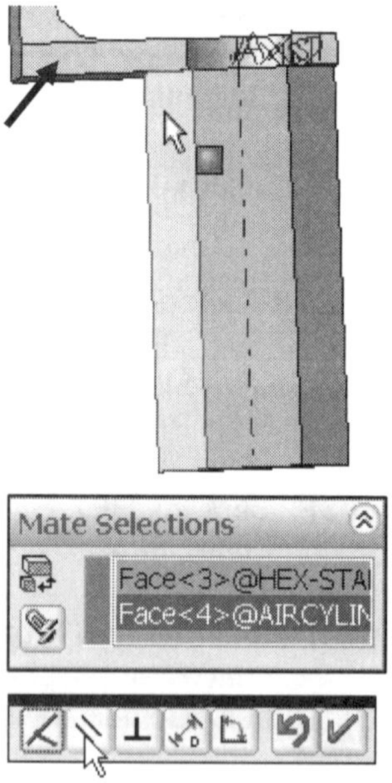

Fit the Model to the Graphics window.

814) Press the **f** key.

815) Click Isometric view.

816) Click **Save**.

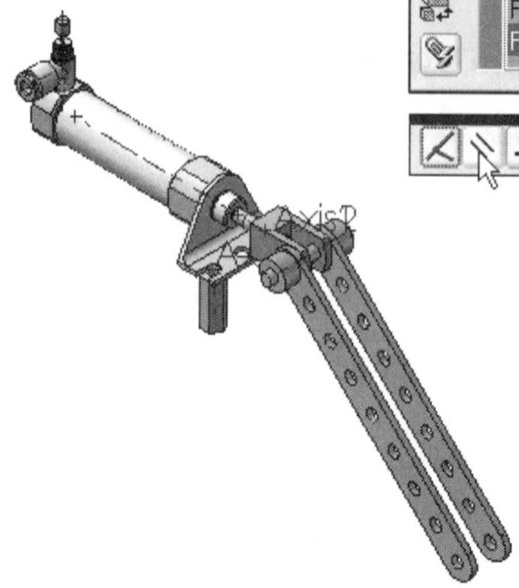

Insert the second HEX-STANDOFF.

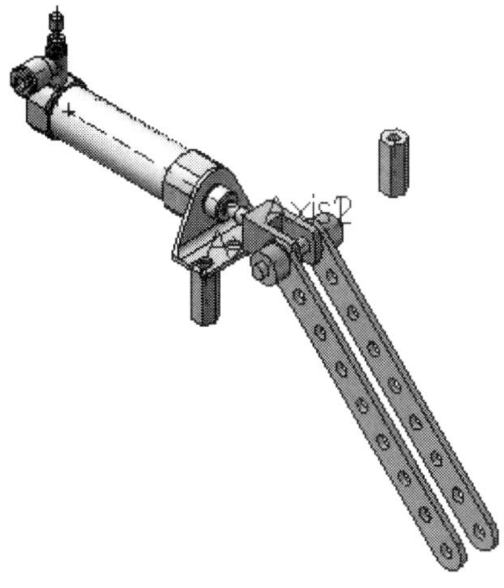

817) Click **Insert Component** Insert Compo... from the Assembly toolbar. The Insert Component PropertyManager is displayed.

818) Click **Browse**.

819) Select **Parts** for Files of type from the SW-TUTORIAL-2007 folder.

820) Double-click **HEX-STANDOFF**.

821) Click a **position** to the right of the right half Slot Cut as illustrated.

Insert a Concentric Mate.

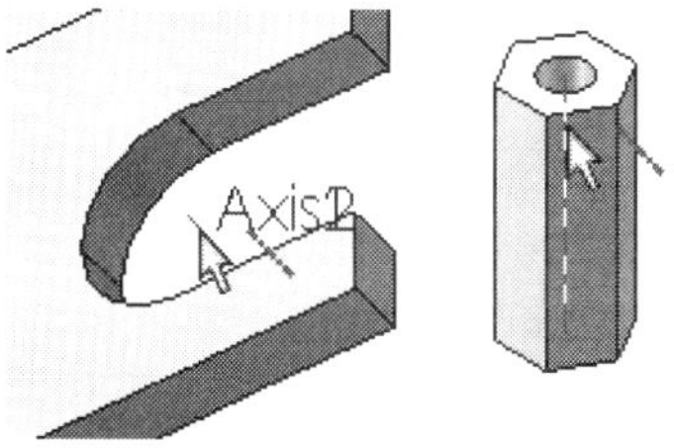

822) Click **Mate** Mate from the Assembly toolbar. The Mate PropertyManager is displayed.

823) Click the **second HEX-STANDOFF** Tapped Hole Temporary Axis.

824) Click the **back half Slot Cut Axis2**. Coincident is selected by default.

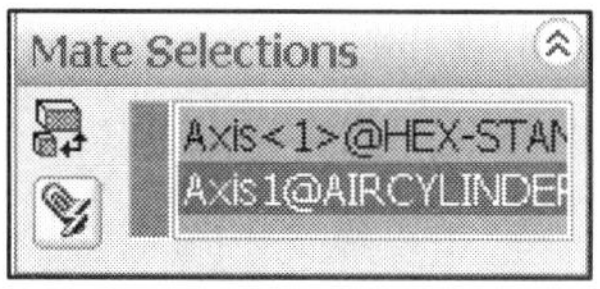

825) Click the **Green Check mark**.

Insert a Coincident Mate.

826) Click the second HEX-STANDOFF top face.

827) Click the **BRACKET bottom face**. Coincident is selected by default.

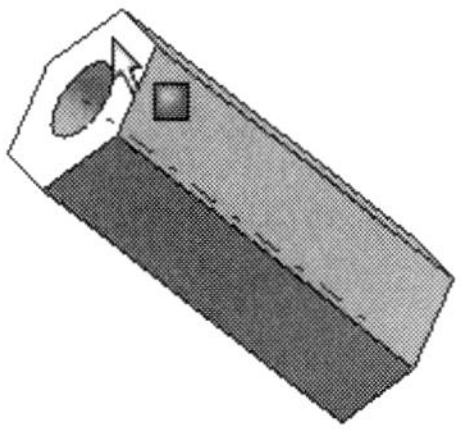

828) Click the **Green Check mark**.

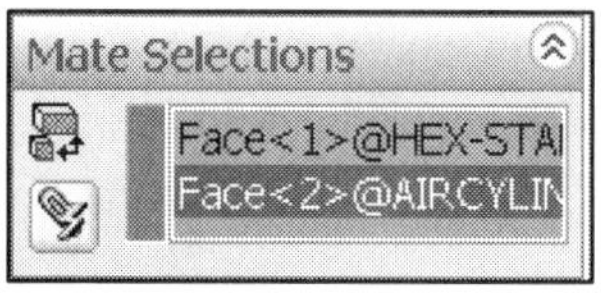

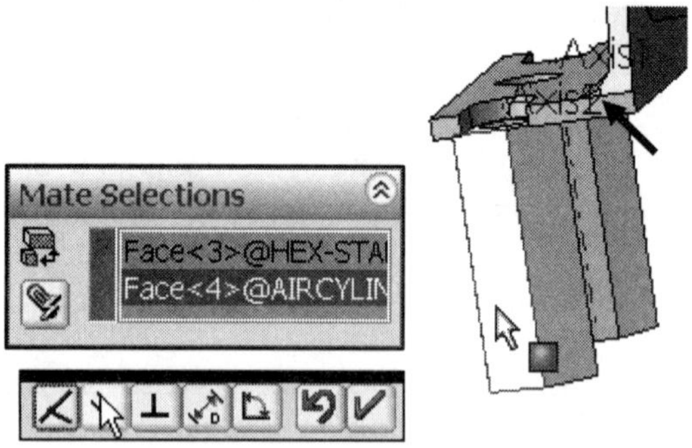

Insert a Parallel Mate.

829) Click the second HEX-STANDOFF face.

830) Click the BRACKET right front face.

831) Click **Parallel**.

832) Click the Green Check mark.

833) Click **OK** from the Mate PropertyManager.

Fit the Model to the Graphics window.

834) Press the **f** key.

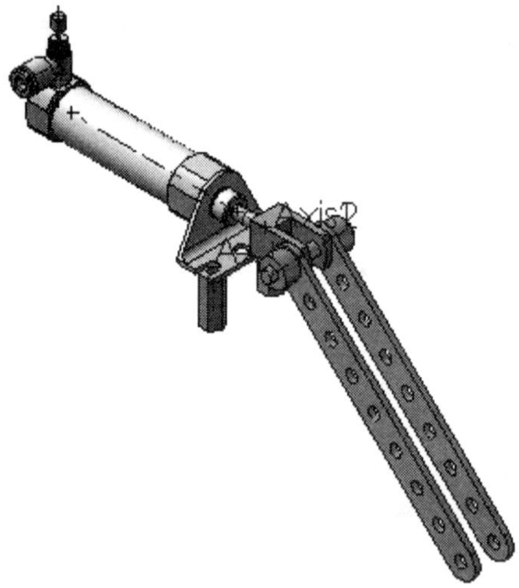

835) Click Isometric view.

836) Click **Save**.

In Exercise 1.3a you created the LINKAGE-2 assembly. Insert the second AXLE. The two SHAFT-COLLAR parts are inserted as an exercise at the end of this Project.

Insert the second AXLE.

837) Click **Insert Component** Insert Compo... from the Assembly toolbar. The Insert Component PropertyManager is displayed.

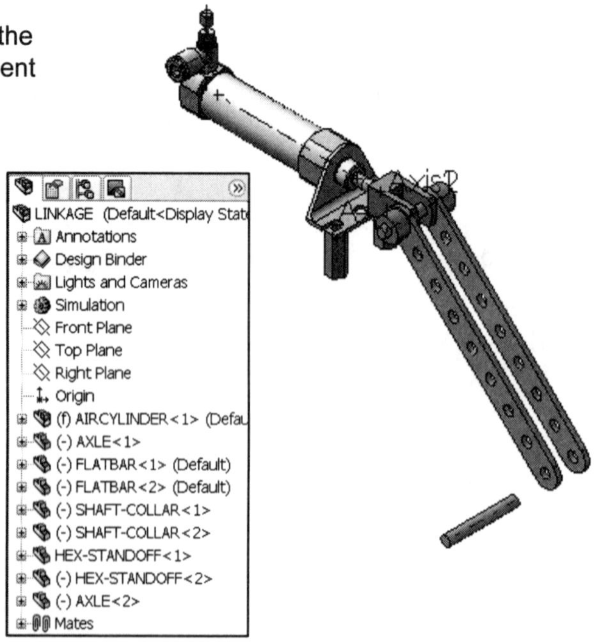

838) Click **Browse**.

839) Select **Parts** for Files of type from the SW-TUTORIAL-2007 folder.

840) Double-click **AXLE**.

841) Click a **position** to the left of the bottom of the FLATBAR as illustrated.

Insert a Concentric Mate.

842) Click **Mate** from the Assembly toolbar. The Mate PropertyManager is displayed.

843) Click the second AXLE cylindrical face.

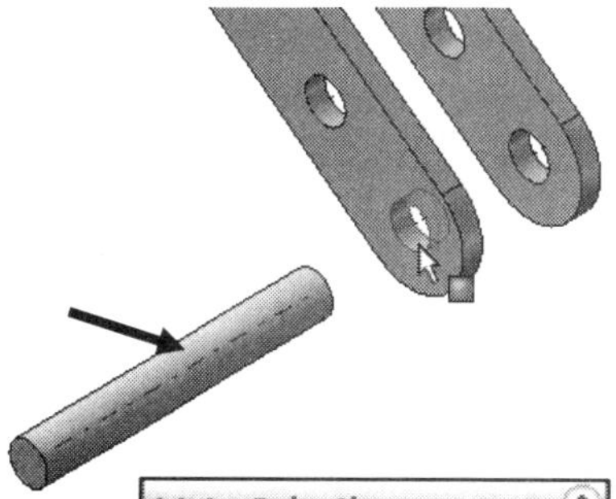

844) Click the **FLATBAR bottom hole** as illustrated. Concentric is selected by default.

845) Click the **Green Check mark**.

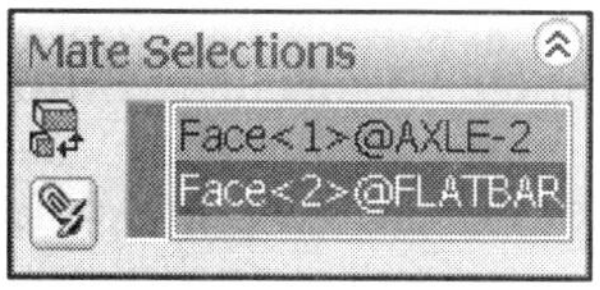

Insert a Coincident Mate.

846) Click the second **AXLE Front Plane** from the fly-out FeatureManager.

847) Click the **LINKAGE assembly Front Plane** from the fly-out FeatureManager. Coincident is selected by default. The selected Front Planes are displayed in the Mate Selections box.

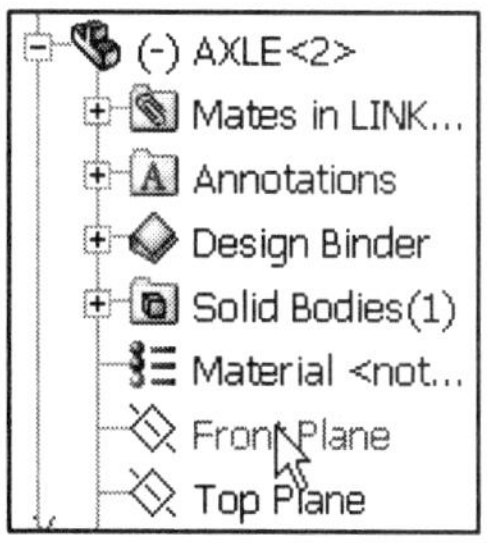

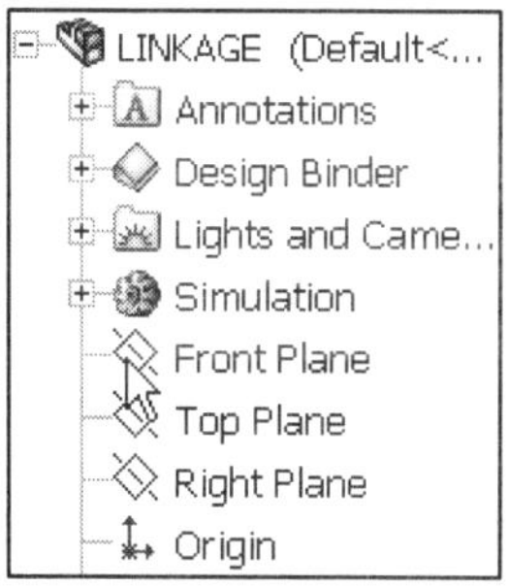

848) Click the Green Check mark.

849) Click **OK** from the Mate PropertyManager.

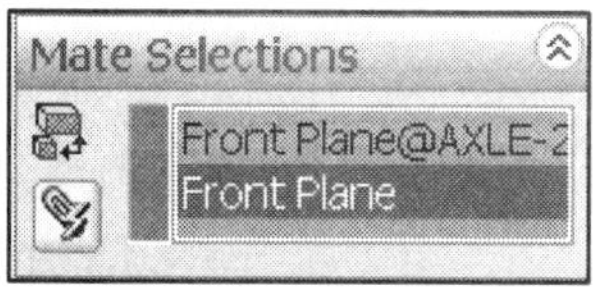

Fit the Model to the Graphics window.

850) Press the **f** key.

851) Click Isometric view.

Save the LINKAGE assembly.

852) Click **Save**.

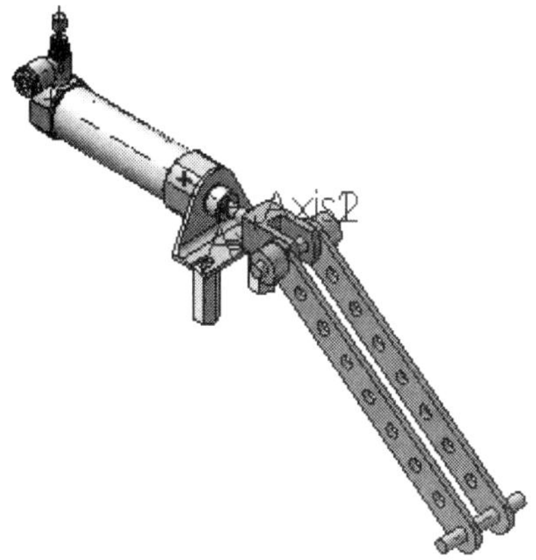

Insert the first SHAFT-COLLAR on the second AXIS.

853) Click **Insert Component** Insert Compo... from the Assembly toolbar.

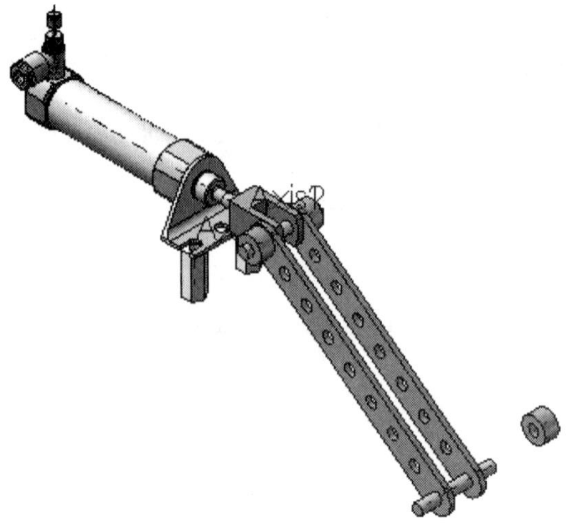

854) Click **Browse**.

855) Select **Part** type from the SW-TUTORIAL-2007 folder.

856) Double-click **SHAFT-COLLAR**.

857) Click a **position** to the right of the second AXLE as illustrated.

Enlarge the view.

858) Click Zoom to Area.

859) Zoom-in on the **SHAFT-COLLAR** and the **AXLE** to enlarge the view.

Insert a Concentric Mate.

860) Click **Mate** Mate from the Assembly toolbar. The Mate PropertyManager is displayed.

861) Click the inside **hole face** of the SHAFT-COLLAR.

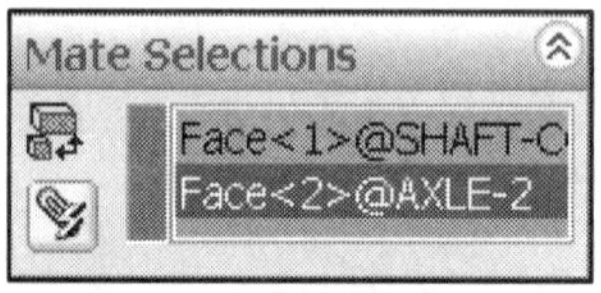

862) Click the **long cylindrical face** of the AXLE. Concentric is selected by default. The selected faces are displayed in the Mate Selections box.

863) Click the Green Check mark ✔.

Insert a Coincident Mate.

864) Press the **Shift-z** keys to Zoom in on the model.

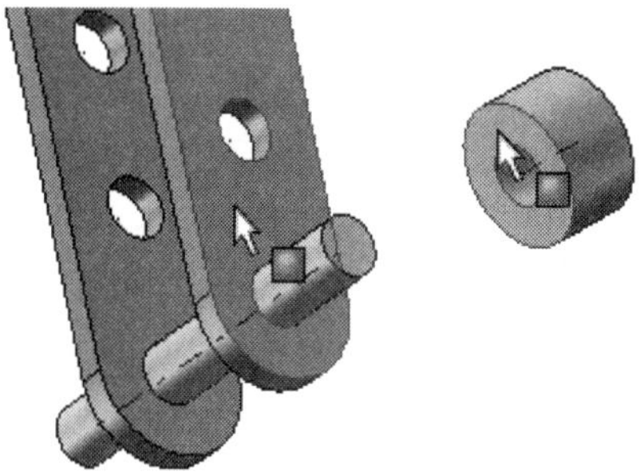

865) Click the **front face** of the SHAFT-COLLAR.

866) Press the **left arrow key** approximately 5 times to rotate the model to view the back face of the first FLATBAR.

867) Click the **back face** of the FLATBAR. Coincident is selected by default.

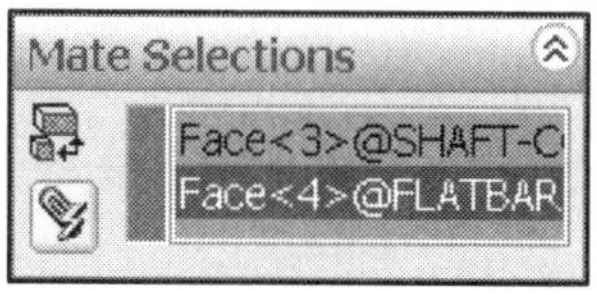

868) Click the Green Check mark ✔.

869) Click **OK** from the Mate PropertyManager.

Display the Isometric view.

870) Click Isometric view.

Insert the second SHAFT-COLLAR

871) Click **Insert Component** Insert Compo... from the Assembly toolbar. The Insert Component PropertyManager is displayed.

872) Click **Browse**.

873) Select **Part** for Files of type from the SW-TUTORIAL-2007 folder.

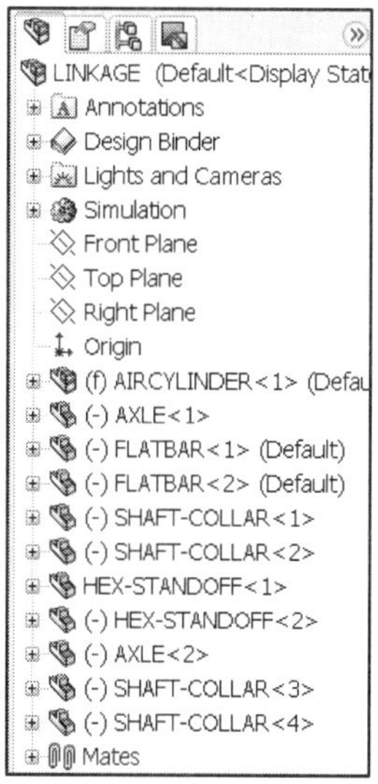

874) Double-click **SHAFT-COLLAR**.

875) Click a **position** on the left side of the AXLE as illustrated.

Enlarge the view.

876) Click **Zoom to Area** on the second SHAFT-COLLAR and the AXLE to enlarge the view.

Insert a Concentric Mate.

877) Click **Mate** Mate from the Assembly toolbar. The Mate PropertyManager is displayed.

878) Click the inside **hole face** of the second SHAFT-COLLAR.

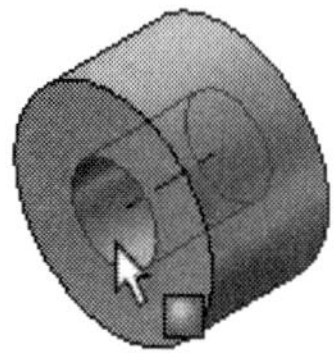

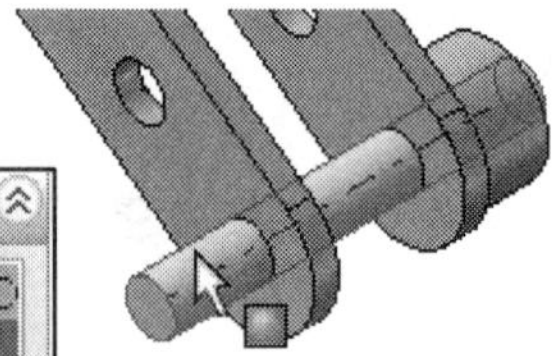

879) Click the **long cylindrical face** of the AXLE. Concentric is selected by default.

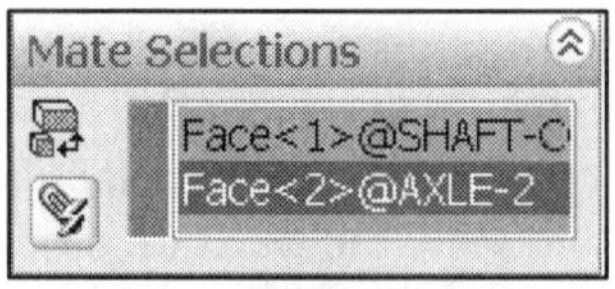

880) Click the Green Check mark ✔.

Insert a Coincident Mate.

881) Press the **f** key to fit the model to the Graphics window.

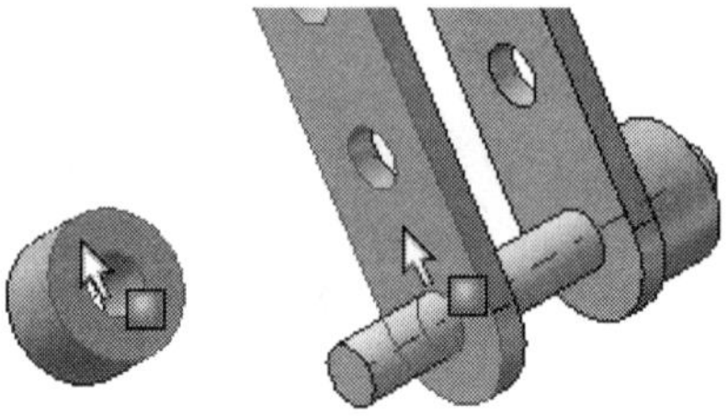

882) Use the **Shift-z** keys to Zoom in on the front face of the second FLATBAR.

883) Click the **front face** of the second FLATBAR.

884) Click the **back face** of the second SHAFT-COLLAR. Coincident is selected by default.

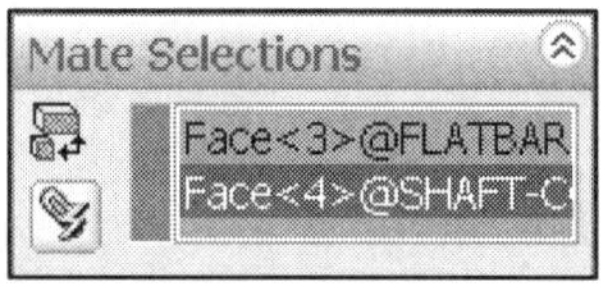

885) Click the Green Check mark ✔.

886) Click **OK** from the Mate PropertyManager.

Display the Isometric view.

887) Click Isometric view.

Save the LINKAGE assembly.

888) Click **Rebuild** from the Standard menu.

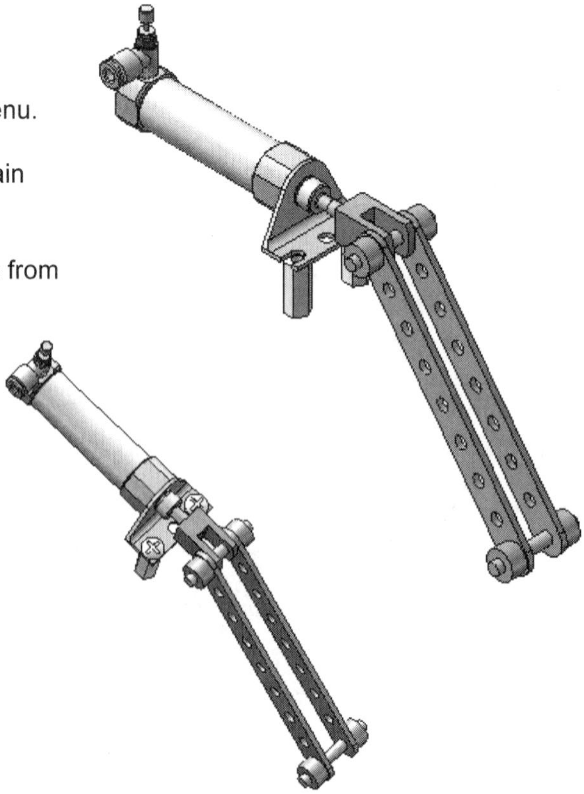

889) Click **View**; uncheck **Axis** from the Main menu.

890) Click **View**; uncheck **Temporary Axis** from the Main menu.

891) Click **Save**. Note: As an exercise, insert SCREWs between the AIRCYLINDER assembly and the two HEX-STANDOFFs.

Activity: PNEUMATIC-TEST-MODULE-Insert LINKAGE Assembly

Insert the LINKAGE assembly into the PNEUMATIC-TEST-MODULE assembly.

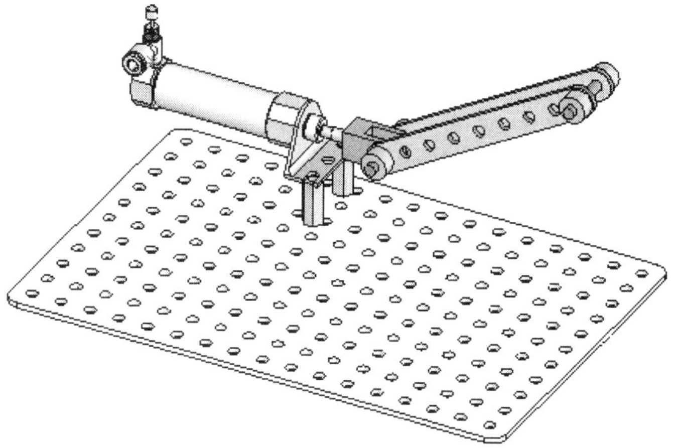

892) Click **Window**, **Tile Horizontally** from the Main menu.

893) Rotate the two **FLATBARs** approximately 45°.

894) Click and drag the **LINKAGE** LINKAGE assembly icon into the PNEUMATIC-TEST-MODULE assembly.

895) Click a **position** above the FLAT-PLATE. **Maximize** PNEUMATIC-TEST-MODULE Graphics window.

896) Click **View**; uncheck **Origins** from the Main menu.

897) Click Trimetric view.

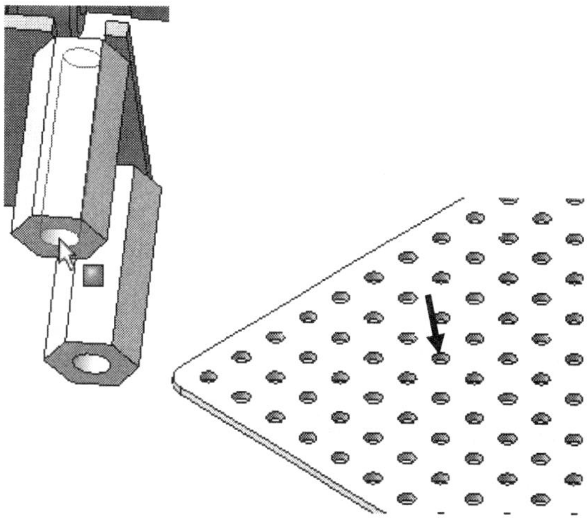

Create a Concentric Mate.

898) Click **Mate** Mate from the Assembly toolbar. The Mate PropertyManager is displayed.

899) Click the Front HEX-STANDOFF Tapped Hole face as illustrated.

900) Click the **FLAT-PLATE Hole** face in the 5th row, 4th column as illustrated. Concentric is selected by default. The selected faces are displayed in the Mate Selections box.

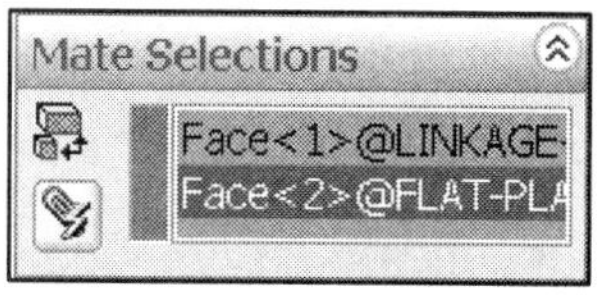

901) Click the Green Check mark.

Create a Parallel Mate.

902) Click the **PNEUMATIC-TEST-MODULE Front Plane** from the fly-out FeatureManager.

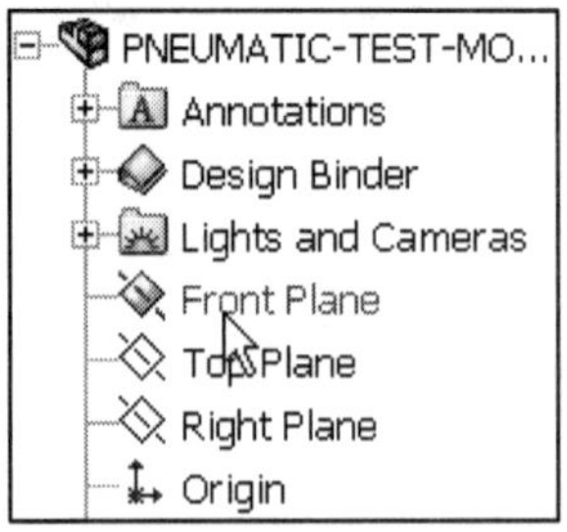

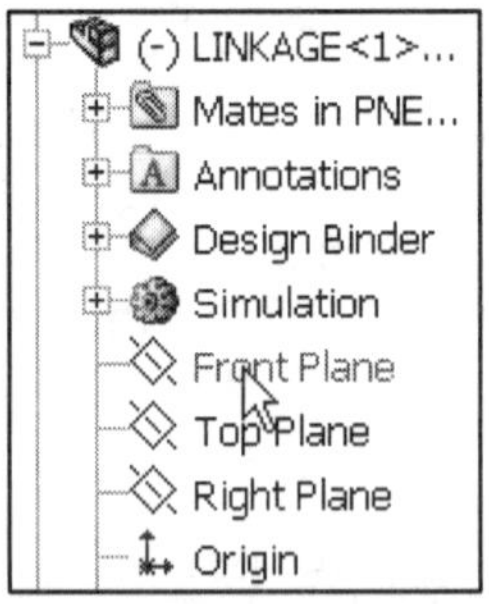

903) Click the **LINKAGE assembly Front Plane** from the fly-out FeatureManager.

904) Click **Parallel**.

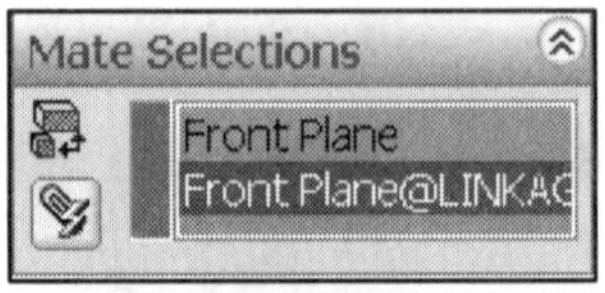

905) Click the Green Check mark.

Create a Coincident Mate.

906) Click the **Front HEX-STANDOFF** bottom face.

907) Click the **FLAT-PLATE top face**. Coincident is selected by default.

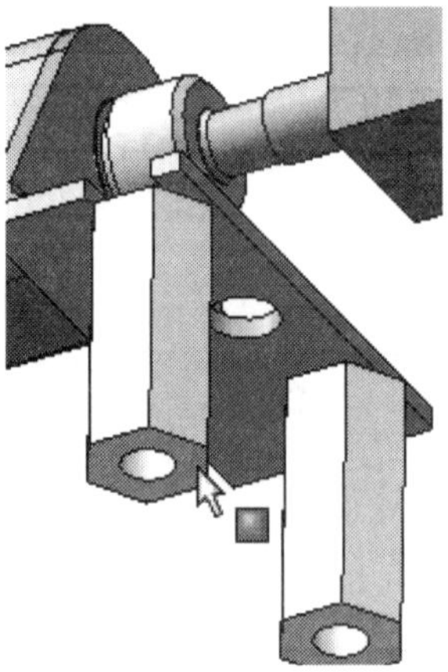

908) Click the Green Check mark.

909) Click **OK** from the Mate PropertyManager.

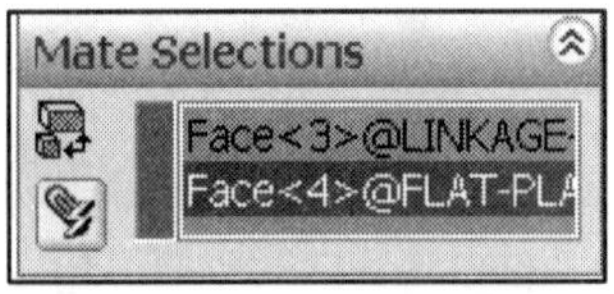

Display the Isometric view.

910) Click Isometric view.

Save the PNEUMATIC-TEST-MODULE assembly.

911) Click **Save**.

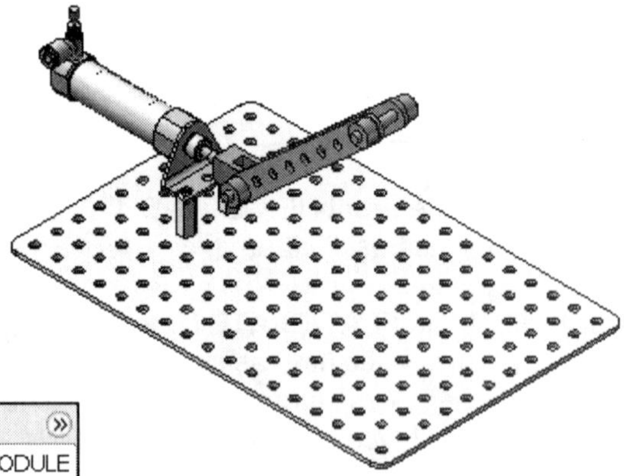

The LINKAGE assembly is fully defined and located on the FLAT PLATE part. Insert the AIR-RESERVOIR-SUPPORT assembly. The AIR-RESERVOIR-SUPPORT assembly was created in the Project 2 exercises. Note: The AIR-RESERVOIR SUPPORT is also located in the book's CD.

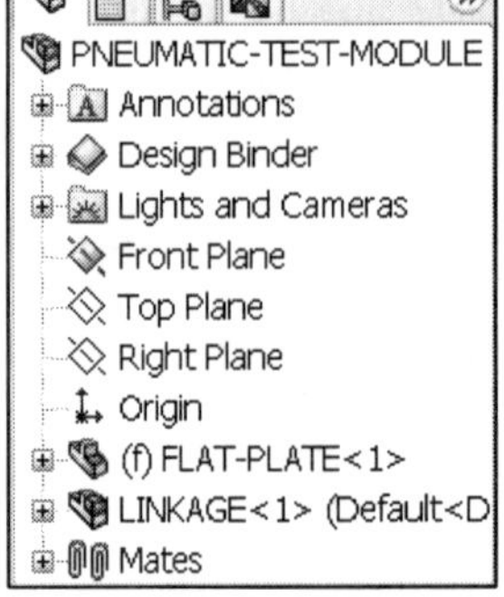

Activity: PNEUMATIC-TEST-MODULE Insert AIR-RESERVOIR-SUPPORT

Insert the AIR RESERVOIR SUPPORT assembly.

912) Click **Insert Component** Insert Compo... from the Assembly toolbar. The Insert Component PropertyManager is displayed.

913) Click **Browse**.

914) Select **Assembly** for Files of type from the SW-TUTORIAL-2007 folder.

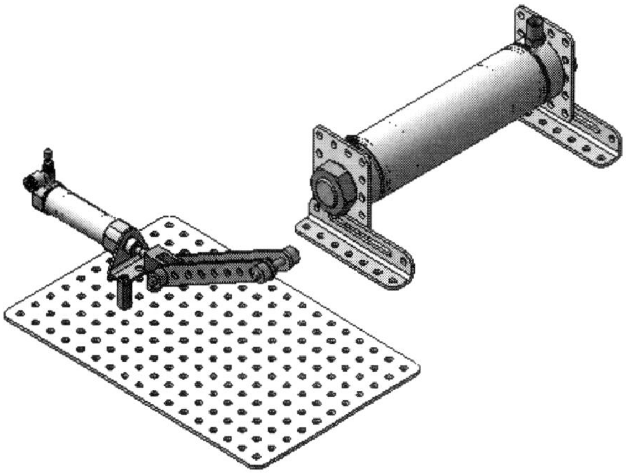

915) Double-click the **AIR-RESERVOIR-SUPPORT**. Note: The AIR-RESERVOIR SUPPORT assembly is supplied on the CD in the book.

916) Click a **position** above the FLAT-PLATE as illustrated.

917) Click **Rotate Component** Rotate Compo... from the Assembly toolbar.

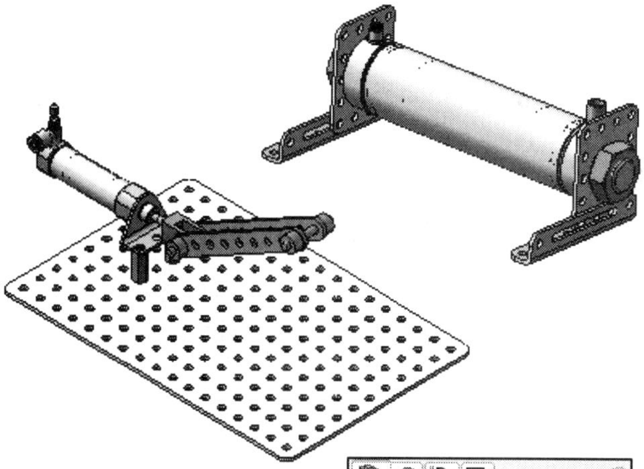

918) Click and drag the **AIR-RESERVOIR-SUPPORT** until the tank is parallel with the AIRCYLINDER as illustrated.

919) Click **Rotate Component** Rotate Compo... to deactivate.

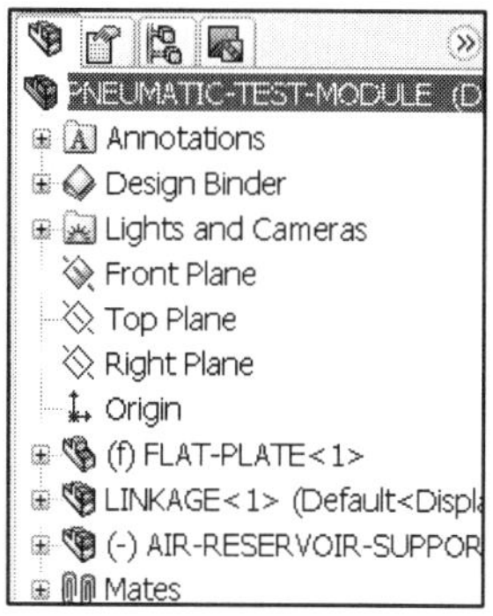

Create a Concentric Mate.

920) Click **Mate** from the Assembly toolbar. The Mate PropertyManager is displayed.

921) Click the FLAT-PLATE back left hole.

922) Click the fourth **ANGLE-BRACKET** hole. Concentric is selected by default.

923) Click the Green Check mark.

Create a Coincident Mate.

924) Click the ANGLE-BRACKET bottom face.

925) Click the **FLAT-PLATE top face**. Coincident is selected by default.

926) Click the Green Check mark.

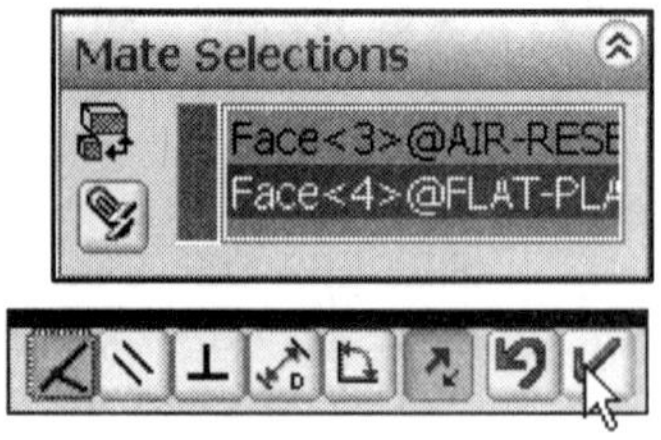

Create a Parallel Mate.

927) Click **Left view**.

928) Click the ANGLE-BRACKET narrow face.

929) Click the FLAT-PLATE narrow face.

930) Click **Parallel**.

931) Click the Green Check mark.

932) Click **OK** from the Mate PropertyManager.

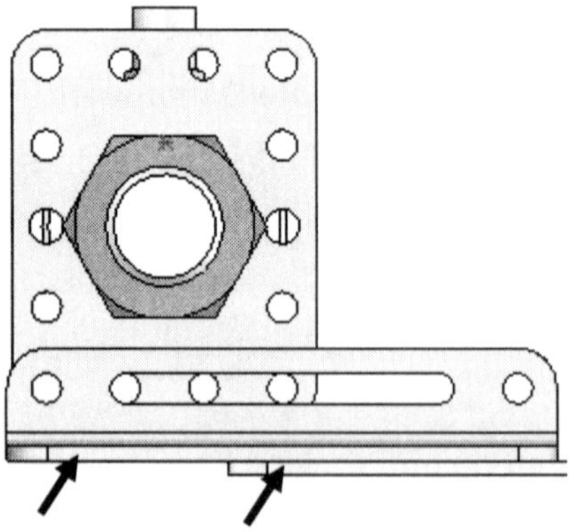

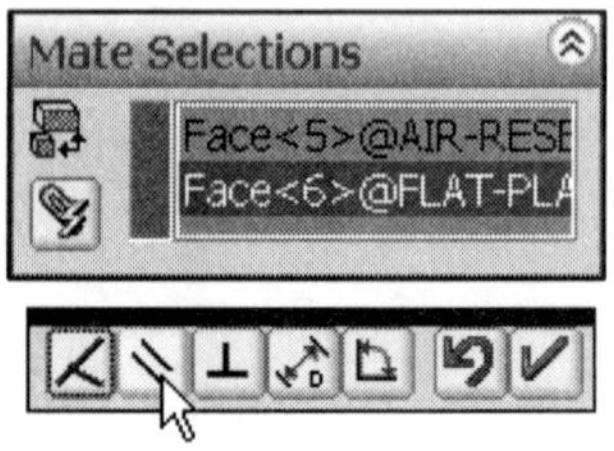

Display the Isometric view.

933) Click Isometric view.

Save the PNEUMATIC-TEST-MODULE assembly.

934) Click **Save**.

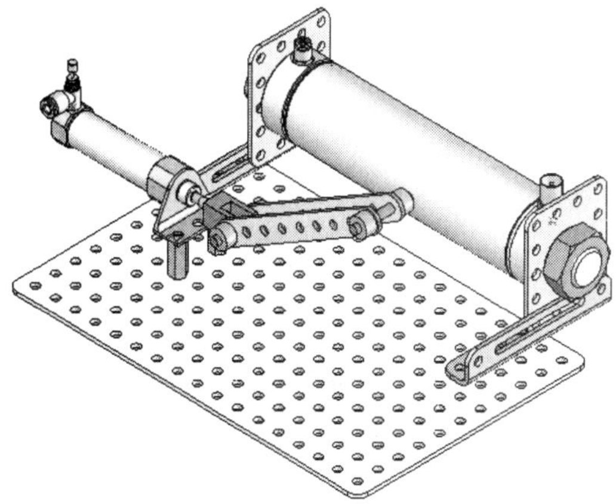

Component Patterns in the Assembly

There are two methods to define a pattern in an assembly.

- Derived.
- Local.

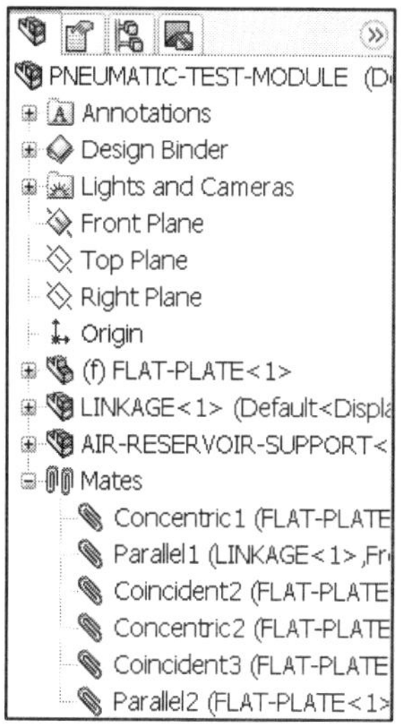

A Derive Component Pattern utilizes an existing feature pattern.

A Local Component pattern utilizes geometry in the assembly to arrange instances in a Linear or Circular pattern.

The SCREW part fastens the ANGLE-BRACKET part to the FLAT-PLATE part. Mate one SCREW to the first instance on the ANGLE-BRACKET Linear Pattern.

Utilize a Derived Pattern to create instances of the SCREW. Suppress the instances.

Utilize a Local Component Pattern to copy the Derived Pattern of SCREWS to the second ANGLE-BRACKET part.

Drag the part by specific geometry to create a Mate.

Activity: PNEUMATIC-TEST-MODULE-Component Pattern

Open the SCREW part.

935) Click **File**, **Open** from the Main menu.

936) Double-click **SCREW** from the SW-TUTORIAL-2007 folder.

937) Un-suppress the **Fillet1** and **Chamfer1** feature.

938) Click **Window**, **Tile Horizontally** to display the SCREW and the PNEUMATIC-TEST-MODULE assembly.

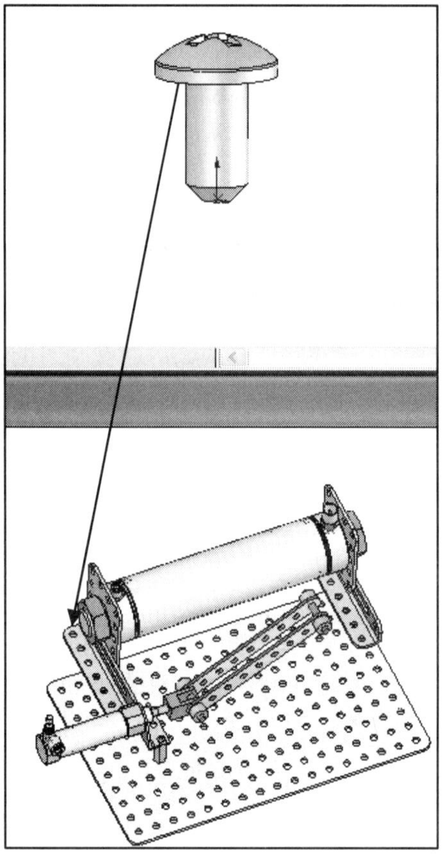

Insert and Mate the SCREW.

939) Click the **bottom circular edge** of the SCREW.

940) Drag the **SCREW** into the PNEUMATIC-TEST-MODULE assembly window. Note: Zoom in on the top circular edge of the ANBLE-BRACKET left hole.

941) Release the mouse pointer on the **top circular edge** of the ANGLE-BRACKET left hole. The mouse pointer displays the Coincident/ Concentric Circular edges feedback symbol.

942) **Return** to the PNEUMATIC-TEST-MODULE assembly window. Click **Left view**.

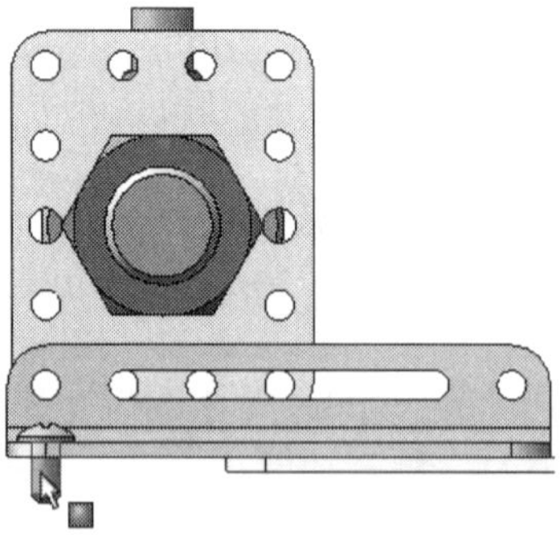

The SCREW part is position in the left hole with a Coincident/Concentric Mate.

Create a Derived Pattern.

943) Click **Insert**, **Component Pattern**, **Feature Driven** from the Main menu. The Feature Driven PropertyManager is displayed. Click the **SCREW** for the Component to Pattern.

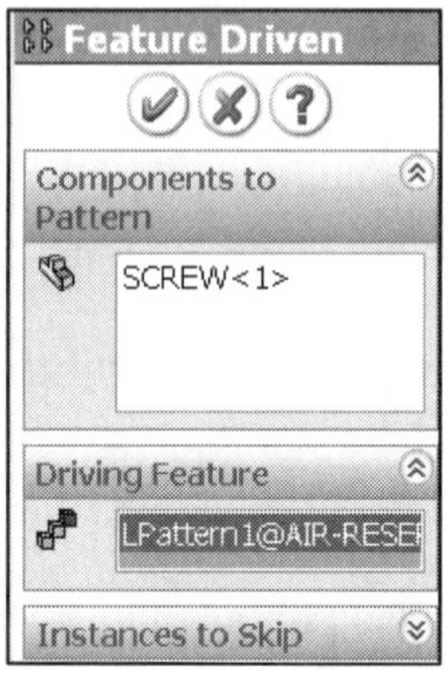

944) Click inside the **Driving Feature** box.

945) **Expand** the AIR-RESERVOIR-SUPPORT assembly in the PNEUMATIC-TEST-MODULE fly-out FeatureManager. **Expand** ANGLE-BRACKET <1>. Click **LPattern1** in the fly-out FeatureManager. The SCREW is the Seed Feature.

946) Click **OK** from the Feature Driven PropertyManager. Six instances are displayed in the Graphics window. DerivedLPattern1 is displayed in the FeatureManager.

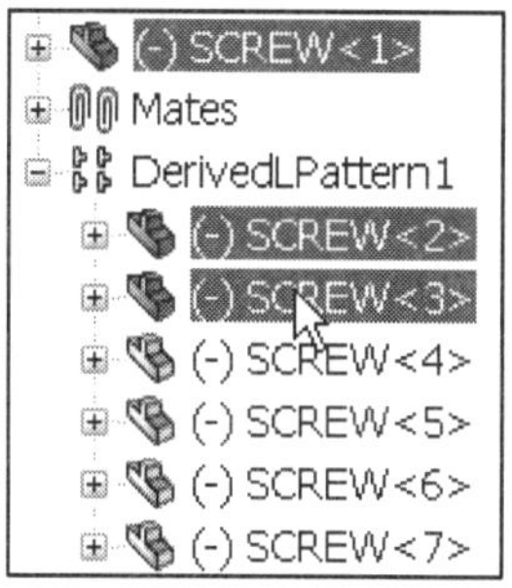

947) Click **SCREW<1>** from the FeatureManager.

948) Hold the **Ctrl** key down.

949) **Expand** DerivedLPattern1 from the FeatureManager.

950) Click the first two entries: **SCREW<2>** and **SCREW<3>**.

951) Release the **Ctrl** key.

952) Right-click **Suppress**. The first three SCREWs are not displayed.

Note: The Feature Driven Property Manager contains an option to skip instances of a component in a pattern.

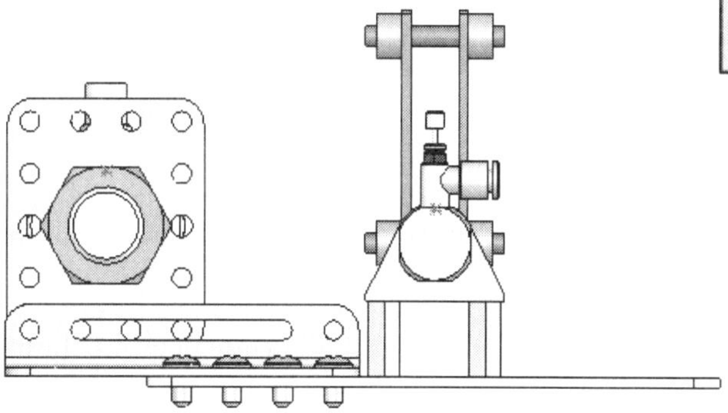

Activity: PNEUMATIC-TEST-MODULE-Local Pattern

Create a Local Pattern.

953) Click **Front view**.

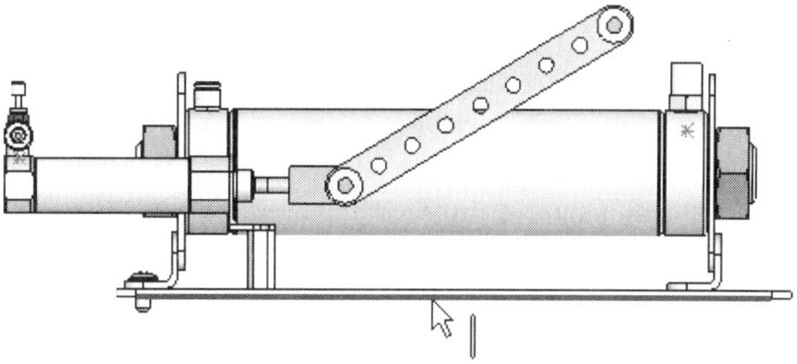

954) Click **Insert**, **Component Pattern, Linear Pattern** from the Main menu. The Linear Pattern PropertyManager is displayed. Click inside the **Pattern Direction** box for Direction 1.

955) Click the long front edge of the **FRONT-PLATE** as illustrated. Edge<1> is displayed in the Pattern Direction box. Enter **177.80**mm, [7in] for Spacing.

956) Enter **2** for Instances.

957) Click inside the **Components to Pattern** box.

958) Click **DerivedLPattern1** from the fly-out FeatureManager.

959) Click **OK** from the Linear Pattern PropertyManager.

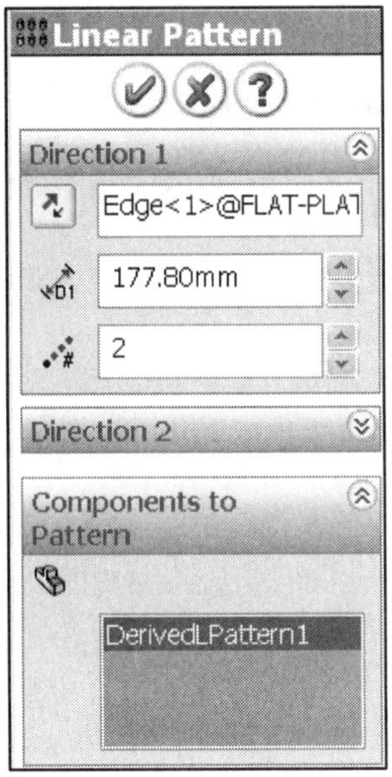

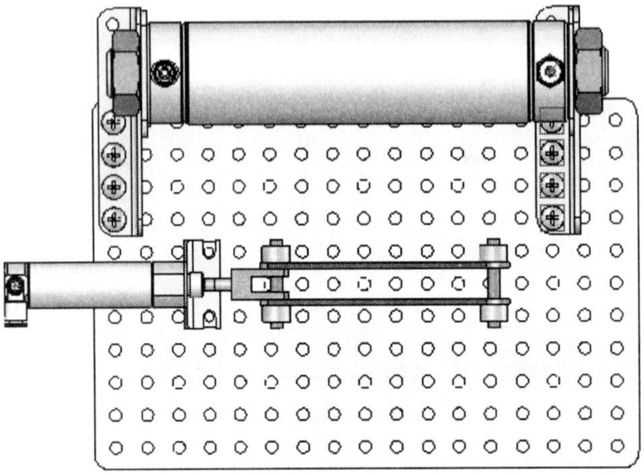

The Local Component Pattern is displayed in the second ANGLE-BRACKET part. LocalLPattern1 is displayed in the FeatureManager.

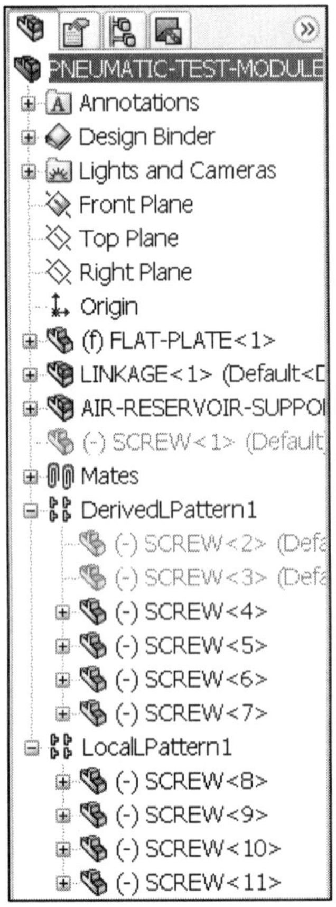

Save the PNEUMATIC TEST MODULE assembly.

960) Click **Isometric view**. View the FeatureManager.

961) Click **Save**.

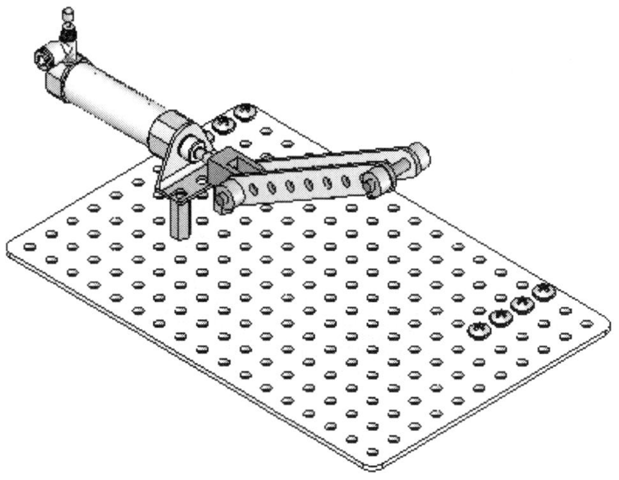

Hide the AIR-RESERVOIR-SUPPORT assembly.

962) Right-click **AIR-RESERVOIR-SUPPORT<1>** in the FeatureManager.

963) Click **Hide** Hide. Note: Utilize Show to display a component that has been hidden.

Hide the LINKAGE assembly.

964) Right-click **LINKAGE<1>** in the FeatureManager.

965) Click **Hide** Hide.

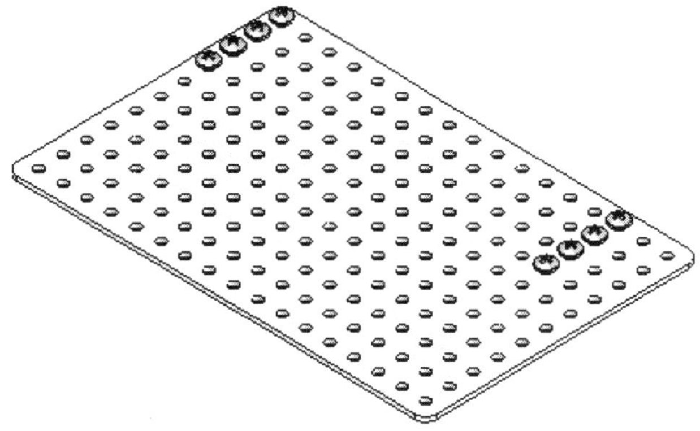

Insert the FRONT-SUPPORT assembly into the PNEUMATIC-TEST-MODULE assembly. Mate the FRONT-SUPPORT assembly to the FLAT-PLATE part.

Utilize the Mirror Component to create a mirrored copy of the FRONT-SUPPORT assembly.

Activity: PNEUMATIC-TEST-MODULE-Insert FRONT-SUPPORT Assembly

Insert and Mate the FRONT-SUPPORT assembly.

966) Click **Insert Component** Insert Compo... from the Assembly toolbar. The Insert Component PropertyManager is displayed.

967) Click **Browse**.

968) Select **Assembly** for Files of type.

969) Double-click **FRONT-SUPPORT**.

Hide the SCREWs in the FRONT-SUPPORT.

970) Click a **position** above the FLAT-PLATE as illustrated.

971) Right-click **FRONT-SUPPORT** in the FeatureManager.

972) Click Open Assembly.

973) **Hide** the SCREW parts and HEX-NUTS if required.

974) Click **Rebuild** from the Standard menu.

975) Click **Save**.

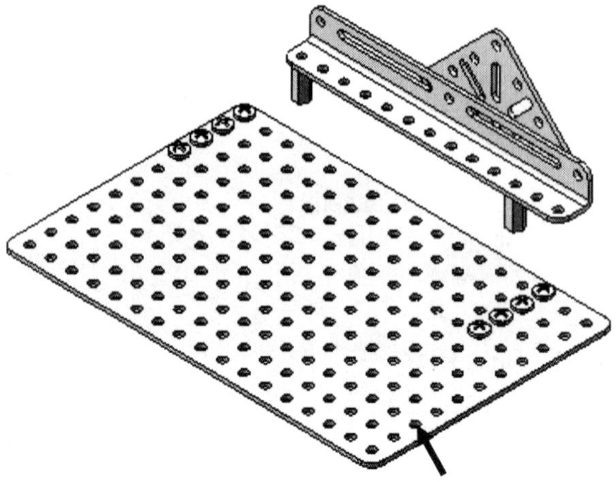

Return to the PNEUMATIC-TEST-MODULE assembly.

976) Press **Ctrl Tab**.

977) Click **Save**.

978) Click **Yes** to the Message, "Save the document and referenced models now?"

The PNEUMATIC-TEST-MODULE is displayed. The SCREW part and HEX-NUT part are hidden in the FRONT-SUPPORT assembly.

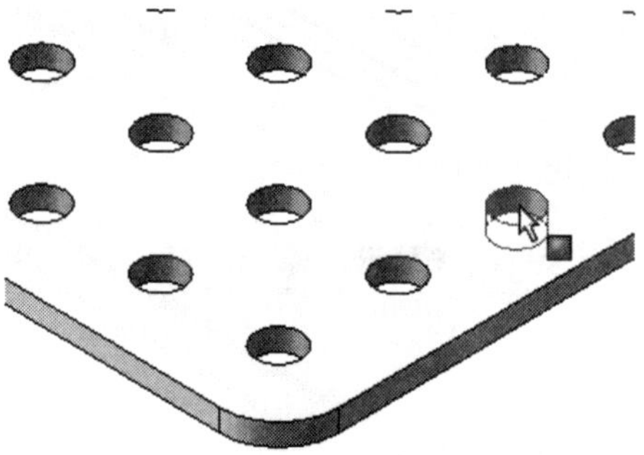

Insert a Concentric Mate.

979) Click **Mate** from the Assembly toolbar. The Mate PropertyManager is displayed.

980) Click the **FLAT-PLATE hole face** in the 3rd row, right most column (17th column).

981) Click the **HEX-STANDOFF Tapped Hole**. Concentric is selected by default.

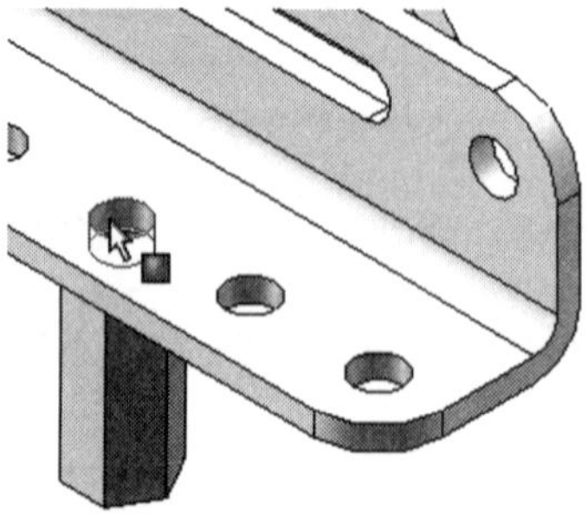

982) Click the Green Check mark.

Insert a Coincident Mate.

983) Click the bottom face of the **HEX-STANDOFF** part.

984) Click the top face of the **FLAT-PLATE**. The selected faces are displayed in the Mate Selections box. Coincident is selected by default.

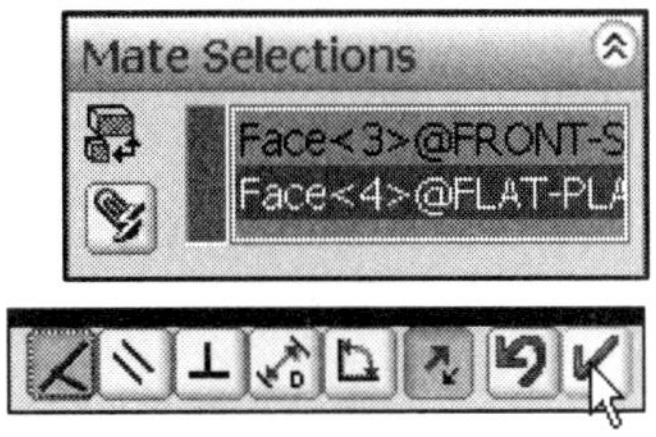

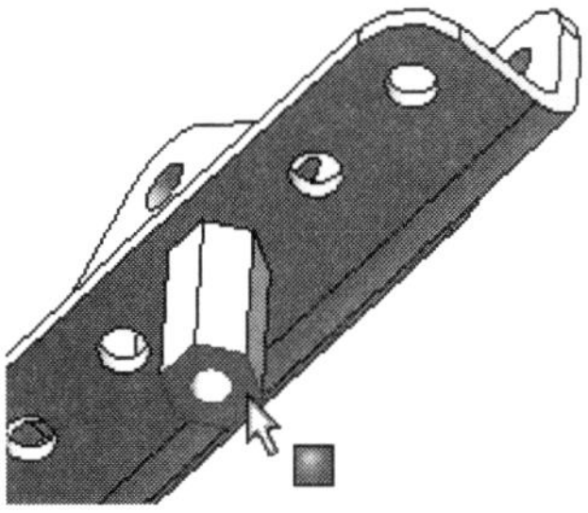

985) Click the Green Check mark.

Insert a Parallel Mate.

986) Click the **FRONT-SUPPORT Front Plane** from the fly-out FeatureManager.

987) **Show** the LINKAGE assembly.

988) Click the **LINKAGE Front Plane** from the fly-out FeatureManager.

989) Click **Parallel**.

990) Click the Green Check mark.

991) Click **OK** from the Mate PropertyManager.

992) **Hide** the LINKAGE assembly.

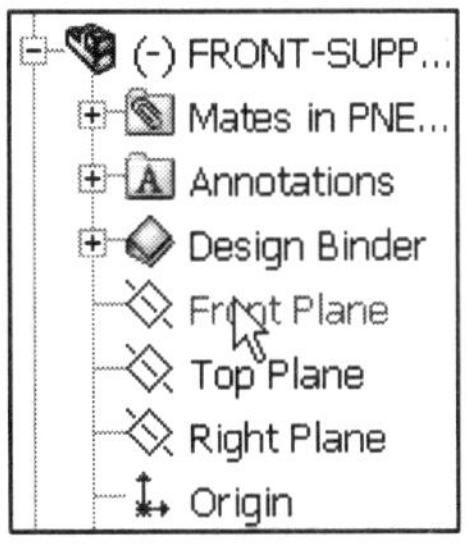

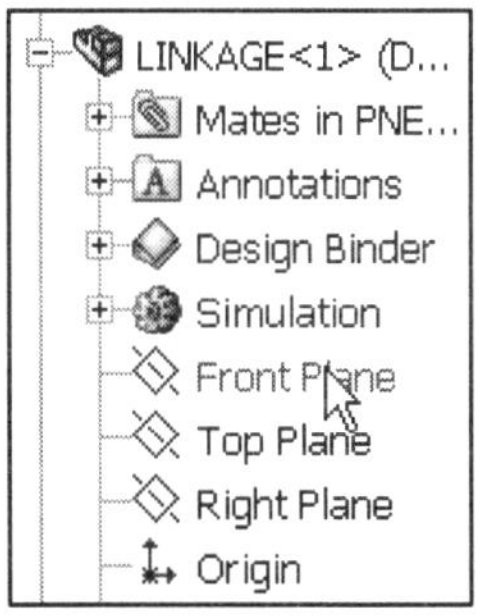

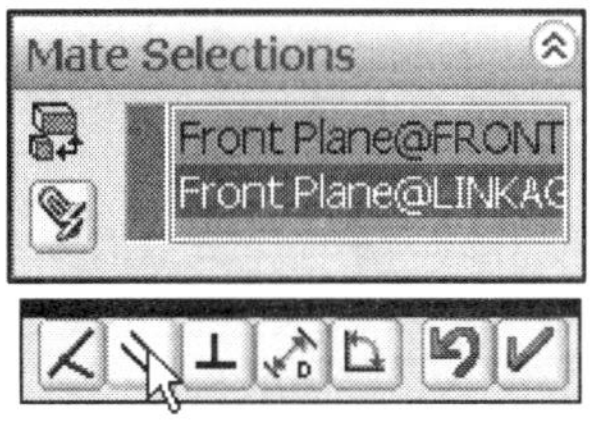

Save the PNEUMATIC-TEST-MODULE assembly.

993) Click **Save**.

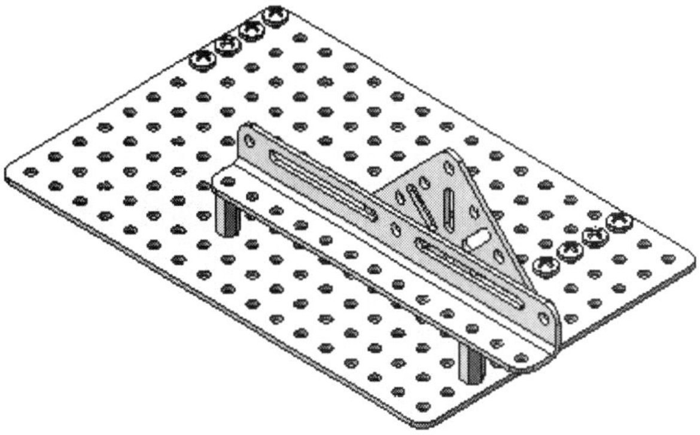

Mirrored Components

Create new components by mirroring existing parts or sub-assemblies. New components are created as copied geometry or mirrored geometry.

A mirrored component is sometimes called a "right-hand" version of the original "left hand" version.

The copied or mirrored component changes, when the original component is modified.

A mirrored component creates a new document. The default document prefix is mirror. A copied component does not create a new document.

Suppressed components in the original sub-assembly are not mirrored or copied. The SCREW parts in the FRONT-SUPPORT assembly are not copied.

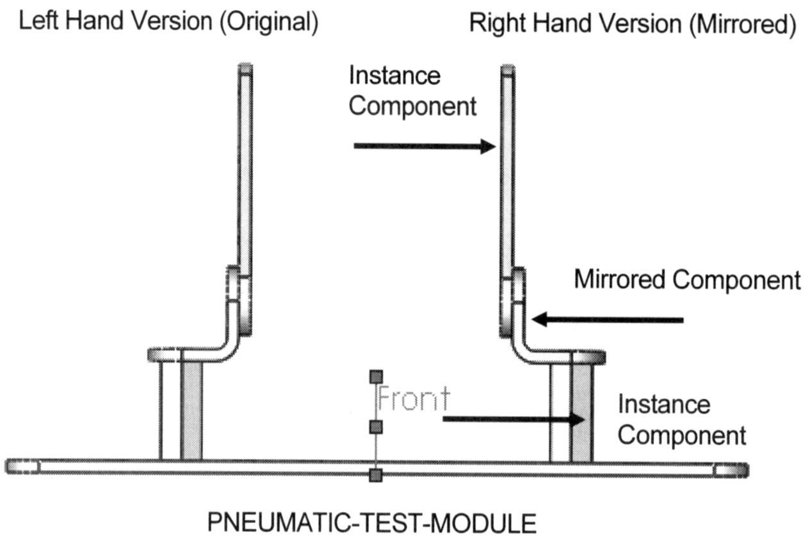

Activity: PNEUMATIC-TEST-MODULE Assembly: Mirrored Component

Insert a Mirrored Component.

994) Click **Insert**, **Mirror Components** from the Main menu. The Mirror Components PropertyManager is displayed.

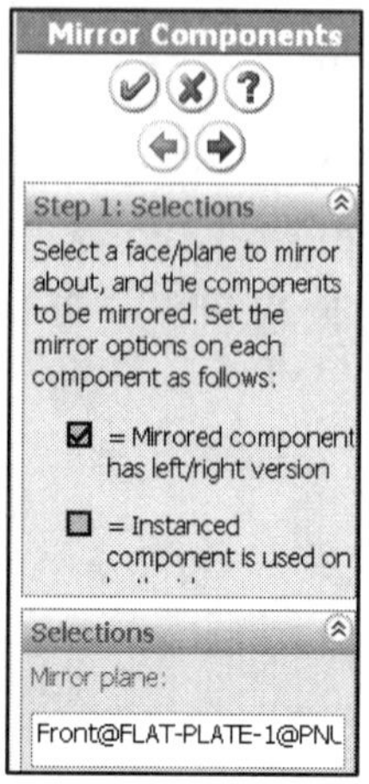

Step 1: The Selections box is displayed. The first Step requires the mirrored plane, the components to mirror, and the components to copy.

995) **Expand** the PNEUMATIC-TEST-MODULE fly-out FeatureManager.

996) Click the **FLAT-PLATE Front Plane**. The Front Plane is displayed in the Mirror plane box.

997) Click the **FRONT-SUPPORT** assembly from the fly-out FeatureManager. The FRONT-SPPORT assembly is displayed in the Components to Mirror box.

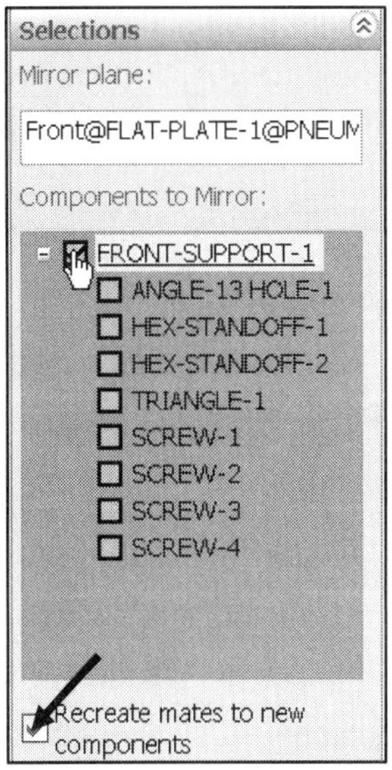

998) **Expand** the FRONT-SUPPORT entry in the Components to Mirror box.

999) Check the **FRONT-SUPPORT-1** box.

1000) Check Recreate mates to new components.

1001) Click **Next**.

Step 2: The Filenames box is displayed. "Mirror" is the default prefix utilized in the mirror part and assembly. MirrorFRONT-SUPPORT is the new assembly name.

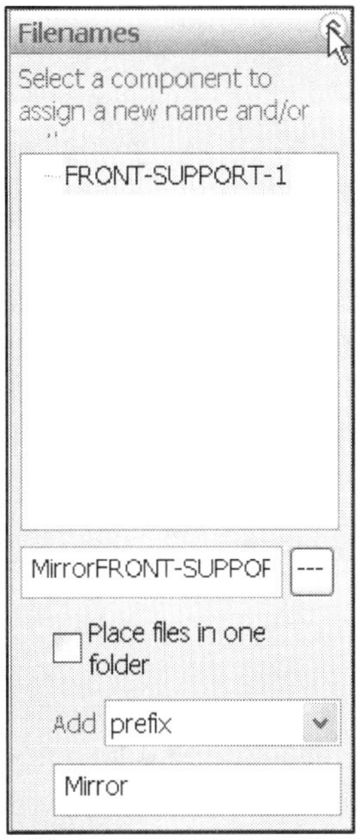

1002) Accept Mirror as the default prefix. Click **Next**.

Step 3: The Orientation box is displayed. The instanced components check box is automatically selected. A preview of the mirrored TRIANGLE and HEX-STANDOFF parts are displayed.

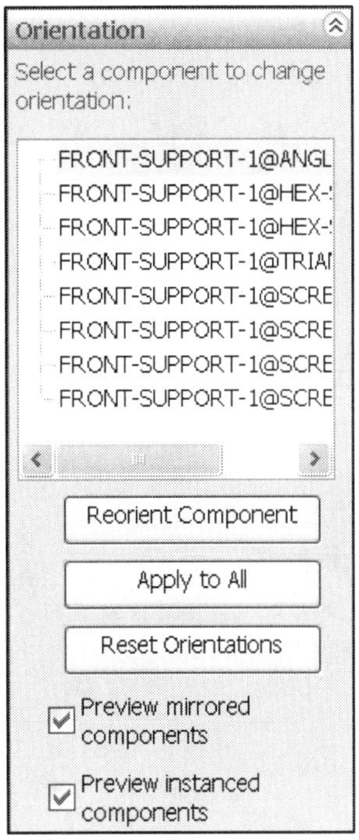

1003) Check **Preview mirrored components**. The ANGLE-13HOLE part is displayed in a preview in the Graphics window.

1004) Click **OK** from the Mirrored Components PropertyManager.

1005) Click **OK** from the New SolidWorks Document dialog box. Assembly is the default template.

Note: Select suppressed components and their Mates to be mirrored in the Components to Mirror box.

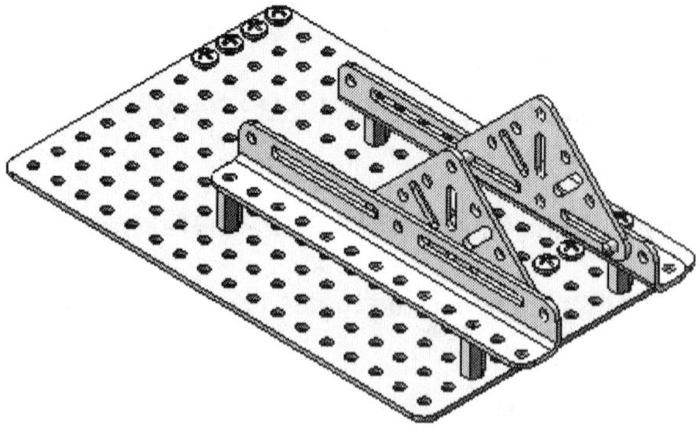

The MirrorFRONT-SUPPORT, TRIANGLE, ANGLE-13HOLE, and SCREW components are mated.

Utilize the Fix option to mate the MirrorFRONT-SUPPORT to its current location in the PNEUMATIC-TEST-MODULE. No other Mates are required.

Activity: PNEUMATIC-TEST-MODULE-Fix the MIRRORFRONT-SUPPORT

Fix the MirrorFRONT-SUPPORT.

1006) Right-click **MirrorFRONT-SUPPORT** from the FeatureManager.

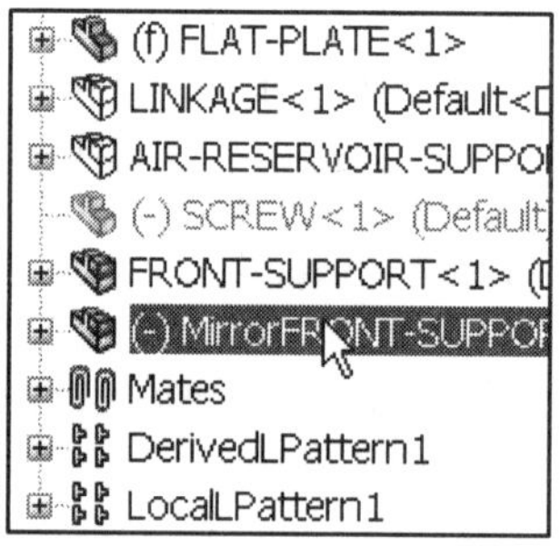

1007) Click **Fix**. The MirrorFRONT assembly is fixed in the PNEUMATIC-TEST-MODULE assembly. The MirrorFRONT-SUPPORT does not move or rotate.

Display the LINKAGE assembly.

1008) Right-click **LINKAGE** in the FeatureManager.

1009) Click **Show**.

Save the PNUEMATIC-TEST-MODULE assembly.

1010) Click **Save** .

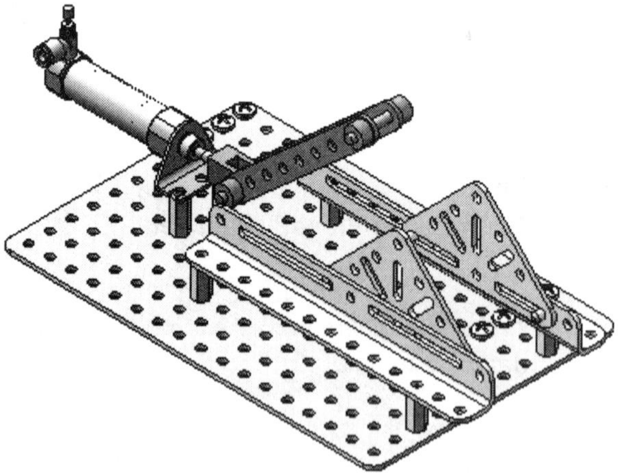

 Reuse geometry in the assembly. Utilize Mirror Component to create a left and right version of parts and assemblies.

Component Properties

Component Properties control the flexibility of the sub-assembly when inserted into an assembly. Components do not translate or rotate after insertion into the assembly.

The FLATBAR parts in the LINKAGE assembly do not rotate after insertion into the PNEUMATIC TEST MODULE assembly. The LINKAGE assembly is in the Rigid State.

Insert the WHEEL-AND-AXLE assembly into the PNEUMATIC-TEST-MODULE assembly. Modify the Mate state of the LINKAGE assembly from the Rigid State to the Flexible State. The LINKAGE assembly is free to rotate.

Modify the Mate State of the AIRCYLINDER assembly from the Rigid State to the Flexible State.

The AIRCYLINDER assembly is free to translate.

Activity: PNEUMATIC-TEST-MODULE Assembly-Insert WHEEL-AND-AXLE Assembly

Insert the WHEEL-AND-AXLE assembly.

1011) Click **Insert Component** from the Assembly toolbar. The Insert Component PropertyManager is displayed.

1012) Click **Browse**.

1013) Select **Assembly** for Files of type.

1014) Double-click the **WHEEL-AND-AXLE** assembly from the SW-TUTORIAL-2007 folder.

1015) Click a **position** above the FLAT-PLATE part as illustrated.

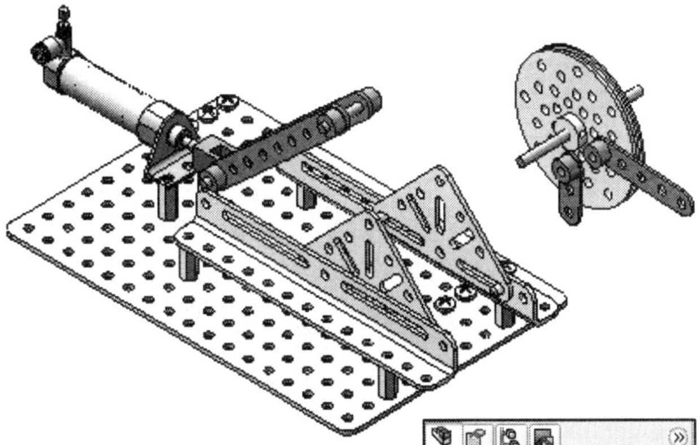

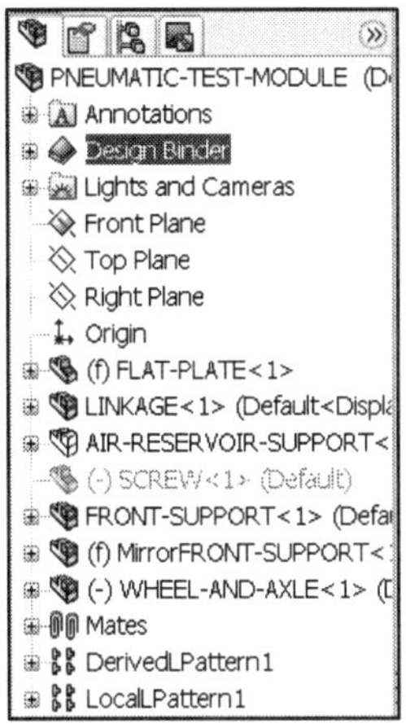

Create a Concentric Mate.

1016) Click **Mate** from the Assembly toolbar.

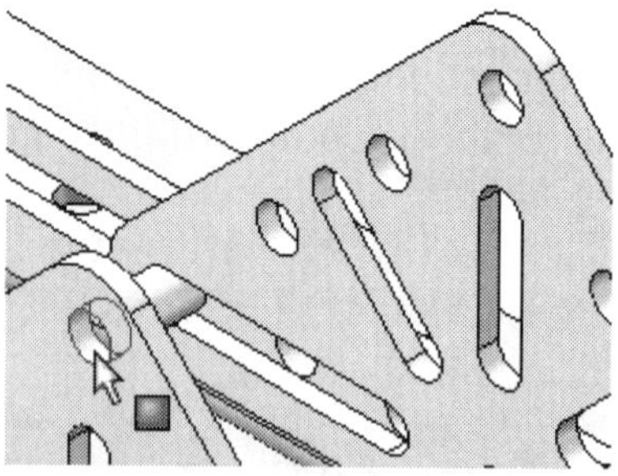

1017) Click the AXLE3000 cylindrical face.

1018) Click the inside **TRIANGLE top hole** face. The selected faces are displayed in the Mate Selections box. Concentric is selected by default.

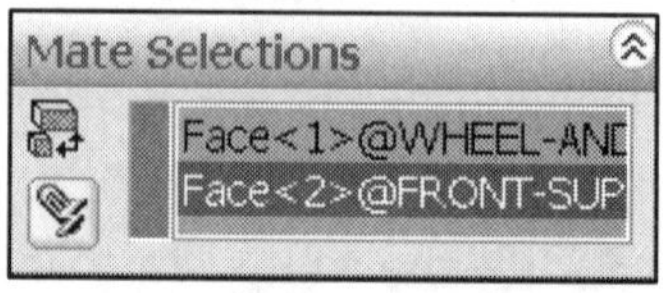

1019) Click the Green Check mark.

Create a Coincident Mate.

1020) Click the **WHEEL-AND-AXLE Front Plane** from the fly-out FeatureManager.

1021) Click the **LINKAGE Front Plane** from the fly-out FeatureManager. Coincident is selected by default.

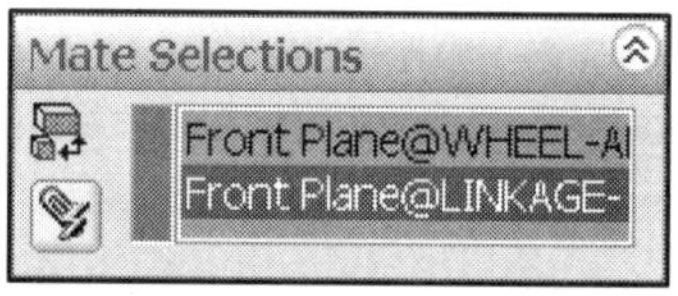

1022) Click the Green Check mark.

1023) Click **OK** from the Mate PropertyManager.

A Concentric Mate is required between the left hole of the FLATBAR-3HOLE and right AXLE of the LINKAGE assembly.

DO NOT INSERT A CONCENTRIC MATE AT THIS TIME!

A Concentric Mate will result in Mate errors.

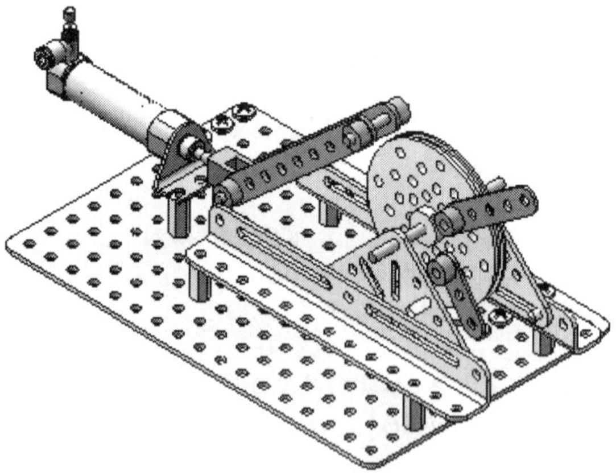

The WHEEL-AND-AXLE is free to rotate in the PNEUMATIC-TEST-MODULE assembly. The LINKAGE assembly interferes with the WHEEL-AND-AXLE. The LINKAGE assembly is not free to rotate or translate. Mate errors will occur.

Sub-assemblies within the LINKAGE assembly are in a Rigid Mate state when inserted into the PNEUMATIC-TEST-MODULE assembly. Remove the Rigid Mate state and insert a Concentric Mate between the LINKAGE assembly and the WHEEL-AND-AXLE.

Activity: PNEUMATIC-TEST-MODULE Assembly-Remove Rigid state

Remove the Rigid State.

1024) Right-click the **LINKAGE** assembly from the FeatureManager.

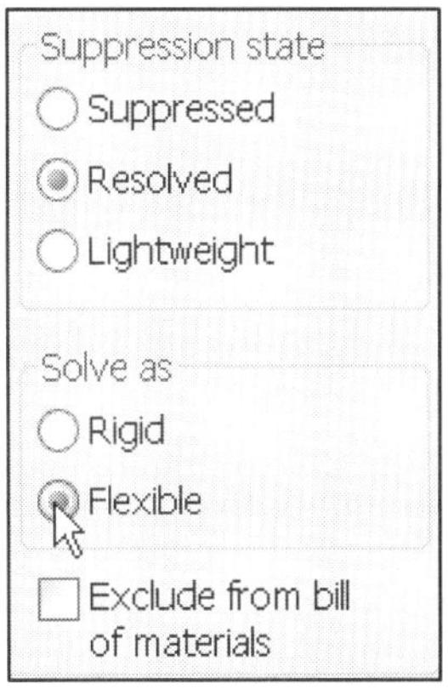

1025) Click Component Properties.

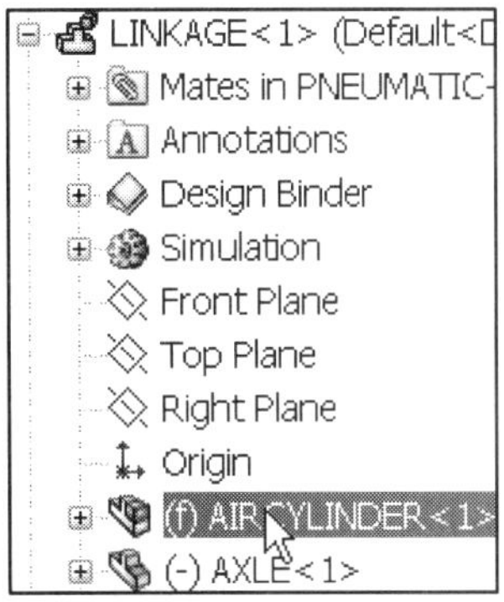

1026) Check **Flexible** in the Solve as box.

1027) Click **OK** from the Component Properties dialog box.

1028) Right-click the **AIRCYLINDER** assembly from the FeatureManager.

1029) Click Component Properties.

1030) Check **Flexible** in the Solve as box.

1031) Click **Flexible** in the Referenced configuration box.

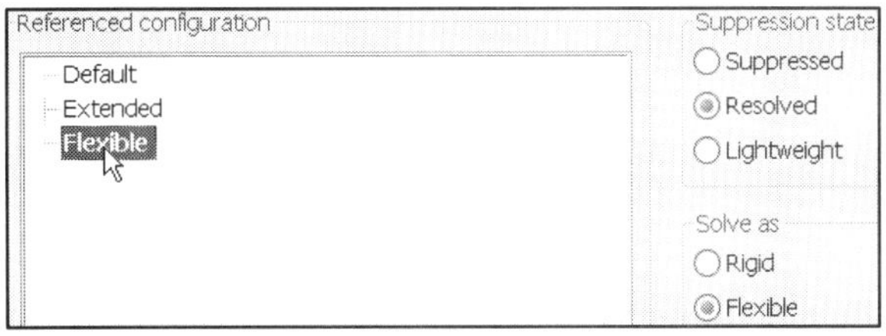

1032) Click **OK** from the Component Properties dialog box.

Hide the FRONT-SUPPORT assembly.

1033) Right-click **FRONT-SUPPORT** from the FeatureManager.

1034) Click **Hide** Hide.

Move the LINKAGE assembly.

1035) Click and drag the **front FLATBAR-9HOLE** downward. The FLATBAR-9HOLE rotates about the left AXLE.

1036) Click a **position** below the WHEEL-AND-AXLE.

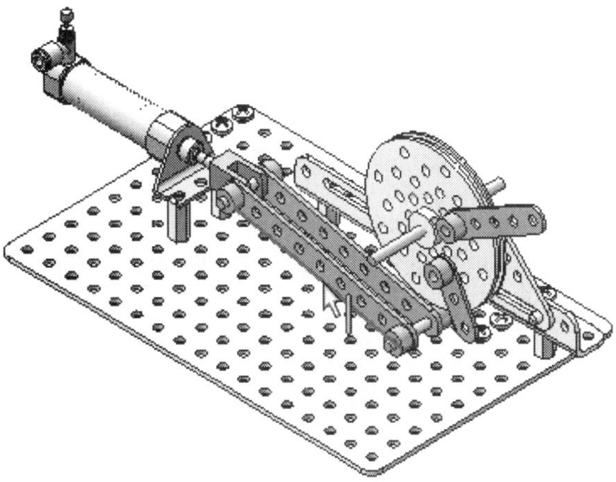

Insert a Concentric Mate.

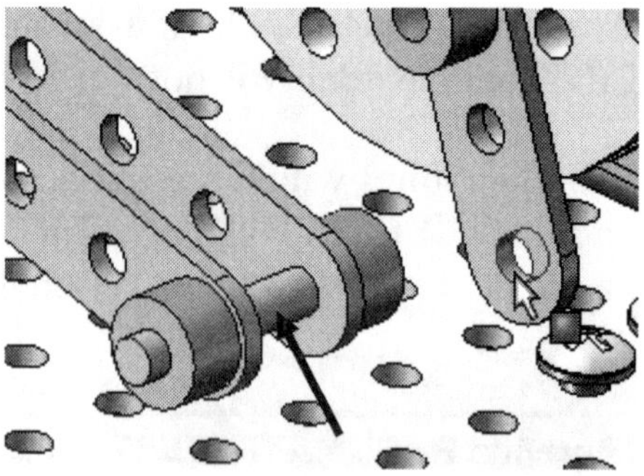

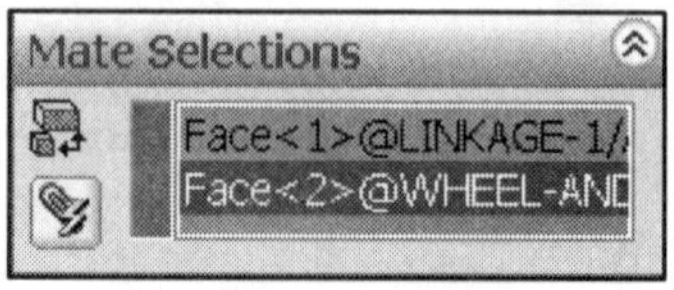

1037) Click **Mate** Mate from the Assembly toolbar.

1038) Click the second bottom **AXLE** face of the LINKAGE assembly.

1039) Click the **left hole** of the FLATBAR-3HOLE. Concentric is the default.

1040) Click the Green Check mark.

1041) Click **OK** from the Mate PropertyManager.

Save the PNEUMATIC-TEST-MODULE assembly.

1042) Click Isometric view.

1043) Click **Save**.

The AIRCYLINDER assembly is inserted in a Rigid state by default. The AIRCYLINDER contains three configurations:

- Default.
- Extended.
- Flexible.

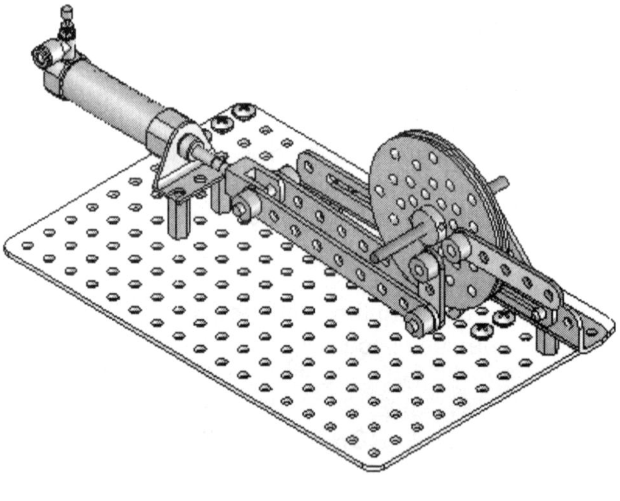

Open the AIRCYLINDER assembly. Modify the configuration to Flexible. Open the LINKAGE assembly. Modify the AIRCYLINDER Component Properties from Default to Flexible.

Activity: PNEUMATIC-TEST-MODULE Assembly-Review AIRCYLINDER configurations

Review the AIRCYLINDER configurations.

1044) Right-click **LINKAGE** from the PNEUMATIC-TEST-MODULE FeatureManager.

1045) Click Open Assembly.

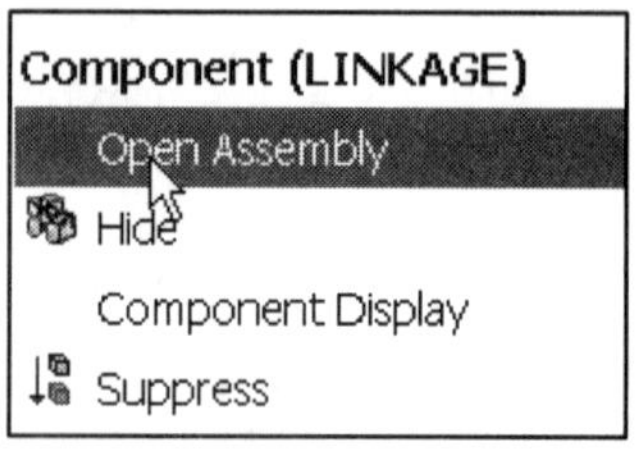

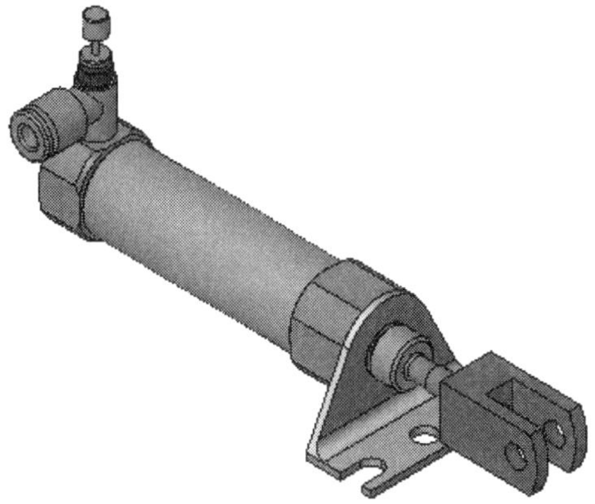

1046) Right-click **AIRCYLINDER** in the LINKAGE FeatureManager.

1047) Click Open Assembly.

1048) Click the **Configuration Manager** tab at the top of the AIRCYLINDER FeatureManager. Three configurations are displayed: Default, Extended and Flexible. Note: The current Default configuration sets the Piston Rod at 0 mm.

Display the Extended Configuration.

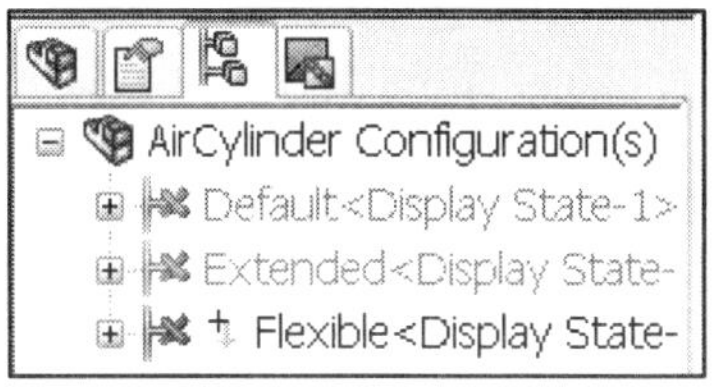

1049) Double-click **Extended**. The Piston Rod of the AIRCYLINDER extends 25mm.

Display the Flexible Configuration.

1050) Double-click **Flexible**. Click the **Rod-Clevis** in the Graphics window.

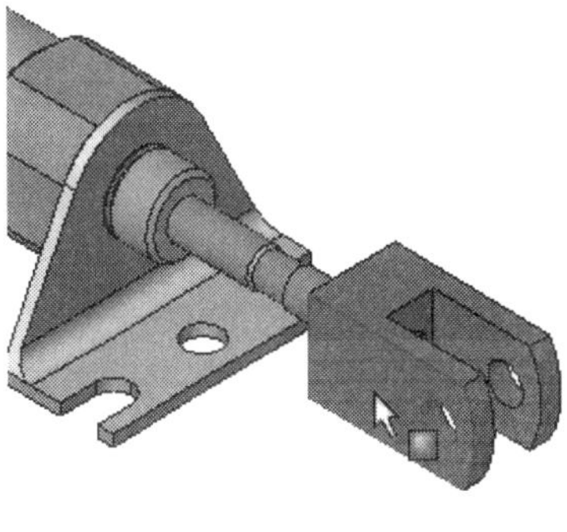

1051) Click and drag the **Piston Rod** from left to right.

1052) Click a **position** near its original location. The AIRCYLINDER remains in the Flexible configuration for the rest of this project.

Update the LINKAGE assembly.

1053) Click **Window**, **LINKAGE** from the Main menu.

1054) The current configuration of the AIRCYLINDER part in the LINKAGE assembly is Default. Modify the configuration. Right-click **AIRCYLINDER** from the LINKAGE assembly FeatureManager.

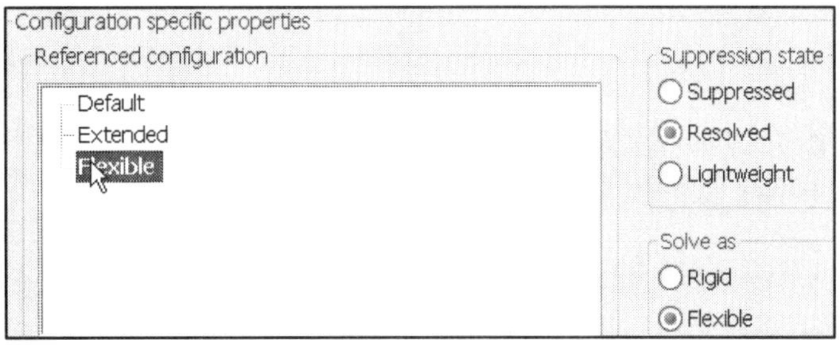

1055) Click Component Properties.

1056) Click **Flexible** for Solve as.

1057) Click **Flexible** for Referenced configuration.

1058) Click **OK**. The AIRCYLINDER displays the Flexible configuration next to its name in the FeatureManager.

Update the PNEUMATIC-TEST-MODULE.
1059) Click **Window**, **PNEUMATIC-TEST-MODULE** assembly from the Main menu.

Move the ROD-CLEVIS.
1060) Click and drag the **ROD-CLEVIS** to the right. The WHEEL rotates in a counterclockwise direction.

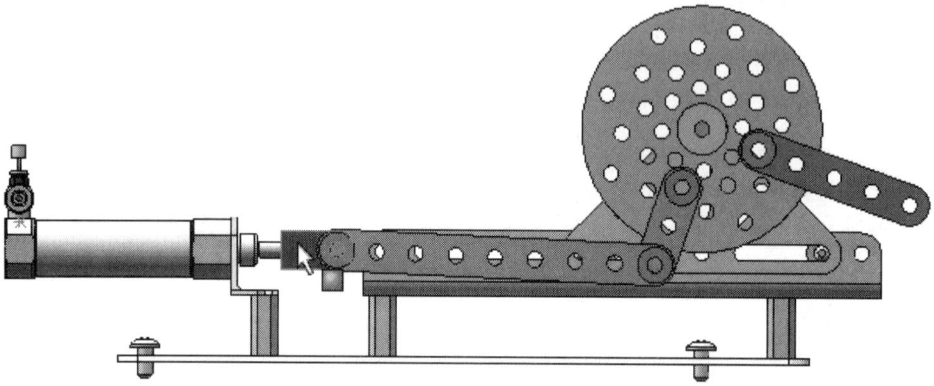

1061) Click and drag the **ROD-CLEVIS** to the left. The WHEEL rotates in a clockwise direction.

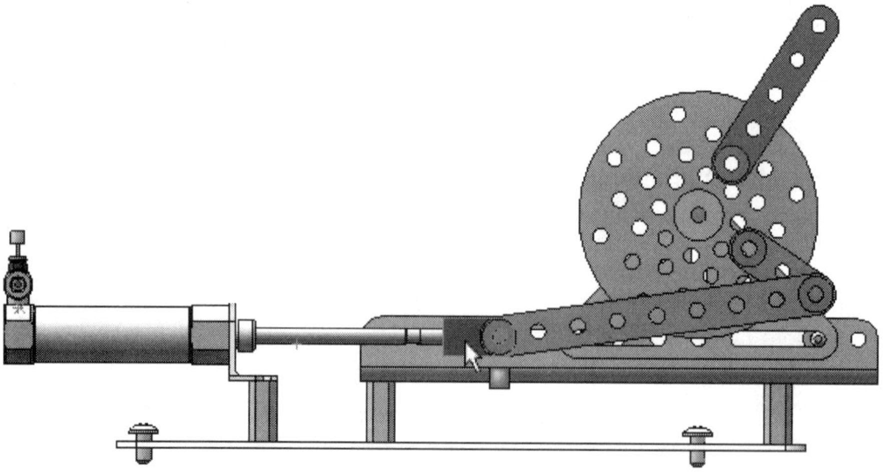

Display the AIR-RESERVOIR-SUPPORT assembly.
1062) Right-click **AIR-RESERVOIR-SUPPORT** in the FeatureManager.

1063) Click **Show**.

Display the second FRONT-SUPPORT assembly.
1064) Right-click **FRONT-SUPPORT** in the FeatureManager.

1065) Click **Show**.

1066) Display the SCREWs in the FRONT-SUPPORT.

Save the PNEUMATIC-TEST-MODULE.
1067) Click Isometric view.

1068) Click **Save**.

1069) Click **Yes** to update referenced documents.

Close All documents.
1070) Click **Windows**, **Close All** from the Main menu.

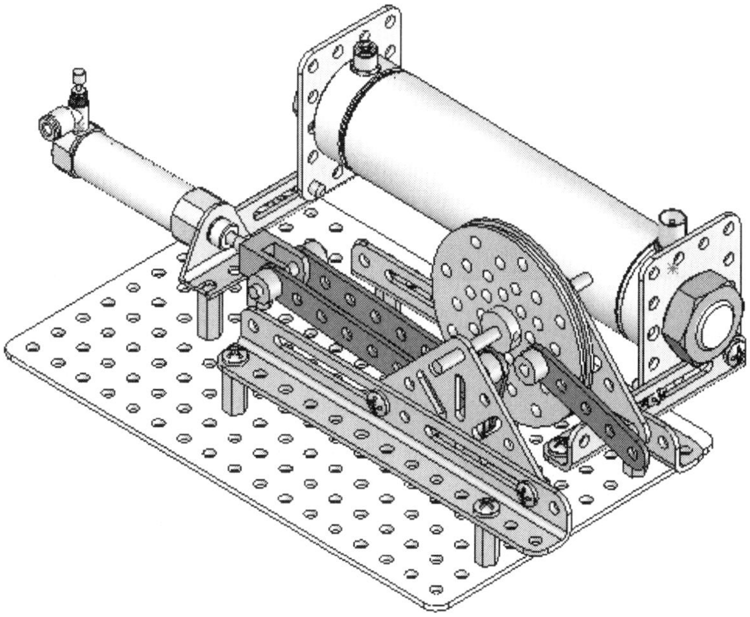

Explore additional parts and assemblies at the end of this project. Add the WEIGHT, HOOK and FLATBAR parts.

Additional details on Show (assembly components), Hide (assembly components), Component (Patterns, Derived), Mirror Component, Configurations, Configuration Manager are available in SolidWorks Help. Select Help, SolidWorks Help topics.

Review the PNEUMATIC-TEST-MODULE Assembly.

The PNEUMATIC TEST MODULE assembly was created by combining four major mechanical sub-assemblies.

The PNEUMATIC TEST MODULE assembly utilized the FLAT-PLATE as the first component. The LINKAGE assembly, AIR-RESERVOIR-SUPPORT assembly, FRONT-SUPPORT assembly and the WHEEL-AND-AXLE assembly were mated to the FLAT-PLATE part.

Work at the lowest assembly level. The LINKAGE assembly required two HEX-STANDOFF parts. The HEX-STANDOFF parts were inserted into the LINKAGE assembly. The LINKAGE assembly was inserted into the PNEUMATIC-TEST-MODULE assembly.

The AIR-RESERVOIR-SUPPORT assembly was inserted into the PNEUMATIC-TEST-MODULE assembly. The SCREW part utilized a Derived Component Pattern and Local Component Pattern to create multiple copies.

The FRONT-SUPPORT assembly was inserted into the PNEUMATIC-TEST-MODULE assembly. The Mirror Component option created a mirrored version of the FRONT-SUPPORT assembly.

The WHEEL-AND-AXLE assembly was inserted into the PNEUMATIC-TEST-MODULE assembly. Component Properties created a Flexible state Mate. The Configuration Manager selected the Flexible configuration for the Air Cylinder assembly.

Create three additional pneumatic sub assemblies utilizing the following components:

- ON/OFF/PURGE VALVE.
- REGULATOR.
- 3WAY SOLENOID VALVE.

Explore these three sub-assemblies in the exercises at the end of this project.

Project Summary

In this project you created six parts. The first three parts utilized new features. The WEIGHT part utilized the Loft feature. The HOOK part utilized the Sweep, Dome and Sweep-Cut features. The WHEEL part utilized the Revolved-Cut feature and Circular Pattern feature.

The second three parts utilized existing parts created in early projects. The HEX-ADAPTER part, AXLE-3000 part and the SHAFTCOLLAR-500 part utilized existing part geometry.

You worked with multiple documents in an assembly. You developed sound assembly modeling techniques that utilized symmetry, component patterns and mirrored components.

The WHEEL-AND-AXLE assembly combined the WHEEL-FLATBAR assembly with the AXLE3000 part, SHAFTCOLLAR-500 part and HEX-ADAPTER part.

The WHEEL-FLATBAR assembly combined the 3HOLE-SHAFTCOLLAR assembly and 5HOLE-SHAFTCOLLAR assembly.

The PNEUMATIC-TEST-MODULE assembly combined four major mechanical sub-assemblies. Organize your assemblies. Create an assembly Layout Diagram to determine the grouping of parts and assemblies.

Project Terminology

Mates: A Mate is a geometric relationship between components in an assembly.

Circular Pattern: A Circular Pattern repeats features or geometry in a polar array. A Circular Patten requires an axis of revolution, the number of instances and an angle.

Component Pattern: There are two methods to define a component pattern in an assembly. A Derive Component Pattern utilizes an existing feature pattern. A Local Component pattern utilizes geometry in the assembly to arrange instances in a Linear or Circular pattern.

Component Properties: The properties of a component, part or assembly are controlled through Component Properties. The Rigid/Flexible Mate State property and Configuration property were explored in this project. Component Properties are used to define visibility and color.

ConfigurationManager: The ConfigurationManager on the left side of the Graphics window is utilized to create, select, and view the configurations of parts and assemblies.

Dome: A Dome feature creates a spherical or elliptical feature from a selected face.

Loft: A Loft feature blends two or more profiles. Each profile is sketched on a separate plane.

Mirror Component: A mirror component creates a mirrored or copied part or assembly. A mirrored component is sometimes called a "right-hand" version of the original "left hand" version.

Replace: The Replace command substitutes one or more open instances of a component in an assembly with a different component.

Revolved Cut: A Revolved Cut removes material. A sketched profile is revolved around a centerline. The Revolved Cut requires a direction and an angle of revolution.

Sweep: A Sweep feature adds/removes material by moving a profile along a path. A basic Sweep feature requires two sketches. The first sketch is called the path. The second sketch is called profile. The profile and path are sketched on perpendicular planes.

Engineering Journal

1. Engineers research, specify and test the components utilized in their designs. The PNEUMATIC TEST MODULE assembly was partially completed in this project. Additional pneumatic components are required.

The Regulator utilizes a plastic knob to control the pressure from the Air Reservoir.

The Knob controls the Pressure at P2 by adjusting the screw loading on the setting Spring. The Main valve is held open, allowing flow from the inlet, P1 to the outlet, P2. When the air consumption rate drops, the force at P2 increases. This increase in force causes the Diaphragm to drop maintaining the constant pressure through the valve.

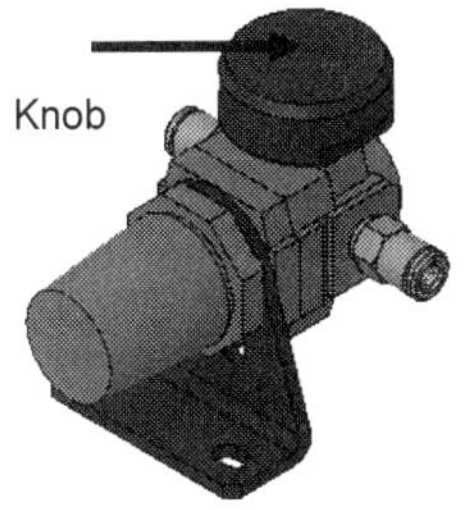

Regulator Assembly Courtesy of SMC Corporation of America

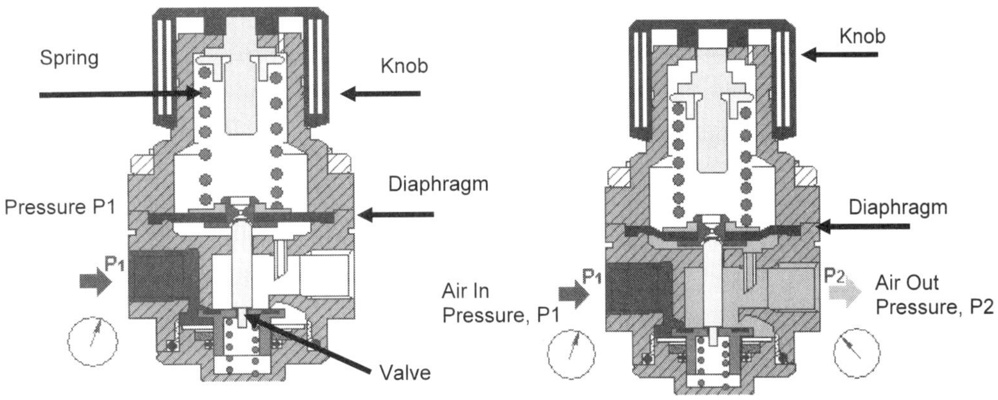

Images Courtesy of SMC Corporation of America

Utilize the World Wide Web to research different types of Air Regulators. What design parameters are required for the Regulator before placing an order to purchase one?

2. Pneumatic Applications.

ON/OFF/PURGE Valve Courtesy of SMC Corporation of America

Plastic components are utilized in a variety of applications. The ON/OFF/PURGE value utilizes plastic components for the Knob and Inlet and Outlet ports.

The ON/OFF/PURGE valve controls the airflow from the Regulator. The valve knob indiates the direction of flow. The valve is Off when the knob is perpendicular to the direction of flow.

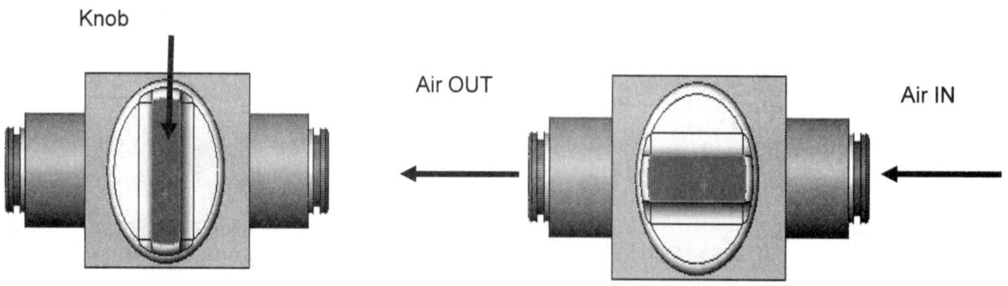

Valve OFF Valve ON

The valve is On when the knob is parallel to the direction of flow.

Write a 2 step operating procedure to instruct your customer how to operate the valve. Indicate the position of the value and the state of the air in each step.

Valve Operating Procedure

1 ______________________________
____
____
2 ______________________________
____

3. Industrial Design and Plastic Manufacturing.

Industrial designers begin with conceptual sketches to develop new products. Notion Development designed an injection-molded bottle for the company, Clubwa.

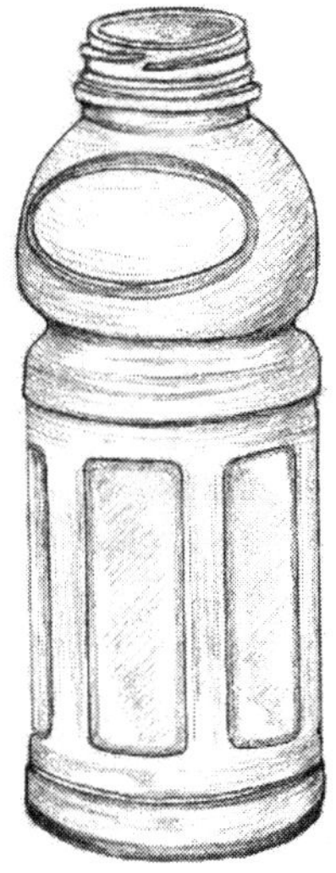

Conceptual Sketch

From the conceptual sketch, the engineer determines the necessary plastic manufacturing processes and materials required to produce the product that the customer wanted.

The bottle is created with a blow mold technique that utilizes the material, polyethylene terephthalate. The pre-form is an injection molded part utilized in the blow mold process. The pre-form is inserted into the blow mold machine to produce the bottle.

The bottle is filled with Clubwa's Oxygenized Elixir at temperatures above 80°C. High temperature reduces bacteria, which increase shelf life of the product.

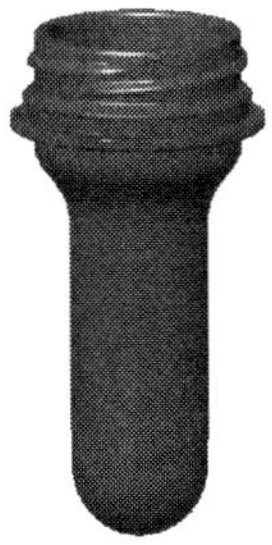

Pre-form Part Injected Molded Part

Clubwa Bottle design by Notion Development

Sketches and Models courtesy of Bob Caldicott, Notion Development for Clubwa.

In hot filling, thermal energy relieves molecular stress, resulting in a loss in volume and a pressurized container. As the product cools, a vacuum is formed inside the container.

Utilize the World Wide Web to determine other products that utilize a blow mold manufacturing process.

4. Sketch FLATBAR Parts.

Sketch the front view of the FLATBAR configurations that contain 11, 13, 15, and 17 holes. Determine the center-to-center distance between the first hole and the last hole for each FLATBAR configuration.

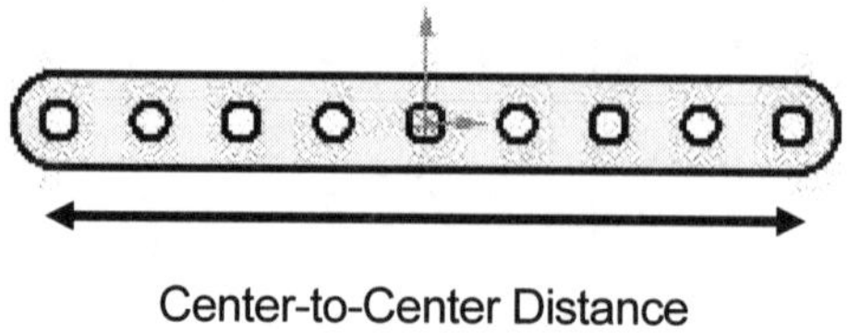

FLATBAR-11HOLE.

FLATBAR-13HOLE.

FLATBAR-15HOLE.

FLATBAR-17HOLE.

Questions

1. What is the minimum number of profiles and planes required for a Loft feature?
2. A Sweep feature requires a ___________ and a ______________.
3. Describe the differences between a Loft feature and a Sweep feature.
4. Identify the three default reference planes in an assembly.
5. True of False. A Revolved-Cut feature requires an axis of revolution.
6. True or False. A Circular Pattern contains only one feature to pattern.
7. Describe the difference between a Sweep Boss/Base feature and a Sweep Cut feature.
8. Identify the type of Geometric Relations that can be added to a Sketch.
9. What function does the Save as copy check box perform when saving a part under a new name?
10. True or False. Never reuse geometry from one part to create another part.
11. Describe 5 assembly techniques utilized in this project.
12. True or False. A fixed component cannot move and is locked to the Origin.
13. Describe the purpose of an assembly layout diagram.
14. Describe the difference between a Derived and Local Component Pattern.
15. Describe the difference between copied geometry and mirrored geometry utilizing the Mirror Component command.
16. True of False. An assembly contains one or more configurations.
17. Review the Design Intent section in the Introduction. Identify how you incorporated design intent into the assembly.
18. Review the Keyboard Short Cut keys in the Appendix. Identify the Short Cut keys you incorporated into this project.

Exercises

Exercise 4.1: WEIGHT-LINK Assembly.

Create the WEIGHT-LINK assembly. Utilize the AXLE, FLATBAR; 7HOLE configuration, HOOK and WEIGHT parts.

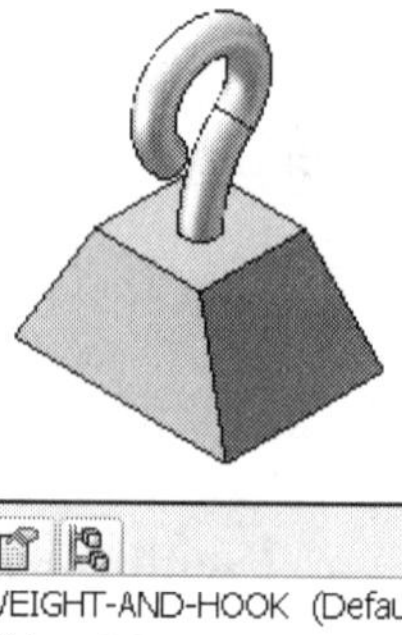

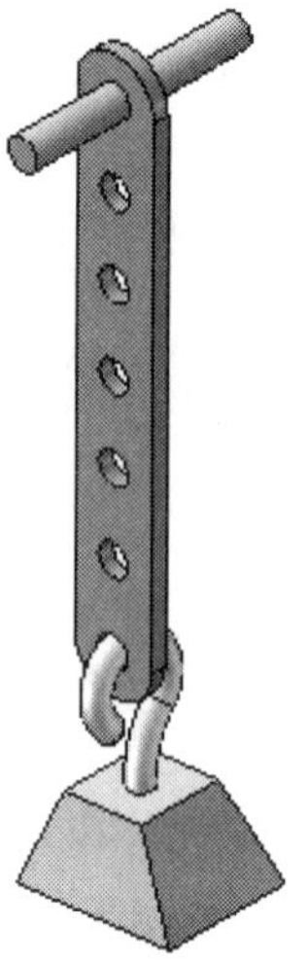

- Create a new assembly named WEIGHT-AND-HOOK using the WEIGHT and HOOK parts.
- Create a new assembly named WEIGHT-LINK. Insert the AXLE, FLATBAR - 7Hole configuration, and the WEIGHT-AND-HOOK assembly.

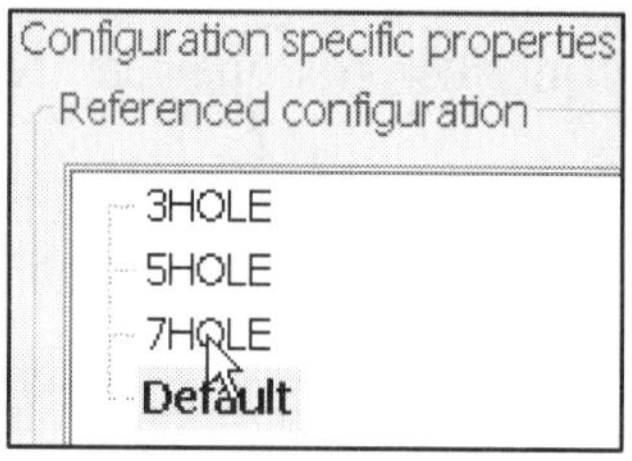

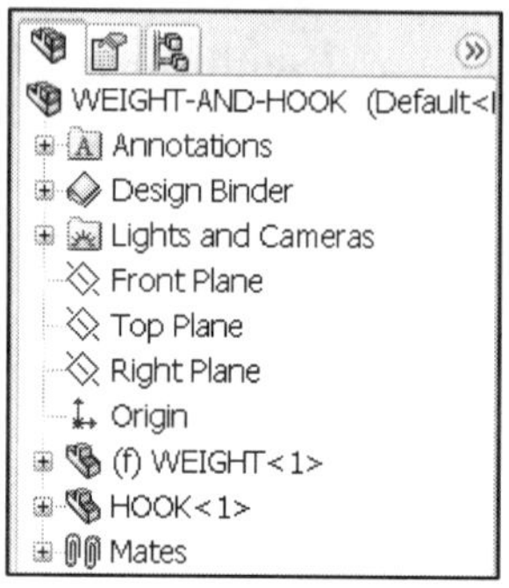

- Insert the correct mates for these two assemblies.

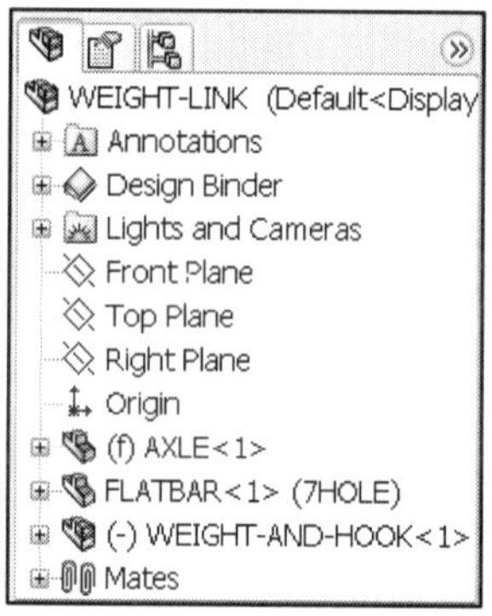

There is more than one mating technique for this exercise. Incorporate symmetry into the assembly. Divide large assemblies into smaller subassemblies.

Exercise 4.2: REGULATOR-STANDOFF Assembly.

The REGULATOR assembly is a pneumatic component. The SMC REGULATOR assembly is available in the pneumtatic component models to download from the CD in the book. The REGULATOR assembly cannot be directly fastened to the PNEUMATIC-TEST-MODULE assembly. The slotted holes in the bracket do not fit directly onto the FLAT-PLATE.

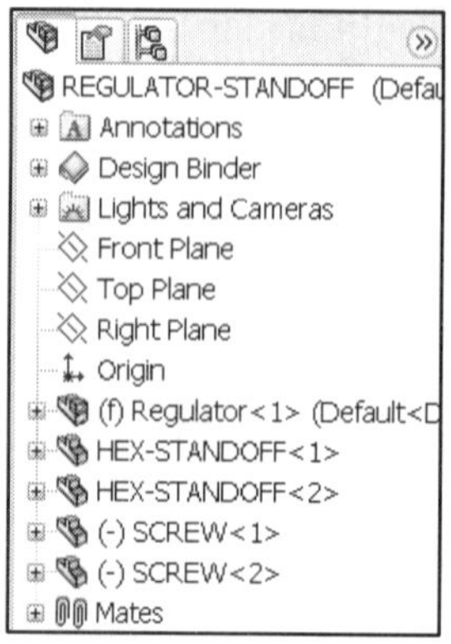

- Insert two HEX-STANDOFF parts. Note: Use the View, Temporary Axis option.
- Insert two SCREWs as illustrated.

Exercise 4.3: VALVE-BRACKET Assembly.

The ON-OFF-PURGE-VALVE assembly cannot be directly fastened to the FLAT-PLATE.

- Create the SERVO-BRACKET part on the Top plane.

The VALVE-BRACKET assembly consists of the ON-OFF-PURGE-VALVE assembly, the SERVO-BRACKET and two HEX-STANDOFF parts.

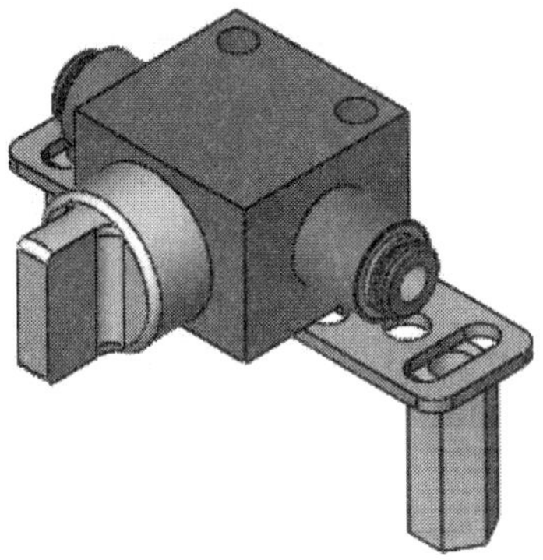

The SMC ON-OFF-PURGE VALVE assembly is available in the pneumtatic component models on the Multimedia CD.

- The Servo Bracket Part is machined from 0.09in, [2.7mm] Stainless Steel flat stock.
- The ∅4.2mm, [.165in] Mounting Holes fasten to the back Slot Cuts of the Servo Bracket.
- The Servo Bracket default units are inches. The Purge-Valve Assembly default units are millimeters.
- Engineers and designers work with components in multiple units such as inches and millimeters. Utilize Tools, Options, Document Properties, Units to check default units and precision.

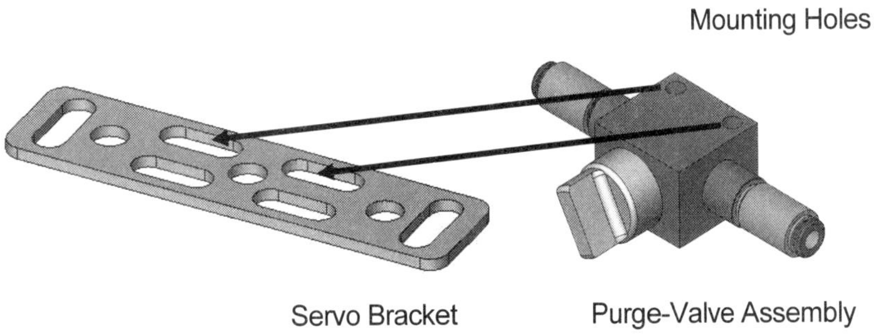

The Servo Bracket Part illustration represents part dimensions, only.

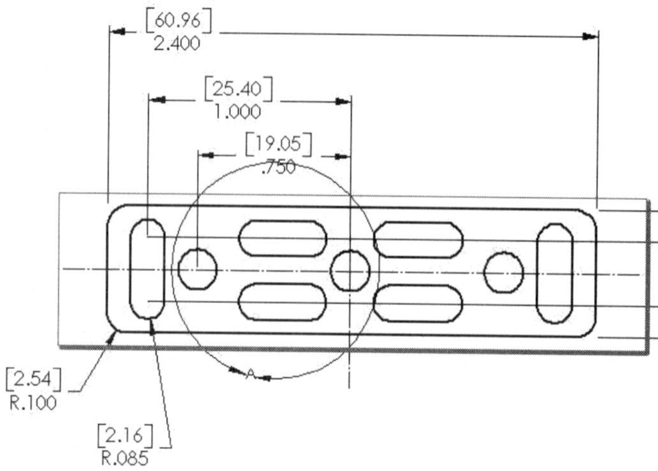

Servo Bracket
Part Dimensions

- Locate the center circle at the part Origin.
- Utilize a Mirror Feature.
- Utilize a Distance Mate to align the Mounting Holes of the ON-OFF-PURGE-VALVE Valve to the Slot Cuts of the Servo Bracket.

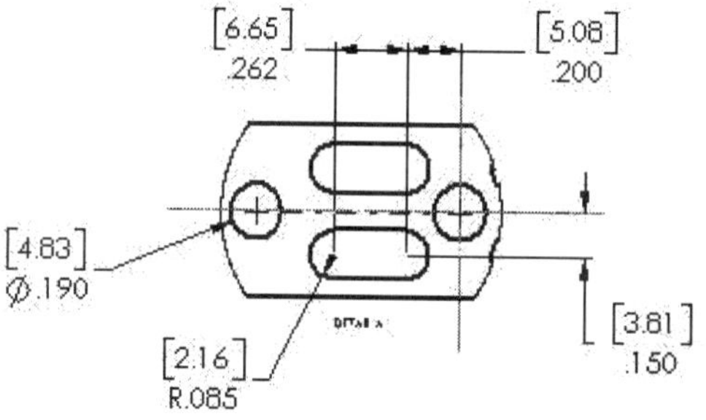

Detail A

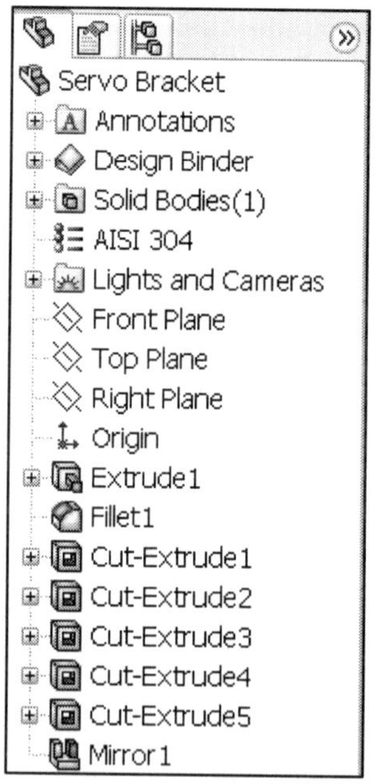

The valve knob indicates the direction of flow. The valve is off when the knob is perpendicular to the direction of flow.

The valve is on when the knob is parallel to the direction of flow.

Review the ON-OFF-PURGE-VALVE Configurations and Mates. The Angle Mate controls the orientation of the Knob.

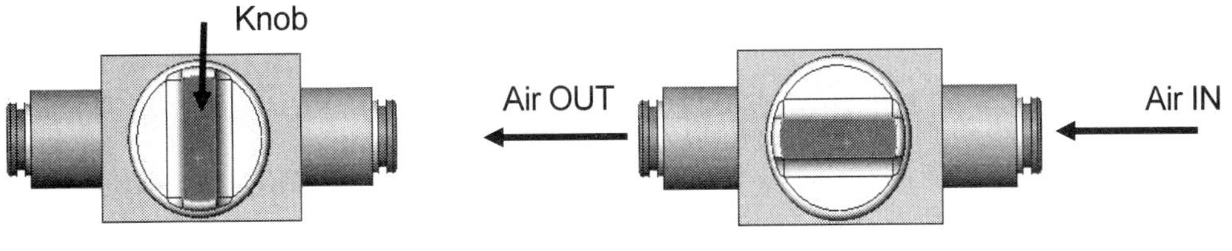

Valve OFF Valve ON

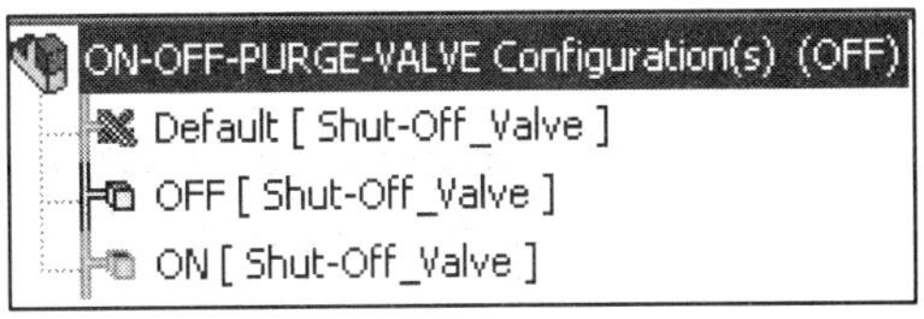

Exercise 4.4: FLATBAR Design Table.

- Create FLATBAR configurations with a Design Table.

The configurations contain 11, 13, 15, and 17 holes.

	A	B	C	D	E	F	G
1	Design Table for: FLATBAR						
2		D1@Sketch1	D2@Sketch1	D1@Extrude1	D1@Sketch3	D3@LPattern1	D1@LPattern1
3	Default	4.000	0.25	0.09	0.19	0.5	9
4	11HOLE	5.000	0.25	0.09	0.19	0.5	11
5	13HOLE	6.000	0.25	0.09	0.19	0.5	13
6	15HOLE	7.000	0.25	0.09	0.19	0.5	15
7	17HOLE	8.000	0.25	0.09	0.19	0.5	17
8							
9							
10							

Sheet1

Exercise 4.5: SOLENOID-VALVE Assembly and PNEUMATIC-TEST-MODULE Assembly.

The 3Way SOLENOID-VALVE utilizes a plastic housing to protect the internal electronic components. The 3Way Solenoid value controls the electrical operation of to the AIRCYLINDER.

The Solenoid acts like a switch. The SOLENOID-VALVE is assembled to the PNEUMATIC-TEST-MODULE with cable ties.

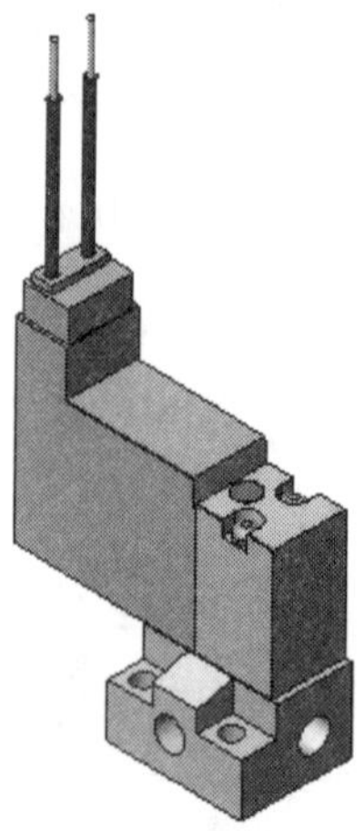

3WAY SOLENOID VALVE
Courtesy of SMC Corporation of America

Insert the following components into PNEUMATIC TEST MODULE assembly:

- SOLENOID-VALVE assembly.
- VAVLE-BRACKET assembly.
- REGULATOR-STANDOFF assembly.
- WEIGHT-AND-LINK assembly.

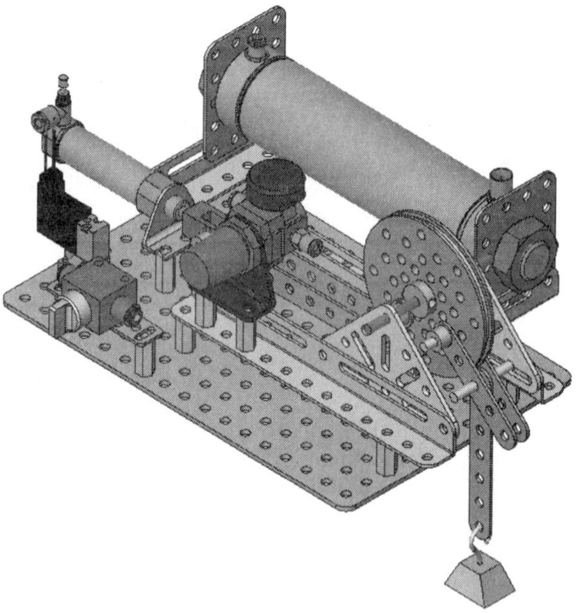

Exercise 4.6: Drive Motor Mount assembly.

- Create the Drive Motor Mount Assembly. The Drive Motor Mount assembly is utilized on a MARS Rover Training Robot (courtesy of Gears Educational Systems). Create the Drive Motor Mount assembly from the components located on the enclosed CD in the book.

- Create an Exploded view that represents how the components would be assembled in manufacturing.

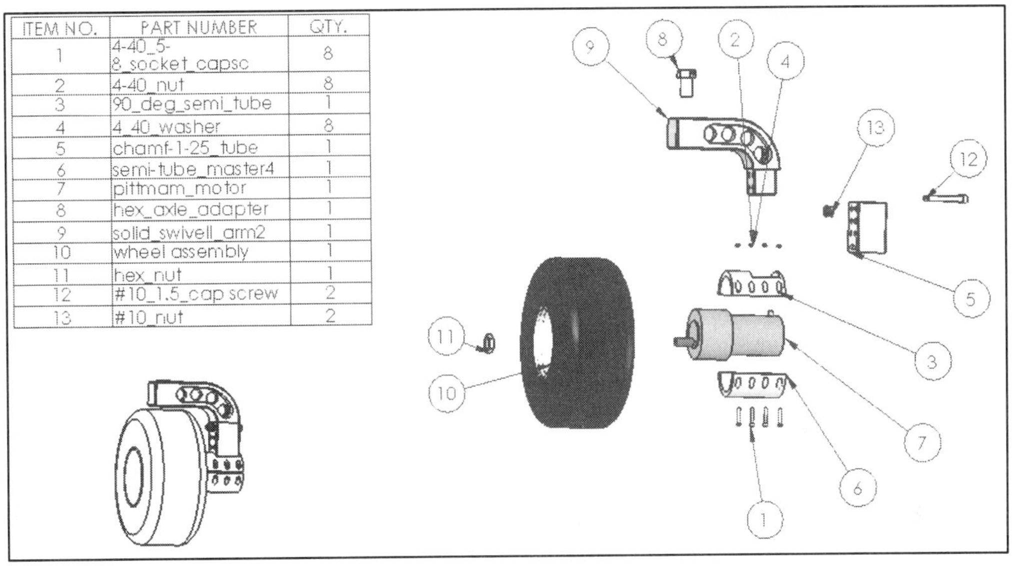

ITEM NO.	PART NUMBER	QTY.
1	4-40_5-8_socket_capsc	8
2	4-40_nut	8
3	90_deg_semi_tube	1
4	4_40_washer	8
5	chamf-1-25_tube	1
6	semi-tube_master4	1
7	pittmam_motor	1
8	hex_axle_adapter	1
9	solid_swivell_arm2	1
10	wheel assembly	1
11	hex_nut	1
12	#10_1.5_cap screw	2
13	#10_nut	2

Exercise 4.7: GEAR-DRIVE Assembly.

Create the GEAR-DRIVE assembly.

The DC Motor shaft drives the 36TOOTH-GEAR. The TIRE, WHEEL, 60TOOTH-GEAR parts are all located on the same axle rod and rotate at the same angular velocity.

The TIRE, 60TOOTH-GEAR, 36TOOTH-GEAR and SHAFT - PLATE2 parts and BearingPlate-Bushing assembly are located on the CD contained with the text. Copy these components to the SW-TUTORIAL file folder.

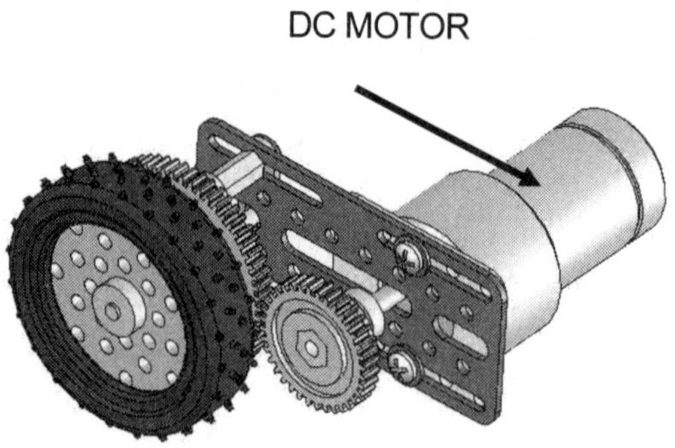

GEAR-DRIVE Assembly
Courtesy of Gears Educational Systems, LLC

You created the other components in the projects and exercises.

Design unknowns:

- The AXLE-ROD length required to mount the WHEEL, TIRE and 60TOOTH-GEAR.
- Clearance distance between the 60TOOTH-GEAR and the WHEEL-TIRE assembly. Stack multiple LARGE-WASHER parts for the clearance distance.
- Mating Distance between the 36TOOTH-GEAR and the 60TOOTH-GEAR.

Utilize your skills to create the following documents:

- Draw an assembly layout listing all parts, sub-assemblies and assemblies on paper.
- In SolidWorks create a top level assembly and sub-assemblies.
- In SolidWorks create a top level assembly drawing and sub-assembly drawings with Bill of Materials.
- In SolidWorks create individual part drawings for machined parts.
- In SolidWorks create exploded view and animation of the GEAR-DRIVE.

Note: Balloons have been enlarged. Actual GearsEds (www.gearseds.com) purchased parts may vary from the model file.

- The IM15-MOUNT PLATE was created in Exercise 2.4.

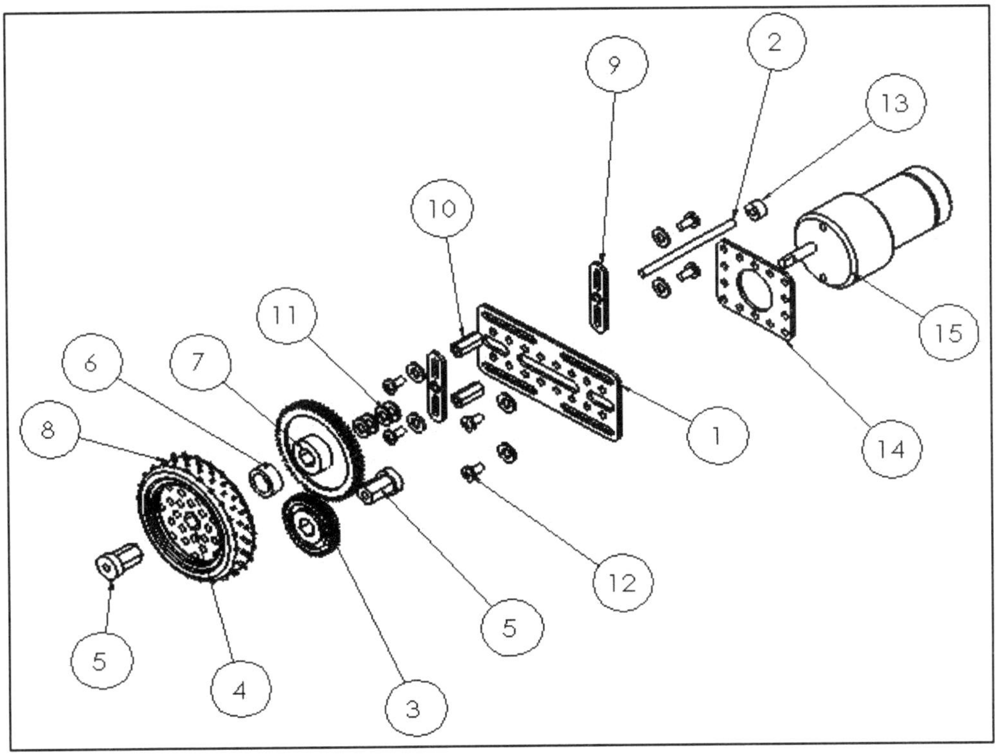

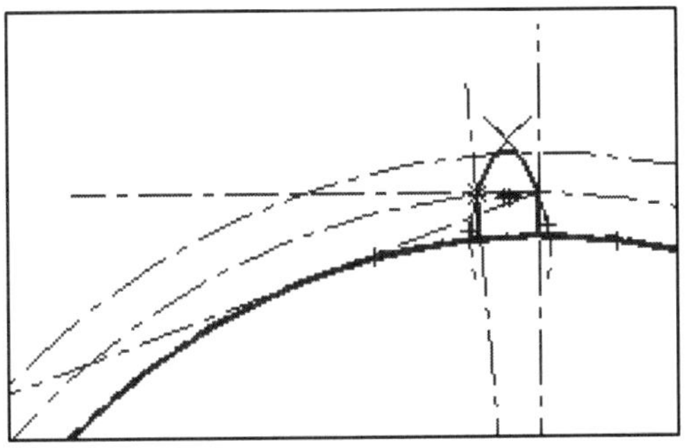

The gears in the assembly utilize imported geometry.

Parts List for GEAR-DRIVE assembly:

ITEM NO.	PART NUMBER:	DESCRIPTION:	QTY:
1	GIDS-SC-10003	SHAFT-PLATE2	1
2	GIDS-SC-10017	AXLE-ROD	1
3	GIDS-SC-60036	36-TOOTH, 24-PITCH GEAR	1
4	GIDS-SC-10014	WHEEL	1
5	GIDS-SC-10013	HEX-ADAPTER	2
6	GIDS-SC-10012-3-16	LARGE-WASHERS	?
7	GIDS-SC-60060	60-TOOTH, 24-PITCH GEAR	1
8	GIDS-SC-10004	TIRE-RUBBER	1
9	GIDS-SC-10010	BEARING PLATE-BUSHING ASM	1
10	GIDS-SC-10015	HEX-STANDOFF	2
11	GIDS-SC-10016-SW	SMALL WASHER ¼ IN	8
12	GIDS-SC-10016-MS	MACHINE SCREW 10-24X3/8	6
13	GIDS-SC-10012-3-16	SMALL SHAFT-COLLAR	1
14	GIDS-SC-10009	IM15-MOUNT PLATE	1
15	GIDS-MC-11515	MOTOR DC	1

Answers will vary. Simplify a large design problem. Create multiple sub-assemblies.

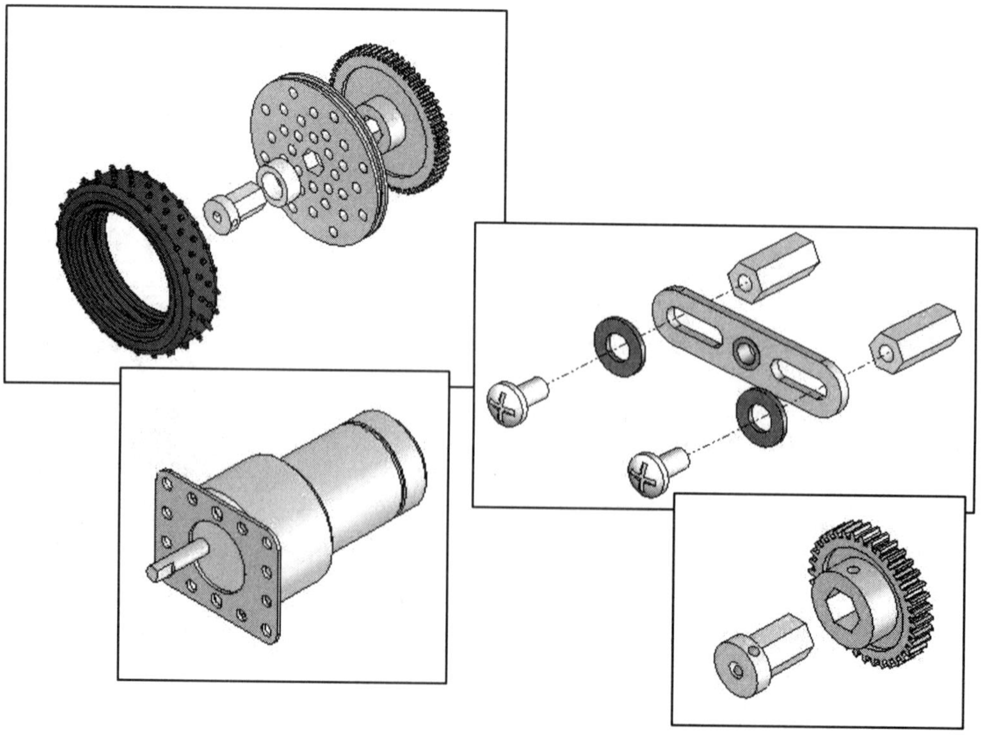

Exercise 4.8: Industry Application.

Automatic Systems, Inc. Kansas City, MO, USA (www.asi.com) designs, manufactures, and installs quality material handling systems.

- Utilize the World Wide Web to investigate the types of industries that require material handling systems.
- Utilize 3DContentCentral to investigate the suppliers of Gearmotors, Bearings and Air Cylinders. Utilize the SolidWorks Manufacturer's Partner Network to determine machine shops and sheet metal shops in your geographical area.
- ASI engineers evaluate their customer's requirements and propose an innovative and cost effective material handling solution. Identify the types of questions you would propose to a potential customer that requires a material handling system.

High Lift Fork Transfer
Courtesy of Automatic Systems, Inc.
Kansas City, MO USA
www.asi.com

Notes:

Engineering Changer Order (ECO)

D&M

Engineering Change Order

ECO # ______________

Page 1 of __

	☐ Hardware		Author
	☐ Software		Date
Product Line	☐ Quality		Authorized Mgr.
	☐ Tech Pubs		Date

Change Tested By

Reason for ECO(Describe the existing problem, symptom and impact on field)

D&M Part No.	Rev From/To	Part Description	Description	Owner

ECO Implementation/Class			Departments	Approvals	Date		
All in Field	☐		Engineering				
All in Test	☐		Manufacturing				
All in Assembly	☐		Technical Support				
All in Stock	☐		Marketing				
All on Order	☐		DOC Control				
All Future	☐						
Material Disposition			ECO Cost				
Rework	☐		DO NOT WRITE BELOW THIS LINE(ECO BOARD ONLY)				
Scrap	☐		Effective Date				
Use as is	☐		Incorporated Date				
None	☐		Board Approval				
See Attached	☐		Board Date				

This text follows the ASME Y14 Engineering Drawing and Related Documentation Practices for drawings. Display of dimensions and tolerances are as follows:

TYPES of DECIMAL DIMENSIONS (ASME Y14.5M)			
Description:	**UNITS: MM**	**Description:**	**UNITS: INCH**
Dimension is less than 1mm. Zero precedes the decimal point.	0.9 0.95	Dimension is less than 1 inch. Zero is not used before the decimal point.	.5 .56
Dimension is a whole number. Display no decimal point. Display no zero after decimal point.	19	Express dimension to the same number of decimal places as its tolerance. Add zeros to the right of the decimal point. If the tolerance is expressed to 3 places, then the dimension contains 3 places to the right of the decimal point.	1.750
Dimension exceeds a whole number by a decimal fraction of a millimeter. Display no zero to the right of the decimal.	11.5 11.51		

TABLE 1 TOLERANCE DISPLAY FOR INCH AND METRIC DIMENSIONS (ASME Y14.5M)		
DISPLAY:	**UNITS: INCH:**	**UNITS: METRIC:**
Dimensions less than 1	.5	0.5
Unilateral Tolerance	$1.417^{+.005}_{-.000}$	$36^{0}_{-0.5}$
Bilateral Tolerance	$1.417^{+.010}_{-.020}$	$36^{+0.25}_{-0.50}$
Limit Tolerance	.571 .463	14.50 11.50

Cursor Feedback

Cursor Feedback provides information about SolidWorks geometry. The following tables summarize cursor feedback. The tables were developed by support engineers from Computer Aided Products, Inc. Peabody, MA. Used with permission.

Sketch Tools:			
	Line		Rectangle
	Circle		Ellipse
	Arc (Centerpoint, Tangent, 3 Point)		Ellipse
	Parabola		Spline
	Polygon		Point
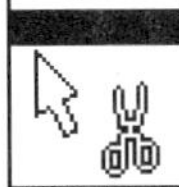	Trim		Extend
	Split line (not possible)		Split line (here)
	Linear step and repeat		Circular step and repeat
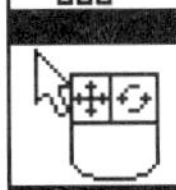	Modify sketch tool		Modify Sketch (Rotate only)
	Modify Sketch (Move / Flip Y-axis)	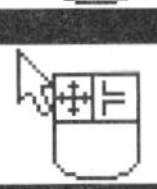	Modify Sketch (Move / Flip X-axis)
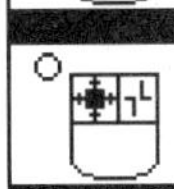	Move Origin of Sketch / Flip both axes		

Cursor Feedback Symbols

Courtesy of Computer Aided Products, Inc. Peabody, MA USA

Sketching relationships:			
	Horizontal		Vertical
	Parallel		Perpendicular
	Tangent		Intersection
	Coincident to axis		Midpoint
	Quarter arc		Half arc
	3 quarter arc		Quadrant of arc
	Wake up line/edge		Wake up point
	Coincident to line/edge		Coincident to point
	3D sketch		3D sketch
	3D sketch		3D sketch
	3D sketch		3D sketch

Dimensions:			
	Dimension		Radial or diameter dimension
	Horizontal dimension		Vertical dimension
	Vertical ordinate dimension		Ordinate dimensioning
	Horizontal ordinate dimension		Baseline dimensioning

Cursor Feedback Symbols

Courtesy of Computer Aided Products, Inc. Peabody, MA USA

Selection:			
	Line, edge		Axis
	Surface body		Select Point
	Select Vertex		Select Endpoint
	Select Midpoint		Select arc centerpoint
	Select Annotation		Select surface finish
	Select geometric tolerance		Datum Target
	Multi jog leader		Select multi jog leader control point
	Select Datum Feature		Select balloon
	Select text reference point	This Field Left Blank	Cursors for other selections with a reference point look similar
	Dimensions		Dimension arrow
	Cosmetic Thread		Stacked Balloons
	Hole Callout		Place Center Mark
	Select Center Mark		Block
	Select Silhouette edge		Select other
	Filter is switched on		

Cursor Feedback Symbols

Courtesy of Computer Aided Products, Inc. Peabody, MA USA

Assemblies:			
	Choose reference plane (insert new component/envelope)		Insert Component from File
	Insert Component (fixed to origin)		Insert Component to Feature Manager
	Lightweight component		Rotate component
	Move component / Smartmate select mode		Select 2nd component for smartmate
	Simulation mode running		
Smartmates:			
	Mate - Coincident Linear Edges		Mate - Coincident Planar Faces
	Mate - Concentric Axes/Conical Faces		Mate - Coincident Vertices
	Mate - Coincident/Concentric Circular Edges or Conical Faces		

FeatureManager:			
	Move component or feature in tree		Copy component or feature in tree
	Move feature below a folder in tree		Move/copy not permitted
	Invalid location for item		Move component in/out of sub assembly

Cursor Feedback Symbols

Courtesy of Computer Aided Products, Inc. Peabody, MA USA

Drawings:			
	Drawing sheet		Drawing view
	Move drawing view		Auxiliary view arrow
	Change view size horizontally		Change view size vertically
	Change view size diagonally		Change view size diagonally
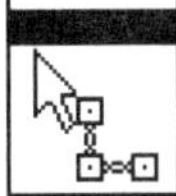	Align Drawing View		Select detail circle
	Block		Select Datum Feature Symbol
	Insert/Select Weld Symbol		Select Center Mark
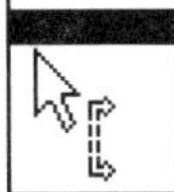	Select Section View	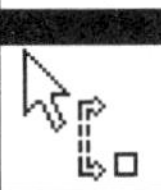	Section view and points of section arrow
	Select Silhouette edge		Hide/Show Dimensions

Standard Tools:			
	Selection tool		Please wait (thinking)
	Rotate view		Pan view
	Invalid selection/location		Measure tool
	Zoom to area		Zoom in/out
	Accept option		

Cursor Feedback Symbols

Courtesy of Computer Aided Products, Inc. Peabody, MA USA

SolidWorks Keyboard Shortcuts

Listed below are the pre-defined keyboard shortcuts in SolidWorks:

Action:	Key Combination:
Model Views	
Rotate the model horizontally or vertically:	**Arrow** keys
Rotate the model horizontally or vertically 90 degrees.	**Shift** + **Arrow** keys
Rotate the model clockwise or counterclockwise	**Alt** + left of right **Arrow** keys
Pan the model	**Ctrl** + **Arrow** keys
Zoom in	**Shift + z**
Zoom out	**z**
Zoom to fit	**f**
Previous view	**Ctrl + Shift + z**
View Orientation	
View Orientation menu	**Spacebar**
Front view	**Ctrl + 1**
Back view	**Ctrl + 2**
Left view	**Ctrl + 3**
Right view	**Ctrl + 4**
Top view	**Ctrl + 5**
Bottom view	**Ctrl + 6**
Isometric view	**Ctrl + 7**
NormalTo view	**Ctrl + 8**
Selection Filters	
Filter edges	**e**
Filter vertices	**v**
Filter faces	**x**
Toggle Selection Filter toolbar	**F5**
Toggle selection filters on/off	**F6**
File menu items	
New SolidWorks document	**Ctrl + n**
Open document	**Ctrl + o**
Open From Web Folder	**Ctrl + w**
Make Drawing from Part	**Ctrl + d**
Make Assembly from Part	**Ctrl + a**
Save	**Ctrl +s**
Print	**Ctrl + p**
Additional shortcuts	
Access online help inside of PropertyManager or dialog box	**F1**
Rename an item in the FeatureManager design tree	**F2**
Rebuild the model	**Ctrl + b**
Force rebuild – Rebuild the model and all its features	**Ctrl + q**
Redraw the screen	**Ctrl + r**
Cycle between open SolidWorks document	**Ctrl + Tab**

Line to arc/arc to line in the Sketch	**a**
Undo	**Ctrl + z**
Redo	**Ctrl + y**
Cut	**Ctrl + x**
Copy	**Ctrl + c**
Additional shortcuts	
Paste	**Ctrl + v**
Delete	**Delete**
Next window	**Ctrl + F6**
Close window	**Ctrl + F4**
Selects all text inside an Annotations text box	**Ctrl + a**

In the Sketch, the Esc key unselects geometry items currently selected in the Properties box and Add Relations box. In the model, the Esc key closes the PropertyManager and cancels the selections.

Windows Shortcuts

Listed below are the pre-defined keyboard shortcuts in Microsoft Windows:

Action:	**Keyboard Combination:**
Open the Start menu	Windows Logo key
Open Windows Explorer	Windows Logo key + E
Minimize all open windows	Windows Logo key + M
Open a Search window	Windows Logo key + F
Open Windows Help	Windows Logo key + F1
Select multiple geometry items in a SolidWorks document	Ctrl key (Hold the Ctrl key down. Select items.) Release the Ctrl key.

Helpful On-Line Information

The SolidWorks URL: http://www.solidworks.com contains information on local resellers, Partners and SolidWorks users groups.

The SolidWorks URL: http://www.3D ContentCentral.com contains additional engineering electronic catalog information.

The SolidWorks web site provides links to sample designs, frequently asked questions, an independent News Group (comp.cad.solidworks) and Users Groups.

Helpful on-line SolidWorks information is available from the following URLs:

- http://www.mechengineer.com/snug/

  News group access and local user group information.

- http://www.nhcad.com

  Configuration information and other tips and tricks.

- http://www.solidworktips.com

  Helpful tips, tricks on SolidWorks and API.

- http://www.topica.com/lists/SW

  Independent News Group for SolidWorks discussions, questions and answers.

Certified SolidWorks Professionals (CSWP) URLs provide additional helpful on-line information.

• http://www.scottjbaugh.com	Scott J. Baugh
• http://www.3-ddesignsolutions.com	Devon Sowell
• http://www.zxys.com	Paul Salvador
• http://www.mikejwilson.com	Mike J. Wilson
• http://www.frontiernet.net/~mlombard	Matt Lombard
• http://www.dimontegroup.com	Gene Dimonte & Ed Eaton

On-line tutorials are for educational purposes only. Tutorials are copyrighted by their respective owners.

INDEX

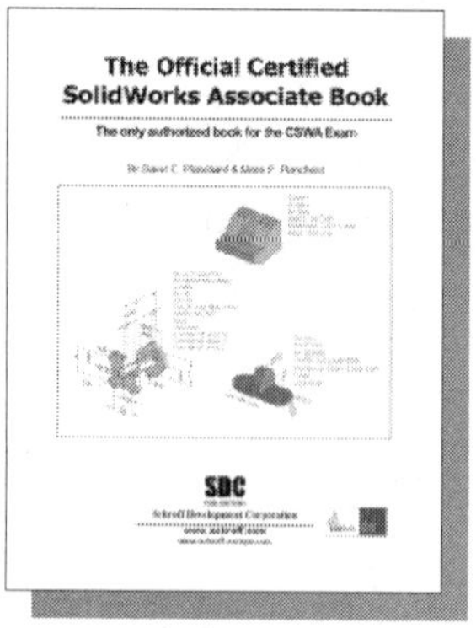

The Official Certified SolidWorks Associate Book

The only authorized book for the CSWA Exam

By David C. Planchard & Marie P. Planchard

INTRODUCTION

The Official Certified SolidWorks Associate CSWA exam book is written to assist the SolidWorks user to pass their CSWA exam. SolidWorks Corporation offers two levels of certification representing increasing levels of expertise in 3D CAD design as it applies to engineering: Certified SolidWorks Associate CSWA, and the Certified SolidWorks Professional CSWP.

The CSWA certification indicates a foundation in and apprentice knowledge of 3D CAD design and engineering practices and principles. The main requirement for obtaining the CSWA certification is to take and pass the three hour, seven question, on-line proctored exam at a Certified SolidWorks CSWA Provider, "university, college, technical, vocational, or secondary educational institution" and to sign the SolidWorks Confidentiality Agreement. Passing this exam provides the student the chance to prove their knowledge and expertise and to be part of a world wide industry certification standard.

Intended Audience

The intended audience for this book and the CSWA exam is anyone with a minimum of 6 - 9 months of SolidWorks experience and basic knowledge of engineering fundamentals and practices. SolidWorks recommends that you review their online tutorials on Parts, Assemblies, and Drawings as a prerequisite and have at least 45 hours of classroom time learning SolidWorks or using SolidWorks with basic engineering design principles and practices.

How This Book is Organized

The CSWA exam is divided into five major categories. Questions in the exam are provided in a random manor. The book is divided into five chapters. Each chapter is aligned to the five categories of the exam and covers the topics described below:

Chapter 1: Basic Theory and Drawing Theory
(2 Questions - 10 Points)

- Understand and apply basic concepts in SolidWorks.
- Recognize 3D modeling techniques
- Identify material, measure, mass properties, and section properties
- Identify and understand the function and elements of a Part and Assembly FeatureManager
- Ability to understand and identify the default Sketch Entity from the Sketch toolbar: Line, Rectangle, Circle, etc.
- Ability to understand and identify the default Sketch tool to from the Sketch toolbar: Entities: Fillet, Chamfer, Offset Entities, etc.
- Knowledge of the available SolidWorks File formats for Input and Export.
- Ability to use the SolidWorks Help topics
- Identify the process of creating a simple drawing from a part or an assembly
- Recognize all drawing name view types:
- Identify the procedure to create a named drawing view
- Specify Document Properties

Chapter 2: Part modeling
(1 Question - 30 Points)

- Read and understand an Engineering drawing document.
- Identify the reference plane, part origin, and applied design intent
- Apply 2D and 3D Sketches
- Build a part from a detailed dimension illustration
- Apply Extruded Boss/Base, Extruded Cut, Fillet, and Chamfer features
- Calculate mass, volume, and material properties for the created model
- Apply geometric relations and dimensions.

Chapter 3: Assembly modeling
(1 Question - 30 Points)

- Specify Document Properties
- Identify the components to construct the assembly from a detailed illustration
- Identify the first fixed component and position
- Build a bottom-up assembly with Standard Mates
- Calculate the center of mass

Chapter 4: Advanced Part modeling
(1 Questions - 20 Points)

- Ability to interpret engineering terminology
- Build an advance part from a detailed dimension illustration
- Edit 2D sketches and features
- Apply Revolved Boss/Base, Revolved Cut, Linear, and Circular Pattern features
- Apply geometric relations and dimensions

Chapter 5: Advanced modeling theory and analysis
(2 Question - 10 Points)

- Knowledge to apply COSMOSXpress to a simple part
- Knowledge of the differences between COSMOSXpress, COSMOSWorks, COSMOSFloWorks, and COSMOSMotion

Why the CSWA Exam?

The 3D CAD world has many different certifications available. Some of these certifications are sponsored by vendors and some by consortiums of different vendors. Regardless of the sponsor of the certifications, most CAD professionals today recognize the need to become certified to prove their skills, prepare for new job searches, and to learn new skills while at their existing jobs.

Specifying a CSWA or CSWP certification on your resume is a great way to increase your chances of landing a new job, getting a promotion, or looking more qualified when representing your company on a consulting job.

To purchase a copy or for more information, please visit
www.schroff.com